JANE'S

FIGHTING AIRCRAFT
OF WORLD WAR I

JANE'S
FIGHTING AIRCRAFT
OF WORLD WAR I

FOREWORD BY JOHN W. R. TAYLOR

STUDIO

PUBLISHER'S NOTE

The editors and publishers of *Jane's Fighting Aircraft of World War I* wish to state that, in reproducing pictures and typematter from wartime editions of Jane's *All the World's Aircraft*, they have done their best to ensure the retention of as much of the original detail of the material as possible. They are aware, however, that some of the original pictures are of poor quality, but since no others are available these have been included in the interests of completeness.

To provide readers with the most comprehensive record of the aircraft that fought aviation's first great War the compiler of *Jane's Fighting Aircraft of World War I*, Michael Taylor, has supplemented the 1919 material by extracting entries on śignificant military aircraft from the 1914, 1916, 1917 and 1918 editions. (There was no 1915 edition.) Pictures missing in the original material have also been supplied from other sources wherever possible.

Jane's Fighting Aircraft of World War I
Originally published by Jane's Publishing Company 1919

All rights reserved

This edition published in 2001 by
Random House Group Ltd
20 Vauxhall Bridge Road
London SW1V 2SA

By arrangement with the proprietor

Copyright © for this edition Studio 1990

ISBN 1 85170 347 0

Printed and bound in Great Britain by
Butler & Tanner Ltd, Frome and London

CONTENTS.

FOREWORD

JANE'S All the World's Aircraft was only five years old when the First World War began. It had already established such a reputation for authenticity that its Founder/Editor, Fred T. Jane, feared that the 1914 edition might be of assistance to Britain's enemies. It was not practicable to scrap the work already done and, in a reasonable period of time, restart page make-up and printing. So, when purchasers opened the book they discovered that pages in the British section that should have carried large illustrations of aeroplanes and airships in service with the Royal Flying Corp and Royal Naval Air Services were sometimes almost entirely obliterated by rectangles of solid black ink.

In a Special Note above his Preface, Jane wrote "On account of the general European War it has been decvided to publish the first edition of this book a month earlier than was originally anticipated. This means that the Italian and United States pages have to go to press imperfectly brought to date. On the other hand, though certain details which would otherwise have appeared are necessarily lacking, the matter collected concerning the principal belligerants is of such a nature that immediate publication seems desirable and to justify the unfinished state of the British pages, from which, for obvious reasons, a good deal has been deliberately deleted."

We shall never know whether the purpose was simply to deny the enemy information on aircraft that some considered to be world-beaters. But Jane could hardly have foreseen that types such as the RFC's B.E.2c, poorly armed and with the emphasis on stability for reconnaissance, would be almost cleared from the sky over the Western Front in France when the Germans introduced their Fokker Eindecker (monoplane), with a forward-firing machine-gun, in the Summer of 1915.

From that time, combat aircraft developed at an astonishing pace. By the end of the war, in 1918, successive generations of single-seat fighters had progressed from having engines capable of producing 80 hp on a good day to engines giving a reliable 200 hp or more. Speeds increased in consequence from 82 mph to nearly 150 mph. Twin forward-firing machine-guns became the normal armament, with up to four guns on some aircraft such as the Sopwith Dolphin.

It is surprising to realise, long afterwards, that the so-called "Fokker scourge" of 1915-16 was accomplished in only ten months by aircraft that weighed only 1,400 lb fully loaded, and of which only some 423 were built. In contrast, nearly 5,500 British Sopwith Camels were produced, and they shot down 1,294 enemy aircraft – more than any other Allied or enemy type – in dogfights that were often decided by their extreme manoeuvrability.

Unlike the present day, when many types of military aircraft remain in first-line service for 20, 30, or more years, some of the best-known types of the 1914-18 period operated for only a year or 18 months before being replaced by something better. As a result, they had long disappeared from assembly factories and from the inventory of squadrons fighting in France when the late Fred Jane's successor, C. G. Grey, compiled the 1919 edition of All the World's Aircraft that forms the basis of this book.

To provide readers with a more comprehensive record of the aircraft that fought aviation's first great war, the compiler of Jane's Fighting Aircraft of World War I has supplemented the 1919 material by extracting entries on significant military aircraft from the 1914, 1916, 1917 and 1918 editions (there was none in 1915). Civilian types have been omitted as irrelevant to this volume.

It has to be remembered that in wartime it is seldom possible to describe in full detail the structures, dimensions, weights, performance and armament of contemporary aircraft built by manufacturers on one's own side. Even the 1919 edition of All the World's Aircraft was compiled partly during the still-desperate closing months of the conflict, with some updating after it ended. So, the descriptions of individual aircraft in this book are, for the most part, based on reports and studies of German aircraft that had been captured (often in a damaged state) by the Allies, and vice versa. They are of considerable historical interest and, although they could not include all the facts and figures that became available later, they provide some of the most detailed descriptions of important aircraft that have ever appeared in any reference book.

In retrospect, it can be seen that the four years and three months of the First World War represented the most significant period in the entire history of aerial warfare.

PREFACE.

BY C. G. GREY, EDITOR OF
"THE AEROPLANE".

WHEN one began the compilation of *"All the World's Aircraft"* for 1919, one did so with a light heart. Though Peace had not been declared, the War was manifestly over, and all lets and hindrances due to the necessary, and one may add, the kindly and sympathetic, censorship of a publication entirely concerned with war material were removed. It was to be assumed that all would be the plainest of plain sailing.

But as the work progressed one found, as many people have found in other occupations, that Peace was by no means an unmixed blessing, and one almost wished for the simple condition of war, when there was a fixed regulation for everything. One began to sympathise with the dog whose muzzle is removed at the end of a prolonged Muzzling Order, and who does not quite know what to do with himself.

During the War it was fairly easy to judge what one might safely put into the book. In these days the difficulty is to know how to get into it all the matter that obviously ought to be in it, for there are limits to the amount of paper and printing which can be expended on a publication of this nature, even at a slightly increased price. Also there are limits to the size of book which a cover will hold without bursting asunder in the midst. Also there are limits to the time which can be allowed for printing and binding if the book is not to consist entirely of ancient history.

Therefore the problem became largely one of what to leave out of the book rather than what to put into it. In order to make room for the mass of illustrations, specifications and technical descriptions which are now available it was necessary to cut out something else. Consequently the whole of what was "Part A" of last year's volume, consisting of the Dictionary, the International Glossary, the Table of Records, and so forth, has been omitted bodily. The Dictionary has been published separately, for the benefit of those who are still unfamiliar with aeronautical phraseology. The whole of the Historical Section has also been eliminated, for if one were to attempt to do justice to All the World's Historical Aircraft one would need a volume nearly as big as this. Also the List of Pilots and the R.A.F. Honours' List have been omitted, for they also have grown to such a size that if they were included most of the Aeroplane Section of the book would have to be excluded.

The removal of all these sections of the previous volume has left room for many more illustrations and descriptions of aeroplanes, airships and engines than have ever appeared in any other publication, but even so the task of compilation has not been easy. Naturally one has wished to give the fullest possible descriptions of British and Allied machines. As a matter of interest, and also of education for our own designers, one has endeavoured to describe as fully as possible the machines of our erstwhile enemies, the Germans.

And here, be it said, there is much to learn from the German aeroplanes and engines. Though British aeroplanes have had the finest performance of any in the world during the war, there are many German machines which beat the majority of our own in pure "eyeability". And it is an axiomatic fact that if an aeroplane *is* right it *looks* right, though it is by no means true that conversely if an aeroplane *looks* right it *is* right. Many German machines *look* right, but are constructionally bad.

It may be noticed that British aeroplanes have during the past two years become more and more "Hunnish" in appearance. Long before the end of the war one of the greatest compliments one could pay an aeroplane was to say that it looked "very like a Hun", and the attitude of mind among aviators which was indicated by this state of affairs showed that the Germans had developed an eye for the aeroplane that looked right. Where they failed was firstly in detail of construction, and secondly in certain points of aerodynamic science which need not be specified, for we are now commercially at war with Germany.

For this reason the German section of this volume is well worth study, and one is glad to acknowledge the fact, that thanks to the enterprise of Mr. Hildesheim, the compiler of the Scandinavian pages of this book, one was able to secure at the last moment before printing a number of photographs of German aeroplanes which have not hitherto been published out of Germany. Taking these in conjunction with the constructional details of German machines which have been reproduced from the reports of the Technical Department, Aircraft Group, Ministry of Munitions, much may be learned about German aircraft design.

As regards the French section, it has been extremely difficult to obtain information from the French firms, chiefly, one believes, because there has been so little new in French design for the past two years. The French aircraft designers and constructors blame *"l'Administration"* for holding back their best designs in the effort to produce enormous output during the last year of the war. The fact remains that during 1918 very little of interest was produced in France.

The British section is naturally the most voluminous of all, but here, the keen enquirer will see serious anomalies. Hardly any details will be found about some machines, and there are profuse descriptions of others. The reader must blame the firms and not the present writer. About the end of 1918 precisely the same letter was sent to each and every firm in the Aircraft Industry asking for information about its products. Some sent full details, with photographs and scale drawings, some sent photographs without descriptions, some sent descriptions without photographs, and some sent drawings without descriptions. Others again sent blue prints of drawings on such a scale that they could not be reproduced. Yet others refused to send any details of their machines, for fear lest their competitors might copy them.

In each case the material available has been used, and one hopes that it has been displayed to the best advantage of the British Aircraft Industry. But the disparity apparent between the information acquired concerning one firm and that acquired from another may be taken as representing the views of the various firms on the desirability of publishing details of their products.

Nevertheless one believes that on the whole the British Industry makes a good display.

An additional difficulty this year has been the fact that one has had to mix together war aeroplanes and commercial aeroplanes. It is true that with about two exceptions all so-called commercial aeroplanes are merely war aeroplanes with a species of conservatory added in which to carry an extra passenger or two, but it would have been distinctly more instructive if it had been possible to separate them. Doubtless this will become possible in future as the design of war aeroplanes diverges from that of commercial aeroplanes. But at present much space is occupied by obsolete war machines, which are included simply because it has not been permissible to publish them sooner, and by peace machines which are merely converted war machines.

A certain amount of extra information has been gathered this year concerning several countries which in previous volumes made but little showing in aeronautics. One is particularly indebted to the Japanese, Swedish and Argentine representatives in this country, and to certain Brazilian naval officers for their kindness in assisting one to procure information concerning aviation in their countries.

Finally one would like a word with one's friends the critics. One's only complaint against them is that they were too kind to the last volume. It is one's ambition to make "All the World's Aircraft" an absolute necessity to anybody who has to do with aircraft in any shape or form, and one would be grateful for any criticisms of this volume, and suggestions for improvements in future volumes which will make the book more valuable and therefore more necessary to the aeronautical world in general.

Meantime one hopes that the professional critics will be moderately pleased with those review copies which they acquire without cost, and that the buyers of the book will feel that it gives them value for their money. One can at any rate assert truthfully, as a certain famous comedian remarked about motoring, that there is nothing like it. — C.G.G.

In August 1914 many people, including Fred T. Jane, believed that airships were the most potent instruments of military flying. Few members of the opposing armies and navies expected aeroplanes to prove of any value except as unarmed aerial cavalry, able to observe the movements of men on the ground and ships over the horizon at sea.

By November 1918, pilots in swift, heavily-armed fighters were shooting each other from the sky; reconnaissance aircraft photographed every move made by unhappy soldiers on and behind the combat areas; bombers rained high explosive and incendiary bombs on battlefield and town alike; the first dive bombers had entered service to demoralise further the infantry in their muddy trenches; torpedo-carrying aircraft had achieved their first modest successes against ships at sea; carrier-based fighters and bombers had, to a large extent, replaced the frail seaplanes of 1914; and long-range flying boats had helped to end the menace of German U-boats around Britain.

Vast new industries had been created, to build a total of 55,093 aircraft in the UK alone during the war years. The Royal Air Force had 22,171 aeroplanes in service and in store in October 1918. The French had 15,342 serviceable aircraft in August 1918; the Germans had about 20,000. The United States had managed to gear itself quickly to build some 15,000 aeroplanes in its 21 months of war, but not one warplane of US design was used operationally except for Curtiss flying boats, the first of which had been bought for the RNAS in 1914.

Even if one was fortunate enough to be offered a reasonably good original copy of the 1919 *All the World's Aircraft* today, it would cost hundreds of pounds and would not contain entries on all the aircraft described in *Jane's Fighting Aircraft of World War I*. This book represents, therefore, a uniquely fascinating addition to the library of anyone with an interest in the history and technology of flight.

AIRCRAFT IN THE WAR.

By Major W. E. de B. WHITTAKER, Late of the King's Regiment and General Staff.

THE last piece in this series was written when the fate of the allies was in the balance. Through the dark days in the spring of 1918 there seemed to be a possibility of final victory falling to the Central Powers. At the best the end might be indecisive and all the blood and treasure wasted to no apparent good.

A brief six months after the most critical period all was over save the talking and the reconstruction. The unity of the Central Powers, so powerful a factor in the continuance and course of the great war, had dissolved, the Kaiser, powerless before the rising disloyalty of his people, had gone sadly into Holland and an armistice giving victory to the allies had been signed by the responsible military authorities.

It is not uncommon in great wars of the past for the culminating effort on both sides to be greater in determination and vigour than any of the earlier stages of hostilities. Waterloo, which ended a quarter of a century of conflict, surpassed in grandeur and decision all the battles of the Revolutionary and Napoleonic eras. The hardest fighting in the American Civil War came at the end. The Russo-Japanese war drew to its close in a blaze of fury which almost rivalled M. Bloch's worst prophecies as to the horrors of modern war. The throw of the dice for the last time is generally for the largest stakes and is directed by a desperation not unallied with tragedy.

In those operations which brought the war successfully to its close the Royal Air Force, the newest of the King's Services, took a primary part. While the Royal Air Force units with the troops in the field carried out their duties with loyalty and efficiency, impressing their personality on the enemy, the Independent Air Force was busily engaged destroying the moral of enemy civilians far behind the battle line by means of bombs distributed impartially by day or by night. At sea the enemy submarine campaign had ceased to be a serious menace to allied shipping almost entirely as a result of the aeroplane, airship and kite-balloon patrols carried out by R.A.F. units attached to the Navy. In each theatre of war the Royal Air Force can regard with pride its fighting records during the first and most vital period of its existence.

RECONNAISSANCE.

In that work which one cannot help regarding as the most important duty which fell to the R.A.F. during the war, the final year of hostilities saw no marked change. The principles of aerial reconnaissance had been well defined in earlier days and experience had shown but little reason for any amendment. The methods and the means employed improved but that is all. The photographs taken were better and the number produced was greater. More efficient wireless equipment was issued and the training and knowledge of pilots and observers showed marked improvement.

The improved types of aeroplanes available for reconnaissance in the latter days of the war extended the area over which it was possible to carry out with a proper degree of security the work of strategical scouting. Before the output and efficiency of aircraft had increased strategical reconnaissance was only possible under conditions of high risk and at great expense in casualties. It is one thing to fly a hundred miles behind the enemy lines on an aeroplane with all the appearance and many of the attributes of a Christmas tree and fitted with an engine on which but little reliance could be placed but there is greater joy and more profit in making the same journey in machines possessing both speed and reliability and equipped in such a manner as to make aerial fighting less one-sided in its results.

Tactical reconnaissance had improved greatly in the later stages of the war as a result of the increased knowledge of both pilots and observers in matters concerning military operations. There is a great art in reading correctly the movements of an enemy and before it can be attained those engaged in the work must have a close understanding of the principles of war and their concrete application. It is not possible to report everything seen—life and a flight are too short for that, but it is necessary to record everything that is of importance. It is not always the obvious that is of value and many a pilot has wasted valuable time to report manoeuvres which in the light of events could be read quite as easily from the ground and from behind the lines.

The value of photography in tactical reconnaissance cannot be overestimated. By its aid a daily map can be prepared and changes in enemy dispositions can be recorded in detail and with accuracy. It provides a check on visual observation and is invaluable in all artillery preparations. During the war aerial photography has grown from an experiment to an exact science. It provides a valuable means of correcting maps in areas where imagination rather than exactitude has directed the delineation of the ground. Some day when the official history of the war is produced it will be possible for the first time in history to illustrate each stage of hostilities by actual photographs taken during the conflict.

ARTILLERY OBSERVATION.

When first it was decided to employ aircraft to "spot" for the guns, the gunner officer was a little sceptical as to the value of aerial observation. Such ideas looked very well on paper, but would they work out equally well in practice? And he was not greatly encouraged by the first experiences of "spotting" during the war. Inexperience coupled with the inefficiency of the aeroplanes in use, made the first observations a little erratic and disconnected. Wireless was not available and the then prevailing method of using Véry light signals was cumbrous and slow. To-day all has changed. Wireless equipment is fitted in all "spotting" aircraft and is dependable and rapid in action. Observers understand their work and are in close liaison with the artillery at all times. No gunner to-day would dream of setting to work without the aid of aircraft when aircraft is available.

A Bristol Two-seater Fighter and Reconnaissance Machine in the air.

A Patrol of Bristol Fighters Starting in Formation.

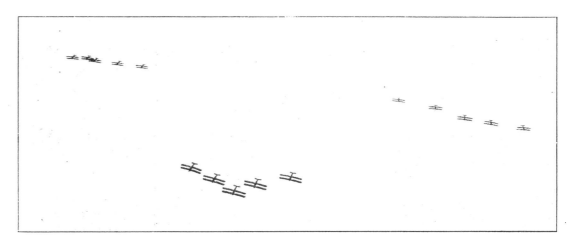

Part of a Squadron of Reconnaissance Machines in Formation.

The introduction of the wireless telephone is another improvement which increases the speed and accuracy of "spotting." It will be possible for artillery brigade, group or battery to communicate direct in open speech with the observers "spotting" for them. There is less chance of error in the conveyance of messages and targets can be changed at will either from the ground or from the air without the delay consequent even in the use of the wireless telegraph. It must be remembered that in the case of the wireless telegraph it was not the custom to fit receiving apparatus in the machines, consequently replies or requests from the ground had of necessity to be sent visually. In any case speech is simpler to the ordinary man than is the Morse Code.

AERIAL FIGHTING.

The production of aeroplanes definitely designed for aerial fighting proceeded with vigour up to the end of the war both in the British and the German armies. Others of the allies on both sides paid attention to this matter but the results were not striking. None compared favourably in all round fighting efficiency with those produced in Germany and England. In the air as on the land

and sea the two great antagonists in the war developed their material of war on similar lines and with almost equal success.

It is a matter of high interest to follow throughout the war the progress of aerial fighting from the days when contests were few and were almost in every case accidental to the last phase when it had become an exact science and was a deliberate and vital part of war. There is not space for any recapitulation of the stages of this progress and it has been done in various manners before but it cannot be stated too often how important in modern warfare is the employment of a strong aerial fighting arm. By degrees the aeroplane is becoming the eyes of an army in the fullest sense of the phrase. Cavalry is restricted in its speed of action and in the area over which it can operate. The tank and the armoured car also adversely affect the operations of the mounted arm. Hence the aeroplane alone can carry out with efficiency and speed the work of scouting. The new principle is accepted and the greatest reliance is placed in the reconnaissance work of the Royal Air Force.

Should aerial reconnaissance fail from any cause there is nothing to replace it with adequacy and the army whose aerial arm has even temporarily been defeated is almost completely blinded. The transition from a great volume of intelligence to an entire lack of information is paralysing in its effect. A force operating entirely in the dark would be less liable to disaster—though victory would not be a common incident—than would a body of troops suddenly deprived of all information.

Thus the maintenance of a strong force of aeroplanes whose sole duty is that of fighting is essential in modern war. More and more will it be necessary to obtain an actual fighting supremacy in the air before the routine duties of the flying service can be carried out. At one time failure in the air was a drawback, an inconvenience which had to be compensated for in other ways, but to-day and in the future the success of a ground operation will depend largely on what happens in the air.

CONTOUR FIGHTING.

The use of aeroplanes in the attack on lines of communications troops, reserves and so on will grow until the tactical conditions of war have undergone fundamental variation. During the actions of the last two years of the war it was common practice for aircraft to be employed on contour fighting against infantry and other arms in the field but the lack of machines and more particularly of specially designed machines, prevented the growth of these tactics to a stage when they would influence the entire movements of an army.

An army strong in itself but harassed continually over all its area of operations by continual attack from low flying aircraft would be unable to carry any detailed plan into effect with that degree of certainty which is essential in manoeuvres on a large scale. The staffs of the army would be unable to work in peace unless buried well below the earth, communications would be constantly interrupted, movements in column would become well-nigh impossible and above all the fighting troops would never be permitted to rest.

Certain important nerve centres of an army could it is true be accommodated in dug-outs sufficiently deeply cut into the ground as to give them comparative safety from aerial attack but it is manifestly impossible to bury an entire army and expect it still to spread terror upon the earth. The obtaining of security by measures of passive defence is clearly limited.

Hence other measures must be taken to prevent ground forces being reduced to impotence by the somewhat impertinent attentions of hostile pilots. There is always a solution to every problem. When the steam engine was first adopted as a means of propulsion in ships there were those who foretold the entire destruction of somebody's navy because of the superior mobility inherent in steam-ships. And destruction would certainly have fallen on any navy which cared to rely entirely on sail power when attacked by ships which owed their ability to manoeuvre to Mr. Watt's curious interest in the eccentricities of a tea kettle. The answer in that case was to adopt similar measures to those of the enemy. And it is invariably so in war. The tank will be countered by the tank as the rifle was met by the rifle. So too must the contour fighting aeroplane be met in its own element by weapons of its own class.

Anti-aircraft guns and machine guns specially equipped for the purpose cannot be an entire answer or even an adequate one. They are not ubiquitous nor is it possible to supply sufficient of them with the necessary personnel to cover all sections of the territory occupied by troops. Therefore it is essential to defend by means of a vigorous aerial offensive. Both sides endeavouring to attain the same ends by the same means will deflect the contour fighting aeroplane from its specified duties to an aerial battle in self defence. Engagements will take place at all levels and in all places.

FUTURE DEVELOPMENTS.

A definite system of strategy and tactics is growing imperceptibly. The time is rapidly approaching when it will be no longer possible for the aerial arm of an army to carry out a series of sporadic raids unrelated to each other in general principles. Every move of aircraft units will be in accordance with the plan and the ultimate purpose will be kept always in sight.

It is a little difficult at this moment to foretell the influence of aircraft on the form of future war. There are some who think that trench warfare will remain the constant habit in great conflicts owing to the necessity of providing adequate cover for vital sections of an army. Trenches are a necessary protection in ground warfare and they are still more necessary when a large proportion of the attack comes from the air. The greatest protection for the greatest numbers is quite a possible theory in the future. There are many attractions in immobile warfare. The preparation of operation orders is simplified, the element of surprise is reduced and the maintenance of communications is not difficult. There is less necessity for quick decision and enemy attacks can more easily be countered in a short space of time.

But trench warfare implies defensive warfare. The duration of hostilities is prolonged and the final victory is rarely decisive. Attrition and weariness determine the period and success is not entirely due to the sword. Victory, if conclusive, should be decided in the field and in action. Its after effects are then healthier and

No. 23 Squadron R.F.C. (Spads) ready to start for the Somme Front on March 23rd, 1918.

A Captured German "Albatros" Single-seater Fighter.

less provocative of future trouble. The starving of a nation rouses the worst spirit of revenge, and sooner or later the world is again bathed in blood because the sword failed in its duty.

Trench warfare simplifies the duties of the aerial arm. There is little difficulty in conducting orderly operations over an extended fortified line. Each change is recorded from day to day and all positions are registered. The daily work proceeds almost as a matter of routine. There is little opportunity for the unexpected

without which life lacks its chief charm. Aerodromes can be maintained in reasonable security and in a degree of comfort which cannot fail to react favourably in the efficiency of pilots and observers. Aeroplanes worked under these conditions can be kept in a constant state of fitness for service. To the aerial arm there are distinct attractions in trench warfare.

It is because of this simplification of the work of aircraft that we imagine future wars will not be immobile in nature and that siege

A Formation of Fokker Biplanes, of the late 1918 period.

warfare will become exceptional. The old days of open contest will return and generalship will once again hold the field. In a war of manœuvre the work of the aeroplane, as shown in Mesopotamia, Palestine and Egypt, will be of the highest importance and will in the hands of an efficient general be a weapon of vast possibilities. But with an increase in the importance of its duties, the aerial arm will meet with far greater difficulties than have been common in the present war. The advanced squadrons must be highly mobile and the quantity of stores carried will of necessity be small. No lengthy

A German Junker-Fokker "Contour-Fighter" or "Ground-Strafer" loading up with food and ammunition for conveyance to German troops in trenches which were cut off from other communication.

Bourlon Wood and the open country to the South of the Bapaume-Cambrai Road, showing the trench lines.

tenure of any aerodrome can be guaranteed and change of position will be constant. Conditions will arise which have not been common in the past.

Strategical reconnaissance will become of first and immediate importance. Information as to enemy movements must then be instantly forthcoming and of high accuracy. One's own movements must be screened by offensive action or by a feint which will draw enemy squadrons over many objectives. Bombing will be arranged as counter measures to enemy tactics with exclusive attention to such moves as are read to be essential parts of a coming attack in the culmination of strategical dispositions which are in successful progress.

In a war of movement, aircraft, even in the vast numbers certain to be employed in future wars, will have no easy task and that reason is one of those which, it seems, may sound the knell of trench warfare.

THE INDEPENDENT FORCE R.A.F.

During 1918, the Independent Force R.A.F., operating in accordance with the plans of the Supreme Command, but a separate entity of the British Armies in the Field, came into its own. Day by day, night by night, in fine or even in stormy weather, the large bombing aeroplanes of this force flew far beyond the enemy lines and past the frontiers into Germany bombing with discrimination, munition areas, rail-heads and dumps, until life in the back areas was deprived entirely of happiness. Many tons of bombs were dropped with startling frequency on such places as the railway triangle at Metz-Sablon and in towns as far removed from apparent danger as Karlsruhe and Cologne.

The moral of the German people was disturbed by this incessant and successful bombardment and the depression and dismay reacted unfavourably on the fighting troops with results which undoubtedly helped in the final collapse of the German arms.

Berlin would have been bombed before the year was out had it not been for hostilities ending with depressing suddenness. Many machines were completed and waiting opportunity, all of which could have reached the enemy capital with comparative ease.

In the previous year and in the first few months of 1918 German bombing squadrons had operated with a high degree of success against the Allies' back areas, attacking dumps, towns, junctions, army and corps' headquarters with equal impartiality. The menace at one time became serious and the damage done was seriously affecting the course of the war.

Night flying units were sent from England to join in the defence, the anti aircraft organisation overseas was improved and was equipped with unwonted liberality, and the advanced fighting squadrons made special preparations to carry the offensive into enemy territory. The new measures were successful and by the summer of 1918 enemy back-area bombing by night had dropped from intensity to a desultory series of rather aimless raids.

A Scene at an Aircraft Depot in France, at which damaged aeroplanes were rebuilt and re-issued to the Mobile Supply Parks nearer the Front Line.

KITE BALLOONS.

A high standard of efficiency in the employment of observation balloons on land had been attained at an earlier stage in the war and few improvements save in detail equipment were made in the last year of hostilities. The use of balloons was understood and their value appreciated in a proper degree. During the final retreat of the Germans on the Western Front many balloon companies achieved fame by the manner in which, undeterred by the heavy risks, they carried their balloons so far forward that they were within reach of enemy rifle fire. The value of the work done during those last days cannot be over estimated and the balloon *personnel* have aided ably in the creation of tradition in the newest of the King's Services. There was at one time a feeling among pilots that the balloon sections were a suitable home for enervated warriors unwilling to face the greater risks of war. The casualty list has supplied an adequate answer and all who know will regard those who have chosen the balloon service as their path in war with the respect due to those who have fought bravely and well.

The use of observation balloons as a part of the balloon apron system is dealt with later in this paper.

The enemy have not neglected balloons in their scheme of war. In fact at one time they made use of an infinitely greater number of observation balloons than did the allies. The duties in both cases were similar, primarily in artillery observations, secondarily in watching and reporting on movements of their own infantry. These balloons were well protected by anti-aircraft guns both small and large, and the work of destroying them was not simple.

ANTI-AIRCRAFT DEFENCES AT HOME AND ABROAD.

At the beginning of the war anti-aircraft defences did not exist in this country and were particularly inadequate in other countries. Firstly there had been no experience on which to base the necessary organisation, and secondarily the necessity of putting all available material into the field prevented the allocation of guns, searchlights and aeroplanes to what then seemed a somewhat problematical duty.

The Zeppelin airship was the only aerial menace to English territory in 1914 and it does not seem to have been considered a formidable enemy in those days. We were all so deeply convinced that the aeroplane was the master of the airship in every way that the possibilities of aerial attack by airship were largely discounted.

With 1915 came a series of Zeppelin attacks growing steadily in intensity as the enemy began to realize not only the inadequacy but the non-existence in any practical sense of anti-aircraft defences in this country. A few isolated guns of small calibre on improvised mountings permitting of high elevation do not and cannot constitute a defence.

In view of the shortage of military *personnel* the Admiralty undertook the aerial defence of London and the Home Counties. Admiral Sir Percy Scott, K.C.B., who had been interested in gunnery, was posted in command. Little however was done to prevent enemy air raids, largely owing to the shortage of material, and in 1916 the War Office took over responsibility for what was in truth a military matter. Squadrons of night flying aeroplanes were at once organised and vulnerable points were protected in some degree by guns and searchlights. In the autumn of that year success was achieved against raiding Zeppelins by aeroplanes and the airship menace ceased for a space. The credit of the organisation which they formed under almost incredible conditions of difficulty, yet supplied the answer to the airship attack, was due to General Headquarters, Home Forces in general and in particular to the Anti-Aircraft Branch of that Headquarters.

In 1917, as was foreseen, attack by aeroplane became common. First in broad daylight, later by night German aeroplanes made a series of air raids over the Home Counties inflicting heavy damage at but little cost in machines or *personnel*. It was considered necessary to form a separate command responsible directly to General Headquarters Home Forces in order to co-ordinate and direct the anti-aircraft defences of London and the South of England. Guns, searchlights and aeroplanes were supplied with a generosity unknown in the earlier stages of hostilities. Guns were disposed in accordance with considered tactical plans and the system of specifically defending vulnerable points was relinquished in favour of a general scheme. Searchlights, highly important in anti-aircraft defences, were sited with the guns and in positions in which they could co-operate effectively with aeroplanes. Night flying aeroplane squadrons were based in areas over which they could patrol without being in danger of injury from the defending shell fire. Each part of the defences was arranged in such manner as to co-operate most easily with other parts of the command. Elaborate communications were established and the system of control was unified while entire discretion was left to subordinate commanders as to action in cases of emergency.

A new form of defence was also devised and produced. The balloon apron which mystified so deeply such of the public as had heard rumours of its existence came to take its effective part in the defences. After rapid experiments, the balloon apron was brought to a stage of usefulness which, if immature, had its very real value in war. The final scheme was that three balloons of the latest type, without car and of any desired dimensions, were placed equidistantly over a space of 1,000 yards. These balloons were connected by a cable to which depended a series of streamers 1,000 feet long. The apron thus constructed was elevated to such a height that aeroplanes flying in its vicinity had perforce to fly at their extreme altitude in order to avoid the risk of entanglement.

The aprons were disposed on sites distributed in vital parts of the London Air Defence Area and all intelligence indicates that their moral effect was considerable among enemy pilots. There are few who fly and would care to travel through a sky dotted with obstructions of this nature. No aeroplanes capable of carrying an effective supply of bombs could fly at a height at which they were immune from risk in regard to balloon aprons. It is always natural to exaggerate the dangers of the entirely unknown and it is possible that raiding pilots had greater fear of balloon aprons than of high explosive shell or aeroplane attack.

The Italian Avorio-Prassone Kite-Balloon, the most efficient kite-balloon of the war. Introduced into the British Services for Balloon-Apron Work.

Another scene at an Aircraft Depot in France, showing Reconnaissance Machines in process of reconstruction.

It is known that enemy aircraft were damaged by these aprons and it is possible that one machine was destroyed through collision with a cable though the final blow was dealt by a defending aeroplane. The aprons covered but a small area in a vast sky and it would be absurd to expect any high rate of positive destruction. Moral effect is in itself a vital asset in war and that the enemy, brave though he undoubtedly was, had no pleasure in encountering aprons is a sufficient gain to the defences.

Incidentally the existence of balloon aprons in a thickly populated area for over eighteen months without the public knowing either their form or uses is proof of the standard of secrecy which can be maintained when necessary in His Majesty's Forces.

Other nations adopted or had adopted systems of balloon screens which were no very close relations to those used in London. Venice, eager to preserve its historic beauty organised an aerial defence of high efficiency, a part of which was a screen of small balloons in single cables. These balloons were independent and were not

ends the contest. At one time it was thought that flying and fighting by night would be highly expensive in *personnel* and machines. Yet in truth the casualties by night have been no greater than those by day. In home defence with many dozens of aeroplanes in the air during any night raid the total casualties in the five years of war can almost be counted on the fingers of the two hands. It was even rare for a machine to be damaged in landing even though emergency landings under conditions of great difficulty were by no means uncommon.

The searchlight, which though a thing of beauty to the public has attracted no great appreciation for its services, is the third essential part of anti-aircraft defences. Here, too, efficiency has greatly increased and the training has improved to such a degree that whereas at one time the illumination of every aeroplane from the ground was a matter of charming accident, to-day aircraft are located and passed from beam to beam with great frequency. Each succeeding year will raise the standard of success until it will be possible to locate and hold all "aircraft" passing over the illuminated areas.

At an Aircraft Depot in France, showing air mechanics endeavouring to start a reconstructed engine in a repaired aeroplane.

The Bow of a German "Giant" Bombing Aeroplane, showing the two pilots, and the position of the Commanding Officer behind them.

connected by aprons. France had a somewhat similar system round various vulnerable points behind the lines.

Germany, never far behind in the great game of war, also protected in this manner many of the towns threatened by aerial attack but in these cases again the balloon apron was not put into use.

It is the fashion in some quarters to scoff at anti-aircraft gunners apparently because enemy aircraft are not destroyed by each round fired. It is a new science vastly different from gunnery in the horizontal plane. Questions of height finding and range finding complicate the issue in addition to a mass of technical troubles unsuitable for discussion in this paper. The four years of war have brought the science from birth to a high stage of efficiency and the public would be surprised, if surprise still exists in humanity, at the successes gained by anti-aircraft gunnery in the war.

The aeroplane is naturally the mainstay of any system of aerial defence. It alone can engage enemy aircraft in any part of the area defended and it alone can continue the fight until success or defeat

But to no branch of the service is all the credit due. The secret of success in anti-aircraft defence is co-operation. The aeroplane, the gun, the heightfinder, the balloon apron, the searchlight and the sound locator have each their respective places in the scheme, but all are inter-dependent. One helps the other and it is the entire united effort which leads on to victory.

Future wars may begin by aerial attack. Commercial aircraft can be converted to war machines in a few hours and consequently all an enemy country's aeroplanes are its potential fleet in War. A swift aerial blow well timed and well placed might cripple the attacked country before mobilisation was completed. The centres of government in a country are no more immune from attack than is the smallest and most remote village.

Hence the importance of fixed anti-aircraft defences will increase in the future and it will probably be necessary to retain a strong force under war conditions.

Anti-aircraft defence in the field has to face very different conditions. The constant change in position of an army in open warfare or even in trench warfare make it necessary for anti-aircraft defences to be highly mobile. The maintenance of communications is a primary difficulty. Efficient communications are naturally of the first importance as an aerial attack may be made at any time and in any place. The anti-aircraft guns in the forward area are subject to constant and often heavy shell fire. Thus frequent changes of position are necessary. Communications also are destroyed with disconcerting regularity. As an instance of the strenuous nature of the life, in one Army alone in France the casualties during one year to the *personnel* manning the anti-aircraft guns in the forward area amounted just to 100 per cent. of their establishment. The route of the attackers can be altered at will, a freedom of movement which is rare in land warfare. Secondly, in a constantly moving number of units it is difficult to keep to the necessary standard of co-operation which must be assured if the defence is to be effective. In attacks on countries such as England or Germany there are certain definite objectives on which the attackers must concentrate if any real damage is to be inflicted. Towns, harbours, dockyards, munition areas and railway junctions each has its attraction to the invading pilot. He has no desire to waste effort by bombing sparsely inhabited areas. The defences have therefore the advantage of knowing what they have to defend, and they know moreover the probable lines of approach of enemy attack.

In the field the position is more difficult. The entire back area of an army is crowded with *personnel*, material and transport. Countless roads and railways feed the front line. There is little that is not of importance and the possibilities of doing damage are limitless. Then to this the troops and guns in the line must be added and it will be seen that the attacking aircraft are rather in the advantage as to the power of inflicting injury on the attacked.

It is manifestly impossible to defend with equal strength the whole of the area now occupied by an army in the field—at least until the relative strength of anti-aircraft defence to other arms be adjusted in the light of future experience in air war. It therefore falls to the

Supreme Command in the Field so to lay out his defences as to protect definite zones over which defending aircraft will endeavour to drive the enemy if the attack is by night or by day.

NAVAL AERONAUTICS.

The aeroplane designed and produced for work over the sea has developed greatly during the past eighteen months until at the present time the seaplane and flying boat are not very far behind the land machine in efficiency. The flying boats of various sizes produced from designs drawn out at Felixstowe have been employed incessantly on patrols over the seas surrounding Great Britain with such success as greatly to reduce the risks to shipping from submarine attack.

The Germans did not devote much time to the development of flying boats but the seaplanes produced by the navy and certain firms which specialised in this work were very effective. In the early part of 1918 the Brandenburg seaplane, a monoplane of somewhat curious design, began to appear in quantities and waged very successful war against our shores and less handy flying boats. Day after day they with other classes of seaplanes crossed to the British coast fighting and destroying all manner of aircraft which they were fortunate enough to encounter. They escorted torpedo carrying seaplanes whose efforts were directed entirely against shipping entering the Thames or the great ports on the East coast.

The Engineers looking out of the forward engine-room window of German five-engined "Giant" aeroplane.

The Engine Arrangement of a five-engined German "Giant" aeroplane.

The answer to the Brandenburg type of machine was presumably found in the use of land machines flying from the decks of ships of war. The higher power of manœuvre inherent in land machines, owing to the lack of floats and the head resistance resulting therefrom and to the necessarily heavier construction of machines destined to alight in the sea, gives them the mastery over the seaplane in action.

It was also common practice for land machines to patrol long distances over the sea despite the high risks attendant on such procedure. The machines employed were not always the most satisfactory type and the patrolling squadrons have paid the price in casualties of their silent and unadvertised work.

During the year the Navy added to its lists two specially designed seaplane carriers, the "Furious" and the "Argus." Originally built as fast cruisers with a long range armament they were adapted shortly after launch to their new work. The upper deck in either case was free from encumbrances—in the "Argus" entirely so and in the "Furious" forward and aft the bridge and funnels. It was intended that aeroplanes should fly from the decks and after the flight alight again on the decks, the ship heading into the wind to simplify the task. In practice it would seem that most pilots preferred to alight in the sea alongside. The machine was then lifted on board and was re-fitted with wings and such other parts as were damaged by the sea water. Pilots are more expensive than aeroplanes and the cost of new wings, tailplanes, etc., is but little in the general expenditure of a great war.

As the high value of the aeroplane in naval warfare began to be understood it became the practice for the bigger ships of war each to carry one or two aeroplanes (not seaplanes). These were launched by the method indicated in the article on the R.A.F. A platform was laid down over two big guns and from this the aeroplane took to flight, the ship steaming into the wind to reduce the necessary run. The aeroplane on the completion of the reconnaissance either alighted in the sea or flew to the nearest land.

Other Navies, the French and the Italian, also employed seaplane carriers but in each case one understands that only flying boats and seaplanes were carried. The land aeroplane was not used. An illustration is given in the Italian section of an Italian seaplane ship with her cargo festooned round her sides.

The Germans apparently made no use of seaplane ships as far as one can gather, though individual ships of war carried aeroplanes on occasion. The Wolff, at one time an elusive terror of the seas, had one or two aeroplanes as part of her equipment though little is known as to when and where they were used. German naval effort except in regard to isolated raiders and to submarines was confined to the North Sea, consequently the airship served the purpose of reconnaissance better than would an aeroplane.

One of the London Balloon-Aprons.

THE AIRSHIP.

The airship improved steadily in so far as Germany is concerned until the armistice stopped all military effort. The principal use of the airship is undoubtedly for naval reconnaissance and for raiding by night. At one time the aeroplane provided a satisfactory answer to airship attack made under cover of darkness as the heights attained by airships were not great—13,000 to 14,000 feet. Towards the end of hostilities the Zeppelin was capable of reaching a height of 20,000 feet and could cruise at that height for lengthy periods. Hence the task of the defences both on the earth and in the air was greatly increased. It is conceivable that raiding under these conditions might have been profitable to the enemy. The attack now known as "The Silent Raid" was arranged in accordance with this principle of flight at extreme altitudes but it failed entirely as a result of the entirely unsuitable weather encountered when at a height of 20,000 feet over England.

Anti-aircraft defence would be quite capable of dealing with the new menace after the necessary modifications in materiel had been made. The chief drawback in home defence during a war in which aircraft were undergoing their first trial, lay in the fact that the best machines were required in the field until construction caught up to the demand.

The British while designing and constructing large rigid airships of the Zeppelin type were unable during the war to produce any which would have been of use in operations. Time sets a limit on all things and war invariably ends when equipment and organisation is about to attain perfection. England made great use of the non-rigid airship which had been developed in this country to a stage not yet attained elsewhere. The small "Blimps" and the larger S.S.'s and North Sea types each proved of high value in sea warfare, though their value in land operations was negligible. No German Submarine Commander had much liking for the airships which dogged his path through European waters.

KITE BALLOONS AT SEA.

The Kite balloon, at one time discredited because it was expected to carry out work for which it was not designed, found one of its

A Brandenburg Seaplane looping over the coast. Machines of this type for a time gave the Germans the Command of the Air over the North Sea.

H.M.S. Furious, Seaplane-Carrier, showing the long forward launching deck.

principal uses in one branch of sea warfare. Towed behind a ship of war it flew as a protective eye over the movements of the great convoys of ships which brought food and men to Europe.

At one time the shipping losses—especially in the Mediterranean which the gallant and resourceful Otto von Hersing had made his hunting ground—rose to a dangerous figure and every plan to reduce them failed or was only of moderate success. The kite balloon was then employed and with almost startling suddenness the losses decreased and convoy after convoy passed from port to port unscathed.

Improvements in design made it possible for these balloons to be drawn through the air at high speeds without resultant instability.

ARMAMENT AND ARMOUR IN AIRCRAFT.

The most common form of armament in British aircraft was a machine gun of the Lewis type, the design of which is peculiarly suitable for aerial work. These guns were mounted in various manners, some fixed rigidly along the fuselage in front of the pilot and firing between the propellor blades by means of special gearing. In this case the aeroplane itself was used in aiming at enemy targets. In the rear seat of two-seaters and in the bows of multiple engined

Little detail is available to those not employed in the Air Ministry as to the manner in which armour was fitted, nor is it possible easily to find what grades or thickness of steel were employed.

The aeroplane of the future, large, swift and easy of manoeuvre, will, when equipped for war, almost certainly be comparatively heavily armoured. Possibly, as in the case of the Navy, the newer theory will be that effective gun power and speed will more than counterbalance the risks attendant on light armouring. The contrary view that increased gun power should be met by increased armour protection may perhaps be held, but one thinks this to be unlikely.

THE END.

The war is over and the lethargy of peace is again with us for a space. The forced progress in aeronautics brought about by the demands of the fighting forces has ceased and the Industry is groping for direction into the necessities of civil aviation.

Little is known as to what can be done or what is required. The time is however comparatively distant when the design of the commercial aeroplane will be so individual in character as to make it of little use for warlike purposes. For years to come the large commercial aeroplane will be a potential bomb dropper possessed of wide range and a high ceiling. Even the fast sporting aeroplanes will not be without value as scouts or as fighting aircraft for the adventurous.

The future is hidden from our sight, but it is almost a platitude to say even at this date that aeronautics will bring about a fundamental change in the daily habits of our lives. We have seen what aircraft can do as a weapon of war while yet in an early stage of development. Can any doubt that the future possibilities of aeronautics in war and peace are so immense as to be beyond all human vision?

H.M.S. Argus, a Seaplane-Carrier in which the funnels are led horizontally aft, thus giving a flush deck.

A British Flying Boat, of the F.2a. type made practicable by Lieut.-Col. John Porte, photographed from another boat.

machines and flying-boats the Scarff rotating mounting was used, the observer thus having a large arc of fire. There was in truth very little difference in the manner of mounting guns in any of the great armies.

The French made extensive use of the Hotchkiss automatic gun which, while not entirely satisfactory in land warfare, did excellent work in the air, and they also used with some success towards the the end of the war a " cannon " of 37 mm. bore, which fired through the airscrew-boss of a geared-down V-type engine.

The German aerial arm used in general either the Spandau or Parabellum machine guns, which resembled closely the Vickers and Lewis machine guns common in Allied armies. The larger German aircraft and contact patrol machines were fitted with a 22 mm. automatic gun firing an explosive or incendiary shell six inches in length. These shells were clipped into chargers holding twelve rounds, the charger sliding into the top of the breech. As in the case of the Vickers gun it is operated by recoil action. This gun which has shown its value during the closing operations of the war is about 3'6" in length, and weighs complete with mounting and one charger, under 100 lbs.

There is evidence that a larger gun is employed in giant aeroplanes but few details have been permitted to leak out as to its form and capabilities.

As the size and reliability of aircraft increases there is little doubt that guns of considerably greater calibre will be fitted. The day is not far off when three inch and larger guns specially designed for the purpose will be mounted in aircraft and will be employed against other aircraft and against land defences. There is naturally no limit to the size of guns which it will be possible to carry at a future date.

As with armament so with armour. Tentative attempts were made in early machines to protect the pilot but the armour in such cases rarely consisted of more than a steel seat-plate which did little more than retard the passage of the projectile without entirely stopping its progress save at extreme ranges and in the case of glancing shot. Machines in the beginning of the war were already sufficiently laden with all manners of instruments and gear without the additional weight even of a small steel plate.

Later, as the efficiency of aircraft increased, efforts were made by the Germans to put adequate armour on the aeroplanes set aside for contour fighting. Such armour was intended only to protect against rifle and machine gun fire and not in any way against anti-aircraft guns. There are no aeroplanes yet in existence capable of carrying armour of such thickness as would deflect or stop shells or large shell fragments.

In the British Forces a certain amount of armour was placed round the engine or engines in some machines, as it was held that the smallest fragment of a projectile often sufficed to put an engine out of action and it was known that many pilots paid special attention to inflicting injury on motors. The engine provides a bigger and not less vulnerable target than does the aviator.

A British Fighting Pilot changing a double Lewis drum on the top gun of an S.E.5a.

THE WORLD'S AEROPLANES.

(Based on the 1919 Jane's All the World's Aircraft, with
additional material from the 1914, 1916, 1917 and 1918 editions)

ARRANGED IN ALPHABETICAL ORDER OF NATIONALITY

(WITH NOTES ON THE DEVELOPMENTS OF NAVAL AND

MILITARY AERONAUTICS IN EACH NATION).

ARGENTINE.

Aerial Journals :—

Boletin del Ae. C. Argentino, Avenida de Mayo, 646, Buenos Ayres. Monthly.

Aerial Societies :—

Aero Club Argentino, Avenida Alvear, 1325, Buenos Ayres.

MILITARY AVIATION.

The Argentine Government decided in 1912, in collaboration with the Aero Club, Argentino, to establish a military flying school and balloon school on a sound basis.

First of all, the military school at Palomar was established and several pilots were trained, the ground at Villa Lugano being used for balloons. It was hoped to have at the end of 1914 a perfectly organised military aviation service.

The Military Aerodrome of El Palomar is equipped with half-a-dozen *Henry Farman* 50 h.p. Gnôme biplanes, for primary training, and about a dozen Blériot and Morane-Saulnier type 80 h.p. Gnôme monoplanes, for advanced training.

Most of these machines were built at the carpentry attached to the aerodrome, only the motors being imported from Europe.

The aerodrome is under the command of Commandante Alejandro Obligado.

The carpentry and repair works are in charge of Sr. Edmundo Lucius.

Fifty-three aero-engines were available on Jan 1st, 1918, in the Argentine.

BEST ARGENTINE FLIGHTS IN 1918.

13th of April : Crossing of the Cordillera de Los Andes by Teniente Luis C. Candelaria, piloting a Morane-Saulnier Parasol of 80 H.P. from Zapala (R. Argentina) to Cunco (Rio de Chile). Distance, 200 km.   Maximum height, 4000 metres.

23rd of May : Flight from El Palomar (Province of Santiago del Estero) to Tucumán on a Voisin, Salmson engine, 140 h.p. Pilot Teniente Benjamin Matienzo ; passenger, Edmundo Lucius. Distance, Palomar to Tucumán and back, total 1400 km. Total time, 12 hours. Mean height, 900 metres.

ARGENTINE FLYING SCHOOLS.

El Palomar. Escuola Militar de Aviación. Director Tet. Coronel Uriburu, actualmente Teniente Coronel ALEJANDRO OBLIGADO.

San Fernando : Civilian School Director-Founder, Aviador Marcel Paillete and Aviador Teodoro Fels

Villa Lugano : Civilian School Director-Founder, Aviador Pablo Castaibert.

Quilmes : Civilian School Director-Founder, Aviador Edmundo Marechal.

José C. Paz : Civilian School Director-Founder, Aviador Luis A. Pardo.

Longchamps : Civilian School Director-Founder, Aviador

ARGENTINE MILITARY AVIATION,

The following have passed through the Military School :—

First Course, begun Nov. 4, 1912 :

Teniente de Navio Melchor Escola, Capitán Raúl E. Goubat, Capitán Anibal Brihuega, Teniente Pedro Zanni, Teniente Baldomero Biedma, Teniente Saturno Perez Ferreyra, Teniente Carlos

ARGENTINE AVIATION.

Gimenez Kramer, Teniente Leopoldo Casavega, Teniente Carlos Ferreyra, Sargento 1° Francisco Sanchez.

Teniente 1° Alfredo Agneta (killed 18 of October, 1914, in an accident in a Nieuport 100 H.P.)

Sub-Teniente Manuel Origone (killed 19 of January, 1913, in an accident on a Blériot 50 H.P. during a flight to Mar del Plata.)

Second Course, begun in August, 1913 :

Capitán Juan M. Pueta, Teniente 1° Elisendo Pissano, Teniente 1° Edgardo Benavente, Teniente 1° Enrique Padilla, Teniente 1° José E. Campos, Teniente 1° Agustin Varona.

Third Course, begun in June, 1914 :

Capitán Angel Zuloaga, Teniente 1° Alberto Gonzales Albarracín, Teniente 1° Antonio Parodi, Teniente 1° Atilio Cataneo, Teniente 1° Mario Godoy, Teniente 1° Julio García Fernandez.

Sargento 1° Ramón Alderete, Sargento 1° Segundo Gomez.

Cabo 1° Abraham Jalil (killed on 27th of November, 1914. Killed while practising on a Farman.)

Fourth Course, begun in August of 1915.

Teniente 1° (Oriental) Cesareo Berisso, Alferez Esteban Cristi.

Sub-Teniente (Reserva) Martín Pico, Sub-Teniente (Reserva) Edmundo Lucius, Sub-Teniente (Reserva) Alfredo Sosa, Sub-Teniente (Reserva) Enrique Molina, Sub-Teniente (Reserva) Enrique Torres.

Fifth Course, begun in September of 1916.

Capitán (Bolivian) José Alarcón (killed on 23rd of January, 1917, while flying for his certificate on a Farman). Capitán (Bolivian) René Parejas, Teniente (Bolivian) Horacio Vasquez, Teniente (Peruvian) Enrique Ruiz (killed on 13th of March, at Mercedes, while flying over the triangular Military Course in a Blériot 50 H.P. No. 111), Teniente (Peruvian) Guillermo Protzel, Guardia Marina (Peruvian) Ismael Montoya, Guardia Marina (Peruvian) Roberto Velazco, Teniente 1° (Argentine) Jorge Manni, Teniente José Rosasco, Teniente Martín Salinas Gomez, Teniente Luis Candelaria, Teniente Benjamin Matienzo, Teniente Valentin Campero, Teniente Argilioo T. Vadela Orito, Teniente Victoriano Martinez de Alegria, Teniente Adolfo C. Udry, Teniente Otón Mantovani, Teniente Florencio D. Parravicini.

Also the following N.C.O.'s :

Sargento 1° Dante Ferrari, Sargento Pedro Mendez, Sargento Próspero Sianja, Sargento Liborio Fernandez, Sargento José A. Sábatto, Sargento Luis T. Romero, Cabo 1° Juan C. Goggi, Cabo 1° Pedro Oyarzabal, Sargento 1° Luis Barruffaldi, Sargento Angel C. Albornóz (killed on 26th of December, 1917, while training on a 50 h.p. Blériot).

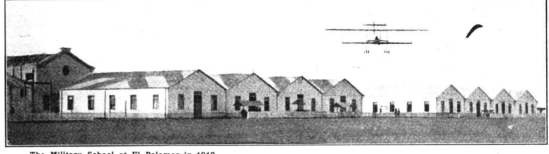

The Military School at El Palomar in 1918.

Officers of the Argentine Air Service—Capitan Anibas Briuhega, Tte. Leopoldo Casavega, Cap. Raul E. Goubat, Tte. Baldomoro Biedma, Tte. Pedro Zanni, Tte. S. Ferreyra.

Officer Pilots of the Argentine Air Service.

Argentine N.C.O. Pilots—Sargente I° D. Ferrari, Sargente Pedro Oyargatal, Sargente I° J. Sabathe, Sargente I° Fernandez, Sargente Luis T. Romere, Sargente I° L. Baruffaldi, Sargente I° Pedro Mondez, Sargente I° P. Seaya, Sargente Juan C. Coggi.

AUSTRO-HUNGARIAN.

The Empire of Austria-Hungary having been broken up into various ungoverned sections, there is now no Air Service or Aircraft Industry to be described. The following matter brings the record of Austro-Hungarian aircraft up to the end of the War.

·MILITARY AVIATION : GENERAL.

In June, 1912, a central aeronautical committee was created, under the presidency of Prince Fürstenberg, to deal with the creation of a national aerial fleet. One of the objects was the perfection of the Austrian machines and factories.

In July, 1913, it was proposed to acquire six *Zeppelins*, to be stationed respectively at Vienna, Budapest, Innsbruck, Prag, Lemberg and Sarajewo.

In February, 1914, the military aviation corps was reorganised and formed into a battalion of four companies stationed at Vienna, Cracow, Sarajewo and Goerz.

In March, 1914, a prize of 12,000 kroner was offered by the Minister of War as follows :—Armed two-seater, gun to have arc of fire 120 degrees, 30 degrees elevation and 60 degrees depression. Useful load 1764 lbs. (800 ks.). Minimum climb 6,500 ft. (2,000 m.) in 45 minutes from times of starting, to alight in ploughed field.

A prize of 13,000 kroner for the machine with the best speed variation.

In June, 1914, the airship *Korting* (*M 3*) was wrecked by collision with an aeroplane. All were killed in both.

ARMY SECTION.

At end of July, 1914, there were :—

60 monoplanes.—*Etrich-Taube, Albatros, Lohner-Daimler.*

50 biplanes.—*Lohner-Daimler* and *Albatros.*

The majority of the aeroplanes used by the Austrians on active service have been of German make, or have been made by Austrian branches of the big German firms, and have frequently had German pilots.

NAVAL SECTION.

A large number of seaplanes were in use. Most of them are of German make, and others built by the Lohner Aircraft Works of Vienna, or by Austrian branches of German firms.

The Austrian naval pilots have done much consistently good flying, from the purely naval point of view.

THE AUSTRO-HUNGARIAN AIRCRAFT INDUSTRY.

(BY A FOREIGN CORRESPONDENT.)

The German journal "Motor" contained recently a report on the Austrian-Hungarian aircraft trade during the War, as rendered below, leaving an impression of the retardment of aeroplane developments in that country too from official Government efforts of pushing their own products, inferior to private results, and showing further that Austria differed in one respect from most other countries, and thus in being not held up in output for lack of aero-engines, but rather from the insufficient number of works turning out planes.

When war started, Austria-Hungary was the least prepared aeronautically of all the big powers, lacking financial support going no further than for a few Etrich "Taube" monoplanes and Lohner "Arrow" biplanes of national manufacture, besides a few German-made aeroplanes. Only the Lohner Body Works and the Albatros and Aviatik branches built aircraft in quantity, and not till during the War the Ufag (Ungarische Flugzeugwerke A. G.) in Assod and the Lloyd Works in Hungary were formed, the former building *Lohner* biplanes under license, the latter the *D.F.W.* type.

So the army authorities required German support highly, a large number of *Albatros, Rumpler* (*RuC1*), *D.F.W.* (*Mars*) and *Aviatik* biplanes being supplied, while the home-produced aero motors, Austro-Daimler and Hiero (by the Ersler, Warschalowski Co.) proved efficient.

The C.O. of the airship department, Colonel Uzelac, had few officer pilots, engaged some German civil aviators, as Kriger (Bill) and conscripted some in the service of German firms, like the Fokker pilot Franz Kuntner and the L.V.G. one, Alois Stiplocheck.

The Russian opponent air service was, however, not too effective for a start, and so the home industry, which proved a necessity, found time to develop. The Lloyd works brought out types of their own, and the Albatros establishment went especially ahead, managed by the former chief engineer, Gabriel, of the Johannisthal plant, thanks to good workmanship.

Large contracts were executed too by Fokker, and thus twelve flight companies had been established when Italy entered the War. The fighting troops were separated from the home, being centralized as a "Flight Arsenal" under the command of Major Leidl.

The Aspern aerodrome, by Vienna, was the chief acceptance point, further ones being erected later at Vienna Neustadt and Budapest.

To introduce new types, the *Brandenburg* biplane was ordered, Commerce Councellor Camillo Castiglione forming a combine of the Hansa, Brandenburg, Vienna Albatros and Ufag concerns, being all turned to the production of Brandenburg aircraft.

The large Skoda works (known for their 305 mm. howitzers) financed the "Oeffag" works in Vienna Neustadt (Oesterreichische Flugzeugfabrik A. G.) which produced a type of their own, as did now the Lloyd works, theirs being also manufactured by Dr. Guttmann's W.F.K. works (Wiener Karosserie Fabrik) changing from body to aeroplane work.

All before-mentioned types did well on active service, which cannot, however, be said of the aircraft designed by Professor Knoller, which was pushed by the Government Factory, and which the Aviatik, Lohner, W.F.K. and Thone & Fiala (a former engineering works), were forced to build against their will. The result was that large sums were expended and several good pilots killed in test flights before the *Knoller* aeroplanes were sent unflown to eternal sleep in the stores.

So far, all aeroplanes had been two-seaters, with the exception of a few *Fokkers*. The Ufag made twin-engined aircraft to Brandenburg pattern and proved a failure, as did a giant aircraft to the design of Professor Dr. Richard von Mieses, of which much was expected, and only cost lots of money.

But the period of aerial engagements came, and the *Brandenburg K. D.* single-seater proved to some extent a success, but was superseded by the *DIII*, borrowed from the German Albatros Company, and built in hundreds for active service by the Oeffag.

Next the Hungarian General Engine Works "Mag" (Allgemeine Maschinen Fabrik), in Budapest, acquired the licence for building *Fokkers*, and not till 1917 did a pure Austrian product put up a good performance, this being the biplane scout of Engineer Berg, at the Vienna Aviatik works, of a speed of 190-200 kilometres per hour and climbing to 3,000 feet in 2¼ minutes, with a 185 h.p. Daimler motor. So the "Berger" commenced, the type being ordered from almost every Austrian and Hungarian aircraft works.

A good single-seater was turned out, too, by the Phönix works, being the new manufacturing establishment of the Austrian Albatros Company, remaining a plant for turning out experimental craft.

During the last part of the War, big aeroplane orders were again given to Germany, more than 100 twin-engined *Gothas* (*GIV*) being ordered from the L.V.G. firm, and some experimental aeroplanes from Rumpler, Pfalz and Fokker.

The Oeffag acquired the rights for the twin-engined *Friedrichshafen*, but Austria broke down so quickly that only some *Gothas* saw active service.

The War did not help the Austro-Hungarian aircraft works to a strong financial position, as neither of the active C. O. of the "Flight Arsenal," Major von Petroczu, nor his successor, Colonel von Prochaska, succeeded in speeding office matters. Thus the works had to wait for months, or even years, to have their accounts paid, the lack of raw materials was in a hopeless position, the lack of skilled workmen felt still more hardly, and private activities were hampered by petty official inspection.

When the War ended, the Government refused to take over half-finished products, or materials only employable in aeroplane construction, in spite of all agreements. The Austrian does not pay any accounts later than August, the works having thus perforce to reduce their staffs, Phönix, for instance, from 1,700 to 100 workmen, while the Hungarian Government continued to pay, but then did not allow any dismissals, the result being only that the men did no work for high wages.

Finally, the Government "Aeraric" aircraft works should be referred to, a giant plant, formed in Fischamend under military control, two more in Aspern and Szeged.

Later, so-called "flight parks" in Vienna Neustadt and Graz-Thalerhof, showing an output of Lohner and Brandenburg biplanes that would have ruined any private enterprize. These establishments were to supply cheap school machines for the training, being exclusively carried out military in 22 "Ersatz" reserve companies, but in fact hampered the school service, being unable to cope with the breakages, and three privately-produced aeroplanes could have been made at the cost of one Government aircraft.

AGO. (Austrian Branch of German Firm.)

THE AGO SEA PURSUIT BIPLANE.

In its general lines this machine does not differ much from all the flying boats of the *Ago* type. It does offer, however, features that are original and worthy of mention. Most striking is the structure of the wing cell in which no wires are employed.

The wing cell may be considered as consisting of two cross-networks, each made up of a front spar and a rear spar and of adjacent struts in inclined planes connecting the spars, all converging toward the centre of the "star" located midway between upper and lower wings. The struts are of polished steel tubing with a fairing of laminated wood less than one mm. thick, providing a good streamlining effect.

General Dimensions.

Span : Upper Plane, 8.00 m.
Span : Lower Plane, 7.38 m.
Chord : Both Planes, 1.50 m.
Gap Between Planes : 1.65 m.
Length Overall : 7.62 m.
Length of Hull : 6.50 m.
Maximum Width of Hull : 1.00 m.
Motor : Warschalowski, 218 h.p.
Propeller : Diameter, 2.72 m.

Control cables to the ailerons pass close to the struts of the turret and lead to the upper plane. Each aileron is about 1.40 m. long and 0.40 m. wide.

The constructional design of the hull, the great care with which the exposed parts have been shaped, the complete covering of cables and control wires, and the streamlined shape of the hull, all show a desire to cut down head resistances as much as possible. Similar care is shown in all details of construction to reduce to a minimum the weight of the machine without detriment to its strength.

The hull is 6½ m. long; width at the step, 0.95 m.; maximum width, 1 m.; distance from bow to step, 3.45 m.; height of step, 0.16 m. The shape of the body with the necessary lining at the bow and because of a careful laying of the side and bottom plating approaches very much the shape of a solid body of fairly good streamline form.

The wing floats are spaced 5 m. apart. They are of streamline section, with flat sides, attached to the planes by means of one forward strut and two rear struts, with cross wire bracing between the struts.

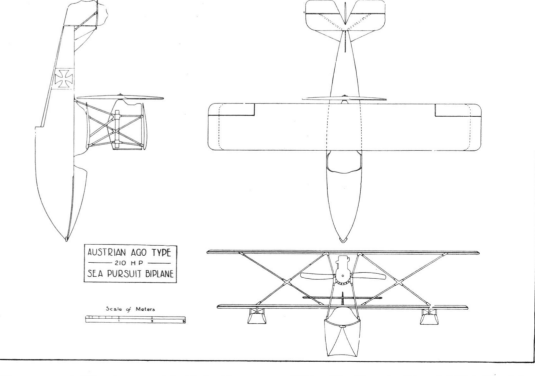

AUSTRIAN AGO TYPE
— 210 H P —
SEA PURSUIT BIPLANE

Scale of Meters

The empennage is 2.38 m. in span, sustained in front by a vertical fin of very thin laminated wood, by two stays and two wire cables.

Control wires of the rudder and elevators run through the fin. The rudder is 1.40 m. high by 0.80 m. wide.

The data given out concerning the motor is as follows :—

"Motor : Hiero Flugmotor, Osterr; Ind. Werke Warschalowski, Eissler and Co. A-G. 6 cylinders; type, HN1096. It develops 218 h.p. at 1,400 r.p.m. Weight, 314 kilos. It is equipped with Bosch magnetos and small starting magnetos. Propeller : 200 h.p. Hiero 6 cylinder; diameter, 2.72 m.; pitch, 2.25-2.40."

A.M.A. Allgemeine Maschinen Aktien Gesellschaft Aircraft department in Budapest, Vaczi-ut 141/43.

ETRICH Pioneer aviator, Igo Etrich, designed a bird-like monoplane as the Taube (Dove), which first flew in 1910. Evolved into a two-seater for military use by 1912, it became widely used by the Austro-Hungarian Air Service and by Germany, in the latter country built by most aircraft manufacturing companies (beginning with Rumpler). Much German construction took place after Igo Etrich waived German licence rights. Other Etrich aircraft followed but the company became part of Brandenburgische Flugzeugwerke in 1914.

LLOYD Aircraft Co., Ltd., Budapest.

Managed by the well-known military pilot Oberlieut. Bier, former director of Deutsche Flugzeug Werke in Liepzig, and building as branch " D.F.W's " under license.

The altitude record with three passengers stands to the credit of Oberlieut. Bier on a *Lloyd* biplane since the Vienna 1914 Meeting.

LOHNER, Jacob & Sons, Aircraft and Body Builders, Vienna.

Creator of the tractor *Arrow* biplane, generally adopted by Germany. Since the Etrich Dove Manufacturing Company is defunct, the only producer of an original Austrian model and chief supplier of the Army with a pre-war yearly output of 100-150 machines.

Piloted by Oberlieut Blaschke, the *Lohner* biplane won second place in the Berlin-Vienna race, 1911, and all later national competitions up to the Schicht circuit, 1914, as well as leading place in the various Vienna meetings.

Features : One single cock-pit for pilot and passenger, the latter sitting behind ; a special tube landing chassis and streamlined front body part and propeller cap, adopted too in the later *Etrich* " Tauben."

Numerous "flying boats" of the types shown herewith have been built by the Lohner firm during the war, and are said to have a very good performance.

A 1915-16 Lloyd Two-Seater Biplane.

Lohner Arrow biplane, Type B, 1913

THE LOHNER TYPE L FLYING BOAT—1915-18.

This is an enlarged machine of the *Lohner* type, retaining the swept back wings, which are typical of the *Lohner* aeroplanes.

There are six steel struts on either side and, two by two, are connected in transverse planes with steel tubes of 40 mm. outside diameter.

General Dimensions.
Span : Upper Plane, 16.20 m.
Length : 10.25 m.
Bomb Carrying Capacity : 440 kg.
Weight Loaded : 1,700 kg.
Maximum Speed : 105 km.p.h.
Motor : Austro-Daimler, 140-160 hp.

In form the ailerons are trapezoidal.

A Lohner Type L Flying Boat.

M.L.F. Motorluftfahrzeug Gesellschaft, Vienna. Oldest Austrian aircraft works, having built *Etrich* dove monoplanes and *Lohner* arrow biplanes, now manufacturing only the latter.

Ö-ALBATROS. Oesterreichische-Ungarische Albatros Flugzeug Werke G.m.b.H., Vienna, XXI Stadlar.

Owned by the former Ober-engineer Gabriel of the Berlin *Albatros* firm. Remained during the war as an experimental plant, with the allied Phönix firm as the production plant.

Ö-AVIATIK. Oesterreichische-Ungarische Flugzeug-fabrik Aviatik, G.m.b.H., Vienna.

Branch of the German firm. Towards the end of the war produced the famous Berg scout to the Oesterreichische Flug-zeugfabrik, A.G., Wiener-Neustadt (known as the *Oeffag*). Founded during the war and financed by the Skoda Works.

OESTERREICHISCHE FLUGZEUG-FABRIK, A.G. Vienna-Neustadt.

Known as the *Oeffag*. Financed by the Skoda Works.

PHÖNIX AEROPLANE WORKS.

Vienna XXI–Stadlau.

Formed during the war by the engineer Gabriel, formerly of the Berlin Albatros Company, who upon the outbreak of hostilities transferred his activities to his native country, starting the Austrian Albatros works and now running the two concerns so that the Phönix firm undertakes the quantity production, while the O-Albatros carries out the experimental work.

A Brandenburg Two-Seater Biplane, built by the " Oeffag " in 1916.

An Austrian AVIATIK biplane, captured by the Italians.   *Reproduced from "La Guerra," the Italian official publication.*

The first Austrian war-product Scout—The Brandenburg K Model and K.B. built by the Phönix Co.

A Phönix D.III 1918 type Single-seater. A Phönix Two-seater is seen in the background.

A Phönix Two-seater C.1 reconnaissance biplane of 1917-18. (230 h.p. Hiero Engine.)

The "Star-Strutter" Brandenburg D.I Scout of 1916-17, built by the Phönix Works.

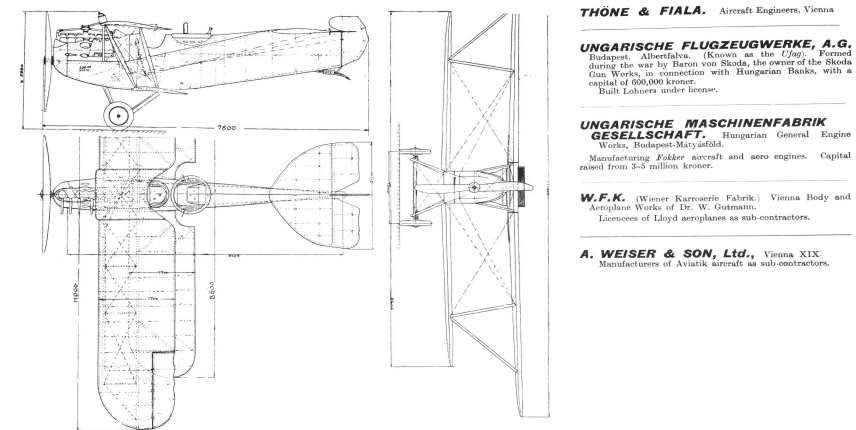

General Arrangement Drawings of the 1918 Phonix C.I reconnaissance Biplane.

THÖNE & FIALA.   Aircraft Engineers, Vienna

UNGARISCHE FLUGZEUGWERKE, A.G.
Budapest. Albertfalva. (Known as the *Ufag*). Formed during the war by Baron von Skoda, the owner of the Skoda Gun Works, in connection with Hungarian Banks, with a capital of 600,000 kroner.
   Built Lohners under license.

UNGARISCHE MASCHINENFABRIK GESELLSCHAFT.   Hungarian General Engine Works, Budapest-Mátyásföld.
   Manufacturing *Fokker* aircraft and aero engines. Capital raised from 3–5 million kroner.

W.F.K.   (Wiener Karroserie Fabrik.)   Vienna Body and Aeroplane Works of Dr. W. Gutmann.
   Licencees of Lloyd aeroplanes as sub-contractors.

A. WEISER & SON, Ltd.,   Vienna XIX.
   Manufacturers of Aviatik aircraft as sub-contractors.

BELGIAN.

Flying Grounds :—(All were in possession of the German Army, but are now reinstated as Belgian aerodromes.)

Berchem—St. Agathe.
Brasschaet (Military).
Camp de Casteau.
Etterbeek, near Brussels.
Kiewit.
St. Job (formerly private property of Baron de Caters).
Tenplaux (Military).

MILITARY AEROPLANES.

At the outbreak of war, the military air force consisted of twenty-four 80 h.p. Gnôme *H. Farman*, also various old school machines.

The military school was at Brasschaet, near Antwerp.

The course was as follows :

1.—*Theoretical Course.*—Lectures on meteorology, structure of aeroplanes, aviation motors, etc.

2.—*Practical.*—This, in addition to flight, consists of dismounting and replacing parts of aeroplanes and aerial motors, all general repairs, erecting hangars and aerial photography.

The school possessed nine hangars, of which three were Bessonneau type, three wooden, and three metal.

For 1913, the sum of £20,000 was expended for purchase of aeroplanes and the establishment of aerial squadrons at Antwerp, Liege, and Brasschaet.

These were organised into six squadrons of four units each. The full complement of each squadron is eight aviators, fifteen to twenty mechanics, etc., and six citizen soldiers.

A small but fairly efficient force had been created. It was almost extinguished. Later on new Belgian pilots were trained in France and England, and were equipped with French machines, largely Moranes, Voisins, Farmans. British machines such as B.Es., R.Es., and Sopwiths have also been supplied to the Belgian Army. On various occasions they have proved a useful adjunct to the Allies' forces operating in Flanders.

AEROPLANE FACTORIES.

Destroyed or adopted by the Germans.

BOLIVIAN.

MILITARY AVIATION.

A start in this direction was made in 1917, when Capts. Jose Alarcon and Renato Parejas, and Sub-Lieut. Horacio Vasquez were sent to El Palomar (Buenos Ayres) for training as aviators.

The first-named officer unfortunately lost his life on Jan. 23rd, 1917, while training, but the two others successfully graduated.

An aero-engine was imported during 1917 from the Argentine, apparently for the purpose of instruction.

CENTRAL AMERICAN, ETC.

General Note.—Nicaragua and S. Domingo have both purchased one or two aeroplanes for their military forces ; but nothing appears to have been done with them.

Gautamela had one aeroplane flown by Nannini, who was appointed military flying instructor.

Cuba had one, flown by Paris.

Two Belgian aviators with a Maurice Farman biplane, equipped for fighting and photography. The camera may be seen on the ground.

CHILEAN.

Aerial Societies:—

Aero Club de Chile, Santiago de Chile.

Aerial Journals:—

Auto y Aero. Santiago de Chile. (Monthly.)

MILITARY AVIATION.

Three engines were imported during 1917 from the Argentine for the construction of training machines.

MILITARY AEROPLANES.

The available force consisted of **18** machines when last communications were received :—

8 *Bleriots*, **4** *Brequets*, **1** *Voisin*, **4** *Sanchez-Besa*, **1** *Deperdussin*.

Aerodrome:—

Lo Espejo. (Four sheds and some portable hangars).

Flying Grounds:—

Lo Espejo. (Military Aerodrome.)

AVIATORS.

Military Flying Corps.

Concha, General, Inspector-Gen. of Aeronautics.	Leon, 1st Lt. A. G., Adjut.
	Larrain, C., Quarter-master.
Donoso, Dr. R. U., Surg.	Prado, Copt. M. V., Commant.

Military Pilots.

Ampuero, Sergt. A.	Page, Sergt. L. O.
Bello, Lt.	Perez, 1st Lt. E.
Cabezas, M.	Rojas, Sergt. F.
Cazarino, Lt.	Torres, 2nd Lt. J.
Conberas, Lt.	Verscheure, Sergt.
Conzalez, Sergt. F.	Valenzuela, 1st Lt. G.
Menadier.	Urgua, 1st Lt. A.

Private.	Killed.
Cadezas, M.	1914.
Donoso, P. L.	Mery, Lieut.
Figuroa.	

Note.—No fresh information has been obtainable during 1919, beyond the fact that in 1917 six Bristol monoplanes with Le Rhône engines of 110 h.p. were sent to Brazil by the British Government in part payment for two battleships building for Chile in British yards at the outbreak of war and taken over by the British Navy. On one of these a Chilean officer flew over the Andes to Argentina.

CHINESE.

FIRST AVIATORS.

Gunn, T. (*Instructor*).	Tsai Tao, Prince	Wee Gee.
Lym, A. (*Instructor*).	Tsing, Col.	Yoa, Lt.
Lee, Y. L.	Poa, Lt.	

MILITARY AVIATION.

In March, 1913, orders were placed for six 80 h.p. *Caudrons*, also for six 50 h.p., and a decision arrived at gradually to acquire a large force. A home-made aeroplane was built at Nanuan, in 1913.

In January, 1914. Art Lym was appointed flying instructor to the Chinese Army.

In the "White Wolf" operations, 1914, four of the *Caudrons* were employed, and found very effective in locating the enemy. No casualties to the machines occurred.

AERODROME.

The military school (*Caudron*) is at Nanyuen, Peking.

The chief instructor is Mr Zee Yee Lee, who learned to fly at the Bristol School on Salisbury Plain.

The Officer Commanding is Sao K. Y. Chen.

Two snapshots at a Chinese Aerodrome near Peking.

BRAZILIAN.

Aerial Societies :—

Aero Club Brazileiro, 31, Rua do Theatre. Rio de Janeiro. Founded 1911.

Aerial Journals :—

Aerophilo (Orgas Official do Aero Club).

Aviacao Nacional Avenida Rio Branco, 110, Rio de Janeiro. (Subscription : 5 milreis per annum, Brazil ; 8 milreis, foreign.) Monthly.

Flying Grounds :—

Ilha dos Euxadas, Bay of Guanabara, Rio. (Naval Air Stations and Flying School).

Aerodromo dos Affonssos, Rio de Janeiro. (Flying Ground, School of the Aero Club.)

Aeroplane Factories :—

Newspapers state that the Brazilian Government has been in " pourparlé " with Italian firms to make a big one in Rio, and the shopwork of the Naval School, Ilha dos Euxados, is fitting for to produce aeroplanes for the Navy.

Airscrew Factories :—

Internacional Fabrica de Helies, 139-145, Rua dos Invalidos, Rio de Janeiro.

NAVAL AVIATION.

Nine naval aviators, graduates of the naval flying school at Euxadas, were sent to England in January, 1917, for a course of advanced training and to be attached to the R.A.F. for war active service.

A number of naval officers also went to Italy for war experience.

MILITARY AVIATION.

This is still in the experimental stage, but plans are maturing for the development of the fifth arm of the Army, and it is contemplated to create in each state of the Union one, or several, federal flying grounds. To hasten this achievement, several state organisations have started public subscriptions tending to present to the federal government a number of military aeroplanes.

A big French commission arrived in Rio last October to create the aviation for the Army.

BRAZILIAN AVIATORS.

The following are the names of the Brazilian aviators (end of 1918) :—

Civil :—Santos Dumont, Edu. Chaves Bergmann, Cicero Marques.

Naval Aviators :

Araujo (O. de, Lieut.), Baudiera (R. V. F., Lieut.), *Barbedo (H. de), *Borges (Leitao), de Lamare (V. B., Lieut.), Epaminondas dos Santos (Sub-Lieut.), Filleto dos Santos (Sub-Lieut.), Godiuho (M. da C., Sub-Lieut.), Possolo (Eugenio), Lieut., killed through collision in the air in Eastbourne. Sá Earp (Fabio de, Lieut.), Silva Junior, Schoreth (Augusto), Lieut. Com.-Mecanico, Trompowsky (Armando), Lieut., Varady (Heitor), Lieut.,

Vasconcellos (M. A. P. de), Lieut.-Com., Victor de Carvalho (Sub-Lieut.), *Vieira de Mello.

* Those marked thus are Army Officers trained at the Naval School.

Machines (types flown in Rio) :—*Curtiss* Flying Boats (seaplane), *Standard* (seaplane), *Farman, Morane.*

Since September of 1918 aviation in Brazil has made great advances, but detailed information is lacking.

INSTRUCTORS AND PUPILS AT THE BRAZILIAN CHIEF FLYING SCHOOL AT ENXADAS.

BRITISH.

MILITARY AERONAUTICS.

THE British Flying Services have grown out of what was originally The Balloon Company, Royal Engineers, therefore it is necessary to deal with Military Aviation first, despite the correct precedence of the older Services. The Balloon Company was first commanded by Colonel Templer, R.E., then by Colonel Capper, R.E. (now Major-General).

In 1908, Colonel Capper did his best to encourage the production of an aeroplane by the late Samuel Franklin Cody, then employed at the Balloon Factory, R.E., at South Farnborough, Hants, on the production of War Kites. Colonel Capper and Mr. Cody had previously produced an airship.

Mr. Cody's aeroplane began to fly in 1909, and in the same year a Wright biplane was also acquired by the Army from the late Hon. Charles Rolls. Mr. Cody then left the Balloon Factory to experiment by himself, during 1910, on Laffan's Plain, Aldershot. Mr. Mervyn O'Gorman was appointed chief of the Balloon Factory.

On March 1st, 1911, The Air Battalion, R.E., was formed, to operate five aeroplanes and one or two small experimental airships.

No. 1 Aeroplane Section of The Air Battalion was formed later, with Captain J. D. B. Fulton, R.F.A., in command, the Airship and Balloon Company being under the command of Major Sir Alexander Bannerman, Bart, R.E. The Aeroplane Section was stationed at Lark Hill, on Salisbury Plain, officers and men living in the Artillery Camp at Bulford. Various French aeroplanes were purchased, including *Farmans, Bleriots,* and *Nieuports,* but no encouragement was given to British enterprise.

In the same year, the Army Aircraft Factory was formed, on what had been the Balloon Factory, R.E., and Mr. Mervyn O'Gorman remained in charge. The chief control of Army aircraft of all kinds was in the hands of Brigadier-General David Henderson, D.S.O., then Director of Military Training at the War Office.

THE FORMATION OF THE R.F.C.

During 1912, various developments took place. The Royal Flying Corps was formed from the old Air Battalion, and General Henderson became Director-General of Military Aeronautics. The Aircraft Factory was exalted into The Royal Aircraft Factory, ostensibly as an experimental workshop, though its subsequent growth before the war was so great as to give rise to the belief that it was intended to build all the Army's aeroplanes there, a belief increased by the fact that hardly any British aeroplanes of designs other than those produced by the R.A.F. were purchased, though a number of French machines were bought. Up to the outbreak of war, all engines on British Army aeroplanes were of French make, except for one or two Austrian engines, but from 1912 onwards, the R.A.F. was endeavouring to produce an aero-engine of its own design.

In the autumn of 1912, a Military Aeroplane Competition, open to the world, was held on Salisbury Plain, and the £5,000 prize offered for this was won by the late S. F. Cody, on a machine of his own make, with an Austro-Daimler engine.

When the R.F.C. was formed, it was supposed to consist of a Naval Wing and a Military Wing, each wing supplying pilots and machines to the other when required. Major F. H. Sykes was appointed Commandant Military Wing, and Captain Sueter, R.N., was made Director of the Air Department at the Admiralty. Also a joint Central Flying School was formed on Salisbury Plain (at Upavon), with Captain Godfrey Paine, M.V.O., R.N., as Commandant, and Lieut.-Col. Cooke, R.A., D.S.O., as Assistant-Commandant. In 1913, Major Hugh Trenchard, D.S.O., Royal Scots Fusiliers, became Assistant-Commandant.

In practice, Naval pilots assisted at Army Manœuvres in 1912 and 1913, but no Army pilots ever took part in Naval Manœuvres. The Central Flying School also held a large

Official Photograph.

THE R.F.C. in 1918. A group of Flying Officers of the R.F.C. on active service. It is stated officially that each of the pilots and observers in this group has brought down at least three German machines. The increasing altitude at which fighting now takes place is indicated by the pseudo-Arctic costumes worn by the crews of fighting machines.

majority of Army pupils, and ultimately became entirely Military.

By the beginning of 1913, the R.F.C. possessed thirteen aeroplanes in flying order—as proved by Mr. Joynson-Hicks, M.P., in the House of Commons early that year. At Army Manœuvres, in the Autumn of that year, something like fifty aeroplanes were got together, including half-a-dozen Naval machines attached to the "White" Army. During this year, the Aeronautical Inspection Department was formed, under Major Fulton, C.B., and became one of the best organised departments in the King's Services. Major Fulton (by then Lieut.-Col.) died in 1916, and his death was the most severe blow the R.F.C. has suffered by the death of any one officer.

THE ESTABLISHMENT.

In 1913, it was laid down that the establishment of the R.F.C. was to consist of seven squadrons of aeroplanes of 12 machines each, with 12 pilots, and a reserve of 12 machines and 12 pilots for each squadron. This figure was never reached up to the outbreak of war. Headquarters were built at Farnborough.

At the beginning of 1914, No. 1. Squadron, R.F.C., was stationed at Farnborough, No. 2 Squadron at Montrose, No. 3 and No. 4 Squadrons at Netheravon, on Salisbury Plain, but all squadrons were still below the establishment laid down.

In June of 1914, a concentration camp of these four squadrons, with the nucleus of a fifth squadron, then in process of formation at Farnborough, was formed at Netheravon. Representatives of all foreign powers, including Germany and Austria, visited the camp. The maximum number of aeroplanes capable of taking the air on one day did not exceed thirty, which may be taken as representing the effective strength of the R.F.C. at the outbreak of war.

WAR.

When war broke out, four squadrons of the R.F.C. were raised almost to establishment—but without the 100% reserve—by calling up civilian pilots who had previously joined the Corps as Special Reserve officers, and by taking over the best machines from the Central Flying School. Brigadier-General Henderson took command in the field. Major Trenchard left the C.F.S. and took command of R.F.C. Headquarters at Farnborough, and Major Brancker acted as Assistant Director at the War Office. A fifth squadron came into being soon after the outbreak of war.

The increase of the personnel of the R.F.C. was begun and continued with energy, and enormous expansions took place. Aeroplanes, chiefly to designs produced by the R.A.F., were ordered in large quantities from firms which, at the outbreak of war, were on the verge of closing down, and all sorts of firms who had never made aeroplanes were induced to come into the Aircraft Industry. Motor firms were turned on to make engines, also largely of R.A.F. designs.

Later on, General Henderson returned from the front, and Major Trenchard, promoted by successive steps to Major-General, commanded until the end of 1917. He has been on various occasions thanked in despatches from the Commander-in-Chief in France for the excellent work done by the R.F.C., under his able leadership.

In 1915, Major Brancker, after seeing active service in France, was promoted to Brigadier-General, and in 1916 was appointed Director of Air Organisation. In April, 1917, he was further promoted to Deputy-Director General of Military Aeronautics, and Lieut.-Col. L. E. O. Charlton, D.S.O., was appointed Director of Air Organisation, with temporary rank of Brigadier-General.

At the end of 1915 and beginning of 1916, agitation was raised in Parliament and out on account of the superiority in speed and climb of the German machines over the British. This agitation was led by Lord Montagu, of Beaulieu, Mr. Pemberton-Billing, M.P., Mr. Joynson-Hicks, M.P., Captain Bennet-Goldney, M.P., and others. As a result, a Committee of Enquiry was appointed to investigate the affairs of the R.F.C., and its report, published at Christmas, 1916, disclosed various defects, many of which have since been remedied. Another Committee visited the Royal Aircraft Factory, at Farnborough, and advised drastic changes, which have been more or less effected.

General Henderson during 1916, had been promoted to Lieut.-General, and had been appointed a member of the Army Council. An enquiry into the administration of the Royal Naval Air Service was refused.

At the beginning of 1917, a fresh agitation arose for the better equipment of the R.F.C., as the Germans had put a number of "destroyers" of a new type into the air towards the end of 1916, which did considerable damage to the older types of British aeroplanes.

During 1915-1916-1917, the whole organisation of the R.F.C. was altered and expanded out of all recognition. The old five squadrons were vastly extended. Wings containing a number of squadrons apiece and commanded by a Lieut.-Colonel were formed. Wings were assembled into Groups, with a full Colonel in command. Groups again were formed into Brigades, each with a Brigadier-General in command. And Brigades were grouped into Divisions, each under a Major-General.

The R.F.C. in France remained during 1917 under the command of Major-General Trenchard. Lieut.-General Sir David Henderson, K.C.B., remained Director General of Military Aeronautics. The Headquarters work of the R.F.C. grew to such an extent that De Keyser's Hotel, at Blackfriars, was taken over, renamed Adastral House, and turned into a species of War Office on its own account during 1916.

Later the administration of the R.F.C. was removed to the Air Board Office at the Hotel Cecil, Strand, W.C., and, as towards the end of 1917 even this proved too small for the various combined departments of the R.N.A.S. and R.F.C. and Ministry of Munitions (all operating under the Air Board, *q.v.*), other premises were also commandeered for the ever-growing mass of officers in home billets.

The growth of the R.F.C. warranted the expansion. Flying schools on a big scale were opened in Canada, in Egypt, and in France.

During the early part of 1917, the Germans, as stated by Mr. Ian MacPherson on March 13th, in the House of Commons, "reinforced and rested during the winter, put up a serious opposition," but, thanks to the high *moral* of the R.F.C. under General Trenchard, the R.F.C. continued to do its Army work. As newer machines of superior types were produced, the Corps regained its mastery in the air, and, despite heavy losses during the fighting at Easter, 1917, before Arras, by the end of the year had definitely established its complete superiority over the enemy.

By April 1st, 1918, when the Royal Air Force came into being, the R.F.C. was incomparably the finest aerial fighting force in the world, and by common consent in the Corps the credit for its efficiency and *moral* was given to General Trenchard.

In July of 1917, Brig.-Gen. Brancker was promoted to Major-General, while holding the post of Director-General of Military Aeronautics, and in September, Brevet Lieut.-Col. (temp. Brig.-Gen.) J. M. Salmond, D.S.O., was promoted to Major-General, on the expansion of the Home Training Brigade to the size of a Division.

In October, Major-General Salmond was made Director-General of Military Aeronautics. Lieut.-General Sir David Henderson being "deputed to undertake special work"—the duty in question being the drawing up of the organisation of the new Royal Air Force. General Brancker was sent to Egypt. Brig.-General Charles Longcroft was promoted to temp. Major-General, Commanding Home Training Division, with Brig.-Gen. Ludlow-Hewitt as Inspector of Training. General Salmond also became a member of the Army Council.

In December, Brig.-General E. L. Ellington was gazetted Deputy-Director-General of Military Aeronautics.

In the last few days of December, Major-General Trenchard, C.B., D.S.O., was promoted to K.C.B., and at about the same date he handed over the command of the R.F.C. in the Field to General Salmond, he himself coming back to England to take over the office of Chief of the Air Staff in the newly formed Air Ministry.

The R.F.C. continued in existence, daily increasing its superiority over the enemy, until March 31st, when it ceased to exist, and became a part of the Royal Air Force, which came officially into being on April 1st.

ANTI-AIRCRAFT DEFENCES.

During the latter part of 1917, great alterations were made in the organisation of the London Air Defence Area by Major-General Ashmore, C.M.G., M.V.O., R.A., formerly a Brig.-General, R.F.C. Proper gun and searchlight co-operation was established. Special "destroyer" squadrons of the R.F.C. were stationed in suitable positions, and operated highly effectively against German raiders. The proof of the efficacy of the organisation was given on Whit Sunday, 1918, when a raiding squadron lost five machines, certainly observed, and probably others which fell in the sea. This proved to be the last German raid over this country. The efficacy of the London Air Defence Area seems to prove that a permanent Air Defence organisation for the whole of the British Isles, concentrated under a single command, is one of the military necessities of the future.

THE R.N.A.S.

Naval flying began in 1911, when three Naval officers and a lieutenant of the Royal Marine Light Infantry were permitted by their Lordships of the Admiralty to draw full pay while being taught to fly at the Royal Aero Club ground at Eastchurch, on three *Short* biplanes lent by Mr. Frank McClean, a member of the Club. Mr. G. B. Cockburn, another member of the Club, gave his services gratuitously as instructor for some six months, while teaching these officers to fly.

When the Royal Flying Corps was formed in 1912, these officers, and some three or four others who had learned to fly at their own expense, were located at Eastchurch as the Naval Wing, R.F.C. An Air Department was formed at the Admiralty, under Captain Murray F. Sueter, R.N., who had already been concerned with airship work. (See Airship Section.)

From this nucleus, the Naval Wing expanded. Coast defence and experimental stations were formed before the war at Calshot, Isle of Grain (Kent), Felixstowe, Yarmouth, and Dundee. Much development and experimentation with seaplanes was carried on.

Seaplanes took part in Naval Manœuvres of 1913, in the North Sea, and many excellent flights far out to sea were made.

On July 1st, 1914, the Naval Wing, R.F.C., became by Royal Warrant the Royal Naval Air Service, and was dissociated from the Army entirely. Captain Sueter was promoted to Commodore.

Prior to this, all the Army airships had been handed over to the Navy, and several military officers who had been concerned with the development of airships went over to the Navy with the ships, and were given rank in the R.N.A.S. corresponding to their R.F.C. rank.

At the Spithead Review in July, immediately before the war, the R.N.A.S. concentrated all its seaplanes at Calshot, about a dozen in all, and all its land-going aeroplanes at Gosport—about another dozen.

After the outbreak of war, many new coast stations were formed and many aeroplanes and seaplanes were ordered. The personnel of the Service was expanded largely, and R.N.A.S. pilots operated all over the world.

During 1917, the R.N.A.S. continued its amphibious duties. The activities of seaplanes, airships, and naval kite-balloons against submarines, became more and more developed, and by the end of the year were having very considerable effect. Seaplanes and airships definitely sank a number of submarines. Convoys of ships escorted by aircraft, and by other ships equipped with kite-balloons, were hardly ever, if at all, attacked by submarines, and it gradually became recognised that here was the real reply to the submarine menace.

R.N.A.S. shore-going squadrons at Dunkerque carried on bombing and fighting expeditions against German forces in Flanders. Fighting squadrons operated with the R.F.C. in France. Bombing squadrons bombed German towns from aerodromes on the Eastern French frontier. Sea and land squadrons operated in the Eastern Mediterranean, in the Red Sea, and in Mesopotamia, in alliance with the R.F.C. During May, 1917, a Naval Handley-Page biplane flew from London to an aerodrome in the Balkans, and thence, after re-fitting, bombed Constantinople with good effect on July 9th.

When the new Air Board was formed at the beginning of 1917, Commodore Godfrey Paine, C.B., M.V.O., R.N., was appointed Director of Air Services by the Admiralty, and was made a member of the Board of Admiralty with the title of Fifth Sea Lord. He remained in command of the R.N.A.S. till it too became merged in the Royal Air Force on April 1st.

KITE BALLOONS.

Kite-balloons, a German invention, were introduced into the Royal Naval Air Service by officers at Dunkirk, who had opportunities of watching the operation of the solitary kite-balloon possessed by the Belgian Army. Several K.B. Sections were formed, and proved so successful that the R.F.C. also adopted kite-balloons, and had a large number in operation by the end of 1916. Kite-balloons were also used largely by the Navy for spotting for Naval guns, the balloons being carried on ships specially fitted out for the purpose.

The uses of kite-balloons have been greatly increased during 1917 and 1918. They were particularly useful in repelling submarine attacks, and it is stated as a fact that no convoy of merchant ships equipped with K.Bs. ever lost a ship, or was ever attacked, whether escorted by destroyers or not.

THE AIR BOARD.

The Air Board came into being on Jan. 2, 1917, with Lord Cowdray, better known perhaps as Sir Weetman Pearson, as President, to control the supply of aircraft for both Services, and to co-ordinate the work of the Services. The Board was composed of Commodore Godfrey Paine, who was also made Fifth Lord of the Admiralty, representing the R.N.A.S.; Lieut.-General Sir David Henderson, representing the R.F.C.; Mr. William Weir, as Controller of Aeronautical Supplies, representing the Ministry of Munitions; and Mr. Percy Martin, as Controller of Aero-Engines, also representing the Ministry of Munitions. Major J. G. Baird was appointed Parliamentary Under-Secretary. The technical departments of the R.N.A.S. and R.F.C. were removed from the Admiralty and Adastral

Officers of the Royal Naval Air Service as they were before the War. *Photograph by F. N. Birkett.*

House respectively, and located at the Hotel Cecil, which was made the Air Board Office, and much of the administrative work of the Flying Services was also transferred to the Hotel Cecil.

Mr. William Weir was knighted on February 11th, and one may safely say that seldom, if ever, has a knighthood been more fully deserved. As Controller of Aircraft Supplies, during 1917, he increased output to an extraordinary extent. To him and to Sir Hugh Trenchard may be ascribed the dominance in the air possessed by the R.F.C. in 1918.

On May 23rd, 1918, the formation of a Civil Aerial Transport Committee, to study after-the-war problems, was announced in the House of Commons. Lord Northcliffe was made Chairman; Major Baird, Deputy Chairman; and among the members were the Duke of Atholl, Lord Montagu, Lord Sydenham, Mr. Balfour Browne, Mr. Berriman, Mr. G. B. Cockburn, Mr. Holt-Thomas, Mr. Claude Johnson, Mr. Joynson Hicks, Mr. Lanchester, Lieut.-Col. O'Gorman, Maj.-Gen. Ruck, Mr. Siddeley, Mr. Sopwith, Mr. H. G. Wells, Mr. H. White-Smith, Mr. Dyson Wilson, Sir Laurence Guillemard, Col. Pringle, Lord Drogheda, Mr. Murray, Sir Thomas Mackenzie, Mr. W. P. Schreiner, Mr. Grindle, Capt. Vyvyan, and General Brancker. The Secretary was Mr. D. O. Malcolm.

Much was expected of the Committee, but little came of it. Various sub committees were formed and met at various times. A voluminous report was issued late in 1918, which gave evidence of much work, which appears to have been of some service to drawing up the Regulations for Civilian flying in 1919.

The Air Board carried on its work very effectively till the end of 1917, when it was superceded by the Air Ministry. Before the end, however, several changes were made. Sir William Weir was made Director-General of Aircraft Production, with all the Technical Department under him. Mr. Henry Fowler, O.B.E. (later K.B.E.) was made Assistant D.G.A.P. Lieut.-Col. Alexander became Controller of the Supply Department, and Lieut.-Col. J. G. Weir, Controller of the Technical Department.

THE AIR FORCE BILL.

The Air Force Bill was introduced in the House of Commons on November 8th, and passed its third reading on November 13th. It passed its third reading in the House of Lords on November 27th, and received the Royal Consent on November 28th, 1917. This Act established the Air Council and the Royal Air Force.

THE AIR MINISTRY.

The Air Council, under the Secretary of State for the Air Force, came into being by an Order in Council of January 2nd, 1918. It was constituted as follows :—

Lord Rothermere—Secretary of State and President of the Council.

Major-General Sir Hugh Trenchard, K.C.B., D.S.O.—Chief of the Air Staff.

Rear-Admiral Mark Kerr, C.B., R.N.—Deputy Chief of the Air Staff.

Commodore Godfrey Paine, C.B., M.V.O., R.N.—Master-General of Personnel.

Major-General W. S. Brancker—Comptroller-General of Equipment.

Sir William Weir—Director-General of Aircraft Production in the Ministry of Munitions.

Sir John Hunter, K.B.E.—Administrator of Works and Buildings.

Major J. G. Baird, C.M.G., D.S.O., M.P.—Parliamentary Under-Secretary of State.

Lieut.-General Sir David Henderson, K.C.B., D.S.O.—Additional Member of Council and Vice-President.

Mr. W. A. Robinson, C.B., C.B.E.—Permanent Secretary to the Council.

Mr. H. W. McAnally—Assistant-Secretary.

Sir Henry Norman was appointed an Additional Member of the Air Council by Lord Rothermere.

Under this arrangement, the Air Council had no representative either on the Board of Admiralty or on the Army Council. However, an officer of the R.N.A.S., Wing-Capt. F. R. Scarlett, D.S.O., was appointed Director of the Air Division at the Admiralty, presumably to act as a link between the Air Council and the Navy. No analogous appointment has been announced at the War Office, but an Army Council Instruction, issued in March, makes it clear that so far as the Army is concerned the Air Ministry has merely to supply men and machines, and that for all practical purposes, when once they are supplied, they then become part of the Army.

On March 15th, it was notified in the *London Gazette* that the Air Force, to be created under the recent Act, was to be known as the Royal Air Force. The name roused considerable comment, as its initials were the same as those of the Royal Aircraft Factory—an institution which was not popular with the Services. At a later date, the name of this institution was changed to "The Royal Aircraft Establishment," to prevent confusion. Mr. Sydney Smith, formerly Chief Inspector of Factories under the Home Office, was appointed Superintendent in March, in succession to Sir Henry Fowler, K.B.E., who had become Assistant D.G.A.P.

On Sunday, April 14th, it was made known publicly that Major-General Sir Hugh Trenchard had resigned his post as Chief of the Air Staff, and that Major-General F. H. Sykes, C.M.G., had been appointed in his stead. The announcement raised the biggest storm in Parliament, and out, ever known in connection with a purely Service appointment, for it was well known that the resignation of General Trenchard was caused by personal disagreement with the Air Minister. No objection was raised to General Sykes, who, though he had not been concerned with aviation for some two years, was recognised as one of the pioneers of Military Aeronautics, but the Services strongly resented the removal of General Trenchard, who was acknowledged to be the soul and inspiration of the R.F.C., and the organiser of victory in the air.

As the result of these changes, Lieut.-General Sir David Henderson also resigned from the Air Council, giving as his reason that he felt himself unable to work with the new C.A.S.

With the R.A.F. in the Field :—A R.A.F. Padre preaching to officers and men of the R.A.F. from the nacelle of a F.E.2b Night-bomber. It will be noted that the men still wore R.F.C. uniform. This custom still prevailed in many parts until the middle of 1919, when nearly all the men were demobilised.

On April 25th, Lord Rothermere resigned his position as Air Minister. Sir William Weir was appointed Air Minister in his stead, and the appointment gave general satisfaction. Sir Arthur Duckham, K.C.B., of the Ministry of Munitions, was appointed to supervise the production of aircraft, in place of Sir William Weir, who, after being made Air Minister, was justly rewarded for his earlier work by being made a Peer of the Realm.

By the end of May, 1918, the affairs of the Air Ministry seemed to have settled down, and the organisation appeared to be working smoothly.

THE R.A.F. IN 1918.

The Royal Air Force came into being officially on April 1st, 1918. It embraces all personnel and matériel of the R.N.A.S. and the R.F.C.

The Home Command was at first divided into five areas, as follows :—

London Area.—Maj.-Gen. F. C. Heath-Caldwell, C.B.

North Eastern Area.—Maj.-Gen. The Hon. Sir Frederick Gordon, K.C.B., D.S.O.

South-Western Area.—Maj.-Gen. Mark Kerr, C.B., M.V.O. (Rear-Admiral, R.N.)

Midland Area.—Brig.-Gen. J. F. A Higgins, D.S.O., R.A.

Scottish Area.—Maj.-Gen. G. C. Caley, C.B. (Rear-Admiral, R.N.)

Maj.-Gen. J. M. Salmond remained G.O.C., R.A.F. in France and Germany, and Maj.-Gen. G. H. M. Salmond—his brother—G.O.C., R.A.F. in the Eastern Areas until June, 1919.

At a later date the North Eastern Area and the Scottish Area were amalgamated into one. A separate Irish Area was also created. An Irish Officer, Brig.-Gen. E. L. Gerrard (Lt.-Col. R.M.L.I.) was made the first G.O.C., Ireland.

Maj.-Gen. Sir Hugh Trenchard, greatly to the satisfaction of the Services, was appointed in May, 1918, to command "an important part " of the R.A.F. in France. After some months it was made known that this was the Independent Force R.A.F., which was formed by Lord Weir to operate independently of the Navy and Army and to carry aerial warfare into Germany.

An important adjunct to the R.A.F. was created in May by the organisation of the Women's Royal Air Force, under the Hon. Violet Douglas-Pennant—as Commandant. The W.R.A.F's are to the R.A.F. what the W.A.A.C.'s are to the Army, and the W.R.N.'s to the Navy. Shortly afterwards Miss Pennant was dismissed, and her dismissal became the subject of a Special Committee of the House of Lords late in 1919.

THE DEVELOPMENT OF THE R.A.F.

Perhaps the most peculiar thing about development of the R.A.F. in 1918 is the fact that no attempt was made to divide it definitely into three distinct branches for Naval, Military, and purely Aerial operations respectively. On the contrary, officers and men of the former R.N.A.S. were deliberately mixed up with those of the R.F.C., and *vice versa*, with, as the natural result, a marked drop in the efficiency of the two branches.

Young officers and men trained for the R.F.C. were drafted to seaplane work, and those trained for the R.N.A.S. were sent to the squadrons in the field. The natural result was that the young men found that, except for the mere fact of being able to fly, all the months they had spent in training had been practically wasted, as the manners, customs and operations of seaplane stations differ entirely from those of squadrons with the Army in the Field, or at aerodromes at home, precisely as the manners, customs and operations of the Navy differ from those of the Army. The experienced air mechanics of the two Flying Services who were mixed up in this way also lost efficiency through having to unlearn what they had previously learned of Service routine and to learn anew the routine of another Service.

This chaotic and inefficient state of affairs occurred because the R.A.F. naturally had no customs or routine of its own, and each individual station, ship, aerodrome, or squadron was run on the lines chosen by its Commanding Officer, according to whether he happened to have been of the R.N.A.S. or of the R.F.C. It was impossible for even the Air Council, if warlike operations were to continue, to be logical and thorough in mixing the two Services, and to complete the job by putting sailors in command in the Field and soldiers in command at sea, so operations at sea, from ships or coast stations, still remained in the hands of R.N. and R.N.A.S. officers, generally down to the grade of Squadron-Commander, and those in the Field were commanded by R.F.C. officers—except for a few R.N.A.S. squadrons which had been specially trained for land fighting and bombing in Belgium.

The result, as might have been expected, was a grave loss in the efficiency of many units. Nevertheless, owing to the enormous numbers of British aviators, as compared with those of the enemy, owing to the marked superiority of British aeroplanes, and owing to the individual skill and bravery of the British aviators, aided by the excellent organising ability of many experienced General Officers in the Field and by the gallant leadership of wing, squadron and flight commanders in action, the R.A.F. on the West and East fronts was more than able to hold that Command of the Air which was won by the R.F.C. in 1917, despite the *dicta* of highly-placed officials who sneered at the idea of the Command of the Air as impossible to achieve.

In the Summer of 1918, His Majesty the King visited his Armies in the Field, and on August 13th, in a letter to Field-Marshal Sir Douglas Haig, he wrote :—" Its prowess and established superiority over the enemy make me proud to be General-in-Chief of this last creation in the fighting forces of the World."

This established superiority was maintained until the end of the War, and for the last two months of fighting, the German aviators were practically driven out of the air.

THE COMMAND IN THE FIELD.

At the date of the Armistice, the R.A.F. with the Army in the Field was commanded by Major-General J. M. Salmond, C.M.G., D.S.O., and his Brigade-Commanders were Brigadier-Generals T. I. Webb-Bowen, C.M.G.; C. A. H. Longcroft, D.S.O.; E. R. Ludlow-Hewitt, D.S.O., M.C.; L. Charlton, C.M.G., D.S.O.; D. le G. Pitcher, C.M.G.; and R. Hogg, C.I.E.

Brigadier-General C. L. Lambe, D.S.O. (Post Captain, R.N.), commanded another brigade (composed entirely of R.N.A.S. shore-going squadrons) in Belgium, but, though operating with the Army at the end of the War, this was theoretically under the Admiral Commanding Dover Patrol.

The Independent Force R.A.F., under Major-General Sir Hugh Trenchard, K.C.B., D.S.O., was operating on the Franco-German frontier, with Headquarters near Neufchateau. This force was still only in process of formation, and consisted of a single brigade, under Brigadier-General C. L. N. Newall. Preparations were well in hand for the bombing of Berlin in November, but the Armistice occurred a few days too soon.

Nevertheless, the I.F., R.A.F., had already had a very considerable effect on the *moral* of civilians in Western Germany, and on that of the German troops in the regions around Metz and Luxemburg, so that it contributed very materially to that break-up on the Western front which was on the verge of occurring when the Armistice was signed just in time to enable the German Army to say truthfully in the future—as we said of our Army after the Retreat from Mons—that though it was a beaten army t was never a broken army.

Major-General W. G. H. Salmond, C.M.G., D.S.O.—elder brother of General J. M. Salmond—continued to command the R.A.F. in the Near and Middle East, his forces being distributed over the Balkans, Palestine, Egypt, East Africa, the Soudan, Mesopotamia and India. Despite the fact that the oldest machines, of types obsolete or obsolescent on the Western Front, were sent to him to be used up, the R.A.F. in those war areas maintained the same command of the air as was held by their better-equipped brethren in the West. Also, a vast training establishment in Egypt maintained a constant supply of well-educated pilots and observers for the Eastern Areas.

The R.A.F. Brigade detached for service with the British Army in Italy was at first commanded by Brigadier-General Webb-Bowen. When that officer returned to command in France (at the special request of General Plumer, it is understood) the command in Italy was taken over by Colonel P. B. Joubert de la Ferté, D.S.O.

SEA WORK.

The sea work of the R.A.F. consisted chiefly of patrolling the coasts of Great Britain, the North Sea, and the Mediterranean, in search of mines and submarines. Some few bomb-raids were made, including one successful one on the Zeppelin sheds at Tondern, in Slesvig, several across the Adriatic on Austrian ports, and some on Turkish positions in Palestine and Asia Minor.

The machines used for coast patrols at home were very largely land-going machines which were unfit for use at the front. They were generally fitted with floatation bags, but frequently not. Many of them fell into the sea and were lost, but in most cases the crews were saved. These crews were generally officers and/or men who had been trained for the R.F.C. and knew nothing about sea work.

Officers of a Unit of the Independent Force, R.A.F., in France, showing the mixture of Naval, Military, and R.A.F. uniforms in vogue on Active Service.

THE R.A.F. AT SEA :—H.M.S. Furious, arranged as a Seaplane Carrier and Aircraft Ship. In the bows may be seen an aeroplane of the type adapted to fly off a ship's deck. Round it is a removable stockade, which acts as a wind-breaker. Aft may be seen an S.S. Airship (or "Blimp"), which has alighted on deck. Forward of the airship is a scaffold arrangement which is intended to act as a screen to prevent aeroplanes which alight on the deck from over-shooting their mark and running overboard.

The North Sea patrols were chiefly done by big flying-boats of the type originated in America by Mr. Glenn Curtiss and developed into highly-efficient flying machines by Lieut.-Col. J. C. Porte, C.M.G. (formerly Lieutenant, R.N.). These are known as *F* Boats, having been produced at Felixstowe, where Colonel Porte was in command of the R.N.A.S. Experimental Station as well as the War Station.

During 1918, the Experimental Station produced, to the designs of Colonel Porte, a triplane flying-boat, with five Rolls-Royce engines. This was, at the end of 1918, the biggest aeroplane in the world.

It was intended originally, when the Armistice was signed, that this boat should fly the Atlantic. The scheme was quashed on the score of expense, though the boat's tests proved that she was capable of carrying fuel for the distance, whether flying from East to West or from West to East.

The speed and lifting power of the "Felixstowe Fury" are both very much higher than would be expected from so big a craft.

DECK FLYING.

The units of the R.A.F. operating with the Grand Fleet developed during 1918 the art of flying aeroplanes off and onto the decks of ships. H.M.S. *Furious*, which had proved to be useless as a super-battle-cruiser, was turned into a seaplane carrier, her forward deck being used as a starting platform and her after deck being rigged up with catching gear, so that ordinary aeroplanes with wheels might alight thereon with comparative success.

H.M.S. *Argus* was constructed with a flush deck along her whole length, her funnels being led horizontally aft to permit of this construction.

A number of battleships and cruisers were fitted with platforms on their gun-turrets, the out-board ends of the platforms resting on the guns, and from these turret-platforms aeroplanes were flown in the manner illustrated. In these cases no provision was made for the machines to alight again, and the plan was that when their flight was finished they should come down in the sea and be picked up as opportunity might serve.

The experiments in "deck-flying," as it was called, which produced these schemes, were chiefly carried out at the R.N.A.S. Experimental Station, Isle of Grain, at first under Wing-Commander John Seddon, and later under Wing-Commanders L'Estrange Malone, Featherstone Briggs, and Harry Busteed.

If these experiments had received more support from their Lordships of the Admiralty in the early and middle days of the War, there is no doubt that bomb-dropping and torpedo-carrying aeroplanes flown from the decks of seaplane-carriers would have played a very important part in the War, for it was a single flight of such machines which destroyed several Zeppelin sheds at Tondern, in Slesvig, in 1918, and all these schemes, now mentioned for the first time in this book, were actually proposed before the War and reached the early stages of experiment in 1915 or 1916. In fact, aeroplanes had been flown off and onto ships by British and American aviators in 1912, and special launching gears for use on ships were illustrated in 1913 or earlier.

An R.A.F. Flying-Boat of Lieut.-Col. Porte's design, and known as the Felixstowe F2a Type, built by various companies. Dazzle-painted, in accordance with Naval custom.

FURTHER HISTORY OF 1918.

On August 22nd, further changes took place in the organisation of the R.A.F. at home. Major-General Sir Godfrey Paine, Master-General of Personnel, was made Inspector-General R.A.F. Major-General W. S. Brancker was appointed M.G.P., and Major-General E. H. Ellington, C.M.G., was appointed Controller General of Equipment.

In September, Mrs. Gwynne-Vaughan, C.B.E., commanding W.A.A.C. in France, was appointed to command the W.R.A.F.,

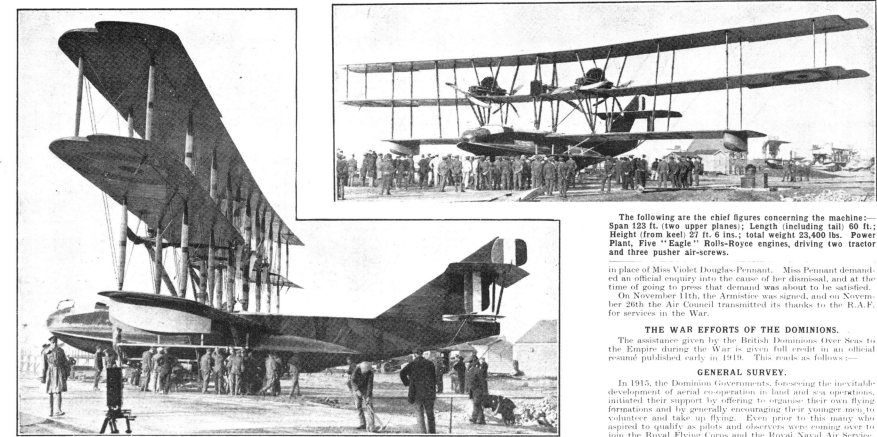

The following are the chief figures concerning the machine:— Span 123 ft. (two upper planes); Length (including tail) 60 ft.; Height (from keel) 27 ft. 6 ins.; total weight 23,400 lbs. Power Plant, Five "Eagle" Rolls-Royce engines, driving two tractor and three pusher air-screws.

Side and Three-quarter Bow View of the Big Porte Boat, known officially as the "Felixstowe Fury."

in place of Miss Violet Douglas-Pennant. Miss Pennant demanded an official enquiry into the cause of her dismissal, and at the time of going to press that demand was about to be satisfied.

On November 11th, the Armistice was signed, and on November 26th the Air Council transmitted its thanks to the R.A.F. for services in the War.

THE WAR EFFORTS OF THE DOMINIONS.

The assistance given by the British Dominions Over Seas to the Empire during the War is given full credit in an official resumé published early in 1919. This reads as follows :—

GENERAL SURVEY.

In 1915, the Dominion Governments, foreseeing the inevitable development of aerial co-operation in land and sea operations, initiated their support by offering to organise their own flying formations and by generally encouraging their younger men to volunteer and take up flying. Even prior to this many who aspired to qualify as pilots and observers were coming over to join the Royal Flying Corps and the Royal Naval Air Service, and during the whole of the War service of the highest value has been performed by pilots from the Dominions who were destined to play an important part in building up and maintaining the air-fighting forces in every theatre of war. The following details give some idea of the extent of the efforts of the principal Dominions :—

AUSTRALIA.

The inauguration of the Australian Flying Corps in 1915 was the result of an offer by the Australian Government to form a flying unit for co-operation with our Indian forces in Mesopotamia. Four flying officers and sixty other ranks arrived at Basra in May, 1915, and took part in the Kut operations. The first complete Australian squadron left Australia for Egypt in March, 1916, and later played an important part in the work of the 40th Wing in the Middle East Brigade. Three additional squadrons were organised for service in France, the first arriving there in August, 1917 ; these were responsible for the destruction of over 400 enemy machines between that time and the signing of the Armistice. Further, four training squadrons were formed in

A " Ship-Plane," flying off a turret platform.

England in which most of the Australian pilots were trained, the entire personnel being drawn from Australia or from the Australian Imperial Forces in France. Some months ago a central flying school was created at Melbourne, and the aeroplane industry has now been definitely established in Australia.

The strength of the Australian Flying Corps in November, 1918, amounting to over 250 pilots and a total personnel of considerably over 3,000, gives an impression of the part played by Australia in gaining aerial supremacy.

CANADA.

In the early days of the War a large number of Canadians came over to join the Royal Flying Corps and the Royal Naval Air Service, and as many as 800 officers and cadets had been enrolled in the former corps up to the time when a training centre for flying cadets was organised in Canada itself. A total of 1,239 Canadian officers have been seconded or attached to the Royal Flying Corps, Royal Naval Air Service, and the Royal Air Force, and, since training in Canada was begun, over 4,000 Canadian cadets have been commissioned in the flying services, while the number of other ranks transferred and subsequently commissioned is about 2,750. Altogether, over 8,000 Canadians have served as officers in our flying services, and at the date of the Armistice there were nearly 2,500 in the Royal Air Force, while 1,200 Canadian cadets were undergoing training in England and in Canada. It may be added that several Canadian firms have maintained a large output both of machines and engines ; Canada was producing, in November, 1918, about 350 light machines and eight large flying-boats per month.

NEW ZEALAND.

Over 300 New Zealanders have served as officers in the British Flying Services during the War, and at the time of the Armistice there were 142 cadets in training.

The Dominion has presented six aeroplanes to the Imperial Government and lent two others.

Since the outbreak of War, two Schools of Instruction in Aviation have been established in New Zealand.

SOUTH AFRICA.

On the outbreak of War many South Africans came to England to take up flying, and by the beginning of 1916 nearly 2,000 were serving in England or Egypt as probationary flight officers. When the 28th Squadron Royal Flying Corps was sent to co-operate with the Forces in East Africa, it was largely composed of South Africans, and came to be known as the South African Squadron.

The total number of South Africans who have been commissioned in the Flying Services is about 3,000, who have taken part in the campaigns in France, Egypt, Palestine, and Africa.

The Colony presented a large number of machines to the Imperial Government during the War.

ASSISTANCE TO THE ALLIES.

The same official resumé gives an account of the assistance given by the R.N.A.S., R.F.C., and R.A.F. to the Allies and the United States. This reads as follows :—

AMERICA.

The Government of the United States has paid a striking tribute to the British Air Service by adopting our system of

An Aeroplane on the Turret of a Warship, showing the out-board portion of the platform folded back. This portion rests on the supports which may be seen fixed to the barrels of the guns.

training. The first 500 American officer cadets to be trained went through the School of Military Aeronautics at Oxford, subsequently graduating at various aerodromes in England. These officers formed the nucleus of American schools which were eventually started both in the United States and in France. In addition to this training of American pilots, 10 American squadrons were partially trained in Canada under a reciprocal agreement whereby Canada obtained the use of certain American aerodromes at seasons when weather conditions rendered some of the Canadian aerodromes temporarily unavailable. Four of these squadrons completed their training in England, and were then attached to the R.A.F. in the field to gain experience under Service conditions for six to eight months. The remaining six went direct to the American authorities in France. In all, about 700 American pilots have passed through our schools and graduated at our aerodromes.

An agreement was also entered into under which a pool of American mechanics up to a maximum of 15,000 at a time was maintained in England. This arrangement was mutually advantageous, as, while relieving the demand for skilled tradesmen in the R.A.F., it also assisted the Americans to train their own squadrons for service in the field. This personnel, coming from America untrained, was attached to training units for three to eight months, being then sent to France from time to time in the form of complete squadrons until a total of 59 squadrons was reached in accordance with the demands of the American Command in France.

We have also supplied large numbers of aeroplanes of modern standard type, and when the question of producing a standardised engine was considered, every facility was given and all our experience placed at the disposal of the American Government, with the result that the Liberty engine was evolved. Some 95 officers were sent out to the United States to assist in an advisory capacity, and a large number of American officers have both visited and undergone courses at most of the schools and training stations of the Royal Air Force. In addition, a very large amount of material, supplies, samples, drawings, and technical information was supplied to both the American Army and Naval Aviation Services.

FRANCE.

We have assisted the French Government to a considerable extent in training her pilots, more especially in aerial fighting. For this purpose four Gosport instructors together with four mono-Avro aeroplanes were sent to France. We have supplied 48 complete machines and various new types of engines to the French Government, and an order for 150 Sunbeam engines is on the point of completion.

About 600 Hythe gun cameras were also supplied during 1917-1918 to the French schools for training purposes.

French officers have constantly visited this country with a view to studying our methods, and have been given every facility for visiting schools, training centres, and technical establishments.

ITALY.

Immediately after the Italian retreat in November, 1917, four British aeroplane squadrons were sent to the Italian Front to co-operate with the Italian Air Service and with the British Forces in Italy ; these four squadrons have been maintained and a fifth squadron has recently been added.

The brief record of the work performed by these squadrons, given in the Appendix, illustrates the valuable assistance they have rendered to our Ally.

During 1918, the Italian Government were supplied with 150 Vickers guns each month, and with upwards of 2,000 Lewis guns.

A number of Hythe gun cameras have been sent out, and between 200 and 300 sights and lenses, as well as photographic chemicals.

BELGIUM.

In 1916, a number of Sopwith 1½ strutters were provided by the R.N.A.S. In 1917, 22 more machines of this type were supplied, and 22 R.E. 8s for artillery co-operation. In 1918, 36 " Camel " and 18 D.H.9 machines were furnished to the Belgian Aviation Corps.

GREECE.

The Greek Government have been supplied with 20 seaplanes, 40 D.H.6 machines and 6 Sopwith " Camels," together with complete equipment and transport, had been allotted and were ready for dispatch, but have been held back owing to the cessation of active hostilities.

RUSSIA.

In 1916, a mission was sent to Russia to assist in training and organising the Russian Flying Corps, and during the latter part of 1916 and during 1917 Russia was supplied with 251 aeroplanes.

In May, 1918, orders were issued for the dispatch of a R.A.F. contingent in conjunction with a special mission which was being sent to Northern Russia to operate from Archangel. The Force consisted of 8 D.H.4 (R.A.F.3a) machines with a complement of personnel and stores. On arrival at Archangel, sufficient machines were collected from those which had previously been sent to Russia to form two squadrons of Nieuports and 1½ strutters.

In August, 1918, reinforcements were dispatched to Archangel, consisting of a proportion of British officers, N.C.Os, and men, a wing headquarters, an Intelligence Section, one flight of R.E.8s, and two Repair Sections for engines and aircraft respectively. On November 12th, 1918, a further reinforcement of six Sopwith scouts and a six months' supply of stores were dispatched.

JAPAN.

Several officers have been undergoing courses on aeroplanes and seaplanes.

BRAZIL.

Seventy-seven complete machines and 100 Le Rhone engines have been supplied.

Several officers have graduated as pilots under the tuition of our instructors. Two flying-boats have been supplied to the Brazilian Government.

ROUMANIA.

Several officers have been given instruction and have graduated as pilots. Twenty Sopwith machines have also been supplied.

Air Ministry, January 1st, 1919.

FIGURES FOR THE FLYING SERVICES.

The tables which follow hereafter give, in easily visible form, some interesting comparative figures illustrating the accomplishments of the Flying Services in the War. They are taken from the official resumé to which reference has already been made.

PERSONNEL.

	August 1914.			December 1916.			December 1917.			October 1918.		
	Officers.	Other Ranks.	Total.	Officers.	Other Ranks.	Total.	Officers.	Other Ranks.	Total.	Officers.	Other Ranks.	Total.
R.F.C.	147	1,097	1,244	5,982	51,915	57,897	15,522	98,738	114,260	..	..	..
R.N.A.S.	50	550	600	2,764	26,129	28,893	4,765	43,050	47,815	..	..	..
R.A.F.	..	..	..	..			..	..	..	27,906	263,842	291,748
Total ..	..	..	1,844	..	..	86,790	..	..	162,075	..	..	291,748

MACHINES AND ENGINES ON CHARGE.

	August 1914.		January 1917.		January 1918.		October 1918.	
	Machines.	Engines.	Machines.	Engines.	Machines.	Engines.	Machines.	Engines.
R.F.C.	179	..	3,929	6,056	8,350	14,755	..	..
R.N.A.S.	93	..	1,567	3,672	2,741	6,902	..	..
R.A.F.	..	..	..	..	..	..	22,171	37,702
Total	272	..	5,496	9,728	11,091	21,657	22,171	37,702

OUTPUT OF MACHINES AND ENGINES.

	August 1914 to May, 1915 (10 months).		June, 1915 to February, 1917 (21 months).		March 1917 to December, 1917 (10 months).		January 1918 to October, 1918 (10 months).	
	Machines.	Engines.	Machines.	Engines.	Machines.	Engines.	Machines.	Engines.
R.F.C.	530	141	7,137	8,917	12,275	..	..	..
R.N.A.S.	No record.	No record.	No record.	No record.	1,246	..	..	..
R.A.F.	..	..	..	..	..	..	26,685	29,561
Total	530	141	7,137	8,917	13,521	13,979	26,685	29,561

EXPANSION OF MOTOR TRANSPORT.

Motor Transport. (All Types.)	R.F.C. Only.				Royal Air Force.
	August 1914.	August 1915.	August 1916.	August 1917.	October 31, 1918.
On charge ..	320	2,469	5,282	8,584	23,260

SQUADRONS MAINTAINED.

	Service.		Training. (1 Training Depot Station reckoned as 3 Squadrons.)		
	August 1914.	October 31, 1918.		August 1914.	October 31, 1918.
Western Front	4 (R.F.C.)	84 & 5 flights	Home	1 (R.F.C.)	174
Independent Force	..	10		2 (R.N.A.S.)	..
5 Group	..	3	Egypt	..	10
India ..	..	2	Canada	..	15
Italy ..	..	4			
Middle East ..	..	13			
Russia	..	½			
Home Defence	..	18			
Naval Units ..	1 (R.N.A.S.)	64			
Total ..	5	198½ & 5 flights	..	3	199

RESULTS OF OPERATIONS IN THE AIR.

	July 1916 to Nov. 11, 1918	January 1, 1918, to November 11, 1918.									
	Western Front.	Independent Force.	Home Forces.	5th Group and Naval Units.	Italy.	Egypt.	Mesopotamia.	Salonika.	Palestine.	India (Aden).	Total.
Enemy aircraft accounted for, i.e., brought down or driven down ..	6,904	150	8	470	405	25	6	59	81	..	7,908
Our machines missing ..	2,484	111	..	114	44	9	13	8	24	..	2,810
Bombs dropped .. (tons)	6,402	540	..	662	59	43	25	130	74	30	7,945
Hours flown ..	889,526	11,784	..	39,102	25,206	7,022	7,862	13,417	21,848	579	1,016,346
Rounds fired at ground targets	10,238,182	353,257	..		222,704	50,937	107,563	193,354	735,550	7,527	11,858,137
Photographs taken ..	401,375	3,682	..	3,440	14,596	8,135	66,720	15,587	27,039	542	501,116
Enemy balloons brought down ..	258	..	..	..	..	..	..	..	..	..	258

NOTE.—Records are not available of the results obtained by Expeditionary Force, Western Front, prior to July, 1916, or by 5th Group and Naval Units, or in Eastern Theatres prior to January, 1918. The absence of these records, however, will not materially affect the totals shown as regards enemy aircraft accounted for, our machines missing, or the weight of bombs dropped, owing to the comparatively recent growth in intensity of aerial fighting and the smaller number of aircraft engaged.

NOTE BY EDITOR OF "ALL THE WORLD'S AIRCRAFT."—It should be noted that the number of British machines recorded as "missing" does not represent our losses as compared with those of the enemy, as it does not include machines shot down in our own territory, or crashed on landing. An official statement published in November, 1918, states that the Total Losses of the Flying Services were 7,589 killed, wounded, and missing, of whom 1,551 officers and 1,129 other ranks were definitely reported as killed.

ROYAL AIRCRAFT ESTABLISHMENT.—(Late Royal Aircraft Factory).

THE F.E. 2b. With Beardmore engine of 120 h.p, fore-runner of the Rolls engined type, which it resembles in general design. This machine, with slight modifications and a 160 h.p. Beardmore engine, was still in use at the end of the war, as a night-bombing machine.

THE F.E. 2b. Viewed from below.

A

AIRCRAFT ESTABLISHMENT, ROYAL. (New name for The Royal Aircraft Factory, South Farnborough.) This establishment was engaged in airship construction and repairs. During the war the Factory has been at work on experiments in various types of aeroplanes, and has been turning out a certain number of spare parts for existing machines. It is not used for the production of aeroplanes in quantities, the designs produced from its experiments being built by numerous "contractors."

As the result of the Air Defence agitations of early 1916, a Committee, composed of Sir Charles Parsons, the late Sir Richard Burbidge, and the late Sir Frederic Donaldson, investigated the management of the Royal Aircraft Factory. In 1916, Mr. Henry Fowler, late of the Ministry of Munitions, and previously Chief Mechanical Engineer of the Midland Railway, was appointed to be Superintendent.

In 1917, Mr. Fowler was created a Knight of the Order of the British Empire, and, as Sir Henry Fowler, K.B.E., he was appointed Assistant Director-General of Aircraft Production under the Air Ministry. Mr. Sydney Smith, formerly Chief Inspector of Factories, took his place as Superintendent.

The R.A.F. "type-letters" have the following significance : —
"B.E." at first indicated "Bleriot Experimental," M. Blériot being credited with having originated the "tractor" type machine. It is now taken to mean "British Experimental."

The original B.E. was designed by and built under the supervision of Mr. Geoffrey de Havilland, now Captain R.F.C., and chief designer for the Aircraft Manufacturing Co., Ltd. A later type of the same general design was numbered "B.E. 2." Developments of this type were the "B.E. 2b," "B.E. 2c," "B.E. 2d," and "B.E. 2e," the two last being built in very large quantities, but the "B.E. 2c" is now chiefly used for school purposes.

The "B.E." general type was also developed along different lines, as the "B.E. 3," "4," "5," "6," and so forth, up to the "B.E. 12," which cannot be here described, as it is in war use. One may perhaps say that it has been successful in destroying Zeppelins, and is very much more powerful than the "B.E. 2c."

"F.E." indicated "Farman Experimental," M. Henri Farman being credited with having originated the "pusher" type. It is now taken to mean "Fighting Experimental." This has been developed along various lines, the "F.E. 2b" being a big fighting machine with a 160 h.p. Beardmore engine, and the "F.E. 2d" still bigger, with a 250 h.p. Rolls-Royce engine. One may state this without giving away secrets, as samples of both types have been captured by the enemy.

The "F.E. 8," on the other hand, is a small single-seat fighting machine.

"R.E." indicates "Reconnaissance Experimental." These also have been developed as "R.E. 2," "R.E. 3," up to "R.E. 7," "R.E. 8," and so forth, with various engines.

"S.E." indicates "Scouting Experimental."

The Royal Aircraft Factory was so known until, on April 1, 1918, the Royal Air Force came into being. In order to prevent confusion over the initials the name of the Factory was then changed to The Royal Aircraft Establishment.

From a German photograph published in various parts of the world.

An F.E. 2d. A photograph from Germany, *via* a neutral country, showing an F.E. 2d. which landed by error at Lille and tried to turn over on reaching the ground. It will be seen that it resembles the F.E. 2b, but it has a 250 h.p. Rolls-Royce engine instead of the 150 h.p. Beardmore.

It is regretted that the only photographs available are those of damaged machines, but the R.A.F. machines, being definitely of Government design, may not be photographed under normal conditions.

A " B.E. 2c." BIPLANE, with Renault engine, built by the Royal Aircraft Factory.

THE B.E. 2d. With 90 h.p. or 100 h.p. R.A.F. engine. Note the petrol tank under the upper plane, and the exhaust pipe projecting upwards.

THE B.E.2e. With 100 h.p. R.A.F. engine. Note the single pair of struts outside the fuselage, the thin aileron strut, and the long over-hang to the upper planes. The pilot sits behind and the passenger in front.

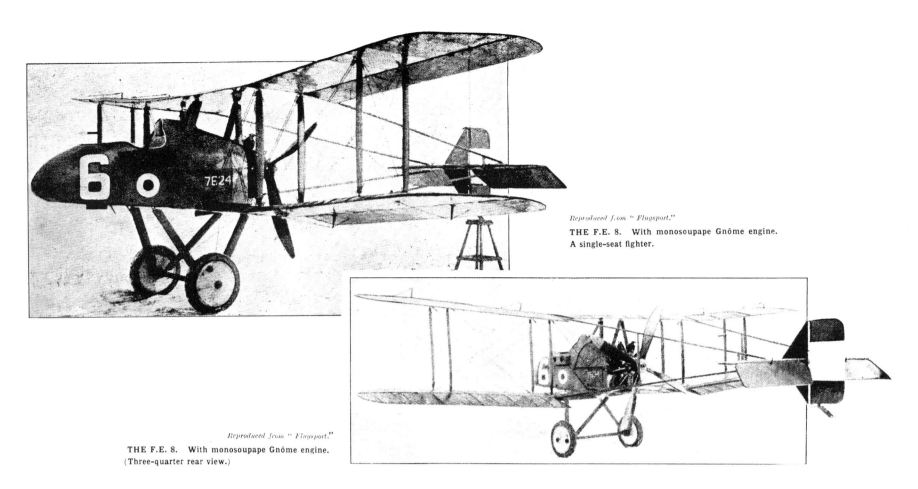

Reproduced from " Flugsport."

THE F.E. 8. With monosoupape Gnôme engine.
A single-seat fighter.

Reproduced from " Flugsport."

THE F.E. 8. With monosoupape Gnôme engine.
(Three-quarter rear view.)

THE R.E. 8. With 130 h.p. R.A.F. engine (Side view.)
This machine was still in use at the end of the war, as an
artillery observation machine and as a night bomber.

THE R.E. 8. With 130 h.p. R.A.F. engine.
Note the big engine, the heavier aileron strut,
and the less overhang to the upper planes
than in the B.E. 2e. The pilot sits in
front, and the gunner has a gun-ring
round the after seat.

(Reproduced from " Flugsport.")

Side view of a S.E. 5 Biplane, captured by the Germans.

THE S.E. 5a.

A Neutral Correspondent writes :—

Following is a translation of the description of the British S.E.v.A. (scouting, experimental) fighting single-seater, published in the March issue of the German Airmen's Journal, " Luftwaffe," reading thus :—

The aeroplane in question was built by Vickers, Ltd., and numbered B.507, wearing further as recognition initial or that of a squadron, an A as well as a white circle. The propeller is marked : S.E.V.A., which leads to the idea that the older model of this same aeroplane type with the 150 h.p. Hispano motor not geared down is called S.E.v.

The biplane has a surface of 22.8 square metres, and both planes, connected with but one pair of struts to each side, have a span of 8.15 metres, and a chord of 1.52 metres, the gap from the top of the fuselage amounting to 0.15 metre.

No arrow-shape prevails. The V-shape of the equal-sized ends of the upper and lower planes mounted on the centre section and respective body rudiments amounts to 1.71 degrees.

The sight field of range is improved by cutting the centre section in the middle and the lower planes near the body.

Above the angle of incidence is 5 deg. mean, below by the body 6 deg., by the struts 5 deg.

Both plane spars show sections of I shape, whereas the longerons of the rudiment pieces, running through the body are steel tubes of 1.75 millimetre thickness, and 45 mm. outer diameter. The plane ribs show the usual construction of most British air craft.

There are no compression struts between the spars, some of the ribs being solid struts instead.

The interior wiring of the planes between the body and the struts is carried out in simple profile wire, that of the overhanging ends of thick-end wire.

A wood strip forms the back edge of the planes. Further, two auxiliary ribs ranging from the leading nose edge to the main spar are arranged between each two ribs.

The fabric is sewed together with the ribs, and is painted yellow below, browned above, as is the fabric of the body. Shoe-eyes are arranged on the underside of the trailing edge of the plane to assess the pressure.

The centre section struts are covered steel tubes. The plane spruce struts rest in long stampings, serving as fixing points of the vertical wiring.

Profile wire is employed for the plane cross wiring with twin wires for those carrying load and single for counter ones.

The two spars of the upper planes are strengthened further between the centre section and the struts with two wires each. Unbalanced ailerons are hinged to the back crossbar of the upper and lower planes.

The body shows the usual strut-cum-wire combination, being rounded above with half-circle frames and fairings, and having three-ply wood planking of 4 millimetre thickness to the pilot's seat. Fuselage longitudinals and struts have sections of I-shape, except the vertical struts behind the pilot's seat, which are worked out round.

The tail-plane is curved to both sides and fixed to the body, so that the angle of incidence can be varied during the flight within the limits + 4.5 deg. and — 3 deg. To this end the front spar is turnable, while the rear spar, with its wiring, is fixed to a tube, arranged shiftable to the body stern post. This tube rests with a piece of thread in a gear nut, again resting in the stern-post fixed, yet turnable.

When the nut is turned from the pilot's seat by means of wheel and cable, the tube is displaced upwards or downwards, transferring thereby the same manoeuvre on the rear spar of the tail plane, and thus its angle of incidence changes.

The elevator hooked to the fixed tail-plane partakes in this movement. The wires for operating the elevator are led through the body and tail-plane, which certainly saves air resistance, yet makes twice a 20 deg. direction change of each wire necessary. Main and tail-planes are equipped with cellon windows, rendering a control of the rollers possible.

The under-carriage shows the normal form. The through-running axle rests between two auxiliary ones. There is no limit of the springing range.

The main petrol tank of 120 litres' capacity is placed behind the motor on the upper fuselage longitudinals. A gravity tank of 17 litres capacity is arranged in the centre section between the leading edge and the main spar. The oil tank of a capacity of 14 litres lies across in the engine frame below the rear edge of the motor.

The fuel suffices for a flight of about two hours duration.

Following instruments are arranged in the pilot's seat :—

To right : A box for the light pistols ; a contact breaker for the self-starter ; a contact breaker for the two magnetos ; a triple led cock for the gravity and pressure petrol ; a triple led cock for the hand and motor air-pump ; a thermometer for the water of the radiator ; the petrol gauge placed on the back side of the main tank, and a manometer for air-pressure.

To left : Gas lever ; lever for regulation of the gas in altitude flights ; lever for operating the radiator blinds, clip for three light cartridges. On the bottom is further arranged a hand-pump for the hydraulic machine-gun gear ; two boxes for drums for the moveable machine-gun and self-starter.

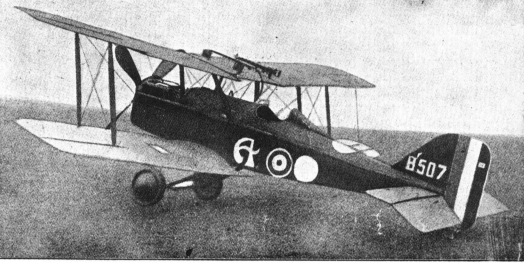

Three-quarter rear view of a S.E. 5 Biplane, captured by the Germans.

The tail skid shows an unusual construction, being arranged turnable behind the stern-post and connected with the rudder cable by intermediacy of springs. A brass skid bow is sprung by means of two spiral pressure springs which are prevented from sideway turning by inserted telescope tubes.

According to the firm's sign board the Wolseley-Hispano-Suiza engine gave the 30th August, 1917, on brake 206 h.p.=203 P.S. at 2005 revolutions. The r.p.m. of the four-bladed airscrew is geared down in the ratio of 4 to 3.

The exhaust gas is led behind the pilot's seat in two tubes to each side of the body. The motor sits so that there is free accessibility after removing the bonnet. The radiator forms the bow of the body.

A cover arrangement makes it possible to uncover the body about half-way from the pilot's seat.

A square windshield of Triplex glass is placed in front of the pilot's seat. Behind it a box is arranged in a queer position to the body with access from outside.

The fixed Vickers' machine-gun lies to left of the pilot inside the body fabric. The cartridge girdle is of metal. The firing of the machine-gun takes place hydraulically by means of a control arrangement, placed in front of the motor and connected with the machine-gun through a copper main, as well as driven from the air screw by a gear set. The firing lever sits on the stick.

On the bow-shaped iron band lying on the centre section rests a Lewis gun, which can be pulled down during the flight to permit vertical firing.

The empty weight of the aeroplane was worked out at 706 kilos, distributed as follows :—

20   Der englische S. E. V. A.-Kampf-Einsitzer   Nr. 5/6

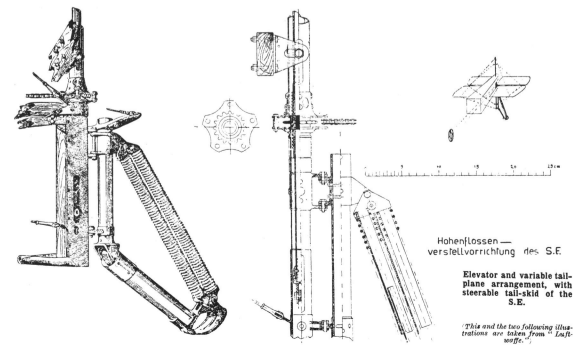

Hohenflossen —
verstellvorrichtung des S.E.

Elevator and variable tail-plane arrangement, with steerable tail-skid of the S.E.

(This and the two following illustrations are taken from " Luftwaffe.")

ROYAL AIRCRAFT ESTABLISHMENT.

Engl. S. E. V. A.

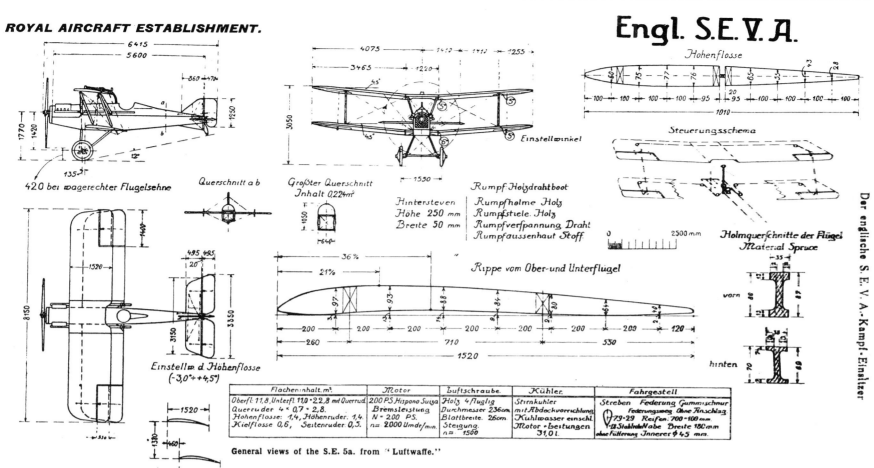

General views of the S.E. 5a. from "Luftwaffe."

	kilos.
Engine	225.0
Exhaust collection	12.0
Self-starter	3.6
Radiator	23.8
Radiator water	31.0
Air screw	26.6
Main petrol tank	17.8
Gravity petrol tank	6.5
Oil tank	3.9
Motor equipment	6.4
Body with seat and plate covers	151.0
Tail-plane angle of incidence change arrangements	1.9
Under carriage	40.8
Tail skid	3.7
Pilotage arrangement	5.4
Planes with wiring	112.2
Vertical and horizontal wiring	21.0
Body equipment	14.0
	706.0

The fuel weight amounts with fully loaded tanks to 111 kilos., so that the total useful load can be calculated at 250 kilos., the total weight working out at 956 kilos.

The load of the planes is thus : $\dfrac{956}{22.8} = 42$ kilos per square metre.

The performance load is then : $\dfrac{956}{200} = 4.78$ kilos per horse power.

The first DE HAVILLAND biplane, the de H.1 or D.H.1, built by the Aircraft Manufacturing Co., Ltd.

AIRCRAFT MANUFACTURING Co., Ltd.

47, Victoria Street, London, S.W. Works : Hendon, London, N.W. This Company, established in 1912 by Mr. G. Holt Thomas, holds all the British rights for the *H. & M. Farman* types.

The Aircraft Mfg. Co., Ltd., under the direction of Mr. Holt Thomas, and with Mr. Hugh Burroughes as General Manager, has tackled the problem of large output with marked success, to a great extent by adopting the French "*système globale*," which consists in having a vast quantity of minor parts made by small firms, under rigid inspection by the staff of the head firm, and assembling them at the firm's own works. In this way all finished products are under the direct supervision of the management, and the sub-contracting firms are responsible, at their own expense, for the quality of the component parts.

During 1914 Mr. Holt Thomas secured the services of Capt. Geoffrey de Haviland, R.F.C., as the firm's designer-in-chief, and has produced the series of extraordinarily successful machines which have made Capt. de Haviland's initials famous.

As a matter of general interest, and for purposes of reference, specifications of the whole of the "De H." series are included in the following descriptions, but no illustrations are given of the older types of this make. These aeroplanes are now known as "Airco" machines.

A DE HAVILLAND single-seat fighting "pusher" biplane, of the D.H.2 or de H.2 type used successfully against the *Fokker* biplane early in 1916, but out-climbed and out-speeded in turn by the later products of both sides, especially by its own designer's newer types.

AIRCO DE H.1.

The first of the series, produced just before the declaration of war, was a two-seater Renault-engined "pusher" machine.

Specification.

Type of machine	Biplane ("Pusher.")
Name or type No. of machine	De H.1.
Span	41 ft.
Gap, maximum and minimum	5 ft. 7 in.
Overall length	28 ft. 11½ in.
Maximum height	11 ft. 4 in.
Chord	5 ft. 6 in.
Total surface of wings, including centre plane and ailerons	409.3 sq. ft.
Span of tail	12 ft. 5½ in.
Total area of tail (empennage)	80.45 sq. ft.
Area of elevators	11.0 sq. ft. each.
Area of rudder	16.15 sq. ft.
Area of fin	4.05 sq. ft.
Area of each aileron	18.0 sq. ft.
Engine type and h.p.	80 h.p. Renault.
Airscrew, diam., pitch and revs.	9.03 dia. ; 9.2 pitch; 870 revs.
Weight of machine empty	1,356 lbs.
Weight of machine full load	2,044 lbs.
Load per sq. ft.	4.99 lbs.
Weight per h.p. full load	25.5 lbs.
Tank capacity in gallons	30 gallons.

Performance.
Speed low down	78 m.p.h.
Landing speed	41 m.p.h.

Climb.
To 3,500 feet	11¼ minutes.

Disposable load apart from fuel	420 lbs.
Total weight of machine loaded	2,044 lbs.

AIRCO DE H.1A.

This was a modified De H.1 fitted with a 120 Beardmore engine in place of the original Renault.

Specification.

Type of machine	Biplane ("Pusher.")
Name or type No. of machine	De H.1a.
Span	41 ft.
Gap, maximum and minimum	5 ft. 7 in.
Overall length	28 ft. 11½ in.
Maximum height	11 ft. 2 in.
Chord	5 ft. 6 in.
Total surface of wings, including centre plane and ailerons	409.3 sq. ft.
Span of tail	12 ft. 3 in.
Total area of tail (empennage)	79.9 sq. ft.
Area of elevators	11.0 sq. ft. each.
Area of rudder	15.6 sq. ft.
Area of fin	4.05 sq. ft.
Area of each aileron	18.0 sq. ft.
Engine type and h.p.	130 h.p. Beardmore.
Airscrew, diam., pitch and revs.	9.03 diam., 9.2 pitch, 1,350 revs.
Weight of machine empty	1,672 lbs.
Weight of machine full load	2,400 lbs.
Load per sq. ft.	5.87 lbs.
Weight per h.p. full load	18.45 lbs.
Tank capacity in gallons	33 gallons.

Performance.
Speed low down	89 m.p.h.
Landing speed	49 m.p.h.

Climb.
To 3,500 ft.	6.45 mins.

Disposable load apart from fuel	420 lbs.
Total weight of machine loaded	2,400 lbs.

AIRCO DE H.2.

The De H.2 was produced in 1915 to meet the need for a high-speed single-seater fighter.

At that time the synchronised machine-gun fire through the airscrew had not been developed in this country, and consequently the high-speed tractor single-seater was of very little use for fighting purposes.

This machine was therefore an attempt to combine a high performance with the unobstructed use of a machine-gun firing straight ahead, which is possible with a machine of the "pusher" type.

In this respect the De H.2 was extraordinarily successful. During 1915 and the early part of 1916 this type of machine gave an excellent account of itself on the Western Front, but was displaced by machines of the "tractor" type when the use of synchronised guns became more general.

Specification.

Type of machine	Biplane ("Pusher.")
Name or type No. of machine	De H.2.
Span	28 ft. 0½ in.
Gap, maximum and minimum	4 ft. 6 in.
Overall length	25 ft. 2½ in.
Maximum height	9 ft. 6½ in.
Chord	4 ft. 9 in.
Total surface of wings, including centre plane and ailerons	228.0 sq. ft.
Span of tail	10 ft. 3 in.
Total area of tail (empennage)	56.5 sq. ft.
Area of elevators	6.8 sq. ft. each.
Area of rudder	13.5 sq. ft.
Area of fin	2.4 sq. ft.
Area of each aileron	9.7 sq. ft.
Engine type and h.p.	100 Gnôme.
Airscrew, diam., pitch and revs.	8.0 dia., 7.7 pitch, 1,350 revs.
Weight of machine empty	896 lbs.
Weight of machine full load	1,320 lbs.
Load per sq. ft.	5.8 lbs.
Weight per h.p. full load	13.2 lbs.
Tank capacity in gallons	22.4 galls.

Performance.
Speed low down	93 m.p.h.
Landing speed	45 m.p.h.

Climb.
To 6,500 ft.	8.40 mins.

Disposable load apart from fuel	213 lbs.
Total weight of machine loaded	1,320 lbs.

AIRCO DE H.3.

This machine, produced in 1915, was never put into service. It is of interest, however, as one of the earliest attempts at building a twin-engined machine and as the ancestor of the De H.10.

Specification.

Type of machine	Biplane "Pusher" (2 engines)
Name or type No. of machine	De H.3.
Span	60 ft. 10 in.
Gap, maximum and minimum	7 ft.
Overall length	36 ft. 10 in.
Maximum height	14 ft. 6 in.
Chord	6 ft. 9 in.
Total surface of wings, including centre planes and ailerons	790.0 sq. ft.
Span of tail	23 ft. 2 in.
Total area of tail (empennage)	164.0 sq. ft.
Area of elevators	25.5 sq. ft. each.
Area of rudder	22.0 sq. ft.
Area of fin	13.0 sq. ft.
Area of each aileron	30.7 sq. ft.
Engine type and h.p.	Two 130 h.p. Beardmore.
Airscrew, diam., pitch and revs.	9.03 diam., 9.18 pitch, 1,400.
Weight of machine empty	3,982 lbs.
Weight of machine full load	5,776 lbs.
Load per sq. ft.	7.3 lbs.
Weight per h.p. full load	22.2 lbs.
Tank capacity in gallons	140 gallons.

Performances.
Speed low down	95 m.p.h.

Climb.
To 6,500 ft.	24 mins.
Landing speed	53 m.p.h.

Disposable load apart from fuel	711 lbs.
Total weight of machine loaded	5,776 lbs.

AIRCO DE H.4.

The De H.4 was the first really high-speed British general utility machine of the medium weight type fitted with a high-power stationary engine. In the original form produced in 1916—fitted with a B.H.P. engine of 240 h.p.—the De H.4 had a speed greater than, and a climb and speed little, if at all, inferior to, that of the best of the rotary-engined single-seater fighters of that date.

It was thus possible to use these machines for reconnaissance and photographic work over the lines without the need for a fighter escort, since their excellent performance and the fact that they were fitted with a gun ring in the after seat in addition to a synchronised gun firing through the airscrew, put them upon at least equal terms with any existing type of enemy fighter.

The later editions of the same type fitted with "Eagle" Rolls-Royce engines, were considerably more valuable, and were extensively used for day-bombing in addition to reconnaissance work.

From a structural point of view this machine is chiefly remarkable for the very extensive use which is made of three-ply wood in the fuselage.

From the nose to aft of the passenger's seat the fuselage is devoid of wire bracing, a three-ply covering serving the purpose. Not only is this the case, but the whole of the engine mountings are built of ply-wood, which takes the place of the metal plates commonly used for such purposes.

It is thus possible to put bullet holes through almost any part of the front end of the fuselage without seriously impairing the strength of the structure—whereas with the usual methods of construction a single lucky shot may destroy an important bracing or cut out the flange of an engine plate, and seriously weaken the structure.

The Aircraft Manufacturing Co.'s De H.3 (2-160 h.p. Beardmore engines).

The De H.4 Biplane, with Rolls-Royce "Eagle" engine, 375 h.p.

Specification.

Type of machine	Biplane "Tractor."
Name or type No. of machine ..	De H.4.
Span	42 ft. 4½ in.
Gap, maximum and minimum ..	5 ft. 6 in.
Overall length	30 ft.
Maximum height	11 ft. 4½ in.
Chord	5 ft. 6 in.
Total surface of wings, including centre plane and aileron ..	434.0 sq. ft.
Span of tail	14 ft.
Total area of tail (empennage) ..	81.1 sq. ft.
Area of elevators	12.0 sq. ft. each.
Area of rudder	13.7 sq. ft.
Area of fin	5.4 sq. ft.
Area of each aileron	20.5 sq. ft.
Engine type and h.p. ..	240 h.p. B.H.P.
Airscrew, diam., pitch and revs.	8.75 diam., 8.2 pitch, 1,355 revs.
Weight of machine empty ..	2,302 lbs.
Weight of machine full load ..	3,400 lbs.
Load per sq. ft.	7.84 lbs.
Weight per h.p. full load ..	14.35 lbs.
Tank capacity in gallons ..	66 gallons.

Performance.

Speed low down	120 m.p.h.
Landing speed	52 m.p.h.

Climb.

To 6,500 feet	8 minutes.
To 10,000 feet	14.10 minutes.
To 15,000 feet	29.15 minutes.
With B.R. engine ..	136½ m.p.h.
To 6,500 feet	5.15 minutes.
To 10,000 feet	9 minutes.
To 15,000 feet	16.30 minutes.

Disposable load apart from fuel .. .. .. 578 lbs.

Total weight of machine loaded .. .. .. 3,400 lbs.

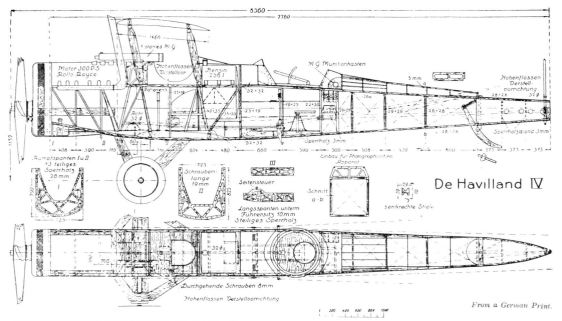

Fuselage Construction of the "Airco" De H.4. light bomber.

From a German Print.

An "Airco" De H.4 (375 h.p. "Eagle" Rolls-Royce) Converted to Passenger Carrying Purposes for use by No 2 Communications Squadron, RAF, to fly between Kenley and Buc during Peace Conference negotiations.

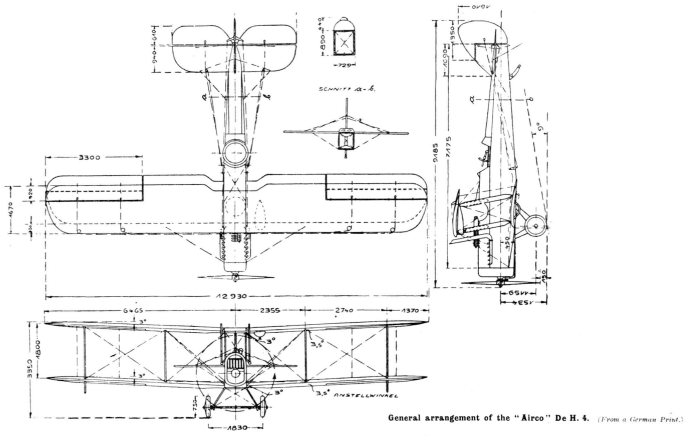

General arrangement of the "Airco" De H. 4. *(From a German Print.)*

AIRCO DE H.5.

This machine, produced late in 1916 and extensively used at the front in 1917, was in the main an effort to produce a single-seater fighter in which the pilot's view upwards and forward was not entirely blanketed by the top wing.

For this reason the top wing was staggered backwards very considerably, and the pilot's cockpit was put beneath the leading edge of that wing. In spite of the loss of efficiency which results from this backward stagger, Capt. De Haviland, by careful attention to the reduction of head resistance and weight, succeeded in producing a machine with a very good all-round performance.

Specification.

Type of machine	Biplane "Tractor."
Name or type No. of machine ..	De H.5.
Span	25 ft. 8 in.
Gap, maximum and minimum ..	4 ft. 9 in.
Overall length	22 ft.
Maximum height	9 ft. 1½ in.
Chord	4 ft. 6 in.
Total surface of wings, including centre plane and ailerons ..	212.1 sq. ft.
Span of tail	8 ft. 4½ in.
Total area of tail (empennage) ..	34.1 sq. ft.
Area of elevators	6.1 sq. ft. each.
Area of rudder	6.3 sq. ft.
Area of fin	2.2 sq. ft.
Area of each aileron ..	11.6 sq. ft.
Engine type and h.p. ..	110 h.p. Le Rhône.
Airscrew, diam., pitch and revs.	8.5 diam., 8.33 pitch, 1,295 revs.
Weight of machine empty ..	1,012 lbs.
Weight of machine full load ..	1,492 lbs.
Load per sq. ft.	7.03 lbs.
Weight per h.p. full load ..	13.57 lbs.
Tank capacity in gallons	25 gallons.

Performance.

Speed at 10,000 feet	102 m.p.h.
Speed at 15,000 feet	89 m.p.h.
Landing speed	50 m.p.h.
Disposable load apart from fuel	260 lbs.
Total weight of machine loaded	1,492 lbs.

Three-quarter Front View of the " Airco " De H. 5 (110 h.p. Le Rhône engine).

AIRCO DE H.6.

The De H. 6 was produced as an elementary training machine for pilots, and, to meet requirements, fundamentally different from those which are desirable in machines for war use.

High performance was not desired, was in fact rather to be avoided. Cheapness and simplicity and strength of construction, together with ease in repair and a low landing speed, were of primary importance.

As a result of these considerations, the De H. 6, vulgarly known alternatively as the " Clutching Hand " or the " Sky Hook " has very few of those rather expensive refinements of form which characterise most modern machines.

It has, in fact, rather the appearance of having been built by the mile and cut off to order, which is, of course, a testimony to the thoroughness with which the desired simplicity has been reached in the design.

Specification.

Type of machine	Biplane "Tractor."
Name or type No. of machine ..	De H.6.
Span	35 ft. 11 in.
Gap, maximum and minimum ..	5 ft. 8½ in.
Overall length	27 ft. 3½ in.
Maximum height	10 ft. 9½ in.
Chord	6 ft. 4 in.
Total surface of wings, including centre plane and aileron ..	436.3 sq. ft.
Span of tail	12 ft.
Total area of tail (empennage) ..	81.0 sq. ft.
Area of elevators	13.0 sq. ft. each
Area of rudder	12.0 sq. ft.
Area of fin	5.5 sq. ft.
Area of each aileron ..	19.0 sq. ft.
Engine type and h.p. ..	100 h.p. R.A.F. 1A.
Airscrew, diam., pitch and revs.	9.085 diam., 10.0 pitch, 1,800 r.p.m.
Weight of machine empty ..	1,460 lbs.
Weight of machine full load ..	2,027 lbs.
Load per sq. ft.	4.64 lbs.
Weight per h.p. full load ..	20.27 lbs.
Tank capacity in gallons ..	26 gallons.

Performance.

Speed low down	66 m.p.h.
Landing speed	39 m.p.h.

Climb.

To 6,500 feet	29 minutes.
Disposable load apart from fuel	360 lbs.
Total weight of machine loaded	2,027 lbs.

A De H. 6 Biplane, with R.A.F. engine (90 h.p.)

AIRCO DE H.9.

This machine is a modification of the De H. 4, intended for bombing work. The main alterations are that the pilot's cockpit has been moved from beneath the centre section to just behind the trailing edge thereof leaving space for bombs in the fuselage, that the engine centre line has been slightly raised and the chassis somewhat shortened, and that the nose radiator has been replaced by a vertical water tank and a radiator in the bottom of the fuselage.

The total weight empty has been reduced by about 100 lbs., the tank capacity is somewhat increased, and the total load carried has been increased by about 500 lbs., at the cost of a slight loss in speed and climb and an increase in the landing speed.

Specification.

Type of machine	Biplane "Tractor."
Name or type No. of machine ..	De H.9.
Span	42 ft. 4⅝ in.
Gap, maximum and minimum ..	5 ft. 6 in.
Overall length	30 ft. 10 in.
Maximum height..	11 ft. 2 in.
Chord	5 ft. 6 in.
Total surface of wings, including centre plane and ailerons ..	434.0 sq. ft.
Span of tail	14 ft.
Total area of tail (empennage) ..	81.1 sq. ft.
Area of elevators	12.0 sq. ft. each.
Area of rudder	13.7 sq. ft.
Area of fin	5.4 sq. ft.
Area of each aileron	20.5.
Engine type and h.p.	240 h.p. B.H.P.
Airscrew diam., pitch and revs...	9.5 diam., 6.9 pitch, 1525 revs.
Weight of machine empty ..	2,200 lbs.
Weight of machine full load ..	3,890 lbs.
Load per sq. ft.	8.95 lbs.
Weight per h.p. full load ..	16.2 lbs.
Tank capacity in gallons.. ..	74 gallons.
Performance.	
Speed at 10,000 feet	110½ m.p.h.
Speed at 15,000 feet	102 m.p.h.
Landing speed..	57 m.p.h.
Disposable load apart from fuel	1,121 lbs.
Total weight of machine loaded	3,890 lbs.

A Standard Type De H.9 (240 h.p. B.H.P. engine).

A De H.9 with a Napier "Lion" engine (450 h.p.)

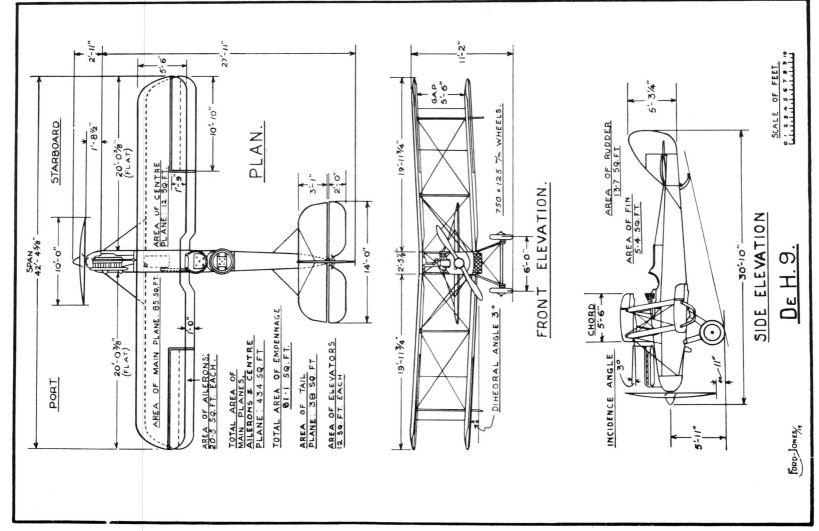

Three-quarter View from Rear—" Airco " De H.9A (400 h.p. Liberty engine).

AIRCO DE H.9.A.

This machine is an enlarged De H. 9, designed for the 375 h.p. Rolls or the 400 h.p. Liberty. The span and the total surface have been somewhat increased, and the nose radiator has returned. Otherwise there is little alteration.

Specification.

Type of machine	Biplane "Tractor."
Name or type No. of machine ..	De H.9a.
Span	45 ft. 11¾ in.
Gap, maximum and minimum ..	5 ft. 6 in.
Overall length	30 ft. 3 in.
Maximum height	11 ft. 4 in.
Chord	5 ft. 9 in.
Total surface of wings, including centre plane and ailerons ..	486.73 sq. ft.
Span of tail	14 ft.
Total area of tail (empennage) ..	80.1 sq. ft.
Area of elevators..	12.0 sq. ft. each.
Area of rudder	13.7 sq. ft.
Area of fin	5.4 sq. ft.
Area of each aileron	18.59 sq. ft.
Engine type and h.p.	375 h.p. Rolls-Royce or 400 h.p. Liberty.
Airscrew, diam., pitch and revs.	10.0 diam., 12.3 pitch, 1,780 r.p.m.
Weight of machine empty ..	2,656 lbs.
Weight of machine full load ..	4,815 lbs.
Load per sq. ft.	9.89 lbs.
Weight per h.p. full load ..	12.8 lbs., 12.03 lbs.
Tank capacity in gallons ..	112 gallons.

Performance.
R.R. engine. Speed at 10,000 feet 110½ m.p.h.
Landing speed .. 59 m.p.h.

Climb.
To 6,500 feet .. .. .. 11 minutes.
To 10,000 feet .. .. .. 20.6 minutes.
Disposable load apart from fuel .. .. .. 1,199 lbs.
Total weight of machine loaded .. .. .. 4,815 lbs.

Note.—If less weight is carried a speed of 125½ m.p.h. is attained at 10,000 feet, and 116 m.p.h. at 15,000 feet.

Another View of the " Airco " De H.9A (400 h.p. Liberty engine).

A De H.9A, with Liberty engine.

The Pilot's and Gunner's Cockpits of a De H.9A, with Napier Lion engine. 450 h.p.

Three-quarter Front View—The De H.9A (Liberty engine).

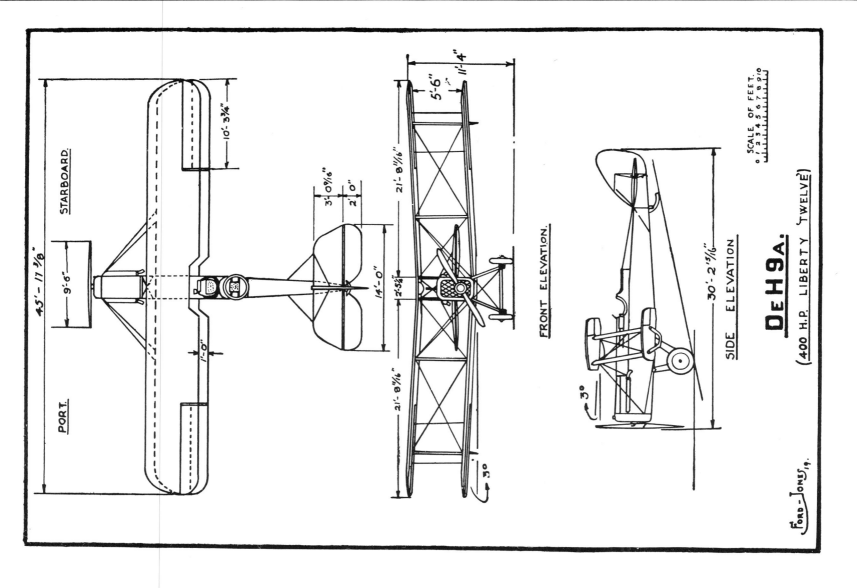

STARBOARD.

PORT.

45'- 11 1/8"

9'-6"

1'-0"

10'- 3 3/4"

3'- 0 9/16"

2'- 0"

14'- 0"

2'- 5 3/4"

21'- 8 11/16"

21'- 8 11/16"

11'-4"

5'-6"

FRONT ELEVATION.

SIDE ELEVATION.

30'- 2 13/16"

3°

3°

SCALE OF FEET.
0 1 2 3 4 5 6 7 8 9 10

De H 9A.
(400 H.P. LIBERTY "TWELVE")

Ford-Jones '19.

AIRCO DE H.10 AND 10A.

The De H. 10 was designed as a high-speed day bomber and made its first appearance towards the end of 1917. As has been already stated, it is essentially a development of the De H. 3, from which it differs in that whereas the De H. 3 was fitted with pusher airscrews, the De H. 10 has tractor airscrews.

The most noticeable feature of this machine is the extremely low position of the fuselage, which is mainly below the bottom wing, and the curious mounting of the engines, overhung from one side of the outer centre section struts

The De H 10 is a somewhat later type of the same machine. They differ mainly in that in the De H. 10 the twin engines are mounted well up in the gap between the planes, and in the De H 10a, the engine nacelles are actually on the bottom plane.

The alterations have resulted in a very marked increase in the speed of the type 10a, accompanied by an increase in the empty weight of the machine of nearly 140 lbs.

Both types proved their qualities on active service, before the cessation of hostilities, and it may be expected that with suitable modifications they will show their value even more fully as commercial machines in the near future.

Specification.

Type of machine	..	Biplane " Tractor."
Name or type No. of machine	..	De H.10.
Span	..	65 ft. 6 in.
Gap, maximum and minimum	..	7 ft.
Overall length	..	39 ft. 7 7/16 in.
Chord	..	7 ft.
Total surface of wings, including centre plane and ailerons	..	837.4 sq. ft.
Span of tail	..	22 ft.
Total area of tail (empennage)	..	144.3 sq. ft.
Area of elevators.. ..	..	16.54 sq. ft. each.
Area of rudder	..	25.75 sq. ft.
Area of fin	..	10.0 sq. ft.

Area of each aileron ..	..	29.5 sq. ft.
Engine type and h.p. ..	..	Two 400 h.p. Liberty.
Airscrew, diam., pitch and revs.	..	10.0 diam., 7.3 pitch, 1,625 revs.
Weight of machine empty	..	5,355 lbs.
Weight of machine full load	..	8,500 lbs.
Weight per h.p. full load	..	10.6 lbs.
Tank capacity in gallons..	..	215 gallons.
Performance.		
Speed low down ..	..	117½ m.p.h.
Speed at 10,000 feet ..	..	115 m.p.h.
Speed at 15,000 feet ..	..	110 m.p.h.
Landing speed.. ..	..	62 m.p.h.
Disposable load apart from fuel	.. ..	.. 1,381 lbs.

Front View of a De H.10 (two 400 h.p. Liberty engines) without wings.

Three-quarter Front View—" Airco " De H.10 (two Rolls-Royce " Eagle " engines, each 360 h.p.)

AIRCO DE H.10 A.

Type of machine	Biplane "Tractor."
Name or type No. of machine ..	De H.10a.
Span	65 ft. 6 in.
Gap, maximum and minimum ..	7 ft.
Overall length	39 ft. 7⁷⁄₁₆ in.
Maximum height	14 ft. 6 in.
Chord	7 ft.
Total surface of wings, including centre plane and ailerons ..	837.4 sq. ft.
Span of tail	22 ft.
Total area of tail (empennage) ..	144.3 sq. ft.
Area of elevators..	16.54 sq. ft. each.
Area of rudder	25.75 sq. ft.
Area of fin	10.0 sq. ft.
Area of each aileron	29.5 sq. ft.
Engine type and h.p.	Two 400 h.p. Liberty.
Airscrew, diam., pitch and revs.	10.0 diam., 7.3 pitch, 1,625 revs.
Weight of machine empty ..	5,488 lbs.
Weight of machine full load ..	8,500 lbs.
Weight per h.p. full load.. ..	10.6 lbs.
Tank capacity in gallons.. ..	215 gallons.

Performance.

Speed low down	128 m.p.h.
Speed at 10,000 feet	124 m.p.h.
Speed at 15,000 feet	117 m.p.h.
Landing speed	62 m.p.h.
Disposable load apart from fuel	1,248 lbs

Three-quarter View from Aft—The De H. 10A (two 400 h.p. Liberty engines).

ARMSTRONG-WHITWORTH

Sir W. G. Armstrong, Whitworth & Co., Ltd., of Gosforth, Newcastle-on-Tyne (Aeroplane Works), and Barlow, nr. Selby (Airship Works).

Captain I. F. Fairbairn-Crawford, who is general manager of the aircraft department, founded the aeroplane department in 1913 and the airship department in 1915. Lieut.-Commander R. G. Lock, R.N., was assistant to the general manager. Mr. F. Murphy is chief designer and works manager of the aeroplane department, Gosforth. Mr. H. H. Golightly is works manager of the airship department, Barlow Aircraft Works, Selby.

Both departments have been working at full pressure during the period of the war, and over 1,300 aeroplanes for military purposes and three large rigid airships for the Navy have been completed and delivered.

The following types of aeroplanes have been delivered :—

B.E.2a., B.E.2b., B.E.2c., biplanes to R.A.F. design.

The 70 h.p., 90 h.p., 120 h.p., and 160 h.p. F.K. type Armstrong-Whitworth two-seater biplanes, which were designed by Mr. Frederick Koolhoven.

A 250 h.p. triplane.

Several 130 h.p. quadruplanes.

220 h.p. B.R.2, F.N. type, single-seater scout biplanes. (The " Armadillo.")

320 h.p. A.B.C., F.M. type, single-seater scout biplanes. (The " Ara.") Etc., etc., etc.

The following Naval rigid airships.

H.M.R.25, with four 250 h.p. Rolls-Royce engines.
H.M.R.29, with four 250 h.p. Rolls-Royce engines.
H.M.R.33, with five 270 h.p. Sunbeam engines.
Cars for fifteen S.S. and coastal type non-rigid airships.
Larger rigid airships are in course of construction and design.

THE ARMSTRONG-WHITWORTH F.K.3.

The Armstrong-Whitworth F.K.3 was designed by Mr. Frederick Koolhoven, and was built at the time when B.E.2cs were being produced in large numbers and was an improvement on this type of machine.

In general appearance there is very little difference from the B.E.2c, the fuselage being of the same long, narrow type, with the exception that the pilot is placed in front of the observer, who is equipped with a swivel gun-mounting.

A 90 h.p. R.A.F. air-cooled engine is carried in the nose.

The undercarriage consists of an axle hinged in the middle to a central skid which is carried in two Vees from the fuselage, the two side struts from the axle being mounted on oleopneumatic shock-absorbers inside the fuselage.

Three-quarter Front View of the Armstrong-Whitworth F.K.3 (90 h.p. R.A.F. Engine).

Three-quarter Rear View of the Armstrong-Whitworth F.K.3 (90 h.p. R.A.F. Engine).

The main planes are staggered with a wide gap, and have two sets of struts on each side of the fuselage. The rudder is balanced. The machine was used on active service for some time, but was eventually used as a training machine in conjunction with the B.E.2c and d.

Specification.

Type of machine	Two-seater Biplane.
Name or type No. of machine ..	Armstrong-Whitworth F.K.3.
Purpose for which intended ..	Sport and Training.
Span	40 ft.
Overall length	28 ft. 8 in.
Maximum height.. ..	10 ft. 2½ in.
Engine type and h.p. ..	90 h.p. R.A.F.
Weight of machine empty ..	1,900 lbs.
Tank capacity in hours ..	3½ hours.

Performance.

Speed at 1,000 feet	.. ..	85 m.p.h.
Landing speed..	..	38 m.p.h.

Climb.

To 10,000 feet in minutes	..	23 minutes.

THE ARMSTRONG-WHITWORTH F.K.8.

The Armstrong-Whitworth F.K.8, also designed by Mr. Koolhoven, was a heavier and improved F.K.3. It had a deeper fuselage, a similar type of undercarriage except that the central skid was cut short in front of the front Vee, and a 120 h.p. Beardmore engine was enclosed in a cowling, with two radiators, one on either side of the fuselage and meeting in the form of an inverted Vee at the upper plane.

There is no centre section, the two upper planes being attached to two inverted Vees over the fuselage.

This machine was used to a large extent on various fronts for contact patrols, artillery spotting, light bombing, photography and reconnaissance work up to the signing of the Armistice, although it was gradually being superseded by machines of improved design.

About half-way through its active service life the F.K.8 was slightly modified by having a Vee-type undercarriage fitted and the engine mounting altered to take a 160 h.p. Beardmore and smaller radiators of improved efficiency, fitted on the sides of the fuselage only. A long exhaust pipe was also added to carry the exhaust fumes well clear of the crew.

Accommodation was made for two guns, camera and wireless installation to be carried.

Specification.

Type of machine	Two-seater Biplane.
Name or type No. of machine ..	Armstrong-Whitworth F.K.8.
Purpose for which intended ..	Military and Commercial.
Span	43 ft. 4 ins.
Overall length	31 ft.
Maximum height.. ..	10 ft. 6 in.
Engine type and h.p. ..	160 Beardmore.
Weight of machine empty ..	2,500 lbs.
Tank capacity in hours ..	3½ hours.

Performance.

Speed at 1,000 feet	..	104 m.p.h.
Landing speed..	..	45 m.p.h.

Climb.

To 10,000 ft. in minutes	..	17½ minutes.

THE ARMSTRONG-WHITWORTH "ARMADILLO."

This machine was designed by Mr. Murphy as a single-seater fighter and was produced about the middle of 1918, the trial flights taking place in September of that year.

The chief characteristics of the machines are a square fuselage and the top plane resting on the upper longerons. Two pairs of interplane struts are fitted on each side of the fuselage.

A 200 h.p. B.R.2 engine is carried in the nose of the fuselage and is enclosed in a circular cowl in the top of which is a peculiar box-like hump, which is actually a continuation of the upper part of the fuselage brought round and finished off on the cowling. In this box-like arrangement are two fixed Vickers guns, mounted to fire through the airscrew with the usual form of fire control gear.

Specification.

Type of machine	Single-seater Biplane.
Name or type No. of machine ..	"Armadillo" (1918).
Purpose for which intended ..	Military and Sport.
Span	27 ft. 6 in.
Overall length	20 ft.
Maximum height.. ..	7 ft. 10 in.
Engine type and h.p. ..	220 h.p. B.R.2 Rotary.
Weight of machine empty ..	1,900 lbs.
Tank capacity in hours ..	2¾ hours.

Performance.

Speed at 1,000 feet	..	140 m.p.h.
Landing speed..	..	55 m.p.h.

Climb.

To 10,000 feet in minutes	..	4½ minutes.

The F.K.8 Type Armstrong-Whitworth Biplane. With 120 h.p. Beardmore engine.

Three-quarter Front View of the Armstrong-Whitworth F.K.8 (160 h.p. Beardmore engine).

Three-quarter Front View of the Armstrong-Whitworth "Armadillo" (220 h.p. B.R.2 Engine).

Front View of the Armstrong-Whitworth "Ara" (320 h.p. A.B.C. Engine).

THE ARMSTRONG-WHITWORTH "ARA."

The Armstrong-Whitworth "Ara," although it was not produced until early this year, was designed as a single-seater fighter, but can be easily adapted as a sporting machine for one who desires something more than the low-powered, slow-speed machines which are being introduced by many firms at the present time.

The fuselage is of square section and carries a 320 h.p. A.B.C. "Dragonfly" engine in its nose, which is covered in by a conical cowl leaving the cylinder heads protruding, a continuation of the cowl forming a spinner on the propeller boss

An ordinary vee-type undercarriage is fitted. The upper plane is placed very low over the top of the fuselage thus giving the pilot an excellent view upwards.

Specification.

Type of machine	Single-seater Biplane.
Name or type No. of machine ..	"Ara" (1919).
Purpose for which intended ..	Military and Sport.
Span	27 ft. 6 in.
Overall length	20 ft.
Maximum height	7 ft. 10 in.
Engine type and h.p. ..	320 h.p. A.B.C. "Dragonfly."
Weight of machine empty ..	1,900 lbs.
Tank capacity in hours ..	3¼ hours.

Performance.

Speed at 1,000 feet ..	150 m.p.h.
Landing speed.. ..	55 m.p.h.

Climb.

To 10,000 feet in minutes ..	5½ minutes.

Three Armstrong-Whitworths. —Two of the F.K.10 Type Quadruplanes and an F.K.8 with a Sunbeam-Coatalen "Arab" Engine. Eight F.K. 10s went to the RNAS for fighting and bombing.

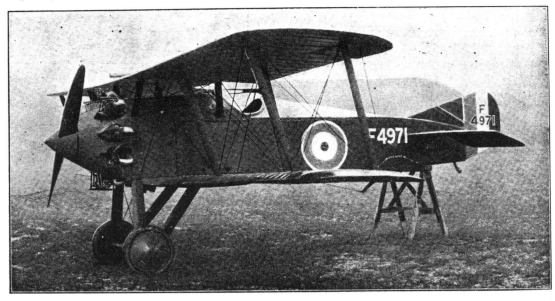

The Armstrong-Whitworth "Ara" 320 h.p. A.B.C. "Dragonfly."

AUSTIN MOTORS, LTD. Northfield, Birmingham.

A motor-car firm which took up the manufacture of aircraft during the war. In addition to numerous machines to Government specifications, have built the machines hereafter described and illustrated to their own designs.

THE AUSTIN "BALL" SINGLE-SEATER BIPLANE.

The *Austin* "Ball" biplane was designed as a single-seater fighting scout to the ideas of the late Capt. Ball, V.C., D.S.O., M.C. The fuselage is very deep, reaching almost to the top plane, and carries in its nose a 200 h.p. Hispano-Suiza engine, which is well cowled in, the radiators being fixed on the side of the fuselage below the front centre section struts.

The planes are unstaggered and of equal length, having one pair of struts on either side of the fuselage. The tail unit is of standard type except that there is no fixed fin area. Undercarriage is of the Vee-type, the axle and wheels being slung at the apex of the Vee with rubber shock absorber. A small tailskid pivoted to an extension of the rudder-post takes the weight of the tail, when the machine is at rest on the ground.

Specification.

Type of machine	Single-seater Biplane, Scout, Fighter.
Name or type No. of machine ..	Austin "Ball."
Purposes for which intended ..	Scouting and Fighting.
Span	30 ft.
Gap	4 ft. 9 in.
Overall length	21 ft. 6 in.
Maximum height	9 ft. 3 in.
Chord	5 ft.
Wing surface	290 sq. ft.
Span of tail	11 ft. 3 in. (over elevators).
Total area of tail	32 sq. ft. (includes elevators).
Area of elevators	8 sq. ft. each.
Area of rudder	8 sq. ft.
Area of Ailerons	7½ sq. ft. each.
Total area of ailerons ..	30 sq. ft.
Engine type and h.p. ..	200 h.p. Hispano-Suiza "V" type, water cooled.
Weight of machine empty	1,426 lbs.
Load per sq. ft.	7 lbs.
Load per h.p.	9.25 lbs.
Tank capacity in hours ..	2 hours.
Tank capacity in gallons ..	Petrol 31½ galls., oil 5 galls., water 9 galls.

Performance.

Speed low down	138 m.p.h.
Speed at 10,000 feet ..	126 m.p.h.

Climb.

To 10,000 feet..	10 minutes.
Total weight of machine loaded	2,075 lbs.

Front View of the Austin "Ball" (200 h.p. Hispano-Suiza Engine).

Side View of the Austin "Ball" Single-seat Fighter.

THE AUSTIN "GREYHOUND."

The *Austin* "Greyhound" represents one of the latest efforts to produce a fast, quick-climbing two-seater, fighting and reconnaissance biplane. In general arrangement it follows standard practice. The fuselage carries in its nose a 320 h.p. A.B.C. "Dragonfly" engine. A conical cowling covers the engine in with the exception of the cylinder heads, the shape of the cowling being preserved throughout the length of the fuselage by fairing. There is almost equal fin area above and below the fuselage. The upper main plane trailing edge is cut away, and the lower plane is of lesser chord than the upper, thereby giving the pilot a good view. Accommodation is made for the machine to carry three guns, camera, wireless, oxygen apparatus and heating apparatus.

Three-quarter Front View of the Austin "Ball" Single-seat Fighter.

Side View of an Experimental Austin Triplane.

Specification.

Type of machine	Two-seater Fighter, Reconnaissance Biplane.
Name or type No. of machine ..	"Greyhound."
Purposes for which intended ..	Fighting and Reconnaissance.
Engine type and h.p.	A.B.C. "Dragonfly," 320 h.p.
Span	Top plane, 39 ft.; bottom plane, 36 ft. 7 in.
Gap	4 ft. $11\frac{7}{8}$ in.
Maximum height..	10 ft. 4 in.
Chord	Top plane, 6 ft. 4.8 in.; bottom plane, 4 ft. 3 in.
Total surface of wings ..	400 sq. ft.
Span of tail	12 ft. 9.5 in.
Total area of tail.. ..	47 sq. ft.
Total area of elevators ..	19.8 sq. ft.
Area of rudder	9.9 sq. ft.
Area of fin	Top, 2.76 sq. ft. bottom, 2.3 sq. ft.
Area of each aileron and total area	Two top, 14.8 sq. ft.; two bottom, 7.8 sq. ft ; total, 45.2 sq. ft.
Weight of machine empty ..	2,050 lbs.
Load per sq. ft.	7.72 lbs. per sq. ft.
Weight per h.p.	10.3 lbs.
Tank capacity in hours ..	3 hours.
Tank capacity in gallons..	Petrol 66 galls., oil 8 galls.
Weight of machine full ..	3,090 lbs. (including guns, ammunition, &c.)

Performance (estimated).

Speed at 10,000 feet	130 m.p.h.
Landing speed..	45 m.p.h.

Climb.

To 10,000 feet..	11 minutes.

Three-quarter Front View of the Austin "Greyhound" 320 h.p. A.B.C. "Dragonfly" Engine.

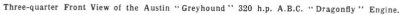

An Austin-built S.E.5a.

AVRO. *Aeroplanes.* A. V. Roe & Co., Ltd., Clifton Street, Miles Platting, Manchester.

A new factory, with its own aerodrome and experimental plant, has been established at Hamble, Hants, where Mr. A. V. Roe is in charge, assisted by his brother, the Rev. E. V. Roe.

The main output of the firm is produced at the Manchester Works.

Mr. H. V. Roe left the firm in 1917 and joined the Royal Flying Corps. He was injured in an accident in the Vosges while night-flying, and has now retired from the aircraft business.

The history of the *Avro* machine commences with the design in 1906 by Mr. A. V. Roe of a biplane, which by leaving the ground at Brooklands, in July, 1908, was the first British aeroplane to fly. In 1909, Mr. Roe flew a triplane with a 9 h.p. J.A.P engine at Lea Marshes. During 1910, Mr. Roe built two more triplanes, fitted with 30 h.p J.A.P. and 35 h.p. Green engines, and flew them at Wembley and at Brooklands.

Early in the summer of 1911 an *Avro* biplane made its first flights at Brooklands, piloted by Mr. Howard Pixton. At this period the embryo " Avro " firm was financed by Mr. H. V. Roe, who owned the firm of Everitt & Co., Webbing Manufacturers, of Manchester.

From this biplane of 1911 the development of the *Avro* machines is to be traced through a very pretty little machine with a 40 h.p. E.N.V. engine, built for Mr. Duigan, the first Australian aviator, an extremely efficient two-seater with a 60 h.p. E.N.V. engine, a series of 50 h.p. Gnôme-engined machines ordered by the War Office, which were actually the first aeroplanes designed and built by a British firm to be delivered to the British Army, to the totally enclosed biplane with the 60 h.p. Green engine which gave so good an account of itself in the British military trials at Salisbury Plains in 1912.

Early in 1913 the famous two-seater *Avro* with an 80 h.p. Gnôme engine made its appearance. This machine—unaltered in all its essential aerodynamic features and in its main dimensions—survives to this day as the *Standard Avro* training machine.

THE AVRO STANDARD TRAINING BIPLANE.

By a process of detailed improvement, which has led to increased strength and greater simplicity, and by the adoption of standardised methods of manufacture, the 80 h.p. machine of 1913 has evolved into the Type 504 K., a machine admirably adapted for the methods of quantity production.

GENERAL REMARKS.

This machine is specially suitable for the purpose of training pilots, and has been adopted as the Standard Training Machine by the Royal Air Force. In the 504 K. Type the nose of the machine has been altered and the engine mounted overhung from the bearers. The machine will now take any of the existing rotary engines up to 150 h.p. This has been accomplished by suitably designing the engine mounting and fitting adaptors to take the different engines. It will be seen that this is a great advantage from the engine supply point of view.

The machine retains its characteristics of simplicity, strength and controllability, and one of its chief advantages is the ease with which it can be repaired at School Workshops where interchangeable spares can be obtained readily.

Specification.

The following tables give the main features of this machine :

Type of Aeroplane ..	..2 Seater Biplane (Training Machine).
Aeroplane Specification	.." Avro " Type 504K.
Engine	..100 Mono Gnôme, 110 Clerget, 110 Le Rhône, or 130 Clerget.
Revolutions of engine for stated b.h.p. ..	..1250 r.p.m.

Estimated speed with full load and with all fittings in position.

Maximum speed for the above horse power and revolutions.

At ground level .. .. .. 95 m.p.h.	
At 8,000 feet .. .. .. 87 m.p.h.	
At 10,000 feet .. .. .. 85 m.p.h.	

Duration of flight at this speed.

At ground level .. .. .. 2 hrs.	
At 8,000 feet .. .. .. 2.14 hrs.	
At 10,000 feet .. .. .. 3 hrs.	
Minimum speed with full load near ground .. .. 40 m.p.h.	
Estimated speed at ¾ power at 8,000 feet .. .. 74 m.p.h.	
Estimated speed at ¾ power at 10,000 feet .. .. 71 m.p.h.	
Estimated duration at ¾ power at 8,000 feet .. .. .. 3.7 hrs.	
Estimated duration at ¾ power at 10,000 feet .. .. .. 4.25 hrs.	

Estimated climb with full load and with all fittings in position.

To 3,500 feet .. .. .. 5 mins.	
To 8,000 feet .. .. .. 10 mins.	
To 10,000 feet .. .. .. 16 mins.	

Seating Accommodation.

Pilot, position ..	Level with trailing edge of lower wing.
Passenger's position	In front of pilot.

Airscrew.

Type .. .. 2 bladed "Avro."	
Pitch (110 Le Rhône) .. .. 8 ft. 8 in.	
Diameter .. .. .. 9 ft. 0 in.	

Overall Dimensions.

Span of upper wings	..	.. 36 ft. 0 in.
Span of lower wings	..	.. 36 ft. 0 in.
Span of tail plane	..	.. 10 ft. 0 in.
Height overall	..	.. 10 ft. 5 in.
Length overall	..	.. 29 ft. 5 in.
Chord top wing	..	.. 4 ft. 9 in.
Chord second wing	..	.. 4 ft. 9 in.
Chord tail plane	..	.. 2 ft. 8⅜ in.
Chord elevator	.. ..	.. 2 ft. 4 in.

Three-quarter front view of the Avro 504K Standard Training Machine.

AVRO 504B Biplane, 80 h.p. Gnome, about to start. This type of Avro was one of the most successful machines in the early days of the war, owing to its durability, speed, and climbing power. It is still one of the most efficient machines for its power, but is, of course, surpassed in actual performance by machines with bigger engines, so is very largely used to-day as a training machine for Service pilots practising cross-country flying before passing on to the higher-powered war machines. It will be remembered that *504As* carried out the first ever strategic bombing raid, on 21 November 1914, when three RNAS aircraft attacked the Zeppelin sheds at Friedrichshafen.

Side view of the Avro 504K Seaplane. This machine is the Standard Training Machine in all essentials, fitted with a float under-carriage.

Details of Weight.

Component.		Weight in lbs.
Tail Unit.		
Tail plane with supports	..	$21\frac{1}{2}$
Elevators	..	12
Rudder with levers and wires	..	$8\frac{1}{2}$
	Total ..	42 lbs.
Main Lift Structure.		
Wings with flaps with centre section	..	$260\frac{1}{2}$
Interplane struts	..	41
Interplane wires	..	$24\frac{1}{2}$
	Total ..	326 lbs.
Alighting Gear.		
Undercarriage with axle and skid	..	65
Main Wheels 100 × 700	..	40
Wing skids	..	2
Tail skids	..	6
	Total ..	113 lbs.
Hull.		
Body and Engine Housing	..	270
Aeroplane control gear and wires	..	30
Other details, flying instruments, lighting set, etc.		25
	Total ..	325 lbs.
Power Plant.		
Engine with magnetos 110 h.p. Le Rhône	..	330
Airscrews, boss and bolts	..	41
Oil tanks, cooler and piping	..	15
Petrol tanks, piping and air pressure system	..	39
	Total ..	425 lbs.

Total weight of machine bare with water in radiators 1231 lbs.

Military Load.
Crew of 2 at 180 lbs. each .. .. 360 lbs.

Weight of Machine in Flying Trim.
(a) Weight of machine bare with water in radiators		1231
(b) Military load	..	360
(c) Petrol $25\frac{1}{2}$ galls.	..	184
(d) Oil 6 galls.	..	54
	Total ..	1829 lbs.

Areas. Wings and Ailerons.
Top	..	173 sq. ft.
Second	..	157 sq. ft.
	Total ..	330 sq. ft.

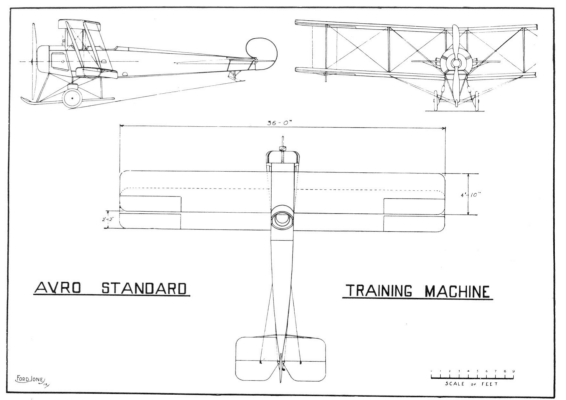

General arrangement of the Standard Avro Type 504 K.

THE AVRO TWO-SEATER FIGHTER.—Type 530.

This machine was originally designed by Messrs. A. V. Roe and Co., in 1915, to meet the needs of the R.F.C. for a fast two-seater fighter. For some reason or other (presumably because it was so much better than the contemporary R.A.F. product—Ed.) the machine did not obtain the approval of the authorities, and has never been put into production.

In its design special attention has been given to securing the best possible view for both pilot and passenger.

The upper centre section is arranged to be level with the pilot's eye, thus obstructing his view to the smallest possible extent. The lower plane is staggered back and gives him a view downwards and forwards at a very steep angle.

The rear gunners' seat is aft of the trailing edge of the lower wing, so that both occupants have a very wide range of vision.

The following tables give the essential details of the machine :—

Specification.

Type of machine	..	Two-seater Biplane.
Name or type No. of machine	..	Avro 530.
Purpose for which intended	..	Fighter or fast two-seater.
Span	..	36 ft.
Gap, maximum and minimum	..	5 ft.
Overall length	..	28 ft. 6 in.
Maximum height	..	9 ft. 7 in.
Chord	..	5 ft. 6 in.
Total surface of wings	..	$325\frac{1}{2}$ sq. ft.
Span of tail	..	12 ft.
Total area of tail	..	52.2 sq. ft. (including elevators).
Area of elevators	..	23.8 sq. ft.
Area of rudder	..	8.8 sq. ft.
Area of fin	..	4.5 sq. ft.
Area of each aileron and total area	4 × 14.5 sq. ft.	58 sq. ft.
Maximum cross section of body	..	14.0 sq. ft.
Horizontal area of body	..	$63\frac{1}{2}$ sq. ft.
Vertical area of body	..	100 sq. ft.
Engine type and h.p.	..	200 h.p. Hispano-Suiza or Sunbeam " Arab."

Airscrew, diam., pitch, and revs.	..	Avro Tractor D. 2.97, p. 2.82; r.p.m. 1,200
Weight of machine empty		1,695 lbs.
Load per sq. ft.	..	8.23 lbs.
Weight per h.p.	..	13.4 lbs. (assuming 200 h.p.)
Tank capacity in hours	..	4 hours at 10,000 ft.
Tank capacity in gallons	..	40 gallons.

Performance.

Speed low down	..	114 m.p.h.
Speed at 10,000 feet	..	102 m.p.h.
Speed at 20,000 feet	..	
Landing speed	..	58 m.p.h.

Climb.

To 5,000 feet in minutes	..	$6\frac{1}{2}$ min.
To 10,000 feet in minutes	..	15 ,,
To 20,000 feet in minutes		Ceiling, 18,000 ft. in 40 mins.
Disposable load apart from fuel	.. ..	574 lbs.
Total weight of machine loaded	.. ..	2,680 lbs.

THE AVRO "MANCHESTER" TWIN-ENGINED BIPLANES.

The two "Manchester" types hereafter described differ mainly in respect of their power plant.

Both have a common origin in the *Avro "Pike,"* a twin-engined three-seater fighter-bomber built and designed for the Royal Naval Air Service by the Avro firm in 1916.

This machine, fitted with two 160 h.p. Sunbeam engines, performed exceedingly well in spite of the insufficient power plant, and was undeniably one of the cleanest twin-engined designs which has yet been produced.

The "Manchester" Mark 1 and 2 machines differ very little in their general arrangements and outline from this original.

One very interesting feature which is shown in the scale drawings reproduced of the Mark 1 machine, is the method of balancing the ailerons which is employed.

To the top of the upper king-post of the top plane aileron a small plane is fixed. When an aileron is pulled down this plane is given a positive incidence by the movement of the king-post, and gives an appreciable lift. As the plane is ahead of the aileron hinge, this lift assists in holding the aileron down, and so partly balances the aileron.

When the aileron is pulled up the balancing plane is given a negative incidence, and exerts the required balancing force tending to hold the aileron up.

Both types are three-seaters with pilot's cockpit under the leading edge of the wings, observer's seat and gun turret in the nose of the fuselage, and a rear gunner's cockpit well aft of the main planes, whence a very wide field of fire is obtained.

THE TWIN-ENGINED AVRO.—"Manchester Mark 1."

Type of machine	Three-seater Twin-engined Biplane
Name or type No. of machine ..	Avro "Manchester Mark I."
Purpose for which intended	Photography, reconnaissance, bombing.
Span	60 ft.
Gap, maximum and minimum ..	7 ft. 3 in.
Overall length	37 ft.
Maximum height	12 ft. 6 in.
Chord	7 ft. 6 in.
Total surface of wings ..	843—30 (area of nacelles).
Span of tail	13 ft.
Total area of tail	82 sq. ft. (including elevators.)
Area of elevators.. ..	32 sq. ft.
Area of rudder	19 sq. ft.
Area of fin	11.7 sq. ft.
Area of each aileron and total area	31 sq. ft.; total 124 sq. ft.
Maximum cross section of body .	14.3 sq. ft.
Horizontal area of body.. ..	80 sq. ft.
Vertical area of body ..	111 sq. ft.
Engine type and h.p.	A.B.C "Dragon-fly"; 320 h.p. at 1,650 r.p.m.
Airscrew, diam., pitch, and revs..	Avro Tractor D. 2.9m., P. 2m., r.p.m. 1600.
Weight of machine empty ..	4,049 lbs.
Load per sq. ft...	8.06 lbs.
Weight per h.p.	10.3 lbs.
Tank capacity in hours ..	5¾ hours, at 10,000 ft. (including climb).
Tank capacity in gallons ..	183 gallons.

Performance.

Speed low down ..	128 m.p.h.
Speed at 10,000 feet ..	122 m.p.h.
Speed at 15,000 feet ..	115 m.p.h.
Landing speed	45 m.p.h.

Climb.

To 5,000 feet in minutes	4½ mins.
To 10,000 feet in minutes ..	11 mins.
To 20,000 feet in minutes ..	Service ceiling, 40 mins.

No bombs carried for this performance.

Disposable load apart from fuel..	1,007 lbs.
Total weight of machine loaded..	6,586 lbs.

THE TWIN-ENGINED AVRO.—"Manchester Mark II."

Type of Machine	Three-seater Twin-engined Biplane.
Name or type No. of machine..	Avro "Manchester Mark II."
Purpose for which intended ..	Photography, reconnaissance, bombing.
Span	60 ft.
Gap, maximum and minimum ..	7 ft. 3 in.
Overall length	37 ft.
Maximum height.. ..	12 ft. 6 in.
Chord	7 ft. 6 in.
Total surface of wings ..	843—26 (area of engine nacelles)
Span of Tail	13 ft.
Total area of Tail	82 sq. ft. (including elevators).
Area of elevators	32 sq. ft.
Area of rudder	19 sq. ft.
Area of fin	11.7 sq. ft.
Area of each aileron and total area	31 sq. ft.; total 124 sq. ft.
Maximum cross section of body..	14.3 sq. ft.
Horizontal area of body.. ..	80 sq. ft.
Vertical area of body ..	111 sq. ft.
Engine type and h.p.	Siddeley "Puma" (boosted); 300 h.p. at 1,600 r.p.m.
Airscrew, diam., pitch and revs. .	Avro Tractor D. 2.9m., P. 2m., r.p.m. 1,600.
Weight of machine (empty) ..	4,574 lbs.
Load per sq. ft...	8.76 lbs.
Weight per h.p.	11.93 lbs. (assuming 600 h.p.)
Tank capacity in hours.. ..	3¾ hrs. at 10,000 ft., including climb.
Tank capacity in gallons ..	116 gallons.

Three-quarter front view of the Avro Two-seater Fighter, Type 530. (200 h.p. Hispano-Suiza).

Performance.

Speed low down	125 m.p.h.
Speed at 10,00 feet.. ..	119 m.p.h.
Speed at 15,000 feet ..	112½ m.p.h.
Landing speed	45 m.p.h.

Climb.

To 5,000 feet in minutes ..	6½.
To 10,000 feet in minutes ..	16½, 15,000 ft. in 32 mins.
To 20,000 feet in minutes ..	Service ceiling 17000 ft. in 43 minutes.
Disposable load apart from fuel	1,614 lbs.
Total weight of machine loaded	7,158 lbs.

Three-quarter front view of the Avro "Pike" (two 230 h.p. B.H.P. engines).

THE AVRO "SPIDER."

The *Avro* "Spider" is one of the very few examples amongst British aeroplanes of the so-called " wireless " type. The wing structure is entirely supported by a triangulated system of steel tubes, and has neither flying nor landing wires.

The front end of the fuselage is identical in all respects with the forward portion of the type 504 *Avro ;* but it has been shortened up aft of the cockpit. The tail unit is also of the same design as that of the standard training machine, so that fittings already being produced in quantity can be used for the whole of this part of the machine.

This machine has been specially designed as a single-seater fighter. Great attention has been paid to the question of view and manœuvrability. It is extraordinarily quick and light on the controls, and in mock flights, for which it has so far been used, has easily out-manœuvred other machines which have been standardised.

Although the first machine has only been fitted with 110 Le Rhône, it is proposed to fit a much higher-powered engine, so as to get a still better performance.

The view in every direction is excellent, as the pilot sits between the main spars of the top plane, and has a perfect view both upwards and downwards, the dimensions of the bottom plane being so small as hardly to obstruct the view at all.

The pilot's cockpit is very roomy and comfortable, and full use can be made of the controls without any obstruction.

The guns are conveniently placed and the ammunition boxes and chutes well arranged.

The engine controls are placed in a convenient position on the pilot's left-hand side, and the hand-pump is in a comfortable position for use.

Front view of the Avro " Spider" Showing the wing bracing system. (110 h.p. Le Rhône.)

Side view of the Avro " Spider." (110 h.p. Le Rhône.)

Specification.

Type of Aeroplane	Single-Seater "Fighter."
Aeroplane specification	Avro "Spider."
Engine	180 h.p. B.R. 2.
Revolutions of engine for stated b.h.p.	1250 r.p.m.

Estimated speed with full load and with all fittings in position.

Maximum speed for the above horse-power and revolutions.

At ground level	124 m.p.h.
At 8,000 feet	121 m.p.h.
At 10,000 feet	122 m.p.h.
At 15,000 feet	115 m.p.h.

Duration of flight at this speed.

At 10,000 feet	2 hrs.
At 15,000 feet	2½ hrs.
Minimum speed with full load near ground	45 m.p.h.

Estimated climb with full load and with all fittings in position.

To 3,500 feet	2·2 mins.
To 8,000 feet	5 mins.
To 10,000 feet	7 mins.
To 15,000 feet	13½ mins.
To 18,000 feet	20 mins.
To 20,000 feet	26 mins.
Pilot, position	Between main spars of top plane.

Air-screw.

Type	"Avro."
Pitch	9 ft.
Diameter	8 ft. 6 in.

Overall Dimensions.

Span of top wings	28 ft. 6 in.
Span of bottom wings	21 ft. 6 in.
Span of tail plane	8 ft. 6 in.
Height overall	7 ft. 10 in.
Length overall	20 ft. 6 in.
Chord top wing	6 ft.
Chord bottom wing	2 ft. 6 in.
Chord tail plane	2 ft. 8 in.
Chord elevator	1 ft. 6 in.

Armament and Military Load.

Pilot's gun	70
Mounting and ammunition box	20
Belt and ammunition, 800 rounds	60
Total Gun Load	150 lbs.
Véry Pistol with cartridges	8
Total reconnaissance load	8 lbs.

Military Load.

Total of Gun, bomb and reconnaissance loads	158
Crew of 1 at 180 lbs	180
Total military load	338 lbs.

Weight of Machine in Flying Trim.

(a) Weight of machine bare	1148
(b) Military load	338
(c) Petrol 26½ gallons	194
(d) Oil 6 gallons	54
Total	1734 lbs.

Areas.—Wings.

Top	122 sq. ft.
Second	45 sq. ft.
Total	167 sq. ft.

Wing Flaps

Top	22 sq. ft.
Total supporting surface	189 sq. ft.

Tail Plane	17.5 sq. ft.
Elevators	11 sq. ft.
Rudder	7.8 sq. ft.

Materials.

Wing spars	Built up spruce.
Wing struts	Steel tubes.
Body struts	Spruce.
Undercarriage	Steel tubes.
Longerons in body	Spruce.
Shock absorber	Rubber cord.
Petrol tank	Behind pilot.
Pressure feed capacity	26½ gallons.
Material	Tinned steel.
Weight empty	20 lbs.

Loading.

Loading on wing surface per sq. ft.	9.15 lbs.
Weight fully loaded per h.p.	9.65 lbs.
Weight carried on tail when in flight	Nil.

Control.

Type of aeroplane controls	Stick and V foot bar.
Position of engine controls	On left hand side of body.
Rudder bar adjustable	
Tail skid controllable	
Load on tail skid when loaded ready for flight	100 lbs.
Tail plane adjustable on the ground but not in the air from pilot's seat	

Bracing.

Wings—(a) Internal	High tensile wire.
(b) External	Steel struts.
Body	High tensile wire.
Undercarriage	Cable.

Undercarriage.

Type	"Vee" Type.
Size of Standard Wheels fitted	700 m/m × 78 m/m

	Top.	Bottom.
Minimum factor of safety—front spars	13	9½
rear spars	13	
Rear wing bracing.		
front struts	6	6
rear struts	6	6
Range of movement of centre of pressure	.20 to .5 of chord.	

B

B.A.T. The British Aerial Transport Company. Head Office, 38, Conduit Street, London, W.1. Works, Hythe Road, Willesden, London, N.W.10.

Founded by Mr. Samuel Waring (now Sir Samuel Waring, Bart.) in 1917, when the firm took over, purely as an experimental works, not as a production factory, the premises in Hythe Road, formerly occupied by the Joucques Aviation Co.

Chief designer, Mr. Frederick Koolhoven, who, in conjunction with M. Béchereau, was responsible for the design of the 1913 "Gordon Bennet" *Deperdussin* monoplane, the first machine to cover 120 miles in an hour. Mr. Koolhoven was also responsible for the design and construction of the British *Deperdussin* machine built for the British Military Trials of 1912, which machine was still flying in 1917, and for a number of the *Armstrong-Whitworth* machines, including the type F.K. 8, one of the very few 1914 designs which continued to be used on active service till the signing of the Armistice.

THE B.A.T. "BANTAM."

The B.A.T. "Bantam" is a small single-seater fighter, and although it was never adopted by the Air Board, it certainly had the finest performance for its type of any machine constructed at the time. The fuselage is of the monocoque type, built up of formers covered with three-ply, dispensing entirely with any form of internal bracing. The main planes have a very small gap, which is practically filled by the fuselage, and the pilot is seated between the centre section spars, with his head protruding above the top plane. The sides of the cockpit are cut away, thus giving him a good view downwards.

Two sets of struts are fitted, one either side of the fuselage. The under-carriage consists of two Vees, one under each of the inner sets of interplane struts. Two tubes hinged to the under side of the fuselage and rubber spring to the Vees form axles for the two wheels.

The armament consists of two fixed Vickers guns fitted low down on either side of the pilot, and firing between the two lower pairs of cylinders.

Specification.

Type of machine	..	Biplane
Name and type No.	..	"Bantam" F.K. 23.
Purpose	..	Single-seater Fighter.
Span	..	25 ft
Gap	..	3 ft. 3½ in.
Overall length	..	18 ft. 5 in.
Maximum height	..	6 ft. 9 in.
Chord	..	3 ft 11¼ in.
Total area of wings	..	185 sq. ft.
Span of tail	..	9 ft. 2 in.
Total area of tail	..	23 sq. ft.
Area of elevators	..	6.3 sq. ft.
Area of rudder	..	4.4 sq. ft.
Area of fin	..	2.85 sq. ft.
Area of ailerons	..	4.5 sq. ft. each; 18 sq. ft. total.
Max. cross sectional area of body		8.7 sq. ft.
Horizontal area of body	..	32 sq. ft.
Vertical area of body	..	30 sq. ft.
Engine type and h.p.	..	A.B.C. "Wasp."
Airscrew	..	"Bat" dia. 7 ft. 10½ in.; pitch 5 ft. 4 in.
Weight of machine empty	..	830 lbs.
Load per sq. ft.	..	7.2 lbs.
Load per h.p.	..	7.85 lbs.
Tank capacity, hours	..	3¼.
Tank capacity, gallons	..	22.
Performance.		
Speed at ground level	..	138 m.p.h.
Speed at 10,000 feet	..	134 m.p.h.
Speed at 15,000 feet	..	127 m.p.h.
Speed at 20,000 feet	..	121 m.p.h.
Landing speed	..	50 m.p.h.
Climb.		
To 5,000 feet in minutes	..	3 mins. 10 secs.
To 10,000 feet in minutes	..	7.20 minutes.
To 20,000 feet in minutes	..	21.48 minutes.
Disposable load from fuel	..	378 lbs.
Total weight of machine loaded	..	1,333 lbs.

THE B.A.T. "BABOON." TYPE F.K. 24.

A small dual control two-seater, designed for training purposes.

Very great attention has been paid in design to ease of manufacture and interchangeability of parts.

As an instance of this it may be noted that ailerons, rudder and elevators are all identical and interchangeable.

The following are the leading particulars.

Specification.

Type of machine	..	Two-seater Biplane (dual control).
Name or type No. of machine	..	B.A.T. F.K. 24 "Baboon."
Purpose for which intended	..	Training.
Span	..	25 ft.
Chord	..	5 ft. 7 in.
Gap, maximum and minimum	..	4 ft. 8½ in.
Stagger	..	Nil.
Dihedral	..	2° upper and lower planes.
Overall length	..	22 ft. 8 in.
Overall height	..	8 ft. 10 in.
Total area of planes	..	259 sq. ft.
Ailerons	..	On upper and lower planes.
Area of each and total area of ailerons		Each 6 sq. ft. Total 24 sq. ft.
Span of tail	..	9 ft. 10 in.
Total area of tail	..	27.75 sq. ft. (including elevators).

Side View of the B.A.T. "Bantam" (A.B.C. 200 h.p. "Wasp" engine).

Area of elevators	..	12 sq. ft.
Area of rudder	..	6 sq. ft.
Area of fin	..	5.25 sq. ft.
Max. cross sectional area of body		7.5 sq. ft.
Side area of body	..	52 sq. ft.
Engine (type and B.H.P.)	..	170 A.B.C. Wasp I.
Revs. at nominal b.h.p.	..	1850 r.p.m.
Propeller (make and type, etc.)	..	B.A.T. 2 blade Tractor dia. 7 ft. 10 in., pitch 5ft.
Weight of machine empty	..	950 lbs.
Load per sq. ft.	..	5.2 lbs.
Weight per h.p.	..	7.95 lbs.
Tank capacity in hours	..	2 hours.
Tank capacity in gallons	..	12 gallons.
Disposable load, apart from fuel		400 lbs.
Armament.		
Weight of Instruments	..	12 lbs.
Total weight of machine fully loaded	..	1350 lbs.
Performance.		
Speed (at ground level)	..	90 m.p.h.
Landing speed	..	40 m.p.h.
Climb.		
To 10,000 feet	..	12 mins.

THE BAT "BASILISK."

The "Basilisk" is a slightly enlarged form of "Bantam." The principal alterations are the installation of the 320 hp. A.B.C. "Dragonfly" engine, an increase in the gap, and the placing of the pilot in rear of the main planes.

Specification.

Type of machine	..	Biplane.
Name and type No.	..	"Basilisk" F.K. 25
Purpose	..	Single-seater Fighter.
Span	..	25 ft. 4 in.
Gap	..	4 ft. 4 in.
Overall length	..	20 ft. 5 in
Maximum height	..	8 ft. 2 in.
Chord	..	4 ft. 6½ in.
Total area of wings	..	212 sq. ft.
Span of tail	..	9 ft. 10 in.
Total area of tail	..	22 sq. ft.
Area of elevators	..	8.3 sq. ft.
Area of rudder	..	4.5 sq. ft.
Area of fin	..	2.6 sq. in.
Area of ailerons	..	7.5 sq. ft. each; 30 sq. ft total.
Max. cross sectional area of body		9.2 sq. ft.
Horizontal area of body	..	29.5 sq. ft.
Vertical area of body	..	47 sq. ft.
Engine type and h.p.	..	A.B.C. "Dragon-fly," 320 h.p.
Airscrew	..	"Bat" dia. 8 ft. 8in.; pitch 8 ft.; 1,650 r.p.m.
Weight of machine empty	..	1,350 lbs.
Load per sq. ft.	..	9.25 lbs.
Load per h.p.	..	5.77 lbs.
Tank capacity, hours	..	32.
Tank capacity, gallons	..	40.
Performance.		
Speed at ground level	..	162 m.p.h.
Speed at 10,000 feet	..	154 m.p.h.
Speed at 15,000 feet	..	141 m.p.h.
Speed at 20,000 feet	..	132 m.p.h.
Landing speed	..	52 m.p.h.
Climb.		
To 5,000 feet in minutes	..	2 minutes.
To 10,000 feet in minutes	..	5 minutes.
To 20,000 feet in minutes	..	16.40 minutes.
Disposable load apart from fuel	..	448 lbs.
Total weight of machine loaded	..	2,085 lbs.

Side View of the B.A.T. " Basilisk " (320 h.p. A.B.C. " Dragonfly " engine).

The B.A.T. " Baboon " Two-seater Training Machine (170 h.p. A.B.C. " Wasp.")

Three-quarter Front View of the B.A.T. " Baboon " Training Machine (170 h.p. A.B.C. " Wasp " engine).

BEARDMORE. Wm. Beardmore & Co., Dalmuir, nr. Glasgow, Scotland. The world-famous firm of engineers and shipbuilders, proposed, just before the war, to construct under license the *D.F.W.* biplane (see GERMANY) fitted with Beardmore Daimler motors.

Mr. G. Tilghman Richards (late lieut. R.N.V.R.) is in charge of the design and technical department of the aircraft works.

In addition to the manufacture of a number of machines of external design, this firm has produced a number of machines of its own design. Particulars of the more important types are given herewith.

THE BEARDMORE BIPLANE W.B. 1.

This was a large two-seater bomber, from which the type W.B. 1a was developed later. The following gives the main particulars of this machine :—

Specification.

Type of machine	Biplane.
Name or type No. of machine	W.B. 1.
Purpose for which intended ..	Bomber.
Span	61 ft. 6 in.
Gap, maximum and minimum ..	7 ft.
Overall length..	32 ft. 10 in.
Maximum height..	14 ft. 9 in.
Chord	7 ft.
Total surface of wings, including ailerons	796 sq. ft.
Span of tail	18 ft.
Total area of tail	106 sq. ft.
Area of elevators	40 sq. ft.
Area of rudder	20 sq. ft.
Area of fin	14.2 sq. ft.
Area of each aileron and total area	28.32 sq. ft., 113.26 sq. ft.
Maximum cross section of body..	15.2 sq. ft.
Horizontal area of body ..	88 sq. ft.
Vertical area of body ..	81.6 sq. ft.
Engine type and h.p. ..	240 h.p. Sunbeam or 230 h.p. Beardmore Adriatic.
Airscrew, diam., and revs. ..	10 ft. 6 in. dia., 1,075 revs. (with Sunbeam).
Weight of machine empty ..	3,410 lbs. (with Beardmore).
Load per sq. ft.	7 lbs.
Weight per h.p.	23 lbs.
Tank capacity in hours ..	7.3 hours.
Tank capacity in gallons..	137 gallons.

Performance.

Speed low down	91 m.p.h.
Landing speed	48 m.p.h.

Climb.

To 5,000 feet in minutes ..	26 minutes.
To 10,000 feet in minutes ..	44 minutes.

Disposable load apart from fuel	1,100 lbs.
Total weight of machine loaded	5,600 lbs.

THE BEARDMORE BIPLANE W.B. 1A.

The *Beardmore* two-seater biplane W.B. 1a. was designed as a long-distance bomber equipped with a 500 h.p. Beardmore Atlantic engine. The main planes are heavily staggered, are of large span, and have four pairs of interplane struts at either side of the fuselage. The pilot and observer are placed very much in rear of the main plane, the pilot being midway between the main and tail planes and the observer is immediately in advance of the fixed fin which emerges from the fairing round the observer's cockpit.

Specification.

Type of machine	Biplane.
Name or type No. of machine	W.B. 1a.
Purpose for which intended ..	Bomber.
Span	70 ft.
Gap, maximum and minimum ..	7 ft.
Overall length	32 ft. 10 in.
Maximum height.. ..	15 ft. 8 in.
Chord	7 ft.
Total surface of wings, including ailerons	946 sq. ft.
Span of tail	19 ft.
Total area of tail	110 sq. ft.
Area of elevators	33.5 sq. ft.
Area of rudder	20 sq. ft.
Area of fin	14.2 sq. ft.
Area of each aileron and total area	29.5 sq. ft., 118 sq. ft.
Maximum cross section of body..	22.5 sq. ft.
Horizontal area of body ..	105 sq. ft.
Vertical area of body ..	131 sq. ft.
Engine type and h.p. ..	Beardmore Atlantic 500 h.p.
Airscrew, diam. and revs. ..	14 ft., 900.
Weight of machine empty ..	4,537 lbs.
Load per sq. ft.	9.4 lbs.
Weight per h.p.	17.3 lbs.
Tank capacity in hours ..	6.5 hours.
Tank capacity in gallons ..	214 gallons.

Performance.

Speed low down	110 m.p.h.
Speed at 10,000 feet	101 m.p.h.
Landing speed	65 m.p.h.

Climb.

To 5,000 feet in minutes ..	12 minutes.
To 10,000 feet in minutes ..	27 minutes.

Disposable load apart from fuel	2,700 lbs.
Total weight of machine loaded	8,900 lbs.

Front View of an early Beardmore Experimental Single-seater Biplane.

Side View of a Beardmore Type W.B.1 "Adriatic" (230 h.p. B.H.P. Engine).

THE BEARDMORE FIGHTER W.B. 2 AND 2A.

The *Beardmore* W.B. 2 is a conventional two-seater fighter equipped with a 230 h.p. Hispano-Suiza engine. The main planes are heavily staggered. The pilot is situated under the trailing edge of the top plane and the observer over the trailing edge of the bottom plane, giving both an excellent view all round.

The type W.B. 2a. is a modified version of this machine fitted with a Beardmore "Adriatic" engine of 230 h.p and with increased tank capacity.

The following tables give the details of both machines :—

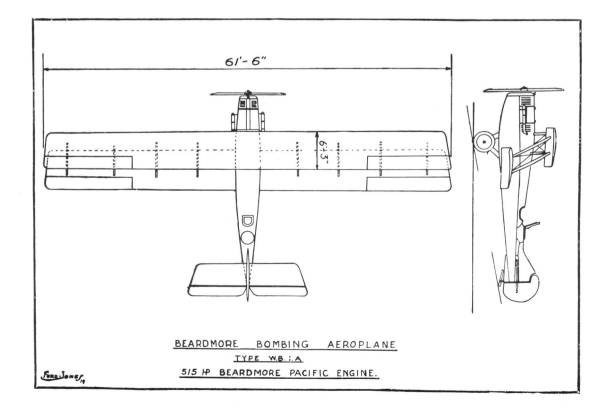

BEARDMORE BOMBING AEROPLANE
TYPE W.B. 1A
515 HP BEARDMORE PACIFIC ENGINE.

Vertical area of body	.. ..	75 sq. ft.
Engine type and h.p.	.. ..	Beardmore Adriatic, 230 h.p.
Airscrew, diam. and revs.	..	10 ft., 1,350 r.p.m.
Weight of machine empty	..	1,650 lbs.
Load per sq. ft.	.. ..	7.6 lbs.
Weight per h.p.	.. ..	11.7 lbs.
Tank capacity in hours	..	4.5 hours.
Tank capacity in gallons	..	75 gallons.

Performance.

Speed low down	..	125 m.p.h.
Speed at 10,000 feet	..	117 m.p.h.
Landing speed ..	..	50 m.p.h.

Climb.

To 5,000 feet in minutes		5 minutes.
To 10,000 feet in minutes		12 minutes.

Disposable load apart from fuel	.. ..	460 lbs.
Total weight of machine loaded	.. ..	2,700 lbs.

THE BEARDMORE BIPLANE W.B. III.

The *Beardmore* W.B. III. was evolved from the *Sopwith* "Pup" in an effort to turn this machine into a ship-plane, the principal modifications being folding planes and a retractable under-carriage, in order to simplify stowage on board ship. The fuselage and tail unit are practically of Sopwith design, the overall length being only slightly increased.

Instead of four short centre-section struts, four long struts, two on either side of the fuselage, are fitted with a short horizontal strut connecting them with the upper longeron of the fuselage. The main planes are unstaggered and hinged at the main rear spar close up to the fuselage.

Two sets of interplane struts are fitted to each set of main planes one set being placed at the inner edge of the plane in order to preserve the truss when the wings are folded.

Ailerons are fitted to upper and lower planes and are operated on the Nieuport principle, the upper and lower ailerons being inter-connected by a strut.

An ordinary Vee-type under-carriage is fitted, the front members of the Vee being hinged, and the rear members equipped with a release device operated from the pilot's seat which allows the under-carriage to collapse into the fuselage, leaving half the wheels exposed. The armament consists of a Lewis gun fitted on a special mounting in front of the pilot's cockpit to allow it to fire through an opening in the centre section.

Particulars of this machine are given in the following table :—

Type of machine ..	..	Biplane.
Name or type No. of machine	..	W.B. III.
Purpose for which intended	..	Ship's Scout.
Span	..	25 ft.
Gap, maximum and minimum	..	4 ft. 9 in., 4 ft. 9 in.
Overall length	..	20 ft. 2.5 in.
Maximum height ..	..	8 ft. 1.25 in.
Chord	..	5 ft. 1.5 in.
Total surface of wings, including		
ailerons	..	243 sq. ft.
Span of tail	..	10 ft. 1 in.
Total area of tail ..	..	34.5 sq. ft.
Area of elevators ..	..	11.5 sq. ft.
Area of rudder	..	4.5 sq. ft.
Area of fin ..	..	3.5 sq. ft.
Area of each aileron and total area	5.75 sq. ft., 23 sq. ft.	
Maximum cross section of body..	4.6 sq. ft.	
Horizontal area of body	..	17 sq. ft.
Vertical area of body	..	39 sq. ft.
Engine type and h.p.	..	Clerget or Le Rhône 80 h.p.
Airscrew, diam. and revs.	..	8 ft. 6 in. ; 1,200 r.p.m.
Weight of machine empty	..	880 lbs.
Load per sq. ft. ..	..	5.3 lbs.
Weight per h.p.	..	16.1 lbs.
Tank capacity in hours	..	2.75 hours.
Tank capacity in gallons..	..	18 gallons.

Performance.

Speed low down	..	103 m.p.h.
Speed at 10,000 feet	..	88 m.p.h.
Landing speed ..	..	40 m.p.h.

Climb.

To 5,000 feet in minutes	..	9 minutes.
To 10,000 feet in minutes	..	24 minutes

Disposable load apart from fuel	.. ..	300 lbs.
Total weight of machine loaded	.. ..	1,290 lbs.

THE BEARDMORE BIPLANE W.B. IV.

The *Beardmore* W.B. IV. is a single-seater ship's scout designed with flotation gear in the fuselage and a dropping under-carriage. In order to keep the size of the flotation gear which is actually built into the fuselage, down to a minimum, the power unit is placed under the centre-section and over the centre of gravity, the pilot being seated in front astride the airscrew shaft in a watertight cockpit.

The under-carriage is of the Vee type and is so arranged that by means of a control in the pilot's cockpit the whole under-carriage can be released.

Two wing-top floats are fitted as additional stabilizers when the machine is resting on the sea.

Specification.

Type of machine ..	.. ..	Biplane.
Name or type No. of machine	..	W.B. IV.
Purpose for which intended	..	Ship's Scout.
Span	..	35 ft. 10 in.
Gap	..	4 ft. 9 in.
Overall length	..	26 ft. 6 in.
Maximum height ..	..	9 ft. 10.5 in.
Chord	..	Top 6 ft. 3 in., bottom 4ft. 9 in.
Total surface of wings, including		
ailerons	..	350 sq. ft.
Span of tail	..	11 ft. 9 in.
Total area of tail ..	..	50.5 sq. ft.
Area of elevators ..	..	24 sq. ft.
Area of rudder ..	..	12 sq. ft.
Area of fin ..	..	8 sq. ft.
Area of each aileron and total area	18.8 sq. ft. each,	
		37 ft. 6 in. total.
Maximum cross section of body..	12.5 sq. ft.	
Horizontal area of body ..	73 sq. ft.	
Vertical area of body ..	51 sq. ft.	
Engine type and h.p.	..	Hispano-Suiza 200 h.p.
Airscrew, diam. and revs.	..	9 ft., 1,500 r.p.m.
Weight of machine empty	..	1,960 lbs.
Load per sq. ft. ..	..	7.5 lbs.
Weight per h.p. ..	..	13 lbs.
Tank capacity in hours ..	..	8.5 hours.
Tank capacity in gallons..	..	37 gallons.

Performance.

Speed low down	..	110 m.p.h.
Speed at 10,000 feet ..	..	102 m.p.h.
Landing speed ..	..	45 m.p.h.

Climb.

To 5,000 feet in minutes		7 minutes.
To 10,000 feet in minutes		18 minutes.

Disposable load apart from fuel	.. ..	340 lbs.
Total weight of machine loaded	.. ..	2,600 lbs.

THE BEARDMORE BIPLANE W.B. V.

This machine was also designed as a ship single-seater fighter, and was of very much the same overall dimensions as the W.B. IV.

Instead of placing the engine over the C.G. and driving the propeller by a shaft passing between the pilot's legs, and designing the fuselage to provide the necessary buoyancy for flotation after alighting on the sea, the conventional engine in front arrangement was adopted, and the necessary buoyancy had to be provided by external air bags.

Specification.

Type of machine ..	..	Biplane.
Name or type No. of machine	..	W.B. V.
Purpose for which intended	..	Ship's Scout.
Span	..	35 ft. 10 in.

The Beardmore Type W.B. III Folding Ship plane (80 h.p. Le Rhône Engine) with wings and chassis folded for stowage.

The Beardmore Ship plane, Type W.B. IV (200 h.p. Hispano-Suiza Engine).

The Beardmore Type W.B. V Ship plane (200 h.p. Hispano-Suiza Engine.

BEARDMORE—*continued*.

THE BEARDMORE BIPLANE W.B. V.—*continued*.

Gap	4 ft. 9 in.
Overall length	26 ft. 7 in.
Maximum height	11 ft. 10 in.
Chord	6 ft. 3 in.
Total surface of wings, including ailerons	394 sq. ft.
Span of tail	11 ft. 9 in.
Total area of tail	50.5 sq. ft.
Area of elevators	24 sq. ft.
Area of rudder	12 sq. ft.
Area of fin	8 sq. ft.
Area of each aileron and total area	18.8 sq. ft. each, 37.6 sq. ft. total.
Maximum cross section of body..	11.5 sq. ft.
Horizontal area of body ..	46.5 sq. ft.
Vertical area of body ..	58 sq. ft.
Engine type and h.p. ..	Hispano-Suiza 200 h.p.
Airscrew, diam. and revs. ..	9 ft., 1,500 r.p.m.
Weight of machine empty ..	1,860 lbs.
Load per sq. ft.	6.33 lbs.
Weight per h.p.	12.5 lbs.
Tank capacity in hours ..	2.5 hours.
Tank capacity in gallons.. ..	37 gallons.

Performance.

Speed low down	112 m.p.h.
Speed at 10,000 feet ..	103 m.p.h
Landing speed	45 m.p.h.

Climb.

To 5,000 feet in minutes ..	6 minutes.
To 10,000 feet in minutes ..	17 minutes.

Disposable load apart from fuel	340 lbs.
Total weight of machine loaded	2,500 lbs.

THE BEARDMORE TORPEDO CARRIER W.B. VI.

The *Beardmore* single seater torpedo-carrying, folding ship-aeroplane, type W.B. VI., was the result of one of the many efforts to produce a satisfactory, fast torpedo-carrier. The general arrangement is on conventional lines, with the pilot well back in the fuselage.

The under-carriage is arranged to permit the stowage and dropping of a torpedo under the centre of gravity.

Specification.

Type of machine	Biplane.
Name or type No. of machine ...	W.B. VI.
Purpose for which intended ..	Torpedo Carrier.
Span	Top 53 ft. 6.5 in., bottom 47 ft. 10.5 in.
Gap	7 ft. 6 in.
Overall length	34 ft.
Maximum height	12 ft. 6 in.
Chord	Top 8 ft. 10 in., bottom 7 ft. 9 in.
Total surface of wings, including ailerons..	796 sq. ft.
Span of tail	15 ft. 9 in.
Total area of tail	80 sq. ft.
Area of elevators	32.4 sq. ft.
Area of rudder	12 sq. ft.
Area of fin	10 sq. ft.
Area of each aileron and total area	47.75 sq. ft. each, 95.5 sq. ft. total.
Maximum cross section of body..	10 sq. ft.
Horizontal area of body ..	62 sq. ft.
Vertical area of body ..	100 sq. ft.
Engine type and h.p. ..	Rolls-Royce Eagle 350 h.p.
Airscrew, diam. and revs. ..	12 ft., 1,080 r.p.m.
Weight of machine empty ..	3,027 lbs.
Load per sq. ft.	7 lbs.
Weight per h.p.	15.6 lbs.
Tank capacity in hours ..	3 hours.
Tank capacity in gallons.. ..	70 gallons.

Performance.

Speed low down	102 m.p.h.
Speed at 10,000 feet ..	91 m.p.h.
Landing speed.. ..	47 m.p.h.

Climb.

To 5,000 feet in minutes ..	15 minutes.
To 10,000 feet in minutes ..	41 minutes.

Disposable load apart from fuel	2,060 lbs.
Total weight of machine loaded	5,637 lbs.

BLACKBURN Aeroplanes.

The Blackburn Aeroplane and Motor Co., Ltd., Olympia, Leeds, and Seaplane Works, Brough and Hull. Mr. Robert Blackburn produced his first machine early in 1910 (see 1911 edition for details). In the latter part of that year he designed the machine which ultimately developed into the *Blackburn* military monoplane. In 1911 other types were produced. The *Blackburn* monoplane was successfully flown by naval officers before the war.

The 80 h.p. *Blackburn* monoplane has done a great deal of work in the past. In October, 1913, one of these machines won the Inter-County 100 Miles "War of the Roses" Air Race for a Silver Challenge Cup presented by the "Yorkshire Evening News."

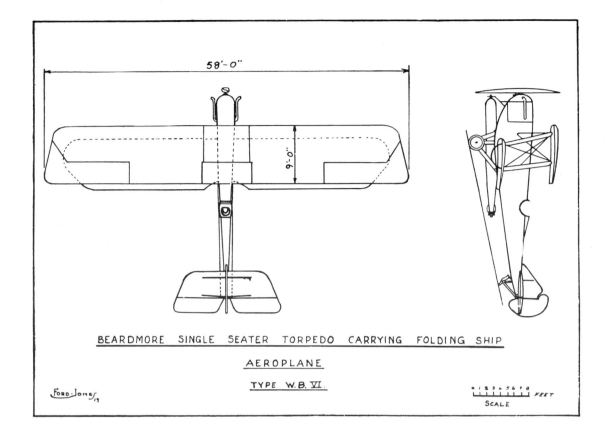

BEARDMORE SINGLE SEATER TORPEDO CARRYING FOLDING SHIP AEROPLANE

TYPE W.B. VI.

A machine of similar type was used in 1914 for passenger flying, and was in use at the end of 1915, fitted with floats and a 100 h.p. Anzani motor, as a school machine on Windermere.

The firm turned out during 1915 a number of B.E. 2c. biplanes and certain seaplanes and other machines for the Admiralty.

The firm's more recent work has been of a nature of high importance to naval and military flying, and is hereafter described.

The active directors of the firm are Mr. Robert Blackburn, one of the pioneers of British aviation, and Mr. Stuart A. Hirst, a well-known Leeds business man, and the combination is proving highly successful.

Mr. Bumpus (late major R.A.F.) and Mr. Harris Booth F.Ae.S. (formerly of the Admiralty), are the chief technical officials of the firm.

THE BLACKBURN "KANGAROO."

The Blackburn twin-tractor biplane was developed from a twin-float twin-engined seaplane built by the Blackburn firm for the Admiralty in 1916–17, of which a specification is given. The machine was afterwards remodelled as a long-distance bomber, and has been used as such, and also to a considerable extent for anti-submarine patrols over the North Sea and elsewhere.

Three-quarter View from the Rear of the Blackburn "Kangaroo" (Two 250 h.p. Falcon Rolls-Royce Engines).

THE BLACKBURN "KANGAROO."—continued.

The central fuselage carries the pilot's cockpit well in advance of the leading edge of the planes and two gunner's cockpits, one right in the nose and the other about midway between nose and tail, well in the rear of the planes. The power units, two Rolls-Royce 250 h.p. "Falcon" engines, are carried (one on either side of the fuselage) in two streamline housings between the first two sets of interplane struts and just above the lower planes.

Under each power unit is a separate Vee-type chassis.

The upper plane has a considerable overhang, braced above from kingposts and below from the base of the outer set of struts. Ailerons are fitted to both sets of planes and are interconnected by a light strut.

The tail unit is of the biplane type with two fins, which are used as a fairing to the intertail struts.

Specification.

Type of machine	Blackburn Twin Tractor.
Name or type No. of machine ..	"Kangaroo."
Purpose for which intended ..	Long Range Bomber.
Span	74 ft. 10¼ in. top; 47 ft. 9½ in. bottom plane.
Gap	7 ft. 3 in.
Overall length	46 ft.
Maximum height	16 ft. 10 in.
Chord	7 ft. 3 in.
Total surface of wings ..	880 sq. ft.
Span of tail	17 ft. 6 in.
Total area of tail ..	143 sq. ft.
Area of elevators	63.5 sq. ft.
Area of rudder	22.5 sq. ft.
Area of fin	25 sq. ft.
Area of ailerons	166.5 sq. ft.
Maximum cross section of body ..	12 sq. ft.
Horizontal area of body ..	105 sq. ft.
Vertical area of body ..	115 sq. ft.
Engine type and h.p. ..	Falcon-Rolls, two 250 h.p.
Weight of machine empty ..	5,150 lbs.
Load per sq. ft.	9.21 lbs.
Weight per h.p.	16.2 lbs.
Tank capacity in hours ..	8 hours.
Tank capacity in gallons ..	230 petrol; 18 oil.

Performance.

Speed low down ..	87 knots.
Disposable load apart from fuel	1,710 lbs.
Total weight of machine loaded	8,100 lbs.

THE "BABY" SEAPLANE.

The "Baby" seaplane traces its origin back to the original Sopwith "Schneider," the winner of the International "Schneider" Cup for hydro-aeroplanes at Monaco in 1914.

Something over a year after the outbreak of hostilities the Air Department of the Admiralty awoke to the fact that a machine of this type might have uses, and, after a few experiments, a number of these machines, somewhat modified, were ordered from Messrs. Sopwith & Co. Ltd., and from a number of other makers. The original machines were all fitted with 100 h.p. monosoupape Gnômes. A later edition was fitted with 110 h.p. Clerget engines.

It was then attempted to use these machines as bomb carriers, with two 65 lb. bombs, with the result that in their overloaded condition they became distinctly unpopular.

Orders for the type were stopped, and a number of experimental machines were ordered from various sources with the idea of supplanting this type of machine.

Before any of the experimental types had reached a production stage an acute shortage of seaplanes, and particularly of seaplanes with any reasonable speed, occurred, and orders for large numbers of the "Baby" type, fitted with 130 h.p. Clerget engines were placed with various firms.

Messrs. Sopwith being at that time extremely busy with single-seater land fighters, the task of carrying out the modifications necessary for the new engine and of issuing all the new drawings was entrusted to the Blackburn Aeroplane and Motor Co.

The machine is of very simple and straightforward construction. The wings are of low aspect ratio, and have a gap less than the chord, and the overall length of the machine has been reduced to a minimum by placing the pilot's feet beneath the carburettor, and bringing the engine very close up to the leading edge of the wings.

In consequence, the machine has a very compact appearance and is extremely easy to manœuvre.

Specification.

Type of machine	Tractor Single-seater Biplane Twin-float Seaplane.
Name or type No. of machine ..	"Baby."
Purpose for which intended ..	Fighting Scout.
Span	25 ft. 8 in.
Gap	4 ft. 6 in.
Overall length	23 ft.
Maximum height	10 ft.
Chord	5 ft. 2 in.
Total surface of wings ..	225 sq. ft.
Span of tail	9 ft. 5 in.
Total area of tail ..	34 sq. ft.
Area of elevators	15 sq. ft.
Area of rudder	7 sq. ft.
Area of fin	4 sq. ft.
Area of ailerons	23 sq. ft.
Maximum cross section of body	10 sq. ft.
Horizontal area of body ..	38 sq. ft.
Vertical area of body ..	42 sq. ft.

Engine type and h.p.	Clerget; 130 h.p.
Weight of machine empty ..	1,226 lbs.
Load per sq. ft.	7.63 lbs.
Weight per h.p.	13.2 lbs.
Tank capacity in hours ..	2½ hours.
Tank capacity in gallons ..	25 petrol; 6 oil.

Performance.

Speed low down	87 knots.

Climb.

To 10,000 feet in minutes ..	35 minutes.
Disposable load apart from fuel	255 lbs.
Total weight of machine loaded	1,715 lbs.

THE BLACKBURN THREE-SEATER SEAPLANE.

Type of machine	Blackburn Twin Seaplane.
Name or type No. of machine ..	S. P.
Purpose for which intended ..	Long Range Bomber.
Span	74 ft. 10½ in. top; 47 ft. 9½ in. bottom plane.
Gap	7 ft. 3 in.
Overall length	46 ft.
Maximum height	16 ft. 10 in.
Chord	7 ft. 3 in.
Total surface of wings ..	880 sq. ft.
Span of tail	17 ft. 6 in.
Total area of tail ..	143 sq. ft.
Area of elevators	63.5 sq. ft.
Area of rudder	22.5 sq. ft.
Area of fin	25 sq. ft.
Area of ailerons	166.5 sq. ft.
Maximum cross section of body ..	12 sq. ft.
Horizontal area of body ..	105 sq. ft.
Vertical area of body ..	115 sq. ft.
Engine type and h.p. ..	Falcon-Rolls, two 250 h.p.
Weight of machine empty ..	5,840 lbs.
Load per sq. ft.	9.78 lbs.
Weight per h.p.	17.2 lbs.
Tank capacity in hours ..	8 hours.
Tank capacity in gallons ..	230 petrol; 18 oil.

Performance.

Speed low down	87 knots.
Disposable load apart from fuel	1,710 lbs.
Total weight of machine loaded	8,600 lbs.

THE BLACKBURN "BLACKBURD."

This machine, designed as a torpedo carrier for use from aeroplane carriers working with the fleet at sea, was designed primarily with a view to ease of production.

The machine is generally on conventional tractor lines, with a chassis designed to allow of the dropping of a torpedo slung beneath the body.

The most noticeable feature, as far as appearance is concerned, is the side elevation of the fuselage, which is of the same depth from the leading edge of the lower wing to the sternpost.

Specification.

Type of machine	Tractor Biplane.
Name or type No. of machine .	"Blackburd."
Purpose for which intended .	Torpedo carrier, for use from ship or land.
Span	52 ft. 6 in.
Gap	7 ft.
Overall length	36 ft. 3 in.
Maximum height	12 ft. 4½ in.
Chord	7 ft.
Total surface of wings ..	709 sq. ft.
Span of tail	17 ft.

Three-quarter View from Rear the Blackburn "Baby" Seaplane (130 h.p. Clerget Engine).

Total area of Tail	82 sq. ft.
Area of elevators	34 sq. ft.
Area of rudder	9 sq. ft.
Area of fin	18 sq. ft.
Area of ailerons	85 sq. ft.
Maximum cross section of body	11 sq. ft.
Horizontal area of body ..	80 sq. ft.
Vertical area of body ..	126 sq ft.
Engine type and h.p.	"Eagle" Rolls-Royce; 350 h.p.
Weight of machine empty ..	3,080 lbs.
Load per sq. ft.	7.53 lbs.
Weight per h.p.	15.3 lbs.
Tank capacity in hours ..	3 hours.
Tank capacity in gallons ..	69 petrol; 9 oil.

Performance.

Speed low down	92 m.p.h.
Speed at 10,000 feet ..	84½ m.p.h.

Climb.

To 5,000 feet in minutes ..	11½ minutes.
To 10,000 feet in minutes ..	33½ minutes.
Disposable load apart from fuel	1,680 lbs.
Total weight of machine loaded	5,340 lbs.

Three-quarter Front View of the Blackburn Torpedo-carrying "Blackburd" (350 h.p. "Eagle" Rolls-Royce Engine).

Three-quarter Front View of the Boulton & Paul "Bobolink" (236 h.p. B.R. 2 engine).

BLÉRIOT & SPAD AIRCRAFT Co., Ltd.

Addlestone, Surrey. British branch of Blériot concern (France). Manager, M. Norbert Chéreau, who has handled Blériot products in England for years. Employed during 1915 chiefly in building "parasol" Blériots, and Arros to order of the War Office.

The S.P.A.D. (Société Pour Aviation et Dérives) was formed by M. Blériot in 1916, in conjunction with M. Béchereau, the designer of the highly successful Deperdussin monoplanes (now defunct) and the Spad biplane, which was produced by the firm, is one of the fastest in the world. The British Blériot concern now embraces both M. Blériot's French concerns.

BOULTON & PAUL, Ltd., Norwich.

Big firm of building constructors. Hence have undertaken with conspicuous success the construction of aircraft to War Office specification. Have developed under the management of Mr. Geoffrey ffiske into one of the most progressive of aircraft firms, and may be regarded as likely to occupy a big position in aviation after the war.

Mr. J. D. North, one of the best-known of British aeronautical scientists, is the firm's chief technician and designer.

The firm has produced the following machines :—

THE BOULTON & PAUL "BOBOLINK."

A small single-seat fighter scout on standard lines, with a high performance. The N-type interplane struts are a characteristic feature.

Specification.

Type of machine ..	Single-seater Biplane.
Name or type No. of machine ..	Bobolink.
Purpose for which intended ..	Fighting Scout.
Span	29 ft.
Gap, maximum and minimum ..	3 ft. 10⅝ in.
Overall length	20 ft.
Maximum height ..	8 ft. 4 in.
Chord	Top plane, 5 ft. 4½ in. ; bottom plane, 4 ft. 1½ in.
Total surface of wings ..	266 sq. ft.
Span of tail	9 ft. 2 in.
Total area of tail ..	30 sq. ft.
Area of rudder ..	10 sq. ft.
Area of fin	2 sq. ft.
Area of ailerons ..	7.5 sq. ft.
Maximum cross section of body	7.5 sq. ft.
Horizontal area of body..	30 sq. ft.
Vertical area of body ..	41 sq. ft.
Engine type and h.p. ..	230 h.p. B.R.2.
Airscrew, diameter and revs. ..	9 ft. 0 in. 1350 revs.
Weight of machine empty ..	1220 lbs.
Load per sq. ft.	7.25 lbs.
Weight per h.p.	8.35 lbs.
Tank capacity in hours ..	2.65 hours.
Tank capacity in gallons ..	38 gallons.

Performance.

Speed at 10,000 feet ..	125 m.p.h.
Speed at 15,000 feet ..	110 m.p.h.
Landing speed ..	50 m.p.h.

Climb.

To 10,000 feet in minutes ..	9½ minutes.
To 15,000 feet in minutes ..	18 minutes.
Disposable load apart from fuel	430 lbs.
Total weight of machine loaded	1920 lbs.

Three-quarter Rear View of the Boulton & Paul "Bobolink."

Front View of the Boulton & Paul "Bourges" Twin-engined Fighting Bomber (two 300 h.p. A.B.C. "Dragonfly" engines)

THE BOULTON & PAUL "BOURGES."

This machine was designed late in the war as a fighter bomber.

Is remarkable for its small overall dimensions.

This machine combines the speed, climb, and manœuvring qualities usually associated with a small single-seat fighter, with the fuel and load capacity expected of a large bomber.

The appended specification gives the leading characteristics :

Specification.

Type of machine	Twin-engined Biplane.
Name or type No. of machine ..	Boulton & Paul P 7. "Bourges."
Purpose for which intended ..	Bomber-fighter.
Span	54 ft.
Gap, maximum and minimum ..	6 ft. 6 in.
Overall length	37 ft.
Maximum height	12 ft.
Chord	Top plane, 8 ft. ; bottom plane, 6 ft. 6 in.
Total surface of wings ..	738 sq. ft.
Span of tail	16 ft.
Area of tail plane ..	96 sq. ft.
Area of elevators ..	96 sq. ft.
Area of rudder	21 sq. ft.

Half-side View of the Boulton & Paul "Bourges" Bomber (two 300 h.p. A.B.C. "Dragonfly" engines).

Area of fin	14 sq. ft.
Area of ailerons	27 sq. ft.
Maximum cross section of body	5.3 sq. ft.
Horizontal area of body..	73 sq. ft.
Vertical area of body ..	140 sq. ft.
Engine type and h.p. ..	2—320 h.p. A.B.C. "Dragonfly."
Airscrew, diameter and revs.	9 ft. 6 in. dia. 1650 r.p.m.
Weight of machine empty ..	3420 lbs.
Load per sq. ft.	8 lbs.
Tank capacity in hours.. ..	9.25 hours.
Tank capacity in gallons ..	190 gallons.

Performance.

Speed at 10,000 feet	124 m.p.h.
Speed at 15,000 feet	118 m.p.h.
Landing speed	50 m.p.h.

Climb.

To 10,000 feet in minutes ..	11 minutes.
To 15,000 feet in minutes ..	21 minutes.
Disposable load apart from fuel	1200 lbs
Total weight of machine loaded	5920 lbs.

BRISTOL. The British and Colonial Aeroplane Co., Ltd., Filton House, Bristol. The first great British aeroplane firm. Founded in 1910, by the late Sir George White, Bart., the pioneer of electric tramways. Have very extensive works on the outskirts of Bristol, where they manufacture "Bristol" aeroplanes of the firm's own design.

Chairman, Mr. Samuel White. Managing Director, Sir G. Stanley White, Bart. Secretary and Director, Mr. H. White-Smith. Works Manager, Mr. Herbert Thomas. Chief designer. Captain F. S. Barnwell, R.F.C.

The Bristol "Fighter" has been recognised, especially by the enemy, as one of the most effective and efficient fighter machines yet produced in any country.

BRISTOL T.B.8.

Two-seat training and coastal patrol biplane of 1913 appearance, using an 80 h.p. Gnôme radial engine. Used by RNAS up to 1916 and also built by Breguet in France (which see for photograph).

BRISTOL SCOUT "D."

The Bristol scout, type "D," now commonly known as the Bristol "Bullet," was produced during 1914 and served with active units of the R.F.C. and R.N.A.S. until 1916. Earlier models of the Scout were the types B (two built and served in France from September 1914) and series production Scout C.

It was originally fitted with an 80-h.p. Gnôme and showed a remarkable performance for its date. At the outbreak of war it was used on service, from time to time being fitted with higher-power engines. When its period of active service work ceased it was adopted as one of the standard training machines in the R.N.A.S. It was fitted with either the 80 Gnôme, 100 Mono Gnôme, 110 Le Rhône, or 130 Clerget engines.

Specification

Type of machine	Single-seater Biplane
Name or type No. of machine ..	Scout D
Purpose for which intended ..	Fighting and Reconnaissance.
Span	24 ft. 7 in.
Vertical gap	4 ft. 3 in.
Overall length	20 ft. 8 in.
Maximum height ..	8 ft. 8 in.
Chord	4 ft. 6 in.
Total surface of wings ..	200 sq. ft.
Area of ailerons ..	23.2 sq. ft.
Area of fixed tail ..	23 sq. ft.
Span of tail	10 ft.
Area of elevators ..	15 sq. ft.
Area of rudder ..	7 sq. ft.
Engine type and h.p. ..	80 h.p. Le Rhône, Gnôme, 100 h.p. Gnôme Mono, 110 h.p. Clerget or 110 h.p. Le Rhône
Airscrew, diam., pitch and revs ..	8 ft. 2½ in. diam., 7 ft. 10½ in. pitch, 1,300 r.p.m.
Weight of machine empty ..	760 lbs
Load per sq. ft.	6.25 lbs.
Weight per h.p.	14.7 lbs.
Petrol tank capacity in gallons ..	27 gallons.
Oil tank capacity in gallons ..	5½ gallons.

1914-15 Type.	A Two-seater Tractor biplane.		C Single-seater Scout Biplane.	
Length ... ... feet (m.)	29¼	8·900	21	6·5
Span ... ... feet (m.)	37¾	11·5	23	7·0
Area ... ... sq. feet (m².)	420	39	185	17
Weight { total ..lbs. (kgs.)	968	440	700	320
{ useful ...lbs. (kgs.)	693	315	330	150
Motor ... ... h.p	80 Gnome		85 Rhone	
Speed { max. m.p.h. (km.)	75	120	100	161
{ min. m.p.h. (km.)	34	56	50	80
Endurance ... ... hrs.	5		2	

A row of "Camels" built by Boulton & Paul, Ltd.

Front View of Bristol Scout, type "D," commonly known as the "Bullet" (80 h.p. Gnôme engine).

Performance.

Speed low down	100 m.p.h.
Speed at 5,000 feet	94 m.p.h.
Speed at 10,000 feet	86 m.p.h.
Landing speed	44 m.p.h.

Climb.

To 5,000 feet	6.5 minutes.
To 10,000 feet	18.5 minutes.
Disposable load apart from fuel	240 lbs.
Total weight of machine loaded	1,250 lbs.

Side view of BRISTOL "Scout," early type.

THE BRISTOL SCOUT, TYPE F.1.

The Bristol scout, type F1, is a recent production of the Bristol firm and was about to be put in production when the Armistice was signed. The fuselage is very deep and carried in its nose a 200 Sunbeam "Arab." The main planes show the principal departure from standard Bristol practice in that the lower plane is of smaller chord than the upper one so as to improve the pilot's range of vision downwards. One set of three struts, in the form of an N, are fitted on either side of the fuselage and are inclined outwards from the base. Ailerons are fitted to the upper plane only. The tail plane and undercarriage are of normal type. Armament consists of two fixed Vicker's guns fitted on top of the fuselage and firing through the propeller with the usual form of fire-control gear. The machine shows a speed of 128 m.p.h. at 10,000 feet, to which height it climbs in 8¼ minutes.

A later edition with a "Cosmos" engine of 315 h.p. has given a much better performance.

Specification.

Type of machine	Single-seater Biplane.
Name or type No. of machine	Scout F.
Purpose for which intended	Fighting and Reconnaissance.
Span	Top 29 ft. 6 in., bottom 26 ft. 2 in.
Gap	5 ft. 1 in.
Overall length	20 ft. 10 in.
Maximum height	8 ft. 4 in.
Chord	Top 5 ft. 7 in., bottom 4 ft. 11 in.
Total surface of wings	260 sq. ft.
Area of ailerons	30 sq. ft.
Total area of tail	15 sq. ft.
Span of tail	10 ft. 6 in.
Area of elevators	14.5 sq. ft.
Area of rudder	5 sq. ft.
Area of fin	4.1 sq. ft.
Engine type and h.p.	200 h.p. Sunbeam "Arab."
Airscrew, diam., pitch and revs.	9 ft. 2 ins., 9 ft., 1,155 r.p.m.
Weight of machine empty	1,300 lbs.
Load per sq. ft.	8.08 sq. ft.
Weight per h.p.	10 lbs.
Petrol tank capacity in gallons	32 gallons.
Oil tank capacity in gallons	5 gallons.

Performance.

Speed low down	138 m.p.h.
Speed at 5,000 feet	135 m.p.h.
Speed at 10,000 feet	128 m.p.h.
Landing speed	49 m.p.h.

Climb.

To 5,000 feet	3.7 minutes.
To 10,000 feet	8.5 minutes.
To 15,000 feet	16 minutes.
Disposable load apart from fuel	450 lbs.
Total weight of machine loaded	2,100 lbs.

Three-quarter Rear View of the Bristol type F.1., Single-seat Fighter. (Fitted with a "Mercury" Cosmos engine of 315 h.p.)

THE BRISTOL M.1C MONOPLANE

Contrary to the usual run of single-seater fighting machines, the majority of which pertain to the biplane breed, the British and Colonial Aeroplane Co., designed a monoplane which possessed a very good all-round performance, and which was used on active service in the Eastern theatre of war with great success.

The fuselage is of circular section, the shape of the cowling being preserved down to the tail plane by fairing composed of formers and laths covered with fabric. A 110-h.p. Le Rhône forms the power unit and a large circular spinner is fixed to the propeller.

The armament consists of one fixed Vickers gun firing through the propeller.

Specification.

Type of machine	Single-seater Monoplane.
Name or type No. of machine	Bristol Monoplane.
Purpose for which intended	Fighting.
Span	30 ft. 9 in.
Overall length	20 ft. 4 in.
Maximum height	8 ft.
Chord	5 ft. 11 in.
Total surface of wings	145 sq. ft.
Area of ailerons	18 sq. ft.
Total area of tail	20 sq. ft.
Span of tail	10 ft. 3 in.
Area of elevators	15 sq. ft.
Area of rudder	4.5 sq. ft.
Area of fin	5 sq. ft.
Engine type and h.p.	110 h.p. Le Rhône.
Airscrew, diam., pitch and revs.	8 ft. 6 in., 8 ft. 11 in., 1,350 r.p.m.
Weight of machine empty	850 lbs.
Load per sq. ft.	8.9 lbs.
Weight per h.p.	10.8 lbs.
Petrol tank capacity in gallons	20 gallons.
Oil tank capacity in gallons	5 gallons.

Performance.

Speed low down	130 m.p.h.
Speed at 5,000 feet	127 m.p.h.
Speed at 10,000 feet	117 m.p.h.
Landing speed	49 m.p.h.

Climb.

To 5,000 feet	3.5 minutes.
To 10,000 feet	9.0 minutes.
To 15,000 feet	19.0 minutes.
Disposable load apart from fuel	260 lbs.
Total weight of machine loaded	1,300 lbs.

Three-quarter Front View of the Bristol Monoplane.

View from Rear—The Bristol Monoplane.

THE BRISTOL F.2B. BIPLANE (FIGHTER)

The Bristol F.2B. biplane, more commonly known as the Bristol "Fighter," was designed as a fighter and reconnaissance two-seater biplane and is the latest development of the earlier F.2A type, with a more powerful engine. The fuselage is square section and tapers to a horizontal knife edge aft. A Rolls-Royce "Falcon" engine is carried in the nose of the machine on steel tube engine bearers, with the radiator in front. Metal cowling covers the front of the fuselage as far back as the front top and bottom centre section struts, and the top of the fuselage back to the pilot's seat. The fuselage is slung midway between the planes, there being both top and bottom centre-sections.

The angle of incidence of the tail plane can be altered from the pilot's seat to offset varying weights carried. Partial dual control is fitted, the control column being duplicated in the observer's cockpit, but for the rudder control instead of the rudder bar two hand-grips are fitted to the rudder control which pass through the observer's cockpit.

The armament consists of one fixed Vickers gun inside the cowling firing through the propeller, and a Scarff mounting round the observer's cockpit which is capable of carrying either a single or twin Lewis guns. The 200-h.p. Sunbeam "Arab" and the 200-h.p. Hispano-Suiza engines have been fitted and used on active service in addition to the Rolls-Royce "Falcon."

Specification

Type of machine	Two-seater Biplane.
Name or type No. of machine	F.2.B.
Purpose for which intended	Fighting and Reconnaissance.
Span	39 ft. 3 in.
Gap	5 ft. 5 in.
Overall length	25 ft. 10 in.
Maximum height	9 ft. 6 in.
Chord	5 ft. 6 in.
Total surface of wings	406 sq. ft
Area of ailerons	52 sq. ft.
Total area of tail	22.2 sq. ft.
Span of tail	12 ft. 10 in.
Area of elevators	23.2 sq. ft.
Area of rudder	7.2 sq. ft.
Area of fin	10.7 sq. ft.
Engine type and h.p.	Rolls-Royce "Falcon III" (275 h.p.); or other engines of Falcon II (220 h.p.), Hispano-Suiza (200 h.p.), Arab (200 h.p.) or Puma (200 h.p.) types.
Airscrew, diam., pitch and revs.	9 ft. 8 in. diam., 9 ft. 4 in. pitch, 1,220 r.p.m.
Weight of machine empty	1,750 lbs.
Load per sq. ft.	6.92 lbs.
Weight per h.p.	10.6 lbs.
Petrol tank capacity in gallons	45 gallons.
Oil capacity in gallons	4 gallons.

Performance.

Speed low down	125 m.p.h.
Speed at 5,000 feet	122 m.p.h.
Speed at 10,000 feet	113 m.p.h.
Landing speed	48 m.p.h.

Climb.

To 5,000 feet	5 minutes.
To 10,000 feet	11.5 minutes.
To 15,000 feet	21.5 minutes.
Disposable load apart from fuel	630 lbs.
Total weight of machine loaded	2,800 lbs.

BRISTOL ALL-METAL M.R.I. BIPLANE.

The Bristol all-metal biplane is more or less an all-metal Bristol "Fighter" with sundry modifications and was designed primarily for use in countries where extremes of heat and cold might have a detrimental effect on woodwork.

Metal has entirely replaced wood in the construction, the fuselage being constructed of aluminium and steel and can be easily dismantled for transport and storage purposes. The wings, which are unstaggered are of all-steel construction. The fuselage is slung between the planes, as in the Bristol "Fighter," but the lower centre section is completely cut away, leaving the two main spar tubes, to which are attached the two lower centre section struts.

Specification.

Type of machine	Two-seater Biplane.
Name or type No. of machine	All Metal M.R.I.
Purpose for which intended	Fighting and Reconnaissance.
Span	42 ft. 2 in.
Gap	5 ft. 11 in.
Overall length	27 ft.
Maximum height	10 ft. 3 in.
Chord	6 ft.
Total surface of wings	458 sq. ft.
Area of ailerons	39 sq. ft.
Total area of tail	27.8 sq. ft.
Span of tail	16 ft. 3 in.
Area of elevators	30 sq. ft.
Area of rudder	8.25 sq. ft.
Area of fin	7.8 sq. ft.
Engine type and h.p.	170 h.p. Wolseley "Viper."
Airscrew, diam., pitch and revs.	8 ft. 10 in. diam., 5 ft. 7 in. pitch, 1,700 r.p.m.
Weight of machine empty	1,700 lbs.
Load per sq. ft.	6.13 lbs.
Weight per h.p.	16.5 lbs.
Petrol tank capacity in gallons	50 gallons.
Oil tank capacity in gallons	5 gallons.

Performance.

Speed low down	110 m.p.h.
Speed at 5,000 feet	106 m.p.h.
Speed at 10,000 feet	98 m.p.h.
Landing speed	47 m.p.h.

Climb.

To 5,000 feet in minutes	8 minutes.
To 10,000 feet in minutes	20 minutes.
Disposable load apart from fuel	630 lbs.
Total weight of machine loaded	2,810 lbs.

Three-quarter Rear View of the Bristol F.2B Two-seater Fighter.

Three-quarter Rear View of second prototype Bristol F.2A "Fighter" with 150 h.p. Hispano-Suiza engine. Production F.2As adopted the 190 h.p. Rolls-Royce Falcon engine.

Side View — The experimental Bristol All-Metal M.R.I. development of the 'Fighter' (200 h.p. Sunbeam "Arab" engine.)

Front View of the Bristol Braemar Triplane. (Four 400 h.p. Liberty engines.)

View from Rear of the Bristol Braemar Triplane.

Maximum height	20 ft. 8 in.
Chord	8 ft. 6 in.
Total surface of wings ..	1,905 sq. ft.
Total area of tail	Top 51.5 sq. ft., bottom 45 sq. ft.
Area of elevators	Top 42.5 sq. ft. bottom 42.5 sq. ft.
Area of rudder	25 sq. ft.
Area of fin	28.2 sq. ft.
Engine type and h.p.	Four Liberty engines, 1,640 h.p. (total).
Airscrew, diam., pitch and revs...	Front (two) 10 ft. 2 in. dia., rear (two) 9 ft. 2 in. dia., front (two) 6 ft. 11 in. pitch, rear (two) 7 ft. 5 in. pitch, 1,750 r.p.m.
Weight of machine empty ..	10,650 lbs.
Load per sq. ft.	8.6 lbs.
Weight per h.p.	10 lbs.
Petrol tank capacity in gallons ..	450 gallons.
Oil tank capacity in gallons ..	40 gallons.
Performance.	
Speed low down ..	125 m.p.h.
Speed at 5,000 feet	122 m.p.h.
Speed at 10,000 feet	113 m.p.h.
Landing speed	55 m.p.h.
Climb.	
To 5,000 feet	6 minutes.
To 10,000 feet	13 minutes.
Disposable load apart from fuel	1,940 lbs.
Total weight of machine loaded	16,500 lbs.

THE BRISTOL TRIPLANE "BRAEMAR" MARK II.

The Bristol "Braemar" was originally designed as a long-distance bomber, but owing to the Armistice coming when it did the machine was never used on active service. It is now being slightly modified to do duty as a passenger-carrier and commercial machine.

It is a four-engined triplane with a single fuselage and with the four engines fixed in pairs tandem-wise driving two tractors and two pushers on either side of the fuselage.

In its original form the fuselage had accommodation for one gunner in the nose, two pilots just in advance of the main planes and another gunner's cockpit midway between the planes and the tail unit. The tail is a biplane with triple rudders.

The main planes are slightly swept back and ailerons are fitted to the two upper planes only.

The main planes are made to fold.

Specification.	
Type of machine	Four-engined Triplane.
Name or type No. of machine ..	Braemar Mk. 2.
Purpose for which intended ..	Bomber or Passenger Carrier.
Span	Top 81 ft. 8 in., centre 81 ft. 8 in., bottom 78 ft. 3 in.
Gap	7 ft. 2½ in.
Overall length	51 ft. 6 in.

Side View of the Bristol Braemar Triplane.

BRITISH CAUDRON Co., Ltd. Cricklewood. Con-

structing *Caudron* Biplanes (single and twin engined), to the designs of the Caudron Frères of Le Crotoy and Paris. The Chairman of the firm is Sir William Ramsay, and the Chief Directors are his son, Mr. E. I. Ramsay, and Mr. J. Hunter.

Photograph by F. N. Birkett.

British-built twin-engine CAUDRON biplane, with 100 h.p. Anzani engines.

DE BOLOTOFF. de Bolotoff Aeroplanes, Sevenoaks, Kent.

Prince Serge de Bolotoff will be remembered as the producer of a curious triplane in the very early days of aviation.

During the war he designed and has built the machine illustrated herewith. This is a two-seater machine of medium size (span about 36 feet), fitted with a 200 h.p. 12-Cylinder "Curtiss" Engine.

No detailed information as to dimensions or performance have been received.

As may be seen, the machine is generally on the lines of the early Albatros biplanes.

Side View of the de Bolotoff biplane.

F

THE FAIREY AVIATION Co., Ltd.

Offices : 175, Piccadilly W.1.   Works : Hayes, Middlesex, and Hamble, Hants.

Founded by Mr. C. R. Fairey in 1916 to develop the manufacture of seaplanes and aeroplanes to his own designs.

Mr. Fairey was one of the earliest British aircraft designers. He was associated in 1910-11 with Mr. Dunne in the construction of the experimental Dunne inherently stable machines, and afterwards with Messrs. Short Bros. at Eastchurch, played a very important part in the practical development of the seaplane.

Mr. Fairey's chief recent contribution to the art of aircraft design is the practical development of the use of trailing edge flaps as a camber changing device. This arrangement permits of the use of heavy wing loadings on an efficient wing section, which, when the flaps are pulled down, and the camber increased, becomes a high lift wing section, and makes it possible to land slowly.

The first machine upon which this device was successfully used was a modified "Baby" Seaplane—later produced by the firm as the "Hamble Baby."

Other types of the firms manufacture are described and illustrated hereafter.

THE FAIREY F2 TWIN ENGINE MACHINE.

The type F2 twin engine machine was one of the earliest of the large twin engine types built. It was designed in 1914, and was flying in 1916. It was actually the first twin engine machine fitted with folding wings.

The following table gives the main particulars :—

Specification.

Type of machine	Land Biplane.
Name or type No. of machine ..	F2.
Purpose for which intended	General.
Span, upper plane overall	77 ft.
Gap, Maximum and minimum ..	6 ft.
Overall length	40 ft. 6¼ in.
Maximum height	13 ft. 5⅝ in.
Chord	5 ft. 6 in.
Total surface of wings ..	718.4 sq. ft.
Span of tail	17 ft. 6 in.
Total area of tail	103.9 sq. ft. (including (elevators).
Area of elevators ..	39 sq. ft.
Area of rudder (2 rudders, 10 sq. ft. each)	20 sq. ft.
Area of fin (2 fins, 10.9 sq. ft. each)	21.8 sq. ft.
Area of each aileron and total area ..	47.8 sq. ft. each ; 95.6 sq. ft. total.
Maximum cross section of body	3 ft. × 2 ft. 6 in.
Horizontal area of body..	97 sq. ft.
Vertical area of body ..	75 sq. ft.
Engine type and h.p. (2 engines)	190 h.p. Rolls-Royce.
Load per sq. ft. ..	6.8 lbs.
Weight per h.p. ..	13 lbs.
Tank capacity in hours ..	3½ hours.

Performance.

Speed low down	81 kts.
Landing speed	38 m.p.h.

Climb.

To 5,000 feet in minutes ..	6 minutes.
Total weight of machine loaded	4880 lbs.

THE FAIREY CAMPANIA Types F16, F17, & F22.

These machines were designed as patrol seaplanes with special reference to the stowage capacity and hatchway dimensions of H.M Seaplane Currier "Campania."

The original F16 was designed for the Rolls-Royce "Eagle" engine.

F17 was a slightly modified version fitted with a more efficient wing section, and a later version of the Rolls "Eagle" engine.

The demand for Rolls "Eagles" at the time was considerably greater than the production thereof, and a further Campania type—the F22 was manufactured, fitted with a 260 h.p. Sunbeam engine.

All these machines were fitted with the *Fairey* variable camber device.

The leading particulars of all three types are as follows :—

CAMPANIA F16.

Type of machine ..	Seaplane.
Name or type No. of machine ..	F16.
Purpose for which intended	Patrol.
Span, upper plane overall	61 ft. 7½ in.
Gap, maximum and minimum ..	6 ft. 6 in.
Overall length ..	43 ft. 3⅝ in.
Maximum height	15 ft. 1 in.
Chord	6 ft. 4 in.
Total surface of wings ..	639.8 sq. ft.
Span of tail ..	13 ft.
Total area of tail	75.1 sq. ft. (including elevators).

ANTE-DATING THE ENEMY.—The Fairey Aviation Co.'s Twin-engined Folding-wing Biplane. Designed by Mr. C. R. Fairey in Dec., 1914; built in the summer of 1916; delivered in the autumn of 1916. It had a remarkably good performance.

Three-quarter Front View of the Fairey Twin-engined Folder Biplane. F.2 type.

Three-quarter rear view of the Fairey Twin-engined Folding Biplane.

A Fairey Campania (260 h.p. "Sunbeam" engine), just before leaving the water.

CAMPANIA F 16.—*continued.*

Area of elevators	.. ..	28.1 sq. ft.
Area of rudder	.. ..	22 sq. ft.
Area of fin	.. ..	14 sq. ft.
Area of each aileron and total area		23.4 sq. ft. ; 46.8 sq. ft.
Maximum cross section of body		3 ft. 6 in. × 3 ft. 1 in.
Horizontal area of body..	..	90 sq. ft.
Vertical area of body	..	88 sq. ft.
Engine type and h.p.	..	250 h.p. Rolls-Royce.
Load per sq. ft.	..	8.6 lbs.
Weight per h.p.	..	22.2 lbs.
Tank capacity in gallons	..	88 gallons.

Performance.

Speed low down	.. ..	72 kts.
Landing speed	.. ..	42 m.p.h.

Climb.

To 5,000 feet in minutes	..	14 minutes.
Disposable load apart from fuel	.. .. ..	1026 lbs.
Total weight of machine loaded	.. .. ..	5500 lbs.

A Fairey Campania just leaving the water.

CAMPANIA F17.

Type of machine	.. ..	Seaplane.
Name or type No. of machine	..	F17.
Purpose for which intended	..	Patrol.
Span, upper plane overall	..	61 ft. 7½ in.
Gap, maximum and minimum	..	6 ft. 6 in.
Overall length	.. ..	43 ft. 0⅝ in.
Maximum height	..	15 ft. 1 in.
Chord	.. ..	6 ft. 4 in.
Total surface of wings	..	627.8 sq. ft.
Span of tail	..	13 ft.
Total area of tail	..	75.1 sq. ft. (including elevators).
Area of elevators	.. ..	28 1 sq. ft.
Area of rudder	..	19 6 sq. ft.
Area of fin	.. ..	16 2 sq. ft.
Area of each aileron and total area		23 4 sq. ft. ; 46.8 sq. ft.
Maximum cross section of body		3 ft. 6 in. × 3 ft. 1 in.
Horizontal area of body..	..	90 sq. ft.
Vertical area of body	..	88 sq. ft.
Engine type and h.p.	..	275 h.p. Rolls-Royce.
Load per sq. ft.	..	8.7 lbs.
Weight per h.p.	..	19.5 lbs.
Tank capacity in gallons	..	88 gallons.

Performance.

Speed low down	..	78 kts.
Landing speed	..	43 m.p.h.

Climb.

To 5,000 feet in minutes	..	12.30 minutes.
Disposable load apart from fuel	.. .. ..	1100 lbs.
Total weight of machine loaded	.. .. ..	5560 lbs.

A Fairey Campania well off.

CAMPANIA F22.

Type of machine	.. ..	Seaplane.
Name or type No. of machine	..	F22.
Purpose for which intended	..	Patrol.
Span, Upper plane Overall	..	61 ft. 7½ in.
Gap, maximum and minimum	..	6 ft. 6 in.
Overall length	.. ..	43 ft. 0⅝ in.
Maximum height	..	15 ft. 1 in.
Chord	.. ..	6 ft. 4 in.
Total surface of wings	..	627.8 sq. ft.
Span of tail	..	13 ft.
Total area of tail	..	75.1 sq. ft. (inc. elevators).
Area of elevators	..	28.1 sq. ft.
Area of rudder	..	19.6 sq. ft.
Area of fin	..	16.2 sq. ft.
Area of each aileron and total area		23.4 sq. ft. ; 46.8 sq. ft.
Maximum cross section of body		3 ft. 6 in. × 3 ft. 1 in.
Horizontal area of body..	..	90 sq. ft.
Vertical area of body	..	88 sq. ft.
Engine type and h.p.	..	250 h.p. Sunbeam.
Load per sq. ft.	..	8.14 lbs.
Weight per h.p.	..	20.1 lbs.
Tank capacity in gallons	..	88 gallons.

Performance.

Speed low down	..	74 kts.
Landing speed	..	40 m.p.h.

Climb.

To 5,000 feet in minutes	..	18 minutes
Disposable load apart from fuel	.. .. ..	1026 lbs.
Total weight of machine loaded	.. .. ..	5329 lbs.

Three-quarter Front View of the Fairey Seaplane. F 127 (N 9). (190 h.p. Rolls-Royce " Falcon " engine.)

THE FAIREY N9 TYPE F127.

The *Fairey* seaplane N9 was built in 1917 as a patrol seaplane for the R.N.A.S.

This machine has one set of struts on each side of the fuselage, and a top plane with a large overhang.

Owing to the Rolls-Royce "Falcon" engine being used in other types of machines in production, this type was never proceeded with. It is interesting to note that the original N9 remained in service to the middle of 1918, and was the first float seaplane to begin an actual flight by being thrown off a warship by a catapult gear.

Specification.

Type of machine	Seaplane.
Name or type No. of machine	F127.
Purpose for which intended	Ship work.
Span	50 ft.
Gap, maximum and minimum	5 ft. 7 in.
Overall length	35 ft. 6 in.
Maximum height	13 ft.
Chord	5 ft. 6 in.
Total surface of wings	420 sq. ft.
Span of tail	13 ft.
Total area of tail	34.2 sq. ft.
Area of elevators	34.2 sq. ft.
Area of rudder	9.8 sq. ft.
Area of fin	8.9 sq. ft.
Area of each aileron and total area	18 ft.
Engine type and h.p.	190 h.p. Rolls-Royce.
Load per sq. ft.	9.08 lbs.
Weight per h.p.	18.15 lbs.
Tank capacity in hours	5¼ hours.
Tank capacity in gallons	70 gallons.

Performance.

Speed low down	78 kts.
Speed at 10,000 feet	74 kts.
Landing speed	38 m.p.h.

Climb.

To 5,000 feet in minutes	9.30 minutes.
To 10,000 feet in minutes	38 minutes.
Disposable load apart from fuel	516 lbs.
Total weight of machine loaded	3812 lbs.

Side View of the Fairey F 127 (N 9).

THE FAIREY Type 3 B.

The Fairey 3B was designed as a bomber with the same fuselage as the N10 but the upper plane was increased in span, and larger floats were fitted. The wings and chassis were interchangeable with those of the original type 3.

Specification.

Type of machine	Seaplane.
Name or type No. of machine	F.III.B.
Purpose for which intended	Sea Bomber.
Span	62 ft. 9 in.
Gap, maximum and minimum	5 ft. 7 in.
Overall length	36 ft.
Maximum height	13 ft.
Chord	5 ft. 6 in.
Total surface of wings	570 sq. ft.
Span of tail	13 ft.
Total area of tail	34.2 sq. ft.
Area of elevators	34.2 sq. ft.
Area of rudder	12.4 sq. ft.
Area of fin	12.4 sq. ft.
Area of each aileron and total area	23 sq. ft.
Engine type and h.p.	260 h.p. Sunbeam.
Load per sq. ft.	8.5 lbs.
Weight per h.p.	18.5 lbs.
Tank capacity in hours	4½ hours.
Tank capacity in gallons	76 gallons.

Performance.

Speed low down	83 kts.
Speed at 10,000 feet	76 kts.
Landing speed	42 m.p.h.

Climb.

To 5,000 feet in minutes	12.30 minutes.
To 10,000 feet in minutes	36 minutes.
Disposable load apart from fuel	1041 lbs.
Total weight of machine loaded	4892 lbs.

The Fairey type 3 B. Seaplane (260 h.p. "Sunbeam" engine).

THE FAIREY Type 3C.

This machine was a further development of the F127 type. Wings and Chassis were still interchangeable with those of the F127 or the type 3B but a more powerful engine—the 375 h.p. Rolls-Royce "Eagle" was installed.

The actual wings were identical with those of the original type 3, and the chassis and floats were those of the type 3B

Specification.

Type of machine	Seaplane.
Name or type No. of machine	F.III.C.
Purpose for which intended	Reconnaissance.
Engine type and h.p.	360 h.p. Rolls-Royce.
Load per sq. ft.	10.6 ins.
Weight per h.p.	14 lbs.
Tank capacity in hours	6 hours.
Tank capacity in gallons	120 gallons.

Performance.

Speed low down	97 kts.
Speed at 10,000 feet	90 kts.
Landing speed	44 m.p.h.

Climb.

To 5,000 feet in minutes	6.40 minutes.
To 10,000 feet in minutes	17.30 minutes.
To 20,000 feet in minutes	
Disposable load apart from fuel	1030 lbs.
Total weight of machine loaded	5050 lbs.

The Fairey type 3 C. Seaplane (375 h.p. Rolls-Royce "Eagle" engine).

FAIREY AVIATION CO.—continued.

THE "HAMBLE BABY" SEAPLANE.

Reference has already been made to this machine. The leading characteristics are as stated :—

Specification.

Type of machine	Seaplane.
Name or type No. of machine ..	F129.
Purpose for which intended ..	Reconnaissance.
Span, upper plane overall ..	27 ft. 9½ in.
Gap, maximum and minimum..	4 ft. 6 in.
Overall length	23 ft. 4 in.
Maximum height	9 ft. 6 in.
Chord	4 ft. 9 in.
Total surface of wings ..	246 sq. ft.
Span of tail	10 ft. 9 in.
Total area of tail	41 sq. ft. (including elevators).
Area of elevators	17 sq. ft.
Area of rudder	6.7 sq. ft.
Area of fin	4.3 sq. ft.
Area of each aileron and total area	14.1 sq. ft. ; 36.4 sq. ft.
Maximum cross section of body	3 ft. 2 in. × 2 ft. 7¾ in.
Horizontal area of body.. ..	39.4 sq. ft.
Vertical area of body	34 sq. ft.
Engine type and h.p.	110 h.p. Clerget.
Load per sq. ft.	7.8 lbs.
Weight per h.p.	17.21 lbs.
Tank capacity in hours ..	3½ hours.

Performance.

Speed low down	.. ..	85 kts.
Landing speed	.. ..	44 m.p.h.

Climb.

To 5,000 feet in minutes	..	8 minutes
Total weight of machine loaded	.. .. ..	1900 lbs.

G

THE GOSPORT AIRCRAFT Co., Ltd.
Gosport, Hants.

The Gosport Aircraft Company was formed early in the War by Sir Charles Allom, of White, Allom & Co., Ltd., who is the well-known owner of racing yachts, and Mr. Charles Nicholson, of Camper & Nicholson, the famous yacht builders, of Gosport.

The firm has constructed a number of flying boats to Government specifications, chiefly F.B.A's of the Norman Thompson type. More recently the firm has built complete, several F5 type boats of the kind developed by Lieut.-Col. John Porte, C.M.G., R.A.F.

Front view of a Fairey type 3 B Seaplane.

Rear view of a Fairey type 3 B Seaplane.

A F.B.A. Flying-boat (100 h.p. Gnome engine), built by the Gosport Aircraft Co., Ltd.

A F5 Flying-boat (2—375 h.p. Rolls-Royce "Eagle" engines), built by the Gosport Aircraft Co., Ltd.

GRAHAME-WHITE. The Grahame-White Aviation Co., Ltd., 32, Regent St., London, W. Works and Flying Ground : Hendon. Founded by Mr C. Grahame-White, the well-known aviator, who in 1909 commenced operations with a school at Pau. Later this was removed to England, and a general agency for the sale of aeroplanes, etc., established. This developed, and early in 1911 the Hendon Aerodrome was acquired, and a factory established, which has grown continually ever since. In April, 1912, a monoplane to special design was completed. By the close of the same year biplanes of advanced design were constructed. In 1913, the firm took up the agency for the *Morane-Saulnier* monoplanes, and had built a large number for the War Office, besides building machines of Government design for the Admiralty.

During 1916, the firm built war machines of various types under official supervision. The aerodrome was taken over by the War Office late in 1916, and all the schools were placed under Government control. Later, they were removed to other flying grounds and the Hendon Aerodrome was devoted entirely to the testing of Government aeroplanes.

Side view of the Grahame White "Ganymede" (3/270 H.P. Sunbeam Maori Engines); and of the Grahame White "Bantam" (80 H.P. Le Rhône)

THE GRAHAME-WHITE E.IV DAY BOMBER "GANYMEDE."

This machine was designed prior to the signing of the Armistice, as a long-range day bomber.

It is of the twin fuselage, three engine type, two motors, one in the front of each fuselage driving tractor air screws, and a third, in the rear end of a central nacelle, driving a pusher air screw.

Particulars of dimensions are given in the following table :—

Specification.

Fitted with three 270 h.p. Sunbeam "Maori" motors.

Type of machine	Twin fuselage, three-engined.
Name or type No. of machine	"Ganymede."
Purpose for which intended	Day Bomber.
Span	89 ft. 3 in.
Gap, maximum and minimum	9 ft. 3 in.
Overall length	49 ft. 9 in.
Maximum height	16 ft.
Chord	10 ft. 3 in.
Total surface of wings	1,660 sq. ft.
Span of tail	29 sq. ft.
Total area of tail	254 sq. ft.
Area of elevators	114 sq. ft.
Area of rudders	50 sq. ft.
Area of fin	30 sq. ft.
Area of each aileron and total area	200 sq. ft.
Engine type and h.p.	3 Sunbeam "Maori," 270 h.p. each.
Airscrew, diam., pitch and revs.	3.140 diam., 2.570 pitch, 1,050 r.p.m.
Weight of machine empty	11,500 lbs.
Load per sq. ft. fully loaded	9.65 lbs. sq. ft.
Weight per h.p. fully loaded	19.7 lbs. h.p.
Tank capacity in hours	9 hours at 10,000 feet.
Tank capacity in gallons	400 gallons.
Performance.	
Speed low down	105 m.p.h.
Speed at 10,000 feet	93 m.p.h.
Landing speed	52 m.p.h.
Disposable load apart from fuel	3,100 lbs.
Total weight of machine loaded	16,000 lbs.

The makers state that the machine had been designed for 3—400 h.p. Liberty engines, which would have increased the speed to 120 miles per hour.

H

HEWLETT & BLONDEAU, Ltd., Leagrave, Beds.

Founded in 1913 by Mrs. Maurice Hewlett, wife of the famous author, and herself the first British aviatrice, in conjunction with M. Gustave Blondeau, one of the earliest French aviators. Constructors of aeroplanes for the Admiralty. Employed entirely on work to Government specifications.

K

KENNEDY.

Kennedy Aeroplanes, Ltd., Cromwell Road, London, W.7.

Mr. C. J. H. MacKenzie-Kennedy.

Mr. Kennedy was one of the pioneers of aviation in Russia, and was largely concerned with the development of the Sikorsky biplane.

Returning to England soon after the outbreak of War, he was responsible for the design of the machine illustrated herewith, which was built by the Gramophone Company, Ltd., at their works at Hayes, and was erected in the open at Northolt Aerodrome, there being no shed in the country sufficiently large to house it.

The machine was equipped with 4—200 h.p. British-built Salmson engines, as the only ones which the authorities would issue, and the power was inadequate for more than straight flights.

The following are the leading dimensions :—

Span	142 ft.
Chord	10 ft.
Gap	10 ft.
Overall length	80 ft.
Maximum height	23 ft. 6 in.
Weight of machine empty	19,000 lbs.
Engine type and h.p.	4—200 h.p. Salmson.

L

LONDON AIRCRAFT Co., Ltd., Urswick Road, Lower Clapton, N.

Manager : Mr. J. S. Morch. Made aeroplanes and parts during the war to official specifications.

The GRAHAME-WHITE Type XV school biplane (1916 type, modified from 1914-15), with 80 h.p. Le Rhône engine. Adopted by the RNAS in early part of war.

A Front View of the Kennedy Giant, with a Bristol "Fighter" alongside.

Side View of the Kennedy Giant (4—200 h.p. Salmson Engines).

The Kennedy Giant being erected at Northolt.

M

MARTINSYDE. Martinsyde, Ltd., Brooklands, Weybridge, and Woking, Surrey.

Were among the pioneers of British aviation, Messrs. Martin & Handasyde having built a monoplane in 1908. Their big monoplanes of 1912 and 1913 flew magnificently, but failed to find approval for Service use.

Early in 1914 the firm built an enormous monoplane to the order of the late Gustav Hamel, who was being backed by Mr. Mackay Edgar, the Canadian capitalist, for the attempt on the trans-Atlantic flight, which was frustrated by the death of Mr. Hamel in the English Channel. The trans-Atlantic *Martinsyde* was designed for a 250 h.p. Sunbeam engine, and the tanks held a ton of petrol.

Late in 1914, the firm produced a small fast biplane "Scout," with an 80 h.p. Gnôme motor, which was an immediate success, and was promptly ordered in large quantities by the War Office. It played an important part in the war in 1915, till the increased speed of the German machines rendered it out of date. It was superseded by a more powerful type of *Martinsyde* scout, fitted at first with a 120 h.p. Beardmore engine and later with a 160 h.p. Beardmore.

As the result of the success of these machines, the firm acquired very big works near Woking, where the output of Martinsydes and other types exceeded anything thought possible before the war.

Since then the firm has produced some of the most valuable fighting machines, and some of those with the highest performance in any belligerent country. The Elephant, intended as a fighter but used mainly as a bomber and reconnaissance aircraft during 1916-17, was built in hundreds.

THE MARTINSYDE F3 & F4 BUZZARD

The *Martinsyde* F3 single-seater scout biplane was designed in 1917, and, although it was far superior to any other machine of the period in speed and climb, was not put into production, owing to the difficulty in obtaining engines, in this case, the Rolls Royce "Falcon," which were earmarked by the Air Ministry for other machines actually in use.

It was then adapted to take the 300 h.p. Hispano-Suiza, and was put into production as the F4, but its appearance on active service was preceded by the Armistice.

The fuselage is very deep and carries enclosed in the cowling twin Vickers sychronised guns. One set of interplane struts are carried on either side of the fuselage, and are splayed outwards from the base.

The pilot is set well back, and fairly high in the fuselage, the upper plane being cut away and the lower plane staggered back, thereby giving him a good view both upward and downward.

THE MARTINSYDE F4.

Specification.

Type of machine	F 4.
Purpose for which intended	Fighter.
Span	Top plane, 32 ft. 9$\frac{3}{8}$ in.; bottom, 31 ft. 2$\frac{3}{8}$ in.
Gap, maximum and minimum	5 ft. 2$\frac{5}{8}$ in.
Overall length	25 ft. 5$\frac{5}{8}$ in.
Maximum height	10 ft. 4 in.
Chord	Top plane, 6 ft. 0$\frac{1}{2}$ in. ; bottom plane, 5 ft. 6$\frac{1}{4}$ in.
Total surface of wings	320 sq. ft. (all in).
Span of tail	11 ft. 1$\frac{1}{2}$ in. (over elevators).
Total area of tail	36$\frac{3}{4}$ sq. ft. (tailplane and elevators).
Area of elevators	8$\frac{1}{4}$ sq. ft. each. Total 16$\frac{1}{2}$ sq. ft.
Area of rudder	9$\frac{3}{4}$ sq. ft.
Area of fin	6$\frac{1}{2}$ sq. ft.
Area of each aileron and total area	Top, 11$\frac{3}{4}$ sq. ft. each ; Bottom, 9$\frac{1}{4}$ sq. ft. each. Total, 42 sq. ft.
Engine type and h.p.	Hispano-Suiza. 300 h.p.
Airscrew, diameter and pitch and revs.	Dia., 8 ft. 8$\frac{7}{8}$ in. ; Pitch, 6 ft. 6 in. ; Revs., 1850 r.p.m.
Weight of machine empty	1710 lbs.
Load per sq. ft.	7 lbs.
Weight per h.p.	7$\frac{1}{2}$ lbs.
Tank capacity in hours	3 hours.
Tank capacity in gallons	43 gallons.
Performance.	
Speed low down	145 m.p.h.
Speed at 10,000 feet	143 m.p.h.
Speed at 20,000 feet	126 m.p.h.
Landing speed	45 m.p.h.
Climb.	
To 5,000 feet	3.0 mins.
To 10,000 feet	6.30 mins.
To 20,000 feet	19.30 mins.
Total weight of machine loaded	2280 lbs.

The Martinsyde F3 Single-seat Fighter (Rolls-Royce "Falcon" engine, 275 h.p.)

The Martinsyde F4 Single-seat Fighter (300 h.p. Hispano-Suiza motor.)

A MARTINSYDE S.1 Scout with 80 h.p. Gnôme engine, and later with 100 h.p Monosoupape Gnômes, one of the most successful small fighting machines of the 1915-16 campaign.

Side View of a Martinsyde "Elephant," one of the most successful machines of 1916-17.

N

NIEUPORT & GENERAL AIRCRAFT Co., Ltd. Cricklewood, London, N.W.

The firm is under the direction of Major Heckstall-Smith late of the Royal Aircraft Factory.

The accompanying photographs illustrate the British Nieuport "Nighthawk" with the 320 h.p. A.B.C. "Dragonfly" engine.

This machine is particularly interesting as having been built to the first specification issued by the Royal Air Force. When the R.A.F. decided that the time had come to concentrate on a limited number of types to finish up the war, they decided to concentrate for a single-seater fighter solely on the *Nieuport* "Nighthawk" for the "Dragonfly" engine.

The reasons why this machine was selected were:—

(1) That it fulfilled the performance required.

(2) That it was fully up to the required strength as demonstrated by loading tests on every part of the machine.

(3) That the general arrangement of the machine gave the very best facilities to the pilot for fighting—namely: for position and accessibility of guns, instruments, etc., and the minimum blind area.

(4) Because the general design of the machine was for quick production and the fact that complete engineering drawings and schedules had been prepared in advance.

The design was carried out by Mr. H. P. Folland, who is the chief engineer and designer to the Nieuport Company. Mr. Folland was assistant chief designer at the Royal Aircraft Factory, where he carried out the designs of F.E.2 and S.E.5.

Prior to the war, when Lieut.-Col. J. E. B. Seely, who was then Secretary of State for War, wished to make a world's record on behalf of the Royal Aircraft Factory, he instructed the superintendent of the R.A.F. to produce a machine for this purpose. This machine was known as S.E 4, and was fitted with 160 h.p. 18 cylinder Gnôme engine. The design of this machine was carried out by Mr. Folland, and the machine was flown by Maj. J. M. Salmond (now Major-General and K.C.B.), and, as mentioned in the House of Commons in 1914, the machine made a speed of 135 m.p.h. and climbed the first 1,500 ft. in one minute.

Major S. Heckstall Smith, general manager of the Nieuport Company, was at that time Assistant Superintendent at the R.A.F., and was largely responsible for such successes as the factory produced. The "Nighthawk" is a marked advance in detail design and construction on any of the R.A.F. work, and both he and Mr. Folland deserve to be congratulated on its production.

As will be seen, the machine somewhat resembles the *Sopwith* "Snipe" in general appearance and dimensions. It is designed as a production job, and a quantity of the fittings which are used in S.E.5s have been worked into the design, because these are stock fittings and can be procured easily and in quantities.

The photographs show that the machine is eyeable, and that it gives one an impression of speed. It will be interesting to notice how the official performance of the machine works out in practice.

THE NIEUPORT "NIGHTHAWK."

During 1918 the firm produced a high-performance single-seat fighter, known as the "Nighthawk," which was ordered on a large scale by the R.A.F. Particulars of this machine are given in the following table:—

Type of machine	Fighting Scout.
Name or type No. of machine	British Nieuport "Nighthawk"
Purpose for which intended ..	Fighting, airship destruction, convoying.
Span	28 ft.
Gap, maximum and minimum ..	4 ft. 6 in.
Overall length	18 ft. 6 in.
Maximum height..	9 ft. 6 in.
Chord	5 ft. 3 in.

Total surface of wings	270 sq. ft.
Span of tail	9 ft.
Total area of tail	28 sq. ft.
Area of elevators	10 sq. ft.
Area of rudder	5 ft 3 in.
Area of fin	5 ft. 2 in.
Area of each aileron and total area	9.3 each; total 37.2 sq. ft.
Maximum cross section of body .	10 sq. ft.
Horizontal area of body	46 sq. ft.
Vertical area of body	49 sq. ft.
Engine type and h.p.	A.B.C. "Dragon-fly," 320 h.p.
Airscrew, diam., pitch and revs...	9 ft. dia.; 7 ft. pitch; 1,650 revs.
Weight of machine empty ..	1,500 lbs.
Load per sq. ft.	7.75 lbs.
Weight per h.p.	6.62 lbs.
Tank capacity in hours ..	3 hours at 20,000 feet.
Tank capacity in gallons ..	40 petrol, 4 oil.
Performance.	
Speed low down	151 m.p.h.
Speed at 10,000 feet ..	140 m.p.h.
Speed at 20,000 feet ..	121 m.p.h.
Landing speed	58 m.p.h.
Climb.	
To 5,000 feet	3 minutes.
To 10,000 feet.. ..	7 minutes.
To 20,000 feet.. ..	20 minutes.
Disposable load apart from fuel	400 lbs.
Total weight of machine loaded	2.120 lbs.

Side view of the British Nieuport "Nighthawk" (320 h.p. A.B.C. "Dragonfly" engine).

P

HANDLEY PAGE. Handley Page, Ltd.

110, Cricklewood Lane, N.W. Flying ground : Cricklewood. Established at the end of 1908. In June, 1909, it was turned into a Limited Liability Co., and after that it was busily employed in producing its own machines, also others to inventors' specifications.

The first successful H.P. monoplane was worth noting as it showed such remarkable resemblance to the German "Taube" monoplanes, which played so important a part in the early portion of the war. The first *Handley Page* tractor biplane was of somewhat similar type.

The biplane was taken over by the Navy at the outbreak of war and was used for instructional flying.

In 1916, the firm produced their now well-known and successful twin-engined heavy/night bomber, the O/100, later developed into the more powerful O/400 type, and in 1918 the four-engined V/1500 type.

The HANDLEY-PAGE G Type biplane, first flown in 1913 and adopted by the RNAS in 1914 for training and home defence.

DESCRIPTION OF THE HANDLEY-PAGE 100 BIPLANE.
1917 TYPE.

The *Handley Page* machine is a twin tractor biplane having in the centre a fuselage, in which is carried the pilot, passengers and fuel, and, when used for military purposes, the guns and bombs.

On either side of the fuselage are the two engine nacelles at 16 feet centres.

The span of the top plane is 100 feet and that of the lower plane 70 feet. Ailerons for lateral balance are fitted to the top plane only and extend for 20 feet from each wing tip inwards.

The machine is of the folding wing type, and, as the planes fold back from the nacelle points, the shed accommodation required is small.

The width of the machine when folded is only 32 feet, the extreme height being 22 feet with the planes extended and 18 feet with the planes folded.

The controls of the ailerons are so arranged that they do not foul the other parts of the machine when the planes are folded back.

The fuselage is 62 feet 10½ inches long. In the extreme nose is the front gunner's cockpit with gun ring and guns. Behind this are situated the pilot's and observer's seats side by side, with the instrument board and controls in front of them. Behind them is the starting platform where all the gear is fitted for starting the engines from the inside fuselage, and here also the bomb dropping control box and sighting apparatus are fitted.

In the central part of the fuselage, between the planes, is the bomb chamber with release gears. This bomb chamber is fitted with apparatus for the dropping of eight 250 lbs. and eight 112 lbs. bombs. Over this bomb-dropping gear are fitted two large fuel tanks.

Behind this section again are the two rear platforms with guns mounted, two above and one below the fuselage.

The machine is fitted with a biplane tail with balanced rudders on either side. The elevators are four in number and are operated by the ordinary control gear lever at the pilot's seat.

The machine has a fuel capacity of 300 gallons (this being sufficient to give the machine an eight hours' radius of action).

The total weight of the machine fully loaded is about 12,000 lbs. Its speed is 95 miles per hour at ground level.

A HANDLEY PAGE 100 BIPLANE ON AN AERODROME IN ITALY. The photograph gives a good idea of the size of the machine.

Three-quarter Front View of a Handley Page 400 Biplane, with Rolls-Royce Engines.

HANDLEY-PAGE TWIN-ENGINED BIPLANE, TYPE O/400.

The general arrangement of the *Handley-Page* O/400 bomber is probably well-known to all by now, so it will suffice to say that the characteristics of the machine are—long fuselage with a biplane tail, twin engines carried in "power-eggs" half-way between the main planes, folding wings, extension to the upper plane fitted with balanced ailerons, and a rather complicated form of under-carriage consisting of three sets of Vees under each power unit, connecting to a short central skid, across the centre of which is a hinged axle. On the end of each axle, outside of the wheel hub, a telescopic strut with an inserted shock-absorber runs upwards to the front spar under the engine struts, which is enclosed.

The main petrol tanks are carried in the upper half of the fuselage between the planes. The accommodation is similar to most twin-engined bombers, viz.:—observer in nose, equipped with Lewis gun on Scarff ring, and bomb sights; the pilot's cockpit, fitted with two sets of controls, just in rear of front observer and aft of main planes, a cockpit for a rear gunner fitted with two swivel gun mountings.

Specification.

Type of machine	Biplane.
Name or type No. of machine ..	O/400.
Purpose for which intended ..	Night bombing.
Span	100 ft.
Gap, maximum and minimum ..	11 ft.
Overall length	62 ft. 6 in.
Maximum height.. ..	22 ft.
Chord	10 ft.
Total surface of wings ..	1,630 sq. ft.
Maximum cross section of body..	6 ft. 10 in. × 4 ft. 9 in.
Engine type and h.p. ..	2 R.R. Eagle VIII (Standard equipment.)
Airscrew, diam., and revs. ..	11 ft., 1,080 r.p.m.
Weight of machine empty ..	8,200 lbs.
Load per sq. ft. fully loaded ..	8.5 lbs.
Weight per h.p.	20 lbs.
Tank capacity in hours ..	8½ hours.
Tank capacity in gallons.. ..	300 gallons.

Performance.

Speed low down	97 m.p.h. fully loaded.
Speed at 6,500 feet	95 m.p.h.
Speed at 10,000 feet	93 m.p.h.
Landing speed..	50 m.p.h.

Climb.

To 5,000 feet	10 minutes.
To 10,000 feet	25 minutes.

Disposable load apart from fuel	3,500 lbs.
Total weight of machine loaded	14,000 lbs.

Alternative Engines.

2 "Liberty's," 2 "Sunbeam Maori," 2 "Sunbeam Cossack," or 2 "F.I.A.T." etc.

The Handley Page Type O/400 (2—375 h.p. Rolls-Royce "Eagle" Engines) with the wings folded.

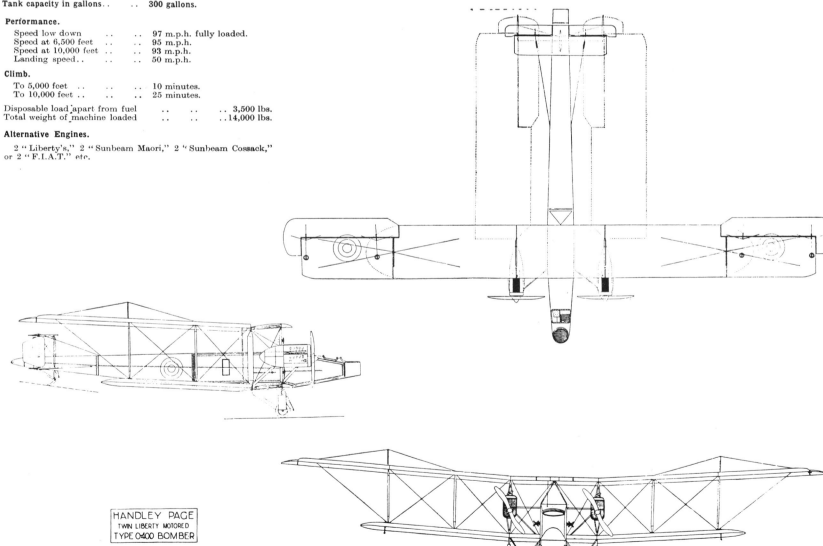

HANDLEY PAGE
TWIN LIBERTY MOTORED
TYPE O/400 BOMBER

Scale of feet

HANDLEY-PAGE FOUR-ENGINED BIPLANE, V/1500.

Tho four-engined *Handley-Page* was a development of the smaller two-engined machine. It was designed principally for night bombing, its most spectacular " engagement " being the bombing of Berlin, which was only forestalled by the signing of the Armistice.

The fuselage remains the same in all its essentials and internal arrangements. The four engines are carried, two tandemwise, on either side of the fuselage, and are not enclosed in any cowling. The upper and lower main planes are of equal span, the upper main plane being flat and the lower plane having a dihedral, and both planes have a decided sweepback. The under-carriage consists of two pairs of Vees under each power unit : the front legs of the Vees carries shock-absorbers enclosed in streamline fairing, the rear members being hinged.

Both the O/400 and V/1500 types can be converted to commercial vehicles by the mere elimination of the military apparatus—bomb gear and guns—and the refitting of the interior of the fuselage for the accommodation of passengers or goods. In the event of passengers, mails and goods all being carried by the same machine, each would be conveyed in a separate compartment.

In addition to the necessary crew of three men, and petrol, oil and water for a non stop flight of 400–500 miles, the nett useful load of each machine would be :—

Type O/400 :—2,700 lbs. of goods or 18 passengers.

Type V/1500 :—10,000 lbs. of goods or 45 passengers.

The external ranges of these machines as commercial vehicles can be regarded as :—

Type O/400 :—800 miles non-stop with useful load of a half ton.

Type V/1500 :—1,300 miles non-stop with useful load of one ton

Specification.

Type of machine ..	Biplane.
Name or type No. of machine ..	V 1500.
Purpose for which intended	Night bombing.
Span	126 ft.
Gap, maximum and minimum ..	15 ft. ; 12 ft.
Overall length ..	62 ft.
Maximum height	23 ft.
Chord	12 ft.
Total surface of wings ..	3,000 sq. ft.
Maximum cross section of body..	8 ft. × 6 ft. 2 in.
Engine type and h.p. ..	4 R.R. Eagle VIII.
Airscrew, diam. and revs. ..	13 ft. 5 in. (tractors) ; 10 ft. 4 in. (pushers). 1,080 ; 1,080.
Weight of machine empty ..	15,000 lbs.
Load per sq. ft. fully loaded ..	10 lbs.
Weight per h.p.	21 lbs.
Tank capacity in hours ..	14 hours.
Tank capacity in gallons..	1,000 gallons.

Performance.

Speed low down ..	103 m.p.h. fully loaded.
Speed at 6,500 feet ..	99 m.p.h.
Speed at 10,000 feet ..	95 m.p.h.
Landing speed.. ..	50 m.p.h.

Climb.

To 5,000 feet	8 minutes.
To 10,000 feet ..	21 minutes.

Disposable load apart from fuel	..	..	7,000 lbs.
Total weight of machine loaded	..	..	30,000 lbs.

Alternative Engines.

4 b.h.p. "Atlantic's," each 500 h.p., or 4 Napier "Lion's," etc.

Three-quarter Front View of a Handley Page Type V/1500 (Four 375 h.p. Rolls-Royce " Eagle " Engines). The standing figures indicate the size of this machine.

PARNALL & SONS (Proprietors : W. & T. Avery, Ltd.), Mivart Street, Eastville, Bristol. Wood-working firm of note. Designing and manufacturing aeroplanes and seaplanes of various designs, for the Air Force.

THE PARNALL "PANTHER."

The Parnall "Panther" was designed as a two-seater reconnaissance ship-plane. It is equipped with a water-tight bulkheaded fuselage, airbags, which are blown up when necessary by the pilot, and a small hydrovane fitted to two struts in advance of the undercarriage to prevent the machine turning over when landing in the sea.

The fuselage is built up of formers and three ply, minus any internal wire tracing (on the German principle), and is made to fold at a point just in rear of the observer's seat. On top of the monocoque fuselage is a huge bulge in which is situated the pilot and observer's cockpits. The elevator controls are carried through the continuation of this hump to the tail, whereas the rudder control runs through a special compartment on the right hand side of the fuselage clear of the bulkheaded portion of the fuselage.

Main planes have no dihedral and have four ailerons inset in the trailing cage. A photograph shows the arrangement of the empennage. A Vee type undercarriage is fitted, the whole being released by the pilot automatically when the air bags are blown up.

Specification.

Type of machine	Two-seater Reconnaissance Ship Aeroplane.
Name or type No. of machine	Parnall "Panther."
Purpose for which intended	Flying off Carrier or Cruiser.
Span	29 ft. 6 in.
Gap, maximum and minimum	6 ft. 3 in. to 6 ft. 2½ in.
Overall length	In flying trim, 24 ft. 11 in.; folded, 14 ft. 6 in.
Maximum height	10 ft. 6 in.
Chord	6 ft. 3 in.
Total surface of wings	336 sq. ft.
Span of tail	12 ft.
Total area of tail	(Tail plane alone), 18.4 sq. ft.
Total area of elevators	(Two, balanced), 19.3 sq. ft.
Area of rudder	4.4 sq. ft.
Area of fin	6.85 sq. ft.
Area of each aileron and total area	Each 11.3 sq. ft., total 45.2 sq. ft.
Maximum cross section of body, including fairing	14.5 sq. ft.
Engine type and h.p.	200 h.p. B.R.2. Actual h.p. about 210 at 1,300 r.p.m.
Airscrew, diam. pitch and revs.	Diam. 2,775, pitch 2,416, 1,300 r.p.m.
Weight of machine empty	1,420 lbs. (production machine).
Load per sq. ft.	7.6 lbs.
Weight per h.p.	12.2 lbs.
Tank capacity in hours	See below.*
Tank capacity in gallons	Petrol 58 galls., oil 10 galls.

Performance.		
Speed, ground	122 m.p.h. approx.	These are
Speed at 6,000 feet	116 m.p.h.	actual
Speed at 10,000 feet	111 m.p.h.	trials
Landing speed	40 m.p.h.	with
Climb.		all up
To 6,000 feet	6 mins., 3 secs.	weight
To 10,000 feet	12 mins., 29 secs.	of 2,480 lbs.

Disposable load apart from fuel	630 lbs.
Total weight of machine loaded	2,560 lbs. (production machine.)

*The makers write :—" This figure is a misleading one, since the consumption in gallons per hour drops steadily with the speed at any given height. It is better to quote *maximum economical mileage*. This is found at approximate 100 m.p.h. when the consumption is 12 gallons per hour at 2,000 feet. Hence *maximum economic mileage* = 480 miles."

Three-quarter front view of the Parnall "Panther" Ship Plane (230 h.p. B.R. 2 engine). The machine is here shown with air bags inflated for flotation purposes, and the hydrovanes on the chassis can be clearly seen.

Three-quarter rear view of the Parnall "Panther," with fuselage folded for stowage on shipboard.

The curious Tail Unit of the Parnall "Panther."

PHŒNIX DYNAMO Co. Ltd. Bradford.

Managing Director. Mr. P. J. Pybus, C.B.E.; Managing Director of Aircraft Department, Capt. J. C. Crawshaw; Aircraft Designer, Mr. W. O. Manning (late lieut. R.N.V.R.), one of the pioneers of British aviation, having been the colleague of Mr. Howard Wright in the experimental work of 1908–09.

Amalgamated with Dick Kerr & Co. and the Coventry Ordnance Co. as the English Electrical Co. The aircraft work of the group is concentrated at the Phœnix Co.'s works.

Manufacturers of land machines and float and boat type seaplanes to Air Ministry and own designs. Speciality: Large flying boats.

THE PHŒNIX "CORK" FLYING BOAT.

One of the most successful of the large type of flying boat.

The machine is a twin-engined boat on well-tried and conventional lines, but special care has been devoted to detail design.

In particular the hull is of excellent form and of very low resistance.

Great attention has been paid to the duplication of all controls, and the whole of the petrol system, including the gravity tanks and the piping, is in duplicate. Both engines can be operated through either petrol system.

A noticeable feature of the later models of this type are the two nacelles mounted behind the rear spar in the upper wings, the occupants of which have an extremely wide angle of vision and of fire for the machine guns with which they are equipped.

Specification.

Type of Machine	Flying Boat.
Name or type No. of machine ..	"Phœnix Cork" P. 5.
Purpose for which intended ..	Submarine Patrol.
Span	85 ft. 6 in.
Gap .. .. { maximum .	10 ft. 6 in.
{ minimum .	10 ft.
Overall length	49 ft. 2 in.
Maximum height	21 ft. 2 in.
Chord	9 ft.
Total surface of wings	1,300 sq. ft.
Span of tail	25 ft.
Total area of tail	200 sq. ft.
Area of elevators	58 sq. ft.
Area of rudder	42 sq. ft.
Area of fin	31 sq. ft.
Area of each aileron and total area	42.75 each ; 85.5 total.
Maximum cross section of body ..	27.75 sq. ft.
Horizontal area of body	202.5 sq. ft.
Vertical area of body	208 sq. ft.
Engine type and h.p.	"Eagle" Rolls-Royce, two 360 h.p.
Airscrew, diam., pitch and revs...	10 ft. diam., 10 ft. p., 1,080 revs. r.p.m.
Weight of machine empty ..	7,000 lbs.
Load per sq. ft.	8.85 lbs.
Weight per h.p.	16.1 lbs.
Tank capacity in hours	8 at full speed.
Tank capacity in gallons ..	360 galls.

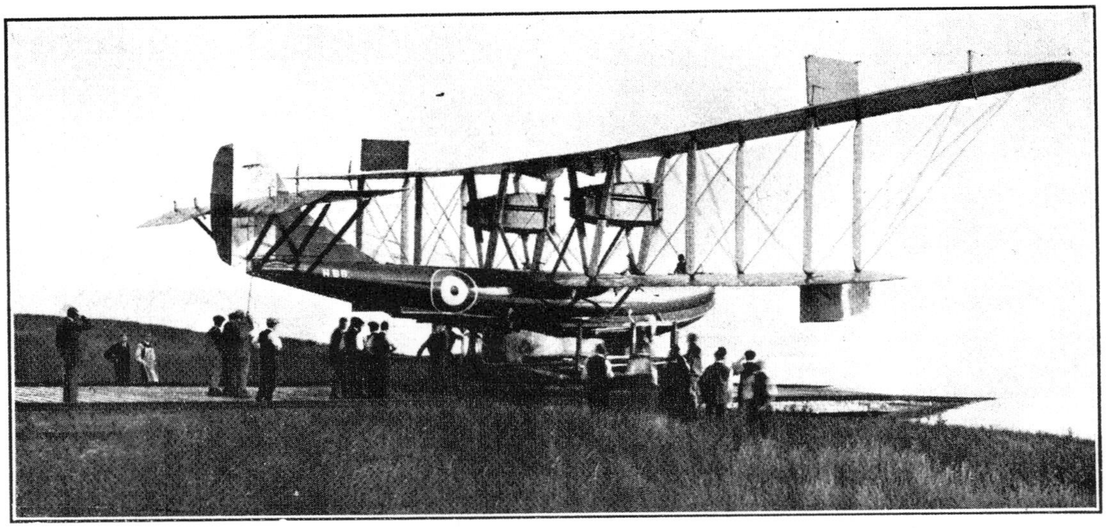

A Phœnix "Cork" Flying-Boat (2—375 h.p. Rolls-Royce engines) on the Slipway.

Performance.

Speed low down	106 m.p.h.
Speed at 10,000 feet	94 miles.
Landing speed	52 m.p.h.
Climb.	
To 5,000 feet	10 minutes.
To 10,000 feet	30 minutes.
Disposable load apart from fuel	2,000 lbs.
Total weight of machine loaded	11,600 lbs.

Armament: 5 Lewis guns and 4—230 lbs. or 2—520 lbs. bombs. Crew, 5,—Pilot, observer, wireless operator, engineer, and gunner.

S

FREDK. SAGE & Co., Ltd. 58-62, Gray's Inn Road, London, W.C., also at Peterborough, and at 5, Boulevard des Italiens, Paris.

An old established firm of shopfitters who took up the manufacture of aircraft during the war of 1914-19.

During the period of hostilities, the Aircraft Department was under the control of Mr E. C. Gordon England, one of the earliest British experimental pilots and constructors. Mr. Clifford W. Tinson was the chief designer, under Mr. England's management, and retains that position at the time of writing.

Mr. England is now a consulting engineer to various aircraft and motor firms.

SAGE I.

Specification.

Type of machine	Biplane.
Name or type No. of machine ..	Sage I.
Purpose for which intended ..	Bombing.
Span	66 ft.
Gap, maximum and minimum ..	7 ft. 2 in.
Overall length	38 ft.
Maximum height	12 ft. 6 in.
Chord	7 ft.
Total surface of wings	778 sq. ft.
Span of tail	17 ft. 3 in.
Total area of tail	44 sq. ft.
Area of elevators	30 sq. ft.
Area of rudder	15 sq. ft.
Area of fin	20 sq. ft.
Area of each aileron	$58\frac{1}{2}$ sq. ft.
Total area of ailerons	117 sq. ft.
Maximum cross section of body	5 ft. × 3 ft. 10 in.
Horizontal area of body	115 sq. ft.
Vertical area of body	132 sq. ft.
Engine type and h.p.	(2) 190 h.p. Rolls.
Airscrew diameter and pitch ..	7 ft. d. × 6 ft. p.
Airscrew revs.	1327 r.p.m.
Weight of machine empty ..	3787 lbs.
Load per sq. ft.	77.71 lbs.
Weight per h.p.	15.8 lbs.
Tank capacity in hours	$5\frac{3}{4}$ hours.
Tank capacity in gallons ..	100 gallons.
Performance.	
Speed low down	93 m.p.h.
Landing speed	52 m.p.h.
Disposable load apart from fuel	500 lbs.
Total weight of machine loaded	6000 lbs.

THE SAGE NO. 2 SCOUT.

The Sage No. 2 Two-seater fighter was designed in the spring of 1916. The pilots and observers seats are enclosed in a Streamline cabin reaching to the upper plane, the top plane being left open so as to enable the observer to use a Lewis gun in a ring mounting on the top plane, for firing over the propeller.

Specification.

Type of machine	Biplane.
Name or type No. of machine ..	Scout.
Purpose for which intended ..	Fighting.
Span	32 ft. $2\frac{1}{2}$ in.
Gap, maximum and minimum ..	5 ft. 6 in.
Overall length	21 ft. $1\frac{5}{8}$ in.
Maximum height	9 ft. 6 in.
Chord	Top plane, 5 ft. ; lower plane, 2 ft. 8 in.
Total surface of wings	168 sq. ft.
Span of tail	9 ft. 5 in.
Total area of tail	20 sq. ft.
Area of elevators	14.5 sq. ft.
Area of rudder	9 sq. ft.
Area of each aileron	$12\frac{1}{2}$ sq. ft.
Total area of ailerons	25 sq. ft.
Maximum cross section of body	3 ft. 5 in. dia.
Horizontal area of body	44 sq. ft.
Vertical area of body	52.5 sq. ft.
Engine type and h.p.	100 h.p. Gnôme.
Airscrew diameter and pitch ..	8 ft. d. × 7 ft. p.
Airscrew revs.	1200 r.p.m.
Weight of machine empty ..	890 lbs.
Load per sq. ft.	9.2 lbs.
Weight per h.p.	15.46 lbs.
Tank capacity in hours	$2\frac{1}{2}$ hours.
Tank capacity in gallons ..	26 gallons.
Performance.	
Speed low down	112 m.p.h.
Speed at 10,000 feet	100 m.p.h.
Landing speed	50 m.p.h.
Climb.	
To 5,000 feet	$6\frac{1}{2}$ minutes.
To 10,000 feet	$14\frac{3}{4}$ minutes.
Disposable load apart from fuel	96 lbs.
Total weight of machine loaded	1546 lbs.
Ceiling	16,000 ft.

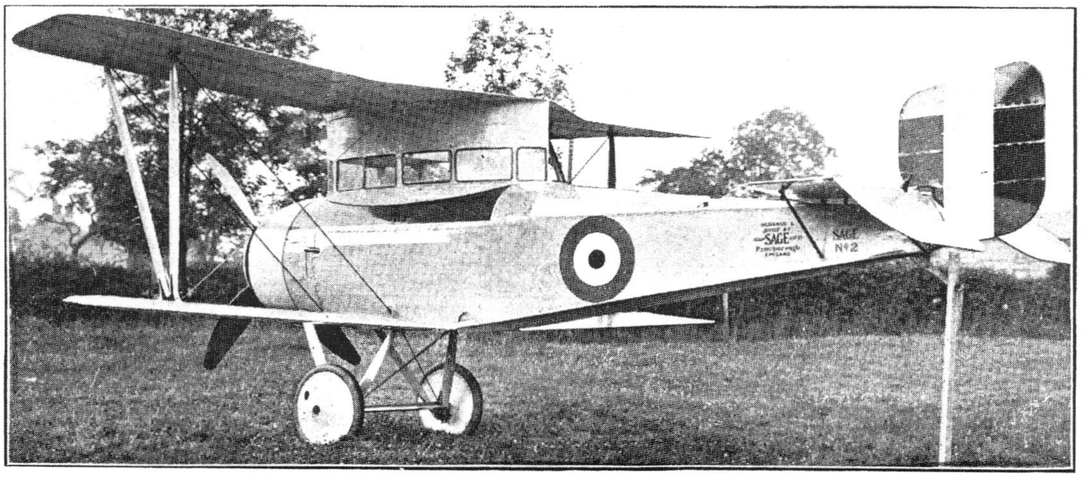

Three-quarter View from Rear—Sage No. 2 (100 h.p. Mono Gnôme engine).

THE SAGE NO. 3 TRAINING BIPLANE.

The *Sage No. 3* was designed in the autumn of 1916 as a primary training machine and was fitted with dual control with a full cut-out gear in the instructor's cockpit. The undercarriage is of the oleo-pneumatic type and has a pair of small wheels mounted on the front Vee in addition to the landing wheels.

Specification.

Type of machine	Biplane.
Name or type No. of machine	Sage 3.
Purpose for which intended	Training.
Span	34 ft. 6 in.
Gap, maximum and minimum	5 ft.
Overall length	26 ft. 6 in.
Maximum height	10 ft. 9 in.
Chord	4 ft. 9 in.
Total surface of wings	330 sq. ft.
Span of tail	11 ft. 4 in.
Total area of tail	26 sq. ft.
Area of elevators	24 sq. ft.
Area of rudder	10 sq. ft.
Area of fin	4 sq. ft.
Area of each aileron	18 sq. ft.
Total area of ailerons	72 sq. ft.
Maximum cross section of body	2 ft. 6 in. × 2 ft. 6 in.
Horizontal area of body	59 sq. ft.
Vertical area of body	78 sq. ft.
Engine type and h.p.	75 h.p. Rolls.
Airscrew diameter and pitch	8 ft. d. × 6 ft. 4 in. p.
Airscrew revs.	1500 r.p.m.
Weight of machine empty	1390 lbs.
Load per sq. ft.	6.25 lbs.
Weight per h.p.	27.5 lbs.
Tank capacity in hours	4 hours.
Tank capacity in gallons	26 gallons.

Performance.

Speed low down	72 m.p.h.
Landing speed	38 m.p.h.

Climb.

To 5,000 feet	20 minutes.
Disposable load apart from fuel	119 lbs.
Total weight of machine loaded	2064 lbs.
Ceiling	9,500 ft.

THE SAGE NO. 4A SEAPLANE.

The *Sage No. 4a* was designed for sea patrol work in June 1917. It is similar to most float seaplanes and is fitted with a 150 h.p. Hispano-Suiza engine which gave the machine a considerably superior performance to any seaplane or flying boat of its power at the time. The *No. 4b* and *No. 4c* were similar to the *No. 4a*, but were fitted with dual control and 200 h.p. Hispano-Suiza and Sunbeam "Arab" engines. The *No. 4c* had staggered planes and folding gear, whilst the *4b* had fixed wings of slightly smaller area and a faster wing section. Both types could be rolled, spun, looped, &c., and have been used for advanced training for seaplane pilots.

Specification.

Type of machine	Seaplane.
Name or type No. of machine	Sage 4a.
Purpose for which intended	Patrol.
Span	34 ft. 6 in.
Gap, maximum and minimum	5 ft.
Overall length	26 ft. 8 in.
Maximum height	11 ft. 3 in.
Chord	4 ft. 9 in.
Total surface of wings	330 sq. ft.
Span of tail	11 ft. 4 in.
Total area of tail	26 sq. ft.
Area of elevators	24 sq. ft.
Area of rudder	9 sq. ft.
Area of fin	7 sq. ft.
Area of each aileron	18 sq. ft.
Total area of ailerons	72 sq. ft.
Maximum cross section of body	2 ft. 6 in. × 2 ft. 5 in.
Horizontal area of body	59 sq. ft.
Vertical area of body	78 sq. ft.
Engine type and h.p.	150 h.p. Hispano.
Airscrew diameter and pitch	9 ft. d. × 7 ft. 3 in. p.
Airscrew revs.	1500 r.p.m.
Weight of machine empty	1620 lbs.
Load per sq. ft.	8.0 lbs.
Weight per h.p.	17.6 lbs.
Tank capacity in hours	4 hours.
Tank capacity in gallons	50 gallons.

Performance.

Speed low down	93½ m.p.h.
Speed at 10,000 feet	81 m.p.h.
Landing speed	50 m.p.h.

Climb.

To 5,000 feet	12 minutes.
To 10,000 feet	25 minutes.
Disposable load apart from fuel	291 lbs.
Total weight of machine loaded	2645 lbs.
Ceiling	13,000 ft.

SAGE 4B.
SAGE 4C.
Specification.

Type of machine	Seaplane.
Name or type No. of machine	Sage Seaplane.
Purpose for which intended	Training.
Span	39 ft. 7¼ in.
Gap, maximum and minimum	5 ft. 3 in.
Overall length	37 ft. 6 in.
Maximum height	11 ft. 7 in.
Chord	5 ft. 3 in.
Total surface of wings	386 sq. ft.
Span of tail	11 ft.
Total area of tail	24 sq. ft.

Area of elevators	21 sq. ft.
Area of rudder	9 sq. ft.
Area of fin	7 sq. ft.
Area of each aileron	21 sq. ft.
Total area of ailerons	84 sq. ft.
Maximum cross section of body	2 ft. 6 in. × 2 ft. 5 in.
Horizontal area of body	56 sq. ft.
Vertical area of body	70 sq. ft.
Engine type and h.p. (4. A.)	200 h.p. Hispano-Suiza ;
(4. B.)	200 h.p. "Arab" Sunbeam.
Airscrew diameter and pitch	9 ft. d. × 7 ft. 9 n. p.
Airscrew revs.	1500 r.p.m.
Weight of machine empty	2100 lbs.
Load per sq. ft.	7.45 lbs.
Weight per h.p.	14.4 lbs.
Tank capacity in hours	2½ hours.
Tank capacity in gallons	35 gallons.

Performance.

Speed low down	97 m.p.h.
Speed at 10,000 feet	94 m.p.h.
Landing speed	45 m.p.h.

Climb.

To 5,000 feet	8 minutes.
To 10,000 feet	21 minutes.
Disposable load apart from fuel	155 lbs.
Total weight of machine loaded	2875 lbs.
Ceiling	15,800 ft.

S. E. SAUNDERS, Ltd. East Cowes, Isle of Wight

Famous makers of motor boats on Saunders' Patent principle. Made the hulls of the original Sopwith "Bat-boats" with marked success, and later specialised on hulls for flying-boats of various types. Took to making aeroplanes complete, and has won a high reputation for excellence of workmanship.

Later produced the famous "Consuta" system of sewing wooden sheets together. This has been used with much success in the hulls of flying boats.

Side view of the Sage Training Machine, Sage 3 (75 h.p. "Hawk" Rolls-Royce engine).

Side View—The Sage No. 4A Seaplane (150 h.p. Hispano-Suiza engine).

SHORT BROS. Works : Rochester, Kent. London Works : Queen's Circus, Battersea Park, S.W. London office : 29/30. Charing Cross, S.W.

The firm of Short Bros., which is the oldest established firm of aeroplane designers and producers in the United Kingdom, was founded by two brothers, Eustace and Oswald Short, in the year 1898, their work for some years being the manufacture of spherical balloons. In 1906 they nearly succeeded in winning the Gordon Bennett Race, and actually gained second place. In 1907 the firm was appointed " Official Aeronautical Engineers to the Royal Aero Club."

The two brothers were joined by their elder brother, the late Horace L. Short, in 1908, and they added to their balloon work the design and manufacture of aeroplanes, for which purpose they established works at Shellness, near Leysdown, in the Isle of Sheppey.

In 1909, a " Short " aeroplane, fitted with a Green engine, won the " Daily Mail's " £1,000 prize for a flight over a closed circuit by an all-British aeroplane, the pilot being Mr. J. T. C. Moore-Brabazon, now Major, R.F.C. The Short Bros. were also the British agents for the Wright Bros.

In 1910 the works were transferred to Eastchurch, adjacent to the Flying Grounds of the Royal Aero Club, and there were produced a series of biplanes with two engines, which were certainly the first multiple-engined aeroplanes in the world. At Eastchurch, Messrs. Short Bros. produced also the three " Short " biplanes on which the four officers first appointed by the Admiralty to the Royal Flying Corps, Naval Wing, were taught to fly.

In 1911 the firm took up the design of seaplanes with which they achieved almost immediate success, and in 1912 a seaplane of their design, piloted by Lieut. (now Colonel) Samson, R.N., rose from the deck of H.M.S. Hibernia, this being the first " heavier-than-air " machine of any kind to achieve this feat.

By the introduction of the " Short " Patent Folding Wing device, in 1913, the firm revolutionised the use of the seaplane, making it possible for seaplanes of large dimensions to be carried in H.M. ships for operations in all parts of the world. The device also brought about an immense saving in the cost of storage of both seaplanes and aeroplanes.

In 1913, finding further development necessary, the firm erected new works at Rochester, which were placed under the charge of Mr. H. O. Short, and devoted almost entirely to the manufacture of seaplanes.

The Short seaplane was the first, and is so far the only seaplane, employed successfully in a Naval Engagement (vide the following extract from an official letter to Messrs. Short Bros.) :—

" . . . the flight made by Flight Lieut. Rutland, with Assistant Paymaster Trewin, as observer, which Sir David Beatty praises so highly, was carried out on a 225-h.p. ' Short Seaplane ' . . ."

Early in the war, a " Short " seaplane achieved the feat of carrying a torpedo into the air, and it has been officially announced that Flight Com. C. H. K. Edmonds, in a " Short " seaplane, succeeded in torpedoing a Turkish transport in the Sea of Marmora.

At the end of 1915, owing to the great development of their business, the firm found it necessary to establish an office in London, and from it the " business " side of their activities is mainly carried on. Mr. J. B. Parker, formerly Assistant-Paymaster, R.N., afterwards one of the best pilots of the R.N.A.S., was appointed to manage this office, having been previously invalided out of the Service before the war.

The firm sustained a grave loss in the death of Mr. Horace L. Short, the eldest of the three brothers, on the 6th April, 1917.

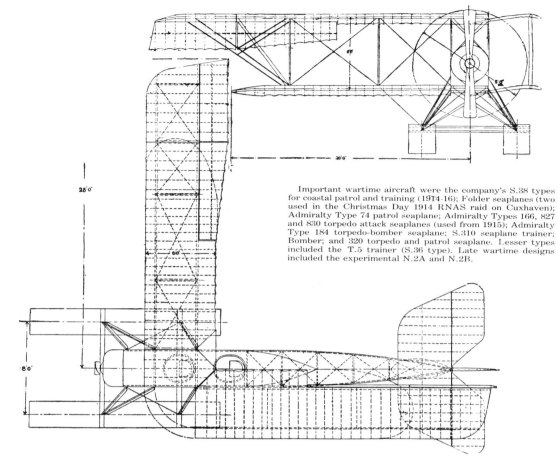

Important wartime aircraft were the company's S.38 types for coastal patrol and training (1914-16); Folder seaplanes (two used in the Christmas Day 1914 RNAS raid on Cuxhaven); Admiralty Type 74 patrol seaplane; Admiralty Types 166, 827 and 830 torpedo attack seaplanes (used from 1915); Admiralty Type 184 torpedo-bomber seaplane; S.310 seaplane trainer; Bomber; and 320 torpedo and patrol seaplane. Lesser types included the T.5 trainer (S.36 type). Late wartime designs included the experimental N.2A and N.2B.

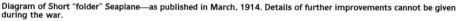

Diagram of Short "folder" Seaplane—as published in March, 1914. Details of further improvements cannot be given during the war.

		S 41. 1913. Hydro Biplane.			S 45. 1913. Military Tractor Biplane.			S 38. 1913. Military Nacelle Biplane.	
		80 h.p. 2-seater.	100 h.p. 2-seater.	160 h.p. 4-seater.	70 h.p. 2-seater.	80 h.p. 2-seater.	160 h.p. 4-seater.	50 h.p. 2-seater.	80 h.p. 3-seater.
Length ... ... feet (m.)		35 _10·67_	39 _11·90_	45 _13·70_	35½ _10·80_	35½ _10·80_	40 _13·70_	35½ _10·80_	35½ _10·80_
Span ... ... feet (m.)		40 _13·70_	50 _15·25_	50 _15·25_	42 _12·90_	45 _13·70_	50 _15·25_	32 _15·85_	52 _15·85_
Area ... ... sq. feet (m².)		390 _36_	...	...	...	...	...	...	...
Weight { Machine ... lbs. (kg.)		1200 _545_	1700 _764_	2000 _909_	1080 _490_	1100 _500_	1890 _860_	950 _432_	1050 _480_
{ Useful ... lbs. (kg.)		771 _350_	...	...	...	...	...	...	...
Motor ... ... h.p.		80 Gnome	100 Gnome	160 Gnome	70 Gnome	80 Gnome	160 Gnome	50 Gnome	80 Gnome
Speed { max. (m.p.h.)		65 _105_	60 _97_	74 _120_	60 _97_	70 _113_	74 _120_	42 _68_	58 _94_
{ min. (m.p.h.)		50 _80_	50 _80_	56 _90_	50 _80_	50 _80_	56 _90_	35 _57_	39 _63_
Endurance ... ... hrs.		4	5	6	5	5	6	4	5
Number built during 1912 ...		...	...	...	...	...	...	...	...

Remarks.—Floats are two long pontoons. Subsidiary floats at tips of lower planes. Small tail float with water rudder. W.-t. compartments to floats. Tandem seated, pilot in front. The observer's seat can accommodate two if necessary. First Short tractor biplane for the Naval Wing, RFC.

Tandem seats, pilot in front. Fittings for maps, etc. Used by Naval Wing, RFC.

Instructional biplane. Tandem seats, pilot in front. An extra passenger can be accommodated. This type is now used in large quantities for school work and instructional flying across country.

The firm has been engaged entirely on machines of their own design to Admiralty order. The date above applies to Short seaplanes which appeared prior to the war, and have been used with marked success during the war.

S 38 type SHORT biplane. 80 H.P. Gnome, largely used for instructional purposes.

SHORT "pusher" biplane—instructional type—taking the air.

SHORT 'folder' seaplanes.

SHORT "folder" seaplane—Sunbeam engine—before launching.

A SHORT Type 184 seaplane with 225 h.p. Sunbeam engine, beached on the bank of the Tigris
for repairs, during the operations against Kut-el-Amara.

The Salmson-engined SHORT Admiralty Type 166 seaplane, illustrated on the following page
is here seen about to get off the water in Salonica harbouir.

SHORT Type 166 seen being lifted out from her shed with wings folded on HMS Ark Royal. The engine
is a Salmson (Canton-Unné) of 130 h.p. The main floats, wing-tip floats and steerable tail floats
may be noted.

Lowering a SHORT Type 166 folding wing seaplane from H.M.S. "Ark Royal,, a seaplane-carrier which has done much work in the Mediterranean.

THE SHORT N2B FLOAT SEAPLANE.

The *Short* N 2 B bombing seaplane is the latest of the many types of float seaplanes produced by Messrs. Short Bros. before and during the war, and used by the R.N.A.S. and subsequently the R.A.F. as sea patrols, etc. The upper main plane has no dihedral and has a slight overhang over the bottom plane which has a dihedral. Two large pontoon floats are fitted to the fuselage by faired struts. The tail unit is on conventional lines except that a very large fin is used in conjunction with a balanced rudder. Wing-tip and tail floats of ample proportions are fitted, the tail float having a small water rudder. The pilot sits under the centre section wherein are carried the petrol gravity tank, and radiator. The observer sits well back and is armed with Lewis Gun carried in a Scarff mounting,

Specification.

Type of machine	Float Seaplane.
Name or type No. of machine	Short N. 2 B.
Purpose for which intended..	Bombing.
Span	55 ft.
Gap, maximum	7 ft.
Overall length	40 ft.
Maximum height	13 ft. 9 in.
Chord	7 ft. 6 in.
Span of Tail	15 ft. 6 in.
Maximum cross section of body	11.5 sq. ft.
Engine type and h.p.	Sunbeam - Coatalen "Maori," 275 h.p.
Airscrew diam.	10 ft. 6 in.
Weight of machine empty ..	3,050 lbs.
Tank capacity in hours ..	4½ hours.
Tank capacity in gallons ..	70 gallons.

Performance.

Speed low down	90 m.p.h.
Speed at 10,000 feet ..	88 m.p.h.

Climb.

To 5,000 ft.	12½ minutes.
To 10,000 ft.	40 minutes.
Disposable load apart from fuel	1,170 lbs.
Total weight of machine loaded	4,800 lbs.

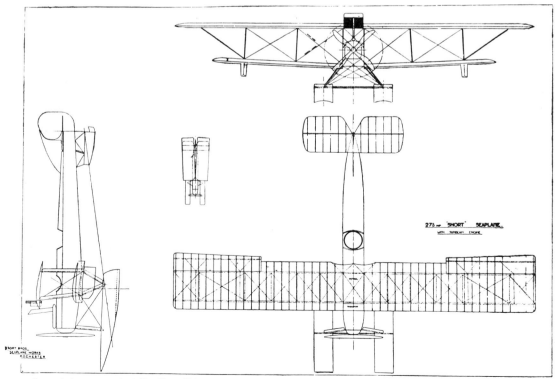

General Arrangement of the Short N 2 B type Seaplane (275 h.p. Sunbeam-Coatalen "Maori" engine).

THE SHORT "SHIRL" TORPEDO-CARRIER.

The *Short* "Shirl" biplane is generally similar to the N2B type seaplane except that a divided wheel and skid chassis is fitted for flying off decks and to allow the stowage of an 18 in. torpedo under the fuselage. The machine is a single-seater, the pilot being situated in rear of the main planes, which are noticeably swept back from the fuselage, and are arranged to fold for stowage on board ship.

Flotation gear in the form of air-bags are carried over the skids and small plane form hydro vanes are fitted to the front of the skids, to prevent turning over when alighting on water.

The machine entered by Messrs. Short Bros. for the transatlantic flight is a modified "Shirl," fitted with somewhat larger wings and tailplane, and an immense petrol tank suspended under the fuselage.

Specification.

Type of machine	Biplane.
Name or type No. of machine ..	"Short Shirl."
Purpose for which intended ..	Torpedo carrying.
Span	52 ft.
Gap, maximum and minimum ..	6 ft.
Overall length	35 ft. 6 in.
Chord	8 ft. upper; 7 ft. lower plane.
Span of tail	15 ft.
Maximum cross section of body..	11 sq. ft.
Engine type and h.p.	Rolls Eagle 8, 400 h.p.
Airscrew, diam.	10 ft.
Weight of machine empty ..	2,850 lbs.
Tank capacity in hours ..	Max. 6½ hours.
Tank capacity in gallons ..	137 gallons.

Performance.

Speed low down	99 m.p.h.
Speed at 10,000 feet ..	97 m.p.h.

Climb.

To 5,000 feet	13 minutes.
To 10,000 feet ..	30 minutes.
Disposable load apart from fuel	2,500 lbs. normal
Total weight of machine loaded	5,950 lbs.

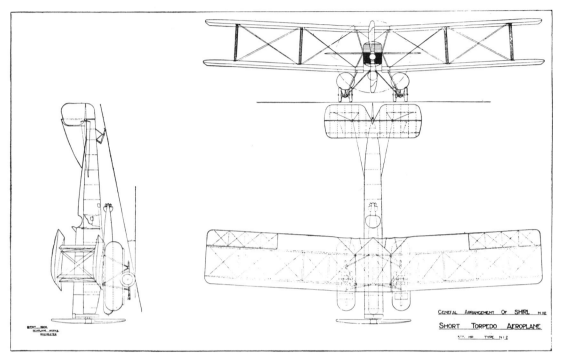

General Arrangement of the Short "Shirl" Torpedo Ship Plane (375 h.p. "Eagle" Rolls-Royce engine).

THE FELIXSTOWE "F3" FLYING BOAT

The F3 Flying Boat designs emanate from the Seaplane Experimental Station, Felixstowe, but it has been built in quantity by Messrs. Short Bros. The boat is of the now well known Felixstowe construction with a wide Vee bottomed planing surface, fitted with two steps. The crew consists of a gunner in the nose, two pilots enclosed in a cabin in advance of the main planes, and a gunners cockpit in the rear of the planes with swivel mountings for Lewis guns firing out of the top and either side of the boat. The top plane has a considerable overhang and is fitted with ailerons of large area. Over the last set of struts are king-posts for bracing the overhang, the intervening space between the front and rear king-posts being covered in to form a fin.

Specification.

Type of machine..	Boat Seaplane.
Name or type No. of machine ..	Felixstowe F 3.
Purpose for which intended ..	Anti-submarine.
Span	102 ft.
Gap, maximum and minimum ..	8 ft. 6 in.
Overall length	49 ft.
Maximum height	18 ft. 9 in.
Chord	8 ft.
Total surface of wings ..	1,413 sq. ft.
Span of tail	22 ft.
Total area of tail	118 sq. ft.
Area of Elevators	67 sq. ft.
Area of rudder	30.3 sq. ft.
Area of fin	37.2 sq. ft.
Area of each ailerons ..	65 sq. ft.
Total area of ailerons ..	132 sq. ft.
Engine type and h.p.	Rolls-Royce Eagle 8 (two) 400 h.p. each.
Airscrew, diam.	10 ft.
Weight of machine empty ..	7,650 lbs.
Load per sq. ft.	842 lbs.
Weight per h.p.	17 lbs.
Tank capacity in hours.. ..	9.7 max.; 5 hours normal.
Tank capacity in gallons.. ..	212 gallons.

Performance.

Speed low down	85 m.p.h.
Disposable load apart from fuel	2,550 lbs.
Total weight of machine loaded	11,900 lbs.

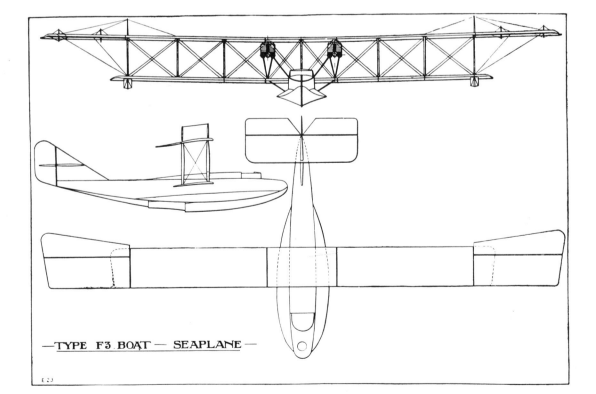

SOPWITH. The Sopwith Aviation Co., Ltd.

Works and offices : Canbury Park Road, Kingston-on-Thames. Established by Mr. T. O. M. Sopwith, the well-known aviator, at Brooklands, Autumn of 1911, where, during 1912, a 70 h.p. tractor biplane and a 40 h.p. biplane were turned out.

The Company is now a private limited company. Directors: T. O. M. Sopwith, C.B.E., M. G. Sopwith, R. O. Cary.

General manager : R. O. Cary.

Secretary : H. P. Musgrave.

Engineering manager : F. Sigrist.

Prior to the outbreak of war the firm had produced machines of extreme interest, and amongst their outstanding performances was the winning of the " Schneider " cup, at Monaco, by Mr. Howard Pexton, on a small seaplane with a 100 h.p. Mono Gnôme engine.

This machine was the direct ancestor of the " Baby " seaplane so largely used by the R.N.A.S, during nearly the whole of the period of hostilities.

Since 1914 the firm have produced a series of machines of the very highest value.

Particularly noteworthy in their line were the famous " 1½ Strutter " produced in 1915, and the Triplane of 1916.

RNAS *Sopwith Tabloids* were the first to bomb Cologne and Düsseldorf, in October, 1914. (The following letter verifies the fact.)

AIR DEPT.,
ADMIRALTY, LONDON, S.W.,
28th December, 1914.

AD5062.

GENTLEMEN,

With reference to the recent attack on the German Airsheds at Cologne and Düsseldorf, carried out by Squadron Commander Spenser D. A. Grey and Flight Lieut. R. L. G. Marix, you may be interested to learn that the machines used were your " Sopwith Tabloid aeroplanes." I take the opportunity of expressing my appreciation of the excellent performance of these machines.

It is reported from Berlin that a new Zeppelin fitted with the latest silent motors, which had just been moved into the shed at Düsseldorf and a Machinery Hall alongside the Airship Shed, were destroyed by Flight Lieut. Marix. The roof of the Airship Shed has fallen in.

I am, Gentlemen,
Yours faithfully,
'(Sd) MURRAY F. SUETER,
Director Air Dept.

In 1917, Captain Beaumont and Lieut. Daucourt, both on *Sopwiths*, bombed the Krupp Works, at Essen.

Later in 1917, Captain Beaumont bombed Munich and afterwards landed in Italy.

Three-quarter Rear View of the Sopwith " Pup " (80 h.p. Le Rhône engine).

SOPWITH " tabloid " scout landing.

Front view of "1½ Strutter" SOPWITH biplane, Clergét engine, 1916 type. Used for fighting, bombing and reconnaisance until early 1918, then becoming a trainer.

Rear view of " 1½ strut " Sopwith biplane, Clergét engine, 1916 type.

A SOPWITH TRIPLANE, of the type eulogised by the German G.O.C. Air Force, Von Hoppner.

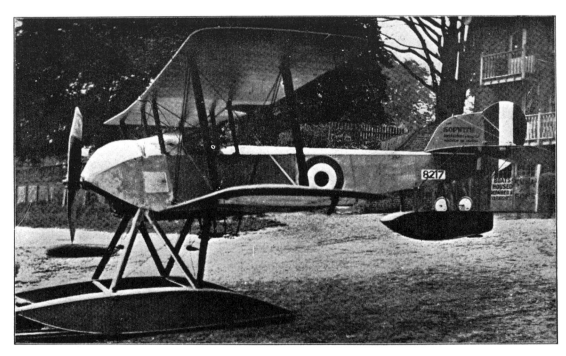

A SOPWITH "BABY" SEAPLANE, of a type much used by the R.N.A.S.

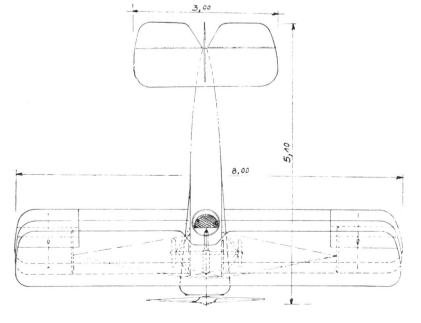

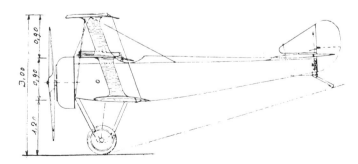

SCALE DRAWINGS OF A SOPWITH TRIPLANE, taken from the German paper "Flugsport."

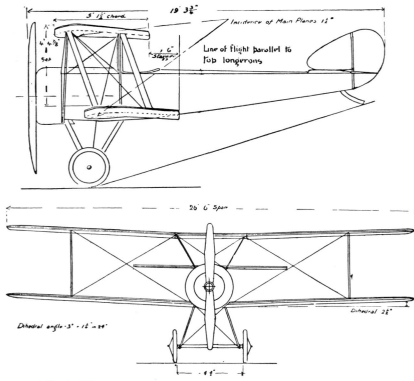

A Hanriot HD-1 Single-seat Tractor Biplane

THE SOPWITH "PUP"

In point of date this machine was intermediate between the 14 "Strutter" and the Triplane. It was a lineal descendant of the original *Sopwith* "Tabloid" of early 1914, and was largely used by the R.N.A.S. from 1916 onwards. During its existence it has maintained the reputation of being one of the most delightful machines to fly that have ever been built. In addition the performance with so low-powered an engine as the 80 Le Rhone, is astonishing.

It is extremely likely that, as a sporting single seater for the pilot owner, this type will maintain its popularity for some time to come.

Specification.

Type of machine..	Single-seater Tractor Biplane.
Name or type No. of machine..	Sopwith "Pup."
Purpose for which intended ..	Fighting Scout
Span	26 ft. 6 in.
Gap, maximum and minimum..	4 ft. $4\frac{7}{8}$ in.
Overall length	19 ft. $3\frac{3}{4}$ in.
Maximum height ..	9 ft. 5 in.
Chord	5 ft. $1\frac{1}{2}$ in.
Engine type and h.p. ..	Le Rhone; 80 h.p.
Tank capacity in gallons	Petrol 18 galls.; oil 5 galls.

Performance.

Speed at 10,000 feet ..	99 m.p.h.

Climb.

To 5,000 feet	7 mins. 40 secs.
To 10,000 feet.. ..	15 mins. 24 secs.
Total weight of machine loaded	1,313 lbs.

THE SOPWITH "CAMEL."

Is generally an enlarged and modified Pup. It was designed specially for high performances and extreme manœuvrability. To obtain these qualities some of the qualities of the "Pup" were necessarily sacrificed, and the machine has a reputation for being relatively—to the original—uncomfortable to fly.

As a single seater fighter however it was a very great success, and did an immense amount of work in 1917.

A distinctive feature of this machine is the great dihedral on the bottom plane, combined with a flat top plane.

A very slightly modified "Camel" with a folding fuselage and fitted with a 150 h.p. B.R.1 Engine was also produced as a "ship plane" fighter.

Specification.

Type of machine..	Single-seater Tractor Biplane.
Name or type No. of machine..	"Camel"—F.I.
Purpose for which intended ..	Fighting Scout.
Span	28 ft.
Gap, maximum and minimum..	5 ft. max; 4 ft. $1\frac{7}{16}$ in. min.
Overall length	18 ft. 9 in.
Maximum height.. ..	9 ft.
Chord	4 ft. 6 in.
Engine type and h.p. ..	Clerget; 130 h.p.
Tank capacity in hours ..	Petrol $2\frac{1}{2}$ hrs.; oil $2\frac{1}{2}$ hrs.
Tank capacity in gallons ..	Petrol 26 galls.; oil $5\frac{1}{4}$ galls.

Performance.

Speed at 10,000 feet.. ..	113 m.p.h.

Climb.

To 5,000 feet	5 minutes.
To 10,000 feet.. ..	12 minutes.
Total weight of machine loaded	1,524 lbs.

Front View of the Sopwith "Camel" type Ship Plane (150 h.p. B.R.1. engine).

The Sopwith "Scooter," a Monoplane "run-about" with a 130 h.p. Clerget.

Three-quarter Rear View of the Sopwith "Camel."

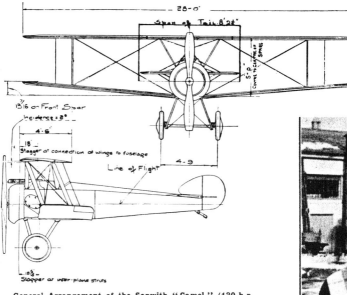

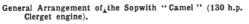

General Arrangement of the Sopwith "Camel" (130 h.p. Clerget engine).

Side View of the Sopwith "Camel" (130 h.p. Clerget engine).

THE SOPWITH "DOLPHIN."

This is another single seater fighter, and retains many distinctively *Sopwith* features.

In appearance however it differs considerably from all previous *Sopwith* Single Seaters.

Unlike its predecessors it is fitted with a stationary water cooled engine.

It has two rows of interplane struts on each side and the top plane is staggered back. The gap is considerably less than in the previous *Sopwith* machines and the fuselage reaches nearly to the centre section.

The pilot's seat is between the rear and front spars of the upper wing, with the pilot's head protruding.

Specification.

Type of machine..	Single-seater Tractor Biplane.
Name or type No. of machine..	"Dolphin"—5 F.I.
Purpose for which intended ..	Fighting Scout.
Span	32 ft. 6 in.
Gap, maximum and minimum..	4 ft. 3 in.
Overall length	22 ft. 3 in.
Maximum height.. ..	8 ft. 6 in.
Chord	4 ft. 6 in.
Engine type and h.p. ..	Hispano-Suiza; 200 h.p.
Tank capacity in hours..	Petrol 2¼ hrs.: oil 2¼ hrs.
Tank capacity in gallons ..	Petrol 27 galls.; oil 4 galls.

Performance.

Speed at 10,000 feet	121½ m.p.h.

Climb.

To 5,000 feet	5 minutes.
To 10,000 feet..	12 minutes.
Total weight of machine loaded	1959 lbs.

Three-quarter Front View of the Sopwith "Dolphin" (200 h.p. Hispano-Suiza engine).

THE SOPWITH "SNIPE."

A further development of the single seat fighter. The rotary type of engine has been installed again, and in general appearance the machine approaches more closely to the earlier *Sopwith* types.

The fuselage is faired out to a circular section, in conformity to the shape of the engine cowl, and the normal stagger forward of the top plane has returned.

Specification.

Type of Machine..	Single-seater Tractor Biplane.
Name or type No. of machine..	"Snipe"—7 F.I.
Purpose for which intended ..	Fighting Scout.
Span	Top plane 31 ft. 1 in.; bottom plane 30 ft.
Gap, maximum and minimum..	4 ft. 3 in.
Overall length	19 ft.
Maximum height.. ..	9 ft. 6. in.
Chord	5 ft.
Engine type and h.p. ..	B.R.; 200 h.p.
Tank capacity in hours ..	Petrol 3 hrs.; oil 3 hrs.
Tank capacity in gallons ..	Petrol 38½ galls.; oil 7 galls.

Performance.

Speed at 10,000 feet	121 m.p.h.

Climb.

To 5,000 feet..	3 mins. 45 secs.
To 10,000 feet..	9 mins. 25 secs.
Total weight of machine loaded	2,020 lbs.

Three-quarter Front View of the Sopwith "Snipe" (230 h.p. B.R. 2 engine).

THE SOPWITH SALAMANDER.

A single seater designed for use against infantry, produced late in the war. Is fitted with protective armour to the cockpit.

Type of machine	Tractor Biplane.
Name or type No. of machine ..	" Salamander."
Purpose for which intended ..	Ground Fighting.
Span	31 ft. 3 in.
Gap, maximum and minimum ..	4 ft. 3 in.
Overall length	19 ft. 6 in.
Maximum height	9 ft. 4 in.
Chord	5 ft.
Span of tail	9 ft. 2 in.
Total area of empennage ..	15 sq. ft.
Area of elevators	11 sq. ft.
Area of rudder	9 sq. ft.
Area of fin	2¾ sq. ft.
Area of each aileron and total area	14 sq. ft. each (4 off).
Engine type and h.p.	200 h.p. BR.
Weight of machine empty ..	1700 lbs.
Load per sq. ft.	9.7 lbs.
Weight per h.p.	11.35 lbs.
Tank capacity in hours ..	1½ hours at ground level
Tank capacity in gallons ..	29 gallons.

Performance.
Speed low lown	125 m.p.h.
Speed at 10,000 feet	117 m.p.h.

Climb.
To 10,000 feet..	17 minutes.
Total weight of machine loaded	2945 lbs.

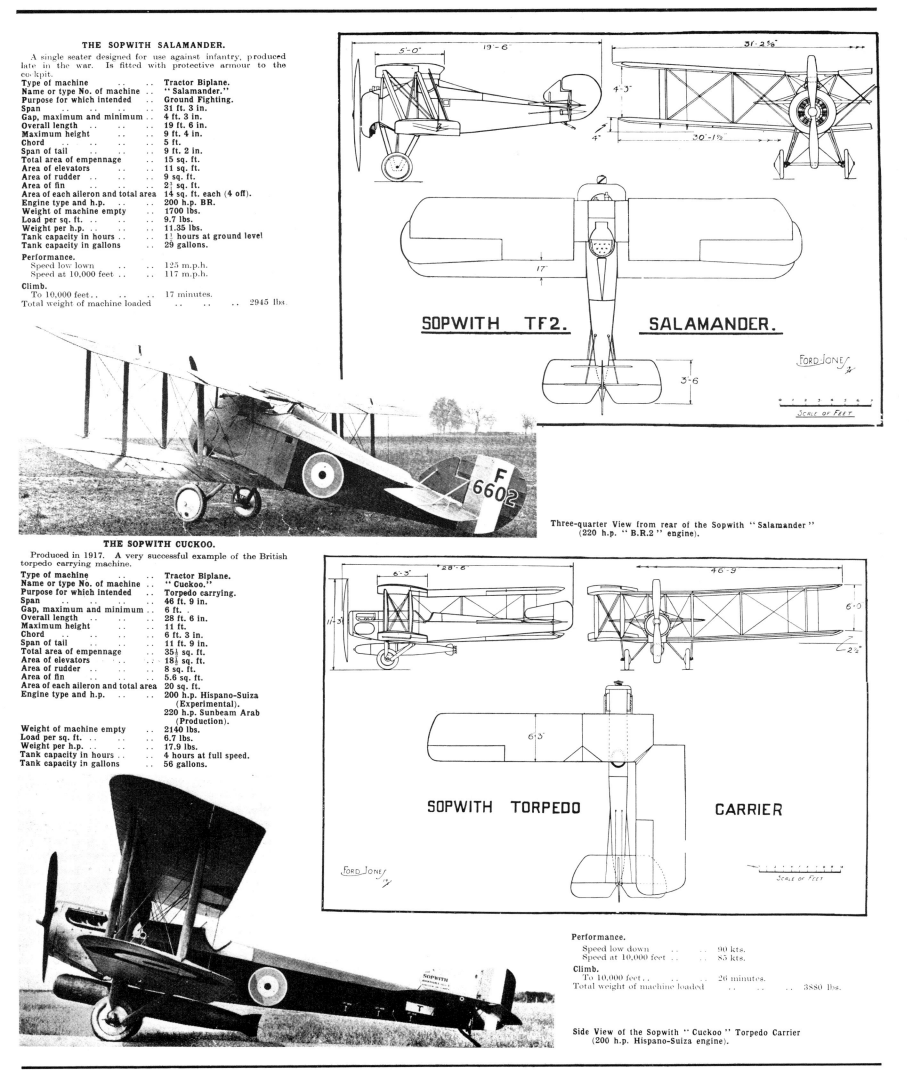

SOPWITH TF2. SALAMANDER.

Three-quarter View from rear of the Sopwith "Salamander"
(220 h.p. "B.R.2" engine).

THE SOPWITH CUCKOO.

Produced in 1917. A very successful example of the British torpedo carrying machine.

Type of machine	Tractor Biplane.
Name or type No. of machine ..	" Cuckoo."
Purpose for which intended ..	Torpedo carrying.
Span	46 ft. 9 in.
Gap, maximum and minimum ..	6 ft.
Overall length	28 ft. 6 in.
Maximum height	11 ft.
Chord	6 ft. 3 in.
Span of tail	11 ft. 9 in.
Total area of empennage ..	35½ sq. ft.
Area of elevators	18½ sq. ft.
Area of rudder	8 sq. ft.
Area of fin	5.6 sq. ft.
Area of each aileron and total area	20 sq. ft.
Engine type and h.p.	200 h.p. Hispano-Suiza (Experimental). 220 h.p. Sunbeam Arab (Production).
Weight of machine empty ..	2140 lbs.
Load per sq. ft.	6.7 lbs.
Weight per h.p.	17.9 lbs.
Tank capacity in hours ..	4 hours at full speed.
Tank capacity in gallons ..	56 gallons.

SOPWITH TORPEDO CARRIER

Performance.
Speed low down	90 kts.
Speed at 10,000 feet	85 kts.

Climb.
To 10,000 feet..	26 minutes.
Total weight of machine loaded	3880 lbs.

Side View of the Sopwith "Cuckoo" Torpedo Carrier
(200 h.p. Hispano-Suiza engine).

THE SOUTH COAST AIRCRAFT WORKS,

Shoreham, Sussex. Telephones : Day Service, 83, Shoreham ; Night Service, 89, Shoreham. Telegrams : " Scaw, Shoreham-by-Sea."

Aeronautical constructional engineers and contractors to the Admiralty and War Office.

STANDARD MOTOR CO., Ltd., Coventry.

Well-known motor manufacturing firm. Have been making aircraft with success for some years.

STANDARD AIRCRAFT MANUFACTURING CO., Ltd. Effingham House, Arundel Street, W.C., and at 28, Bow Common Lane, E.

Made aeroplanes and parts to official specifications.

Part of a week's output of the Standard Motor Co

SUPERMARINE.

The Supermarine Aviation Works, Ltd.

Registered offices and works : Southampton. Flying water and slipways : Woolston.

Designers of the *Supermarine* aeroplanes and flying boats. Founded in 1912, by Mr. Noel Pemberton Billing, then known as a pioneer of aviation, and as a motorist and yachtsman.

Before the war, he built some very interesting experimental flying-boats, some of which were ordered by Germany before the war, but were not delivered.

The Supermarine Works worked during the war on Admiralty designs, but built some experimental machines.

The name of the firm was changed during the war from Pemberton Billing, Ltd., to The Supermarine Aviation Works, Ltd., and Squadron-Commander Pemberton Billing ceased to have any connection with it.

The directors are : Capt. A. de Broughton (late R.F.C.), Mr. C. Cecil Dominy and Mr. Hubert Scott-Paine, the last-named being managing director.

The firm has of late been devoted chiefly to the construction of seaplanes of various types, all with marked success.

The following details concern the firms' experimental machines of 1916 to 1919, which it is permissible to describe.

Front View of a Supermarine " Baby " Flying-Boat (150 h.p. Hispano-Suiza engine).

SUPERMARINE BABY.

Type of machine	Single-seater Flying-boat.
Name or type No. of machine ..	Supermarine " Baby."
Purpose for which intended ..	Single-seater Seaplane Fighter.
Span	30.5 ft.
Gap, maximum and minimum ..	
Overall length	26.3 ft.
Maximum height	10.6 ft.
Chord	5.5 ft.
Total surface of wings ..	309 sq. ft.
Engine type and h.p. ..	150 h.p. Hispano-Suiza.
Weight of machine empty ..	1699 lbs.
Load per sq. ft.	7.5 lbs. per sq. ft.
Weight per h.p.	15.5 lbs. per h.p.
Tank capacity in hours ..	3 hours.
Performance.	
Speed low down	117 m.p.h.
Landing speed	57 m.p.h.
Disposable load apart from fuel	627 lbs.
Total weight of machine loaded	2326 lbs.

Side view of the Supermarine " Baby " with wings folded.

Side View of the " Night Hawk " Quadruplane, built experimentally by the Supermarine Company, to the designs
of Flight-Lieut. N. Pemberton Billing, R.N.

SUPERMARINE "NIGHT HAWK" QUADRUPLANE

Designed and built for night-flying and cruising. Fitted
with two Lewis guns mounted fore and aft and one two-
pounder Davis gun ; six double trays of Lewis gun ammunition
and ten rounds of ammunition for Davis gun, the latter being
fitted with double parallel sliding bed, permitting practically
any arc of fire.

The machine was also fitted with a separate twin A.B.C.
air-cooled petrol engine and dynamo. A searchlight, which
was hung in gimbals, permitting complete range of light ;
wireless telegraphy ; nine separate petrol tanks with patent
change gear, enabling any number of tanks to be used or
dis-used in case of tanks being punctured by gun-fire.

All the controls, pipes, etc., belonging to engines, were laid
outside the fuselage in specially constructed armour-plated
casings.

Accommodation was also fitted for bunking room, enabling
one hand to sleep or rest.

The whole wood members of the fuselage were heavily
taped and fabriced, to reduce the trouble of splinters in case
of crashes.

This machine was flown on several occasions at Eastchurch
by Mr. Prodger, where the contract speed and landing speed
were established. The engines, however, were under-powered,
and after alterations to the propellers, it was decided by the
Authorities to discontinue any further experiments.

NAVY "PUSHER" SEAPLANE

Pusher seaplane, built to Admiralty design, fitted with
130 h.p. Smith. This machine was completed and flying
eight weeks after receipt of drawings. The nacelle is boat-
built, with the lightest wooden construction known, the whole
nacelle weighing 85 lbs.

Three-quarter Rear View of a " Pusher " Seaplane, built by the Supermarine Co.

Three-quarter Rear View of a Supermarine-built A.D Flying Boat of 1917 (prototype), with gunner in tandem in front of pilot.
Pemberton-Billing went on to construct 27 for RNAS.

SUPERMARINE—*continued.*

A.D. FLYING BOAT.

This machine, with the exception of the hull, was completely re-designed by the firm and fitted with Hispano-Suiza engine. It carried 4½ hours' fuel, wireless gear, Lewis gun and ammunition, pilot and passenger, sea anchor, ground anchor, 40 fathoms of line, etc. It is believed to have put up new world's records for flying-boats in March, 1917.

SUPERMARINE PUSHER SCOUT, 1916.

(Commonly called the "Push-Prodge.")

Re-designed from original, and fitted with 100 h.p. mono-soupape engine; 3½ hours' fuel capacity; Lewis gun and ammunition.

Speed : 98 m.p.h.

Climb : 6,000 ft. in 8½ mins., 15,300 in 40½ mins.

T

TARRANT, W. G.

Tarrant, W. G., Offices : Clock House, Arundel Street, W.C. 2. Works : Byfleet.

A firm of building contractors. The close proximity of the works to Brooklands track led to frequent resort thereto by those of the early inhabitants of that place who required timber or woodwork for repairs, etc., to aeroplanes. It was therefore not unnatural that on the outbreak of War Mr. Tarrant should have turned some of his plant onto aircraft construction.

V

VICKERS.
Vickers, Ltd., Vickers House, Broadway, Westminster.

Aviation Department founded in 1911, under the control of the late Major H. F. Wood, 9th Lancers. Capt. P. D. Acland is now in control. The firm's Commercial Aviation Dept. is under the control of Brig.-General Caddell.

Originally the firm acquired the sole British rights in the R.E.P. machines of M. Robert Esnault Pelterie. Starting from this basis the department under Major Wood developed the series of machines with which the name of Vickers is associated.

The Vickers "gun bus," originally produced in 1913, was the only practicable fighting machine in the possession of the R.F.C. at the outbreak of war, and rendered invaluable services during the first six months of hostilities.

DESCRIPTION OF VARIOUS MACHINES DESIGNED AND BUILT BY VICKERS LTD.

F.B.9. PUSHER BIPLANE.

Developed from the successful F.B.5 "Gun bus" that used a 100 hp Monosoupape Gnôme engine and was employed as a fighter-scout from 1914-16.
Pilot and gunner observer placed in tandem.
Fitted with various rotary and fixed radial engines.
Armament : Lewis gun on ring mounting.
One of the best fighting machines of its time.

Model and date.				1914. Fighting type biplane.	
Length	...	...	feet (m.)	27½	*8·23*
Span	...	...	feet (m.)	37	*11·28*
Area	...	... sq. feet (m².)		385	*36*
Weight ... {	total, lbs. (kgs.)			1760	*799*
	useful, lbs. (kgs.)			900	*408*
Motor	...	...	h.p.	100 Monosoupape	
Speed ... {	max. m.p.h. (km.)			70	*110*
	min. m.p.h. (km.)			45	*70*
Endurance	...	...	hrs.	4½ hours	

Remarks, Notes and Details.—Climbing capacity of 150 feet per minute fully loaded. Radius of action 300 miles, and carries (including pilot, passenger and gun,) 300 rounds of ammunition. Fuselage of high tensile steel.

This machine has been designed entirely for offensive action in the air against other aeroplanes. For this purpose the gun is mounted in the front of the machine where it has a clear field of fire. The firer has also a perfectly clear view, and is sheltered from all wind by the design of the cowl.

Side View of the " P.B. Push-prodge," a small fast biplane, built by the Supermarine Co. to the designs of Flight-Lieut. Pemberton-Billing, R.N. The machine was, with a 100 h.p. Mono-Gnôme, the fastest biplane of its day, and was regarded as a " pushed projectile," hence its nick-name.

Front View of the Vickers Single-seat Fighter, type F.B. 16H. (300 h.p. Hispano-Suiza engine.)

Front View of 1916 type Vickers fighting biplane, with Monosoupape Gnôme or 110 hp Le Rhône engine. (Type F.B.9)

F.B.12C. PUSHER BIPLANE. SINGLE SEATER.

Fitted with various rotary and fixed radial engines.
Armament : One or two elevatable Lewis guns firing forward.

Three-quarter Rear View of Vickers' Single-Seater Pusher Fighter. (Type F.B.12.C.)

F.B.14. TRACTOR BIPLANE.

TWO SEATER RECONNAISSANCE.

Pilot and gunner observer placed in tandem.

Fitted with various line and V type engines.

Armament : One Vickers gun firing forward, with Vickers' synchronised firing gear. One Lewis on ring mounting at rear.

Three-quarter Rear View of Vickers' Two-Seater Fighter and Reconnaissance Biplane. (Type F.B.14.)

F.B.19. TRACTOR BIPLANE. SINGLE SEATER.

Fighter of 1916 appearance, capable of 109 mph. Only 36 built for RFC and used in Palestine, Russia, Macedonia and in UK for home defence. Fitted with 110 h.p. Clerget or Le Rhône rotary engine.

Armament: One Vickers' gun with Vickers' synchronised firing gear.

Front View of Vickers' Single-Seat Fighter. (Type F.B.19.)

THE VICKERS F.B. 16 H.

The Vickers F.B. 16 H. is a single-seater fighting Scout type. The planes are rather heavily staggered and fitted with two pairs of interplane struts either side of the fuselage. No centre section is fitted, the planes being fixed direct to the inverted Vee type pylons in front of the pilot's seat. The upper plane is well cut away over the pilot's cockpit to give a clear view upwards.

The tail-unit consists of a large fin and unbalanced rudder and a tail plane and divided elevator, the fin and tail plane being well braced above and below with Rafwire lacing.

The elevator controls are outside the fuselage.

The armament consists of two fixed Vickers guns which are fitted inside the fuselage synchronised to fire to the propeller.

Specification.

Type of machine..	Tractor Biplane, single-seater
Name or type No. of machine ..	F.B. 16 H.
Purpose for which intended ..	Fighter.
Span	T. 31 ft.; b. 30 ft.
Gap, maximum and minimum ..	45 ft.
Overall length ..	21 ft. 8 in.
Maximum height.. ..	8 ft. 1 in.
Chord	T. 5 ft. 4 in.; b. 4 ft. 2 in.
Total surface of wings ..	272 sq. ft.
Span of tail .. .	11 ft.
Total area of Tail ..	33.8 sq. ft.
Area of elevators	15.3 sq. ft.
Area of rudder	6.5 sq. ft.
Area of fin	7 sq. ft.
Area of each aileron and total area	$2 \times 9.5 + 2 \times 6 = 31$ sq. ft.
Maximum cross section of body..	8 sq. ft.
Horizontal area of body ..	36 sq. ft.
Vertical area of body ..	57 sq. ft.
Engine type and h.p. ..	Hispano-Suiza; 300 h.p.
Airscrew, diam., pitch and revs..	8 ft. diam., 6 ft. pitch, 1,875 r.p.m.
Weight of machine empty ..	1,636 lbs.
Load per sq. ft..... ..	8.45 lbs.
Weight per h.p. (300 h.p.) ..	7.65 lbs.
Petrol	Oil
Tank capacity in gallons..	Petrol 40 galls;] oil 5 galls.

Performance.

Speed low down ..	147 m.p.h.
Speed at 10,000 feet ..	140 m.p.h.
Speed at 20,000 feet ..	
Landing Speed.. ..	53 m.p.h.

Climb.

To 5,000 feet	3.3 minutes.
To 10,000 feet ..	7.8 minutes.
To 20,000 feet.. ..	23.5 minutes.
Disposable load apart from fuel (including crew) ..	327 lbs.
Total weight of machine loaded	2,300 lbs.

THE VICKER'S "VAMPIRE."

The Vickers "Vampire" is a small single-seater pusher biplane designed primarily for trench fighting.

The small nacelle is directly under the undersurface of the upper plane and is connected to the lower plane by short struts. The tail booms are fitted at the ends of each of the rear inner interplane struts and are parallel in plan view but, in elevation, converge at the fixed tail plane. The chassis is of the customary Vee-type rubber sprung.

Specification.

Type of machine	Pusher Biplane, single-seater
Name or type No. of machine ..	"Vampire" B.R. 2
Purpose for which intended ..	Trench fighting.
Span	Top 31 ft. 6 in.; bot. 27ft. 6 in.
Gap, maximum and minimum ..	52 in.
Overall length ..	22 ft. 11 in.
Maximum height.. ..	9 ft. 5 in.
Chord	Top 5 ft. 6 in.; bot. 4 ft. 6 in.
Total surface of wings ..	267 sq. ft.
Span of tail ..	12 ft. 3 in.
Total area of tail ..	38 sq. ft.
Area of elevators ..	16 sq. ft.
Area of rudder	6.7 sq. ft.
Area of fin	6.4 sq. ft.
Area of each aileron and total area	$(2 \times 12) + (2 \times 6) = 36$ sq ft.
Maximum cross section of body..	7.6 sq. ft.
Horizontal area of body.. ..	16.6 sq. ft.

Side View of the Vickers Single-seat Fighter, type F.B. 16H.

Three-quarter Front View of the Vickers' "Vampire" (200 B.R. 2 engine).

Side View of the Vickers' "Vampire" Single-seat Fighter.

THE VICKERS "VAMPIRE."—continued.

Vertical area of body	24.5 sq. ft.
Engine type and h.p. ..	B.R. 2; 200 h.p.
Airscrew, diam., pitch, and revs.	8.75 ft., 9 ft., 1,300.
Weight of machine empty (including 500 lbs. steel armour) ..	1,870 lbs.
Load per sq. ft.	9.1 lbs.
Weight per h.p. (228 h.p.) ..	10.7 lbs.
Tank capacity in gallons	Petrol 29 galls.; oil 6 galls.

Performance.

Speed low down	121 m.p.h.
Speed at 10,000 feet ..	115 m.p.h.
Landing speed.. ..	54 m.p.h.

Climb.

To 5,000 feet	5 minutes.
To 10,000 feet	12 minutes.
Disposable load apart from fuel (including crew) ..	568 lbs.
Total weight of machine loaded	2,438 lbs.

VICKER'S "VIMY" TWIN-ENGINED BIPLANE.

The Vickers "Vimy" biplane was designed as a long-distance bomber, and, following the usual practice in twin-engined machines, has a single fuselage, carrying the pilot and two gunners, one in the nose and the other just aft of the trailing edge of the main planes.

The engines are housed in "power-eggs," each containing one complete power unit with its respective petrol and oil tanks, carried halfway between the planes, one on either side of the fuselage.

Under each engine-housing is a separate under-carriage consisting of two vees of steel tube, between which an axle and two wheels are slung on shock-absorbers.

To prevent the machine standing on its nose after too fast a landing, a skid is fitted under the nose of the fuselage.

Four large balanced ailerons are fitted to the main planes. The empennage consists of a biplane tail unit with two unbalanced elevators, and turn rudders with no fixed fin-area.

It was on a Rolls-Royce engined Vickers "Vimy" that Capt. John Alcock, D.S.C. and Lieut. Arthur Whitten Brown made the first direct flight across the Atlantic ocean.

The following specifications give particulars of this machine fitted with various types of engine :—

THE VICKERS "VIMY."—(Fiat Engines.)

Type of machine	Twin-engine Biplane.
Name or type No. of machine ..	"Vimy" Fiat
Purpose for which intended ..	Bombing.
Span	67 ft. 2 in.
Gap	10 ft.
Overall length	43 ft. 6½ in.
Maximum height ..	15 ft. 3 in.
Chord	10 ft. 6 in.
Total surface of wings ..	1,330 sq. ft.
Span of tail	16 ft.
Total area of tail	177.5 sq. ft.
Area of elevators ..	63 sq. ft. (total).
Area of rudder	21.5 sq. ft. (total).
Area of fin	None.
Area of each aileron and total area	60.5 sq. ft.; 242 sq. ft.
Maximum cross section of body..	3 ft. 9in. by 3 ft. 9 in.
Horizontal area of body ..	125 sq. ft.
Vertical area of body ..	120 sq. ft.
Engine type and h.p. ..	Fiat A/12/Bis.
Airscrew, diam., pitch and revs...	9.4 ft. dia., 5.85 ft. pitch, 1,700 revs.
Weight of machine empty ..	6,426 lbs.
Tank capacity in gallons ..	Petrol 170 galls.; oil 17 galls.

Performance.

Speed low down	98 m.p.h.
Speed at 5,000 feet ..	96 m.p.h.
Landing speed.. ..	53 m.p.h.

Climb.

To 5,000 feet	14 minutes.
To 10,000 feet	45 minutes.
Disposable load apart from fuel	2,479 lbs. (including crew of 3)
Total weight of machine loaded.	10,300 lbs.
Load per sq. ft.	7.75 lbs.
Weight per h.p.	17.2 lbs.

Front View of a Vickers' "Vimy" Bomber. (two Fiat engines, type A. 12 Bis).

Three-quarter Front View of a Fiat-engined Vickers "Vimy" Bomber.

Three-quarter view from Aft of a Vickers "Vimy" Bomber (Fiat engines).

THE VICKERS "VIMY."—(Hispano-Suiza Engines)

Type of machine.. ..	Twin-engine Biplane.
Name or type No. of machine..	"Vimy" Hispano.
Purpose for which intended ..	Bombing.
Span	67 ft. 2 in.
Gap	10 ft.
Overall length	43 ft. 6½ in.
Maximum height	15 ft. 3 in.
Chord	10 ft. 6 in.
Total surface of wings ..	1330 sq. ft.
Span of tail	16 ft.
Total area of tail	177.5 sq. ft.
Area of elevators	63 sq. ft. (total).
Area of rudders	21.5 sq. ft. (total).
Area of fin	None.
Area of each aileron and total area	60.5 sq. ft.; 242 sq. ft.
Maximum cross section of body.	3 ft. 9 in. by 3 ft. 9 in.
Horizontal area of body ..	125 sq. ft.
Vertical area of body ..	120 sq. ft.
Engine type and h.p. ..	Two 200 h.p. Hispano-Suiza.
Airscrew, diam., pitch and revs. .	9.25 ft. dia. 5 ft. pitch, 2,100 revs.
Weight of machine empty ..	5,420 lbs.
Tank capacity in gallons ..	Petrol 91; oil 14

Performance.

Speed low down	90 m.p.h.
Speed at 5,000 feet ..	87 m.p.h.
Landing speed ..	51 m.p.h.

Climb.

To 5,000 feet	23.5 minutes.
Disposable load apart from fuel	2,900 lbs. (including crew of 3)
Total weight of machine ..	9,120 lbs.
Load per sq. ft.	6.85 lbs.
Weight per h.p.	22.8 lbs.

THE VICKERS "VIMY."—(Rolls-Royce Engines)

Type of machine	Twin-engine Biplane.
Name or type No. of machine ..	"Vimy" Rolls.
Purpose for which intended ..	Bombing.
Span	67 ft. 2 in.
Gap	10 ft.
Overall length	44 ft.
Maximum height	15 ft.
Chord	10 ft. 6 in.
Total surface of wings	1,330 sq. ft.
Span of tail	16 ft.
Total area of tail	177.5 sq. ft.
Area of elevators..	63 sq. ft. (total).
Area of rudder	21.5 sq. ft.
Area of fin	None.
Area of each aileron and total area	60·5 sq. ft.; 242 sq. ft.
Maximum cross section of body..	3 ft 9 in. by 3 ft. 9 in.
Horizontal area of body	125 sq. ft.
Vertical area of body	120 sq. ft.
Engine type and h.p	Two 350 h.p. "Eagle Mark VIII" Rolls-Royce.
Airscrew, diam., pitch, and revs .	10.5 ft. dia., 9 ft. 11 in. pitch, 1,950 revs.
Weight of machine empty ..	7,100 lbs.
Tank capacity in gallons.. ..	Petrol 452; oil 18.
Performance.	
Speed low down	103 m.p.h.
Speed at 5,000 feet	98 m.p.h.
Landing speed..	56 m.p.h.
Climb.	
To 5,000 feet	21.9 minutes.
Disposable load apart from fuel.	2,010 lbs. (including crew of 3)
Total weight of machine loaded .	12,500 lbs.
Load per sq. ft.	9.4 lbs.
Weight per h.p.	17.8 lbs.

Side View of a Vickers "Vimy" Bomber (two 375 h.p. Rolls-Royce "Eagle" engines).

THE WESTLAND AIRCRAFT WORKS,

Yeovil, Somerset.

Branch of famous engineering firm of J. B. Petter.

Under the management of Mr. R. A. Bruce, M.I.M.E., A.M.I.C.E., M.Sc., formerly of British and Colonial Aeroplane Co., Ltd., and previously connected with the Brennan Torpedo and Brennan Gyroscopic Monorail.

During the period of hostilities the firm built numerous machines to the specifications of the Air Department, Admiralty, and have in addition produced the machines hereafter described to their own designs.

THE WESTLAND "WAGTAIL."

The Westland "Wagtail" was designed in answer to a general demand for a fast, quick-climbing, general utility single-seater fighter.

It conforms in general arrangement with most other machines of this type.

The pilot's view is very good both upward and downward, more than half the centre section being left open. Main planes of equal span are fitted, the upper plane having a dihedral of 5 degrees, whereas the lower plane is flat, i.e., no dihedral.

THE WESTLAND "WAGTAIL."
Specification.

Type of machine		Single-seater Tractor Scout. Aeroplane.
Name and type No. of machine ..		Westland "Wagtail."
Purpose for which intended ..		High altitude fighting.
Span		23 ft. 2 in.
Gap ..	maximum .	At outer strut 4 ft. 6 in.
	minimum .	Centre section 4 ft.
Overall length		18 ft. 11 in.
Maximum height		8 ft.
Chord		4 ft. 6 in.
Total surface of wings		190 sq. ft.
Span of tail		7 ft. 10¾ in.
Total area of tail, incldg. elevators		25 sq. ft.
Area of elevators		9.5 sq. ft.
Area of rudder		4.4 sq. ft.

Area of fin.	2.1 sq. ft.
Area of each aileron	6 sq. ft.
Total area of ailerons	24 sq. ft.
Maximum cross section of body..	7.1 sq. ft.
Horizontal area of body	29.3 sq. ft.
Vertical area of body	36.5 sq. ft.
Engine type and h.p.	170 b.h.p. "Wasp" Fixed Radial.
Airscrew, diam., pitch and revs. .	Pitch 2070 m/m., diam. 2590 m/., revs. 1,900.
Weight of machine empty ..	965 lbs. (including 219 lbs. for fuel and oil).
Weight of machine empty (without fuel and oil). ..	746 lbs.
Load per sq. ft.	Fully loaded 7 lbs.
Weight per h.p.	7.7 lbs.
Tank capacity in hours	2½ hours at 15,000 feet.
Tank capacity in gallons.. ..	Petrol 26 galls.; oil 3 galls.

Three-quarter View from rear of a Westland "Wagtail" Single-seat fighter.

Performance,		
Speed at 10,000 feet		125 m.p.h.
Landing speed..		50 m.p.h.
Climb.		
To 5,000 feet		3½ minutes.
To 10,000 feet..		7½ minutes.
To 17,000 feet..		17 minutes.
Disposable load apart from fuel	365 lbs.	Pilot . 180 lbs. Two guns, gear & 1,000 rounds . 160 ,, Oxygen . 25 ,,
Total weight of machine loaded		1,330 lbs.

Side View of the Westland "Wagtail" Single-seater fighter. (170 h.p. A.B.C. Wasp engine).

WESTLAND SEAPLANE N16.

The Westland seaplane N16 is a small single-seater seaplane fitted with two pontoon floats and a large single tail float, and was designed as a fighter and light bomber for use from seaplane carrier ships.

The fuselage is of normal type, with a pronounced bump in the fairing ahead of the pilot's seat. In this bump is fitted a fixed synchronised Vickers gun.

In order to reduce the space for stowage on board ship, the main planes are made to fold. Both upper and lower planes are of equal span, and two sets of interplane struts are fitted on each side.

The wings are fitted with trailing edge flaps along the whole span, giving a variable camber, which is controlled from the pilot's seat.

Ailerons are fitted to both upper and lower wings.

The Westland N17 seaplane is exactly the same except that the main floats are increased in length, slightly turned up at the rear and no tail float is fitted.

Specification.

Type of machine	Single-seater Tractor Seaplane Scout.
Name of type of machine ..	Westland Seaplane N.16.
Purpose for which intended ..	Fighter Scout, capable of getting off deck of ships.
Span	31 ft. 3½ in.
Overall length, fuselage horizontal	25 ft. 3½ in.
Overall length resting on tail float	26 ft. 5½ in.
Maximum height ,, ,,	11 ft. 2 in.
Chord	5 ft.
Total surface of wings, includes centre sections ..	278 sq. ft.
Span of tail	11 ft.
Area of tail plane	24.5 sq. ft.
Total area of tail, incldg. elevator	42 sq. ft.
Area of elevators	17.5 sq. ft.
Area of rudder	7.5 sq. ft.
Area of fin	6.8 sq. ft.
Area of each outer aileron ..	9.9 sq. ft.
Total area of ailerons ..	39.6 sq. ft.
Maximum cross section of body ..	10¾ sq. ft.
Horizontal area of body ..	44 sq. ft.
Vertical area of body ..	55 sq. ft.
Engine type and h.p.	Air-cooled rotary B.R.1; 150 b.h.p.; 1,240 r.p.m.
Airscrew, diam., pitch and revs. .	Diam. 2,650 m/m., pitch 2,650 m/m., 1,240 r.p.m

Wing section	R.A.F. 14. Variable camber device.
Weight of machine empty, without fuel and oil	1,460 lbs.
Weight of machine empty, but with 268 lbs. for fuel and oil ..	1,728 lbs.
Load per sq. ft.	7.7 lbs. sq. ft. fully loaded.
Weight per h.p.	14·2 lbs.
Tank capacity in hours ..	2½—3 approx. ground level.
Tank capacity in gallons ..	Petrol 30 galls.; oil 5 galls.
Performance.	
Speed low down	108 miles per hour.
Landing speed	50 m.p.h. with no flaps : 45 m.p.h. with flaps.

Climb.	
To 5,000 feet	10 minutes.
To 10,000 feet	28 minutes.
Disposable load apart from fuel	405 lbs.
Total weight of machine loaded	2,133 lbs.

Pilot . .	180 lbs.
Bombs & Gear	150 ,,
Gun and 250 rounds.	60 ,,
Sundries .	15 ,,

Three-quarter Front View of the Westland Seaplane N.16 (150 h.p. B.R.1. rotary engine).

WHITE.
J. Samuel White & Co., Ltd., shipbuilders and engineers, East Cowes, Isle of Wight. London office : 28, Victoria Street, S.W.

This well-known firm of torpedo craft builders, etc., formally opened an aviation department on 1st January, 1913, with Mr Howard T. Wright as general manager of the Aviation Dept., and designer.

Eleven Wight Pusher Seaplanes built for Admiralty for reconnaissance. Two served on the seaplane carrier HMS *Ark Royal*. One 200 h.p. Salmson engine, offering a speed of 72 mph. Details of the firm's latest products are prohibited owing to the firm being employed on work for the Air Ministry. The Aircraft Department has, since 1917, been under the management of Mr. C. Compton Paterson, one of the pioneers of aviation in the North of England and in South Africa.

Type 840 TRACTOR SEAPLANE

Length : 41 ft.
Span : 61 ft.
Surface : 568 sq. ft.
Weight empty : 3408 lbs.
Useful load : 1045 lbs.
Engine : 225 h.p. Sunbeam.
Speed : 81 m.p.h.
Endurance : 4 hours.

A Wight Type 840 tractor seaplane, built by J. Samuel White. Used by RNAS on anti-submarine patrol between 1915-17.

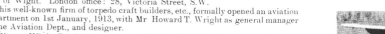

			1913. Navy 'plane.		1914. Wight seaplane.	
Length	...	feet (m.)	30	9·15	33	10·05
Span	...	feet (m.)	44	13·40	63	19·20
Area	...	sq. feet (m².)	500	46½	730	67½
Weight	... {	total ...lbs. (kgs.)	2000	907	3400	1542
		useful .. lbs. (kgs.)	650	295	2600	1179
Motor	...	h.p.	160 Gnome		200 Salmson	
Speed	... {	max. m.p.h. (km.)	70	115	75	47
		min. m.p.h. (km.)	35	57	35	22

Remarks.—Hydro-biplane, with Howard T. Wright patent aeroplanes to give wide range of speed. Two patent hydro floats, 21 feet (6'40 m.) long, three steps on each.

WARING & GILLOW Ltd.
Hammersmith, W.

Well known business and manufacturing firm, making aeroplanes and parts to official specifications.

1914 WIGHT Pusher seaplane.

Australian Commonwealth.

VICTORIA.

In January, 1913, the Australian Flying Corps was instituted, as a part of the citizen forces.

The force was then designed to consist of 4 officers, 7 warrant officers and sergeants, 32 mechanics.

The school is at Point Cook, Werribee, Victoria. Course includes — mechanics of the aeroplane, aerial motors, meteorology, aerial navigation by compass, aerial photography, signalling, etc.

The first commanding officer was Captain Henry Petre, R.F.C., lent to the Australian Commonwealth Forces. In his absence on active service, Captain Eric Harrison, late of the British and Colonial Aeroplane Co., Ltd., commanded.

An engine-Instruction Class in progress at the Commonwealth Central Flying School at Point Cook.

Early in 1916 it set about providing the personnel, including mechanics and transport drivers, for a complete squadron up to the "establishment" of a squadron of the Royal Flying Corps. Since then a number of full squadrons have been supplied to the R.F.C. and have distinguished themselves greatly on active service.

Several aeroplanes have been built by the mechanics of the School, chiefly of "box-kite" biplane type, and the first aero-engine built in Australia was produced by the Sydney Tarrant Motor Proprietary Co., in September, 1915.

The machines at the Werribee School were mostly *B.E.*'s and *Bristol* box-kites, but various *Maurice Farmans* and *F.E.*'s have been added. Major Harrison (formerly Capt. as mentioned above) was in command at the signing of the Armistice, and later came to England to acquire the latest available knowledge of aeronautical developments.

The Government policy is to encourage the production of aircraft and parts thereof by indigenous firms.

Privately owned aeroplanes have been imported by Mr. Hordern (*Maurice Farman* seaplane), Mr. Delfosse Badgery (*Caudron*), and by various foreign aviators who gave exhibitions.

NEW SOUTH WALES.

A new Military School was opened on Aug. 28th, 1916, by the New South Wales Government, at Richmond, near Sydney.

This school is equipped with American *Curtiss* biplanes.

The chief instructor is Mr. W. J. Stutt, formerly of the British & Colonial Aeroplane Co., Ltd. (Bristol), and later of the Royal Aircraft Factory, Farnborough himself an Australian.

QUEENSLAND.

A group of aeronautical enthusiasts enrolled themselves in November, 1915, under the title of "The Queensland Volunteer Flying Civilians."

This body built a biplane, somewhat on *Caudron* lines, for training purposes, at Hemmaut, near Brisbane.

Later several of them joined the British Flying Service, four receiving commissioned rank in the R.F.C. and four becoming air mechanics, R.F.C.

CANADA.

MILITARY AVIATION.

In June, 1914, two officers of the Ottawa defence force were sent to Salisbury Plain for instruction, in connection with the proposed establishment of a flying corps, but nothing came of this beginning.

In 1915 a Flying School was started by a Canadian branch of the American Curtiss Co., under the management of the first Canadian pilot, Mr. J. A. D. McCurdy. Here a number of Canadians were trained to fly. Others were trained at Ithaca, New York, at a school founded by the Thomas Bros., two Englishmen from the Argentine, who had started an aeroplane factory there.

In 1917 the R.F.C. opened an official flying school in Canada and here a large number of Canadians were taught to fly by British instructors.

During the winter the bulk of the *personnel* of the school moved to Fort Worth, Texas, U.S.A., but those who remained achieved remarkable results by flying off the snow in standard type military machines mounted on ski instead of wheels, thus proving the possibilities of aeroplanes in winter in snow-covered country.

Canadian pilots in both the R.N.A.S and R.F.C. have done excellent work and have won many decorations, including two V.Cs. Altogether some 14,000 Canadians have become pilots in the Flying Services.

Late in the war an attempt was made to establish a Canadian Naval Air Service, but this was apparently washed out on the signing of the Armistice. The formation of a Canadian Air Force has now been undertaken.

Early in 1919 an Act was passed in the Canadian House of Commons setting up an Air Board, to control flying in Canada.

Various activities are being undertaken in Canada, but at the time of going to press they are all somewhat nebulous, and no actual Air services are being run. It is noteworthy that Canadian railways are taking Parliamentary powers to run air services as tributaries to the railway lines.

A syndicate, largely of American origin, has bought up a number of Canadian military training aeroplanes of American design and is endeavouring (May 1919) to sell them to Canadians, but as they are only elementary training vehicles they cannot be expected to be of use on regular air services.

AERIAL SOCIETIES.

The Aero Club of Canada, Toronto. Which represents the Royal Aero Club of Great Britain and Ireland, in issuing aviators' certificates, &c.

The Aeronautical Society of Canada, c o. M. P. Logan, 99, Gloucester Street, Toronto.

McGill Aviation Club, McGill University, Montreal.

MANUFACTURE.

The Canadian Curtiss Aeroplane Co., Ltd., of Toronto was the first Canadian firm to manufacture aircraft. It was working on large contracts for the British Navy and Army, and has produced land-going aeroplanes and seaplanes (flying-boat type), with two or more engines apiece.

Later the Polson Ironworks Co., of Toronto, began to build aeroplanes, and their first production (in 1916) was a biplane with an American Sturtevant engine. The fuselage of this machine was built entirely of steel tubing. The machine was taken to the United States for test, and gave good results, but one gathers that the firm has given up aircraft work.

The only other firm of which one can learn is :—

CANADIAN AEROPLANES, Ltd.

Toronto, Ont.

President : Sir William Baillie. Chief Engineer : F. G. Ericson.

This firm was organised late in 1916 to supply a portion of the demand of the British Empire and her Allies for aeroplanes and seaplanes, particularly for training and anti-submarine defence. At the time the Armistice was signed, Canadian Aeroplanes, Ltd., were producing 350 training aeroplanes of the Canadian Avro and Curtiss types and eight F.5 L. flying boats per month. The company was then employing 2,300 workers.

The whole of the share capital of the company was vested in the Imperial Munitions Board, which advanced a million dollars to finance the initial operations of the firm.

CANADIAN TRAINING AEROPLANE (Modified Curtiss J.N.4.)

General description.

Wing area, including ailerons	358.9 sq. ft.
Wing span overall (top)	43 ft. 7$\frac{7}{16}$ in.
Wing span overall (lower)	33 ft. 11$\frac{1}{4}$ in.
Wing chord	59$\frac{1}{2}$ in.
Overall length of machine	26 ft. 10$\frac{1}{2}$ in.
Net weight machine empty	1,170 lbs.
Gross weight per sq. ft. of surface, including ailerons	5.1 lbs.
Gross weight, machine and load	1,850 lbs.
Dihedral angle	1 degree.
Sweepback	0 degree.
Stagger	9$\frac{1}{2}$ degrees.
Curtiss Model O.X. Engine	**90 B.H.P.**
Weight of engine	**350 lbs.**
Weight per h.p.	**3.88 lbs.**
Bore and stroke	**4 × 5.**
Normal speed at full motor load	**1,400 r.p.m.**
Provided capacity, fuel tank	**37 gallons.**
Fuel consumption per hour, throttle wide open	**8.37 gallons.**
Fuel consumption per hour, average flight	**6 gallons.**
Oil consumption per hour	**$\frac{1}{2}$ gallon.**
Provided oil capacity, crankcase	**4 gallons.**

Performance.

Horse power at 1,400 r.p.m.	90 h.p. rated.
Speed, maximum	85 m.p.h.
Speed, minimum	40 m.p.h.
Climb in 10 minutes	4,000 feet.
Useful load	680 lbs.

Distribution of useful load (may be changed if desired).

Fuel	200 lbs.
Water	35 lbs.
Oil	30 lbs.
Pilot	175 lbs.
Passenger and other load	240 lbs.
	680 lbs.

Maximum tank capacity at full motor load		4.4 hours.
Tank capacity for ordinary service flight		6.2 hours.
Maximum tank capacity for duration flight		9 hours.

NEW ZEALAND.

Little flying was done in New Zealand until the outbreak of war. One *Bleriot*, 80 h.p., was presented in 1913 to the New Zealand Government by the *Standard*, London.

Mr. Scotland imported a *Caudron* biplane and flew in 1915.

The most notable New Zealand pilot of the early days, was Capt. J. J. Hammond, who, flying on active service for a considerable time, was employed in experimentally testing new types of aircraft. He was killed in 1918 while flying an American aeroplane in the United States.

New Zealand has contributed largely by voluntary subscriptions to the purchase of aeroplanes for the R.F.C. and has supplied a relatively large number of pilots to the Flying Services during the war. These have nearly all received their initial training at either Walsh Bros. School at Auckland, or at the Canterbury School.

THE NEW ZEALAND FLYING SCHOOL (WALSH BROS. & DEXTER, LTD.), AUCKLAND, NEW ZEALAND.

Walsh Brothers (Leo A. and Vivian C.) having been interested in the early developments of flying, purchased sufficient materials from Howard Wright, England, in 1910, to enable the construction of a biplane to be commenced in Auckland in August of that year.

On Jan. 1st, 1914, a successful flight was made by V. C. Walsh—the first to be made in New Zealand—on a seaplane. Adverse weather conditions and minor adjustments delayed progress to a certain extent, but the pilot having demonstrated the stability of the machine and the success of the design generally, commenced carrying passengers on March 14th, 1915.

Upon the outbreak of hostilities, the brothers, fully believing that aircraft would play a most important part in the war, devoted themselves entirely to the completion of the flying boat and subsequent experiments in connection with learning to operate it. Having successfully overcome the initial difficulties, and proved both machine and pilot capable of use in the training of aviators for war service, the brothers urged the New Zealand Government to recognise the importance of the work.

At the time the importance of military aviation did not appeal to the N.Z. Authorities. The brothers therefore cabled the Royal Aero Club asking for certificates to be issued to pupils in New Zealand who were able to comply with the usual conditions.

Owing to the recognition of their efforts by the Royal Aero Club, the brothers were able to inform the Imperial Government that they were in a position to train and despatch suitable candidates for the Royal Flying Corps possessed of certificates issued by the Royal Aero Club. (There being no Naval Establishment in New Zealand, the military authorities did not care for candidates leaving the dominion to enter any other than a shops, and an ample supply of engines, spares, and construction materials to be carried out. At the time of the signing of the Armistice the equipment included :—

Two twin-float hydro-aeroplanes, equipped with six-cylinder 125 h.p. A 5 Hall-Scott motors.

One *Walsh* flying boat (nearing completion) equipped with a six-cylinder 125 h.p. A 5 motor, Hall-Scott.

One *Walsh* flying boat equipped with a four-cylinder 100 h.p. A 7a motor, Hall-Scott.

One *Walsh* flying boat (the original flying boat), previously equipped with a 70 h.p. Anzani motor, and now fitted with a four-cylinder 100 h.p. A 7a motor, Hall-Scott.

One *Walsh* flying boat (for solo work) fitted with 70 h.p. Anzani motor.

One *Curtiss* flying boat equipped with 90 h.p. OX 5 Curtiss motor.

Although the school is only on a small scale, it represents a considerable expenditure of energy and unremitting work in overcoming the many handicaps that have had to be surmounted, and no little credit is due to the members of the school staff, who have loyally and enthusiastically supported the founders in their efforts to promote aviation in this dominion generally, and in particular to aid in contributing to the winning of the War in the Air.

As regards the *personnel* (members of the staff) :—Leo A. Walsh, Director of the School and Managing Director of the

Part of the Staff and Equipment of the New Zealand Flying School at Auckland, N.Z., in 1918.

The machine was completed by January, 1911, and on Feb. 5th (1911), V.C. Walsh made a short flight. The incident was naturally of great interest to the builders, inasmuch as it was the first flight to be made in this dominion.

The machine was equipped with a 60 h.p. E.N.V. motor (British), which ran excellently.

In connection with the early experiments in learning to operate this machine, it was soon found, by hard experience, that the English design of undercarriage was quite unsuitable for the rough ground used as a flying field.

After having made good progress in gaining knowledge of the control of the machine in the air, the pilot (Vivian) had the ill-luck to capsize the 'plane when running on the ground at high speed just preparatory to taking off. The short skids caught in a depression, and the pilot fortunately crawled out of the complete wreckage unhurt.

Several months were then occupied in re-building the machine completely, and further trials were commenced. Good progress was being made when developments occurred which brought the experiments to a close.

In common with most pioneers of aviation at the period mentioned, financial assistance had been obtained from other parties, and the brothers met with the usual discouraging demands for speedy recoupment for the outlay incurred. Impossible flight and financial conditions were imposed by the financiers—a not uncommon proceeding in other parts of the world during the early days—and a breach of relations followed, resulting in a complete loss to the brothers of all financial interests in their handiwork. The machine in other hands promptly came to grief, and was damaged beyond repair.

The difficulties surrounding the operation and construction of this first machine were accentuated by the difficulty of obtaining not only information on the art of flying, but most necessary materials to repair breakages, on account of the great distance separating the local experimenters from other centres of flying activities. With no assistance obtainable from anyone versed in flying to fall back upon, it was naturally a case of feeling the way step by step. Incidentally, it may be mentioned that the brothers' financial resources were extremely limited, and on many occasions their enthusiasm was sorely taxed in consequence.

This set-back did not have the effect of causing the brothers to lose interest in the progress of aviation. They determined to tackle it from a different angle, and in August, 1913, commenced the building of a flying boat of their own design. As the construction of a shed in which to carry out building operations, and the actual building of the machine could only be done in the brothers' spare time, progress was naturally somewhat slow, and although on the outbreak of war every effort was made to accelerate the completion of the machine, it was not until Dec., 1914, that the flying boat was ready for trials.

military branch of the service, thus the apparent anomaly of men trained upon seaplanes entering the R.F.C.)

After the exchange of various communications, the Imperial Government notified the brothers that suitable candidates for the R.F.C. from New Zealand would be accepted, and that the usual Imperial grant of £75 towards the expense of qualifying would be available to accepted candidates, and that all expenses in connection with transport to England and training charges subsequently would be borne by the British Government.

It was not until October, 1915, that arrangements could be completed to enable the brothers actively to engage in the training of men destined for the Imperial Air Service.

The *Walsh* flying boat, equipped with a 70 h.p. Anzani motor, was used in the early training operations. Subsequently a *Caudron* biplane, fitted with a 60 h.p. Le Rhone motor, was purchased. Floats were built at the school and the machine converted to a hydro-aeroplane. Good progress was made with these two machines, but the difficulty of obtaining spares for the motors frequently hampered operations.

A *Curtiss* 90 h.p. flying boat was later added to the equipment, and two of the pupils trained by V. C. Walsh joined the staff in order to assist in the training work.

The initial preparation of candidates for the Imperial Air Service created interest throughout the dominion, and the school had considerable difficulty in coping with the increasing number of applicants for admission, many of whom being young men ineligible for enlistment in the N.Z. Forces on account of their youth, but who were eager and anxious to serve their country in some capacity, and who recognised that an opening was available to serve in the R.F.C.

The difficulties and delays experienced in obtaining suitable materials and engine spares interfered very materially with the school work from time to time. Many spares and replacements had to be made in the school workshops. Notwithstanding these somewhat frequent delays and interruptions, a steady supply of certificated men were leaving for England, and the demand for tuition constantly increased.

Mr. R. A. Dexter, of Auckland, N.Z., has been associated with the brothers Walsh since 1914. The financial assistance and support given by this gentleman was of great assistance in enabling the brothers to bring the construction and operation of the flying boat built in that year to a successful issue. The efforts of the founders to establish the school were helped by the financial support of Mr. Dexter.

The continued expansion of the undertaking necessitated further capital being provided. A limited liability company was formed at the latter end of 1917, and in a short time the capital was fully subscribed by well-wishers of the school throughout the dominion.

The strengthening of the financial resources enabled the construction of further machines, provision of additional work-

Company; Vivian C. Walsh, Chief Pilot and Works Manager; M. Matthews, P. R. Going and G. B. Bolt, Flight Instructors; R. Johnston, Mechanical Instructor.

Many of the ex-pupils have done excellent work at the Front. Although the school records are not complete, information has been received of the following decorations awarded to ex-pupils, details of which may, doubtless, be found in the Honours List :—

Major K. L. Caldwell, M.C., D.F.C. (succeeded to the command of the 74th Squadron after Major Bishop).

Captain C. G. Callender, Order of the Silver Crown of Italy (recently O.C. 1st School of Aerial Gunnery, Hythe).

Captain M. C. McGregor, M.C., D.F.C. (for some time in the 85th Squadron, Major Ball's).

Captain H. W. Collier, M.C. (squadron unknown).

Captain W. W. Cook, M.C. (squadron unknown).

Captain H. F. Drewitt, M.C. (squadron unknown.)

Capt. R. B. Bannerman, D.F.C. and Bar (squadron unknown).

Several other ex-pupils have made excellent fighting pilots, and may have gained distinction that we are not aware of. The foregoing honours list may be incomplete, and the men mentioned may have been awarded further decorations of which the firm have no record.

In proportion to the numbers trained at this school, the progress as military aviators of ex-pupils has been a record of achievement, and all concerned with the institution are naturally very proud of this fact.

THE CANTERBURY AVIATION CO.

The Canterbury (N.Z.) Aviation Company, Ltd., was formed in 1917 to equip and run a flying school in Canterbury. Ground was secured at Sockburn, four miles or so out of Christchurch, and a *Caudron* with 60-h.p. Anzani imported. Later other machines were also imported and much good training work was done.

Mr. Hill, who learned to fly at Hendon, was engaged as instructor and manager, He was killed in an accident in 1918, but the school instruction is being carried on by his former pupils.

Since the cessation of the war the number of pupils has fallen off considerably, but it is believed that the return of New Zealand aviators from the war will give a fresh impetus to flying.

The immediate difficulty in the way of flying in New Zealand is that all engines have to be imported, and considerable delay is, therefore, inevitable in obtaining engines and spares.

New Zealand affords great opportunities for aviators, especially for flying-boat services round the coast, which, owing to indented nature, provides excellent harbours.

INDIA.

Military Aviation.—A large number of officers belonging to the Indian Army have qualified as pilots. A flying school was started at Sitapur, but on the outbreak of war all the officers came to England and joined up with the R.F.C. These officers have all distinguished themselves by good work. Apparently the Sitapur School and one at Lahore are now in operation. Many aerodromes exist along the North-West Frontier.

A detachment of the R.F.C. came into action late in 1916 in operations against troublesome hill tribes. The aeroplanes were used largely as actual weapons of offence, with bombs and machine-guns, as well as being used for reconnaissance, and their presence had very considerable effect in subduing the trouble.

R.A.F. detachments played a highly important part in the attack by Afghan troops in May, 1919. Bomb raids were made on Kabul, Jellalabad, and other important Afghan towns, as well as on camps and on troops on the march. So great was the effect of these aerial attacks that after a few days of them the Amir of Afghanistan sued for peace.

Private Aviation.—In the past, two or three home-made machines appeared, and one or two were imported, but all are now extinct, as private flying is prohibited.

THE UNION OF SOUTH AFRICA.

Military Aviation.—Officers of the Union Defence Force were trained in England by the R.F.C. in 1914. Some of them served in Flanders early in the war, and afterwards were formed into a South African Aviation Corps, which was built up of mechanics from the Royal Naval Air Service and untrained men from South Africa. Certain R.N.A.S. officers were also lent to the S.A.A.C. The Corps did excellent work in German S.W. Africa, and afterwards came to England where most of it was absorbed into the R.F.C. At a later date a portion of it was used in East African operations, where the South African Squadron, comprising a large proportion of Boers as well as Anglo-South Africans, under Major Wallace, D.S.O., a South African pilot, has won considerable distinction. Boer officer-aviators in the R.F.C. have also distinguished themselves highly in France and elsewhere.

Private Aviation.—John Weston is a qualified pilot, and imported sundry aeroplanes to the Orange Free State, besides building some machines there. He has been on active service, at first with the S.A. Flying Corps, then with the R.N.A.S., and later as an R.A.F. officer, since the outbreak of war.

In 1912, Capt. Guy Livingston (later Brig. General R.A.F.) went to South Africa with Mr. Compton Paterson and Mr. E. F. Driver, and organised exhibition flights all over Cape Colony, the Transvaal and the Orange Free State. These exhibitions, which were later continued by Mr. Paterson alone, did much to influence the Government in forming the South African F.C. Mr. Paterson also established a school at Kimberley where he gave their first instruction to Major Wallace (mentioned above) and various other South African officers who have since distinguished themselves highly.

A number of Aeroplanes have been presented to the Royal Flying Corps by the Overseas Club as the result of subscriptions raised in British Colonies and Dependencies, such as the West Indies, the Malay States, East Africa, &c.

BULGARIAN.

In the Balkan War, 1912-13, Bulgaria hastily organised an aviation corps, the pilots being chiefly foreigners, French, Russian, Italian, and British,—but no Germans. The observers were generally Bulgarian officers. This corps, though necessarily lacking in military organisation, proved very useful on several occasions. After that war, aviation was neglected till the Great War began. The corps was then reorganised, with German assistance.

Military Aviators.—The early Bulgarian aviators were trained in France and England, and latterly a number of Bulgarians were trained in flying and observing in Germany. The Bulgarians themselves do not seem to be able to fly with any skill.

Early Military Aeroplanes.—(Monos.) *Bleriot* and *Bristol*.

(Biplanes) *Albatros*, *Farman*, and *Bristol*.

During the 1914-1918 war the aeroplanes used by the Bulgarian Army were all of German or Austrian make, and appear to have been piloted by Germans or Austrians, judging by captures made in the Balkan war area.

DANISH.

(Scandinavian pages Revised by E. Hildesheim, B.A.)

Aerial Societies:—

Det Danske Aeronautiske Selskab, 34 Amaliegade, Copenhagen.

Aerial Journals:—

Auto : 12, Rosengaarden, Copenhagen.
Motor : 42 Vimmelskaft, Copenhagen.

AVIATORS.

(The numbers are, when not otherwise stated, those issued by the Danish Aero Club).

Svendsen (1)	Lünd-Hansen (29)	O. F. Möller (55)
Thorup (2)	Foltman (30)	G. Erlind (56)
Nervö (3)	Bjarkow (31)	H. J G. S. Erlind (57)
Nielsen (4)	Buhl (32)	W. G. G. H. Watervall
Severinsen (5)	Engberg (33)	(58)
Ullidtz (6)	Larsen (34)	C. Bohnstedt Petersen
Ussing (7)	Sætter-Lassen (35)	(59)
Christiansen (8)	Eivil (36)	C. J. L. Jansen (60)
Laub (9)	Koch (37)	
Prince Axel (10)	Möller-Jörgensen (38)	Pollner (German
Grut (12)	Sörensen (39)	certificate No. 657)
Hammelev (13)	P. F. Yde (40)	Leth-Jensen
von der Maase (14)	A. J. Rasmussen (41)	(French certificate)
Kofoed-Jensen (15)	A. Andersen (42)	Kraüse-Jensen
Waage-Jensen (16)	J. G. Johansen (43)	(French certificate)
Caspersen (17)	H. I. Hansen (44)	Willing-Nielsen (killed
Ekman (18)	K. U. Hansen (45)	on voluntary service
Gundel (19)	E. Hildesheim (46)	in France, March,
Jörgensen (20)	R. Houndinghouse	1918)
Erlind (21)	Jensen (47)	Hildesheim (Swedish
Ehlers (22)	R. Ziemsen (48)	certificate No. 120)
Hansen (23)	V. A. C. Arndal (49)	Christoffersen
Stockfleth (24)	C. C. J. Förslev (50)	(American certificate,
Friese (25)	R. Rasmussen (51)	killed 1916).
Flor-Jacobsen (26)	H. R. M. Herschind (52)	Uffe (killed on voluntary
Holfelt (27)	K. R. K. Höyer (53)	service in France,
Bildsöe (28)	L. Sörensen (54)	11/9/1915).

Killed.

1913. 10/10.	1918.
Birch	Kabell
	Larsen
1915. 27/7.	Ekmanen
Hoeck	Ubbesen
	Caroc
	Friese
1917. 27/6.	
Hammelev	1919
Stockfleth	Flohr-Jacobsen

Flying Grounds:—

Christianshaven by Copenhagen.
Lundtofte.
Avedöre.
Viborg.

Army Aeroplanes:—

Caudron, Henry and *Maurice Farman. H. Morane-Saulnier,
N. & W., Scea, Vickers.*

Navy Aeroplanes:—

Flying boats, 100—200 h.p. } Danish construction.
Seaplanes   160   „   }

Naval Air Stations:—

Copenhagen, harbour and sheds.
Slipshavn, shed.

Aircraft Companies:—

NIELSEN & WINTHER A/s, Oresundsvej, Copenhagen.
VIKING AEROPLANE & MOTOR CO., 2, Toldbodgade,
Copenhagen.

A DANISH SERVICE FLYING BOAT, photographed from another aeroplane.

Front View of Nielsen & Winther Nieuport type Chaser Biplane.

For the countries, CENTRAL AMERICAN, CHILIAN,
and CHINESE, see pages immediately
following Austro-Hungarian.

Three-quarter Rear View of Nielsen & Winther Nieuport type Chaser Biplane.

A Nielsen & Winther Seaplane.

A Danish Government biplane, designed and built in the Government Workshops.

A Danish Flying Boat built by the Danish Navy.

A Danish seaplane, built by the Danish Navy.

FRENCH.

FRENCH MILITARY AND NAVAL AVIATION.

(By JEAN LAGORGETTE.)

Military aviation in France dates from 1910. Up to then, outside four balloon sections organised by Colonel Hirschauer, a few soldiers—some of them officers—interested themselves personally and individually in the testing and piloting of aeroplanes.

On January 1st, 1910, the Aero Club of France instituted the regulations concerning pilots' certificates, and it is in January and February, 1910, that the birth of military aviation may be placed, by the formation of the first "phalanx" of military aviators. A number of officers who had passed for their certificates took part in various tests, such as the Circuit de l'Est, and did splendid performances, in spite of frequent disaster.

THE FIRST MILITARY USE OF AEROPLANES.

In September, 1910, there took place the first aerial manœuvres in Picardie, and as a result of the experience it was concluded that avions (military aeroplanes) could be used in war, and that it was important to develop their employment.

On October 20th, 1910, General Roques was nominated to the new post of Permanent Inspector of Military Aeronautics (Inspecteur Permanent de l'Aéronautique Militaire).

In 1911, there were numerous fine performances, the first regional schools for military aviation were formed, then came regional manœuvres, flights by escadrilles [An escadrille does not quite correspond to a British squadron.—Ed.] under Colonel Etévé, the Paris-Rome flight and the European Circuit by Naval Ensign Conneau, the Grand Manœuvres of 1911, cavalry manœuvres at the Camp de Mailly, competitions for the test of co-operation of aeroplanes and artillery, and finally the Military Competition, in which the machines had to satisfy arduous conditions.

The Department of Inspection of Military Aeronautics was created under the Minister of War, and was placed under the control of General Roques, later himself Minister of War. The flying personnel was recruited in various Arms and was not organised into a special Corps. It was without distinct organisation, but it had modified autonomy. The matériel depended at the same time on the artillery and on the engineers.

THE RECONSTRUCTION OF 1912.

On February 2nd, 1912, M. Millerand, Minister of War, co-ordinated this embryonic organisation, of which he maintained the general lines. He created a special bureau attached to the engineers to deal with matériel. He created aviation parks, central and secondary, with sheds for the machines. The first of these parks was installed in March, at Verdun, with repair shops, stores, etc.

At the end of February, the Association Générale Aéronautique took the initiative in organising a National Subscription to present to the Army aeroplanes, landing grounds with sheds, and funds for instruction. It was seconded by Le Comité National Pour L'Aviation Militaire, under the presidency of Sénateur-aviateur Reymond and by the Press generally.

At the end of March, M. Millerand, Minister of War, fixed the rules for the recruiting of personnel. Colonel Hirschauer was then nominated Permanent Inspector of Aeronautics, and on June 29th, 1912, the Women's Aero Club, known as the Stella, presented to him a flag for the aeronautic troops.

PROGRESS IN 1912.

In the second half-year of 1911, the number of pilots and pupils were 120, and between them they had covered a distance of 300,000 kilometres in that period. At the end of June, 1912, there were 250 aviators, or more than double the number, and in this first half-year they had covered 650,000 kilometres.

Commencing with June 25th, 1912, the test for military aviation certificates became more rigorous. It included a triangular voyage of 200 kilometres in two journeys or more; two voyages of 150 kilometres in a straight line, and 45 minutes flying at a height of at least 800 m. The commissaries at the start and finish were agreed upon by the Aero Club of France.

At this time, M. Michelin, the famous tyre manufacturer, with his usual foresight, presented a handsome prize for a competition for bomb dropping.

THE AERONAUTICAL ESTABLISHMENT.

On August 28th, 1912, a decree by the President of the Republic created ten Aeronautic Sections, composing (with seven companies already existing) three Groups forming Aviation Corps—the first at Versailles, the second at Reims, and the third at Lyon.

Headquarter's Staff was composed of Lieut.-Col. Bouttieaux (1st Group); Lieut.-Col. Breton (2nd Group); and Lieut.-Col. Estienne (3rd Group). An administrative personnel was included in the scheme.

Lieut.-Col. Voyer was nominated Director of Aeronautical Matériel at Chalais-Meudon, which became ultimately the S.F.A. (*Service des Fabrications de l'Aeronautique*). [This corresponded almost exactly in its scheme, and in its ultimate effect with the Royal Aircraft Factory at Farnborough.—Ed.]

NAVAL AERONAUTICS.

Naval aeronautics were organised as from March, 1913, and comprised a double system of observation with airships and hydro-aeroplanes—one section for the Mediterranean and the other for the Ocean.

A MODIFICATION OF 1913.

On April 22nd, 1913, a new decree was issued, modifying the organisation of military aeronautics, notably the attributes of the Permanent Inspector. He was now charged first as Inspector of technical affairs, personnel, and materiel, and secondly to direct the formation of the personnel and to command the schools.

In October, 1913, the direction of military aeronautics was confided to General Bernard, who militarised the Service, and the office of Permanent Inspector passed from Colonel Hirschauer to Colonel Romazotti.

The Permanent Inspector, theoretically powerful, could not in fact manage the aeronautic finances. The duty of the Inspector was to keep in touch with the resources and progress of aeronautics in general, but it was the Fourth Directorate (The Engineers) who managed the finance which was voted, and the Aeronautical Section, created in February, 1912, by M. Millerand in the Fourth Directorate, had not the necessary personnel to bring its task to a satisfactory issue. A central organisation was necessary, which had to be an autonomous directorate. Its rôle was to put order into the multiplicity of little institutions not organised. (See report of M. Bénazet in the Chamber of Deputies, November 17th, 1913.)

THE DEVELOPMENTS OF 1914.

In January, 1914, at the moment when Senateur Reymond (who later fell on the Field of Honour), was criticising severely the Military Aeronautical Service, a presidential decree instituted a Superior Council for military aeronautics. This was charged with co-ordinating the efforts of public services and private initiative for aeronautical progress and in the military application thereof.

On February 21st, 1914, M. Noulens, Minister of War, approved a decree separating aerostation (that is airships and balloons) from aviation (aeroplanes). He suppressed the old Directorate of Aeronautical Matériel and transformed the establishment at Chalais-Meudon. He replaced the services of the Directorate of Matériel by special autonomous establishments as follows:—

1.—The Central Establishment for Aerostation Matériel, comprising all the services of military aerostation, such as the laboratory of aerology and of telephotography.

2.—Le Service des Fabrications de l'Aviation (S.F.A.), comprising the purchases for military aviation, and the workshops for motor repairs. It controlled in a permanent fashion the construction of machines in the constructors' works, and not only the reception of finished machines.

[Incidentally, this Establishment, before it was reformed towards the end of 1917, had done serious harm to the French Service d'Aviation Militaire.—Ed.]

3.—The Aeronautical Laboratory—Chalais-Meudon.

4.—The Aviation Laboratory—Vincennes.

These last two were to carry out practical experiments.

A NEW TECHNICAL ESTABLISHMENT.

Another decree of the same date created another autonomous establishment; La Section Technique de l'Aviation Militaire (S.T.A.), which has become during the war La Section Technique de l'Aeronautique (S.T. Aé.), now including aerostation. This was charged with theoretical studies under Commandant Dorand.

An Inspectorate of Aviation Matériel was attached for the administration of the S.T.A. [This corresponded pretty well to the British A.I.D. and operated in a very similar manner.—Ed.]

THE DUTIES OF THE INSPECTORATES.

The two Inspectorates depended upon the Minister—that is to say, on the Directorate of Aeronautics at the Ministry of War. Their attributes were, notably, consolidation of technical instruction; the allotting of certificates; control of aerial service; the checking of matériel in service and in reserve; the study on the spot of technical observations and the consideration of extension or creation of aviation centres.

The Technical Inspector of Aviation was besides charged with the higher direction of the schools.

The old Permanent Inspectorate of Aerostation matériel was transformed into a Technical Inspectorate, the two Permanent Inspectors, Col. Caron for aviation, and Col. Romazotti for aerostation, became Technical Inspectors.

The Directorate of Aeronautics at the War Ministry existed, crowning the two branches, but it could not assure unity of views, or avoid friction, complications and delays. This was at the period when, on February 25th, England handed over her seaplanes and airships to the Navy and kept the heavier-than-air machines for the Army.

FRENCH NAVAL AVIATION.

In France, Parliament having voted thirty million francs for Naval aviation, M. Monis, Minister of Marine, allotted eight and a half millions of it to the first year, 1914.

On March 13th of that year, two Naval officer aviators, Ensigns de l'Escaille and Destrem, made the sea crossing from France to Corsica on a seaplane.

For the first time, from May 15th–19th, seaplanes participated in Naval manœuvres, notably at Bizerte. (Ensigns Delage, de l'Escaille, etc.)

The Naval centre at Fréjus—St. Raphael was reserved for tests, studies, and instruction in Naval aeronautics, and two other centres were then to be created, but delays occurred, money was not voted, programmes were not realised.

According to a French communiqué, in August, 1914, Naval aviation was possessed of 8 experimental hydravions and an effective total of 200 men.

On the 1st October, 1918, French Naval Aviation comprised 1,264 avions or hydravions, of which 870 were on active service, the balance being used at the Schools for training, etc.

There were also 58 airships and 198 kite balloons and 11,000 men.

During the last year of the war only,—from November 1st, 1917, to November 1st, 1918,—the Naval avions accomplished 70,700 hours' flying and had covered 3,721,670 miles, and the airships in the same Service had done 13,152 hours' flying and had covered 523,970 miles.

These figures give an idea of the effort accomplished by the Franco-British Services in the fight against German submarines for the defence of the coasts and for the spotting of mines.

On October 1st, 1918, the distribution of French Naval Aircraft on active service was as follows:—

Station.	Aeroplanes and Seaplanes.	Airships	Kite Balloons.
Dunkirk to Cherbourg	168	21	22
Brittany	104	11	39
The Loire to the Bidassoa ..	74	7	21
French Mediterranean Coast ..	110	4	41
Corsica	38	2	—
Portugal	16	—	—
Algeria and Tunis	176	11	31
Morocco and Senegal	44	—	—
Corfu	54	3	12
Ægean Sea	86	—	32

MILITARY PROGRESS.

Always recruiting and instruction progressed well; military pilots became experts to such an extent that the War Ministry had to forbid aerobatic flying, in the hopes of reducing breakages due to inexperience or imprudence.

THE OUTBREAK OF WAR.

Immediately on mobilisation, August 1st, 1914, aerial navigation was forbidden, except by the Military.

Alongside the Directorate of Aeronautics at the Ministry of War, where General Hirschauer had succeeded General Roques, a new organisation—which made a twelfth Directorate—was formed. This was the Directorate of Aeronautics at Army Grand Headquarters. This was confided to Commandant Barés, himself a pilot, who remained in office for three years. With him was Commandant Girod, Captains de Goys (aviator), Jaillet (airship pilot), Tulasne, etc.

Commandant Girod became ultimately a Colonel, and in 1917 Commandant Du Peuty controlled this important Service. At the moment of writing, Colonel Duval is at the head, with Commandant Dorsemaine as chief assistant.

Also there was a great development in the military aeronautical repair workshops under Commandant Duperron, which at the end of 1917 were under Commandant Laroche.

A group of French officer-aviators and N.C.O. aviators, on active service.

HOME DEFENCE & DEVELOPMENTS BEHIND THE FRONT.

As a result of incursions by German avions, there was created a special Aeronautical Service for the "Entrenched Camp of Paris," at first under the orders of Commandant Girod, and later under Commandant Leclerc.

For the formation of pilots, the development of schools became necessary. An Inspectorate was created under Commandant Girod, and this was ultimately transformed into a Directorate of Schools and Aviation Depots. There Lieut.-Col. Girod continues to command with his usual zeal.

Under a decree of August 21st, 1915, the pre-war organisation which existed theoretically, but greatly developed, was somewhat modified. Aerostation, which owed its pre-eminence to its age and importance of its Service more than to the complexities of its duties, had the first place, and after a period of separation, aviation and aerostation tended to re-unite. A report of the Ministry of War had shown the importance at the Front of aerostation, kite balloons, etc., the relation of the numerous studies common to aviation and aerostation, particularly those concerning armament, munitions, explosives, optical apparatus, etc., and demonstrated the extension to both services of questions concerning meteorology, photography, etc.

In consequence, La Section Technique de l'Aviation (S.T.A.) became and has remained La Section Technique de l'Aéronautique (S.T.Aé.) with extended attributes. It remained under the command of Colonel Dorand, but his personnel, reduced in 1914 to a few officers, developed till it included some hundreds of soldiers.

At the beginning of 1918, Colonel Dorand took the new post of Inspecteur-Général des Etudes et Expériences Techniques, while Commandant Caquot, the inventor of the sausage-balloons which bear his name, replaced him at the head of the S.T.Aé.

REFORM OF THE TECHNICAL BRANCH.

The same decree of August 21st, 1915, suppressed the Inspectorate of Aviation Matériel, The Aeronautic Laboratory, and the Aviation Laboratory. The General Inspectorate of Aeronautical Matériel was re-established in October, 1916, under Commandant Raymond Sée, formerly Assistant to Colonel Duperron, Director of Repair Workshops of the Aerostation branch at St. Cyr.

Also, it is known that the Aéro-technic Institution at St. Cyr, founded by M. Deutsch de la Meurthe, and presented by him to the University of Paris, has now been placed for the duration of the war at the disposition of the Military Authorities represented by the Section Téchnique.

THE POSITION AT THE END OF 1915.

Thus, at the end of August, 1915, the special establishments for Military Aeronautics comprised :—

1.—Schools and aviation depots, divided into three groups.
2.—Central Establishment for Aerostation Matériel.
3.—Le Service des Fabrications de l'Aviation Militaire (S.F.A.).
4.—La Section Technique de l'Aeronautique Militaire (S.T.Aé.).

Each of these groups were under an officer of superior rank—that of Colonel.

Commandant Dorand had, until then, commanded la Section Technique de l'Aviation, but it was Lieut.-Col. Fleuri who took over the direction of the Section Technique de l'Aeronautique, retaining under his authority Commandant Dorand so far as aviation was concerned.

[This was at the moment when the extension of naval aeronautics in England resulted in the creation of a Director of Air Services, under Admiral Vaughan Lee, while Commodore Sueter, formerly Director of the Air Department, became Superintendent of Aircraft Construction.—Ed.]

A little later, the French Government decided on the creation of an Under-Secretariat of State for the Fifth Arm. General Hirschauer, Director of Aeronautics, was placed at the disposal of the Commander-in-Chief, and took a command at the Front. A member of Parliament, M. René Besnard, a talented young lawyer, was placed at the head of the new Department, and took the title of Under Secretary of State for Aeronautics.

Specialists, those interested, the Press and public opinion had already given voice over a "crisis in aviation," and apparently were under the illusion that with the stroke of a pen one man could transform the whole situation from top to bottom. In spite of all his goodwill and his activity, M. René Besnard could not hold the superhuman role which had been thrust upon him, but nevertheless he made several happy decisions, some of which—thanks to the slowness of official methods—only bore fruit after his disappearance.

M. Besnard wished to rely upon the counsels of recognised authorities. At his proposal, the Ministry of War instituted a Consulting Committee on Military Aviation, of which the General Secretary, Lieut.-Col. Mayer, was at the same time the Chief of the Cabinet of the Under-Secretary. The first meeting took place on October 21st, 1916. Col. Bouttieaux was attached to the Under-Secretary, as formerly to General Hirschauer, and very little of the Personnel of the Directorate was changed.

M. Painlevé, as Minister of War, retained M. Besnard in the Under-Secretariat.

On November 22nd, the Service of Personnel and Matériel of the S.F.A. took the name of the Service Industriel de l'Aeronautique Militaire (S.I.A.M.) and was attached directly to the Under-Secretariat under Col. Gerard. He was replaced at the head of the S.F.A. by Lieut.-Col. of Artillery Raibaud, while at the S.T.Aé. Lieut.-Col. Fleuri was replaced by Battery Commander of Artillery Lafay, who retained Commandant Dorand for special aviation service. M. Lafay soon resigned because of illness, and Commandant Dorand, now promoted to Lieut.-Col., became again Director of the S.T.Aé., which he founded in 1914.

In turn, Colonels Stammler, Bertrand and Richard, in 1917, were appointed to Chalais-Meudon.

At the end of a few months, a new press compaign resulted in the resignation of M. Besnard and his replacement by Col. Régnier, Director of Aeronautics at the Ministry of War, with Commandant Faure as second in command. There was less talk about "an aviation crisis" in the papers, and the task of Col. Regnier was executed in silence and without abuse—or at any rate with much less abuse than formerly.

THE 1917 ALTERATIONS.

As soon as General Lyautey was appointed Minister of War, he interested himself in obtaining the best possible Aeronautical Services, and in assuring unity of views and of control, as well as a more close linking up between the branches of the different Services and the Armies in the Field. To this praiseworthy end the decree of February 12th, 1917, created for the duration of the war a General Directorate of Aeronautical Services, which was placed under Brigadier-General Guillemin of the Artillery.

As the direct representative of the Minister, he was able to establish a complete link with the Naval Aeronautical Service and with Allied Armies. He had under his authority the Director of Aeronautics, who was still Col. Régnier. He had power on all the Fronts ; he was able to learn the needs and desires of the Armies ; to make decisions concerning construction and organisation of new units ; to dispose of troops and matériel ; to direct the research of instructors ; to intensify production and to ensure economy.

[It was at this period that Lord Cowdray became President of the Air Board in England.—Ed.]

A QUICK CHANGE PERIOD.

This Directorate only lasted for a few days. About April 1st, following on a change in the Government, the Under-Secretariat for Aviation was re-established and was given to M. Daniel Vincent, a former aeroplane observer. Col. Régnier remained for a long time as his Assistant.

There was then created an Inter-Allied Aeronautical Service, under the direction of M. P. E. Flandin, a Deputy, and a former pilot.

On June 15th, 1917, M. Daniel Vincent created an inter-ministerial Commission for civil aeronautics, under the Presidency of M. d'Aubigny, Deputy—analogous to the British Civil Aerial Transport Committee.

Following on another ministerial crisis, M. Dumesnil replaced M. Vincent, and was still in office in April, 1918.

THE IMPORTANT ALTERATION.

The principal modification of the interior organisation of Military Aeronautical Services took place in November, 1917. The Service of Aviation Construction (which was more or less the development of the original S.F.A.), with the organisations dependent thereon, was placed thenceforth under the direction of the Ministry of Armament—M. Loucheur.

Maritime Aeronautics, which up to then had been independent, was re-united with Military Aviation in the hands of the Under-Secretariat for Military Aeronautics, and this itself was joined to the Ministry of Armament to assure in concert with him the efficiency of the S.F.A.

The same ministerial decision nominated M. Gille, chief engineer of naval construction, as Chief of the Central Office of the S.F.A., at the Ministry of Armament and War Material.

A decree of the same date nominated as Director of Military Aeronautics Lieut.-Col. Paul-Francois Dhé, replacing Lieut.-Col. A. E. Greffart. Also the Under-Secretary of State nominated as Chief of his Cabinet, Col. Lalanne, a pilot aviator.

GENERAL REFLECTIONS.

Such, up to April, 1918, was the organisation of Military Aeronautics in France. This disquisition may be a trifle confused and may not seem to disclose a clear line of evolution. This is due to successive modifications in a multitude of organisations created without an inclusive plan before the war, merely as immediate needs demanded. The whole organisation is an empirical product of variable necessities, and not the result of an elaborate project. Possibly it is none the worse for that.

The attachment of Military Aeronautics to the Ministry of Armament at first excited considerable agitation, because it seemed to break up the unity of Military Aeronautics, but aviation depends on the Ministry of War as well as the Ministry of Armament, and on certain sides it concerns the Navy. Meanwhile, in practice, the system has not presented any great inconvenience. Institutions are worth what the men in them are worth.

CHANGES IN 1918.

The principal change during 1918 in the personnel of the Service d'Aviation Militaire has been the suppression of the Under-Secretariat of Aeronautics following on the resignation of M. Dumesnil in consequence of bad health. He was replaced by a Director of Aeronautics attached to the Ministry of War despite which fact he has up to the present also controlled Civil Aeronautics, the administration of which remains under military authority. The first Director of Aeronautics has been Colonel Dhé, formerly collaborating with the Under Secretary.

On the 20th April, 1919, he was replaced by General Duval.

THE PERSONNEL OF THE SERVICE.

As regards the Personnel of the French Aviation Services, in which the conditions of test are becoming more strict, it is to be noted that up to 1915 the Aero Club of France allotted the civil certificates—that is to say, certificates of the Fédération Aeronautique Internationale (F.Aé.I.).

These certificates, for which the tests took place on a track or aerodrome, constituted a kind of first degree, nevertheless, they sufficed for more than one civilian pilot early in the war to qualify him as a military pilot. As to the military certificate, it was allotted for a series of more difficult tests across country and observation by officers, or by civilians appointed by the Aero Club. In the first instance, the certificate was delivered direct by the Military Authorities, and in the second on the proposal of the Aero Club.

Since 1915—from which time the aerodromes were crowded—there have been no civil certificates, but the Aero Club, by way of compensation, allots its pilot's certificate, when so desired, to all holding the military certificate, as the latter have to satisfy more rigorous conditions.

At the beginning of the war the Service d'Aviation Militaire was possessed of 21 escadrilles of which the total effectives including pilots, observers and mechanics was only 4,343 persons. At the signing of the Armistice the French Army included 6,000 avions, 6,417 pilots, and 1,682 observers. The total effectives of the aeronautical troops exceeded 80,000 men.

THE AERO CLUB DE FRANCE.

Meantime, the Aero Club of France has played its part. It has supplied a vast amount of information ; it has acted as an intelligence office, and has rendered many services to the Military Authorities, especially at the beginning of the war ; and it has published illustrations of Allied and enemy avions, booklets, and so forth. As a source of propaganda and education, it has been of high value.

The number of certificated pilots has grown, not in arithmetical progression, but in geometrical progression. According to *L'Aérophile*, of November, 1917, one sees that from 900 pilots in 1912, the number grew to 2,700 at the end of 1915, to 5,000 at the end of 1916, and to 7,700 towards October, 1917. As to the actual figures of pilots on Active Service, this of course must remain unknown to the public.

The number of Aviators' certificates delivered to the Aero Club of France has grown from 1,718 at the beginning of the war to 15,845 at the end of March, 1919.

LOSSES.

During the war 1,215 French aviators have been killed for certain.

Added to these must be 1,344 aviators reported as missing, which only signifies that it has not been possible officially to discover the cause of their death.

Thus there are 2,559 aviators killed.

Besides this there have been 2,843 wounded.

This total of 5,400 and odd killed and wounded represents a considerable proportion of the effectives of aviation.

Among the pilots, most of the distinguished civil aviators of the past have in turn disappeared, such as Gilbert, Garros, Védrines, etc. The younger "Aces" who came into being during the war have also lost many of their best, such as Guynemer, Maxime Lenoir, Chaput, etc., but France still has the "Ace of Aces" of all the belligerent Armies, René Fonck, and a constellation of young pilots whose sole desire is to surpass their predecessors.

It is estimated that 2,049 enemy avions have certainly been brought down by French aviators, but there is reason to believe that the official statistics are incomplete, and that this figure has been considerably surpassed without counting the doubtfuls.

AN IMPRESSION OF RESULTS.

As regards the results achieved by the French Aviation Service, according to an official communiqué, during 77 days from December 1st, 1917, to February 15th, 1918, in spite of this being the worst period of the year for weather, the French avions made 22,518 flights, either chasing, bombarding, artillery observing, infantry contact, or reconnaissance. 104 enemy avions were brought down during the same period, of which 39 fell in the French Lines, and only 38 French machines were lost, either behind the French Lines or in enemy territory. 1,400 photographic flights were made, and during these 21,328 photographs were taken. Such is a fine record for the worst period of the year, and may give some impression of what is done in the periods when weather and daylight permit greater activities.

B

BLÉRIOT Aeroplanes. L. Blèriot, "Blériot-Aeronautique," 39, Route de la Révolte, Paris, Levallois. Flying grounds: Buc, Pau, and Brooklands (England). L. Blériot began to experiment in 1906, along Langley lines. By 1909 he was one of the leading French firms; and the first cross Channel flight was made by him on July 9th, 1909.

At the beginning of war the *Blériot* "Parasols," which afford the pilot a perfectly clear view below him, did much valuable reconnaissance work. The "tandem" type also did much good work. Later, these machines were found to be too slow for modern requirements, and the Blériot works at Buc and in Paris were turned on to produce various other types of machines required by the French Government.

Details of 1914 standard types:—

		XI 1-seater.		XI.—2 2-seater.		XI.—2 Hydro		39 Armoured		43 2-seater.	
Length	… … feet (m)	25½	7·80	27½	8·400	29½	9	20¼	6·15	20	6·12
Span	… … feet (m)	28	8·50	33¾	10·350	36¼	11·05	33	10·10	33	10·10
Area	… … sq. feet (m².)	150	14	215	20	226	21	205	19	207	19·3
Weight … {	unladen, lbs. (kgs.	660	300	770	350	1100	500	925	420	770	350
	useful …lbs. (kgs.	330	150	607	275	550	250	385	175	607	275
Motor	… … … h.p.	60 { Gnome Le Rhone		80 Gnome		80 Le Rhone		80 Gnome		80 Gnome	
Speed … {	max. m.p.h. (km.)	68	110	75	120	68	110	78	125	78	125
	min. m.p.h. (km.)	…		…		…		…		…	
	asc. f.p.m. (m.)	490	150	230	70	197	60	328	100	470	143
Endurance	… … hrs.	…		…		…		…		…	

Note.—The monos., as usual, are of wood construction; wheels only for landing. Rectangular section bodies. Warping wings, elevator in rear. Hydros fitted with self-starters.

Blériot PARASOL reconnaissance machine of 1914-15.

Type XI—2. Standard "tandem" military monoplane developed from the single-seat Type XI. Blériot monoplane used (alongside a B.E.2a) on the very first RFC reconnaissance over German lines, 19 August 1914.

BOREL. G. Borel & Cie, 25 rue Brunel, Paris. Established 1910. Capacity: about 25 machines a year.

Model.		1913. Monoplane.	1913. Monocoque racer.	1913. Hydro-mono. 2-seater.
Length	… …	22 feet (6·70 m.)	19 feet (5·80 m.)	27 feet (8·30 m.)
Span	… …	30 feet (9·15 m.)	26 feet (8·00 m.)	37 feet (11·25 m.)
Area	…	152 sq. ft. (14 m².)	116 sq. ft. (11 m²)	237 sq. ft. (22 m².)
Weight {	total	530 lbs. (240 kgs.)	608 lbs. (276 kgs.)	880 lbs. (399 kgs.)
	useful …	287 lbs. (130 kgs.)	…	…
Motor	… …	50 Gnome	80 Gnome	80 Gnome
Speed	… (p.h.)	71 m. (115 km.)	94 m. (150 km.)	62 m. (100 km.)

Note.—The monocoque is of wood and steel construction, the others wood only. The monocoque has coque body. the others ordinary rectangular section. Floats of the hydro as illustrated. For the rest the ordinary mono. is practically on the same lines as the 1912. Some 8 Borel seaplanes in RNAS service at start of war and others in French use. Two-seat ship spotter.

Hydro-avion.

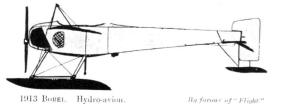

1913 BOREL. Hydro-avion.   *By favour of "Flight"*

The Type 14 A.2 Bréguet Bomber with 300 h.p. Renault Engine.

BRÉGUET. Soc. Anonyme des Ateliers d'Aviation, Louis Bréguet. Paris office : 25, Boulevard Jules Sandeau. Head office : Velizy per Chaville (S-et-O). Aerodrome : Villacoublay.

Owned and directed by M. Louis Bréguet, one of the great pioneers of French aviation. M. Bréguet was one of the first designers to produce a satisfactory tractor biplane.

Has always specialised on steel construction. Made the best seaplane of 1913. Built in collaboration with the Bristol Co. in 1914. One of his machines won its class in the "Concours des Avions Puissants" in 1915.

THE BRÉGUET BIPLANE, TYPE 14 A.2.

Type of machine	Bréguet Biplane.
Name or type No. of machine ..	14 A.2.
Purpose for which intended ..	Reconnaissance, photography and artillery spotting.
Span	14.364 metres.
Overall length	9 m.
Maximum height	3.3 m.
Total surface of wings	49 sq. m.
Engine type and h.p.	300 h.p. Renault.

Performance.
  Speed low down .. .. .. 190 kms. per hour.
Climb.
  To 5,000 metres in 21 minutes 45 seconds.
  Ceiling at 6,100 metres.

THE THREE-MOTORED BRÉGUET—Three 250 h.p. Renault Engines. Flew for three hours at a height of 2,500 metres with a load of 1200 kilogrammes.

Military 2-seater. 1914 type with rigid wings and ailerons. Used for reconnaissance at start of war by French, British and Italian services. RFC nickname "Tin Whistle". 110 h.p. Slamson-Canton-Unné radial engine, offering 68 mph.

Bristol T.B.8 Biplane built by the Bréguet firm.

THE BRÉQUET BIPLANE. Type M.5 bomber. Winner of the competition for high-powered Avions in Oct., 1915 and much used for night-bombing in 1916-17. Developed from earlier Br M.4 light bomber with similar 220 h.p. Renault engine, itself an improved Br M.2 type (200 h.p. Canton-Unné) of 1915.

THE BRÉQUET TYPE 14 B.2.

(Translated by a Neutral Contributor).

In a German technical journal, the automobile and aerotechnical paper "Der Motorwagen," an extensive description of the *Breguet* 14 *B.2* biplane, with a 300 h.p. Renault engine, is to be found in the issues of July 30th and Aug. 10th.

THE WINGS.

This biplane, characterised by two sets of struts, is produced almost exclusively of aluminium, and is intended for bombing purposes. The upper planes have a backwards stagger of 0.21 m. and a span of 14.4 m., and are mounted on a cabane frame, while the lower planes have a span of 13.77 m.

Both upper and lower planes have large cuttings at the fuselage and their arrow shape amounts to 175 deg. The angle of incidence of the upper planes is 4.5 deg. in the middle and 2.5 deg. at the ends, that of the lower ones decreasing from 3 deg. to 2 deg.

The spars of both planes are drawn aluminium tubes of rectangular section 65.6 × 34.6 mm. The thickness of the walls of these tubes amounts in the inner section of the upper plane to 2.6 mm., elsewhere to 1.6 mm. The rear spar grows thinner towards the wing tips till the thickness of the edge, where auxiliary spars with ash bands of 6 mm. thickness and 3 mm. three-ply wood glued to both sides are provided. At the points of juncture and at the end of the stampings the spars are strengthened by ash pieces, in some instances of I shape. A socket of 20 cm. length, made of welded sheet steel of a thickness of 1.5 mm. is provided at the strut ends of the upper planes and at the strut bases. These sockets and the wooden linings are held in position by iron tube rivets.

The main spar of the upper plane is strengthened in the interior section of a pine support of a thickness of 10 mm. being fixed to one side of the spar by means of small brass screws. The spars of the upper planes are equipped with compression supports at the joints of the two sets of struts and the lower planes for the outer strut set, the support being an aluminium tube of the diameters 30 and 27 mm. exterior and interior. Further there are two aluminium ribs of a width of 40 mm., one at the beginning of the ailerons and one by the bomb store in the lower plane. The interior wiring consists of single wire.

The ribs are very strong. They have a depth of 2 mm. above, of 1.9 below. A web provided with weight diminishing holes is glued between the longitudinals of three-ply wood, 3 mm. thick. On both sides of the spars as well as at five points between them the flange is strengthened by glued and nailed birch laths and wrapped bands. The ribs are arranged loosely on the spars. The ribs lie parallel to the axis of longitude, forming in relation to the spars an angle corresponding with the arrow shape. They are connected with each other by means of the veneer planking, reaching on the upper side from the leading edge from the main spar, as well as by the leading and trailing edges. Further they are connected by two bands, lying behind each other and alternately wound from above and below the ribs. The distance between them amounts to 40 mm. Forward and in front of the rear spar more 4 mm. thick auxiliary ribs of plywood are arranged. To reinforce the aerofoil, thin birch ribs reaching to the trailing edge are screwed to the rear of the ribs on the underside.

The yellow-white coloured fabric is sewed to the ribs and secured with thin nailed strips where exposed to the airscrew draught. The provision of hooks and eyes on the under side of the planes behind the leading edge and in front of the trailing edge is to permit the draining off of moisture.

Only the upper planes are provided with ailerons, attached direct to the rear spar.

The part of the lower plane lying behind the rear spar is hinged along its total length and is pulled downwards by means of 12 rubber cords fixed on the under side of the ribs, the tension of these can be adjusted by means of screws, an automatic change of the aerofoil corresponding with the load and speed thus results with an easier control of the aeroplane with and without a load of bombs. The stampings for the hinges of the ailerons and the flexible lower plane pieces embrace the spars and are connected with them by means of bolts passing right through. The spars have no linings at these points.

The construction of the stampings of the spars is very simple. Several sheet steel pieces with corresponding angle pieces are fixed to the spars with two screws penetrating them.

The interplane struts are made of streamlined aluminium tubes with aluminium sockets in both ends. The inner struts are further strengthened by the insertion of riveted U iron. The aluminium employed has a strength of 40 kg. per sq. mm. with a stretching of 18 per cent.

The 4.5 mm. thick load carrying cables are double, the space between them being filled by a wooden lath. In the same manner the landing wires as well as those crossing from the upper planes forward and backwards of the fuselage are arranged, being wires of a thickness of 2½ mm. that are connected with the stampings and the turnbuckles in a primitive way by means of eyes and spiral wire pushed over. To give a better support to the lower planes, being much stressed by the bomb store, the load-carrying cables are in the inner section led to the stampings on the main ribs arranged by the bomb-store, and thence downwards to the landing gear. The rear spar of the upper planes is also provided with a cable to the fuselage between the cabane and strut.

The stampings for the fixing of the wiring is constructed very simply. A bent sheet metal of U form and with drilled holes for the bolts carries the nipples of the eyebolts.

THE FUSELAGE.

The canvas-covered body consists almost exclusively of aluminium tubes that are riveted with welded steel tube sleeves and spanned with wire. Only at specially stressed points in the front part have steel tubes been employed. The upper and lower sides of the fuselage are rounded by the employment of fairings.

The engine rests on aluminium U bearers that are supported by riveted aluminium struts. Two pairs of large view traps are provided below the seats of the pilot and observer, and are operated by cable by the observer.

THE UNDERCARRIAGE.

The very strong landing gear has three pairs of struts of aluminium streamline tubes, strengthened by U irons riveted in, and resting below on horizontal steel tubes. The wheel shaft rests in an auxiliary one of steel sheet in U shape welded on. The back root points of the struts are connected by means of a second steel tube auxiliary shaft, welded on, and by a tension band lying behind. A diagonal wiring is further provided horizontally in the auxiliary shaft level. The streamlining of the shafts is cut out in the middle behind the front auxiliary shaft to improve the sight downwards. There is only a diagonal wiring to the fuselage in the level of the middle struts.

The ash tail skid hangs in rubber springs from the fuselage and is strengthened in the rear end by a covering of a rectangular aluminium tube. Its wire stay is supported in the rear stem by a spiral spring. Leaf springs are further fixed to the end of the skid.

Tail plane, rudder and elevator are of welded thin steel tubes.

The aeroplane is equipped with complete dual control. The control in the observer's cockpit can be removed.

The ailerons are interconnected. The twin control cables run behind the rear spar of the lower planes to two direction changing rollers resting on a shaft. Here they part and are led as separate wires of thickness of 2 mm. to the uuderside of the ailerons. In the upper planes the ailerons are connected by control cables, governing two levers in each side. The ailerons are balanced and welded to a common shaft.

According to a label on the aeroplane the performance of the 12-cylinder Renault engine of V type is 300 h.p. at 1500–1600 normal r.p.m. The engine is the same as the 260 h.p. model, the increase in horse-power being the result of the employment of aluminium pistons and a greater number of revolutions. The engine drives the two bladed airscrew direct. The exhaust going inwards is led above the upper planes by a collector.

The aluminium radiator forms the front part of the fuselage, and is divided in the middle, each row of cylinders having thus its own cooling system with a separate water-pump.

THE PETROL SYSTEM.

Two gravity tanks of 130 litres capacity each are positioned behind the motor. As their underside lies only little above the carburettors an auxiliary tank of 5.6 litres capacity is provided in front of each carburettor behind the engine, the petrol being led on to the tank from the carburettor. These tanks fill themselves by gravity in horizontal or descending flight from the main tanks. Whereas, if the main tank may be unable to supply any more petrol in climbing, the auxiliary ones then feed the carburettor. Check non-return valves are mounted in the piping to prevent the petrol from running back into the main tanks.

As there is by this arrangement a petrol quantity of 11.2 litres in front of the carburettors without any possibility of being cut off, grave accidents may occur by carburettor fires.

The petrol level in the main tanks is indicated electrically by pressing a contact. A hard rubber tube is mounted in each tank inside a tube and wound with a resistance wire of 0.4 m. thickness, above which a cork float with contacts moves. An oil tank of 18 litres capacity is mounted on the right side of the engine. The fuel suffices for a flight of about 2½ hours' duration under ground conditions.

THE INSTRUMENTS.

On the instrument board, protected by a large Triplex safety glass, in aluminium framing, is mounted a tachometer, a watch, altimeter, two cooling water thermometers, the pressure buttons and the indicator arrangement of the petrol height with the dry cell battery lying behind, and the compass. To right of the pilot is to be found the manipulation of the radiator-blinding arrangement, the starting magneto, the petrol start spray pump, oil and petrol stop-cocks, as well as the connections for the illumination for night flying and for wireless. To left are the levers for the gas throttle, the spark timing, the regulation of extra air supply, the magneto switch, as well as a petrol stop-cock.

The observers' cockpit is arranged in the middle of the turning and raising machine-gun ring mounted on the top of the body. The seat is hinged so that the observer may sit either high or low on the bottom of the fuselage. The mounting of Cellon windows in both sides gives him an outside view. The bottom is of steel tube girder work, the sight being thus unhindered downwards when the sight-trap is opened by means of the cables arranged to right of the seat. On the right fuselage wall the bomb-dropping mechanism is mounted; to left levers connected with gas lever and magneto switch in the pilot's cockpit. To both sides are connections for wireless.

The aeroplane is equipped with illumination for night flying and with position lights on the outer struts. Under the root points of the front struts hanging provision for the mounting of searchlights is further to be found. The current for the light and the wireless is produced by a dynamo, which is mounted on a seat below the fuselage and driven by a propeller.

To left on the outside of the body a fixed machine-gun for the pilot is mounted, being operated from the camshaft of the left row of cylinders.

The observer is armed with two machine-guns clutched together and mounted on a raising and turning ring. As the ring is mounted high, the firing range forward is good.

The bomb store is mounted in the inner section of the power planes with a capacity of 16 small bombs, arranged hanging in two rows of eight. In the dropping operation the two bombs, lying behind each other, are released, at the same time, by a camshaft lying in front of the main spar. The camshafts are connected by chain drive with a shaft in cross position in the fuselage with a grooved pulley mounted, driven by a strong rubber cable. Another chain drive connects this shaft with a gear wheel mounted to right of the seat of the observer, on the shaft of which a locking quadrant as well as a transmission gear for the stretching of the rubber chord is keyed on. To load the bomb store the chain wheel is first by means of the crank-handle in the observers' cockpit turned till the locking engages again after revolution. When the rubber cord is thus much stretched the bombs are hung in. When the upper gear wheel is now released by pulling the locking lever for bomb-dropping, the stretched rubber cord starts turning the shaft lying across in the fuselage as well as the camshafts of the bomb stores, so that all bombs are released by one revolution. To enable a timing of the bomb dropping a glycerine brake cylinder, with adjustable throttle valve, is mounted in the chain drive leading upwards. Being connected with the inner bomb pairs and fixed to both sides of the seat, two special cables make the dropping of these four bombs possible, independently of the rest.

One aeroplane has further had a hanging provision for two large bombs mounted inside the cockpit to right of the seat of the pilot. The cables run to the observer.

The aiming arrangement is mounted inside the observer's cockpit on a swivelling arm on the left body side.

The empty weight of the aeroplane was fixed at 1,215 kg. A notice on the rudder gives the weight of the fuel at 216 kg., that of the normal useful load to 514 kg. and the maximum useful load at 614 kg. Reckoning with the normal load the total weight of the aeroplane loaded is thus 1,915 kg., corresponding with a load on the planes of 40 kg. per sq. m., as well as a performance load at 300 h.p. of 6½ kg. per h.p.

CHARACTERISTIC FEATURES.

Beside the usual backwards stagger to be found on other aeroplanes the following features should be emphasised : the high fuselage with the right-angled rudder and forward sharp rounded keel fin, the landing gear with three pairs of struts and a right-angled cutting of the streamlining of the shafts, the small arrow-shape of the trapeze-shaped planes with the sharp and large cuttings, the bomb stores projecting forwards in front of the planes, the triangular-fixed tail plane, the divided elevator, with cornered balance, as well as the dihedral upper planes and horizontal lower ones.

Specification.

Type of machine	Bréguet Biplane.
Name or type No. of machine ..	14 B.2.
Purpose for which intended	Day Bomber.
Span	14,364 metres.
Overall length	9 m.
Maximum height.. ..	3.3 m.
Total surface of wings ..	51 sq. m.
Engine type and h.p. ..	300 h.p. Renault.
Weight of machine empty	1,127 kilos.

Performance.

Speed low down .. .. 185 kms. per hour.

Climb.

To 5,000 m. in 47 min. 30 secs.
Ceiling at 5,750 metres.
Disposable load apart from fuel 882 kilos.

Armament : One gun in front (synchronised), 2 guns aft. 300 kilos. of bombs.

The Bréguet Biplane type 14 B.2 (300 h.p. Renault engine).

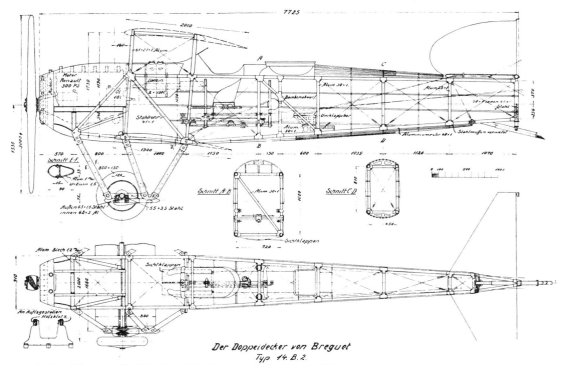

Sectional Plan and Side Elevation of the Fuselage of the Bréguet Biplane. Type 14 B.2.

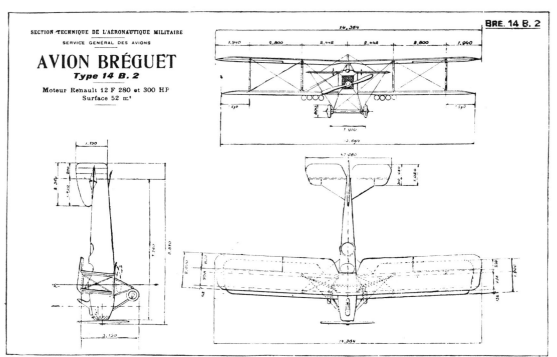

General Arrangement Drawing of the 14 B.2 as issued by the Bréguet firm.

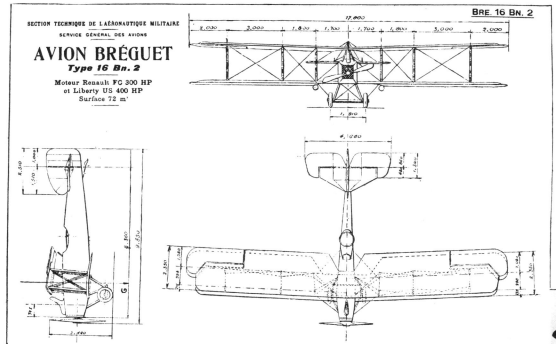

SECTION TECHNIQUE DE L'AÉRONAUTIQUE MILITAIRE
SERVICE GÉNÉRAL DES AVIONS

AVION BRÉGUET
Type 16 Bn. 2

Moteur Renault FC 300 HP
et Liberty US 400 HP
Surface 72 m²

BRE. 16 BN. 2

THE BRÉGUET BIPLANE, TYPE 16 B.N.2.

Type of machine	Two-seater Tractor Biplane.
Name or type No. of machine ..	16 B.N.2.
Purpose for which intended ..	Night Bomber.
Span	17 metres.
Chord	2.35 m.
Overall length	9.55 m.
Maximum height	3.42 m.
Total surface of wings ..	73.5 sq. m.
Span of tail	4.66 m.
Engine type and h.p. ..	Renault 300 h.p. or Liberty 400 h.p.
Airscrew	3.42 m. diam.
Weight of machine empty ..	1,265 kilos.

Performance.

Speed low down	.. ..	160 kms. per hour.

Climb.

To 4,000 metres in 51 minutes 10 seconds.
Ceiling 4,600 metres.

Disposable load apart from fuel : machine gun aft, and 550 kilos. of bombs=1130 kilos.

THE BRÉGUET BIPLANE, TYPE 17 C.2.

Type of machine	Bréguet Biplane.
Name or type No. of machine ..	17 C.2.
Purpose for which intended ..	Two-seat Fighter.
Span	14,280 metres.
Overall length	8.1 m.
Maximum height ..	3.42 m.
Total surface of wings ..	45.3 sq. m.
Engine type and h.p. ..	450 h.p. Renault.

Performance.

Speed low down	.. ..	225 kms. per hour.

Climb.

To 5,000 m. in 24 mins. 51 secs.
Ceiling at 7,000 metres.

Armament : Twin synchronised guns in front ; two guns aft. One gun firing below fuselage.

The Bréguet Biplane, type 17 C.2 (Renault 450 h.p. engine)

C

CAUDRON. René Caudron, Issy-les-Moulineaux. (Seine).

School : Le Crotoy (Aerodrome de la Baie de la Somme).

The *Caudron* has proved on active service to be one of the most useful French aeroplanes. It has been largely used for artillery control and for bomb-dropping, because of its great weight-lifting capacity, and its imperviousness to bad weather. Other firms whose own designs have not been successful have been turned on by the French Government to build *Caudrons*.

THE CAUDRON R.II TWIN-ENGINED BOMBER.

Type of machine	Caudron Twin Tractor.
Name or type No. of machine	R. II.
Purpose for which intended ..	Bombing.
Span	17.92 m. top ; 16.9 m. bottom plane.
Overall length	11.25 metres.
Maximum height ..	2.70 metres.
Engine type and h.p. ..	Hispano-Suiza, two 200 h.p.
Weight of machine empty ..	1,422 kgs.
Tank capacity in litres ..	220.

Performance.

Speed low down	.. ..	190 k.p.h. full ; 95 k.p.h. throttled.
Speed at 2,000 metres	..	185 k.p.h.
Speed at 3,000 metres	..	180 k.p.h.
Speed at 4,000 metres	..	173 k.p.h.
Speed at 5,000 metres	..	167.3 k.p.h.

Climb.

To 2,000 metres in 8·10 minutes.
To 3,000 metres in 14·3 minutes.
To 5,000 metres in 39 minutes.

Disposable load apart from fuel	..	..	..	405 kgs.
Total weight of machine loaded	..	..	..	2,167 kgs.

The Caudron Type R.II bomber, reconnaissance and escort biplane of 1918. (2—200 h.p. Hispano-Suiza engines.)

	G 4. Twin-Engine With Tail Booms.	R 4. Twin-Engine With Fuselage.
Length	7.3 m.	11.75 m.
Span	16.88 m.	21.13 m.
Area	36.796 sq. m.	72.4 sq. m.
Weight { machine ...	820 kgs.	1,680 kgs.
{ useful	500 kgs.	620 kgs.
Motor ... ... h.p.	Two 80 h.p. Le Rhônes	Two 140 h.p. Hispano-Suiza
Speed—max. m.p.h. (km.)	130 k.p.hr.	143 k.p.hr.

THE R4 TYPE CAUDRON, with Two 140 h.p. Hispano-Suiza Engines. Used for reconnaissance before R.II became available.

1917 Model.	G 3. 2-Seater.
Length	6.4 m.
Span	13.4 m.
Area	27 sq. m.
Weight { machine ..	418 kgs.
{ useful ..	290 kgs.
Motor .. .. h.p.	100 h.p. Anzani
Speed—max. m.p.h. (km.)	108 k.p.hr.

THE G3 TYPE CAUDRON, with 100 h.p. Anzani Engine, widely used for reconnaissance and training from 1914.

Twin-engine CAUDRON G.4 biplane. Two Le Rhône engines of 80 h.p. each. Machine fitted with mitrailleuse. This type, with these or with two Anzani engines of 100 h.p. each, was widely operated during 1915-16 as a bomb-dropper and as a fighting machine, later being used for reconnaissance and training.

THE CAUDRON. TYPE G.6.
Specification.

Type of machine	Twin-engined Biplane.
Name or type No. of machine ..	Caudron G6.
Span	17.21 m.
Overall length	8.6 m.
Maximum height	2.95 m.
Total surface of wings	39.7 sq. m.
Engine type and h.p.	2—80 or 110 h.p. Le Rhone.
Weight of machine empty ..	850-940 kgs.
Load per sq. m.	34-36.3 kgs.
Weight per h.p.	6-7.3 kgs.

Performance.

Speed low down	152 km.p.h.

Climb.

To 2,000 metres	9 mins.
To 3,000 metres	18 mins.
Disposable load apart from fuel	500 kgs.

Three-quarter View, from rear, of the experimental Caudron, Type C.23 Twin engined night bomber.

A Twin-engined Caudron Biplane of the tail-boom type, known as G.6. (2—110 h.p. Le Rhone engines.)

D

DEPERDUSSIN. Etablissements Deperdussin, 19 rue des Entrepreneurs, Paris. Established 1910. This firm broke up on the arrest of M. Deperdussin in 1913, but the receiver carried on the works, and these are now employed in building to French Government requirements. The machines are now known as the *S.P.A.D.* (Société Pour les Appariels Deperdussin).

1914 types.			Monocoque. single-seater.		2-seater.		Hydro.	
Length	...	... feet (m.)	19¾	6·02	24	7·30	29	8·85
Span	...	... feet (m.)	21¾	6·60	36¼	11·00	44¾	13·60
Area	...	... sq. feet (m².)	97	9	226	21	301	28
Weight	{ total, lbs. (kgs.)		991	450	1050	475	1380	625
	{ useful, lbs. (kgs.)		419	190	550	250	771	350
Motor	...	... h.p.	160 Le Rhone		80 Gnome		100 Gnome	
Speed	{ max., m.p.h. (km.)		131	210	105	170	75	120
	{ min., m.p.h. (km.)		...		56	90	53	85
	{ asc., f.p.m. (m.)		...		247	75	164	50
Endurance	...	... hrs.	...		...		...	

Notes.—Wood construction. Lateral control by warping. Mounted on wheels without skids. Fabric: "Monodep."

Armed monoplane with machine-gun arranged to fire over the propeller (1914 type).

DONNET.

Hydravions J. Donnet, 57, Rue de Villiers, Neuilly-sur-Seine. Works : 13a rue Levallois-Prolongé, Levallois-Perret, and at Sidi Abdallah, Ferryville, Tunis. (Manager at Ferryville : M. P. Jeltés.)

DONNET FLYING BOAT.

Type of machine	Donnet Flying Boat.
Name or type No. of machine	Type D.D., 200 h.p.
Purpose for which intended	Bombardment.
Span	16.80 m.
Gap	1.83 m.
Overall length	9 m. 50.
Maximum height	3 m.
Chord	Top plane, 2 m. ; Lower plane, 1 m. 45.
Total surface of wings	53 sq. m.
Span of tail	3 m. 20.
Total area of tail	7 sq. m.
Area of rudder	1.20 sq. m.
Area of each aileron	2 sq. m.
Maximum cross section of body	1 m. 20.
Engine type and h.p.	200 h.p. Hispano-Suiza.
Weight of machine empty	950 kgs.
Tank capacity in hours	4 hours.
Tank capacity in litres	140 each (two tanks).
Performance.	
Speed	130 km.p.h.
Landing speed	80 km.p.h.
Climb.	
To 1,000 metres	6.30 mins.
To 2,000 metres	15 mins.
Disposable load apart from fuel	650 kgs.
Total weight of machine loaded	1,800 kgs.

Three-ply wood central float or boat, so constructed that fixed tail fin forms part and whole with it. Two small three-ply floats at wing ends. Seat for pilot and observer side by side. Third seat for gunner in front. Several watertight compartments.

DORAND.

Biplanes designed by Colonel Dorand, of the Section Technique d'Aviation, and built under his instructions, at the Government establishment at Chalais-Meudon, which corresponds to the Royal Aircraft Establishment at Farnborough.

THE DORAND RECONNAISSANCE BIPLANE.

Type of machine	Two-seater Reconnaissance Biplane.
Name or type number of machine	A.R.
Purpose for which intended	Reconnaissance.
Span	13.3 metres.
Gap, maximum and minimum	2 m. to 1.825 m.
Overall length	8.225 m.
Total surface of wings	50.36 sq. meters.
Engine type and H.P.	8 cyl. Renault, 190 h.p.
Weight of machine empty	890 kgs.
Load per sq. metre	7 kgs.
Tank capacity in litres	170.
Disposable load apart from fuel	300 kgs.
Total weight of machine loaded	1330 kgs.

"Flugsport" for Aug. 14th describes the *Dorand* biplane, explaining that this machine is known as "A.R." or "A.L.D." according to its equipment with a Renault or a Lorraine-Dietrich engine. The machine described, naturally one captured from the French, bears the description, "A.R.," and the number 309. The letter "A" indicates that it is a Reconnaissance machine.

The empty weight of the aircraft is 890 kilos. A note on the rudder gives the weight of the fuel (poids combustible) as 140 kg. and that of useful load (poids utile) at 300 kg., the total load working thus out at 1,330 kg. As the planes have an area of 50.36 square metres, the loading of the planes is thus $\frac{1330}{50.36} = 26.40$ kg. per sq. m., and the engine performance $\frac{1330}{190.36} = 7$ kg. per h.p.

The main object of the design seems to have been the production of a light aeroplane with fairly high wing loading. The construction of component parts, such as stampings, has, therefore, been kept simple and light.

Three-quarter Front View of the Donnet Flying-Boat (200 h.p. Hispano-Suiza engine.)

Side View of the Donnet Flying-Boat.

Three-quarter Front View of the Dorand Biplane, type A.R., with 200 h.p. Renault engine (running).

Side View of the Dorand Biplane, type A.R., with 200 h.p. Renault engine. The group in front include, from left to right, Commandant Maurer, Colonel Dorand, and Commandant Lepère—(all wearing caps).

DORAND—*continued.*

Weights.	Kg.
Engine	245
Cooling water ..	25
Airscrew	22
One main petrol tank ..	22.5
One auxiliary petrol tank	2
One oil tank	2
Engine equipment, exhaust collector body with tools ..	244.5
Landing gear ..	60
Control arrangement ..	6
Planes	234.5
Rudder and elevator ..	26.5
Empty load ..	890
Total weight ..	1330

Load (Approximately).	Kg.
Pilot and observer ..	150
Armament	75
4 bombs @ 12 kg. ..	48
Wireless and photography equipment ..	27
182 lit. petrol ; 7 lit. oil	140
	440

Note painted on the rudder :
"Useful load" .. .. 300 kg.
Fuel .. .. .. 140 kg.
Average useful loading of the planes : 4.65 kg. sq. m.

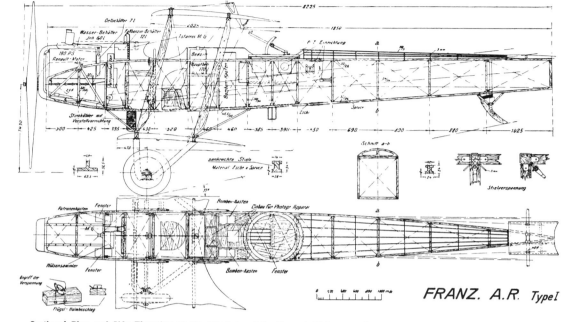

FRANZ. A.R. Type I

Sectional Plan and Side Elevation of the Fuselage of the Dorand Biplane. (This and the illustrations on the following page are taken from the German paper "Flugsport.")

F

FARMAN. Aeroplanes.

Henri and Maurice Farman. 167, Rue de Silly, Billancourt (Seine). *School :* Buc, près Versailles and Etampes. Depôts : Buc, Etampes (Seine and Oise). Camp de Chalons—Reims. Boulogne s mer. Established by H. Farman in 1908. M. Farman established works a little later. In 1912 the two brothers combined. Present works were opened in January, 1912.

Various *Farman* machines did good work early in the War, notably the "short-horn" *Maurice Farman* and the Salmson-engined *Henry Farmans.*

An interesting type is a combination of the "Henri" and "Maurice" Farman characteristics, and on this account it is commonly known among British aviators as the "Horace."

The aeroplane factory of Henri and Maurice Farman, at Billancourt (Seine), is said to be able to produce machines of various types at the rate of ten every day. The factory is two miles long, and, with its extensive facilities and a force of 5.000 employees, the Farman establishments produce all parts of the aeroplane at the Billancourt factory, including all the woodwork and metal parts.

The illustrations and descriptions which follow relate to various types produced during the War.

1914 models.			H. Farman. F-20.		H. Farman. F-22.		H. Farman. F-22. hydro.		H. Farman. F-23.		H. Farman. F-23. hydro.		H. Farman. F-24. one-seater.		M. Farman. S-7.		M. Farman. S-8. hydro.		M. Farman. S-9. hydro.		M. Farman. S-11.	
Length	...	... feet (m.)	26¼	8·06	29	8·80	29	8·80	29	8·80	29	8·80	28¾	8·75	37¼	11·52	32	9·74	30½	9·35	31	9·48
Span	...	... feet (m.)	44¾	13·60	51	15·58	51	15·58	59½	18·08	59½	18·08	37¾	11·50	51	15·52	62½	19·02	56	17·00	53	16·13
Area	...	... sq. feet (m².)	375	35	494	46	494	46	537	50	537	50	279	26	580	54	730	68	644	60	612	57
Weight	total ...lbs. (kgs.)		804	365	849	385	1135	515	860	390	1330	605	640	290	1280	580	2130	967	1660	755	1215	550
	useful ...lbs. (kgs.)		606	275	716	325	606	275	880	400	606	275	385	175	607	275	881	400	607	275	660	300
Motor	...	... ... h.p.	80 Gnome		80 Gnome		80 Gnome		80 Gnome		120 Gnome		80 Gnome		70 Renault		100 Renault		70 Renault		70 Renault	
Speed	max. m.p.h. (km.)		65	105	62	100	56	90	56	90	65	105	68	110	59	95	62	100	56	90	62	100
	min. m.p.h. (km.)		...		..		...		...		...		...		...		...		...		...	
	asc. f.p.m. (m.)		235	71·5	205	62·5	164	50	164	50	164	50	410	125	164	50	164	50	164	50	205	62·5
Endurance	...	... hrs.	...		...		...		...		...		..		...		...		...		...	

Notes.—The hydro-avions are fitted with two narrow floats without steps. Wood and steel construction ; ailerons inter-connected. Type "F-20": two skids and four wheels. All other types : four wheels only.

Notes.—Wood construction ; ailerons inter-connected. Type "S-7" has elevator forward. All other types have none. All hydros are fitted with two narrow floats without steps, four wheels and two skids for landing.

M. FARMAN.

The M.F.11 "shorthorn" MAURICE FARMAN, with 100 h.p. Renault engine of 1914. Used for bombing, artillery observation, reconnaissance, infantry contact patrols and training.

Side View of a "Horace" Farman of the F.40 reconnaissance-bomber series, combining the characteristics of the Henry and Maurice Farman types. 160 h.p. Renault engine, allowing 84 mph.

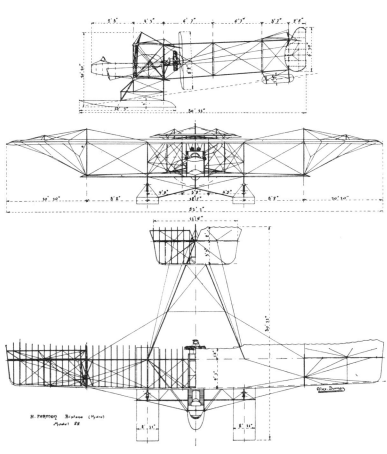

H. FARMAN "F-22." Hydro.

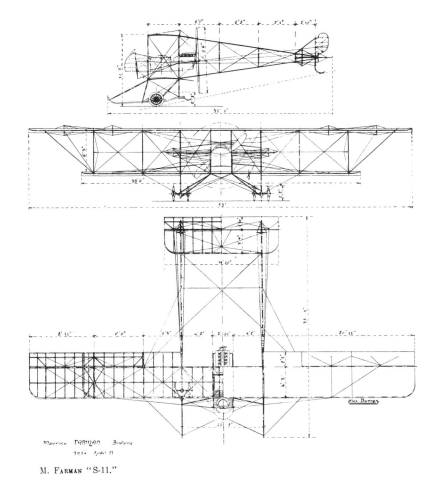

M. FARMAN "S-11."

THE FARMAN. TYPE 50BN2.
Specification.

Type of machine	Twin-engined Tractor. Biplane.
Name or type No. of machine	Farman. Type 50BN2.
Purpose for which intended ..	Night Bomber.
Span	Top plane, 22.85 m. ; Bottom plane, 20.4 m.
Overall length ..	10.92 m.
Maximum height	3.3 m.
Chord	2.35 m.
Total surface of wings ..	100 sq. m.
Span of tail	5.76 m.
Engine type and h.p. ..	2—240 or 275 h.p. Lorraine Dietrich.

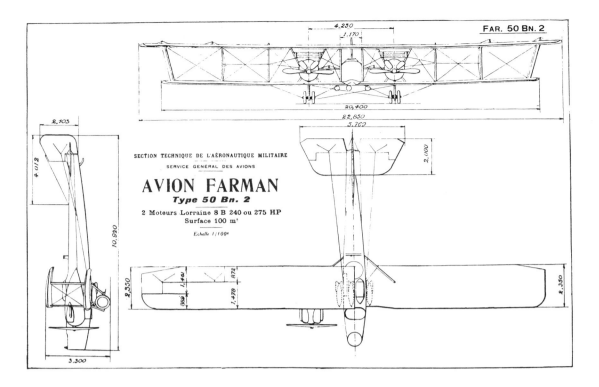

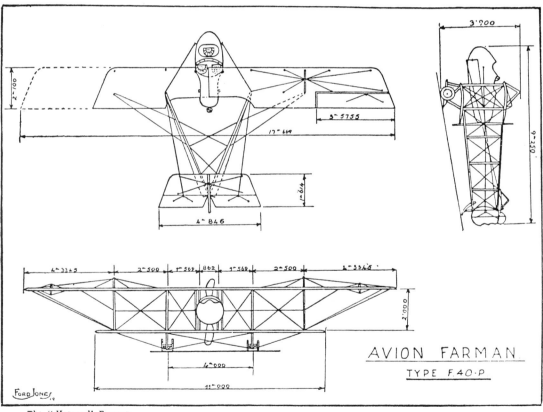

The " Horace " Farman.

F.B.A. Franco-British Aviation (Société Anonyme), Paris.

Founded 1914, by Lieut. Jean de Conneau, of the French Navy (better known as André Beaumont, winner of the Paris-Rome, Circuit-European, and Circuit of Britain races), and M. Schraeck, of the French Wright Company, to work to patents pertaining to the *Donnet-Lévêque* and *Artois* flying boats.

Equipped with Monosoupape Gnôme, Clerget and Hispano. Suiza engines, these boats have been proved to be very fast and suitable for high-speed coastal flying.

They were largely used by all the Allied Naval Air Services for fighting over water and did very good work.

No recent particulars have been received.

An F.B.A. flying boat on the water. Actually in the service of Italy. *Reproduced from "La Guerra," the Italian official publication.*

HANRIOT.

Hanriot & Cie, 84, Avenue des Moulineaux, Billancourt, Seine.

Founded during the war by M. Hanriot, who had retired from aviation before the war. Made a number of Sopwith machines for the French Government (1½-Strutters), and also designed and built a single-seat biplane fighter as the HD-1. Powered by a 120 h.p. Le Rhône 9Jb rotary engine and armed with a single Vickers gun, it attained 114 mph. Some higher-powered examples followed. A few served with the French Navy in 1918 but the Italian and Belgian air forces received 831 and 125 respectively from 1917.

Type of machine	Single-seat Tractor Biplane
Name or type No. of machine ..	Hanriot HD-1
Purpose for which intended ..	Fighting Scout
Span	8.70 m.
Overall length	5.85 m.
Empty weight	412 kg.
Speed	183 km.p.h.

L

LETORD.

Société d'Aviation Letord, Paris.

A manufacturing firm founded by the aviator Letord.

Has for some time been manufacturing twin-engined biplanes, originally notable for the backward stagger of the wings. This characteristic has disappeared in a later type.

Letord Types 1, 2 and 4 were for reconnaissance; Types 3, 5, 7 and 9 for bombing. The most important of these was the Type 5, of which 51 appeared between 1917-18.

THE LETORD. TYPE 5.
Specification.

Type of machine	Twin-engined Tractor Biplane.
Name or type No. of machine ..	Letord. Type 5.
Purpose for which intended ..	Bomber.
Span	18 m.
Overall length	11.17 m.
Maximum height ..	3.7 m.
Total surface of wings ..	62.2 sq. m.
Engine type and h.p. ..	240 h.p. Lorraine Dietrich.
Load per sq. m.	38.96 kgs.
Weight per h.p.	5.0 kgs.
Tank capacity in hours ..	3 hours.

Performance.

Speed at 2,000 mteres ..	160 km.p.h.
Disposable load apart from fuel	548 kgs.
Total weight of machine loaded	2,423 kgs.

Side View of the Letord Twin-Engined Biplane, type V.

The Letord type V Twin-Engined Bomber.

THE LETORD. TYPE 9B.N.2.
Specification.

Type of machine	Twin-engined Tractor Biplane.
Name or type No. of machine ..	Letord. Type 9B.N.2.
Purpose for which intended ..	Night Bomber.
Span	25.94 m.
Overall length	14.95 m.
Maximum height ..	4.26 m.
Total surface of wings ..	135 sq. m.
Engine type and h.p. ..	2—350 h.p. Liberty.
Weight of machine empty ..	40.9 kgs.
Load per sq. m.	7.88 kgs.
Tank capacity in hours ..	6 hours.

Performance.

Speed at 2,000 metres ..	145 km.p.h.	
Disposable load apart from fuel	.. ..	1,243 kgs.
Total weight of machine loaded	.. ..	5,521 kgs.

Three-quarter Front View of the Letord Type 9 Night Bomber.

LÉVY.

Hydravions George Lévy, 4, Rue de Cormeilles, Levallois, Paris.

Lévy built 100 GL40s (R for Renault engine) for the French in 1918.

THE GEORGES LÉVY. TYPE R FLYING BOAT.
Specification

Type of machine	Three-seater Flying Boat. Type R.
Span	Upper plane, 18 m. 50; Lower plane, 12 m. 00.
Overall length	12 m. 40.
Maximum height	3 m. 85.
Total surface	68 sq. m.
Engine type and h.p. ..	Renault, 300 h.p.
Weight of machine empty ..	1450 kgs.
Disposable load	1,000 kgs.

Performance

Speed	145 km.p.h.

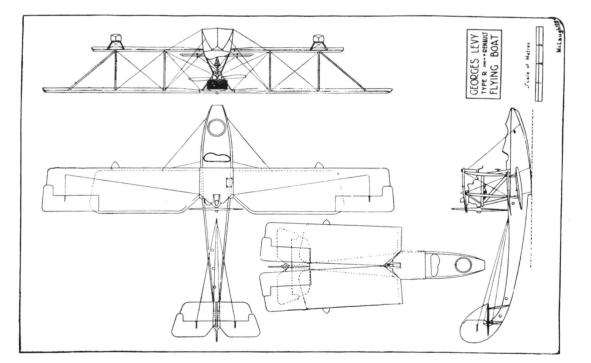

M

MOINEAU.

M. Louis Moineau, the famous pilot of Bréguets before the War, turned constructor in 1915.

In 1916-17 he produced the curious biplane illustrated herewith.

It is driven by a Salmson-Canton-Unné engine, placed with its shaft thwart-wise of the fuselage. Each end of the shaft drives a cross-shaft to a bevel gear at the intersection of the cross-bracing of the wings, so that the engine drives two air-screws, one on each side of the machine.

A gunner sits in front of the engine, and has a very big arc of fire. Another gunner sits behind the pilot.

The machine flew, but was never put into production.

The Salmson-Moineau Biplane of 1916.

MORANE-SAULNIER. Aeroplanes. Morane-Saulnier, Soc. de Constructions Aéronautiques, 205, Boulevard Pereire, Paris. School : Villacoublay.

The Morane machines, particularly the Parasol monoplanes, rendered great services during the earlier part of the War.

The firm has since turned out a number of biplanes, including certain two-engined machines. Among the final Morane-Saulnier war machines was the AI parasol fighter, put into production for service in 1918 as the Type 27 and Type 29. Type 27 C1 achieved 130 m.p.h. (210 km per hour).

THE MORANE SAULNIER. TYPES 27C.1 & 29C.1.

Type of machine	Single-Seater Parasol Monoplane.
Name or type No. of machine ..	Morane-Saulnier. 27C.1, single gun. 29C.1, two guns.
Purpose for which intended ..	Fighting Scout.
Span	8.72 m.
Overall length	5.7 m.
Maximum height	2.4 m.
Chord	2.013 m.
Total surface of wings ..	13.5 sq. m.
Span of tail	2.7 m.
Engine type and h.p. ..	160 h.p. Mono. Gnôme.

THE MORANE SAULNIER. TYPE C.2.

Type of machine	Two-seater Tractor Biplane.
Name or type No. of machine ..	Morane Saulnier. Type C.2.
Span	11.726 m.
Gap	1.7 m.
Overall length	8.345 m.
Chord	1.9 m.
Total surface of wings ..	41 sq. m.
Span of tail	3.66 m.
Engine type and h.p. ..	420 h.p. Bugatti.
Airscrew, diameter	3.1 m.

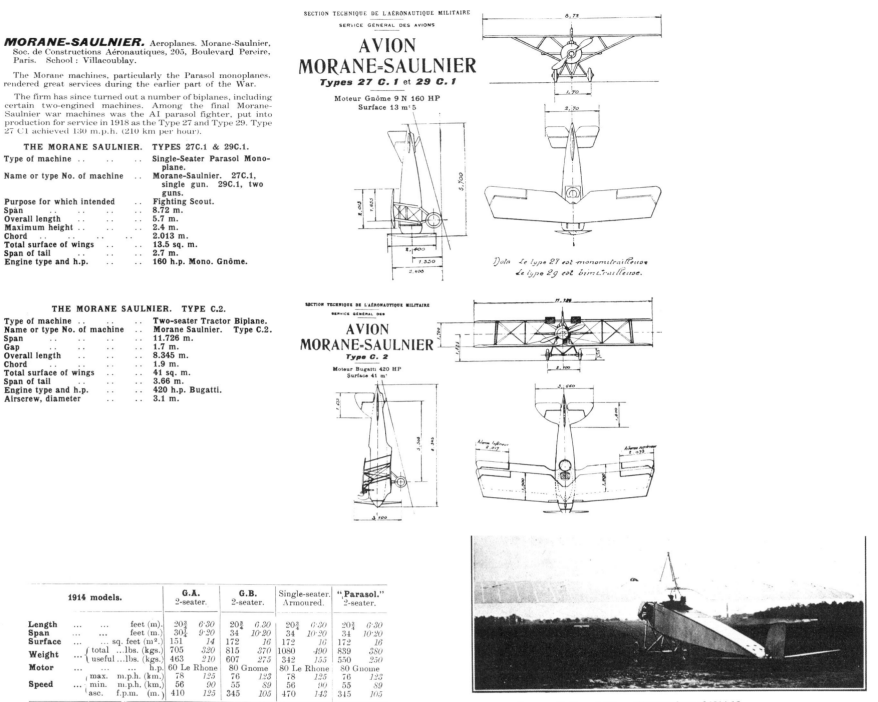

1914 models.		G.A. 2-seater.		G.B. 2-seater.		Single-seater. Armoured.		"Parasol." 2-seater.	
Length	... ... feet (m).	20¾	6·30	20¾	6·30	20¾	6·30	20¾	6·30
Span	... ... feet (m).	30¼	9·20	34	10·20	34	10·20	34	10·20
Surface	... sq. feet (m²).	151	14	172	16	172	16	172	16
Weight	{ total ...lbs. (kgs.)	705	320	815	370	1080	490	839	380
	{ useful ...lbs. (kgs.)	463	210	607	275	342	155	550	250
Motor	... ... h.p.	60 Le Rhone		80 Gnome		80 Le Rhone		80 Gnome	
Speed	{ max. m.p.h. (km.)	78	125	76	123	78	125	76	123
	{ min. m.p.h. (km.)	56	90	55	89	56	90	55	89
	{ asc. f.p.m. (m.)	410	125	345	105	470	143	345	105

In each case **body** is of rectangular section, wood, mounted on wheels only. Lateral control, warping.

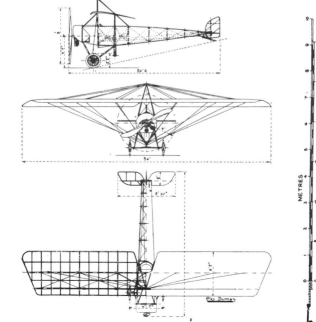

MORANE-SAULNIER Type L "Parasol" monoplane of 1914-16.

A MORANE-SAULNIER Type N *"monoplan de chasse"* or "destroyer."—1914-16 type, with monocoque fuselage. 80 h.p. Gnôme or Le Rhône engine, allowing 102 mph.

The 1916 Model Parasol (Type P) has a Le Rhône engine of 110 h.p. It has been largely used by both the French and British Armies in 1916-17. It resembles the 1915 Type LA reconnaissance and fighting parasol but is marginally larger, also retaining LA-type aileron control instead of the earlier L's warping control.

The speed is about 156 kms. (97 miles) per hour.

The surface is 18 sq. metres.

Weight loaded 731 kg.

The tanks contain 102 litres of petrol and 20 litres of oil. Suitable for about 2¾ hours' flying.

The type is chiefly used in the French Army for short reconnaissance and artillery observation. It carries one fixed Vickers and one free firing Lewis gun.

Three-quarter Rear View of the Type P. Morane-Saulnier '' Parasol.'' Note the ailerons : unusual in a monoplane.

Three-quarter Front View of the Type P. Morane-Saulnier '' Parasol.''

MORANE BIPLANE. Type Bimoteur "S" presented for trial February, 1916, with stationary cylinder Renault engines of 250 h.p. each. Not put into production.
Speed: 145 kms. (96 miles) per hour. 3-seats. Useful load: 1,200 kilos. Weight: 3,000 kilos. Span: 26 m. Surface: 108 sq. m.
(Dimensions and performance practically identical with that of the Gothas of 1917.)

Front View of Morane Biplane, Type Bimoteur "T". First flown in 1914, it was not put into production for reconnaissance until 1916. 80 h.p. Le Rhônes.
Speed: 156 km.p.h. (97 m. per h). Span: 17.65 m (57 ft. 11 in). Ceiling: 4,500 m. Useful load 640 kilos.

Three-quarter Rear View of twin-engined Morane. Type "T."

MORANE-SAULNIER—continued.

Type B.B.— (two-seater) reconnaissance and escort
Biplane. 110 h.p. Le Rhône engine.
Speed: 90 m.p.h. Used by the British Flying Services
from Nov., 1915, to end of 1916.

Three-quarter Rear View of a
Morane-Saulnier Biplane.

N

NIEUPORT. Soc. Anonyme des Etablissements Nieuport, 46, 48 and 50, Boulevard Gallieni, and 15, Rue Camille Desmoulins, Issy-les-Moulineaux (Seine). *School:* Villacoublay (Seine and Oise). Established 1910 by the late Edouard de Nieport, commonly called Nieuport.

The *Nieuport* biplane has been one of the greatest successes of the war, owing to its high speed and quickness in manœuvre. The lower plane in this type is so small that the machine is really a "parasol," with half a plane attached to give girder formation to the wing bracing. It is frequently called the "one-and-a-half plane."

Major Nieuport models were the 10 and 12 fighter and reconnaissance biplanes; 11, 16, 17, 21, 23, 24, 27 and 28 fighters. Of less importance were the 14 bomber of 1916 and 29, the latter coming too late in the war. Major 28 user was the American Expeditionary Force in 1918.

THE NIEUPORT. TYPE 28C.1.

Type of machine	Single-seater Scout.
Name or type No. of machine	Nieuport. 28C.1.
Span	Top plane, 8.16 m. ; Bottom plane, 7.77 m.
Overall length	6.3 m.
Maximum height	2.3 m.
Chord	Top plane, 1.3 m. Bottom plane, 1.0 m.
Total surface of wings	16 sq. m.
Span of tail	2.8 m.
Engine type and h.p.	160 h.p. monosoupape Gnôme.
Airscrew, diam.	2.5 m.

Side View of the Nieuport Type 28C.1 Single-seat Fighter (160 h.p. Monosoupape Gnôme Engine).

Three-quarter Front View of the Nieuport Type 28C.1 Single-seat Fighter (160 h.p. Monosoupape Gnôme Engine).

TYPE XXIII

Length: 5.97 m.
Span: 8.15 m.
Surface: 15 sq. m.
Maximum weight: 535 kg.
Useful load: 185 kgs.
Engine: 120 h.p. Le Rhône.
Maximum speed: 150 km.p.h.

CHARACTERISTICS:
Square fuselage, rigid tail, skid.
Vickers synchronised gun.

TYPE XXVII

Length: 5.84 m.
Span: 8.18 m.
Surface: 15 sq. m.
Maximum weight: 585 kg.
Useful load: 185 kgs.
Engine: 120 h.p. Le Rhône.
Maximum speed: 187 km.p.h.

CHARACTERISTICS:
Streamlined fuselage.
Spring tail skid.
Vickers machine-gun synchronised with the air-screw.

The fore-part of a Nieuport 17 "destroyer" (1916-17 type.)

A NIEUPORT "biplan de chasse" or "destroyer" (1916-17 type).
The mounting of the gun on the top plane is of interest.

*Reproduced from " La Guerre Aérienne," Paris.
from a French military photograph.*

1914 Monoplanes.			2-N. 1-seater.		X. 2-seater.		X. hydro.		XI. 50.		XI. 80.	
Length	...	... feet (m.)	23½	7·15	27	8·26	27½	8·40	21¼	6·49	21¼	6·49
Span	...	... feet (m.)	28¼	8·65	40½	12·32	41	12·50	27¼	8·32	31¼	9·52
Area	...	sq. feet (m².)	150	14	247	23	252	23·50	150	14	172	16
Weight {	machine, lbs. (kgs.)		529	240	880	400	1058	480	595	270	660	300
	useful ...lbs. (kgs.)		352	160	704	320	630	290	385	175	405	225
Motor	...	... .. h.p.	30 Nieuport		80 {Gnome Le Rhone Clerget		80 Le Rhone		50 Gnome		80 Gnome	
Speed {	max. m.p.h. (km.)		68	110	72	115	65	105	68	110	72	115
	min. m.p.h. (km.)		...		...		...		...		...	
	asc. f.p.m. (m.)		...		328	100	216	66	410	125	544	166

A type XXIII Nieuport in the air.

Notes.—In each case the body is of rectangular section, ash and spruce. Fixed tail plane with two elevators in rear. Warping wings. Type "XI" fitted with two wheels only. All other types fitted with standard type of skid.

The monoplanes are now obsolete, except for "hydros," which still exist. The new biplane, whose dimensions must not be given, has been one of the great successes of the war, owing to its high speed and quickness in manœuvre. The lower plane in this type is so small that the machine is really a "parasol" with half a plane attached, to give girder formation to the wing bracing. It is frequently called the "one-and-a-half-plane."

Rear view of the type XXIII Nieuport.

Three-quarter rear view of the type XXIII Nieuport.

Front view of the type XXVII Nieuport.

Side view of the type XXVII Nieuport of 1917-18.

A Nieuport Scout, with the Prieur Incendiary Rockets in position.

An Experimental Nieuport, with Hispano-Suiza Engine.

R

R.E.P. Cabinet á Etudes en Recherches Techniques. Robert Esnault-Pelterie, 37, Rue des Abondances, Boulogne sur Seine (Seine). *School*: Buc. One of the earliest established French firms. The first to go in for steel construction.

The *R.E.P.* "parasols" proved to have excellent climbing and weight lifting power, and so did well early in the war.

Of late, M. Esnault-Pelterie has been engaged on experimental designs, and his works have been employed on special work which cannot be described.

S

SALMSON.

Société des Moteurs Salmson, Billancourt, Seine.

Aircraft factory, allied to the famous aero-engine firm, constructors of the Salmson-Canton-Unné engines.

Have built various aeroplanes on which to demonstrate the firm's engines, and have achieved remarkable results.

M. Salmson is a great engineering employer, and has spent a fortune on experimental work with aero-engines and aircraft generally.

THE SALMSON S.A.L. 2-A. 2.

Type of machine	Biplane.
Name or type No. of machine ..	S.A.L. 2-A. 2.
Span	11 m. 75.
Gap	1 m. 700.
Length overall	8 m. 500.
Maximum height	2 m. 900.
Chord	1 m. 676.
Surface of wings	37.27 sq. m.
Surface of tail	4.20 sq. m.
Surface of rudder	1.25 sq. m.
Surface of each aileron and total area	$2.7 \times 4 = 5.08$ sq. m.
Fuselage section (maximum) ..	1 m. 25 × 1 m. 75.
Engine type and h.p. ..	Salmson Z9. 250 h.p.
Airscrew, diam.	2 m. 75.
Pitch	2 m. 100.
Weight of machine empty ..	834 kgs.
Weight per h.p.	5.5 kgs.
Tank capacity in litres ..	Petrol, 265 litres. Oil, 47 litres.
Performance.	
Speed at ground level ..	187 km.p.h.
Speed at 3,000 m. ..	175 km.p.h.
Climb.	
To 2,000 m.	11 mins.
To 3,000 m.	$17\frac{1}{4}$ mins.
To 5,000 m.	$40\frac{1}{4}$ mins.
Weight of machine in flying order	1,380 kgs.

Three-quarter Front View of the Salmson type S.A.L. 2-A. 2. (250 h.p. Salmson engine).

SCHMITT.

Paul Schmitt, 39, Route de la Révolte, Levallois Perret (Seine).

Constructors of the *Paul Schmitt* biplanes, in association with the Morane Saulnier firm.

The first machine produced before the outbreak of war was notable chiefly for its ability to give variable angle of incidence to the main planes.

During 1916 and 1917 the firm has built war aeroplanes of more orthodox types.

M. Paul Schmitt has experimented since 1904 with large kites and gliders, and has been concerned with flying since 1909. He has invented, constructed, and tuned up various types of aeroplanes of destructive kinds.

In 1910, he experimented with a biplane without a fuselage or tail, analogous to the *Dunne*, but of a different shape. It had variable incidence, weighed 1,000 kilos, and had a 70 h.p. engine.

In 1913, M. Schmitt exhibited at the Paris Aero Show his fuselage biplane, three-seater, with variable incidence. It was bought by the French Army.

At the beginning of 1914, his pilot, M. Garaix—since fallen on the field of honour—put up, on the *Paul Schmitt* biplane, 42 World's Records, which stand to-day in 1918, so far as single-engined machines are concerned, and barring records put up by multi-engined types such as the *Caproni* and *Handley Page*. These included height, speed, duration and distance, with four to nine passengers.

M. Schmitt was winner of the Concours Pour La Securité (Safety Competition) in 1914.

He also came out first in the French competition for high powered aeroplanes in 1915.

During the war, after serving as a bomber-machine-gunner, he built several types of aeroplanes, specially for bombing, and a hydro-aeroplane for the United States. His three-seater with two gunners was the leading machine of its class.

It is claimed that the fuselages of these machines, of steel tube, cannot get out of truth. The controls are of a special type, dating back to 1913. Comparing these machines with the *Albatros*, it is seen that both fuselages terminate in a triangle running into a T-shape for tail and rudder-post, the rudder being above the tail and in front of it, thus giving special solidity at this vital point. In both machines the rudders and elevators are balanced. In both there is a vertical surface under the fuselage. In both the elevator is a single flap, and is not in the usual two pieces. Thus it appears that the *Albatros* designer has profited by study of the *Paul Schmitt* design.

In 1917, the *P. S.* biplanes (bombers) carried two machine-guns, and carried several hundreds of kilos of bombs, with fuel for many hours' flying. With this big load, the "ceiling" of the machines was well over 4,000 m. (13,000 ft.).

The chief characteristic of all the *P. S.* machines is the variable incidence of the main planes, which permits good balance between 0° and 12°. The main cellule is a single block, solid on the four centre-section struts—of steel tube—which can rotate round a central horizontal pivot. The rotation is controlled by a wheel and chain.

This permits the pilot to adjust the angle of incidence to suit his load and speed, while keeping the fuselage always at its correct flying angle, either for climbing, fast flying, or slow landing.

The *P. S.* machines have always been fitted with fixed-cylinder engines, first a Salmson radial, and later V-type Renault.

SPAD.

SPAD. The Spad (Société Pour Aviation et ses Dérivés) is the old Deperdussin firm, founded in 1910, and revived in the first year of war by a company, at the head of which is M. Blériot.

Address :—Société SPAD, 19, Rue des Entrepreneurs, Paris ; also at Quai de l'Industrie, Juvisy, near Paris.

A *Deperdussin* monoplane, designed by M Bécherau and M. Koolhoven, covered 124·8 miles in one hour, flying round a 20 kilometre circuit, in August, 1913, and numerous others of his designs had notable success.

To preserve the organisation and collected talent of the firm, M. Blériot took it over soon after the outbreak of war, and it was then known as the Société Pour les Appareils Deperdussin, hence the initials Spad, which have since taken on a new meaning, namely, Société Pour Aviation et Dérivés.

The new *Spad* biplanes, the product of M. Bécherau's mature genius, are in the very front rank for speed and climbing power, and are recognised as among the finest "*aéroplanes de chasse*," or "destroyers," of the war.

Three-quarter Rear View of Paul Schmitt biplane. Note the wheels in the centre section for the operation of the ailerons.

Side View of a Paul Schmitt tractor biplane. Type VI, of 1916.

A Paul Schmitt hydravion, built in 1916 for the United States Government.

Side view of a Spad Biplane (from a German photograph of a captured example).

THE SPAD. TYPE 7.
Specification

Type of machine	Single-seater Tractor Biplane.
Name or type No. of machine ..	Spad. Type 7.
Purpose for which intended ..	Fighting Scout.
Span	7.82 m.
Overall length	6.10 m.
Maximum height	2.35 m.
Total surface of wings ..	18 sq. m.
Engine type and h.p.	175 h.p. Hispano-Suiza.

Side View of a British two-seater Spad XI, captured by the Germans. Developed from the Spad VII, it achieved 175 km.p.h. on a 235 h.p. Hispano-Suiza engine.

From a German photograph.

A general view of a Spad XIII in the air.

THE SPAD. TYPE 12.
Specification

Type of machine	Single-seater Tractor Biplane.
Name or type No. of machine ..	Spad. Type 12.
Purpose for which intended ..	Fighting Scout.
Span	8.00 m.
Overall length	6.40 m.
Maximum height	2.30 m.
Total surface of wings ..	20 sq. m.
Engine type and h.p.	220 h.p. Hispano-Suiza.

THE SPAD. TYPES 13 AND 17.
Specification

Type of machine	Single-seater Tractor Biplane.
Name or type No. of machine ..	Spad. Types 13 and 17.
Purpose for which intended ..	Fighting Scout.
Span	8.20 m.
Overall length	6.30 m.
Maximum height	2.30 m.
Total surface of wings ..	20 sq. m.
Engine type and h.p.	235 h.p. Hispano-Suiza.

Near View of the "Front-gun" Spad A.2 fighter with the gunner in place. The position seems unenviable, despite the wire guard. A.2s and a few later A.4s served briefly with French and Russian forces.

Rear View of a British two-seater Spad, captured by the Germans.

From a German photograph.

T

TELLIER.

Etablissements Tellier, Quai de Seine, Argenteuil, Seine et Oise.

Famous boat-building firm which produced many famous racing motor-boats and hydroplanes.

Built very successful monoplanes in 1910 and 1911, when M. Dubonnet, the well-known French sportsman, took an interest in the firm.

Gave up aeroplane work before the War, but took to making flying-boats soon after War broke out. Towards the end of the War, a number of these boats, of the type illustrated, and fitted with "Maori" Sunbeam engines, did remarkably good work on anti-submarine patrols.

A Tellier Flying-Boat with "Maori" Sunbeam-Coatalen Engine, 350 h.p.

The Power Plant Instalment of a "Maori" Sunbeam in a Tellier Flying-Boat.

A Tellier Flying-Boat (350 h.p. Sunbeam-Coatalen "Maori" Engine) about to take off.

V

VENDÔME.

M. Vendôme, one of the earliest of French constructors, produced in 1916 a machine somewhat after the style of the *Moineau.*

In the fuselage, one on each side, were two Monosoupape Gnôme engines, each driving a shaft to a bevel gear, which in turn drove a tractor airscrew. Thus the machine had two rotary engines turning in opposite directions, which would give it considerable lateral stiffness (though not stability), owing to their gyroscopic action.

A gunner sat in the nose of the machine and another behind the pilot.

As in the case of the *Moineau*, it was never put into production.

The Vendôme Biplane of 1916 (2—100 h.p. Gnome Engines.)

VOISIN. Aeroplanes Voisin, Boulevard Gambetta, Issy-les-Moulineaux, (Seine).

Associated with the Etablissements Ch. Lefevre & Cie. Société Anonyme, with capital of 3,000,000 francs.

Paris Office : 105, Rue St. Lazare, Paris.

The oldest aeroplane firm in the world, founded by the Brothers Voisin, in 1905.

Voisin Types 1 to 10 (excluding 7 and 9) were used throughout the war for bombing, ground attack and fighting. All had the pusher-engined layout. Final Types 8 and 10 equipped 26 French squadrons, plus others went to the American Expeditionary Force.

Three-quarter Front View of a Voisin "Avion Canon" in the air.

1914 models.			Type III	
Length	... ...	feet (m.)	31½	9.60
Span	... ...	feet (m.)	52½	16.00
Area	...	sq. feet (m².)	452	42
Weight ... {	total ...lbs.(kgs.)		3,030	1,370
	useful ...lbs.(kgs.)		992	450
Motor	... ...	h.p.	130 Canton-Unne	
Speed ... {	max. m.p.h. (km.)		68	110
	min. m.p.h. (km.)		31	50
	asc. f.p.m. (m.)		657	200

Voisin III light bomber of 1914, with a Canton-Unné engine. A Type III was the first French aircraft to bring down a German aircraft, on 5 October 1914.

Notes.—Steel construction. *Control :* ailerons and rear elevator. Landing gear : four wheels.

These machines, now generally fitted with Salmson engines, have done an immense amount of work in the war, being capable of carrying big weights, either of bombs, or machine-gun and ammunition. Towards the end of 1915 the need for higher speeds and climbs put this particular type somewhat out of date.

1917 MODEL.—TWO-SEATER NIGHT BOMBER.

Length : 10 m.
Span : Upper plane, 18 m.
Span : Lower plane, 17 m.
Surface of Wings : 63.2 sq. m.
Weight of machine, empty : 1,400 kgs.
Useful load : 650 kgs.
Motor : 280 h.p. Renault.
Speed : Maximum, 130 k.p.h.
Speed : Minimum, 70 k.p.h.
Climbing speed : 4,000 metres in 45 minutes.

1917 MODEL.—TWO-SEATER GUN CARRIER.

This machine has similar characteristics to the night bomber. It is fitted with a 47 millimetre gun.

CHARACTERISTIC FEATURES :

Steel construction control by ailerons and rear tail unit.
Four-wheeled landing carriage.
This type is fitted indifferently with Peugot, Panhard, and Fiat motors.

THE STANDARD TYPE VIII VOISIN "Avion Canon." Much used for reconnaissance.

THE VOISIN 4-ENGINED BIPLANE. TYPE 13.

Specification.

Type of machine	4-engined Biplane.
Name or type No. of machine ..	Voisin. Type 13.
Purpose for which intended ..	Night Bomber.
Span	Top plane, 30 m. ; Bottom plane, 24.162 m.
Chord	3.00 m.
Total surface of planes	155.686 sq. m.
Tank capacity in kgs.	1,100 kgs.
Engine type and h.p.	4—230 h.p. Hispano-Suiza.
Airscrews, type	Lumière.
Weight per h.p.	6.19 kgs.
Weight per sq. metre	36.53 kgs.

Performance.
Speed	146 km.p.h.

Climb.
To 3,000 metres in minutes ..	30 mins.
Useful load	1,300 kgs.
Total weight of machine loaded	..5,700 kgs.

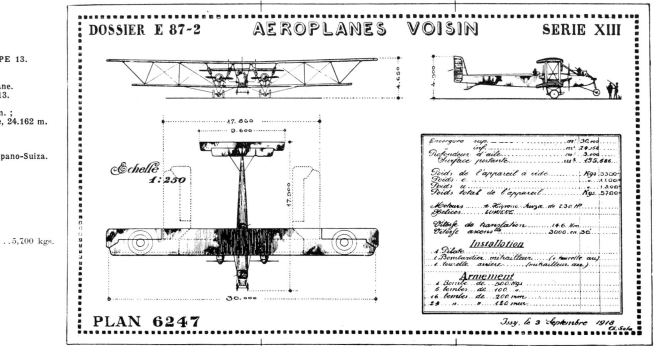

General arrangement of a four engined Night-Bomber slightly modified from the type B12.

VOISIN—*continued.*

THE VOISIN TWO-SEATER NIGHT BOMBER.

Type of machine	Voisin—Bombardement de Nuit.
Purpose for which intended ..	Night bombing.
Span	18 metres top; 17 metres bottom plane.
Overall length	10 metres.
Total surface of wings ..	63 sq. metres.
Engine type and h.p... ..	280 h.p. Renault.
Weight of machine empty ..	1,400 kgs.
Performance.	
Speed	130 k.p.h. max.
Climb.	
To 4,000 metres in 45 minutes.	
Disposable load apart from fuel .. .. .. 650 kgs.	

THE VOISON. TYPE 12 B.N.2.

Specification.

Type of machine	Four-engined Biplane.
Name or type No. of machine ..	Voisin. Type 12 B.N.2.
Purpose for which intended ..	Night bombing.
Span	30.6 m. Folded, 16.6 m.
Overall length	16.6 m.
Maximum height	4.3 m.
Chord	2.7 m.
Total surface of wings ..	145 sq. m.
Engine type and h.p. ..	4—220 h.p. Hispano-Suiza.

Side View of the Voisin Type 12 B.N.2 (Night Bomber) (4—220 h.p. Hispano-Suiza Engines).

The Voisin Single-engined Bomber Type 10 (490 h.p. Liberty Engine).

GERMAN.
GERMAN MILITARY AVIATION.

A group of German officer aviators in front of one of their machines on Active Service.

Aerial Societies :—

Aero Klub (Imperial), 3, Nollenderfplatz, Berlin. Sec.: H. Von Frankenberg und Ludwigsdorf.

Automobil-und Flugtechnische-Gesellschaft (E. V.) Nurnberger Platz 5, Haupyverein Berlin, Hochster Str. 1, Bezirksverein Frankfurt a. M. Neuer Wall 44, II, Hamburg.

ARMY GENERAL.

The Army law of 1914 provided £400,000 (80 million marks) for Army aviation (including dirigibles), in addition to a considerable share of the £4,000,000 which was to be spread over a period of five years.

The Army aerial force was commanded by 2 inspector generals. The aviation force was put at 4 battalions. In 1916, the Army Aviation Service was placed under a separate "Intendantur." The officer commanding having the grading of the Commander of an Army Corps.

Headquarters: Berlin. *Stations*: Aachen, Allenstein, Cologne, Darmstadt, Doebritz, Freiburg, Graudenz, Hannover, Insterburg, Jüterbog, Koenigsberg, Metz, Posen, Strassburg, Zeithain, etc.

The scheme was complete by the end of the year 1914.

The Army Flying Schools then in operation were :—

Darmstadt (3, Kompagnie Flieger Bataillon 3).
Döberitz (1 und 2 Kompagnie Flieger Bataillon 1).
Freiburg (3 Kompagnie Flieger Bataillon 4).
Germersheim (Kgl. Bayernsche Heeresversvaltung).
Graudenz (2 Kompagnie Flieger Bataillon 2).
Hannover (2 Kompagnie Flieger Bataillon 2).

Jüterbog (Truppenkommando).
Köln (1 Kompagnie Flieger Bataillon 3).
Königsberg (3 Kompagnie Flieger Bataillon 2).
Metz (2 Kompagnie Flieger Bataillon 4).
München-Oberschleissheim (Kgl. Bayernsches Flieger Bataillon).
München-Oberwiesenfeld (Kgl. Kommandatur).
Posen (1 Kompagnie Flieger Bataillon 2).
Saarbrücken (Kgl. Preussische Heeresverwaltung).
Schneidemühl (Kgl. Preussische Heereverwaltung).
Strassburg (1 Kompagnie Flieger Bataillon 4).
Zeithain (3 Kompagnie Flieger Bataillon 2).

ARMY AEROPLANES.

The early growth of the aeroplane force may be seen from the following notes :—

Bought in 1913 **120 monoplanes** (*Albatros, Aviatik, Bristol, D.F.W., Fokker, Gothaer, Jeannin, Rumpler*).

120 biplanes (*A.E.G., Albatros, Aviatik, Bristol, D.F.W., Euler. L.V.G., Otto*).

Bought in 1914-15 or ordered sufficient to replace all the 1913 machines. The scheme then was to provide 1000 machines, all of more or less standard *Taube* type (monoplanes) or *Arrow* type (biplanes). Practically all war machines were at first of the *Arrow* type. These were afterwards replaced by higher powered machines with straight planes, which were almost indistinguishable from British tractor biplanes.

Under the 1914 regulations, military machines had to comply with the following conditions :—

1. Must be of entirely German manufacture, with ample and comfortable seating accommodation for pilot and passenger.

2. Design must permit of fitting bomb droppers and photographic apparatus.

3. Speed capabilities must not be less than 90 kilometres (56 m.p.h.)

4. Dimensions must not exceed 49 feet span (14·50 m.), 39 feet long (12 m.), 13 feet high (3·50 m.), and the motor not more than 100 h.p.

5. Minimum endurance, 4 hours.

Since then, speed, climbing capacity and endurance have all increased notably.

A comparison of the German programme for each year with the British programme shows how much more clearly the German Government realised the importance of Military Aviation than did the British Government of the period.

WAR SERVICE.

From time to time, despite the calls on the German Flying Service on other fronts, the German aviators have held a limited superiority over the French and British on the West Front, owing to their rapidity in placing new types of machines in the air in quantities.

At the end of 1915, a number of picked pilots, notably Capt. Immelmann and Capt. Bölcke, mounted on *Fokker* monoplanes, were able to inflict considerable damage on the slower flying and climbing British and French reconnaissance machines of the period. They had the advantage of always flying over their own territory, being on defensive work, and so could carry light loads of petrol, thus adding to both their speed and manoeuvrability. When their operations were checked by superior British machines, and after the deaths of Immelmann and Bölcke the Germans lost their superior defensive power, and by the Battle of the Somme, in the Autumn of 1916 they were markedly inferior.

Soon afterwards the Germans produced the single-seater Albatros type of machine—which included besides the *Albatros*, such machines as the *Roland*, the *Pfalz*, the *Halberstadt*, and the *Fokker* biplane. The chief exponent of this type was Rittmeister (Cavalry Captain), Freiherr Manfred von Richthofen, formerly of Bölcke's *Fokker* monoplane squadron. He developed the "Circus" idea to a fine art, and himself scored 80 aerial victories before being killed on April 21st, 1918. He deserves to be remembered as the first of the really great Jagdstäffel, or "Chaser Formation" leaders.

The victorious career of the German Circuses was checked about the middle of 1917 by the advent in quantities of *Sopwith* "Camels" (single-seaters), and of *Bristol* "Fighters," big two-seaters. By the end of 1917 the British Royal Flying Corps had established a marked superiority over the Germans in the air, and by May, 1918, the British—including the Australian Flying Corps—practically held the mastery in the air. This mastery was fully maintained until the end of the war. The ingenuity of the German designers seemed to have departed and the output of their constructors did not seem to increase. Consequently in quantity and quality the German aeroplanes were utterly outclassed by the British aircraft industry.

1917 was also remarkable for the introduction of the *Gotha* twin-engined bombers. These machines were first tried on defenceless Bucharest early in 1917, and thereafter a raid was tried on Salonika—which lost the Germans two *Gothas* in a day. During the rest of the year the *Gothas* gave much of their attention to bombing London, and occasionally Paris. These machines, and their bigger descendants the "Riesenflugzeugen" —or "Giant Flying Machines"—also bombed Dunkerque, Calais, Boulogne and other towns behind the Allies' lines, but after one or two attempts at day-light raiding, they confined their operations entirely to night-flying.

During the early part of 1918 the Germans introduced armoured machines for "contour fighting," or "ground-strafing"—as it is more commonly called, but these were not very successful.

After July, 1918, the whole *moral* of the German Air Service fell to pieces, and the British, French and American aviators had matters almost entirely their own way.

THE REORGANISATION OF THE GERMAN FLYING CORPS.

The following article by "Austerlitz" (a well-known cosmopolitan writer), sets forth clearly the organisation for the German Flying Corps in 1917, which organisation was retained till the end of the war :—

The Allied offensive of the Somme, in July, 1916, proved beyond doubt the overwhelming superiority of the Royal Flying Corps and of the French *Aviation Militaire* over the aerial forces of the enemy. During the preliminary stages of that battle a powerful aeroplane barrage of the Allies effectually prevented enemy aviators from crossing our lines to discover our preparations ; in addition to this strategical blinding, the enemy's artillery was also deprived of its *eyes*, all of its kite-balloons being either destroyed or driven down by Allied aviators. German army orders, found on officers taken prisoner, acknow-

ledged with great frankness the inferiority of their air service, and directly ascribed to it the costly defeat the enemy suffered.

Since then, however, the enemy has furnished a very considerable effort, with a view of re-establishing the aerial situation in his favour, and this effort, pragmatised by an ambitious building programme, eventually resulted in a complete reorganisation of the German Flying Corps.

This reorganisation, which now appears to be completed, affected both the tactical formation and the *materiel*. There are at present four major tactical formations within the German Flying Corps ; these are :—

(1) Army squadrons (Armeeflieger-Abteilung).
(2) Army corps squadrons (Truppenflieger-Abteilung).
(3) Pursuit squadrons (Jagd-Staffeln).
(4) Battle wings (Kampf-Geschwader).

1. The *Army squadrons* are placed under the direct orders of the O.C. the aviation service of each army ; they are primarily employed for strategical reconnaissances, but may sometimes be detailed on photographic work and even bombardments.

The *machines* forming the Army squadrons all belong to a standard model in which only minor details may vary, as a certain latitude is given the contractors in this respect. The machines are two-seater tractor biplanes of from 41 to 45 feet span, and are fitted with a stationary Benz or Mercédès engine developing from 225 to 240 horse-power. Their horizontal speed is from 100 to 105 miles per hour.

The *armament* consists of (1) two machine guns, one of which is mounted on a fixed emplacement in front of the pilot, and fires through the propeller by means of a synchronising device ; the other machine gun is mounted *en barbette*, aft of the pilot, on the observer's seat ; (2) one or two bomb gears, munitioned with four or six bombs.

The firms building this type are the L.V.G., the D.F.W., the Aviatik, and the Albatros. The latter firm has, however, recently produced a more powerful model, which is fitted with a 260-h.p. Mercédès engine, and develops a horizontal speed of 115 miles per hour. The climbing speed is said to be 6,600 feet in 9 minutes, fully loaded. It is confidently expected that eventually all the machines of the Army squadron type will be fitted with the new 6-cylinder, 260-h.p. Mercédès engine, which is, though but slightly heavier, much more reliable than the 8-cylinder, 240-h.p. model. As the engine base of both models has the same width, only slight alterations would be necessary to fit the above described type of machine with the 260-h.p. model, although the wing area would probably have to be somewhat increased. It is worth noting that in 1916 the standard 150-h.p. two-seater tractor biplane was similarly modernised when it was fitted with the 175-h.p. Mercédès.

2. The *Army-Corps squadrons* are assigned to individual army corps, and are, as a rule, commanded by a captain who is placed directly under orders of the second bureau of the army corps staff. Their chief function is tactical reconnaissance, photography, gun spotting, and, during active operations, contact patrol work between the units engaged in an advance.

The army-corps squadrons are equipped with machines which are in every way similar to those forming the Army squadrons, except for a smaller power plant which endows them with lesser speed. Such are, at present, the two-seater tractor biplanes built by A.E.G., Albatros, Aviatik, L.V.G. and Rumpler, which have a span of from 39 to 43 feet, and are fitted with a 6-cylinder, 175-h.p. Mercédès engine. The horizontal speed is from 90 to 95 m.p.h.

The armament is the same as on the army squadron type. Provision is made on these machines for the quick exchange of the bomb gear against a radio installation or a photographic apparatus.

3. The *Pursuit Squadrons* are assigned to individual armies in numbers varying in accordance with needs. Although their principal function is the defence of the army corps squadrons engaged in tactical reconnaissance work, they are also employed in some instances, on convoy duty with bombers and for the destruction of Allied kite-balloons.

There appear to be, at present, on the Western front, about 40 pursuit squadrons, each of which consists of 12 machines. In some instances two or more squadrons are combined into Pursuit Wings which are placed under the leadership of particularly capable chiefs ; these units are not permanently assigned to particular sectors, but are entrusted with special missions according to needs. Such are the now celebrated "travelling circuses" of Von Bulow and Von Richthofen. These special wings generally scour the Western front for Allied machines, travelling up and down the line from Nieuport to Belfort.

A number of pursuit squadrons are detached to the local defence of important German towns, in particular at Metz, Strasbourg, Mulhouse, Friedrichshafen, Stuttgart, Essen, Cologne, and Treves.

The pursuit squadrons are equipped with one-seater biplanes of from 28 to 30 feet span which are fitted with a 175-h.p. Mercédès engine driving a tractor screw. The horizontal speed of these machines is from 110 to 125 miles per hour ; they are principally built by Albatros, Fokker, L.T.G. (Lufttorpedo-Gesellschaft), and Roland.

The armament consists of two Spandau machine-guns, mounted "fixé" in front of the pilot, which are synchronised to fire either simultaneously or alternately through the propeller. No bomb gear is provided.

The older pursuit machines, such as the Halberstadt, with a 120-h.p. Argus engine, the Rex, with a rotary 100-h.p. Rex engine, and the Fokker, with a 100-h.p. rotary Oberursel (German Gnôme), all of which are tractor biplanes, appear to be employed, at present, chiefly on the "easier" Eastern front.

4. The *Battle wings* are placed under the direct orders of General Headquarters, and are not, as a rule, permanently assigned to particular sectors.

These wings consist of from 40 to 50 machines, and are subdivided into four or five squadrons. The machines are mostly Gotha twin-pusher biplanes, which have a span of 78 feet, and are fitted with two 260-h.p. Mercédès engines.

A certain number of bomber squadrons are, however, equipped with A.E.G. twin-tractor biplanes and a huge Rumpler bomber was to have been placed in commission. The Germans had no mean hopes of this machine, particularly as regards speed and climb.

There are, at present, three battle wings in commission. Wings No. 1 and No. 2 are mobile formations, each of which disposes of a special railway train for the transport of the *matériel* and the *personnel*. These wings are assigned by General Headquarters, from time to time, to such sectors as may require the co-operation of a powerful bombing unit.

Wing No. 3 is stationed in Belgium, and appears to be chiefly entrusted with expeditions against Great Britain. This wing consists of Squadrons No. 13, 14, 15, 16, and 17, all of which are equipped with Gotha bombers.

A GERMAN "CIRCUS" OF ALBATROS SINGLE-SEATERS GETTING READY TO START. Note the "sugar-stick" stripes, by way of camouflage, of the machine near the right end of the picture.

GERMAN NAVAL AVIATION.

NAVY GENERAL.

The 1913 expenditure on naval aviation (including airships) was £250,000 (50 million marks), plus a portion of the special expenditure.

NAVAL FLYING SCHOOLS AND STATIONS.
Kiel.   Putzig b. Danzig.   **Wilhelmshaven.**

Stations are also known to have existed at Heligoland, Langeoog, and Cuxhaven, and at numerous points along the North Sea and Baltic Coasts. Antwerp, Ostend, and Zeebrugge in Belgium also contain German Naval Air Stations.

NAVY AEROPLANES.

Early in 1914 the total effective force was 36 seaplanes as follows:—

1912 { **4 monoplanes** (*Rumpler*).
{ **10 biplanes** (4 *Albatros*, 2 *Curtiss*, 4 *Ewer*).

1913 { **2 monoplanes** (*Rumpler*).
{ **30 biplanes** (*A.G.O., Albatros, Avro, Curtiss, Wright*).

Total **14** old and **32** new machines.

In 1914, a *Wight* seaplane and a *Sopwith* "bat-boat" were bought in England, and a large number of German seaplanes were built.

1914-1915 { Since war broke out it is known that a very large number of seaplanes have been added for patrol work, and for co-operation with fast ships at sea.

1915-16-17 { The German Naval Air Service has increased consistently. German seaplanes are constantly met and fought over the coast of Flanders, and have made frequent raids on the Kentish coast. Seaplanes have also been reported along the Baltic coast, and from Denmark and Holland. Seaplanes have been picked up far out in the North Sea, and have been reported as taking part in Naval actions far from the coast. Seaplane stations are known to exist at Ostend, Zeebrugge, on the Frisian Islands, on Helgoland and on the Island of Sylt, as well as on the Baltic.

The most notable exploit by a German seaplane during 1917-18 was in connection with the cruise of the "Wolf," the famous commerce-destroyer which did so much damage in the Indian Ocean. This ship carried a seaplane, known as the "Wölfchen," or "Little Wolf," and on many occasions this machine discovered victims for her mother-ship. She was brought home safely.

During 1917 and early 1918 seaplane patrols were frequently met in the North Sea by British seaplanes, and a number of actions were fought, in which several German machines were brought down. German seaplanes also took part in all Naval actions during the year, except at night.

During the summer of 1918 the German seaplanes, chiefly Brandenburgers and Rumplers (q.v.), obtained a distinct superiority over British seaplanes in the North Sea, owing to the fact that they were small, very fast, and quick in manœuvring, and were opposed to big slow flying-boats carrying heavy loads of petrol for long patrols. The British Authorities had discouraged the production of fast fighting seaplanes, and consequently none were available to counter the German Navy's attacks.

The British losses in big boats and also in airships became so heavy that ultimately the Navy was forced to move in the matter, and when the Armistice was signed the balance of fighting power was on the point of being redressed.

A

A.E.G.   Allgemeine Elektricitäts Gesellschaft

This big electric company, which also owns and runs the N.A.G. motor works, building up to 1914 Wright and own design aero engines, formed an aircraft branch at Henningsdorf by Berlin, in 1913, the position of which may be compared with the aircraft works of British firms like Vickers and Armstrong-Whitworth, in that they strengthened by their influential financial backing behind them the whole aircraft trade at a time when the latter was looked upon as very problematic by the financial world, and thus not worth investing into.

The activities of the A.E.G. aircraft works have always been confined to military aviation, its flying being open only to and supplied by army pupils, and its aeroplanes never being entered for civil flying competitions.

Steel-built aircraft was always specialised in, the first biplane turned out being of general tractor outlines, the folding of the planes along the fuselage being similar to the British *Short* device.

The well-known former Wright pilot, Schauenberg, was employed, and an A.E.G. biplane entered for the 1914 Prince Henry flight under his pilotage. Schauenberg has been accidentally killed in the firm's service during the war.

The A.E.G. also turned out what was, up to its time, the only successful monoplane flying boat.

A.E.G. G type bombers were operational from 1915 onwards, starting with the G.I. The most important version was the G.IV. Other A.E.G. aircraft were B and C types for observation and reconnaissance, JI and JII armour-plated biplanes for close support and patrol, and the single R.I large four-engined bomber of 1918.

Types of German Naval pupils at the Lübeck Naval Flying School. It will be noted that these pupil-pilots are of non-commissioned rank, contrary to British custom, where almost all pilots are officers.

THE A.E.G. SINGLE-ENGINED BIPLANE, TYPE C.IV.

The biplane illustrated, as is the case of all machines built by this firm, is constructed entirely of steel tube autogenously welded, save for the greater part of the ribs and the leading edge of the wings. The lower wings have a span of 12.55 ms. (42 ft.), which is nearly equal to that of the upper wings, 13 ms. (43 ft.), the length of the machine is very small, being only 7.15 ms. (23 ft.).

The wings are set at a slight dihedral, namely, 2.5 degrees, or 125 mms. The centre section of the top plane, which is reminiscent of certain English machines, is supported by a splayed-out cabane, and there are two rows of interplane struts on either side.

The planes are washed out at the tips. Their incidence is 3 degrees for a little more than a third of the span, and 2 degrees

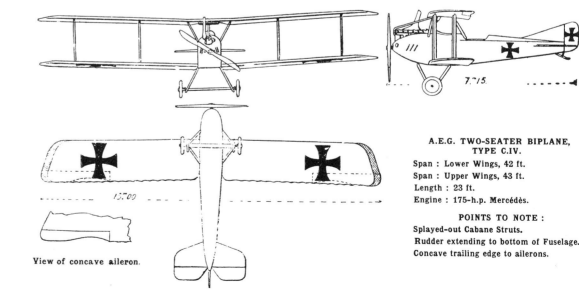

View of concave aileron.

A.E.G. TWO-SEATER BIPLANE, TYPE C.IV.

Span : Lower Wings, 42 ft.
Span : Upper Wings, 43 ft.
Length : 23 ft.
Engine : 175-h.p. Mercédès.

POINTS TO NOTE :
Splayed-out Cabane Struts.
Rudder extending to bottom of Fuselage.
Concave trailing edge to ailerons.

near the external struts which diminishes still further towards the extremity of the wings.

The gap is 1.87 ms. at the front struts, and 1.89 ms. at the rear struts, and exceeds in an unusual manner the chord of the planes, which is 1.65.

The dimensions of the steel interplane struts are as follows :— the internal struts, 66 mms. by 31 mms. ; the external struts, 62 mms. by 25 mms., and they are mounted at their bases on cones topped by balls.

The wing surface is 39.5 sq. ms. (260 sq. ft.), which includes the ailerons.

The wings are of trapezoidal form, but the ailerons have a peculiar form, their rear edge being very concave, which reminds one somewhat of the ancient Taube.

The wings and ailerons are entirely constructed of tube work, save for the leading edge and the secondary ribs in a manner similar to that which is found in the Rumpler. The main spars are of 40 mms. steel tube with tubular distance pieces, and the principal ribs are also made of flat tube work. In the lower wings there is arranged a pair of small tubes as guides for aileron cables. The trailing edge of the wings is formed by steel wire. There is a certain amount of flexibility in the trailing edge.

The ailerons are attached by three hinges to a false wooden spar, the surface of each being 5 sq. ms.

In each wing two of the cross anti-drift wires are cable and one a piano-wire, attached, as are those in the fuselage, by a link similar to those in the chain of a bicycle to lugs welded to the angles of the tubes. At their point of intersection they are joined in a manner similar to that employed in the bracing between the interplane struts, being in the form of an X à la Rumpler. The fabric is painted green and brown.

The elevator flaps have the appearance of a rounded polygon. The rudder, which is nearly triangular, is preceded by a fixed triangular fin. These controls are not balanced. A rather exceptional feature in a modern German aeroplane.

The fixed tailplane has a surface of 1.8 m. The elevators are 1.32 m. The fixed fin is 0.7 m., and the rudder is 0.63 m.

The angle of incidence is adjustable from 2.4 deg. to 4.55 deg.

The fuselage is constructed entirely of straight steel tubes, the surface thereof being slab-sided, but there is a rounded cowl in front, made of three-ply, with fabric on its sides. The streamline fairing on top of the fuselage is formed of three-ply placed on arches.

The two engine bearers, which are made of square steel tube, are supported in front each by two oblique tubes, placed one above, the other below.

The fuselage terminates suddenly at the rear with a vertical strut, and is overloaded with tubes and lugs. It is covered with fabric, which laces underneath.

Behind the motor is placed the pilot, who sits over the petrol tank, and behind him is the passenger's seat, which can be slid along a pair of " U "-shaped rails.

The landing carriage does not differ from others, except for its shock absorbers, which consist of heavy coil springs (6 kgs.), which are attached to three long transverse steel members—an axle of 55 mm. diameter, and a distance piece in front and behind, all of which, together, make a streamline. The tail skid is massive and well sprung.

The motor is a 6-cylinder Mercedès of 175 h.p.

The propeller is a " Wolf," 2.8 m. diameter and 1.8 m. pitch, constructed of alternate layers of ash and walnut, or walnut and mahogany.

An oblique funnel projecting from the fuselage makes it possible to replenish the petrol tank from the ground, without getting into the machine.

There is a water reservoir in the central section of the upper plane to the left of the axis of the machine. The radiator itself is of honeycomb type.

The exhaust pipes unite in a common vertical cylinder.

The armament consists of two machine-guns, one firing through the propeller, the other being placed in the passenger's cockpit.

There is a bomb-rack in the passenger's cockpit to take four bombs, placed one above the other.

REPORT ON A.E.G. G-TYPE BOMBER, G.105.

[For the following report the Editor is indebted to the Technical Department of the Air Ministry.]

This machine was brought down by anti-aircraft fire at Achiet-le-Grand on 23/12/17.

On a label protected by celluloid, mounted on a tube in the nacelle, is the legend—" Abnahme am (Accepted on) 10/11/17."

This machine, whilst carrying a similar power plant, is very different in construction from the *Gotha* type, which also embraces the *Friedrichshafen Bomber* reported on in I.C. 619.

Whereas the latter is generally constructed of wood, ply wood being used to a very large extent throughout, in the *A.E.G.* steel is almost universally employed, not only in regard to the fuselage, nacelle, subsidiary surfaces and landing gear, but also in the wings themselves.

Needless to say, acetylene welding is freely resorted to throughout the construction, which, however, appears to be far from light.

On the whole, the *A.E.G.* aeroplane, judged by contemporary British standards of design, is decidedly clumsy, not only in detail work, but also in appearance. The performance is poor.

The leading particulars of the machine are as follows :—

Weight empty : 5,258 lbs.
Total weight : 7,130 lbs.
Area of upper wings : 395.2 sq. ft.
Area of lower wings : 335.2 sq. ft.
Total area of wings : 730.4 sq. ft.
Loading per square foot of wing surface : 9.77 lbs. per sq. ft.

THE SMALL A.E.G. TWO-SEATER, with 175 h.p. Mercédès engine.

Area of ailerons, each : 17.9 sq. ft.
Area of balance of aileron : 1.8 sq. ft.
Area of tail plane : 34.0 sq. ft.
Area of fin : 11.5 sq. ft.
Area of rudder : 20.8 sq. ft.
Balanced area of rudder : 2.6 sq. ft.
Area of elevators : 31.2 sq. ft.
Balanced area of elevators : 3.6 sq. ft.
Horizontal area of body : 206.4 sq. ft.
Vertical area of body : 209.2 sq. ft.
Total weight per horse power : 13.7 lbs. approx.
Crew—pilot and two passengers : 540 lbs.
Armament : 2 guns.
Engines : 2—260 h.p. Mercédès.
Petrol capacity : 123 gallons=861 lbs.
Oil capacity : 11 gallons=110 lbs.
Water capacity : 13 gallons=130 lbs.

Other dimensions are also shown on the drawings at the end of the Report.

PERFORMANCE.

(a) CLIMB, 5,000 FT. IN 10.3 MINS.
Rate of climb at 5,000 ft.—390 ft. per min.
Climb, 9,000 ft. in 23.4 mins.
Rate of climb at 9,000 ft.—235 ft. per min.

(b) SPEED AT HEIGHTS.
Level to 5,000 ft.—90 miles per hour approximately.
At 9,000 ft.—86 ,, ,, ,, ,,

(c) LANDING SPEED.
The aeroplane is best landed at a speed between 75 and 80 miles an hour ; after flattening out it sinks to the ground quickly and pulls up rapidly.

(d) CONTROL.
1. Lateral—Good.
2. Elevators—Bad, especially when landing.

NOTE.—It is stated that it is not advisable to fly this machine without a passenger in the front seat.

CONSTRUCTION.

The wings are of characteristic form. The central portion consists of a rectangular centre cell permanently attached to the fuselage. The lower wings support the engines. In this centre cell the planes are set horizontally. At each side of it the lower main planes are swept upwards with a vertical dihedral of 2.75°, the top planes being kept flat, and both main planes are swept backwards in the horizontal plane to an angle of 4° for the bottom plane and 3° for the top plane. As the central portion of the upper main plane has 4 inches of negative stagger relative to the bottom plane, this difference in angle brings their tips practically vertically over one another. The angle of incidence attains a maximum of 4° at the base of the engine struts, i.e., 7 ft. 10¾ inches from the centre. At the second strut the angle is 3½° and at the end strut 2¼°. These angles are painted in circles on the surface of the planes, evidently for the convenience of riggers. The camber of both planes is washed out gradually towards the tips.

The main spars are kept parallel throughout the whole of their length and are attached to the central cell by means of pin joints, similar to those on the *Friedrichshafen*. The ribs are of solid wood. It is rather notable in comparison with other German machines of all types that ply wood is almost entirely absent. In the *A.E.G.* construction the rib webs are perforated and strengthened by wooden uprights at intervals and are glued into a grooved flange. The ribs are placed 300 mms.—325 mms. apart—and are not directly or firmly attached to the spars on which they are a relatively loose fit. Passing through the ribs of the bottom plane and extending from their junction with the centre section to the extreme outside strut are two steel tubes, approximately 17 mms. in diameter, which act as housings for the aileron control wires. These tubes are very strong, and it is thought possible that they are also counted upon to lend rigidity to the wing structure.

Front View of the A.E.G. G.IV Bomber. 1918 type.

The leading edge, which is of the usual semi-circular section, acts as a distance piece, as also does the wire trailing edge. Thirteen inches in front of the last-named is a stringer formed of a steel rod. Apart from this, the spars are the only longitudinal members of the wings. Between the main ribs are false ribs running from the leading edge to a point a few inches behind the leading spar and applying only to the upper surface.

The lower plane is covered as to its upper surface with sheet metal immediately under the engines, whilst between them and the fuselage is fixed a strip of corrugated aluminium which acts as a footway. The fabric is attached in the usual manner and is stitched to the ribs both top and bottom. The two surfaces are stitched together behind the metal rod which acts as a stringer, and by this means the actual trailing edge wire is relieved of a certain amount of tension. The wing structure is internally braced by means of steel tubular cross-pieces and stranded cables. A single fitting is employed for the attachment of the interplane struts and for that of the bracing tubes. It is a tight fit on the spar, to which it is fixed by a bolt, and is formed with an extension lug which acts as an anchorage for the bracing tube, whilst a sideways extension of the same lug carries an eye for the bracing wire. It is provided with a cup-shaped upper extension, into which there is screwed a steel dome which carries the ball of the strut socket fitting and also acts as a wiring plate for the interplane bracing wires.

The fabric is run into the space between the upper and lower flanges of this fitting, the whole making a very neat job.

STRUTS.
These are of streamline section steel tube and of uniform dimensions throughout. The section is 92 mms. long by 48 mms. broad. The ends are sharply tapered down, and into them is welded a cupped ferrule which drops onto a ball, and is there held in position by a cotter-pin. This joint gives a considerable range of lateral freedom, as is the usual practice on machines of German design.

FUSELAGE.
The whole of the fuselage is built up of steel tubes welded together. It is of plain rectangular section and the cross tubes are attached directly to the main booms without the intervention of any clips.

Under the nacelle, and in the neighbourhood of the main petrol tanks and the bomb racks, the fuselage is reinforced with thin tubular steel tie-rods.

The upper booms of the fuselage are provided with sockets for the inclined struts of the central cell. The fitting consists of two circular steel plates welded into position to form an integral part of the frame joint, the front one of these flanges being provided with lugs for the anchorage of bracing cables. The inclined struts are secured by a ring of short set screws wired together as shown. If appearances are to be trusted, this form of attachment, whilst being strong and convenient, is excessively heavy. Unlike the practice which is pursued in the *Friedrichshafen Bomber*, wherein the main frame consists of three separate sections, that of the *A.E.G.* is in one piece from stem to stern. The longerons are 30 mms. in diameter and the transverse members 30 mms., these dimensions being retained up to the extreme tail end. The nose part of the frame is covered in with three-ply wood, but behind this a double covering of fabric is used, under which the tubular construction is completely hidden. Behind the after cockpit a single covering only is adopted and laced the whole of its length so that it is removable in its entirety.

ENGINE STRUTS.
These are of streamline steel tubing and embrace joints of a somewhat similar type to those used on the interplane struts; that is to say, a certain amount of free movement is provided. The mounting of the engines is clearly shown in the front and side elevations. In front there are four struts which converge to a joint on the leading spar, whilst at the rear there are two struts which meet at a joint on the trailing spar.

The bell-shaped housing attached to a cup on the spar joint contains a ball-ended set screw which screws into the foot of the four struts which are here united by welding. The inclined transverse struts are taken from the spars to the engine mounting and cross struts from thence again to the upper booms of the fuselage. In order to provide simplicity of erection these subsidiary struts are provided with a means of adjustment. At one end they terminate in a ball-ended set screw screwed into the tapered end of the strut and secured by a lock-nut.

ENGINE MOUNTING.
The engine bearers are of steel rectangular section, measuring 40 mms. high by 30 mms. broad, with a wall thickness of approximately 2 mms. These bearers are welded to the struts which support them, and for the greater part of their length are reinforced by a system of tubular tie-rods also welded in position. Box attachments welded to the engine bearers, are provided for the crankchamber holding-down bolts. The engine is not directly mounted on the steel bearers, but upon ½-inch wooden washers. Owing to the deformation inseparable from so much welding, the engine mounting is of very clumsy appearance, and, in fact, the quality of welding does not appear to be up to previous German standards, but the construction would appear to be light.

ENGINE FAIRING.
As shown in the photographs, the engines are almost completely enclosed in a fairing composed of detachable aluminium panels. The necessary framework and clips are provided for panels totally enclosing the engine, but it would seem that this bonnet right over the heads of the cylinders has been discarded. The tubular framework which supports the panels is an elaborate piece of work comprising a multiplicity of welded joints. It consists of 16 mm. tubes, to which are attached lugs for carrying the necessary turn-buttons. The framework is made in two halves so as to be easily detachable, and a joint for that purpose is made. It will be noticed that a narrow slot for the exit of air passing over the engine is provided at the rear end of the engine egg, an opening of somewhat similar dimensions being between the two halves of the radiator.

ENGINES.
The engines are the standard 6-cylinder 260-h.p. Mercédès. These engines are fully described in the Engine Section and no important novel points are adopted.] A new shape has been adopted for the exhaust pipe, and this is clearly shown in one of the photographs—an inverted cone is placed in the belled mouth of the pipe. The usual water-pump greaser is fitted and worked by a lever in the pilot's cockpit. It is of rather less clumsy design than that of the *Friedrichshafen*, but employs the same principle. The throttle is interconnected with the ignition advance.

A small fitting, the purpose of which is not clear, is fixed to the carburettor, and consists of a bell-shaped cover over the top of the float chamber, not directly connected thereto, but supported on a bracket clipped to the main water pipe. The bell is free to slide up and down the stem of the bracket, on which it is a very loose fit, but is prevented from falling over the float chamber by a small washer. It is conjectured that this fitting may have for its purpose the prevention of petrol having access to the hot exhaust pipe in the event of the machine turning over. Between the bell and the float chamber is a clearance of about ¼-inch.

PETROL SYSTEM.
There are two main tanks, each of 270 litres = 95 gallons total capacity, and these are placed under the pilot's seat in the main cockpit. Two subsidiary tanks, used solely for starting purposes and giving a gravity supply, are mounted in the centre section of the top main plane and are of roughly streamline form. Beneath them is a small cowling containing their level gauges, which are visible from the pilot's seat.

On the right hand side of the main cockpit is fitted a hand-operated wing pump, the object of which is to draw petrol from either of the main tanks and direct it to the gravity tanks. Pipes from all four tanks are taken to a distributing manifold on the dashboard, and by means of seven taps thereon the supply of petrol can be directed from any one of the tanks to either engine or both. Two additional taps are provided on the wing pump so that the fuel for the gravity supply can be drawn from either main tank as required. It would appear that most of the various troubles associated with this form of tap have been overcome, as they show no signs of leaking or sticking. The level of the main tanks is indicated on the dashboard by two Maximall gauges. Those attached to the gravity tanks are made by Laufer and employ the static head principle. They read up to 45 litres each, from zero to this figure being given by one and a half complete revolutions of the indicating hand.

PETROL PRESSURE SYSTEM.
The usual pressure pump is mounted on each engine and pipes therefrom are led to a mainfold mounted on the dashboard. This is also connected to a large hand pump on the right hand side of the pilot's seat. Gauges reading the pressure from each engine pump are provided, and there is also a blow-off tap for relieving the pressure of the whole system.

OIL SYSTEM.
This is the usual system as fitted to all 260-h.p. Mercédès engines. The main supply of oil is carried in the crank-chamber sump and is continually being refreshed by a small additional supply of fresh oil drawn from an external tank. This tank has a capacity of 5 gallons, is of rectangular shape, and is mounted at the side of the engine nearest to the fuselage. It is provided with a visible glass level over which is a celluloid covered window let into the engine fairing, so that the oil level is visible from the pilot's seat.

RADIATOR.
Each radiator is composed of two halves bolted together. The space between the two halves is partially covered with a sheet metal panel pierced with a hole 1ft. 6in. high by 4in. wide. The radiator is not actually honeycomb, though presenting that appearance. It consists of a series of vertical tubes with transverse gills. Each radiator cell measures 2ft. 3½in. high by 7½in. wide, and has a uniform depth of 4in. Each complete radiator is provided with two shutters of roughly streamline section. These, when fully closed, cover over about one-third of the radiating surface.

They are controlled from the pilot's seat by two levers which work them through universally jointed rods.

ENGINE CONTROL.
The throttle levers are of the plain twin variety. They are placed close together so as to be easily worked either in unison or separately. The connections between the levers and the carburettor are made as simple as possible, and the levers operate the throttle through a couple of universally jointed rods which extend from each side of the body to the engine eggs.

Three-quarter Front View of the A.E.G. G.IV Bomber. 1918 type.

Side View of the A.E.G. G.IV Bomber. 1918 type.

Tail Planes.

The fixed horizontal tail planes are notable for their extremely bold curvature, both top and bottom. The framework consists entirely of welded steel tubing. The leading edge of the tail plane is mounted so as to be adjustable in case of necessity, a simple bracket being used for this purpose. This is welded on to the fuselage upright at each side and strengthened with a transverse stay. It allows the tail plane leading edge to be fixed in one of three positions. The trailing edge of the tail plane is supported each side by a streamline section steel tubular strut.

Fin.

The fin, like the fixed tail plane, has also a very strongly marked streamline section at the base, tapering off to flat at the top, where it abuts against the balanced portion of the rudder. At this point its framework, which is of light steel tube, is made rigid by a couple of tubular stays bracing the rudder post to the sides of the fuselage.

Rudder and Elevators.

These organs are built up of steel tubular framework and present no points of special interest, except that in the case of the rudder that part which is above the fixed fin is made of grooved section.

Ailerons.

As may be seen from the plan view of the complete machine, the shape of the ailerons is somewhat unusual. These are applied to the top plane only and have a chord which reaches its maximum at their extreme ends and its minimum in the centre of their length. For what purpose this peculiar shape is adopted is not clear. The framework of these ailerons is welded steel tubing, and the control crank is fitted in such a way as to lie partially hidden in a slot in the main plane. This crank is built up of welded sheet steel, an elliptical hole being cut in the trailing edge of the main plane for the passage of the forward wire.

Control.

The main control consists of a wheel mounted on a pivoted lever, the wheel operating the ailerons by means of a drum and cables, which pass direct over pulleys and along tubes running parallel with the wing spars and then over inclined pulleys up to aileron cranks. The wheel column is pivoted to a long crossbar extending the whole length of the fuselage and carrying at each end cranks for the elevator control wires which at intervals are carried through fibre guides socketed to the frame. The cranks of the elevators are concealed inside the rear end of the fuselage, whilst those of the rudder (which is fitted with duplicate cranks and wires) are external. A modified dual control is fitted, which allows the assistant pilot to work the elevator and rudder only. For this purpose, a socket is mounted on the pivot bar into which can be inserted a plain steel tube, which is normally carried in clips behind the pilot's back. A second rudder bar is carried under the dashboard, and can readily be dropped into position into a square socket partially sunk into the floor of the cockpit and connected to the pilot's rudder bar by cranks and a link.

Personnel.

Seats are provided for a crew of four, who are carried as follows :—

One in the front cockpit.
One in the pilot's seat.
One at the pilot's side.
One in the rear cockpit.

All can, if necessary, change places whilst the machine is in the air. Between the front cockpit and that of the pilot a sliding panel is provided through which the gunner can crawl. The seat at the side of the pilot folds up and slides back into a cavity under the coaming of the nacelle and when in this position allows access down a narrow and inclined passage-way to the rear cockpit. The machine can hardly have been designed to satisfy the requirements of the average pilot in regard to view, as from the pilot's seat it is very difficult to see the ground properly, on account of the position of the lower main plane and the width of the fuselage.

Armament.

Two Parabellum guns are mounted, one in the front cockpit and one in the rear, and provision is made for mounting a third or for transferring one of the others on the floor of the rear cockpit, so that it can fire backwards and under the tail of the machine. For this purpose, a large trap door is provided in the floor of the fuselage, behind the rear cockpit. This trap door has celluloid windows and is normally kept closed by springs. It is lifted up by a small hand winch fitted with a ratchet. It is of passing interest to note that whereas in the *Friedrichshafen* a similar trap door was kept open by means of springs, in the *A.E.G.* springs are used to keep the door closed. In the front cockpit the gun is supported on a carriage which runs round a partially circular rail which is strongly supported from the fuselage by a framework of steel tubes Forming part of this frame is an inclined steel tubular column, the base of which is fitted in a swivel bearing in the floor of the cockpit, and on this is mounted an adjustable seat for the gunner. A toothed rack runs round the rail and engages with a spur pinion driven by a hand wheel so that the gunner, when occupying his seat, swivels himself round as well as the gun. The vertical swivel of the fork-ended gun carrier is locked by a ball-ended lever and a similar lever is employed for locking the carriage itself to its rail.

This action is accomplished by a cam device which depresses the roller of the carriage and squeezes the rail section between the roller and an adjustable set screw which normally just clears the groove on the under side of the rail. In order to prevent the forward gunner from shooting the tractor screws, preventative shields of light steel tube are carried between the upper edge of the forward cockpit and the inclined struts of the centre section. These impose a limit to the travel of the gun. In the rear cockpit the gun mounting is U-shaped in plan form, and here again the principle of a carriage running on a rail and driven by a spur gear meshing with a toothed rack is employed, though in this case the gunner's seat does not revolve with the gun. The carriage is of a somewhat similar type to that used in the front cockpit, but the method of locking it is different. The rail is provided with grooves both above and below, there being two rollers at the top and one underneath. Normally, when the gun carriage is free, the latter is clear of the rail, but when the locking mechanism is brought into action it is forced upwards so that the rail is gripped between the rollers, thus avoiding any possibility of shake at this point, and at the same time a positive lock is obtained on a second rail carried below the first. When the ball-ended hand lever is tightened, its effect is to squeeze the lower rail between two jaws. The movable jaw is, however, connected up by a link to a small cam, the base of which abuts against the foot of a fork-ended rod which carries the lower roller and is free to move up and down in a guide, to the base of which the cam is pivoted. By this means a very secure and rapid locking device is obtained. In the front of the rear cockpit, a locker is provided which would be capable of holding ammunition, and beneath this a series of racks.

Bombing Gear.

Three racks for holding twenty-five pounder bombs are installed on the machine ; two side-by-side on the left side of the rear cockpit, and one on the right side of the petrol tanks in the space between the pilot's and rear cockpits. This rack is covered by a detachable wooden lid which acts as the floor of the narrow gangway mentioned above. Underneath the centre of the nacelle, provision is made for carrying two or more large bomb racks, which, however, were not in use on this machine. Underneath the lower main plane, two at each side of the nacelle, are fixed bomb clips which are capable of supporting bombs roughly 8 inches in diameter. They are held in position by a belly-band consisting of two steel strips. Eleven-and-a-half inches in front of this clip is a bracket suitable for a circular section of 4 inches in diameter, and 13½ inches in the rear of the clip is a second bracket suitable for a 5 inches diameter section. The bomb would thus appear to be 50 kilogrammes. At their fixed end they are supported on a crosshead. This in turn is carried on a bracket clipped to a steel tube running parallel to the wing spars and braced thereto by tubular steel girders. The crosshead is free to swivel on the bracket against the action of a coiled spring, which, when the bomb has been released, twists the crosshead round against a stop, so that the belly-band is forcibly swung round and now faces the direction of flight, instead of lying edgewise on to it. The ends of the steel strips are swivelled on the crosshead, and here again coil springs are used, so that the tendency is for the belly-band to be held flat against the lower surface of the bottom main plane, and out of the way of the other clip.

When the bombs are in position, the rings which are fitted on the free end of the belly-band are caught between the jaws of a trigger mechanism. This device is carried on the same tube which supports the crossheads, as already mentioned. Lying parallel to this tube and between it and the leading spar is a control rod fitted with two levers which are connected respectively to the two bomb trip gears, and this rod is operated by a quadrant lever mounted in the front cockpit. In order to allow one trip gear to be worked at a time, the link of the outer trip is provided with a slot where it is pivoted to the trigger release. On working the lever in the cockpit, therefore, its first action up to half way over the quadrant is to release the bomb nearest the nacelle; whilst a further movement releases the outer bomb.

An exactly similar method is employed for operating the bombs carried underneath the other wing. The levers in the front cockpit are all mounted on a common bracket built up of steel tubes, and are arranged as follows :—First, there are the two levers which control the two bomb magazines in the rear cockpit. These are provided with thimbles and chains, so that they cannot be operated accidentally. Next a single lever, which controls the larger bomb clips on the right wing. These are capable of being secured by split pins inserted in their quadrants. Next, there is a lever which in this particular machine was furnished with no action at all, but is evidently designed for manipulating the large bomb carriers when these are installed. Behind it are, first, a single lever for the left hand outer bomb clips, and, finally, the lever for working the bomb magazine on the right hand side of the nacelle.

Landing Gear.

The landing gear of the *A.E.G.* bomber is simply an elaboration of that which has become practically a standard fitting on single and two-seaters, except that in this machine the gear is in duplicate. It consists of two axles carrying two wheels a-piece, and suspended from pairs of V struts. One pair is connected to the spars of the centre section immediately underneath the engine strut sockets, and the other to the spars midway between this point and the fuselage and at the same point from which diagonal struts are taken from the spars to the engine mounting and nacelle. This, together with the wire bracing of the landing gear struts, provides a completely triangulated construction. The struts are, however, connected by ball joints similar to those used with the engine struts, so that in case of strain a certain amount of free movement can take place. The pairs of V struts carry at their foot a hollow steel crossbar having the section of a trough, and in this lies the axle which connects the two wheels.

The fixed beam has forward and rearward extensions, at each end of which are anchored the ends of the batteries of coil springs which act as shock absorbers, and at their other ends are hooked to a horn plate on the wheel axle. Each battery of springs, of which there are four to each axle, consists of 18 springs. A yoke of stranded steel cable restricts the movement of the axle beyond a certain limit. The tyres are 32 ins. × 6 ins. = 810 × 150. A tail skid of massive proportions is used.

Wireless.

The machine is internally wired for wireless, and a special dynamo for supplying current for this purpose and also for heating is installed on the right hand engine. This dynamo bears the following inscription :—

Telefunken.
J. P. Flieg. C 1916. Type D.
Alternating current 270 watts. 5 amperes. 600 frequency.
Continuous current 50 volts. 4 amperes. r.p.m. 5,400.

The dynamo is mounted on brackets acetylene-welded to the steel engine bearers, and is normally completely enclosed in a detachable fairing. The dynamo drive embraces the pulley, which is a standard fitting on the 260-h.p. Mercédès, but in this particular case the clutch gear whereby the driving pulley can be disconnected from the engine as required, appears to have been discarded. Two sets of wires are taken from the dynamo inside flexible metal conduits to a pair of plugs situated at the junction of the fuselage and the right hand lower main plane. Here they terminate in plug sockets, so designed that the plugs cannot be inserted wrongly. One of these wiring circuits appl es to the heating system, and wires for this purpose are carried to points in all three cockpits, whilst the other circuit is for wireless and terminates in a plug adaptor in the rear cockpit. No wireless instruments were fitted. Two plug sockets for the pilot's cockpit and one for the forward gunner. A small plate on the pilot's dashboard carries the following inscription, but no definite information is given :—

F. T. Fitting. W/T Set.
Aeroplanes.
Type 94. NY 1125/16.
Fitting, No. 85a.
Driving propeller. Type. Direct coupling.
Length of aerial wires — — — —
Telefunken transmitter— — — metres.
Huth transmitter — — — — metres.
D transmitter. — — — metres.
G transmitter. — — — metres.

Three-quarter Front View of the A.E.G. G.IV Bomber. 1918 type.

In addition to these two circuits, there is a lighting installation in conjunction with a battery carried in a box in the rear cockpit. From here, wires are taken to each cockpit and also to the tail and via the leading edge of the upper plane to the extreme outside strut of each wing. On these struts red and green lights are carried. Inspection lights are provided at convenient points in each cockpit over the dashboard, instruments, etc.

For the most part the lighting wiring is contained inside a light celluloid conduit.

INSTRUMENTS.

These comprise twin engine revolution counters, twin air pressure gauges for the petrol supply, electric thermometer, altimeter, petrol level gauges, etc. All of these are of recognised types and call for no detailed description.

CAMOUFLAGE.

This machine is camouflaged in six different colours on a uniform system covering every portion. The colours are arranged in hexagons measuring roughly 18in. across the flats, and the colours are sage green, reddish mauve, bluish mauve, black, blue and grey. These colours are not flat washes, but are softened by being stippled and splashed with paint of a lighter tone. Considerable care appears to have been taken with this camouflage scheme, which is presumably effective.

FABRIC AND DOPE.

The fabric throughout is of good quality and the dope acetate of cellulose.

AIRSCREW.

Diameter 10ft. 3.8in.
+ .20in.
Pitch 59.3in.

The following table gives the thicknesses of the various laminæ used in construction of the airscrew. The laminæ are numbered from the trailing to the leading edge.

No.	Material.	Tickness in inches.
1	Walnut	.73
2	Mahogany	.80
3	,,	.80
4	,,	.80
5*	,,	.80
6	,,	.80
7*	,,	.40
8*	,,	.40
9	,,	.80
10	Walnut	.83

*These laminations were of a quite different kind of mahogany, probably African.

Only one airscrew has been seen and dimensioned. Thus it is unknown whether all airscrews would have laminæ of similar thicknesses and of similar timbers. There is no apparent reason why these laminæ should be of different thicknesses. It is surmised that either the enemy is short of timber or that he has a highly scientific reason for so doing that we do not know. The port and starboard airscrew rotate in opposite directions.

W. G. A.,
March, 1918.

THE A.E.G. J TYPE ARMOURED BIPLANE

[The following Report on the A.E.G. Armoured Biplane is published by kind permission of the Technical Department of the Air Ministry, to whom the thanks of the Editor are due.]

This machine was brought down by an R.E.S. of the 21st Squadron, near Hinges, on May 16th, 1918.

It bears the date February 3rd, 1918, stamped on the main planes, and also on portions of the fuselage, and is the first of its type to have been secured.

This aeroplane is designed for the purpose of carrying out offensive patrols against infantry, and is furnished with armour, which affords protection for its personnel. This armour appears, however, to be more or less experimental.

In general construction it closely follows the lines of the A.E.G. Twin engined Bomber G.105, reported on in I.C. 607, though the arrangement of the power plant is, of course, entirely different.

A steel tubular construction is used practically throughout. The machine was badly crashed, and some details are, therefore, not available; but the General Arrangement Drawings at the end of this report may be regarded as substantially accurate.

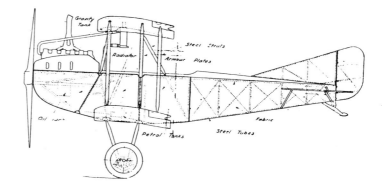

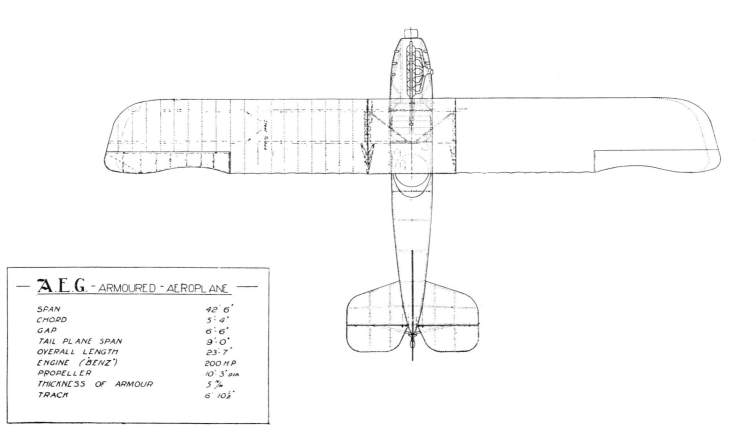

A.E.G. - ARMOURED - AEROPLANE	
SPAN	42' 6"
CHORD	5' 4"
GAP	6' 6"
TAIL PLANE SPAN	9' 0"
OVERALL LENGTH	23' 7"
ENGINE ('BENZ')	200 H.P.
PROPELLER	10' 3' DIA
THICKNESS OF ARMOUR	5 m/m
TRACK	6' 10½"

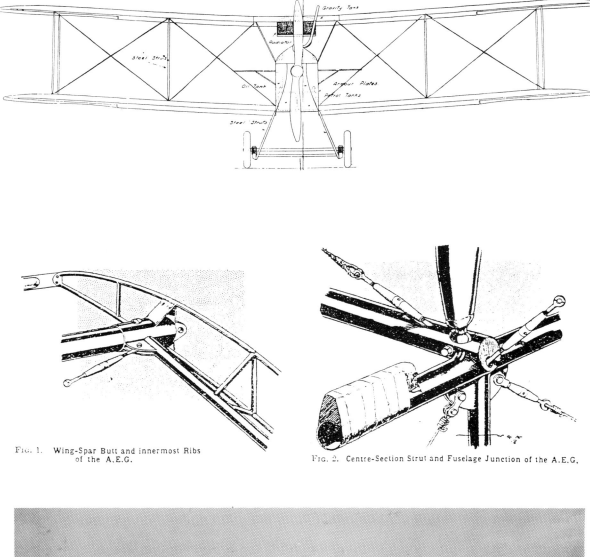

Gravity Tank

Radiator

Steel Struts

Oil Tank

Armour Plates

Petrol Tanks

Steel Struts

FIG. 1. Wing-Spar Butt and innermost Ribs of the A.E.G.

FIG. 2. Centre-Section Strut and Fuselage Junction of the A.E.G.

The leading particulars of the machine are as follows :—

Area of upper wings	..	..	.. 190.4 sq. ft.
Area of lower wings	..	..	.. 168 sq. ft.
Total area of wings	..	..	.. 358.4 sq. ft.
Area of upper aileron	..	..	.. 11.2 sq. ft.
Area of lower aileron	..	..	.. 10 sq. ft.
Area of tail plane	..	..	.. 9.4 sq. ft.
Area of fin..	..	..	.. 7.6 sq. ft.
Area of rudder	..	..	.. 6 sq. ft.
Horizontal area of body..	..	..	.. 48.6 sq. ft.
Side area of body..	..	..	.. 54.8 sq. ft.
Cross sectional area of body	..	..	.. 14.4 sq. ft.
Area of side armour	..	..	.. 33 sq. ft.
Area of bottom armour ..	..	..	.. 29.4 sq. ft.
Area of armour bulkhead	..	..	.. 10.4 sq. ft.
Engine, 200 h.p. " Benz."			
Crew—pilot and gunner ..	..	..	.. 360 lbs.
Armament—three guns.			
Petrol capacity	..	..	.. 38 gallons.
Oil capacity	..	..	.. 3 gallons.

CONSTRUCTION.

WINGS.

The manner in which the wings are constructed is exactly as shown in the report of the A.E.G. Bomber—*i.e.*, the spars consist of two steel tubes 40 mm. in diameter by 0·75 mm. thick. At their ends the upper and lower surfaces of the spars are chamfered away, and flat plates welded in position, so as to provide a taper within the washed-out portion of the wing tips. The wings were, unfortunately, so badly damaged that no accurate drawing of their section can be taken, but there is evidence that this very closely follows the section of the bomber, which has already been published. The ribs are of wood, and between each main rib is placed a half-rib joining the front spar to the semicircular section wooden strip which forms the leading edge. The wing construction is strengthened by two light steel tubes passing through the ribs close behind and parallel to the leading spar, which are used for housing the aileron control wires. The bracing against drag consists of wires and transverse steel tubes welded in position. At the inner end of the wings special reinforced ribs of light gauge steel tube are provided. The method of construction at this point is clearly shown in Fig. 1, which also indicates the manner in which the bracing tube is welded to a socket driven on the main spar. The spars are attached to the fuselage by plain pin joints.

CENTRE SECTION.

The centre section of the upper surface is constructed in a similar manner to that of the wings, except that it is considerably reinforced, and the spars are larger in diameter. The leading spar has a diameter of 51 mm. and the rear spar 45 mm. The centre section is secured to the fuselage by a system of stream-lined steel struts, the feet of which terminate in ball-ends dropped into sockets and there bolted in position.

The centre section contains an auxiliary gravity petrol tank, and also the radiator, and is, therefore, substantially braced with steel tube transverse members.

The wings are set with a dihedral angle of approximately 6 deg.

AILERONS.

The aileron framework is of light steel tube throughout, the tube forming the trailing edge being flattened into an eliptical section. The ribs are fixed by welding. The framework of the ailerons on the upper wing is reinforced by diagonal bracing of light tube.

STRUTS.

These are of light steel tube streamline in section, tapered at each end, and terminating in a socket which abuts against a ball-headed pedestal carried on the wing spars ; through the socket and the ball is passed a small bolt. The manner in which this attachment is carried out is exactly similar to that described in the report on the A.E.G. Bomber.

FUSELAGE.

The whole of the fuselage is built up of steel tubes welded together, and having affixed at their junctions sheet steel lugs, which serve as the anchorage for the bracing wires. The diameter of the longerons and of the frame verticals is 20 mm., except the last three members adjacent to the tail, of which the diameter is 16 mm. The welding throughout the fuselage appears to be of very high quality. In Fig. 2 is illustrated a joint which occurs in the fuselage immediately in front of the pilot's cockpit. The longeron is, from this point to the rear of the gunner's cockpit, fitted with a wooden strip taped in position. This joint shows the method in which the cross bracing wires are furnished with an anchorage. In one or two points in the frame construction the bracing wire lies in the some plane as the transverse tube, and to allow for this a diagonal hole is drilled through the tube, and filled in with a small steel tube welded in place.

ENGINE MOUNTING.

This consists of a triangulated arrangement of steel tubes carrying hollow rectangular section steel bearers, on which the crank chamber is slung. The bearers are well trussed both in the vertical and horizontal planes, and are shown in dotted lines in the General Arrangement of Drawings. The engine bearers themselves are 2 mm. in thickness, and have an approximate section of $2\frac{1}{16}$ ins. by $1\frac{1}{2}$ in.

TAIL.

The empennage possesses no particular points of interest, the frames having the usual tubular framework. The tail plane is not fitted with any trimming gear, but a method of adjustment is provided. This is shown in Fig. 3, which is self-explanatory. The diagonal struts which proceed from the base of the fuselage

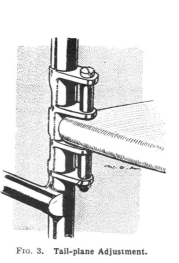

FIG. 3. **Tail-plane Adjustment.**

FIG. 4. **Tail-stay Adjustment.**

FIG. 5. **Rudder-post Arrangement.**

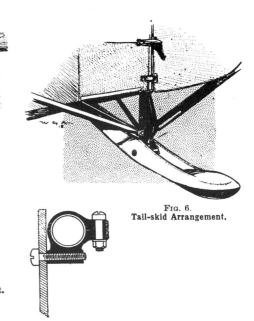

FIG. 6.
Tail-skid Arrangement.

FIG. 7. **Method of Attaching Armour.**

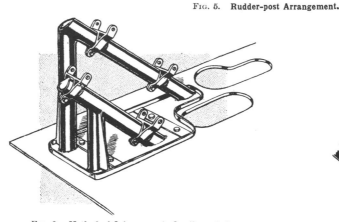

FIG. 8. **Method of fixing guns to fire through floor.**

FIG. 9. **Triggers for fixed guns.**

to the tail plane spar are fitted at each end with a method of adjustment (shown in Fig. 4), allowing them to be extended as required according to the particular socket, which is used to carry the leading edge of the tail plane. Neither the elevators nor the rudder are balanced. The rudder post is mounted on the end of the fuselage (as shown by Fig. 5), in which it will be seen that the vertical frame tube of the fin is very stoutly attached to the frame by a triangulated foot.

LANDING GEAR.

This is of the usual A.E.G. type, and is furnished with shock absorbers consisting of metal coil springs in direct tension, as is clearly shown in the General Arrangement Drawing.

The landing carriage axle has a diameter of 55 mm. The landing carriage struts, which are of similar section to those used between the planes, measures 70 mm. by 37 mm. At their upper ends they are furnished with ball and socket attachments similar to those of the interplane struts.

The wheels are fitted with 810 by 125 mm. tyres, and the track is 6 ft. $10\frac{1}{2}$ ins.

The tail skid is unusually heavy, and it is a built-up construction of welded sheet steel. It is mounted on a stout tail post, which is reinforced by four stream-line steel diagonals. The forward end of the tail skid projects inside the fuselage, and is there provided with four steel springs at direct tension. A sketch of the tail skid is given in Fig. 6.

CONTROL.

This consists of the usual double-handled lever mounted on a transverse rocking shaft, which carries the elevator control cranks at each end. The upper ailerons are worked positively by wires which pass over pulleys on the wings spars at the outer struts, the outer and lower ailerons being connected by a stream-line steel tubular strut.

ENGINE.

The 200 h.p. Benz engine possesses no new features, and has already been made the subject of an exhaustive report.

PETROL SYSTEM.

Underneath the pilot's seat are the two main petrol tanks, each of which contains 80 litres (equals 16 gallons). These tanks are of brass, and are fitted with Maximall level indicators. The gravity tank, containing 27 litres (equals $5\frac{1}{2}$ gallons), is embedded in the centre section of the upper plane, where it forms the leading edge on the left-hand side. The tank is made of lead-covered

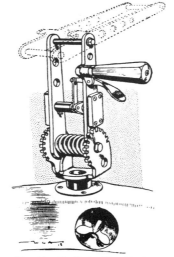

FIG. 10. **Cradle for Movable Gun.**

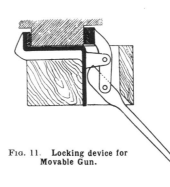

FIG. 11. **Locking device for Movable Gun.**

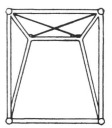

FIG 12. **Method of Fuselage Bracing.**

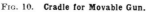

steel. Cocks are provided, so that either the gravity tank or the pressure tanks, separately or together, can feed the carburettor.

It is of interest to note that the chamber which is used in connection with the Benz petrol supply system is not, as is usually the case, contained in the main tank, but is a separate fitting mounted on the side of the engine.

RADIATOR.

The radiator is of the Daimler-Mercédès type, measuring $32\frac{1}{2}$ ins. long by $11\frac{1}{2}$ ins. high and 6 ins. deep. This is fitted with imitation honeycomb tubes, of which there are 118 running vertically, each being fitted with 48 gills. The radiator is carried in a steel cradle, into which it is easily inserted from above, and this in turn is supported on specially built-up steel ribs. It is placed so that the tank, which forms the upper part of the radiator, lies about flush with the centre section of the top plane. The shutter or flap for controlling the water temperature is made of 3-ply-wood stiffened with a light steel framework, and is mounted immediately behind the radiator, being worked by a handle within reach of the pilot. This handle is provided with a rack and pawl device. The shutter is $3\frac{3}{4}$ ins. deep, and is capable, therefore, of covering up about one-third of the total radiator surface. It will be noted that the position of the shutter behind the radiator is unusual.

ARMOUR.

Protection for the pilot and gunner is afforded by armour, which is shown in the General Arrangement Drawing in thick lines. There are three panels at each side and three panels at the bottom of the fuselage, an armour bulkhead being placed at the rear of the gunner's cockpit to protect him from behind. The armour is 5.1 mm. thick, and its total area is 105.8 sq. ft. The weight of the armour is thus approximately 860 lbs.

Careful tests have been made to ascertain the effectiveness of this armour, and the following table gives the ranges at which these plates are safe or unsafe against penetration by bullets of various types. These figures may be taken as correct within the limit of a practical firing test.

Ammunition.	Angle to Normal Degrees.	Safe Range. Yards.	Unsafe Range. Yards.
German A.P.	0	—	600
	15	500	400
	30	400	300
Mark VII. P.	0 probably	700	600
Armour piercing	15	400	300
	30	300	200
German Spitze	0	150	100
	15	100	50
	30	50	
Mark VII.	0	50	
	15	50	
	30	50	

The armour is undoubtedly too light to afford protection against British armour-piercing bullets fired from the ground at a lower height than 500 feet, while a machine armoured with it would have to fly at, at least, 1,000 feet to be safe from all but a very low percentage of hits.

The armour does not appear to have been employed, as it might well have been, in a structural capacity—i.e., it is simply an attachment to the framework, to which it adds no material strength. Its appearance seems to point to the fact that it had been added by way of experiment, and that it was of a more or less makeshift character. It had, for instance, evidently been necessary to open out existing holes and cut new holes in the course of erection. The armour is attached by setscrews to clips clamped on the fuselage members, as shown in Fig. 7.

In this machine the pilot is not provided with a gun, but the observer has to control three, of which two (Spandau) are fixed on the flooring of his cockpit, whilst the other (Parabellum) is carried on a rotable mounting.

With regard to the fixed guns, these are secured to a couple of tubular steel brackets, mounted as shown in Fig. 8. The oval-section steel tubes, of which these brackets are composed, are welded to a light steel base, which forms a sort of tray, and is in turn bolted to the armour forming the cockpit floor.

Adjacent to these two guns, which fire forward at an angle of 45 deg., is a bracket carrying the belts of ammunition, which are fed from a large rotating drum.

In the right-hand front corner of the pilot's cockpit floor is a circular hole which he would appear to use for sight purposes.

The fixed guns are controlled by Bowden wires and triggers mounted on a diagonal frame member, convenient to the gunner's right hand, as shown in Fig 9.

The movable gun is of the Parabellum type, and the mounting is of the usual built-up wood variety. The gun-cradle is, however, novel, the fixture for this purpose being illustrated in Fig.10. It appears to be rather more handy than the usual German device, but is by no means lacking in weight. The vertical carrier is swivelled at its base, and is secured in position by sliding bolts engaging with teeth cut in the turned-up base plate. These sliding bolts are worked by a direct acting thumb lever. The turn-table is made of a single hoop of wood reinforced at the point where the gun is mounted by glued-on strips of plywood. The locking device is as shown in Fig. 11.

The transverse bracing in the immediate rear of the gunner's cockpit, at which point is mounted the armour bulkhead, suggests that it was the original intention for this aeroplane to carry a gun or guns firing downwards and backwards through a hole in the fuselage. The transverse arrangement of steel tubes and bracing wires is shown in Fig. 12.

The machine is fitted with the usual wireless leads and apparatus for heating, the dynamo being carried on a bracket attached to the fuselage immediately in front of the pilot's seat, where it is directly driven from the engine through a hand-controlled clutch. No wireless fittings, other than the dynamo leads, were found.

The instruments fitted to this machine possess no new features of interest.

The fabric throughout is of good quality, but the dope appears to have been badly applied, as in many points it had completely peeled off the fabric.

The colours used are dark purple and dark green, and in contra-distinction to the usual method by which they are arranged in well-defined polygons, are applied so as to give a cloudy effect and appear to have been sprayed on.

The wing spar yields the following analysis :—

Carbon	..	..	.098 per cent.
Silicon	..	..	.011 per cent.
Sulphur	..	..	.017 per cent.
Phosphor	..	..	.014 per cent.
Manganese	..	..	.461 per cent.
Chromium	..	..	.036 per cent.

AGO. Flugzeugwerke G.m.b.H. Johannisthal by Berlin.

Works just outside the main entrance to the flying ground. Said to be financed by the A.E.G.

Being originally a branch of the Otto Company in Munich (taking its name *Ago* from the initials of Aerowerke Gustav Otto). Managed by Germany's fourth certificated aviator, Baron Ellery von Gorrissen, winner of the Emperor's first aviation prize for an altitude flight, and an early holder on *Ago* of the world's record with six passengers. Rejoices also in a feminine director, Frau Wörner, who before the war did much flying as a passenger.

In later years, various fine flights, including records, were put up by Schüler, who flew alternatively the *Ago* and *D.F.W.* biplanes.

Even when the mother firm abandoned the pusher type, the Ago Company devoted still to it among a few others, employing the Swiss designer Haefeli, formerly of Farman Bros.

On the outbreak of war, the Ago Company was largely engaged on experimental work with land and sea aircraft. A small biplane " chaser " was turned out early in the war.

Aeroplanes built by the Aktien Gesellschaft Otto are not seen at the front in large numbers. In addition to the large twin fuselage machine, which has not been very successful, the firm constructs general purpose two-seater machines of medium size, with two pairs of interplane struts on either side of the fuselage, and small single-seat biplanes, with one pair of struts on either side.

These last machines differed from the *Nieuport* in that they had a dihedral to the upper plane, but the wings were not swept back. The chord of the lower wings was small, and, therefore, they appeared to be narrow. The struts were parallel and not V-shaped as in the *Nieuport*. The type is now extinct.

Some time ago German aero papers illustrated the twin-fuselage *Ago* in the illustrations of *Ago* battleplanes rendered here.

They represent two different models, varying chiefly in wing spread. Both biplanes are twin-bodied pushers with Farman type nacelles. The smaller one does apparently not exceed the wing span of a normal-sized tractor biplane, and has but one set of struts to each side beyond the two oval ones, carrying the bodies, the chief object of which seem to yield that pusher type a better longitudinal stability than afford the general Farman tail-booms, for they carry no engines or passengers, and are apparently made of two parts, with a longitudinal vertical division.

The struts are combined by single wire crosses, the nacelle is supported by two inclined struts from the leading edge of the upper plane to the middle of the nacelle, between the two seats, and the tail skids end with the metal scoops, first applied to the middle skid of the Nieuport monoplane.

The second *Ago* twin-bodied battleplane is identical in design and construction, and apparently in the size of the various parts even, but for the larger wings, are almost doubled in span, with three sets of struts to each side, and the four-wheel landing chassis of *Voisin* type.

One imagines that the real reason for the two so-called " bodies " is the theory that two good stout streamlined built-up tubes will be less vulnerable, and will offer less head-resistance than four thin tailbooms with the usual network of wires. The idea seems quite sound, and, properly carried out, it might produce the much-desired high-speed " pusher " biplane, especially in large sizes, where one could fit an enormous engine.

Three-quarter Front View of an Ago C.IV armed reconnaissance Biplane of 1917. Note the tapered wing and the single strut between the outer pair and the fuselage.

Side View of the Ago C.IV armed reconnaissance Biplane, with tapered wings and single intermediate strut.

Ago CII reconnaissance biplane of 1915 (two 220 h.p. Benz IV engines

Ago DV3 unarmed single seat scout of 1915 (100 h.p. Uberursel Ur I rotary engine). Prototype only, achieving 150 km.p.h.

An Ago Flying Boat of 1918 type.   Note the various wing-struts.

An Ago Seaplane of 1918 type.

ALBATROS WERKE. G.m.b.H. Johannisthal by Berlin.

Works and civil flying school at the aerodrome. Military flying, aerodrome and repair works plant at Schneidemühl.

Austrian Branch, The Oesterreichische Albatros werke, G.m.b.H. (see AUSTRIA).

One of Germany's most important aircraft works, established 1910 by building *Farman* type box kites (later with nacelle) and Gnôme engined Antoinette monoplanes by license. One of the first exponents of Albatros aircraft was Brunhüber, who put up a rather astonishing record with three passengers on a 50 h.p. Gnôme engined *Albatros* box kite (with combined lever and wheel control), disappearing soon afterwards from civil aviation, being put in charge of the Doeberitz Army Flying School.

In 1911 a biplane of "Taube" outlines was produced, a graceful machine, being exhibited at the French aero show of the year. It was one of the first examples of employing inclined struts, but did not prove successful.

Germany's then most successful pilot, Hellmuth Hirth, joined the Albatros Company as a director, end of 1912, which resulted in a "Taube" monoplane being turned out.

In one of these the Benz aero engine, which went just from the design room to the Kaiser prize, was tried out, first in school work, then in a non-stop three hours' passenger's flight by Hirth from Johannisthal to the entrance of the Benz motor works in Mannheim.

A star pilot of quick rise and fall, Alfred Pietschker, piloted the *Albatros* box kite to victory in the Johannisthal autumn flying week, 1912, and carried out a three hours' round Berlin flight, but with his death the following day on a self-designed monoplane, the type disappeared.

Hirth gained considerable success with a "Taube" waterplane (combined wheel and two-float chassis) at the Boden See, and first place in the Italian seaplane circuit 1913, while Thelen, whose performances on a huge-spanned, two-float *Albatros* box kite were considerable at the first German seaplane competition (Heiligendamm, 1912), later achieved equal results with *Albatros* tractor seaplanes and further competed with the French passenger record specialist, Garaix, in performing various altitude world record flights with three and four passengers.

Late in 1913, the new *Albatros* tractor biplane was produced, the lamp in the underside of the fuselage of which was prophetic of the 1914 duration performances of Landmann and Boehm in 21 hours' and 24 hours' flights.

Hirth put up a fine flight in the Monaco rally, 1913, on this machine too by his Gotha-Marseille flight, and a remark in a report of this flight by the former monoplane pilot is interesting, saying "Most astonished I was by the surplus power (of the 150 h.p. Benz engine) and the climbing capacity, compared with the heavy-loaded "Taube" monoplanes."

In the 1914 Vienna meeting, Hirth and Von Loessl, again on 150 h.p. Benz-engined *Albatros* biplanes captured the altitude records with two and three passengers.

Albatros biplanes have been largely used in the war, at first as rather slow two-seater fighting machines, and reconnaissance types.

At the end of 1916 there came a very small *Albatros* single-seater with an engine (Benz or Mercédès) of some 175 h.p., and with this little "destroyer" much damage was done to the Allies' aeroplanes, until it was met and defeated by still faster British and French machines.

The speed of this little *Albatros* was computed to be between 120 and 130 miles per hour at its best height.

Front View of the D III Type Albatros Chaser.

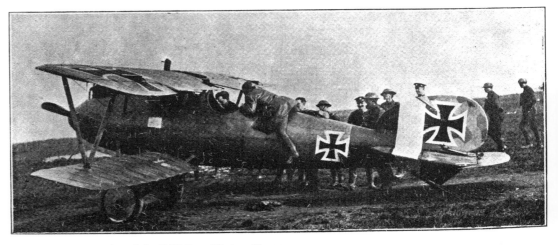

Three-quarter rear view of the D III Type Albatros Chaser.

Albatros-built Etrich Taube.

ALBATROS B.I. biplane, with 100 h.p. Mercédès motor. (on view in the "Place" and Nancy, after being brought down by a French aviator.)

Two types of ALBATROS biplane. Above, the earlier type, and below, the type largely used on active service in 1915.

Side view of the C III type, "General Purpose" ALBATROS biplane, 1916-1917.

Reproduced from L'Aérophile from a French military photograph.

The control wheel and instrument board of a C III type ALBATROS, showing radiator in upper plane and compass upside down just below it.

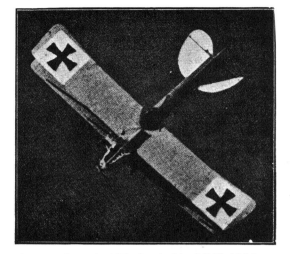

View from above of a C III
type ALBATROS biplane.

*Reproduced from "L'Aérophile," from
a photograph taken by a French
military aviator.*

The exhaust pipes, with machine gun below, and engine cowl of the C III type
ALBATROS.

ALBATROS—*continued*.

1915-16 type.   (128 h.p. Mercédés).

Span (upper wing)	..	..	13.10 m. (43′).
Span (lower wing)	..	..	11.30 m. (36.9′).
Length	..	..	7.9 m.
Total surface	..	..	40.2 sq. m.
Gap	..	..	1.57 m.

C. III type 1916-17.   (170 h.p. Mercédés).

Span	..	..	11.75 m. (35′).
Length	..	..	7.9 m.
Total surface	..	..	37.5 sq. m.
Gap	..	..	1.55 m.
Total height	..	..	1.8 m.
Empty weight	..	..	857 kgs.
Weight (all on)	..	..	1353 kgs.
Top speed	..	..	140 k.p.h.
Climb	..	..	1000 m. in 9 min.
Climb	..	..	2000 m. in 22 min.
Ceiling with full load	..	..	3700 m.
Useful load	..	..	496 kgs.

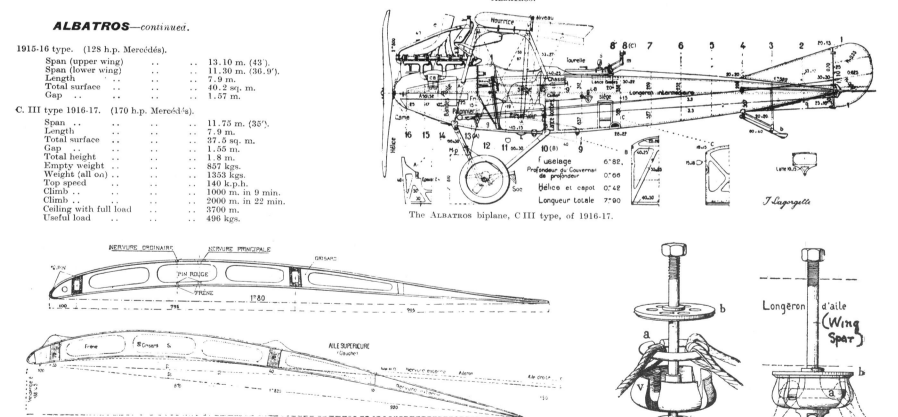

The ALBATROS biplane, C III type, of 1916-17.

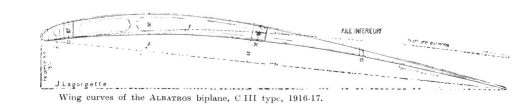

Wing curves of the ALBATROS biplane, C III type, 1916-17.

Method of attaching interplane struts and bracing cables
to main spars on the C III type ALBATROS.

THE ALBATROS D I TYPE.

The aircraft which was known to the Allies' aviators as the German Spad is a tiny single-seater *Albatros*, which shares, however, beyond the name none of the features of former products of that aircraft works. The almost equal-sized wings are nearly 9 metres in span, they are neither V nor arrow-shaped, and have a single set of struts on each side. The body is "whale"-shaped, and an enclosed stationary engine is employed.

The *Albatros* differs from the *Spad* in having the general round tail plane of recent *Albatros* aircraft, the rudder being further in front of the elevator, and as almost none of its features are to be found in older German biplanes, it looks most like the small *Ago* single-seater biplanes.

The wings are a little V-shaped, but not of arrow shape, both wings being of equal chord, and possessing the same gap in their whole length. There are trailing ailerons, as on the ordinary *Albatros*, further, one single or two pairs of masts to each side beyond the four inclined legs of the cabane.

The body with tail and landing chassis are as on the *Nieuport*.

A fixed engine is employed, running in an almost hemispherical cowl, and the propeller is provided with a cap.

The petrol tank is placed behind the engine.

CHIEF DIMENSIONS

Span (upper plane)	8.6 m.
Span (lower plane)	8.05 m.
Chord	1.62 m.
Gap	1.515 m.
Length over all	7.3 m.
Length of fuselage	6.5 m.
Length of elevator	.5 m.
Length of propeller cap	.3 m.
Height to top of wings	2.9 m.
Height to top of propeller circle	3.1 m.
Ailerons each (top plane only)	2.38 m.
Ailerons chord tapering	.41 m. to .52 m.
Total surface of wings	25 sq. m.
Total surface of wings (upper plane)	13.5 sq. m.
Total surface of wings (lower plane)	11.5 sq. m.
Surface of Tail plane	1.4 sq. m.
Surface of Elevator	1.1 sq. m.
Surface of fin (upper)	.55 sq. m.
Surface of fin (lower)	.25 sq. m.
Surface of rudder	.55 sq. m.
Motor (Mercédés)	160–170 h.p.
Armament	2 machine guns, converging fire.
Speed (estimated)	115–120 m.p.h.

Side view of ALBATROS destroyer, type D I, 1916-17.

Back view of the D I type ALBATROS destroyer.

Reproduced from " L'Aérophile," from a French military photograph

Three-quarter front view of the D I type ALBATROS destroyer.

Reproduced from " L'Aérophile," from a French military photograph.

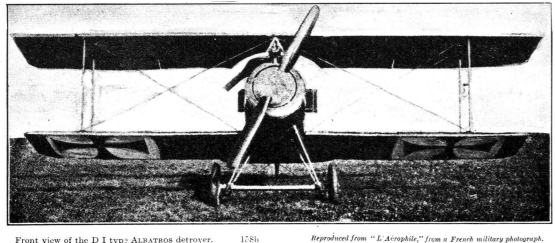

Front view of the D I type ALBATROS destroyer. 158b

Reproduced from " L'Aérophile," from a French military photograph.

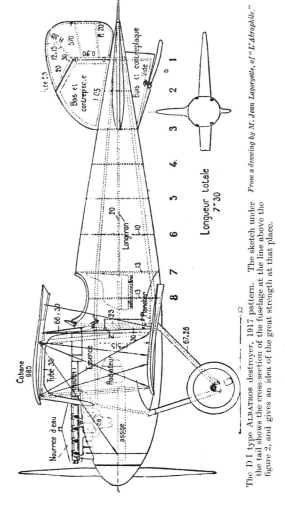

The D I type ALBATROS destroyer, 1917 pattern. The sketch under the tail shows the cross-section of the fuselage at the line above the figure 2, and gives an idea of the great strength at that place. *From a drawing by M. Jean Lagorgette, of "L'Aérophile."*

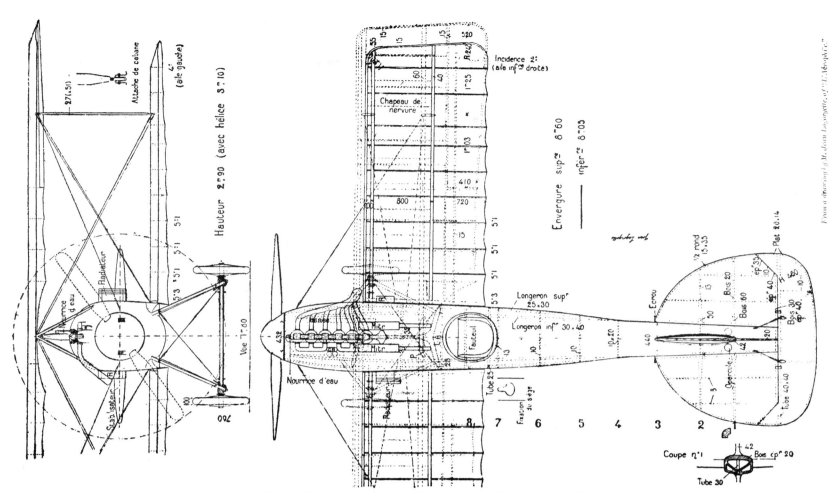

The D I type ALBATROS destroyer, 1917 pattern. (The sketch alongside the tail shows the cross-section of the fuselage at the line opposite the figure 1.)

THE ALBATROS D III.

M. Jean Lagorgette in " L'Aerophile " gives some interesting details of the Albatros single-seater fighter, new style, which is known as the D III, or more commonly in the R.F.C. as the " V strut " type. The machine is the same as that seen in the famous photograph of Capt. Baron von Richthofen's " Circus," in the last issue of " All The World's Aircraft."

This machine is a tractor scout type biplane, developed from the D I 1916 model, described in " The Aeroplane " of March 21st, 1917, and from D II. A number of examples, which had mostly been placed on service in February last, were captured in April.

The control surfaces, fuselage, landing-carriage, motor and armament (two fixed machine-guns firing forwards, with a synchronising gear), remain similar to those of types D I and D II. The three-ply wood of the fuselage is varnished a clear yellow, while the colour of the wings and control surfaces remains green and dark brown.

The differences, most of which are in the wings, are entirely inspired by the Nieuport biplane, of which this machine is a species of caricature, and causes danger of confusion. It is, therefore, the more necessary that the type should be studied carefully, apart from the importance of the machine itself.

As in the Nieuport the upper wings have no dihedral and are much greater in chord than the lower wings, which appear to be much thinner in every way, and are of a span nearly equal to the upper wings. The wings are staggered and have a single pair of struts in the shape of a fore and aft " V " on each side.

But the points of differences from the Nieuport are that the wings are not swept back, and that the outer edges are very oblique, giving the wings, whether viewed from above or below, a trapezoidal outline with rounded edges. The ailerons are markedly projecting and washed out.

Above all, the control surfaces are different. The large shovel-shaped fixed tail plane and elevator are entirely without break in outline. The fixed fin and rudder form an unbroken curve over the top of the fuselage.

The cabane is very spread out at the top. And finally, the fuselage—setting aside its colour—is different, being of monocoque form, with a revolving cowl in front, and an enormous projecting fixed motor, whose sound is quite different from the rotary.

The span of the upper wings is 9.03 m. (about 30 ft.) from the tips of the ailerons, 8.63 m. along the rear spar, and 7.55 m. along the front spar.

The span of the lower wings is 8.75 m. (about 29 ft.), each wing being 3.94 m., with an interval for the fuselage of 0.865 m.

The chord of the upper wings is 1.5 m. (about 4 ft. 11 in.) at the centre, increasing to 1.75 m. (about 5 ft. 8 in.) towards the tips, the depth of the ailerons increasing from 0.3 m. to 0.55 m.

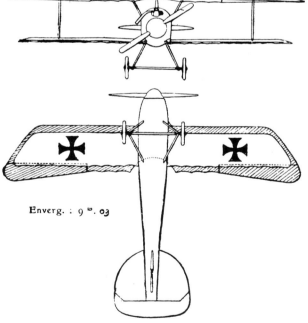

Enverg. : 9 m. 03

The gap between the leading edges of the main planes is 1.5 m. at the fuselage and decreases towards the tips because of the dihedral on the lower plane.

The stagger is 0.22 m. between the upper and the lower leading edges, and is a little less than that between the trailing edges, in an inverse direction ; thus the centre lines of the upper and lower wings nearly coincide when viewed from the side.

The interplane struts are " V " shaped, formed by two tubes soldered (or welded) together at the base, where they join the lower wing.

The bracing of the wings fore and aft is secured on either side by a cable running nearly horizontally between the nose of the machine and the bases of the " V " struts.

The main spars in the upper plane run continuously along the whole span. The centre of this plane has a semi-circular

THE D III ALBATROS.

Span.—Upper Wing 9.03 m. (30 ft.).

Span.—Lower Wing 8.75 m. (29 ft.).

Chord.—Upper Wing 1.5 m. (4 ft. 11 in.).

Gap.—1.5 metres (4 ft. 11 in.).

Stagger.—0.22 metre (9 in.).

POINTS TO BE NOTED.—Upper and Lower Span almost equal. Projecting Ailerons. Dihedral to Lower Plane only. Rudder and Fin entirely above Fuselage. Tiny Fin below Fuselage. Solid Elevator with balanced projections. Rounded Fuselage, with pot on Propeller.

Motor.—Fixed Mercédès, 175 h.p.

section cut away behind the rear spar, 0.48 m. deep by 1.35 m. wide, to allow the pilot to see upwards.

The fixed tail plane still has a chord of 1.62 m. and a span of 2.4 m. (including the width of the fuselage), and the elevator is 0.51 by 2.4 m.

The line of flight is 17 mm. above the middle of the third pair of longerons, which run along half-way up the side of the fuselage, and which support the horizontal stabilising plane.

As in D II, the motor is a 175-h.p. Mercédès (No. 26,786, etc.), with an " Axial " propeller, 2.73 m. diameter, and a pitch of 2.20 m. The radiator, however, is now of the flat tube type, is placed in the upper plane, instead of honeycombs on the sides, and there is no longer a water reservoir on the motor.

The weight of the machine empty is 670 kilogs. (1.470 lbs.). The useful load, in addition to fuel, 135 kilogs. (297 lbs.).

THE ALBATROS 225-H.P. TWO-SEATER BIPLANE.

The following description, translated from an article in "L'Aérophile," by M. Jean Lagorgette, is of interest, because it portrays a general purpose aeroplane which is typical of recent German practice.

This machine is in many respects similar to the Albatros single-seater. The machine examined by M. Lagorgette was constructed by the Bayerische Fleugzeug-Werke Gesellschaft, of Munich.

The span of this machine is 12.6 m. (41 ft. 6 in.), span of lower plane, 12.2 m. (40 ft. 4 in.); total length, 8.5 m. (28 ft.); total height, 3.3 m. (10 ft. 9 in.).

The wings are nearly equal in size. They are not staggered, and slightly trapezoidal. There are two pairs of steel tube interplane struts on either side. The ailerons do not project beyond

A SINGLE-SEATER ALBATROS, with 8-cylinder 250 h.p. Mercédès engine, and geared-down airscrew. This type has been replaced by the D IV type with a 6-cylinder 260 h.p. engine.

THE NOSE-PIECE OF AN ALBATROS with 8-cylinder 250 h.p. Mercédès engine, and geared down air-screw.

the trailing edge. Instead, they taper gradually towards their outer edges. They are partly balanced, a compensating extension projecting into the wing, in front of the axis of the aileron, as can be seen in the diagram.

The gap between the wings is 1.8 m. (6 ft.).

The wings are constructed of wood in a manner similar to that of Albatros C III and D II.

The outline of the horizontal tail-plane is that of a rounded spade. The fixed plane is built in two halves, one on either side of the fuselage, is very thick, and is constructed of timber and covered with three-ply. The elevator is in one piece, and its two compensating flaps embrace the sides of the fixed plane.

The vertical tail members, are placed entirely above the fuselage and behind it, and have a similar appearance to those of the single-seater Albatros, with a rounded upper edge, but it is slightly longer in proportion. The fixed fin is permanently built into the fuselage in the manner of the Perry-Beadle flying-boat.

The fuselage tapers gradually until it becomes a horizontal knife-edge, without any vertical projection. The section is rectangular, with a streamline top. There are four longerons of square section. As in all new German aeroplanes, the fuselage is covered with three-ply, and varnished as in the C III and other early models.

A revolving pot is attached to the propeller.

The landing carriage is ordinary; one pair of wheels and two steel tube Vs, the wheel base being 2 m. (6 ft. 7 in.).

There is a plough brake and an ordinary tail skid.

The motor is a fixed Benz of 225-h.p., which gives 1,415 r.p.m.

It is not geared down. Two large and heavy radiators are placed one on either side of the fuselage. The petrol tank serves as the pilot's seat.

The armament consists of two machine-guns, one fixed on the side of the motor, and firing through the propeller, the other on a rear gun ring. Two bomb-releases are carried in the passenger's cockpit between the floor boards and the bottom of the fuselage.

Side View of a captured Albatros Type D.V. (photographed in April, 1918).

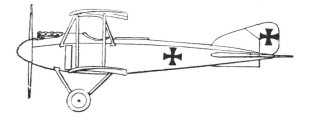

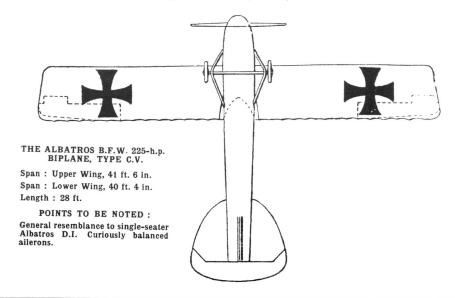

THE ALBATROS B.F.W. 225-h.p. BIPLANE, TYPE C.V.

Span : Upper Wing, 41 ft. 6 in.
Span : Lower Wing, 40 ft. 4 in.
Length : 28 ft.

POINTS TO BE NOTED :

General resemblance to single-seater Albatros D.I. Curiously balanced ailerons.

One of only three Albatros C.IX Type Two-seater biplanes built in 1917, with arrow-shaped wings and curious strutting arrangements.

THE ALBATROS D.XI SCOUT.

The single streamlined and outwards inclined strut idea has been carried out with the clear object of minimising the interplane connection head resistance, and in conjunction with the inclined struts from the interplane strut bottom joint to the upper fuselage longitudinals doing altogether away with wiring. The *Albatros* strut form was first seen in the fashion of the 1916-17 L.F.G. Roland whale effort, while the two inwards inclined struts appear to be of usual streamline shape.

The body nose and the fairly forward position of the *Albatros* gives the impression of a rotary engine installation.

One fails to see immediately the object of advancing the fin and balanced rudder on the *Albatros*.

The tail fin and undivided balanced elevator is similar to the one of the biplane scout of the same firm.

The Albatross D.XI, flown in 1918 but not put into production.

THE ALBATROS G.III "GROSSFLUGZEUG" medium bomber, a twin-engined type which has not become familiar on active service.

AVIATIK. Automobil & Aviatik A.G.

Formed 1910, by Georg Chatel and Germany's most successful pilot of that date, Emil Jeannin, to sell Peugeot motor cars and build *Farman* box-kite type biplanes and *Hanriot* monoplanes by license. Works at Mülhausen in Alsace. Aerodrome : Habsheim.

While the box-kite type nacelled biplane was still used, Faller put up a number of duration records with four, five, six and seven passengers. The early monoplanes were very clumsy, but when the 1913 tractor arrow biplane was produced, fine performances were achieved by Ingold with a 16 hours' flight, and by Stoeffler in various distance flights across Germany, foremost his record of 2,100 km. in 24 hours, in September, 1913.

The fate of the Aviatik aircraft works since the outbreak of war has been tossed about. As an instance of German thoroughness it is worth quoting the preparation for this munition factory that it was moved in the days of mobilizing by rail to prearranged works at Breisgau, not to be exposed to likely French attacks on Alsace, as wise was, Châtel being killed with his wife, in his villa at Mülhausen, by a long range shell in the early fights there (Jeannin having long ago left the Aviatik Co. to form his own firm).

Allied raids found the Breisgau works, and the next move to Freiburg was still within the range of French aviators. Yet finances do not seem to have suffered for the income of 1914-15 was 800,000 marks, by a joint stock capital of 1,000,000 marks.

At present the Aviatik plant is installed at the Leipzig-Heiterblick aerodrome of the Leipziger Luftschiffhaten und Flugplatz Gesellschaft at Mockau, where it is managed by Ernest Stoeffler, the famous pre-war long-distance flier.

AVIATIK (Late 1916 Type).

Span: Top Plane, 40 ft. 8 ins.
Span: Bottom Plane, 35 ft. 5 ins.
Chord: 6 ft. 1 in.
Gap: 6 ft. 4 ins.
Total Surface: 430.5 sq. ft.
Ailerons (Top Planes only): 7 ft. 4 ins. × 2. ft 5 ins. (17.2 sq. ft.)
Tail Plane (semi-circular): 4 ft. 10 ins. × 9 ft. 2 ins.
Elevators (two semi-oval): 4 ft. 3 ins. × 2 ft. 2 ins.
Fixed vertical fin (triangular): 5 ft. 1 in. × 2 ft. 5.5 ins.
Rudder: 3 ft. × 2 ft. 3 ins.
Surface of elevator: 12.1 sq. ft.
Surface of fixed tail plane: 35.3 sq. ft.
Surface of rudder: 6.45 sq. ft.
Angle of incidence of main planes: 4.38°.
Length of fuselage: 21 ft.
Total length of machine: 26 ft.

IMPORTANT FIGURES.

The total weight of the *Aviatik* of 1916 is the same as that of the *L.V.G.*, and about the same as that of the *Rumpler*.

Weight of the body (including radiator, tanks, and pipe lines) ..	757 lbs.	
Weight of the wings..	308 lbs.	
,, struts..	28 lbs.	
,, propeller	42 lbs.	
,, engine	673 lbs.	
,, cooling water	55 lbs.	
Total weight empty ..		1,863 lbs.
Weight of fuel	418 lbs.	
Useful weight—pilot, passenger, armament, accessories, etc.	550 lbs.	
Total load ..		968 lbs.
Total load ..		2,831 lbs.
Weight per sq. ft. of sustaining surface ..		6.81 lbs.

Speeds.	Test in France.	From German source.
Maximum speed at sea-level ..	82 m.p.h.	
Minimum speed at sea-level ..	49 m.p.h.	
Speed at 1,000 m.	79 m.p.h.	83 m.p.h.
Speed at 2,000 m.	74.5 m.p.h.	80.7 m.p.h.
Speed at 3,000 m.	66 m.p.h.	
Climb to height of 500 m... ..		4 min. 30 sec.
Climb to height of 1,000 m. ..		9 min. 30 sec.
Climb to height of 2,000 m. ..		21 min. 30 sec.
Climb to height of 3,000 m. ..		47 min. 30 sec.

Supplies carried for 4 hours and 30 minutes' flight.

The "ceiling" of the machine is at 3,500 m., or nearly 11,500 ft., with a useful load of 720 lbs. German pilots have, however, affirmed that they have climbed as high as 15,750 ft. with their observer and 18.5 gallons of gasolene.

Aviatiks with Benz and Mercédès motors of 220 h.p., differing from the 170 h.p. in cylinder bore only, were said to be in building, in 1917, with two machine-guns, one of which was to fire through the propeller. They were expected to have a speed of 93 miles per hour at a height of 2,000 m.

The fore part of the 1915-17 type Aviatik C.I armed reconnaissance biplane.

Reproduced from "L'Aérophile," from a French military photograph.

Single example of the Aviatik Type D.II Single-seater Biplane.

Single example of the Aviatik D.VI Single-seater Scout (1918). (195 h.p. geared Benz engine).

An Aviatik Twin-engined Biplane, Type G1. (2—230 h.p. Benz engines.)

AVIATIK B.II reconnaissance biplane of 1915, as arranged for road transport.

The prototype Aviatik Type C VIII Biplane of 1917, using a 160 h.p. Mercedes D.III engine.

An Aviatik CIX Biplane of late 1918 design. Evidently an attempt to use the characteristics of the "Bristol Fighter." (200 h.p. Benz IV engine). Two built.

Experimental Aviatik C.V. of 1917 with "gull" upper wings (180 h.p. Argus As III engine). Embodies Vee-strut Warren Type wing-bracing.

B

BAVARIAN RUMPLER WORKS, Munich. (Branch of the Johannisthal firm.)

B.F.W. Bayerische Flugzeug Werke, Fürth.

One of the newcomers to the German aircraft trade during the war. The Gothaer Waggon Fabrik partook in the formation of the new company, so it may be assumed that the aeroplanes of the latter's aircraft department are produced by license.

It is also known that the Bayerische Company has been making *Albatroses* (*see Albatros.*).

The city of Fürth gratis supplied an area of 300,000 square metres for works site and testing ground.

BLEICHERODER AEROPLANE TRADE Co., Ltd. Near Harz.

Contractors to the German and Austrian War Offices and Admiralties.

BRANDENBURGISCHE FLUGZEUGWERKE.
See Hansa und Brandenburgische Flugzeugwerke.

B.F.W.-built 1913 Etrich Taube.

D

DEUTSCHE BRISTOL-WERKE FLUGZEUG.
Ges.m.b.H., see Halberstadter Flugzeugwerke.

D.F.W. Deutsche Flugzeug Werke, formerly "Mars, G.m.b.H.," Lindenthal by Leipzig.

Formed in 1910, by Commercial Counsellor Bernhard Meyer, who died during the war, after having, like the late Sir George White, of Bristol, established an important factor in his country's war needs by his keen faith in the future of aviation. Other concerns of Herr Meyer were the seaplane works at Lubeck-Travemünde, the Jeannin Company, and sundry motor firms.

Austrian branch "Lloyd Flugzeugwerke G.m.b.H.," Budapest.

At one time turned out *Maurice Farman* biplanes, later a *Jeannin* copied "Steel dove," and producing a characteristic bodied aircraft, winning, as monoplane, the 1913 Prince Henry trophy, and flying much in the first Balkan War, on Turkish side, as biplane. This machine was constructed under the direction of Ober-Lieutenant Bier, the famous Austrian pilot, and was known as the "Mars." With the design was associated Mr. Cecil Kny, who was well-known in the British Aircraft Industry, and who has been interned—being an Austrian subject—during the war.

In 1914, the D.F.W. company was busy turning out a number of successful types, one of their biplanes, with a 150 h.p. Benz motor winning the "three-cornered flight," and the standard 100 h.p. Mercédès-engined type putting up the world's altitude record of 25,750 feet shortly before outbreak of war, piloted by Oelerich.

On the outbreak of war the performance of the 150 h.p. aircraft (Benz, Mercédès or Rapp motors) were: 110 kms. per hr. max. and 57½ min., fully loaded for 300 miles, flying with pilot and passenger. Among many prototype warplanes built up to 1918 were included the single R.I and two R.II giant bombers of 1917-18, used operationally (at least the R.I) on the Russian Front.

D.F.W. wartime aircraft included the B.I, B.II, C.I and C.II reconnaissance and training biplanes; C.IV, C.V and C.VI reconnaissance and army co-operation biplanes; and R.II and R.I four-engined heavy bombers.

Model and Date.				D.F.W. Steel "Taube." Military. 1914.	
Length	...	...	feet (m.)	32¾	10·00
Span	...	...	feet (m.)	46½	14·20
Area	...	...	sq. feet (m².)	366	34
Weight	{ total ... lbs. (kgs.)			1370	620
	{ useful ... lbs. (kgs.)			...	...
Motor	...	...	h.p.	100 Mercedes	
Speed	{ max. m.p.h. (km.)			...	...
	{ min. m.p.h. (km.)			72	115
Number built during 1913	...			about 80 all told.	

FRONT VIEW OF THE CAPTURED D.F.W. AVIATIK IN PARIS.—The shape of the nose shows clearly how the Germans obtained better propeller efficiency than we did, and also how, by fitting their radiators directly in the slip stream, they managed to run big engines with small radiators. These points contrasted favourably with our own contemporary methods.

Steel "Taube."

Back view of D.F.W. B.I biplane, Reconnaissance and School type, nicknamed the "Banana" type owing to the wing shape.

A D.F.W. D.II Class experimental Single-seater Biplane of 1918.

CHIEF DIMENSIONS: B.I

Span (upper plane)	..	14·15 metres.
Span (lower plane)	..	13·63 metres.
Length (over all)	..	8·4 metres.
Height (over all)	..	3 metres.
Engine, Mercédés	..	100 h.p.

Side view of D.F.W. B.I biplane, Reconnaissance and School type, 1914-16.

THE D.F.W. TYPE CV.

The Deutsche Flegzeug Werke Gesellschaft was well-known in peace-time for its somewhat ungraceful aeroplanes, some of them with crescent-shaped wings, and others with arrow-shaped wings similar to those of the Austrian Lohner biplanes.

This firm has since produced a somewhat different machine, which, according to M. Lagorgette of "L'Aerophile," was in favour in Germany, and was not only constructed in the firm's own works, but also in those of the Aviatik und Automobil Aktien Gesellschaft, at Leipzig-Heiterblick.

The C.V reconnaissance, photographic patrol and artillery observation biplane went into service in 1916 and lasted the war, proving a widely built and highly successful machine.

The wings have a dihedral, but are not swept back. The span of the lower wings (12.85 m. or 42 ft. 5 in.) is nearly equal to that of the upper wings (13.27 m. or 43 ft. 6¾ in.).

The ends of the upper planes are oblique, those of the lower planes retreating and rounded.

Their maximum chord is 1.75 m. (5 ft. 9 in.). The total lifting surface is about 42.5 sq. m. (421 sq. ft.). The gap is considerable, namely, 1 7 m. (5 ft. 7 in.), which gives the machine a tall appearance.

The wings progressively wash out from root to tip. The lower wings have an incidence of 6 deg. near the fuselage as far as the third rib. This decreases to 4.3 deg. at the 13th rib, which is placed 0.4 m. beyond the external struts.

The incidence of the upper plane is 5 deg. from the cabane to the sixth rib, and 3.3 deg. at the 13th rib, where the aileron commences. The incidence on the right and left wings is uniform.

The cabane is of traditional D.F.W. type, trestled-shaped, and constructed of four struts 1.25 m. long.

Above the cabane is a central wing section, 13 centimetres wide, to which the upper main planes are attached, and which contains a small reservoir holding about 3 litres.

There are two pairs of struts on each side of the fuselage.

The distance between the front and rear spars, and consequently between front and rear interplane struts, is 0.76 m., considerably less than half the chord of the wing. The spars taper considerably towards the ends, and are lapped with fabric.

In addition to the four cables which connect the wing attachments on the cabane and the fuselage to the summits and bases of the inner struts, there is a cable which runs between the top of the front chassis strut and the top of the rear inner interplane strut.

The rectangular ailerons are 2.45 m. by 0.5 m., with rounded ends. Their frame is metallic, as are the frames of the fixed tail planes.

The control planes preserve the appearance of the early models. The fixed stabilising plane is 1.72 m. long and is supported by two tubes, and together with the elevator flaps has a heart-shaped appearance, with a span of 3 m. The rudder, fixed vertical fin, and the end of the fuselage together present the contour of a spatula, a trifle elevated.

The controls differ, however, from earlier models, in that the elevator flaps and the rudder are balanced by triangular extensions which conform to segments cut from the fixed planes.

The fuselage terminates in a vertical knife-edge, rather shallow in depth. The section is rectangular with rounded edges.

As in earlier models, it is entirely covered with three-ply, which is painted with green and brown camouflage streaks. The underneath of the wings is a bright yellow. The rest of the machine is green and brown.

The nose of the machine, and its propeller pot, are somewhat pointed, thus avoiding blanketing the centre part of the propeller.

The landing-carriage is standard, the wheelbase being 2 metres wide. The suspension is rubber cord. The cross-axle is streamlined. There is cable cross-bracing between the front chassis struts. There is a claw brake.

The motor is a fixed Benz, giving 228 h.p. at 1,410 r.p.m. The cylinders are almost entirely enclosed in a special cowl.

The propeller, a 3-metre "Wotan," is made of ash and walnut in alternate layers.

The radiators are placed on the sides of the fuselage, where they form rather deep projections (14 cm.), and are 75 cm. high and 21 cm. from front to back. Their base is found between the front chassis strut and the leading edge of the lower wing. They are made by Hans Windhoff.

The water reservoir on top of the engine is triangular like that in the Albatros D.I.

The pilot sits upon the petrol tank, which also forms a back and arm-rest. He has a machine-gun placed to the right of the motor.

The passenger sits behind, surrounded by a gun-ring.

There is only one bomb-release for six bombs, placed one above another.

The full weight is 1,470 kg (3,240 lb), of which, 300 kgs. (600 lbs.) is useful load.

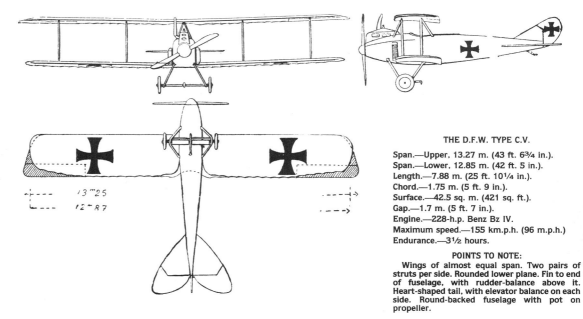

THE D.F.W. TYPE C.V.

Span.—Upper, 13.27 m. (43 ft. 6¾ in.).
Span.—Lower, 12.85 m. (42 ft. 5 in.).
Length.—7.88 m. (25 ft. 10¼ in.).
Chord.—1.75 m. (5 ft. 9 in.).
Surface.—42.5 sq. m. (421 sq. ft.).
Gap.—1.7 m. (5 ft. 7 in.).
Engine.—228-h.p. Benz Bz IV.
Maximum speed.—155 km.p.h. (96 m.p.h.).
Endurance.—3½ hours.

POINTS TO NOTE:
Wings of almost equal span. Two pairs of struts per side. Rounded lower plane. Fin to end of fuselage, with rudder-balance above it. Heart-shaped tail, with elevator balance on each side. Round-backed fuselage with pot on propeller.

THE LATEST D. F. W. BIPLANE—TYPE C 37 III.

Specification.

Span	Upper plane, 13.27 m. ; Lower plane, 12.8 m.
Chord	1.75 m.
Maximum height	3.252 m.
Overall length	7.825 m.
Weight of machine empty	970 kgs.
Useful load	460 kgs.
Engine type and h.p.	200 h.p. Benz.

Performance.

Speed	155 k.p.h.

Climb.

To 1,000 metres	4 mins.
To 2,000 metres	9½ mins.
To 3,000 metres	16½ mins.
To 5,000 metres	49 mins.
Useful load	460 kgs.
Total weight of machine loaded	1,430 kgs.

A D.F.W. type C.37 iii.

E

EULER. August Euler, Niederrad bei Frankfurt a.M.

Germany's first certificated aviator. Acquired the German license for *Voisin* biplanes, and long stuck, alone in Germany, faithfully to the Gnôme engine.

On a modified pusher biplane, Prince Henry of Prussia took his certificate and carried out a 50 km. flight.

The newer *Euler* tractor biplanes were copies of the *L.V.G.*, and no special aircraft or activities of the Euler company has been heard of during the war. Since the Armistice the photograph shown below has been obtained but without any specification.

The plant of the Euler firm at Frankfurt is a fine one, in white appearance, with five sheds (one letter of the word Euler on each of them), a picturesque flower bed produced in the form of a 7-cylinder Gnôme, and a white propeller, and the level flying ground is fenced.

An Euler "D" class Single-seater Scout.

F

FOKKER. Fokker Flugzeugwerke, Schwerin-Gorries in Mecklenburg.

Fokker, a skilful Dutch pilot, had a monoplane built by Goedecker, of inherent stable **V** shape, without warping, which he then manufactured at the Johannisthal aerodrome by the Fokker Aeroplanbau, G.m.b.H.

This monoplane was difficult to handle, even by clever pilots, and Fokker himself had a narrow escape during one of the early flying weeks at Johannisthal, when, during an altitude flight, he had a nosedive, and his passenger, a German flying officer was killed. Credit must, however, be given for the feminine altitude record of 6,600 feet by the Russian aviatrice Miss Galanchikoff, with a lady passenger.

The military authorities ordered Fokker to abandon this model, when he left the Johannisthal aerodrome, where his daring bankings were admired, for a private aerodrome at Schwerin-Gorries with a slipway to the sea. Here he produced his flying boat, as he intended, according to his advertising, to cater for water flying, "the noblest sport."

Yet matters turned out different. Early in 1914 a modified *Morane* type of machine was produced, on which Fokker himself gave looping exhibitions during the three-cornered and Prince Henry flights, when its climbing capability was admired.

This feature led to quantity manufacture early in the war, when the Allies had not too plenty of aircraft, so that the Fokker campaign cost for some months, starting October, 1915, some loss of "*Fokker* Fodder," most of the German star turns, who manned the *Fokkers*, going however out in the end, like Boelcke, Immelmann, Wintgens, etc.

Fokker has not only taken over the large Schwerin piano works, but has formed a company for the manufacture of machine guns.

Below are given some details of *Fokker* war aircraft, samples of which have been captured as biplane and monoplane and triplane.

At the end of the war the *Fokker* biplane (Type D.7) was the best single-seat fighter in the German Air Service.

The Family Tree of the Fokker Firm.

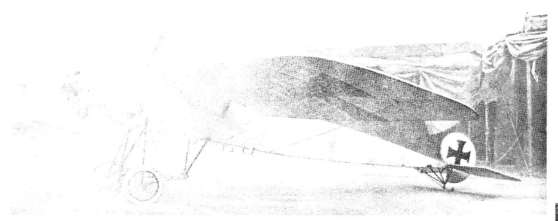

A FOKKER Monoplane, 1914-15 type, with Uberursel motor. One of the earlier examples of the type which has proved so redoubtable as a "destroyer."

A FOKKER B Type biplane, 2-seater, with 100 h.p. rotary Uberursel engine. This particular machine is here seen in a valley of the Carpathians, having been lent to the Austrians. The Austro-Hungarian forces used Fokker Bs from 1915 for reconnaissance and training.

THE FOKKER Dr.I TRIPLANE

A good deal has been heard of late of the new *Fokker* triplane which is apparently being much used by the German fighting pilots. This machine is obviously copied from the *Sopwith* triplane, and is a German attempt to produce a small quickly-manœuvrable machine, apparently specially for fighting at the lower altitudes, owing to the fact that the very high-powered *Albatros* chasers with their heavy fixed-cylinder engines are, in spite of their high speed, at a distinct disadvantage in the type of rough-and-tumble fight between a number of aeroplanes at the same time, which is commonly known in the R.F.C. as a dog fight.

The *Albatros* seems to depend for its effect on one rush, generally in the form of a dive from above, but it is unable to spin round, or loop, or turn in the same small radius which is possible to the lighter and lower-powered British fighting machines. Hence, the introduction by the Germans of this new triplane.

The following description of a captured *Fokker* of the new type is taken from an article by M. Lagorgette in the first March issue of " L'Aérophile."

M. Lagorgette writes more or less as follows :—

The enemy triplane is in effect a copy of the *Sopwith* triplane. The analogy between the two machines is very great, but there are, all the same, differences ; thus, the disposition of the wings is the same in the two types, but the form and dimensions differ considerably.

In the *Fokker* the three planes have neither a dihedral nor an arrow angle. They are staggered vertically, and the spans are unequal, growing smaller from the top plane to the lowest. In form they are rectangular.

The upper plane alone—which is the largest—has ailerons which project beyond the wing-tips.

The main spar is 7 ms. in length. Adding the width of the ailerons, one obtains the total span of about 7.6 ms.

The top plane being cut away in the middle to a considerable extent enables the pilot to see easily above him.

The middle plane, situated 0.75 ms. below the top plane, has a span of about 6.4 ms. The butts of the spars are attached to the fuselage on a level with the top of the cockpit.

The lowest plane which is again 0.75 m. below the middle plane, is fixed to the base of the fuselage, and consists of two wings, each 2.5 ms. in length.

The chord of all three planes is the same—about 1.2 ms.—and on each side, there is a single interplane strut which is very wide and holds both spars of each plane.

The remarkable thing about the machine, however, is that there are no cables, nor any other form of tension members to the wings. The centre section struts, or cabane, diverge from the fuselage to the top plane, as in various other types of German machines when viewed from front or rear, but when viewed broadside these struts converge, forming an inverted V.

CONTROLS.—The skeleton of the control members is metallic. The rudder is balanced, and is of the familiar *Fokker* type without a fixed fin. The elevator is, however, quite different from the ordinary *Fokker* practice. There is a large fixed tail-plane in the form of a triangle with the outer corners cut away to make room for the forward-projecting balanced sections of the elevator, the tail-plane and elevator together forming a large triangle with rounded corners.

FUSELAGE.—The fuselage is a girder construction of steel tubes covered with fabric. According to usual *Fokker* practice it is hexagonal in form, but ends up with a vertical stern-post, contrary to the usual *Fokker* practice in which the fuselage terminates with a horizontal bar similar to the *Morane*.

ENGINE.—The engine is an Oberursel rotary of 100 to 110 h.p., which is now practically a Le Rhône instead of being, as formerly, a Gnôme. The airscrew is an " Axial," with a diameter of 2.6 ms.

UNDERCARRIAGE.—This is of the usual type, but has a very deep streamlined axle. It is furnished with two relatively large wheels, 710 mm. by 85 mm. placed 1.6 ms. apart.

The streamlining of the axle is, in fact, so deep that it forms a fourth lifting surface.

ARMAMENT.—Two fixed Spandau machine-guns are carried, firing through the airscrew either together or separately. They are put in action by the motor, and are controlled by Bowden wire.

Apart from this particular machine, the Fokker Company construct other triplanes of greater span. The Germans state that these machines can climb to 4,500 ms. (practically 15,000 ft.) in 17 minutes. It is also stated that the late Rittmeister Baron von Richthofen used one of this type.

THE FOKKER SINGLE-SEATER BIPLANE—TYPE D.7.

The British No. of the machine illustrated is B/2B 14 and the German No. is Type D.7 F.N. 1,450 ; maker's No. 2,455.

It was brought down north of Hazebrouck on June 6th, 1918, by a British S.E.5a, and is a single-seater fighter.

The principal dimensions are as follows :—

Span	..	..	..	..	29 ft. 3½ ins.
Chord (upper wing)	..	..	..	5 ,, 2½ ,,
Chord (lower wing)	..	..	..	3 ,, 11¼ ,,
Overall length	..	..	..	22 ,, 11½ ,,
Gap	..	..	..	..	4 ,, 2 ,,
Area of Upper Wings (with Ailerons)	..	140.7 sq. ft.
,, ,, Lower Wings	..	..	78.3 ,, ,,
,, ,, Aileron (one only)	..	..	5.7 ,, ,,
,, ,, Balance of Aileron	..	..	.5 ,, ,,
,, ,, Horizontal Tail Plane	..	..	21.1 ,, ,,
,, ,, Elevators	..	..	15.2 ,, ,,
,, ,, Balance of Elevator	..	..	1.1 ,, ,,

Front View of the Fokker Triplane.

Side View of the Fokker Triplane.

Rear View of the Fokker Triplane.

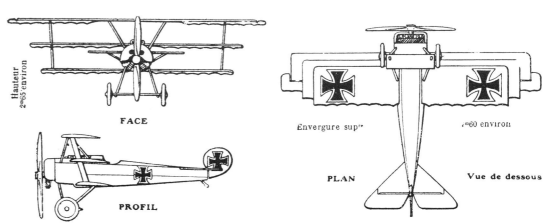

Hauteur 2ᵐ65 environ

FACE

PROFIL

Envergure supᵣₑ

1ᵐ60 environ

PLAN

Vue de dessous

General Sketches of the Fokker Triplane by M. Lagorgette.

Area of Fin	2.8 sq. ft.	
„ „ Rudder	5.9 „ „	
„ „ Horizontal Area of Body..	35.6 „ „	
„ „ Vertical Area of Body ..	58.6 „ „	
„ „ Plane between Wheels	12.4 „ „	

This aeroplane presents features of very great interest, whether viewed from the standpoint of aerodynamic design or of actual construction. The machine which has been the subject of investigation was, unfortunately, rather extensively damaged, thus making absolute accuracy of description difficult, and trials of performance impossible.

A similar machine has, however, being tested for performance by the French authorities, who have issued the following report :

Altitudes.	Time of climb.	Speed at this height.
1,000 metres (3,281 ft.)	4 mins. 15 secs.	116.6 m.p.h.
2,000 „ (6,562 „)	8 „ 18 „	114.1 „
3,000 „ (9,843 „)	13 „ 49 „	109.7 „
4,000 „ (13,124 „)	22 „ 48 „	103.5 „
5,000 „ (16,405 „)	38 „ 5 „	94.9 „

There are many points in which there is distinct divergence from accepted German, and tendency towards British, practice. The undercarriage, position of radiator, and aileron control levers, or kingposts, are examples.

This fact is some indication that the designer of this machine has approached the various problems and compromises which confront one who sets out to create such a machine, with a quite open mind, and, if this be allowed, there is a very strong case for a thorough investigation of those features which are in contradiction to contemporary British practice. These points include the wing design, which is without any external bracing, but of especially deep section ; the steel-tubular fuselage, and the peculiar bracing of this member.

There is nothing to prevent the adoption of the first and last features : but it should be pointed out with regard to the steel work that experienced welders have expressed the opinion that this art has been developed by the enemy to a high degree of efficiency. Indeed, the welding is sufficiently good to give rise to the belief that new methods, involving radical changes, have been adopted.

*The following data regarding weights is taken from a French source :—

Weight of fuselage, complete with engine, etc...	1322.2 lbs.	
„ „ upper wing with ailerons	167.2 „	
„ „ lower wing	99.0 „	
„ „ fin and rudder..	6.6 „	
„ „ fixed tail plane	17.6 „	
„ „ elevators	9.9 „	
	1622.5 lbs.	

A different French report gives the following figures, which are taken from inscriptions found on one of the Spandau guns on a captured *Fokker* of the same type :—

Weight (empty)	1,540 lbs.	
Permissible load (useful load and fuel)	396 lbs.	

* The schedule of principal weights given is the result of weighing the actual components mentioned, which were taken from the aeroplane allotted G 2B 14.

WINGS.

As in the *Fokker* triplane, the extreme depth of wing section and the absence of external bracing are distinctive features. Both upper and lower wings are without dihedral, and are in one piece. The way in which the lower wings are fitted into their place is described in detail under the heading " Fuselage." Both upper and lower chords are set parallel to the crankshaft, i.e., at no angle of incidence. and the inscription " Angle of incidence, o°" is painted on the upper plane.

WING CONSTRUCTION.

In sharp contradistinction to the fuselage, which is constructed of steel, even including members where wood is almost universally used, the wings contain no metal parts, if we exclude strut fittings and other extraneous features. There are no steel compression members, but where the internal wiring lugs occur, special box-form compressed ribs are fixed. The leading edge is of very thin three-ply, which has a deeply serrated edge finishing on the main spar (Fig. 2). The ribs are of three-ply, and are not lightened, although holes are, of course, cut where necessary, to accommodate the control and bracing wires. A rib from the top centre section, and one from the root of the lower wings, are both drawn to scale in Fig. 1.

The extreme thinness of the three-ply has given rise to a new method of fixing the flanges on the ribs. Instead of grooved flanges tacked on so that the tacks run down the length of the three-ply, two half flanges of approximately square section are tacked together horizontally with the ply sandwiched between (see Fig. 2).

SPARS.

As may be seen from the various sections drawn to scale in Figs. 3 and 4, the spars are made up of fairly narrow flanges at top and bottom, joined on either side by thin three-ply webs. They are placed approximately 30 cms. apart. The flanges are made of Scots pine and consist of two laminations. The three-ply has the two outer layers of birch and an inner ply, which is probably of birch also.

The three-ply webs are tacked on to the flanges, and fabric is glued over the joint. The cement is an ordinary gelatine glue.

The spar webs are glued to the flanges by a waterproof casein cement which is proved to contain gelatine, while the plywood adhesive—also a casein cement—is waterproof and of sufficiently good quality to withstand four hours' immersion in boiling water.

A side view of the Fokker D.VII (D.7) Biplane, showing the curious strut arrangement.

Front view of the Fokker D.VII (D.7) Biplane.

The trailing edge is of wire, and tape crosses from the top of one rib to the bottom of the next in the usual way. This tape lattice occurs about half-way between the trailing edge and the rear spar.

Fig. 3 shows the sections of the front and rear upper plane spars, taken in the centre section and at the interplane struts, while Fig. 4 gives the corresponding lower spar sections.

The ribs are stiffened between the spars by vertical pieces of wood of triangular section. There are two such pieces on each rib in the upper plane, and one in the lower plane.

All the woodwork of the wings is varnished, and fabric is bound round the flanges of the ribs and glued to the top and bottom of the spars.

The workmanship is decidedly good, and the finish neat and careful.

SCHEDULE OF PRINCIPAL WEIGHTS.

	lbs.	oz.
Upper wing, complete with ailerons, pulleys, bracing wires, fabric and strut fittings	156	0
Lower wing (no ailerons fitted), complete with strut fittings and fabric	97	0
N strut between wings	6	9
Straight strut, between fuselage and trailing spar of upper wing	2	8
Aileron frame, with hinge clips, without fabric ..	4	8
Rudder frame, with hinge clips, without fabric ..	4	11
Fin frame, without fabric	1	14
Tail planes (complete in one piece), without fabric ..	12	6
Elevators (complete in one piece), without fabric ..	11	2
Radiator, empty	48	0
Undercarriage strut, each	2	10
Undercarriage axle, with shock absorber bobbins ..	18	2
Bobbin, each	0	7
Shock absorber, each	3	9
Undercarriage (complete), without wheels and tyres, and without plane, but including struts ..	29	4
Aluminium tube, forming rear spar of undercarriage plane	1	8
Wheel, without tyre and tube	11	8
Tyre and tube	9	4
Tail strut	1	15
Fabric, per square foot, with dope	0	1
Bottom plane compression rib	0	15
Bottom plane ordinary rib	0	11
Top plane, ordinary rib, at centre of plane ..	1	0
Bracket, with bolts, attaching top plane to fuselage struts	1	11
Main spar, top plane, including fillet for ribs, per foot run in centre	1	12

Owing to tapering ends the average weight per foot of the spars will be slightly less than this figure.

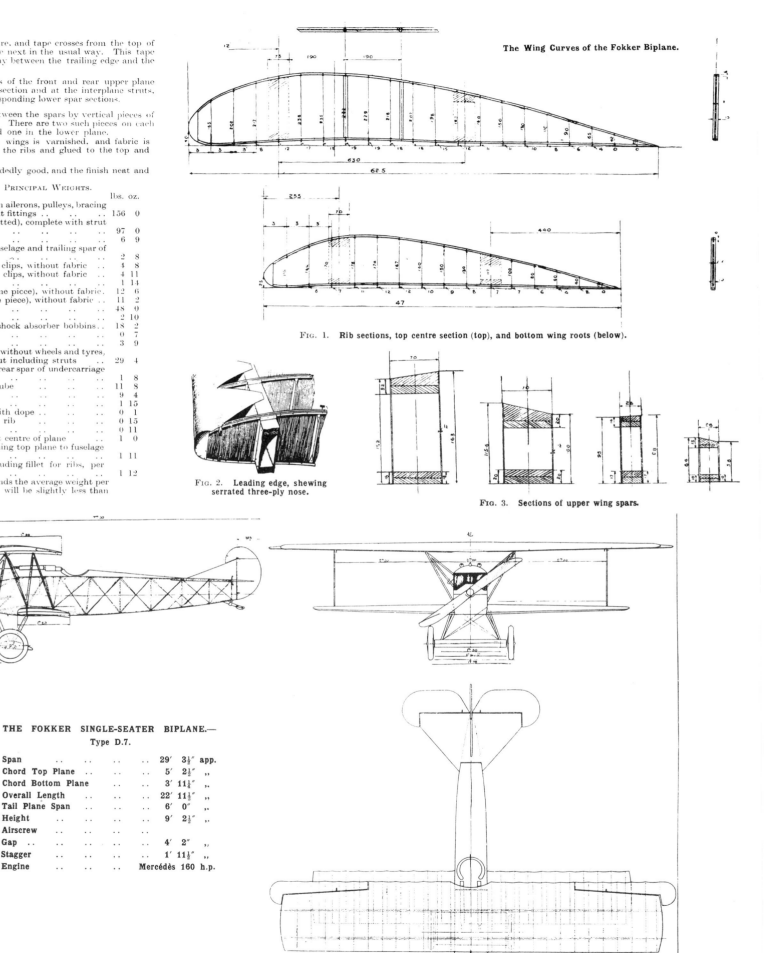

The Wing Curves of the Fokker Biplane.

FIG. 1. Rib sections, top centre section (top), and bottom wing roots (below).

FIG. 2. Leading edge, shewing serrated three-ply nose.

FIG. 3. Sections of upper wing spars.

THE FOKKER SINGLE-SEATER BIPLANE.—
Type D.7.

Span	..	..	..	..	29′ 3½″ app.
Chord Top Plane	..		..	..	5′ 2½″ ,,
Chord Bottom Plane	..		..	..	3′ 11¼″ ,,
Overall Length	..		..	..	22′ 11½″ ,,
Tail Plane Span	..		..	..	6′ 0″ ,,
Height	..	..	..	..	9′ 2½″ ,,
Airscrew	..	..	..	..	
Gap	..	..	..	..	4′ 2″ ,,
Stagger	..	..	..	..	1′ 11½″ ,,
Engine	..	..	..	..	Mercédès 160 h.p.

FOKKER D.7 *continued.*

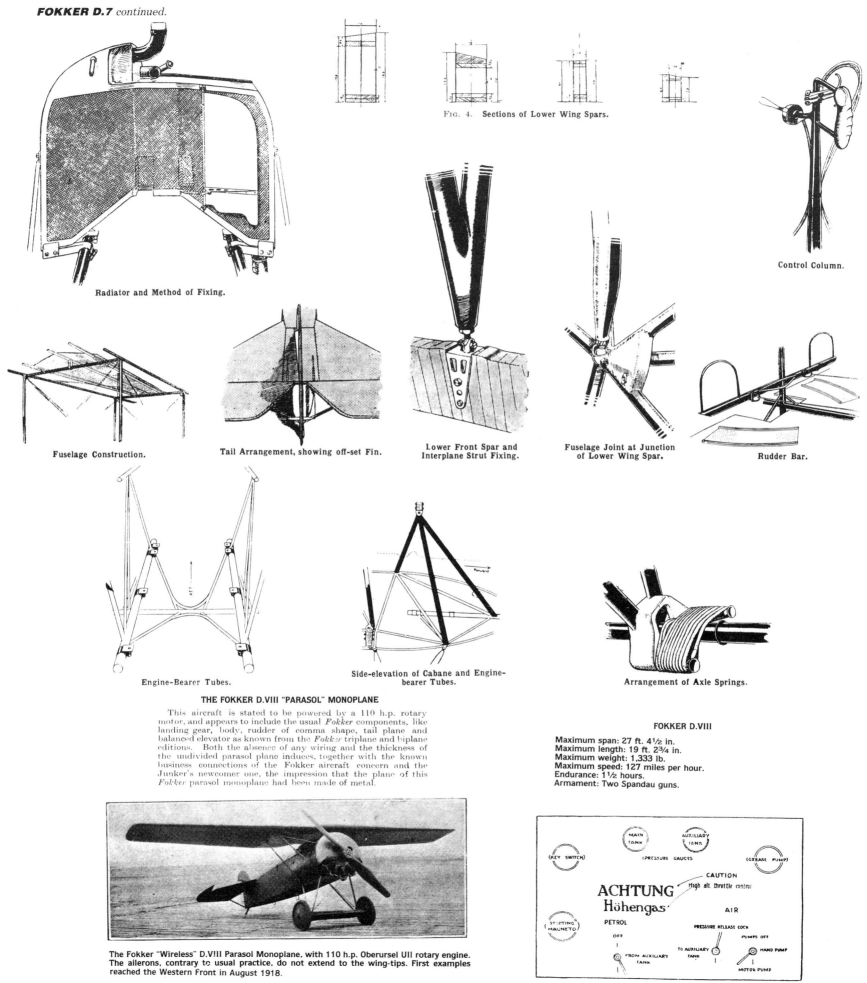

FIG. 4. Sections of Lower Wing Spars.

Radiator and Method of Fixing.

Control Column.

Fuselage Construction.

Tail Arrangement, showing off-set Fin.

Lower Front Spar and Interplane Strut Fixing.

Fuselage Joint at Junction of Lower Wing Spar.

Rudder Bar.

Engine-Bearer Tubes.

Side-elevation of Cabane and Engine-bearer Tubes.

Arrangement of Axle Springs.

THE FOKKER D.VIII "PARASOL" MONOPLANE

This aircraft is stated to be powered by a 110 h.p. rotary motor, and appears to include the usual *Fokker* components, like landing gear, body, rudder of comma shape, tail plane and balanced elevator as known from the *Fokker* triplane and biplane editions. Both the absence of any wiring and the thickness of the undivided parasol plane induces, together with the known business connections of the Fokker aircraft concern and the Junker's newcomer one, the impression that the plane of this *Fokker* parasol monoplane had been made of metal.

FOKKER D.VIII

Maximum span: 27 ft. 4½ in.
Maximum length: 19 ft. 2¾ in.
Maximum weight: 1,333 lb.
Maximum speed: 127 miles per hour.
Endurance: 1½ hours.
Armament: Two Spandau guns.

The Fokker "Wireless" D.VIII Parasol Monoplane, with 110 h.p. Oberursel UII rotary engine. The ailerons, contrary to usual practice, do not extend to the wing-tips. First examples reached the Western Front in August 1918.

Instrument Board of Fokker Monoplane.

FRIEDRICHSHAFEN.

FRIEDRICHSHAFEN. F.F. Flugzeugbau Friedrichshafen, Bodensee. Branch of the Zeppelin Airship Building Company, formed in 1912.

Up to the outbreak of war, devoted solely to the construction of seaplanes, built in few numbers and many forms under Curtiss influence, as single or twin-float seaplanes and flying boats, all pushers.

Performed well (putting up a passenger's duration world's record under the Swiss Gsell's pilotage) at Bodensee, and in long cross-river flights—up the Elbe and Rhine.

During the war the German aviation writer and engineer, Roland Eisenlohr, joined the F.F. Company as designer and both land and sea-going aircraft were produced.

Friedrichshafen concentrated mainly on the production of G type multi-engined bombers and FF 33, FF 49c and later patrol seaplanes, although it did also build single-seat fighters and single-engined bombers.

THE 450-h.p. FRIEDRICHSHAFEN G.II BIPLANE

The French technical journal, "L'Aérophile," has published an interesting description by M. Jean Lagorgette of a three-seater Friedrichshafen biplane, captured in 1917 by the French, near Verdun. Other specimens have been captured on the Macedonian front.

M. Lagorgette points out that the Flugzeugbau Friedrichshafen Gesellschaft, m.b.H.—a branch of the Zeppelin Company—has for a long time specialised in the construction of single and twin-engined seaplanes, the location of their works on Lake Constance making this very natural.

One of the principal changes is the use of arrow-shaped wings, a return to an early German principle.

The machine is of what is sometimes called the "general purpose type."

The dimensions are considerably less than those of the Gotha:—

Length, 11 metres (36 ft.). Height, 3.6 m. (11.7 ft.). Span, top plane, 20.3 m. (66 ft.); lower plane, 18.85 m. (61.2 ft.). Chord of planes, 1.8 m. to 2.3 m. (5.9 ft. to 7.5 ft.).

The gap is 1.95 m. (6.2 ft.). The total surface of the wings is 70 sq. metres (695 sq. ft.).

The wings are set at a dihedral and are slightly swept back, with the exception of the fixed centre section; the top and bottom members of which are slightly unequal, because of the arrangement of the "V" supports of the motors. There is a very slight stagger to the planes, which are oblique at their extremities.

The ailerons are set into the planes, and project outwards at the tips. They have also a slight "balanced" projection into the plane.

A considerable portion of the trailing edge in the centre of both planes is cut away to allow clearance for the airscrews.

The distance between the two main spars, and consequently between the front and back interplane struts, is 1 metre (3.25 ft.).

The spars in the centre section are constructed of steel tube. Those in the outer sections are made of wood. The cabane consists of four vertical struts.

Contrary to Gotha practice, the ribs are parallel with the axis of the machine.

Each aileron has at its extremity a balanced part in front of its hinge. The span of each aileron is 3.8 m. (13.3 ft.), the surface being about 2.3 sq. m. (22 sq. ft.).

The horizontal tail members are 3.95 m. span, and 3.65 m. in length, and have an irregular polygonal shape like that of certain 1914 Albatros machines.

As in nearly all German machines, the tail controls are balanced, and are constructed of tube work. The balance portion of the rudder is 1 m. × 0.25 m.

The fuselage is of the ordinary rectangular type, the upper surface being horizontal when in flight. The maximum height is 1.27 m., the width being 1.2 m.

A Friedrichshafen Single-seater Fighter.

The Friedrichshafen Seaplane, Type FF67, used extensively in the North Sea; operating from land stations and also seaplane carriers.

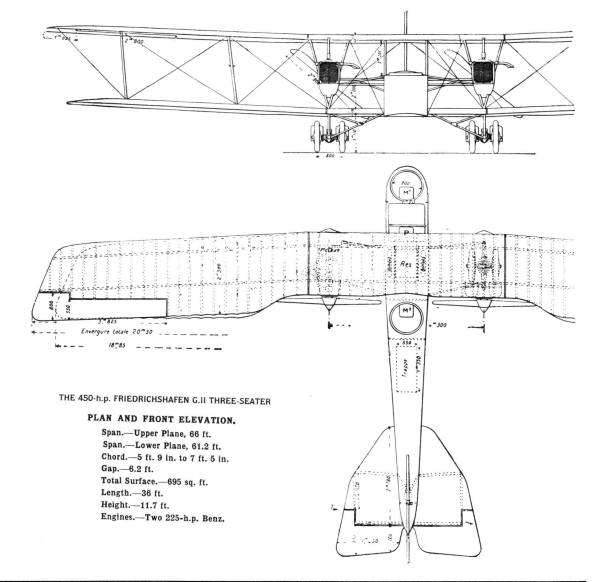

THE 450-h.p. FRIEDRICHSHAFEN G.II THREE-SEATER

PLAN AND FRONT ELEVATION.

Span.—Upper Plane, 66 ft.
Span.—Lower Plane, 61.2 ft.
Chord.—5 ft. 9 in. to 7 ft. 5 in.
Gap.—6.2 ft.
Total Surface.—695 sq. ft.
Length.—36 ft.
Height.—11.7 ft.
Engines.—Two 225-h.p. Benz.

The fuselage is constructed in two portions for ease of transport, the joint being in line with the trailing edge of the planes, so that the rear gun-ring comes away with the tail end of the fuselage, leaving a compact central section.

The landing-carriage is not characteristic of German aeroplanes generally. Underneath each motor is a pair of 965 mm. wheels, mounted on a common axle, giving a track of 0.8 metres. sprung by elastic cord from a large streamlined horizontal skid.

The motors are mounted between two pairs of "V" struts at a distance of 2.1 metres from the centre of the machine, and are linked to the fuselage by three nearly horizontal tubes. The Benz engines have six cylinders each. One, numbered 22799, gave 226 h.p. at 1,410 r.p.m. No. 25344 gave 221 h.p. at 1,400 r.p.m.

The airscrews, trade-mark "Imperial," are 2.9 m. in diameter.

The petrol tank and the two independent gravity tanks in the upper plane have a capacity of about 550 litres.

	kgs.		lbs.
Weight of machine, empty......	2,200	=	4,840
Useful load	520	=	1,180
Fuel load	432	=	940
Total	3,152	=	6,960

This represents 45 kgs. per sq. metre or 10 lbs. per sq. ft., and 7 kgs. (15.4 lbs.) per horse-power.

Three-quarter Front View of a Friedrichshafen G.III Bomber.

The Friedrichshafen G.IV twin-engined Tractor Biplane, Type FF62 of 1918. (2—260 h.p. Mercedes engines.) It will be noticed that the projecting bow for the gunner has disappeared and that this machine is a Twin Tractor instead of a pusher.

G

GEEST. Br. Geest Flugzeugbau G.m.b.H., Berlin-Oberschoneweide.
Formed in 1915 with a capital of 80,000 marks for the manufacture of aircraft, chiefly aeroplanes of inherent stability by Geest shaped planes, similar to the *Radley* "gull wing" monoplane.

GERMANISCHE FLUGZEUGWERKE.
Leipzig.
Formed during the war, producing aircraft of general German tractor type. Has taken over the sheds left at the aerodrome of that city, and runs a flying school, open to private pupils.

GOEDECKER. Goedecker Aircraft Works, Niederwallauf-on-Rhine.
Produced an early interesting, steel-built "Taube" (named *The Storm Bird.*)
Of small importance, being rather a flying school, building its own machines. Reported, without proof, to manufacture during the war a copy of the *Avro* biplane, shot down at Friedrichshafen during the British attack on the Zeppelin Works there.

GOETZE. Commandit Gesellschaft Richard Goetze.
Running four works: I and II at Treptow, Elsenstrasse 106-7; III in Berlin, Schlesische Strasse 26; and IV at the Johannisthal aerodrome, entrance VI.
A firm of new date, which has apparently turned out no design of its own. From the papers it appears that the Goetze Company turn out aeroplanes as sub-contractors.

GRADE. Hans Grade Flieger Werke, Bork, Flugplatz Mars. Post: Bruck in der Mark.
Hans Grade was the first German to fly in a self-designed triplane with an engine (two-cycle) of his own design. Won the Lanz prize of 40,000 marks. (*See Historical Section.*)
The position of the Grade Aircraft Works is unique, having been run on a commercial scale by private support alone.
In spite of all efforts—Grade flew voluntary in the Sachsen manœuvres and designed a nacelled and military control model—the military authorities would never accept his parasol monoplane with hanging warp control.
The highest percentage of pupils trained on one type stands to the credit of the *Grade* monoplane, many of the present German pilots having had their first experience on it. The general development of later years in military direction and some fatal accidents, after long avoidance of same, have restricted the importance of the Grade works.
In 1914, a looping model monoplane was turned out with double chassis, on which the first German looping flights were made.

GEEST Möwe monoplane of 1914. "Inherently Stable" (alleged). 100 h.p. Mercedes engine.

GEEST Möwe monoplane (rear view).

A Germania Biplane.

A Germania Single-Strut Biplane of the " C " Class, with a curious circular-shaped radiator.

GOTHA. Gothaer Waggonfabrik A.G. Aircraft department.
Running the Duke Carl Edward flying school at own aerodrome by Gotha.

The Gotha Company did not go through the early days of
aviation, but as a capital potential firm secured success by
manufacturing large quantities of proved sound aeroplane
models and by engaging first-class pilots for them—Ernst
Schlegel winning 1st prize of 60,000 marks in the National-
flugspende competition.

During the war the Gotha Company has partly floated other
aircraft firms.

Gotha seaplanes were developed early. An early war product
was the small rotary-engined and Morane-bodied *Falke* (Falcon)
single-seater biplane, influenced by and an answer to the Allies'
scouts. A big twin-engined "pusher" bombing biplane has
since been produced, and has been largely used in raids on
England.

Model and date.	"Taube." L D 1913.		"Taube." L E 1913.		Biplane L D 1. 1914		Biplane L D 2. 1914		Waterplane W D 1. 1914	
Length ... ... feet (m.)	33½	10·22	28¼	8·6	28¼	8·6	27¾	8·5	34½	10·5
Span ... ... feet (m.)	47¼	14·4	46½	14·2	47¼	14·5	39⅓	12·0	49¼	15·0
Area ... sq. feet (m².)	323	30·0	301	28	533	50	430	40	576	54
Weight { machine,lbs.(kgs.)	1543	700	1323	600	1477	670	1212	550	1631	740
useful ...lbs.(kgs.)	882	400	882	400	1102	500	838	380	992	450
Motor ... ... h.p.	100 Daimler-Mercedes		100 Daimler-Mercedes		100 Daimler-Mercedes		100 Gnome		100 Gnome	
Speed max. m.p.h. (km.)	62	100	72	115	70	110	75	120	56	90
Number built	...		...		...		...		...	

GOTHA LE "Taube" monoplanes of 1913-14 used for scouting.

THE TWIN-ENGINED GOTHA G.IV BIPLANE

The following description of the Gotha bomb-dropper is taken from "L'Aérophile," M. Jean Lagorgette having been given an opportunity of inspecting a recent capture :—

The span is 23.7 m. (77 ft.) and the length 12.45 m. (40 ft.).

The machine under discussion was a three-seater brought down by the late Capitaine Georges Guynemer. M. Lagorgette says that it does not give one the impression of being well tuned-up, and apparently the design has been modified without being remodelled. Without doubt, in the course of its construction, he says, several inspirations were imbibed from the Handley Page 500-h.p. Rolls-Royce 30 metre biplane captured by the Germans.

WINGS.—These are nearly equal in span, with projecting ailerons ; there is a slight dihedral, but no stagger ; there is a slightly arrowed shape, and the wings are nearly rectangular, and are cut away to a considerable extent along the centre part of the trailing edge so as to make room for the pusher air-screws.

The ailerons are balanced, an angular portion extending past the wing tips and forwards acting as a compensator or balance. There are three pairs of struts on each side, besides those supporting the engines.

The elevator and fixed tail-plane have a semi-hexagonal plan view. The rudder is nearly rectangular, with a balanced portion projecting above the triangular fixed fin.

The fuselage is mounted on the lower wings and is rectangular in section, and of three-ply in front. The gunners, both front and rear, can fire downwards through trap-doors. In a compartment between them are three bomb releases. One pair of wheels are placed under each of the two motors, which are stationary Mercédès of 260 h.p. with six cylinders. The two airscrews are pushers, contrary to the usual German principle.

The height of the machine is 3.85 m. (about 12 ft.).

The span of the lower wings is 21.95 m., nearly equal to that of the upper plane (23.7 m.), which includes the width of the ailerons, which are only on the upper planes.

The chord of the upper wings (2.3 m.) is slightly greater than that of the lower (2.2 m.) and they narrow gradually.

The gap is 2.17 m.

The total surface 95 square metres.

The length of the ailerons is 3.85 m. For 3.37 m. they increase in depth from 0.67 m. to 0.82 m. ; for 0.48 m. they are 1.32 m. deep, where the overhanging section of the aileron is made deeper so that it will act as a counterpoise. The surface of each aileron is 3 square metres.

The upper plane consists of two halves, which are attached to the cabane, which is trestle-shaped. The lower plane has a long central section without dihedral or sweep back, which goes underneath the fuselage and at its extremities supports the motor units.

The attachments consist of simple wires with turnbuckles.

The spars are of I section with three-ply on the sides. They are cross-strutted by tubes.

The ribs indicate nothing new. They do not extend to the leading edge, which is attached solely by its own edges. Being at right-angles to the leading edges, which form a " V," they are not parallel to the axis of the machine.

For this reason the three pairs of struts which are found outside each motor have the peculiarity that the rear struts are not situated immediately behind the front struts, but, nevertheless, the streamline section of each faces the line of flight.

The fabric of the wings and of the tail is unbleached linen.

THE TAIL.—The fixed stabilising plane, or tail-plane, consists of two nearly triangular halves, the two elevator flaps are nearly rectangular, but taper slightly in width towards the centre.

The fixed tail-plane is triangular, held at four points, and extends to the rear of the fuselage, and behind that, above the level of the fuselage, is found the rudder, a rectangular member, the top portion extending forwards as a compensator.

THE FUSELAGE.—This is a single body of rectangular shape, with a three-ply nacelle which is very prominent in front. There are four ash longerons, with formers, or cloissons, on ash frames, with stringers to support the fabric.

The arrangement of the nacelle is not symmetrical. The front passenger sits nearly on the centre line of the machine, but the pilot with his controls, a wheel operating a chain and a rudder-bar, is placed to the left, which leaves on the right a passage which makes it possible to move from front to back of the nacelle.

Behind him are two bomb releases, pigeon-holes, etc. Still farther back is the seat of the rear passenger, and behind him a big depression in the floor, with a sloping vaulted arch along the bottom of the fuselage, which permits the after-gunner to fire right along the bottom of the tail at any attacking machine.

Behind the passenger two transverse tubes support two machine-guns, one above the fuselage, the other near the floor, making it possible to fire both above and beneath the fuselage.

THE LANDING CARRIAGE.—This consists of two wheels under each engine, each supported by a pair of " V " tubes and a cross axle.

The motors are placed 2.1 metres on each side of the centre line of the machine, in two large and high nacelles, which are surmounted by strong cabanes.

MOTORS.—The bore of the six-cylinder 260-h.p. Mercédès motor is 160 mm., the stroke 180 mm. The effective h.p. is 258 to 260 at 1,400 r.p.m. The fuel consumption is 76 litres of petrol and 5 litres of oil per hour.

Each cylinder, precisely similar in appearance to the 175-h.p. type, is isolated, with its own water-jacket connected by a joint to its neighbour, and fixed separately to the crankcase, the six cylinders being in line.

A single carburetter, instead of the duplex pattern on the 175-h.p., and the two separate carburetters on the 235-h.p. models, feeds the six cylinders.

GOTHA LD biplane, probably of LD7 type of 1915 (120 h.p. Mercedes D.II engine)

A specially high speed GOTHA LD5 scouting single-seater of 1914, with 100 h.p. Uberursel engine.

GOTHA G. IV — *continued*

Two magnetos are driven by the vertical shaft which operates the camshaft. There are two plugs per cylinder and four valves. A half-compression device is fitted for easy starting.

There is a honey-comb radiator in front of each motor, and a petrol tank in each engine nacelle.

ARMAMENT.—The armament consists of three machine-guns, one in front in a turntable ring, which will fire through a hemisphere in front and a little over, above, and below. A second gun is mounted, as in the Aviatik, upon a transverse tube at the top of the fuselage, and behind the rear passenger, which can fire nearly vertically above and nearly perpendicular below the machine.

A third, mounted similarly upon a transverse tube near the floor of the machine at the edge of the arched opening, makes it possible to fire underneath the vaulted fuselage, or obliquely to the sides, or to the rear.

The bomb-dropping instruments carry 14 bombs in all. One in the front of the fuselage, an affair with spring jaws, contains two bombs lying longitudinally.

Two others placed between the pilot and the rear passenger contain six bombs each, piled one upon the other in a rectangular chamber, so arranged that as the lowest bomb is released, it is followed successively by the other bombs.

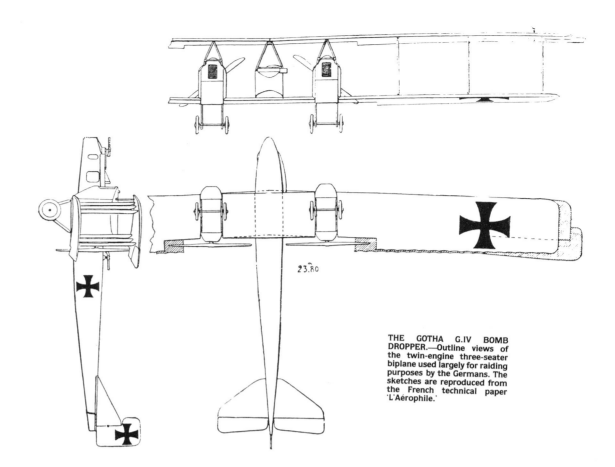

THE GOTHA G.IV BOMB DROPPER.—Outline views of the twin-engine three-seater biplane used largely for raiding purposes by the Germans. The sketches are reproduced from the French technical paper 'L'Aérophile.'

'THE GERMAN BOMBER.—A twin-engined Gotha biplane. The balanced ailerons and rudder are noteworthy.

A Gotha G.V Bomber as seen from above, with its handling crew resting in a trench behind it and on the ground round it.

A Gotha Bombing Squadron about to start.

GOTHA BROUGHT DOWN BY FRENCH A.A. FIRE NEAR CROCHTE ON JULY 4th-5th, 1918.

(probably G. Vb type)

The general construction of this machine appears to be similar to that described above in most respects, except for three modifications, which are worthy of note :—

1. A biplane tail unit.· It is similar in design to that of the *Handley-Page*, and embodies two fins on either side of the fuselage between the planes of the tail. The rudders are hinged to the trailing edges of these fins. The measurements of the tail unit are as follows :—

Top elevator span ..	..	..	5 ft. 7 ins.
Top elevator chord	..	..	2 ft. 7 ins.
Bottom elevator span	..	..	5 ft. 3 ins.
Bottom elevator chord	..	..	1 ft. 6½ ins.
Balance piece	..	..	11½ ins. by 10¾ ins.
Gap ..	..	..	2 ft. 9½ ins.
Bottom tail planes each average fore and aft measurement	..	..	2 ft. 5 ins.
Span along trailing edge, each	..		4 ft. 2 ins.
Top tail plane, average fore and aft measurement..	..	..	2 ft. 5 ins.
Span along trailing edge ..	..		8 ft. 10 ins.

This tail unit would appear to have been adapted in order to give the after gunner a better chance of attacking chasing aeroplanes, as the span is considerably smaller than that of the monoplane tail. It is constructed throughout of steel tubing.

2. Extensions are fitted to the top ailerons. It would appear from these that the *lateral control of the Gotha* has been found insufficient.

3. The undercarriages are arranged in a similar manner to those of the *Friedrichshafen*, that is to say, there is a two-wheeled undercarriage underneath each engine, and a third two-wheeled axle mounted on to the fore part of the fuselage; the wheels throughout are of equal size, carrying 810 by 125 mm. tyres.

The General Scheme of the Gotha Gun-Tunnel.

Three-quarter Front View of a Gotha G.V. Bomber.

Three-quarter Rear View of a 1918 type Gotha G.V. Bomber.

A Gotha G.L. VIII Twin-engined Tractor Biplane of late 1918 design, showing the abolition of the front gunner-observer's cockpit.

A Twin-engined Gotha WD.11 Seaplane of 1917 of the Pusher Type.

An early Gotha WD.2 reconnaissance Twin-float Seaplane supplied to the Turkish Navy about 1915.

A Twin-engined Gotha W.D.14 torpedo-attack Seaplane of the Tractor Type.

H

HALBERSTADT.

Halberstädter Flugzeugwerke G.m.b.H. Works and aerodrome at Halberstadt by Harz.

Formerly known as Deutsche Bristol Werke manufacturing for 1914 a "Taube" with the Rover patent tube-shaped wooden body.

Changed during the war into above name, the *Halberstadt* 1915 biplane being, as most of the German aeroplanes, under English and French influence, and in reality a compound of *Bristol, Avro* and *Morane,* with either rotary or stationary motor. D type fighters served between 1916 and 1917 (D.I to D.V).

During 1917 and 1918 the Halberstadt firm produced some of the best two-seaters of the war, as the CL.II and CL.IV for ground attack and escort and C.V for long-range photographic reconnaissance.

THE HALBERSTADT CL.II TWO-SEATER GROUND ATTACK AND ESCORT FIGHTER

This machine is a two-seater. It was brought down at Villers Bocage, by Lts. Armstrong and Mert on an *R.E.8* on 9/6/18. The machine is marked "Type H.S. C.L.2," and bears the military number C.L.2, 15,342/17. The date of construction 14/4/18, is stamped on various parts. On the side of the fuselage is the following inscription:—

Leergewicht (weight unladen), 796 k.g.
Nochstbelastung (useful weight), 370 k.g.
Einschl Vollen Tank. (Including full tanks).

There is also a red line about 30 inches long drawn at both sides of the fuselage, showing the horizontal in the normal flying position.

General Details.

The *Halberstadt* represents, in all probability, the high water mark of a two-seater German aeroplane construction, as it is not only well and strongly constructed, but its general behaviour in the air is good according to modern fighting standards.

Its general design will be gathered from the drawings at the end of this report and also from the photographs. Constructional details are dealt with by sketches.

Span of upper plane	35 ft. 3¼ in.
Span of lower plane	34 ft. 11 in.
Chord of upper plane	5 ft. 3¼ in.
Chord of lower plane	4 ft. 3¼ in.
Gap, maximum	4 ft.
Gap, minimum	3 ft. 8½ in.
Dihedral angle of lower plane	2°
Horizontal dihedral of main planes	4°
Total area of main planes	310 sq. ft.
Area of each aileron	11.6 sq. ft.
Area of aileron balance	2.0 sq. ft.
Load per square foot	8.2 lbs.
Area of tail planes	13.6 sq. ft.
Area of elevator	12.4 sq. ft.
Area of fin	6.4 sq. ft.
Area of rudder	7.9 sq. ft.
Area of rudder balance	1.0 sq. ft.
Maximum cross section of body	8.8 sq. ft.
Horizontal area of body	44.0 sq. ft.
Vertical area of body	52.8 sq. ft.
Length over all	24 ft.
Engine	180 h.p. Mercédès.
Weight per h.p. (180)	14.07 lbs.
Capacity of petrol tanks	34 gallons.
Capacity of oil tanks	4 gallons.
Crew	Two.
Guns	1 fixed and 1 moveable.
Military load on test	545 lbs.
Total load on test	2,532 lbs.

Performance.

Speed at 10,000 ft., 97 m.p.h., 1,385 r.p.m.

	Mins.	Sec.	Rate of Climb in Ft. Min.	Indicated Air Speed.
Climb to 5,000 ft.	9	25	440	69
Climb to 10,000 ft.	24	30	240	64
Climb to 14,000 ft.	51	55	80	58

Service ceiling (height at which climb is 100 feet per minute), 13,500 feet.

Estimated absolute ceiling, 16,000 feet.

Greatest height reached, 14,800 feet in 64 minutes 40 seconds.

Rate of climb at this height, 50 feet per minute.

Stability and Controllability.

This machine cannot be considered stable. There is a tendency to stall with the engine on, and to dive with the engine off. Directionally, owing to the propeller swirl, the machine swings to the left, but with the engine off is neutral.

Pilots report the machine light and comfortable to fly. The manoeuvrability is good, and this feature, taken in conjunction with the exceptionally fine view of the pilot and observer and the field of fire of the latter, makes the machine one to be reckoned with as a "two-seater fighter," although the climb and speed performances are poor judged by contemporary British standards.

Principal Points of the Design.

Single bay arrangements of wings.
Conspicuous set back of the main planes.
Empennage free from wires.
Fuselage tapers to a horizontal line at the rear in direct contradistinction to the usual German practice.
Pilot's and observer's cock-pit constructed as one.

A general view of the Two-seater Halberstadt CL.II.

A rear view of the Halberstadt CL.II showing tail plane arrangement.

Construction.

Wings.

The upper wings are supported by a large centre section having a span of 6 ft. 3 in. This centre section is at right angles to the centre line of machine, but at each side of it; the wings are thrown back with a horizontal dihedral of 4 degrees. The lower wings are smaller in chord and very slightly smaller in the span than the upper, and are fixed direct to the lower surface of the fuselage, and it is, to be noted that where the trailing edge joins on to the fuselage it is shaped so as to avoid a surface of discontinuity at the root of the wing. This is done by smoothly turning upwards the trailing edge.

The actual construction of the wings is of considerable interest, especially on account of the novel type of spar which is employed. This applies to both the upper and the lower planes. The front spar measures 2¾ inches by 1 inch and at the butt is placed about 4 inches from the leading edge. It is of "I" section, but is left full at such points as those at which internal bracing wires are fixed. This spar is connected to the leading edge by means of ply-wood, both top and bottom.

It will be seen that on the upper surface the ply-wood is extended rearwards for a distance of some 4¾ inches from the centre of the spar, and terminates in a small transverse flange about ½ inch deep. This construction furnishes a leading edge

Gunner-observer on a Halberstadt, equipped for Contour-fighting, with hand-grenades.

of great rigidity and strength, and at the same time it would also appear to be light in weight.

In the case of the rear main spar, the main member is of "O" or box section, and is built up of two pieces let into one another in a rather unusual manner. This is clearly shown in the drawing. Both at the top and bottom of the spar, thin strips of wood are used to cover the glued joint, and on this is tacked, both above and below, a flat length of ply-wood 7 inches wide which overhangs the main member of the spar an equal distance at each side.

This ply-wood web is flanged at each end with strips of wood glued in position, and on these strips are fitted small corner pieces which serve to support the ribs. The latter are also of ply-wood, to which are glued and tacked rails of solid wood, top and bottom.

A notable point of the wing construction is the fact that steel tubes are not used as the compression members of the internal bracing, as is the common practice. These members are made of box form ribs which occur at intervals along the spars. Adjacent to the root of the wing a very large reinforced box rib occurs.

The absence of steel tubes considerably simplifies the attachment of the bracing lugs to the spar. It will be noticed that it is of a very simple form, and in this respect it is characteristic of the design of the aeroplane on the whole, which, from this point of view, is far less elaborate than the majority of German designs and appears to be in many ways more practical, especially having regard to quantity production.

SCHEDULE OF PRINCIPAL WEIGHTS.

	lbs.	ozs.
Total weight .. ..2532 lbs.		
Upper wing, complete with aileron, aileron rod, drag bracing, and strut attachments, but without lift bracing wires and fabric	62	6
Lower wing, as above (no aileron fixed)	52	8
Aileron complete, without fabric	7	12
Aileron bar, with flange	4	0
Interplane strut, front, without bolts.. ..	3	3
,, ,, rear ,, ...	3	14
Centre section, complete, with radiator and gravity tank, aileron control crank, and bracing wires ..	101	0
Fixed tail plane (each), with fabric	7	8
Rudder, complete, with fabric	7	8
Elevator, complete, with hinge clips and fabric ..	12	0
Fin, complete, with fabric	9	6
V centre section strut	2	7
Straight centre section strut	3	7½
Undercarriage, complete, with struts and bracing, wheels, tyres, and shock absorbers ..	102	0
Shock absorber (multiple coil spring type), each ..	4	6
Axle, with shock absorber bobbins and caps ..	14	8
Wheel, with tyre	20	4
Tyre and Tube	8	12
Wings, leading spar, per foot run	1	4
Wings, trailing spar, per foot run	0	14½

HISTORICAL NOTE.

The present *Halberstadt* fighter is a development of the earlier single-seater, an example of which was brought down on 29·10·17. In the latter case ash was used to a fairly large extent, both in the fuselage and wings, but in the more modern design spruce is exclusively adopted. The rear spar was of the ordinary "I" Section type without three-ply reinforcement. The fuselage, of somewhat similar shape, was fabric covered. Balanced elevators and rudder were fitted, but no fixed tail plane or fin. The arrangement of the centre section, with tank and radiator, was substantially the same. Double bays of interplane struts were adopted, but the struts themselves were of the welded-up tapered pattern. The ailerons were controlled by wires and not, as in the present example, positively. Both planes had the same chord and the upper wings had an overhang. The weight of the complete machine, without pilot, was 1,778 lbs.

HALBERSTADT TWO-SEATER, TYPE C.L.IV.

This machine, which is allotted G.5Bde. 22, landed near Chipilly on Aug. 23rd, 1918. Dates stamped on the main planes give the date of construction as July, 1918.

It is very similar in design and construction to the *C.L.II* type, which has already been fully reported upon (I.C.642), but many detail differences are incorporated.

Below is a comparative list of the principal dimensions of both *C.L.II* and *C.L.IV* types.

		C.L.IV	C.L.II
Span of upper plane	.. ..	35 ft. 2¼ ins.	35 ft. 3½ ins.
Span of lower plane	.. ..	34 ft. 9¼ ins.	34 ft. 11 ins.
Chord of upper plane	.. ..	5 ft. 2⅝ ins.	5 ft. 3½ ins.
Chord of lower plane	.. ..	4 ft. 3½ ins.	4 ft. 3½ ins.
Gap, maximum	.. ..	4 ft. 4 ins.	4 ft. 0 ins.
Gap, minimum	.. ..	4 ft. 0 ins.	3 ft. 8½ ins.
Dihedral angle of lower plane	..	2 degs.	2 degs.
Horizontal dihedral of main planes		4 degs.	4 degs.
Total area of main planes	..	308 sq. ft.	310 sq. ft.
Area of each aileron	.. ..	12 sq. ft.	12 sq. ft.
Area of aileron balances ..	..	2.0 sq. ft.	2.0 sq. ft.
Area of tail planes	.. ..	16 sq. ft.	13.6 sq. ft.
Area of elevator	.. ..	13.6 sq. ft.	12.4 sq. ft.
Area of fin ..	.. ..	11.4 sq. ft.	6.4 sq. ft.
Area of rudder	.. ..	7.9 sq. ft.	7.9 sq. ft.
Area of rudder balance	..	1.0 sq. ft.	1.0 sq. ft.
Horizontal area of body	..	36 sq. ft.	44 sq. ft.
Vertical area of body	..	41 sq. ft.	52.8 sq. ft.
Length overall	.. ..	20 ft. 11½ ins.	24 ft. 0 ins.

		C.L. IV.	C.L. II.
Engine	.. .. ..	180 Merc.	180 Merc.
Capacity of petrol tanks ..		34 galls.	34 galls.
Capacity of oil system ..		4 galls.	4 galls.
Crew	..	Two.	Two.
Guns	..	1 fixed and 1 moveable.	

WINGS.

The wings, both in disposition and construction, are substantially the same as in the former machine. The characteristic wash-out at the root of the lower planes is even more pronounced than was the case in the *C.L.II* machine. It will be seen from the photograph that the rear spar is bent and twisted by this wash-out. The exact shape of the trailing edge of one of the lower planes is shown in the scale drawings.

Fig. 1 gives a section of the upper wing drawn to scale, and Fig. 2 a comparison of the upper aerofoil of the *C.L. IV.* with the *R.A.F.* 14 section, which is dotted. From Fig. 1 it will be noticed that the three-ply surrounds to the spars are still employed. They are drawn to scale in Fig. 3.

The ailerons remain unaltered in the *C.L.IV* machine, and this is also true of the interplane and centre section struts.

The attachment of upper wings to centre section and of lower wings to fuselage are unaltered, except that the tube which, in the earlier machine, passed right across the fuselage and connected the spars of the port and starboard lower wings is no longer found.

SCHEDULE OF WEIGHTS, HALBERSTADT, C.L.IV.

	lbs.	ozs.
Body, with undercarriage, engine, Spandau gun, petrol tank, gauges and controls	1,220	0
Engine (dry), 180 Mercédès	635	0
Upper wing, complete (no bracing wires)	70	8
Lower wing, complete (with bracing wires).. ..	64	0
Centre section, complete (with struts and wiring)..	108	8
Gravity petrol tank	11	4
Radiator	36	0
Centre section strut (Vee)	5	3
Centre section strut (straight)	2	4
Interplane strut (front), with cable	4	8
Interplane strut (rear), with cable	4	0
Undercarriage, complete, approximately	112	0
Shock absorber (one)	4	6
Axle, with bobbins and caps	14	8
Wheel, complete with tyre	20	4
Tyre and tube	8	12
Leading spar of wings (per foot run)	1	4
Trailing spar of wings (per foot run)		14½
Tail plane and elevator (covered)	25	0

Radiator in Upper Plane.

Passenger's Gun-ring.

Fig. 1. Wing Rib of C.L.IV type.

Fig. 2. Wing Section of C.L.IV with "Raf 14" section shown dotted.

UPPER WING – FRONT SPAR   UPPER WING – REAR SPAR

Fig. 3. Three-ply reinforcements of C.L.IV type wing spars.

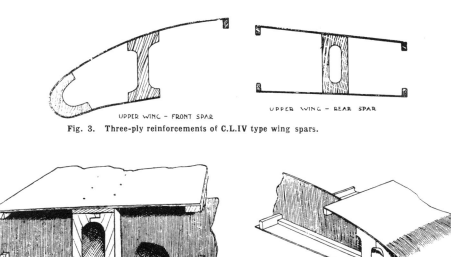

Rear Spar of C.L.2 type.   **Front Spar of C.L.2 type.**

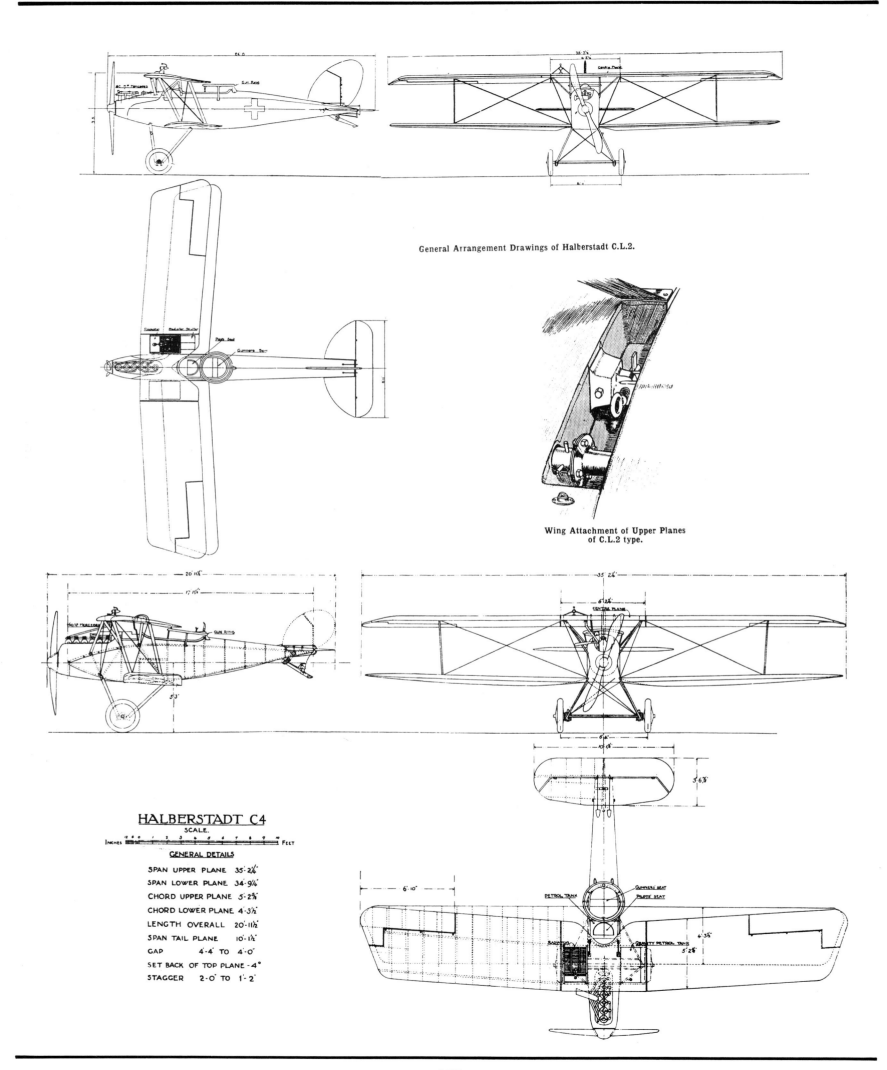

General Arrangement Drawings of Halberstadt C.L.2.

Wing Attachment of Upper Planes
of C.L.2 type.

HALBERSTADT C4

SCALE.

INCHES |⎯⎯⎯⎯⎯⎯⎯⎯⎯⎯⎯⎯⎯⎯| FEET

GENERAL DETAILS

SPAN UPPER PLANE 35'-2⅜"
SPAN LOWER PLANE 34'-9¼"
CHORD UPPER PLANE 5'-2¾"
CHORD LOWER PLANE 4'-3½"
LENGTH OVERALL 20'-11½"
SPAN TAIL PLANE 10'-1½"
GAP 4'-4" TO 4'-0"
SET BACK OF TOP PLANE -4°
STAGGER 2'-0" TO 1'-2"

THE HALBERSTADT FIGHTER.

"L'Aerophile" for June 15th contains a dissertation by M. Jean Lagorgette upon the Halberstadt single-seater fighting biplane, type D.

M. Lagorgette states that the Halberstadt Company, of Halberstadt, modestly call themselves "cherished of the premier aviators of the war," and that their machines seem to be more in vogue on the British front than on the French front, if one can judge from the number which have been destroyed.

The single-seaters have a length of 7.3 metres (25 feet).

The upper plane has a span of 8.7 metres (28 ft.), and slightly larger than the lower plane (7.85 m.). The wings are set at a dihedral angle, are washed out, and are noticeably staggered, the lower wings being staggered 0.45 m., which assists the view ahead.

The wings are not swept back, and are nearly rectangular. The ailerons, which are on the upper planes only project slightly, and are washed out, rising at the tips, as in other German biplanes. They are hinged on a secondary spar placed behind the rear main spar.

The chord of the wings is 1.56 m.; surface, 24.5 sq. m. (256.5 sq. ft.); gap, 1.3 m. The upper wings are not very distant from the top of the fuselage.

There are two pairs of interplane struts on each side of the fuselage, inclined towards the front. These struts are made of streamline tube, which terminate at their extremities in perforated heads, which are pinned between the walls of a fork joint fixed to the main spars, on which they pivot. In this way, the upper plane, by a movement through a parallelogram may, without the removal of the struts, be folded in line with the lower plane, for ease in transport.

This system is all the more advantageous, because there is no necessity for readjustment when re-assembling; to release the cables, which operation is necessary, there is no need to unscrew the strainers, it suffices to unfasten the quick release attachments

(similar to those in the L.V.G.), which connect certain cables to the bases of the interplane struts. Those cables, which do not have to be detached, are fixed to a ring contained in the base of the strut (as in the early Albatros).

This base is sloped by a block of wood to give it the inclination necessitated by the stagger of the wings.

The piano-wire cross bracing, which composes the internal strengthening of the wings, is fixed to long wiring plates, bolted to the inner surface of the spars. The main spars are of I section, and the cabane connects the upper pair with the fuselage. The centre section of the wings is covered with three-ply.

The lower spars terminate with a morticed butt, which meshes with a metal tenon built into the fuselage, and to which it is pinned by a bolt and cotter. This system, imitated from certain French machines, now tends to predominate in German aeroplanes, because it is very simple, and can easily be taken down, and is capable of manufacture on a larger scale than the older complicated attachments, specially constructed for each type of machine.

The section of the wing is well curved and very concave, as is common to all German machines, even when intended for speed, and they are also very heavy. The trailing edge is rigid.

The fuselage and wings of a captured Halberstadt D.III single-seat Fighter of 1916 (120 h.p. Argus As II engine).

HANNOVERSCHE. Hannover, Waggonfabrik, Aktien, Gessellschaft, Hannover-Linden.

Formed during the war for the manufacture of waggons and aircraft. Made a small series of two-seat ground attack and fighter biplanes of the general type shown in the following illustrations. All but the second series of CL.Vs featured biplane tails, the idea being apparently to give plenty of tail control, while at the same time keeping the tail narrow so that the after gunner is not "blinded" by a big tail-plane.

THE HANNOVERSCHE CL.IIIA BIPLANE

The machine illustrated was brought down by anti-aircraft fire, near Lestrem, on March 29th, 1918. As will be seen from the photographs, it is of highly characteristic design, and possesses numerous features of interest.

On labels protected by celluloid, and on the upper surfaces of the wings and fuselage, are identification marks with the date 15/2/18, showing that this machine is of recent construction.

Generally speaking, the construction is of wood throughout, steel being used sparingly, except in the interplane struts, landing chassis struts, centre section and some details of the tail.

Judging by contemporary British standards of design, the *Hannoversche* biplane reaches a fairly high level, the construction throughout being sound, and the finish quite good.

The performance of the machine is not by any means bad.

The leading particulars of the machine are as follows:—

Weight empty	1,732 lbs.
Total weight	2,572 lbs.
Area of upper wings	217.6 sq. ft.
Area of lower wings	142.4 sq. ft.
Total area of wings	360.0 sq. ft.
Loading per sq. ft. of wing surface	7.29 lbs.
Area of aileron, each	16.4 sq. ft.
Area of balance of aileron	1.6 sq. ft
Area of top plane of tail	10.0 sq. ft.
Area of bottom plane of tail	19.2 sq. ft.
Total Area of tail plane	29.2 sq. ft.
Area of fin	6.5 sq. ft. approx.
Area of rudder	6.4 sq. ft.
Area of elevators	22.0 sq. ft.
Horizontal area of body	53.2 sq. ft.
Vertical area of body	91.6 sq. ft.
Total weight per h.p.	14.3 lbs. per h.p.
Crew	Pilot and Observer.
Armament	1 Spandau firing through propeller. 1 Parabellum on ring mounting.
Engine	Opel Argus, 180 h.p.
Petrol capacity	37½ gallons.
Oil capacity	3 gallons.

Side view of the Hannoversche CL.IIIA Biplane.

Front view of the Hannoversche Biplane.

Three-quarter rear view of the Hannoversche Biplane.

PERFORMANCE.

(a) Climb to 5,000 ft. .. .. 7 mins.
  Rate of climb in ft. per min.. 590.
  Indicated air speed .. 68.
  Revolutions of engine.. .. 1,495.
(b) Climb to 10,000 ft. .. .. 18 mins.
  Rate of climb in ft. per min... 340.
  Indicated air speed .. 65.
  Revolutions of engine.. .. 1,475.
(c) Climb to 13,000 ft. .. .. 29 mins. 45 secs
  Rate of climb in ft. per min.. 190.
  Indicated air speed .. 62.
  Revolutions of engine.. .. 1,445.

SPEED.

At 10,000 ft. 96 miles an hour ; Revolutions, 1,565.
At 13,000, 89½ miles an hour ; Revolutions, 1,520.
Service ceiling at which rate of climb is 100 ft. per min. 15,000.

Estimated absolute ceiling .. 16,500.
Greatest height reached .. .. 14,400 in 39 mins. 10 secs.
Rate of climb at this height .. 120 ft. per min.
Air endurance .. .. .. About 2½ hours at full speed at 10,000 ft., including climb to this height.
Military load .. .. .. 545 lbs.

STABILITY.

The machine is nose-heavy with the engine off, and slightly tail-heavy with the engine on. It tends to turn to the left with the engine on.

CONTROLLABILITY.

The machine is generally light on controls, except that the elevator seems rather insufficient at slow speeds. It is not very tiring to fly, and pulls up very quickly on landing.

VIEW.

The view is particularly good for both pilot and observer. The former sits with his eyes on a level with the top plane, and also enjoys a good view below him on account of the narrow chord of the lower plane.

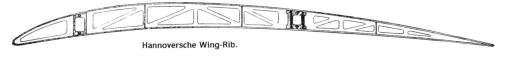

Hannoversche Wing-Rib.

Tail of the Hannoversche.

Undercarriage of the Hannoversche.

Construction.
WINGS.

The general arrangement of the *Hannoveraner* wings is somewhat reminiscent of the R.E.8, except of course, that the bottom planes have no ailerons. The upper wings are practically flat in end elevation, but the lower have pronounced dihedral angles of 2.7 deg., and are set with a positive stagger of 2 ft. 7½ ins. The chord of the upper plane is 5 ft. 10¾ ins., and that of the lower plane 4 ft. 3 ins. In flying position, therefore, the trailing edge of the lower plane is slightly in advance of that of the upper plane. The angles of incidence marked on the manufacturer's rigging diagram, which is fixed to the side of the fuselage, and stamped on the fabric of the wing, are as follows :—

Lower wings .. .. .. 5½ deg. at fuselage.
                       5 deg. at struts.
Top wings .. .. 5 deg. throughout.

The lower wings are carried direct from the bottom edge of the fuselage, the roots of the upper planes being carried on a rigidly constructed centre section, which embraces the radiator and the gravity feed petrol tank. The rearward portion of the centre section is cut away immediately over the pilot's seat, and at this point the wing is about 1 ft. above the upper surface of the fuselage. The lower plane has no very pronounced wash-out, but this feature is more noticeable in the upper plane, and is enhanced by the design of the ailerons, the tips of which are set at a slightly negative angle. This gives the characteristic German appearance to the aeroplane when seen in flight. In contrast with that of the majority of German aeroplanes, the wing section is rather flatter than usual.

The Pilot's Office in the Hannoversche Biplane.

A Hannoversche reconnaissance Biplane, Type C.L.V. (second series), with large single wooden streamline struts and a monoplane tail.

A Hannoversche Biplane, Type C.L.IV, with curious strutting arrangement. (300 h.p. Maybach engine.)

Radiator and Gun-Emplacement.

Rear Gun Attachment and Ring.

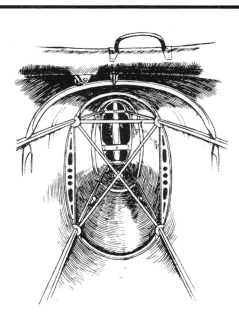

Interior of Fuselage, looking aft.

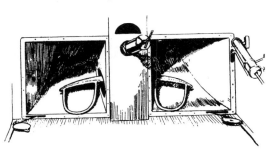

Rudder-Bar Arrangement.

Centre-Section Strut Arrangement.

Method of Attaching Struts.

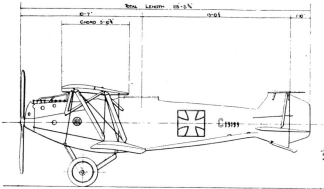

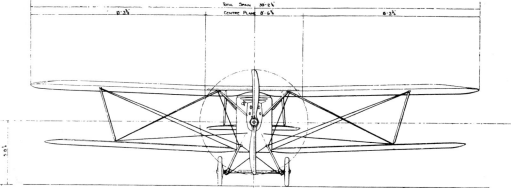

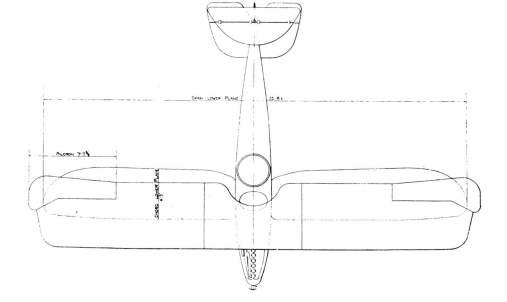

HANNOVERSCHE BIPLANE

Span			39′ 2¼″
Span, Lower Plane ..		..	36′ 8½″
Chord		..	5′ 10¾″
Gap	(about)		5′ 3″
Tailplane Span ..	(Upper)		6′ 9″
Tailplane Span ..	(Lower)		8′ 0″
Overall Length		..	25′ 5½″
Engine (Opel-Argus) ..		..	180 h.p.
Propeller..		..	9′ 4″
Track		..	6′ 0″

HANSA. Hansa & Brandenburgische Flugzeugwerke A.G., Brandenburg on Havel, Berlin-Rummelsburg and Hamburg-Wandsbech.

With a capital of 1,500,000 marks, and a staff of 1,000 workmen in Autumn, 1915, these works were then the biggest concern in the German aircraft industry. Manufacturing at Brandenburg, repair works at Rummelsburg and Fuhlsbüttel. Military flying schools for German and Austrian pupils, at Briestly, by Brandenburg and at Fuhlsbüttel aerodrome, near Hamburg.

The German Aero Company, Ltd. was formed in March, 1915, with a capital of 450,000 marks, chiefly by the Austrian Commercial Councillor Castiglioni, the first director of the concern, and also founder of and controlling the Hungarian Aircraft Works, and by the German aircraft manufacturer Trinks, for the building of *Lohner* biplanes in Germany under license.

On the 7th September, 1915, the stocks were raised to one million and a half marks, and the above name taken by the amalgamation of the Hansa Aircraft Works, Karl Caspar, Hamburg (a former branch of the Gothaer Waggonfabrik), and of the Brandenburgische Aircraft Works, into which the Etrich Works at Libau, and the branch company, the Sports Flieger Flying School at Johannisthal had been transformed.

The chief designer of Hansa & Brandenburgische Flugzeugwerke was Engineer Director Hunkel, formerly of the Albatros firm, who brought out the 160 h.p. Mercédès engined tractor biplane, on which the Austrian chief pilot of the company, Reiterer, put up various passenger altitude record flights, but was killed.

The Hansa-Brandenburg Aircraft Co. was one of the three main suppliers of German sea-going aircraft, including the CC flying-boat of 1916 appearance and a range of biplane and monoplane patrol, fighter, reconnaissance and torpedo attack floatplanes. Landplanes included the D unarmed scout of 1914 appearance, D.I fighter of 1916, C.I reconnaissance-light bombing two-seater, and G.I twin-engined bomber.

THE BRANDENBURG SEA MONOPLANE.

The later *Brandenburg* W.29 seaplane to land in a Danish harbour, as illustrated, bore evidence of the development in the German seaplane line, and the sea monoplane, dealt with here, is the last word in German naval war aviation.

This craft was known for some time to be in existence and at the disposal of Captain Lieut. Christiansen, for North Sea service of the Zeebrugge squadron under his command. It is easily seen that the object strived at has been to obtain a seaplane mount approaching land scouts in controllability, which end, however, renders the aircraft apparently difficult to handle, and thus confines its pilotage to skilled hands.

A comparison shows the biplane and monoplane seaplanes to have the fuselage with the features of raised body curve and tail plane fixing, and rudder form and the floats-cum-strut chassis as identical components. Too, the lower planes of the biplane appear to be in the same position as the wings of the monoplane with its aileron and exterior control cables, and the lower wing strut support of the monoplane is another instance proving the requirements of skilled handling not to have plane damage as the result of a hard descent.

An excellent view and fire range of both pilot and observer will clearly be seen to be attained, besides a live craft, and the weight of the floats may to some extent bring the centre of pressure in approach of the point of gravity.

HANSEATIC AEROPLANE WORKS, CARL CASPAR.

An early German pilot of pluck, Carl Caspar, in spite of a heavy fall by entangling in cables on an overland flight in mist, consistently partook in the various German competitions, such as the Prince Henry, Johannisthal, Round Berlin, East German meetings, and others, with various success.

With headquarters in Hamburg, he founded a flying school at the Fuhlsbüttel drill ground there.

In the last years before the war, he piloted a *Gotha* "dove" and won the £2,500 prize as third best flight in the "National-spende" overland competition as best achievement. He himself started the manufacture of similar "Hansa" tauben.

During the war, Caspar has himself been on active service, and is said to have been the first German aviator to pay the British islands an air visit, by route of Dover as the usual port of call.

His aircraft works was, in 1915, combined with the Brandenburg company, but separated again later. The Hanseatic Aeroplane Works, Carl Caspar, were then run on a successful scale with a capital of £150,000, no news being to hand of the aircraft turned out.

HANUSCHKE. Hanuschke, Bruno, Flugzeugbau, Johannisthal bei Berlin.

A young and early designer and skilled pilot of parasol monoplanes. His last machine before the war was a *Morane* imitation, and later activity has not been heard of.

J

JATHO. Hannoverische Flugzeugwerke, G.m.b.H., Carl Jatho, Hannover, Vahrenwalderstrasse.

Carl Jatho was one of the German aviation pioneers, and for many years has produced experimental aeroplanes. Since the formation of the above company has concentrated on steel monoplanes, the last dove-designed being fitted with zanonia and arrow-shaped wings, but nothing was reported of business activity before or during the war.

A front view of the Brandenburg W.29 Sea Monoplane of late 1918.

Side view of the Brandenburg W.29 Sea Monoplane.

A Brandeburg W.12 Sea Biplane of 1918.

JEANNIN.
Jeannin, Emil, Flugzeugbau, G.m.b.H., *Steeldove* and *Race* monoplane manufacturing works, and flying school at Johannisthal, bei Berlin.

Formed by the early successful German aviator Jeannin, on his leaving the Aviatik Company.

The racing monoplanes of *Nieuport* outlines first produced brought the German pilots to fatal accidents, a steel "Taube" being then built, in a rather original edition, which was one of the fastest German aircraft on account of its flat wing section.

During the war the firm has been turned into the Nationale Flugzeug Werke (see latter), under new management, Jeannin leaving.

JUNKERS-FOKKERS WORKS, Ltd.
Dessau.

One of the most interesting new formations of 1917. Has a capital of £75,000. Founded by the co-operation of the well-known concerns of the aeroplane manufacturer, Fokker, and the Diesel engine manufacturer, Junkers.

The subtitle of "metal aeroplane building" indicates, possibly, the field of activity.

THE JUNKER ALL-METAL (ALUMINIUM) MONOPLANE.

The same comments as applied to the *Brandenburg* sea mono-plane scout, may be employed on this monoplane version of the foregoing biplane of the *Junker* company, the more, as in this instance there are no heavy floats to bring the point of gravity within approach of the centre of pressure. The body is of monocoque appearance with pronounced streamlining behind the pilots and looks as are the planes, provided with large trailing curved ailerons, the divided triangular tail fin and the undivided balanced elevator to be made of corrugated aluminium.

The fuselage ends with a point of sheet metal, and the rudder, of sharp-cornered shape, is attached unsupported to the stern post. What looks like a wire post is to be seen on top of the right plane, but not on the left. A car type radiator is employed, as is a stationary engine and an old-time backwards led exhaust pipe collector. Besides the usual V-shaft rest, the landing gear comprises a forward converted, narrow and streamlined V strut set and two inclined ones of circular tubes, meeting in the middle below the fuselage.

[NOTE.—There is no recent information concerning the Hanuschke, Jatho, Jeannin or Krieger firms, which in any case are of little note. The accompanying information is retained merely for purposes of record.—Ed.]

Side view of the Junkers J.I all-metal low-level close support and reconnaissance biplane of 1917 appearance.

The Junkers J.7 experimental all-metal fighter of 1917, developed into the operational D.I of 1918.

A rear view of the Junkers J.7 Monoplane.

Three-quarter front view of the Junkers J.I Biplane.

Front view of the Junkers J.I Biplane.

The All-Metal Wireless Junkers CL.I ground attack and escort monoplane of 1918.

K

K.K. Karl Krieger, Berlin-Johannisthal.

The Emperor's former car driver, pilot designer of speedy German monoplanes. Has during the war produced the first modern type parasol aircraft in Germany.

KONDOR. Flugzeugwerke, G.m.b.H.
Works at the Gelsenkirchen-Rotthausen aerodrome.

Formed by the aviator Joseph Suvelack, who has brought out various monoplanes, biplanes and seaplanes.

Killed on active service on an *Albatros* biplane in combat with British aircraft.

The designer Westphael has apparently during the war joined the firm, producing now a tractor biplane, 160 h.p. Mercédès motor, on which an altitude record with four passengers was established at Johannisthal.

Wartime aircraft included the W.1 two-seat biplane of 1915 and a string of D Type biplane fighters. Its final product was the E3 (E111) built for an October 1918 fighter competition.

The Kondor E 111 Wireless Parasol Monoplane. (140 h.p. Oberursel rotary engine), which is said to give a speed of 195 kms. per hour and a climb of 5,000 metres in 16 minutes.

Three-quarter Rear View of the Kondor D VI Biplane. (140 h.p. Oberursel Ur III rotary engine.) The elimination of the centre section, in an endeavour to improve the pilot's vision, should be noted.

The Kondor E 111a " Wireless " Parasol Monoplane (200 h.p. Goebel rotary engine) which gives a speed of 200 kms. per hour and a climb of 5,000 metres in 11 minutes.

Front View of the Kondor D VI Biplane. (200 h.p. Goebel rotary engine).

L

L.F.G. ROLAND. Luft Fahrzeug Gesellschaft m.b.H.
City office : Berlin W. 62, Kleiststrasse.

Builds *Parseval* airships at Bitterfeld, aircraft works at Adlershof, the latter were almost completely burned down on September 6th, 1916.

The early type aeroplanes were a " Taube " monoplane with elevator tail and an "Arrow" biplane, on which Bruno Langer put up the first German duration record of 14 hours in 1914.

A tractor biplane of general type was manufactured during 1914-15, while the 1916-17 model possess the features given below.

As the pre-war and early war monoplanes of Germany were generally nomenclatured " Tauben " (doves), owing to their zanonia back-swept shaped planes, the latest German fighting biplanes (like *Roland, Halberstadt*, and so on) are likely to be named " Walfische " (whales), as their aspect comes to them from the big front part of the body, which houses the 160 h.p. or 220 h.p. motor.

The *Roland* is the name of aircraft manufactured by the Luft Fahrzeug Gesellschaft (L.F.G. by initials), at Adlershof, successors of the old German Wright Aeroplane Co., and thus not to be confused with the L.V.G. Co. at Johannisthal (Luft Verkehrs Gesellschaft, or Air Traffic Co.).

Operational warplanes included the C.II of 1916-17 use, and D series fighters (D.I, D.II, D.III and D.VI).

L.F.G. ROLAND C.II

The details of the C.II given here are based on a machine captured on March 24th 1916. This *Roland* biplane was a two-seater with the passenger behind, the main dimensions being :—

Span of planes, 10.3 metres (33 ft 9 ½in).
Chord of planes, 1.60 metres (about 4 ft. 6 in.).
Gap of planes, 1.55 metres (about 4 ft. 6 in.).
Length, 7.70 metres (25 ft. 3 in.).
Maximum weight, 1,284 kg. (2,831 lb.).
Engine, 160 h.p. Mercedes.
Propeller, length, 2.70 metres (about 9 ft.).
Propeller, pitch, 1.85 metres (about 5 ft. 6 in.).

Only the upper planes had ailerons, which were worked in the ordinary way. There were two hollow longitudinal spars, the front one 85 mm. by 25 mm. the back one of 100 mm. by 62 mm. measures, having a gap of 60 centimetres, the latter being almost in the middle of the plane.

The upper planes are cut away above the fuselage to add to the view and field of firing. The sides are also perforated with windows. This fuselage was of oval monocoque shape.

The plane mounting is on a single cabane, not a pair, one each side—as on the small *D.F.W.* of 1914.

The landing chassis is ordinary with a claw-brake.

The armament is a Parabellum gun mounted on a gun-ring.

As to performance, the following figures are available:—

Rise to 500 metres (about 1,500 ft.) in 4 minutes; to 1,000 metres (about 3,000 ft.) in 8 minutes; to 1,500 metres (about 4,500 ft.) in 14 minutes; to 2,000 metres (about 6,000 ft.) in 22 minutes. Maximum speed is 165 km.p.h. (102 miles per hour).

A curious ROLAND C.II reconnaissance and escort two-seater biplane of 1916-17, with pilot and passenger above the upper plane. It will be noted that the "single strut" idea is not new in Germany. The engine is a 160 h.p. Mercedes D.III. Its body arrangement recalls Mr. R. F. Macfie's design of 1911.

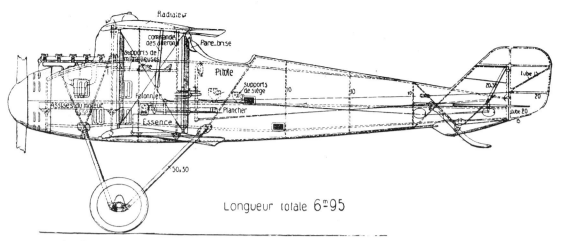

Longueur totale 6ᵐ95

Side Elevation of the Roland Single-Seater.

THE ROLAND SINGLE-SEATER FIGHTER.

L'Aérophile for May, 1918, gives the following particulars of the *Roland* single-seater fighter. For this information and the accompanying drawings one is indebted to the editor of that excellent paper.

The single-seater *Roland Biplane D II.*, which first made its appearance in March, 1917, is once more frequently encountered by French pilots, chiefly in the Eastern sectors.

The dimensions of the machine are as follows :—

Span, upper plane	..	..	..	..	8.90 m.
,, lower	..	..	..	..	8.50 m.
Total length	..	..	..	..	6.95 m.
Height	..	..	..	..	2.95 m.

Its weight, 827 kgms., is slightly greater than that of the *Albatros D III.* The lifting surface being 23 sq. m., the load carried per square metre of surface being 36 kgs. (about 7.3 lbs. per square foot).

THE FUSELAGE.

The construction of the fuselage is worthy of special notice. It is built entirely of plywood, covered with fabric, monocoque fashion, and has an oval section finishing up with a vertical knife edge at the stern-post.

The construction is of the lightest, the framework consisting merely of extremely thin longerons extending the whole length of the fuselage.

Rigidity is due only to two plywood partitions uniting the middle of the top half with the middle of the bottom half. The total thickness of the six layers of the plywood is only 1½ millimetres. At the rear of the pilot's seat one can count only four thin layers.

Between the pilot's seat and the engine there is a superstructure to the fuselage which thins itself at the top to a fin 11 m. thick, to which is attached the radiator and the upper plane.

The centre section of the upper plane is hollowed out to provide space for the radiator. This arrangement replaces the cabane.

One finds on the lower part of the fuselage two shoulders, one on either side, to which are fixed the lower planes.

At the rear the tail skid, built of timber and shod with metal, penetrates the fuselage through a kind of swelling, reminiscent of Nieuport practice.

The pilot is seated high up, his view being assured by two wind-screens placed one on each side of the central ridge. The field of view ahead is very obstructed, and visibility is not so good as in other machines.

THE UPPER PLANES.

The planes are trapezoidal in plan, unequal in span, without stagger or dihedral, but swept back 1½°. Their chord is uniformly 1.45 m., and their gap 1.34 m.

The ribs are perpendicular with the leading edge, and, as each strut of a pair is attached to a common rib and the wings are swept back, the struts are not exactly one behind the other.

The upper planes are formed on two spruce spars placed .83 m. apart, the front one being .13 m. from the leading edge.

There are twelve ribs which are placed .37 m. apart and are interspaced with laths 10 mm. wide, running from the leading edge to the rear spar.

The distance between the main spars is maintained by four compression members of steel tube. These tubes are 25 mm. diameter and are placed at equal intervals of 1.30 m. ; and are cross-braced by piano-wire 3mm. thick. Two fabric strips between the leading edge and the front spar, and two others between the front and rear spars alternately pass from one rib to another, over and under.

Certain angles in the wing frame are kept very rigid by plywood angle pieces.

The ailerons, which are fitted to the upper planes, do not project and are unbalanced. A strip of plywood placed over the fabric protects the aileron hinge at its attachment to the rear spar.

Along this line the aileron measures 1.82 m. It is .42 wide. Its axis is a 30 mm. tube. The aileron cranks are operated by two vertical tubes, Nieuport fashion.

In the upper left hand wing is found a gravity feed petrol tank.

The upper planes are attached directly to the highest part of the fuselage with the help of a special bolt which recalls the system of attachment described on the *L.V.G. C.IV.* type.

THE LOWER PLANES.

The structure of the lower wings is like that of the upper wings. The spars are disposed in the same way, and consequently maintain the same distance between one another. There are ten ribs to each wing, of which nine are .01 of a metre and the last .025 of a metre thick. Between each of them there is also a light lath 10 mm. thick. The bracing is the same as in the upper wings, except that the struts, made of four steel tubes, are slightly different, the first being of 20 mm. and the three others of 25 mm. From the first to the second is 1.17 ms., from the second to the third 1.13 ms., and from the third to the fourth 1.11 ms.

The lower wings are fixed up against the rudimentary planes on each side of the base of the fuselage.

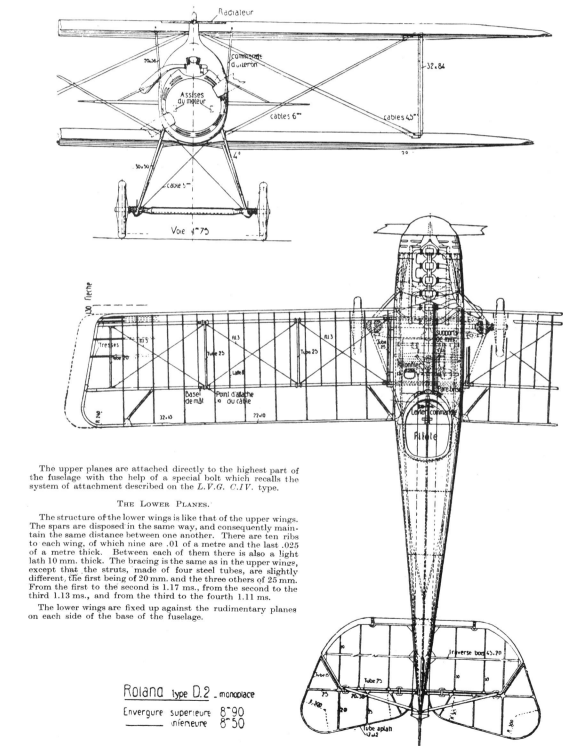

Roland type D.2 _monoplace

Envergure	supérieure	8ᵐ90
	inférieure	8ᵐ50

In rigging one notices an incidence of 4 degrees at the second rib and 3 degrees at the seventh. The interplane struts are of tube of .025 ms. diameter, placed inside a streamline of wood, which gives them a depth of .09 ms.

TAIL.

The whole tail unit has the aspect of a trapezium with at the base a large triangular piece of small depth cut out.

The fixed tail plane is of wood, and the two balanced members forming the elevator are entirely of metallic construction.

The leading edge of the fixed tail plane is of wood hollowed on the inside. A piece of wood, which traverses the fuselage and sticks out .5 m. on each side of it, is embedded in the hollowed part of this leading edge, and thus ensures absolute rigidity.

Two struts of streamline tube running from the top of the fin to the angle of the elevator assist still further this rigidity.

The rudder is almost rectangular in form, with rounded angles. It is balanced by a triangular part prolonging the fin, of which the leading edge is similarly oblique.

The rudder is built of tubing and the fin is of 3-plywood, forming part of the fuselage.

The control cables of the elevator are concealed inside the fuselage, and the control cables of the rudder only come out of the fuselage about 1 metre from the end.

MOTOR.

The single-seater *Roland D.II* is fitted with a Mercédès engine of 160 h.p. of a type already described. As well as the supplementary tank placed in the upper left plane, it has a tank 70 by 70 by 25 placed under the rudder bar.

ARMAMENT.

There are two Spandau machine-guns operated by the motor. They are placed one on each side of the engine inside the fuselage, from which they only protrude at the front.

UNDERCARRIAGE.

This is formed of two tubular V's held together by two cross cables. Their point of attachment corresponds exactly to the base of a partition of the fuselage. The axle is placed between two tubes and is enclosed in a streamline casing. The wheel track is 1.75 m. The wheels are 760 by 100 and the springing is of rubber cords.

It has been said that the *D.II Roland*, owing to its light construction, often suffers from a deformation of its fuselage and is very apt to spin. No test of this machine having yet been possible, this opinion cannot be based on the evidence of our own aviators. It is, however, certain that this machine, which was quite a new idea at the time of its creation, has been among the best of the German chaser machines, and was still in use in May, 1918, in certain of the enemy escadrilles.

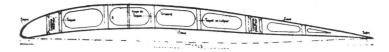

Rib Section.

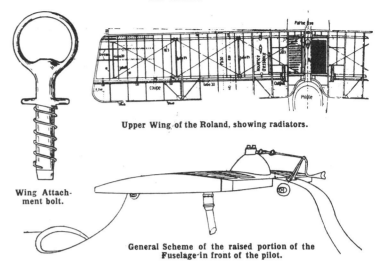

Wing Attachment bolt.

Upper Wing of the Roland, showing radiators.

General Scheme of the raised portion of the Fuselage in front of the pilot.

A Roland Single-seat fighter of 1918, Type D VIb. (150 h.p. Benz Bz IIIa engine). Went into production for the German air force and navy. Achieved 114 miles per hour.

An Early (1917) experimental Roland Triplane, Type D IV. First L.F.G. Roland with the wooden clinker-built fuselage. (160 h.p. Mercédès engine.)

An Experimental Roland Type D.XV Single-seater Biplane. (160 h.p. Mercédès engine.) This machine was the 2,000th war aircraft turned out by the Roland factory.

A Roland Single-seater "Wireless" Biplane, Type D.XV in third prototype form. (190 h.p. B.M.W. engine.)

A Roland Single-seater Fighter, Type D XIV. (160 h.p. Goebel engine.)

A Roland Type D.XVII Single-seater "Wireless" Monoplane. (185 h.p. B.M.W. engine.)

An early (1915) Type, Twin-propeller and Single-engined Roland Biplane, Class G I. (260 h.p. Maybach engine.) Remained a prototype.

Second to last Roland fighter was the experimental Type D XVI. (160 h.p. eleven-cylinder Siemens-Halske Sh III engine.)

A Roland experimental Single-seater Biplane, Type D VIb. (190 h.p. Benz engine.)

LINKE-HOFFMAN. Werke, Breslau.

Little is known of this firm, which was not much heard of till the Armistice, when certain illustrations of its products appeared in the German Press.

It is stated that none of its products have been used in any war area.

The Four-engined, Single Airscrew Linke-Hoffman R.II prototype bomber of 1918.

Linke-Hoffman R.I of 1917, using four 260 h.p. Mercedes D.IVa engines carried inside fuselage. Remained a prototype bomber.

L. T. G. The Luft Torpedo-Gesellschaft, Johannisthal, bei Berlin.

The Luft Torpedo-Gesellschaft, of Johannistal, a company which has recently been established, manufactures a seaplane fighting aeroplane, called the FD.1, nearly similar in appearance to the Albatros fighter.

The wings have no dihedral nor are they swept back, and the chord of the lower planes is slightly less than that of the upper.

The upper wings meet the top of the fuselage.

On either side there is one pair of interplane struts; placed closely one behind the other (the rear spar has behind it more than half of the wing), and the struts approach one another slightly towards their bases.

The ailerons do not project, and are compensated by a forward projection, as in other new German machines.

The tail planes are like those of the Albatros fighter. The rudder and fixed fin are similarly placed above the fuselage, but are slightly more oval.

The landing-carriage, especially its rear members, is placed somewhat farther forward than usual. The propeller has a revolving pot. The motor is a 150 h.p. Benz Bz III. Six went to the German Navy in 1918.

L.V.G. Luft Verkehrs Gesellschaft m.b.H. Works and civil flying school at Johannisthal aerodrome. Military flying school at private aerodrome in Koslin, in Pommern.

One of Germany's largest aircraft works, if not the largest one. It is situated at the Johannisthal aerodrome, by the *Zeppelin* and *Parseval* airship sheds, of which the latter serves as its giant erecting shop, as the firm ran in its early days an air traffic service with *Parseval* airships, from which the name of Air Traffic Co. Ltd. was taken.

Having hitherto chiefly produced *Farman* box kite types, the company acquired in 1912 the service of the Swiss engineer, Franz Schneider, who had helped to design the various *Nieuport* monoplanes.

On being appointed a director of the L.V.G. firm, Schneider brought out, first, a monoplane following closely on the lines of *Nieuport* practice, which, however, proved unsuccessful, so long as only stationary motors were manufactured in Germany, but with an 80 h.p. German Gnôme motor won second prize in the three-cornered flight, 1914, and first prize in an attached competition classified by horsepower, and then a biplane which has set the standard to the general German military tractor type. It secured the three first places in the 1914 Prince Henry flight, and has been built under license by Otto, in Munich, for the Bavarian army and has been copied by Euler (see both).

Herr Schneider has now left the firm, and has started a factory of his own.

The L.V.G. Two-seater Biplane. Type C.V.

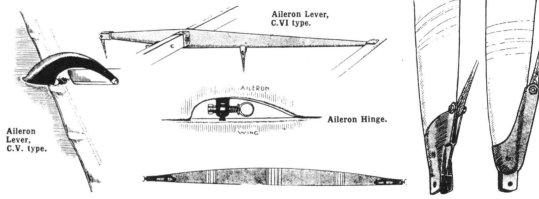

Aileron Lever, C.VI type.

Aileron Lever, C.V. type.

Aileron Hinge.

Interplane Strut, C.V. type.

Strut Sockets, C.VI type.

Type.	L.V.G. B.I Biplane.		L.V.G. Monoplane.
Length ... ... feet (in.)	25	7	No data available
Span ... ... feet (in.)	47	8½	
Area ... ... sq. feet	431		
Weight ... { total, lbs.	1,683		...
{ useful lbs.	...		...
Motor ... ... h.p.	100 Mercedes		80 Oberursel
Speed ... ... m.p.h.	63	110	...
Number built during 1912 ...	...		...

L.V.G. monoplane showing distinct Nieuport characteristics.

Notes.—Against the German army tractor biplanes can be said that the view and bomb dropping facilities of the observer are not the best.

Accompanying war device, shewn apparently on an L.V.G. biplane, allows the bombs to be dropped clear of the planes.

L.V.G. B.I reconnaissance biplane of 1914-15, unarmed and using either a 110 h.p. Benz or a 100 h.p. Mercedes engine.

A slightly different type of L.V.G. showing a crude bomb-shoot by which hand-dropped bombs are prevented from hitting the wings.

The gun-ring and cockpits of an L.V.G. C.II reconnaissance and general purpose biplane of 1916-17 use, captured by the French. 160 h.p. Mercedes D.III engine, allowing 81 miles per hour.

French military photograph, reproduced from "L'Aérophile."

An L.V.G. C.II biplane, 160 h.p. Mercédés engine of 1916 type. Note the
radiator built into the centre sections of the wings.

*Reproduced from " L'Aérophile"
from a French military photograph.*

THE L.V.G. TWO-SEATER BIPLANES.

The following illustrations and notes are concerned with two
L.V.G. biplanes, of which one is of the *C.V.* type, while the
other, a *C.VI.* type machine, is of later design, embodying
certain alterations and improvements. The *C.V.* machine is
allotted G/3BDE/5, and the *C.VI.*, which was brought down
near Proven, on Aug. 2nd, 1918 by two *S.E. 5's*, piloted by
Lieuts. Gordon and Gould, is allotted G/2Bde/21.

Any description which follows and is not definitely stated to
apply to either model must be read as appertaining to the
C.VI. type.

The *C.V.* machine was only slightly damaged and has been
put into flying order, but the *C.VI.* has suffered severely, and
it must be stated that on this account the G.A. drawings at the
end of this report are not guaranteed to be of absolute accuracy
in every respect. The greatest care has, however, been taken
in their preparation, and only features of rigging such as
dihedral and stagger (besides the tail planes, which are in a
very fragmentary condition) are at all doubtful. In matters of
detail the drawings are accurate.

Some leading particulars of both machines are given
below:—

	C.V. Type.	C.VI. Type.
Weight empty	2,188 lbs.	2,090 lbs.
Total weight	3,141 lbs.	3,036 lbs.
Area of upper wings (with ailerons)	238.4 sq. ft.	196.0 sq. ft.
Area of lower wings	190.4 sq. ft.	160.0 sq. ft.
Total area of wings	428.8 sq. ft.	356.0 sq. ft.
Loading per sq. ft. of wing surface	7.3 lbs.	8.5 lbs.
Area of ailerons, each	13.6 sq. ft.	11.2 sq. ft.
Area of balance of aileron ..	.4 sq. ft.	0.6 sq. ft.
Area of tail plane..	21.6 sq. ft.	28.0 sq. ft.
Area of fin	5.2 sq. ft.	*5.2 sq. ft.
Area of rudder	6.8 sq. ft.	*6.8 sq. ft.
Area of balance of rudder ..	·6 sq. ft.	*.6 sq. ft.
Area of elevators	20.8 sq. ft.	16.0 sq. ft.
Area of balance of elevator (one)	1.2 sq. ft.	.8 sq. ft.
Total Weight per h.p.	13.7 lbs.	13.2 lbs.
Crew	2—Pilot and Observer.	
Armament	1 Spandau & Parabellum gun	
Engine	230 h.p. Benz.	
Petrol capacity	52½ gals.	52½ gals.

* Assumed same as C.V. Type.

WINGS.

There are several important differences between the arrangement of main planes of the two models, as will be seen by referring
to the General Arrangement Drawings.

The wings of the *C.V. L.V.G.* are without stagger, and are not
swept back, and both upper and lower planes are set at a dihedral
angle, this being 1 deg. for the upper and 2 deg. for the lower
wings. The lower planes are smaller all round than the upper,
and have rounded tips. The upper planes only have ailerons,
which are of equal chord throughout their length, and are balanced.
These planes also follow what was, until recently, the usual enemy
practice, by being joined at their roots to a central cabane. There
is, therefore, no horizontal centre section in this aeroplane, except
for the 3-ply box (about 4 in. wide), which surrounds the horizontal tube of the cabane. For improving the view, the upper
plane is cut away over the pilot's cockpit. Relative to the crankshaft the upper wing has a constant angle of incidence of 5 deg.
That of the lower wing is the same, except at the tip, where the
angle is washed out to 4 deg., and at the root to 4½ deg.

Rear and front views of the L.V.G. Biplane. Type C.V.

Both upper and lower wings are attached to the body by the same general means, this being adapted to the particular positions and conditions of each joint. In the case of the upper planes, the cabane has lugs welded to its upper side at both ends. The same type of hinge pin is used for all wing joints, and for the aileron hinges also. It consists of a short length of steel tube, carrying at one end some form of stop, and at its other end a slot in which a short rectangular piece of steel is free to rotate, the steel piece being pivoted at its centre. Thus, when the steel piece is placed parallel to the tube, the whole fitting can be passed through any hole which accommodates the tube, but when the piece is placed at right angles to the tube axis, the tube cannot be withdrawn through a small hole. A helical spring ensures that the steel piece shall be pressed against the hole, and not be free to slip into the parallel position.

The lower wing attachments are very similar. Figures show respectively the front and rear joints, and this plan has not been changed on the *C.VI.* type of *L.V.G.*

In the later model—The *C.VI.*—the planes are of the same general shape, but important changes are remarked. The radiator has been removed from the position it occupied on the *C.V.* (see G.A. Drawings), and is now built into the horizontal centre section. It is, of course, common German practice to build the radiator into the upper plane, and such a position is not incompatible with the cabane type of centre section strutting. This is particularly true when—as is the case in the *L.V.G.*—a service petrol tank is supported by the upper plane, and can be made to balance the radiator. It is clear, therefore, that the alteration in design from the cabane system to the centre section system has not been made solely to accommodate the radiator.

So far as may be judged from the machine in its present condition, the *C.VI.* has a positive stagger of 10 in., and both upper and lower planes have a similar dihedral angle, viz., 1 deg. Ailerons are still fitted to the upper plane only, but are not balanced in this model. The upper and lower wing sections of the *C.VI.* model are shown in a figure, and another gives the *C.VI.* upper wing section with the R.A.F. 14 section superimposed. The R.A.F. 14 section is dotted.

Front and three-quarter front views of the L.V.G. Biplane. Type. C.VI. Note the absence of balanced extension on the ailerons and the different nose-piece.

Three-quarter rear view of the L.V.G. Biplane Type C.VI.

Schedule of Principal Weights (C.VI Type).

	lbs.	ozs.
Fuselage, without undercarriage, engine or centre section	440	0
Lower wing, covered complete (no ailerons)	76	12
Upper wing, covered complete (with ailerons)	85	4
Centre section without struts or cable	64	0
Centre section N strut	5	8
Interplane strut, each	3	11
Aileron, covered, each	8	4
Balanced elevator, covered, complete in one piece	14	8
Undercarriage, comprising:—		
2 Vees, bare	29	1
2 Wheels, with tyres	55	8
2 Axle caps, with pins	0	6
2 Shock absorber bobbins	1	4
2 Shock absorbers	17	6
Axle and fairing	23	2½
Compression tube in front of Axle	3	0
2 Bracing wires, with strainers	2	0
4 Ferrules	0	10
Undercarriage, complete	132	5½
Tail skid, bare	4	6
Brass oil tank, with 20 ins. copper pipe	9	7
Ammunition magazine (aluminium)	5	0
Exhaust pipe	16	4
Spinner	2	9
Dynamo, without airscrew	23	12

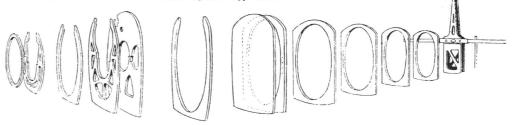

Fuselage Formers and Tail Post of C.V. type.

L. V. G. SCOUT. D.V. TYPE.

In this *L.V.G.* the streamlining embraces both the interplane and plane-cum-fuselage connecting twin struts, of more or less V structure. The inner set is provided with a round cutting in the streamlining. The steepness, though not markedly whale type, camouflaged body of the *L.V.G.* may be the result of the employment of a powerful stationary motor. The chord of the lower plane of the *L.V.G.* looks large for a scout; the rudder asks for comment. Considering the large impulses on a scout rudder from hard work the unsupported position seems daring. The hinged fixed plane and elevator position of the *L.V.G. Scout* is that of the *Brandenburg* seaplane fashion.

The L.V.G. D.V. prototype slab-sided fighter of 1918.

An L.V.G. Single-seater Scout produced towards the end of the War, presumably of the D.VI. class. Final LVG fighter of the war (195 h.p. Benz Bz IIIb.)

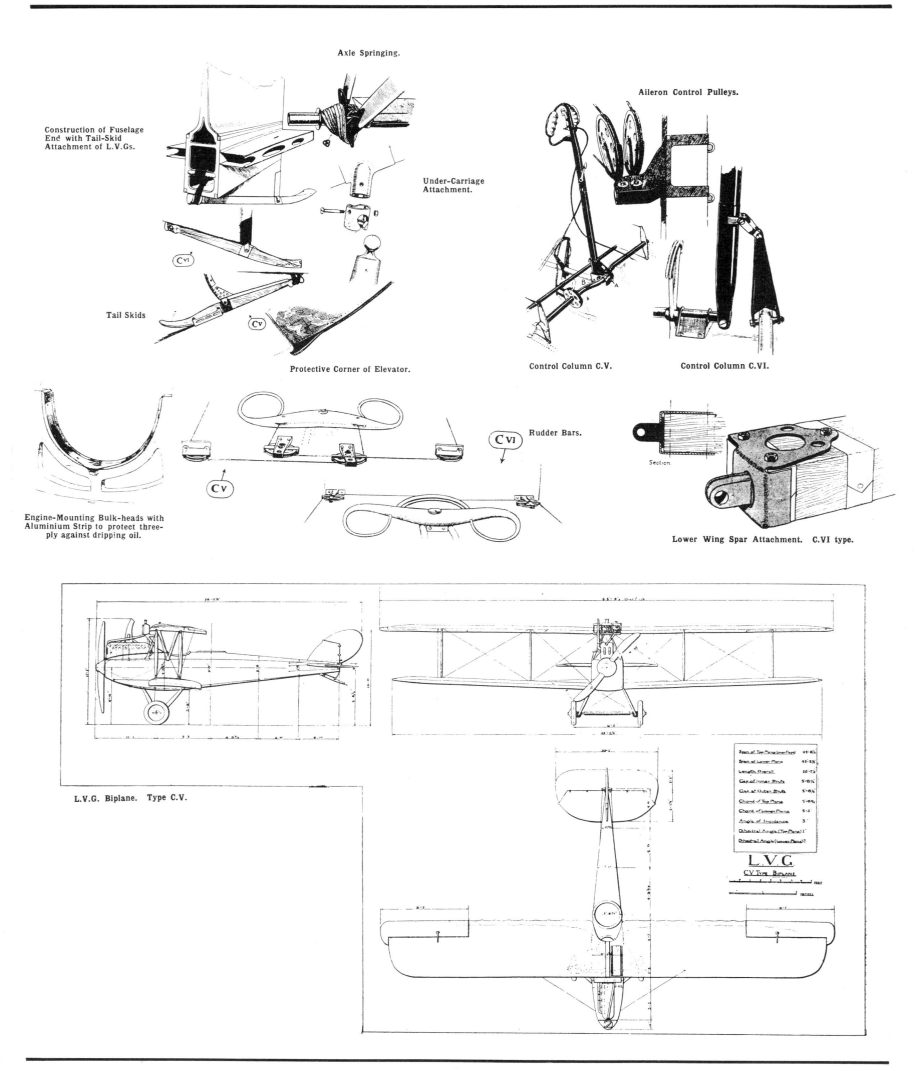

Axle Springing.

Aileron Control Pulleys.

Construction of Fuselage End with Tail-Skid Attachment of L.V.Gs.

Under-Carriage Attachment.

Tail Skids

Protective Corner of Elevator.

Control Column C.V.

Control Column C.VI.

Engine-Mounting Bulk-heads with Aluminium Strip to protect three-ply against dripping oil.

Rudder Bars.

Section

Lower Wing Spar Attachment. C.VI type.

L.V.G. Biplane. Type C.V.

L.V.G.
CV TYPE BIPLANE

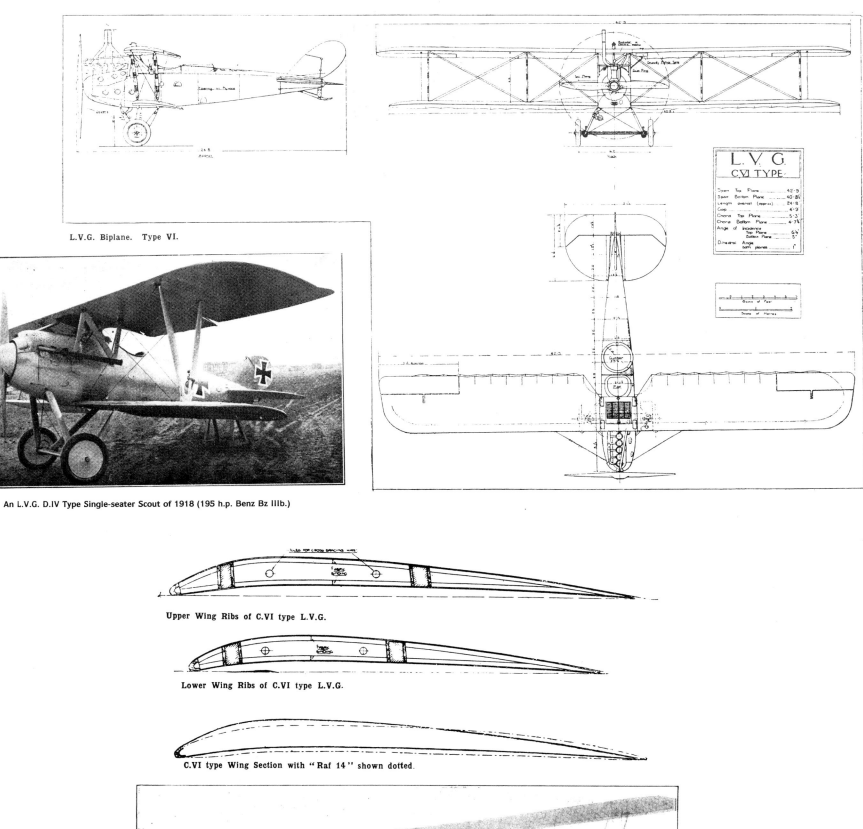

L.V.G. Biplane. Type VI.

L. V. G.
C.VI TYPE

Span Top Plane	42.9
Span Bottom Plane	40.8½
Length overall (approx.)	24.8
Gap	4.9
Chord Top Plane	5.3
Chord Bottom Plane	4.7½
Angle of Incidence Top Plane	6½°
Bottom Plane	5°
Dihedral Angle both planes	1°

An L.V.G. D.IV Type Single-seater Scout of 1918 (195 h.p. Benz Bz IIIb.)

Upper Wing Ribs of C.VI type L.V.G.

Lower Wing Ribs of C.VI type L.V.G.

C.VI type Wing Section with " Raf 14 " shown dotted.

An L.V.G. G.III Twin-engined Tractor Triplane. Note, as in the Friedrichshafen and the Gotha the "sawed-off" nose. Appeared at end of war (two 245 h.p. Maybach Mb IV engines). The G.I biplane bomber (prototype only) had appeared in 1915.

M

"M.B." Melli Beese. This female aviator, with her husband, Charles Boutard, ran a flying school as a limited company at Johannisthal.

They manufacture a two seater *M.B.* "Taube" with 100 h.p. Mercédès for their own school work, a *M.B.* single-seater "Taube" as a sporting mount, equipped with a 50 h.p. Gnôme or Anzani, yet both types only on a small scale, and produced just prior to the war for Warnemünde seaplane meeting a flying boat with a 200 h.p. Mercédès engine mounted in the main float, with a reducing bevel drive of the propeller.

No fresh information.

MERCÉDÈS-DAIMLER.

Mercédès-Daimler Motorcar Gesellschaft. Aeroplane Works : Singelfingen.

The famous builders of aero-engines. During the War, extended their activities to the building of aircraft. No other information is available beyond the illustrations attached and the inscriptions thereto.

MERCUR. Flugzeugbau G.m.b.H., Berlin. Joint stock : 60,000 mark. Not known to produce a model of its own. Likely sub-contractors.

A Mercédés-Daimler L.6 fighter of 1918, using 185 h.p. Daimler D.IIIb engine. Six built as D.Is.

A Mercédés-Daimler Single-seater "Wireless" Parasol Monoplane, Type L 11, with curiously-shaped wing-tips. 185 h.p. Daimler D.IIIb engine.

A Mercédés-Daimler Single-seater Biplane, No. 9. One only, with 185 h.p. Daimler IIIb engine.

N

NAGLO.

Naglo Yard, Wein Meisterhorn, Pickelsdorf-Spandau, nr. Berlin.

As far as can be ascertained, this firm's activities have been purely experimental, and the quadruplane illustrated is their only known product.

N.F.W. National Flugzeug Werke, G.m.b.H. Works and a military flying school at the Johannisthal aerodrome, bei Berlin.

Into this the former Jeannin Company was transformed on June 15th, 1915, being taken over by Counsellor Bernhard Meyer (see D.F.W.)

A tractor biplane of the general German army type is being manufactured, and the military school of flying is run on large lines with a staff of 120 men at that date.

An Experimental Naglo Quadruplane.

Seating arrangement and wing fitting of N.F.W. B.I biplane of 1915 (120 h.p. Argus As II.)

O

OTTO Werke, München 46, Gustav Otto, Aircraft Works, Neulercherfeld-strasse 76.

Flying schools at Oberwiesenfeld and Puchheim. 600 workmen.

As the biggest South-German aircraft works, the Otto Company has always been the chief contractors of the Bavarian army, alone to have own flying service within the Imperial German air service.

The early German pilot, Gustav Otto, manufactured first a *Henry Farman* shorthorn type, on which the Emperor's first aviation prize was won in an altitude flight by Baron von Gorrissen in the Johannisthal Spring Meeting, 1911, later one of Germany's first tractor biplanes, on which a four passengers' duration world's record was put up, then the characteristic nose-nacelled pusher biplane, which, when abandoned, was still manufactured by the Johannisthal branch, the Ago Company.

The license for building *L.V.G.* biplanes to the Bavarian army was obtained in 1914.

During the war, tractor biplanes of own and conventional type have been produced, and, as in the case of the early aircraft, Otto engines have been employed now of 200 h.p., 8-cylinder vertical type.

In 1916 the Otto Works were taken over by the big German engineering firm, Maschinenbau Augsburg-Nürnberg (building the M.A.W. Diesel engines of the German submarines), and the name being changed into Bavarian Works, light cars being now even manufactured beside aeroplanes and aero engines.

P

PIPPART-NOLL. Flugzeugbau-Mannheim.

Of small importance. Building in 1914, on a small scale, the *P.N.* 1913 steel "Taube," had steel cables instead of the usual bridge building below the planes, with a U chassis and a drop-like body.

No fresh information.

PFALZ. Flugzeugwerke G.m.b.H., Speyer on Rhine.

(Founded by the brothers Everbusch, one of whom has fallen on active service.)

Building, prior to the war, a military model, similar to the *Ago* pusher biplane, doing 120 km. with a 100 h.p. Rapp motor.

Little was heard of this aeroplane from Germany, but Bruno Büchner carried out the African flight Swakopmund-Karibib with a passenger, and the post for the latter city on a *Pfalz* biplane, which was together with Truck's *Aviatik* biplane used on the German side in the South-West African campaign.

During the war, a *Pfalz* fighter monoplane has been produced, similar in appearance to the *Fokker,* but sometimes with two machine guns fixed for firing through the propeller instead of the latter's one.

Scout biplanes constructed by this firm have recently been captured.

Front view of the Pfalz Single-seater D.III Type.

Three-quarter rear view of the Pfalz Chaser. D.III Type.

The PFALZ E.V monoplane.—This machine closely resembles the fixed engine *Fokker.* Not all of the 20 ordered were built. 100 h.p. Mercedes D.I engine, allowing 103 m.p.h.

THE PFALZ D.III SINGLE-SEATER (G. 141).

This machine landed in the British lines near Bonnieul, on Feb. 26th, 1918. It is a single-seater scout of interesting design. The number D.3, 4184/17 is painted on the fuselage. From its light construction and clean design, and from the great amount of care that has been taken to keep the fuselage of very good streamline shape and so free from irregularities, it appears to be the result of a serious attempt to produce a scout machine with good performance.

In this connection the actual performance of the aeroplane as given below is especially interesting and instructive.

Some leading particulars follow :—

Weight empty	1,532 lbs.
Total weight	2,056 lbs.
Area of upper wings	151.6 sq. ft.
Area of lower wings	88.4 sq. ft.
Total area of wings	240 sq. ft
Loading per sq. ft. of wing surface	8.56 lbs.
Area of aileron, each	10.25 sq. ft.

PFALZ D.III – *continued*

Area of balance of aileron			0.6 sq. ft.
Area of tail plane			12.1 sq. ft.
Area of fin			2.8 sq. ft.
Area of rudder			6.0 sq. ft.
Area of elevators			12.7 sq. ft.
Total weight per h.p.			12.84 lbs.
Crew			1.
Armament			2 Spandau guns firing through propeller.
Engine			160 h.p. Mercédès.
Petrol capacity			21½ gallons.
Oil capacity			4 gallons.

PERFORMANCE.

(a) Climb to 5,000 ft.		6 min. 55 secs.
Rate of climb in ft. per min.		605.
Indicated air speed		73 m.p.h.
Revolutions of engine		1,330.
(b) Climb to 10,000 ft.		17 min. 30 sec.
Rate of climb in ft. per min.		360.
Indicated air speed		67 m.p.h.
Revolutions of engine		1,310.
(c) Climb to 15,000 ft.		41 min. 20 sec.
Rate of climb in ft. per min.		110.
Indicated air speed		50 m.p.h.
Revolutions of engine		1,280.

SPEED.

At 10,000 ft.		102½ m.p.h.
At 15,000 ft.		91½ m.p.h.
Service ceiling at which rate of climb is 100 ft. per min.		15,800
Estimated absolute ceiling		17,000.
Greatest height reached		15,000 ft
Rate of climb at this height		110 ft. per min.
Air endurance		About 2½ hours.
Military load		281 lbs.

STABILITY AND MANŒUVREABILITY.

This machine is reported to be stable laterally and unstable directionally and longitudinally. It answers well to all controls, much better than does the *Albatros D.5*, but tends to turn to the left in flight. It is not tiring to fly, and is normally easy to land. Though the tail skid is of the non-steering type, no difficulty is found in directing the machine on the ground.

VIEW.

As may be expected from the shape and disposition of the wings, the view is excellent in all directions—except, perhaps, on a downward glide, when the top plane interferes to some extent.

WINGS

The wings and wing bracing are a copy of the *Nieuport* practice. The top plane is in one piece, and has no dihedral angle. The smaller type lower planes have a dihedral angle of 1 deg.

In flying position the leading edge of the upper plane is 15 inches in front of the leading edge of the lower plane.

Ailerons are fitted to the upper wings only, and both upper and lower planes have the characteristic wash-out at the tips.

WING CONSTRUCTION.

The spars of this machine are well worthy of attention. The webs are made of a thick central core of good straight grained wood, covered on each side with one layer of extremely thin 3-ply. The 3-ply stiffens up the webs against buckling inwards, thus enabling thinner webs to be used than if not reinforced. The flanges are spindled to give good glueing area and fillet, and diaphragms are fixed at each rib to transmit the sheer stress across the spar. This is a good feature, and might with advantage be incorporated in all box spars.

The ribs are built up in the usual way of 3-ply and flanges, and are of light construction.

Rear view of the Pfalz Chaser, D.III type.

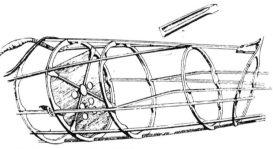

Fuselage Construction, D.III.

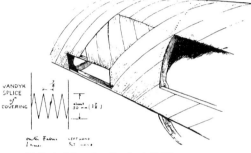

Method of Covering Fuselage, D.III.

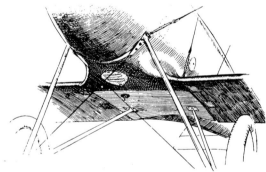

Undercarriage Arrangement, D.III.

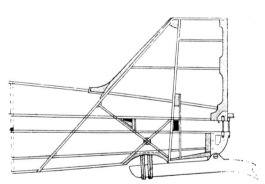

Rear End of Fuselage showing method of building the Fin and of attaching the Tail-Skid, D.III.

Front Spar Construction, D.III.

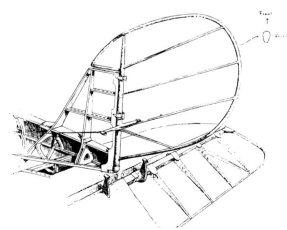

Construction of Tail Unit, showing Rudder, part of Elevator and Fin, D.III.

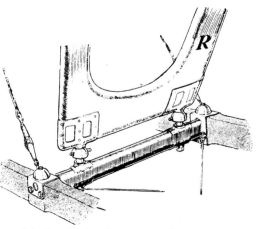

Interplane Strut and Mounting, D.III.

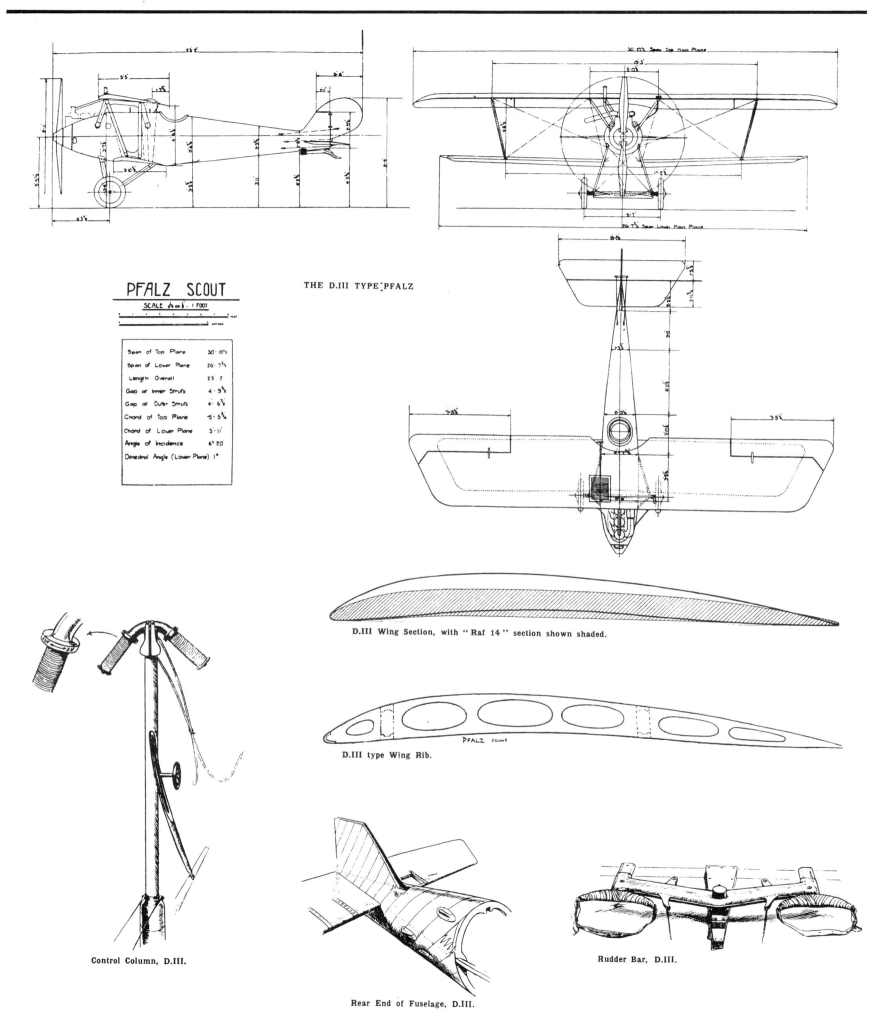

PFALZ SCOUT

SCALE ¼ in = 1 FOOT

Span of Top Plane	30· 10½
Span of Lower Plane	26· 7¾
Length Overall	23· ?
Gap at Inner Struts	4· 9½
Gap at Outer Struts	4· 6½
Chord of Top Plane	5· 5½
Chord of Lower Plane	3· 11
Angle of Incidence	6° 20
Dihedral Angle (Lower Plane)	1°

THE D.III TYPE PFALZ

D.III Wing Section, with " Raf 14 " section shown shaded.

D.III type Wing Rib.

Control Column, D.III.

Rear End of Fuselage, D.III.

Rudder Bar, D.III.

THE PFALZ (D. XII) SINGLE-SEATER FIGHTER.

This aeroplane, which was allotted G/H.Q/6, was brought down near Dury, on 15/9/18 ; by Lt. Cameron (No.1 Squadron) and Capt. Staton (No. 62 Squadron).

Although in construction it is strongly reminiscent of the Nieuport-like type of *Pfalz* the design of this machine is entirely new, and is of considerable interest.

GENERAL DESIGN.

As will be seen from the general Arrangement drawings, the *D.XII Pfalz* has a car-type radiator in front of the engine, and wings which have two bays a side. The lower planes are faired off into the body in the characteristic *Pfalz* way, but the fin, which in the earlier model was built of 3-ply as an integral part of the body, is now a separate fitting.

Area of upper wings (without ailerons)	104.8 sq. ft.
Area of lower wings (both) ..	117.6 sq. ft.
Area of aileron (one only) ..	8.4 sq. ft.
Area of balance of aileron ..	0.8 sq. ft.
Area of elevators (each)	8.4 sq. ft.
Area of balance of elevator (one)	0.6 sq. ft.
Area of rudder	8.8 sq. ft.
Area of balance of rudder ..	0.4 sq. ft.
Area of tail plane (both sides) ..	16.0 sq. ft.
Area of fin	4.4 sq. ft.
Area of body (horizontal) ..	32.8 sq. ft.
Area of body (vertical) ..	53.6 sq. ft.
Engine	180 h.p. Mercédès.
Petrol capacity	18¾ gallons.
Guns	Two Spandau (fixed).

The portion of body 3-ply which bears an inscription regarding weight and permissible load is missing.

WINGS.

The flat upper plane is built in one piece as before, but the centre section contains neither gravity tank nor radiator, and the tips are no longer heavily raked. The two ailerons of high aspect ratio, are very similar to those of the *D.VII Fokker*, as are the placing of the radiator and the form of the interplane struts.

The lower planes, which are attached to a kind of centre section that may be said to grow out of the body, are of the same chord as the upper plane, and only slightly shorter in span. The lower planes possess a dihedral angle, in this case of 1½ deg., and the two pairs of interplane struts on each side slope outwards.

The attachments of the lower plane to the body are unchanged.

A lug on the fuselage has a circular-section base round which the open end of the tube on the spar fits, while the lug itself is pinned into the fork on the spar in the usual manner. Both front and rear spars are attached in this way.

A figure shows the upper aerofoil section compared with that of the *R.A.F. 14*, which is shown dotted. It will be noticed that the two sections approximate more closely than was previously the case.

The wing construction of upper and lower planes is similar. Each lower wing contains 11 ribs, spaced at equal intervals of approximately 13¼ ins. The wood leading edge of the plane is not of the usual " C " section, but is more solid. The spars retain the former *Pfalz* design, but the section is of a squarer shape than formerly, and the flanges are not spindled. The upper and lower plane spars are exactly similar. As those points where the strut attachments occur, the spars are solidified by the insertion of small blocks of wood. The various components of the spars are very strongly glued together with a casein cement, and fabric is glued round the whole.

The tape lattice work that was found in the old-type *Pfalz* between the spars, and between the rear spar and trailing edge is no longer present, but a vertical rectangular-section strip of wood lies parallel to the rear spar between that member and the trailing edge, and strips of wood are tacked on to the leading edge, and on to the two spars, and finish just behind this strip. These false ribs are placed midway between the true ribs, and the space between each false and true rib is again bisected by another strip. These pieces simply pass from the leading edge to just behind the front spar, and are built up with a vertical strip so that the whole is of T section. The ribs are of a 2 mm. 3-ply, with flanges tacked on in the usual way, and are lightened. The trailing edge is of wire and each rib has fabric sewn over it. There are 12 steel compression tubes in the upper plane, and five in each of the lower planes. The bracing varies from steel tie rods of 5 mm. diameter to 12-guage piano wire.

PROPELLER.

This is of Heine make, No. 26,206 ; diameter 2.780 m., pitch 2.000 m. It has eight laminations of mahogany and walnut.

SCHEDULE OF PRINCIPAL WEIGHTS. (*D.XII* TYPE.)

	lbs.	ozs.
Fuselage, without engines, guns, auxiliary tank or oil tank, but with main tank and tail skid ..	257	0
Starboard lower wing, with control cables but no bracing wires. Only one side fabric covered ..	46	0
Upper wing, with bracing wires, but only one side fabric covered	127	0
One centre section M strut	7	4
Radiator	44	8
Brass oil tank	5	1
Auxiliary petrol tank	7	8
One outer N strut	8	9
Fin (covered)	3	2

The latest type Pfalz Biplane in use at the end of the war, Type D.XII.

Three-quarter front view of a wrecked Pfalz D.XII Single-seater Fighter.

	lbs.	ozs.
One inner N strut	10	6
Aileron (covered)	7	12
Aileron hinge rod	0	8
3-ply tail plane (partly estimated).. ..	19	0
Aluminium rose cowl	3	14
Cockpit cowl and padding	2	6
One aluminium side cowl	2	12
Ammunition magazine	7	12
Two clutches for synchronising gear ..	5	13
Two gun channels	5	5

The weights of the various components of the earlier *Pfalz*— the *D. III* type—make an interesting comparison, and are given below :—

	lbs.	ozs.
Fuselage, without engine, guns, or empennage, but with tanks and all fittings	295	0

	lbs.	ozs.
One lower plane, covered, but without bracing wires..	49	0
Complete upper plane, covered, with ailerons, bracing wires, radiator, and gravity tank ..	225	0
One centre section strut	9	6
Radiator	37	3
Brass oil tank	3	2
One U interplane strut	8	13
Aileron, covered	10	14
Fixed tail planes, without fabric ..	14	9
Aluminium spinner	1	7
Cowl behind spinner	2	13
Exhaust pipes..	11	8
Tail skid, bare	5	0
Elevator, without fabric	9	0
Rudder, with fabric	6	13

Wing Section of the D.XII Pfalz, with " Raf 14 " section shown dotted.

Wing Structure of the D.XII Pfalz.

A Pfalz 1917 Type Rotary-engined Triplane. Perhaps ten built after tests in October 1917.

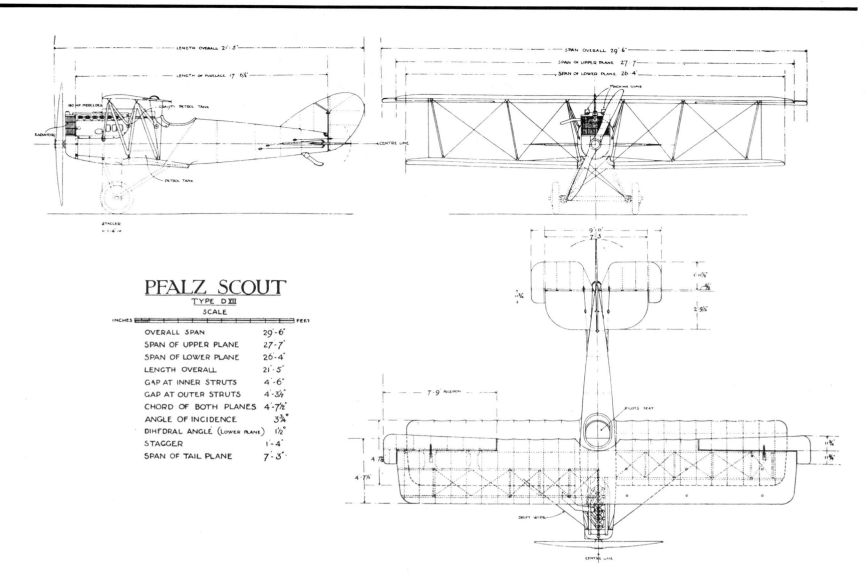

PFALZ SCOUT
TYPE D XII
SCALE

OVERALL SPAN	29'-6"
SPAN OF UPPER PLANE	27'-7"
SPAN OF LOWER PLANE	26'-4"
LENGTH OVERALL	21'-5"
GAP AT INNER STRUTS	4'-6"
GAP AT OUTER STRUTS	4'-3½"
CHORD OF BOTH PLANES	4'-7½"
ANGLE OF INCIDENCE	3¾°
DIHEDRAL ANGLE (LOWER PLANE)	1½°
STAGGER	1'-4"
SPAN OF TAIL PLANE	7'-3"

R

REX. Flugmaschine Rex Gesellschaft m.b.H., Cologne on Rhine. Aircraft works at 1, Antwerpener Street, flying school at the Wanne-Herten aerodrome.

Formed during the war by Dr. Friedrich Hansen, formerly of the Statax Engine Co., London, for the building of light destroyer aeroplanes of English-French features (*Bristol* and *Morane*).

THE REX FIGHTING BIPLANE.

The chaser-biplane, constructed by the Rex Company of Cologne is not definitely known to have been used on active service on the Western Front.

The information available shows it to be a single-seater fighter of the D.II type.

The machine offers a striking resemblance to the Nieuport, the more especially because the lower wings have a span slightly less than that of the upper wings (about 9 metres), and a much smaller chord. In fact, the lower plane is smaller and lighter in all its aspects.

Contrary to Nieuport practice, the lower wings have no dihedral, and it is almost certain that they are not swept back. The upper wings are trapezoidal in plan view.

There is only one pair of interplane struts on either side of the fuselage, which are arranged "V" fashion as in the Albatros D.III.

The upper wings are placed very close to the fuselage, and are attached to a central section, which is supported by short splayed-out struts reinforced with wire bracing.

The elevating planes are placed in line with the axis of the motor, and have no incidence.

The rudder is very tall, and is believed to be placed entirely above the fuselage, as in the Albatros fighter.

The fuselage is a three-ply monocoque, with projecting flats for the attachment of the lower wings.

The landing-carriage is ordinary "V" type, with cable cross bracing.

The Rex is apparently always fitted with a rotating monosoupape Rex engine (Gnome type), and carries a machine-gun placed to the right and synchronised with the motor.

This machine may be distinguished from the Albatros D.III by the absence of a dihedral to the lower plane.

RUMPLER. Werke G.m.b.H. Formerly E. Rumpler, Luftfahrzeugbau. Works and flying school at Johannisthal aerodrome by Berlin. Military flying school at Moncheberg.

The start of the first aircraft works in Germany is characteristic of German business procedure. The former engineer of the Daimler Motoren Gesellschaft, E. Rumpler, was charged by the German Aero Club with issuing a book of aviation—somewhere in 1908—for the material of which he wrote to and was supplied by trade and inventors of all countries. Acquired the German license for building the *Etrich* "Taube," on which Hirth attained his early successes, winning the Upper Rhine, Prince Henry, the München-Berlin and Berlin-Vienna flights, the latter on a special race dove.

Controversies arising between Rumpler and Etrich, the latter dropped the German patent rights, which led to the general adoption of the "Taube" type by almost every aircraft works in Germany.

Hirth left, and Rumpler lost much in influence. Linnekogel put up further altitude records on the new *Rumpler* monoplane, of modified "Taube" design, in that the plane underbridge was abandoned and the back-swept elastic wing tips replaced by usual ailerons of same shape.

The same body, canvas covered over steel tubes, was employed in the first *Rumpler* biplane, on which Basser performed his 18 hours' duration record and the passenger overland flight Berlin-Budapest-Sofia-Constantinople non-stop, excepting the three capitals.

During the war this biplane has been produced as a seaplane, earlier efforts in this field being the *Rumpler* flying boat, an intermediate between the *Curtiss* and *F.B.A.* types and the ordinary "Taube" design, only with a two-floats landing gear.

During the war Rumpler produced G type twin-engined bombers (from 1915), several ply-skinned single-seat fighters (the D.I. may have become operational in time for war use), and seaplane versions of the C types.

THE TWO-SEATER RUMPLER BIPLANE (Type C.IV.).

(260 h.p. Mercédès Engine).

This machine, which was used by the enemy from 1917 onwards, differs from the C.III of 1916-17 and later C.V. of 1918 by having a B/C.I type of triangular fin plus rudder tail unit.

The general shape and disposition of the wings is maintained, including the characteristic sweep-back of the main planes, and

Front view of the Rumpler, C.IV. type, biplane.

Three-quarter rear view of the Rumpler (C.IV. type).

Rumpler 1914 Military Mono.

Rumpler Flying Boat.

EARLY RUMPLER MODELS

Type.				Military Monoplane. 1914.		Military Biplane. B.I		Flying Boat.	
Length	...	...	ins	27	8·3	27	7	49	15
Span	...	...	ins	46	14	42	7	33	10
Area	...	...	sq. feet	301	28			537	50
Weight	...	{ empty... lbs.		1323	600	1,653		...	
		useful lbs.		440	200	485		...	
Motor	...	...	h.p.	100 Mercedes		100 Mercedes		150 Benz	
Speed	...	...	m.p.h.	75	120	90		...	
Endurance	...	...	hrs.	...		...		4½	

Note.—The flying boat has one main staggered float of a length of 8·15 m. by 1·4 m. max. beam, a cubic capacity of 7 m³, and a weight of 140 kgs., the step being 18 m. high.

Early form of RUMPLER B.I type military biplane, which just before the war broke various distance and duration records, including an 18 hours non-stop flight by Herr Basser, and a flight from Berlin to Constantinople, stopping only at Vienna, Sofia and Bucharest. Herr Basser is seen in the pilot's seat above.

GERMAN AEROPLANES

Side view of a RUMPLER C.I type two-seat general-purpose biplane captured by the French. The C.I was an improved armed version of the B.I and was operational from 1915-17, then as a trainer. 160 hp Mercedes engine usually allowing 95 m.p.h.

From a French military photograph, reproduced from "L'Aérophile."

the fitting of ailerons to the upper planes only. However, the fin of the C.IV gives way to a rounded rudder only tail on the C.V. Some important particulars follow:—

Weight empty (but with water)	2439 lbs.
Weight, fully loaded	3439 lbs.
Total Military load	545 lbs.
Span (upper)	41 ft. 6 ins.
Span (lower)	40 ft.
Chord (Upper)	5 ft. 8 ins.
Chord (lower)	4 ft. 4 ins.
Sweep back	3 degrees.
Dihedral	$2\frac{1}{2}$ degrees.
Area of upper wings (with ailerons)	217.6 sq. ft.
Area of lower wings	146 sq. ft.
Area of ailerons (each)	15.3 sq. ft.
Total area of main planes	363.6 sq. ft.
Loading per sq. ft. of wing surface	9.5 lbs.
Area of tail plane	22 sq. ft.
Area of fin	4 sq. ft.
Area of elevators	20.8 sq. ft.
Area of rudder	6 sq. ft.
Total weight per h.p.	13.2 lbs.
Petrol capacity	59 gallons.
Oil capacity	3 gallons.
Water capacity	10 gallons.
Endurance	About 4 hours.

PERFORMANCE.

	ft.	m.p.h	revs.
Speed at	10,000	100.5	1510
Speed at	15,000	87	1390

Rate of climb in ft. per

	ft.	m. s.	min.	revs.
Climb to	10,000	16 0	400	1375

Service ceiling, 15,500 ft. (estimated).
Estimated absolute ceiling, 17,500 ft.
Greatest height reached 15,300 ft. in 38 min. 25 secs.
Rate of climb at this height is 125 ft. per min.

CONTROL.

Longitudinal (elevators), good.
Lateral (ailerons), very heavy and very ineffective.
Directional (rudder), moderately light and quite effective.
It is reported that the machine is tiring to fly owing to the very poor lateral control; that it is nose-heavy, and rather liable to get into a spin.

AIRSCREW.

The airscrew is an "Axial," No. 6987, diameter 3,150 mm., pitch 1,830 mm. It is secured to the crankshaft by eight bolts, an extra pair being fitted between two of the pairs of the usual six.

Rear view of the C.IV. type Rumpler.

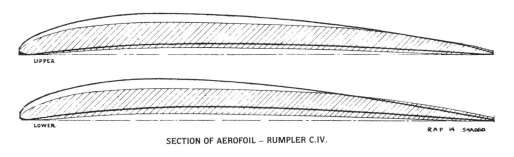

SECTION OF AEROFOIL – RUMPLER C.IV.

"Raf 14" Wing Section shown shaded.

RUMPLER—continued.

Tail and Fin Bracing of the Rumpler. Note the saw-teeth on the low tail stay tube to prevent mechanics from lifting the machine by this tube.

Engine Emplacement in the C.IV. Rumpler.

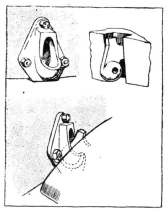

Cup and ball coupling of Upper Wing, C.IV.

Radiator and Shutter of the Rumpler C.IV.

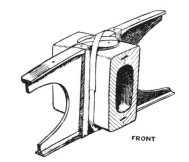

FRONT

Front Spar of C.IV.

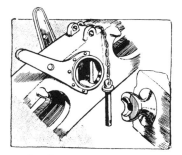

Coupling of Lower Wing, C.IV.

Strut and Bracing-Wire Attachment.

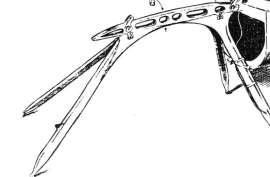

SECTION

Cabane and Radiator Attachment.

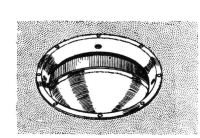

Well for Compass.

Piano-stool Seat for Gunner.

Axle Attachment.

Under-Carriage Strut Junction.

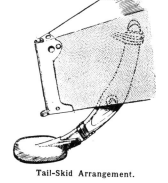

Tail-Skid Arrangement.

AILERON WIRES

ELEVATOR WIRES

Control Cross-Bar.

Rudder-Bar.

DETAILS OF RUMPLER C.IV. TYPE.

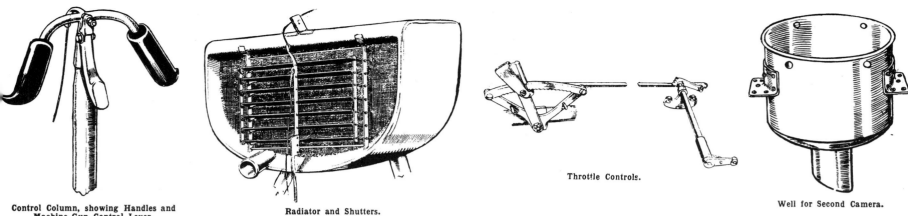

Control Column, showing Handles and
Machine-Gun Control Lever.

Radiator and Shutters.

Throttle Controls.

Well for Second Camera.

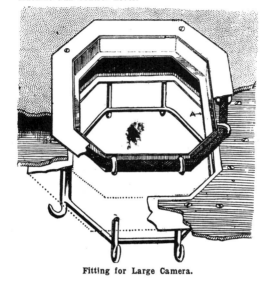

Fitting for Large Camera.

The Latest Rumpler C.X Type Two-seat Biplane. (240 h.p. Mercedes MbIV.) Note the crossed interplane struts—a fashion now
becoming prevalent in Germany. Prototype of 1918 only.

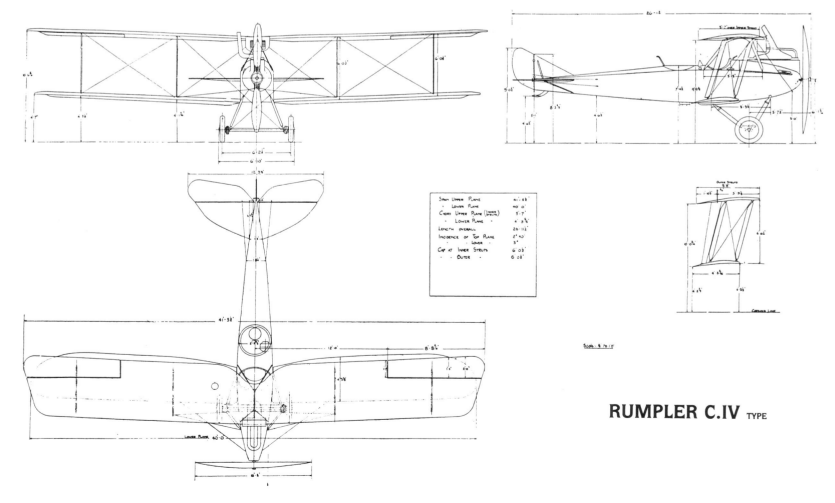

RUMPLER C.IV TYPE

S

SCHÜTTE-LANZ, LUFTSCHIFFBAU.

Aeroplane works : Zeesen, nr. Konigswusterhausen.

The well-known airship building firm. Commenced to build aeroplanes early in the War. It seems probable that no Schütte-Lanz aeroplanes passed far beyond the experimental stage—as they have not been heard of at the front.

The accompanying photographs are given because, although some of them are of type of 1914-15, they have never yet been illustrated in Great Britain.

An early (1914-15) Schütte-Lanz Experimental Type G.I Twin-engined Biplane, possessing many features betraying its relationsh[ip] lighter-than-air craft. Two 160 h.p. Mercedes D.III engines.

A Schütte-Lanz Dr.I Single-seater Triplane Scout. 160 h.p. Mercedes D.III engine. Based on D.I biplane design.

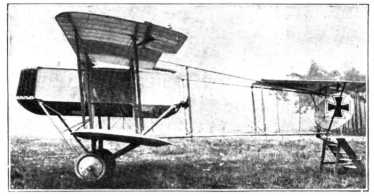

An Early (1914-15) C.I Type Schütte-Lanz Pusher Biplane. One built with 160 h.p. Mercedes D.III engine.

Schütte-Lanz Single-seater D.III Fighter of 1917-18.

SIEMENS-SCHUCKERT. Berlin.

One of the many branches of the great Siemens electrical firm, which had world-wide ramifications before the war.

The Siemens "Grossflugzeug," or "Big Aeroplane," which is illustrated herewith, is said to have been succeeded by the Siemens "Riesenflugzeug," or "Giant Aeroplane," a species of Super-Gotha, with four or six engines.

The firm built an experimental airship some years before the war, but never built aeroplanes until recently.

THE SIEMENS-SCHUCKERT AND SIEMENS-STEFFEN GIANTS.

(A Description by a Neutral Correspondent).

The efforts of the Siemens-Schuckert Company, confined, like the aircraft branch of its great competitor the A.E.G. concern, apparently to military requirements with a determination of staying with the aircraft department in the business line by catering for the requirements of commercial aviation to come, appear in two editions resulting, both of which appear more workmanlike than the Staaken biplane, which is to the air traffic aeroplane as the pre-war Sikorsky was to the Handley Page.

The one Siemens-Schuckert giant illustration looks as having suffered from the retoucher's hand. Judging from the right side of the view, the aircraft appears to be equipped with four engines, two motors, apparently of V types, may be Körting model, driving tractor screws to each side. Though the motor mounting is not visible, one motor looks as if installed on the fuselage with the screw in an impossible position for revolving. The skid rudiments act probably as mudguards and so as to prevent the wheels of the weighty aircraft from sinking into muddy ground.

The name of Steffen combined with Siemens in the other product may be that of the flying officer, known as a pre-war daring lieutenant pilot. The idea of the designers with the split body relates undoubtedly to the stability ; the other feature is the nose stepping, looking almost too prominent to be radiators, so one may have a guess at some blinding armourment for engine or engines and crew. The nearest struts to the body are carried out as double V rests for the shafts of the two screws, being driven by transmission from inside the fuselage. The landing gear is like those found in the various models in the German G class.

A Four-engined Siemens Schuckert Biplane bomber of 1915, with 110 h.p. Mercedes engines. The first multiple-engined machine built by this firm.

An early type of Siemens-Steffen Giant Aeroplane. Probably the second four-engined bomber designed by Forssmann and flown in September 1915. Featured an enclosed cabin.

A further feature is the appendicitis (presumably the writer means "attachment") combined with two struts to the ailerons and recalling the Curtiss interplane ailerons from the days of the Wright patent flights.

THE SIEMENS-SCHUCKERT BIPLANES.

To judge from general appearance, the D4 model looks the older, with its numerous interplane cross wiring. The form of the cabane struts here and of the interplane ones of the other scout edition are similar to the familiar construction from the Pfalz biplane. So far as can be seen, both Siemens biplanes are provided with balanced ailerons at both planes, as well as with balanced rudders and elevators. The D4 machine is equipped with a four-bladed screw, being, in fact, the result of an attachment of two, and rotary motors being employed the broad form from the body nose is given, the other model looking, with its monocoque fuselage and striking streamlining aft the pilot's head, altogether the more finished. In this connection due attention may be paid to the news in the book on rotary aero engines of the Swedish aircraft manufacturer, Dr. Thulin, as source that the associated Siemens and Halske concerns have for some time manufactured a rotary motor with cylinder and crankshaft rotating in opposite directions, with the same r.p.m. of 900. The airscrew is mounted on the crankshaft, and the advantage to be obtained is that the screw gives by a fairly low number of revolutions a better effect without the employment of reduction gear, all while the chargings and accordingly the power development is the effect of the relative low number of revolutions. Yet at the same time the low number of r.p.m. has a bad influence on the air-cooling of the motor.

SABLATNIG. Aircraft works.

Being of the first batch of pilots to be trained in Germany on the *Wright* biplane, the Austrian *Sablatnig* achieved special results in passenger altitude records on the peculiar arrow biplane of the Union Works.

His own aircraft works were formed during 1917 with a capital of £25,000.

SCHNEIDER. Franz. Aircraftworks. Siegefeld in Spandau.

The Swiss engineer, Schneider, was the chief collaborator of Nieuport, and on being engaged in 1912 by the German L.V.G. Company, his first effort was to produce a monoplane of those characteristic lines.

Later he produced the 100 h.p. *L.V.G.* tractor biplane, which was the originator of that German class which has played an important part before and during the war.

Though no informing news is available, one is apt to believe the designer to continue his activities in his own work in the line started.

SCHWADE. Schwade & Co., Erfurt.

Before the war built *Henry Farman* type biplanes. Reports of later activities not to hand.

SCHULZE. Gustav, Aircraft Works, Burg by Magdeburg.

Run on similar, but smaller lines to the Grade Co. of pupil training. Not heard of during the war years.

SIGISMUND. Friedrich Prince Sigismund of Prussia, Danzig.

Forbidden by his father to fly either as pilot or passenger, he turned his interest in aviation to the design of various monoplanes, which he built at his own small works in Danzig, where he also ran a flying school for gentlemen aviators. His racing type monoplane, 100 h.p. Mercédès, named *Bull Dog*, was flown with some success in various competitions during 1914 by Stiefvater, who was killed early in the war in a test flight near Berlin, though no news is to hand of his mount, nor of further activities of the principal aircraft during the war.

During the war, both Prince Friedrich Sigismund and his brother Carl Friedrich, received permission to go on active service in the air force, where, shortly after a flight of the two brothers from Doeberitz to Hannover and return, the latter was wounded and shot down in the British lines during a fighting trip on an *Albatros* scout, and died shortly afterwards.

An early type of Siemens-Schuckert Giant Aeroplane of the 'R' series, flown from 1915. The engines are within the fuselage and drive both airscrews through clutches and a gear box.

The Siemens-Schuckert D.IV.

Rear view of Siemens-Schuckert of another Type.

A Siemens-Schuckert Monoplane, with a rotary engine. Twenty E.Is were ordered in 1915.

The experimental Sablatnig C.II Two-seater Tractor Biplane C II. (240 h.p. Maybach Mb IV engine.)

A Sablatnig Two-seater Tractor Biplane, Type C I. (180 h.p. Argus engine and later a 230 h.p. Benz engine.)

An 160 h.p. Benz-engined Sablatnig Seaplane of SF 5 (1917) type, largely used by the German Navy.

A Sablatnig SF 4 experimental Single-seater Triplane Scout Seaplane.

U

UNION.
Flugzeugwerke G.m.b.H., Berlin, S.W., 48, Friedrichstrasse 235.

Flying school at Teltow aerodrome. On the *Union-Arrow* biplane, system Bombard, with the lower planes swept upwards, various passenger records were set up with a 120 h.p. Austro-Daimler engine, and looping demonstrations carried out in 1914 by one of the present German star turns, Höhndorff, with a biplane, equipped with a rotary Oberursel motor.

URSINUS.

The *Ursinus* is said to have been built to the designs of Oskar Ursinus the Editor of the German paper, "Flugsport."

The German idea was to have the twin-engine drive concentrated as much centrally as possible, raising the fuselage and having the tractor screw tips almost touching, with the object of improving the control of large aircraft.

The experimental biplane was built at the Barmstadt Air Station, and the type was next put into production at the Gotha Works, both as a land and seagoing model.

THE URSINUS GUH G.I. HYDRO-AEROPLANE at rest.

The early Ursinus GUH G.I. twin-engined bomber. It was produced at Darmstadt in 1914. Later it was built under licence by the Gotha company first as a land machine and later as a seaplane with 2-100 h.p. motors, which were subsequently replaced by more powerful power units.

Z

ZEPPELIN.

Zeppelin Works : Lindau, v Staaken.

The famous Zeppelin airship firm very early in the War took up the development of aeroplanes and seaplanes through the medium of the F.F. Friedrichshafen Flugzeugbau, under whose name will be found a description of the Friedrichshafen product.

At a later stage the parent company itself, at its Lindau and Staaken works, devoted itself to the building of aeroplanes, particularly those of the "Giant" type, and certain of their products are described and illustrated hereafter.

THE FOUR-ENGINED ZEPPELIN BIPLANE.
The following description of a four-engine Zeppelin is due to M. Jean Lagorgette, and is based on an examination of the *debris* of a machine which was captured, in a badly damaged condition, on the French front on June 4th, 1918 :—

Overall Dimensions.
In reality the total height is 6.4 ms. of which 1.5 m. is under the fuselage and 4.4 m. between the wings in the centre section. Total length, 22 ms. Total span, 41 ms.

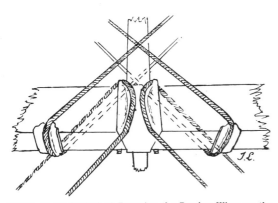

Sketch of the Method of Fastening the Bracing Wires on the Wing-spars of the Zeppelin Four-engined Biplane.

The Wing Form.

FORM.—The span of the lower wings is equal to that of the upper wings and the chord is the same except for a difference of some centimetres in the centre section. There is no stagger.

The upper wings have no dihedral, the lower wings only being so provided, and they also only have a dihedral outside the base of the cabanes which carry the engines, but what there is is accentuated. From 4.4 ms. at this point the gap decreases to 3.6 ms. at the tips, or .8 ms. decrease in a little less than 16 ms., or almost 5 centimetres per metre.

The two planes indubitably are arrow-shaped only as to the leading edge, and in a somewhat marked manner. The whole recalls the form of the L.V.G. of 1913-17, and not that of the earliest Morane-Saulniers, of which the L.V.G. was the inverse.

From 4.5 ms. at the axis of the machine and as far as the summits and bases of the engine cabanes, the chord decreases to 3.5 ms. at the tips, or 1 m. of arrow in about 17 ms.— that is to say, about 6 cms. per metre. As to this arrow of the two planes, it is no less certain than as regards the V of the lower wings that it begins only at 110 mms. from the exterior bases of the cabanes and at 100 mm. from the summits. Beyond these points the gap of the wings is then at each point a little greater or a little less than their chord, and the average gap is equal to the average chord.

All these dimensions are, besides, confirmed by the height of the interplane struts as to the dihedral, and by the length of the compression tubes between the spars as to the arrow—that is to say, in plan and front elevation.

The trailing edge of the wings seen in plan is, as distinct from the leading edge, a straight line. The wing tips are slightly oblique and rounded.

INCIDENCE AND WING SECTION.—The incidence of the wings from the axis of the machine to the engine cabanes is determined by the two following points. The lower longerons of the fuselage being horizontal in front, the lower side of the front spar of the lower wing rests directly on their upper surface, while the upper side of the rear spar only comes flush with the upper surface of the fuselage longeron. This is to say, the angle of the under surface of the wings between the spars is fixed by the depth of the rear spar—that is to say, about 160 mms.

The incidence is thus approximately 0.45 ms. in the 4.5 ms. of the total chord, or about 1 in 10.

Even if with the idea of simplification, and, contrary to the rule of nearly all German biplanes, the angle of incidence does not diminish from the middle of the machine to its extremities, the difference in level between the leading edge and the trailing edge would decrease progressively in the same direction, since the wings narrow towards the tips. But as it seems certain that the curves of the wings are more accentuated towards the centre of the machine than at 15 ms. from the centre, I have

Experimental Zeppelin CL.II all-metal Two-seater Biplane of 1917.

A 1918 Zeppelin D.I All-metal Wireless Scout. One 185 h.p. BMW IIIa engine.

taken the curve illustrated, it is possible that the angle of incidence decreases correspondingly with the concavity of the wings.

Wing Structure.

WING SPARS.—There are two principal spars which are true girders, a third spar, the shape of a gutter placed on its side, holds the ribs .75 ms. from their ends. In the upper planes this only runs as far as the beginning of the ailerons. The aileron spar, also of a gutter section, supports the aileron hinge and is placed about a metre from the trailing edge.

Both of the true wing spars cross the fuselage at their different levels. The front spar on top of the lower fuselage longeron to which it is held by eight bolts. The rear spar comes flush with the longerons to each of which it is united by a heavy spar-box of a T shape, which spar-box also serves for the fixing of the rigging cables.

By this continuity across the fuselage it is possible to dispense with special compression tubes, and the position of the leading spar of the wing permits the existence below it of the metal cross-bracing of the fuselage, while the rear spar itself fulfils the purpose of a similar cross member.

Each of the spars is composed in the course of its length of three pieces, each in a straight line. The rear spars are assembled all three in a straight line, but the front spars, outside the engine cabanes, are set back in the arrow shape, and as regards the lower wings, both spars are assembled to give a dihedral.

Thus the centre part of the spars which traverse the fuselage are a single piece in a straight line without either arrow or dihedral as far as the outside of the engine cabanes.

As may be seen in a Fig., each spar forms a double box composed of seven grooved pieces assembled, glued and reinforced on the two sides by one or two layers of ply-wood, then wrapped with fabric in a spiral before placing the ribs in position. At the points of attachment and at the centre they are left solid. The upper spars, as well as being larger, especially the rear spar, are made of ash, and the lower ones of spruce.

RIBS.—Outside the central fixed part where they are perpendicular to both edges, the ribs form with the leading edge and with the front spar an angle clearly obtuse on the side of the fuselage and acute on the opposite side, while they are perpendicular to the rear spar and trailing edge. The same also is true of the compression tubes situated between the bases of the interplane struts.

The construction of the ribs recalls that of the Handley Page, also of certain Albatroses, and specially that of the framework of the Zeppelin airships, as may be seen by comparing the sketches.

There are top and bottom flanges glued and nailed to a central web, also in spruce, which is bedded into the flange. Webs in the form of double laths unite the opposite flanges, and in the case of those in compression are made into boxes by the addition of three-ply strips (Fig. 3). They are disposed in zig-zags and fixed to the web of the rib by duralumin rivets.

All these wooden elements are glued. The ribs are nailed to the spars. Everything except the ply-wood is made of spruce. The trailing tip of the rib is sheathed in a sort of square thimble of thin brass. The trailing edge of the wing is held by a simple piano wire which goes through this thimble.

The distance between the ribs, which is enormous, varies from .565 m. to .43 m. It is less in the vicinity of the airscrews.

Between two neighbouring ribs a flat lath, 15 by 10 mm., extends to the leading edge above the front spar to maintain the shape of the fabric.

On top of each rib the fabric carries a strip of braid glued outside. It is fixed to the ribs by a thread which passes over this tape and on top of the lot is glued a strip of fabric 3 to 4 cm. in width.

Between the spars two series of bands pass alternatively over and under the ribs of the flanges to which they are nailed, maintaining the position of the ribs laterally. Exactly in the middle between the interplane struts two ordinary ribs are much closer together than the others, being .15 m. apart. They maintain the distance between the longerons against the compression which is exercised by the secondary cross-bracing in the vicinity of these ribs.

BRACING.—The wings have a double system of cross-bracing, one between the bases of the struts, which is very long and consists of thick cables, and the other is in simple 3 mm. piano-wire joined by the ends of the twin ribs which are placed halfway between the struts.

These wires, by a curious disposition in crossing the spars, penetrate through them obliquely, and they are connected to a simple nut and bolt arrangement. In the spruce block situated in the exterior angle between the rib and spar they are fixed solely by the pull of the turnbuckle.

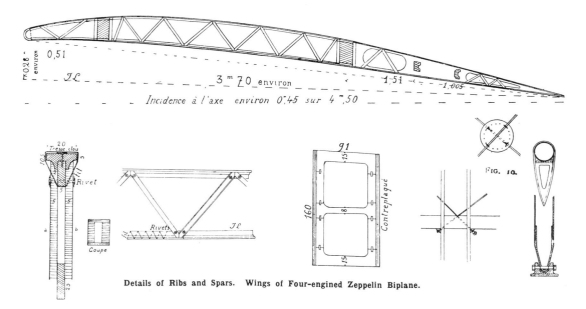

Details of Ribs and Spars. Wings of Four-engined Zeppelin Biplane.

The long cable bracing is fixed to the extremities of the compression tubes. This extremity is fixed to the spar by two lateral lugs, pierced with holes, to which are attached the cables and wires of the cross-bracing.

COMPRESSION TUBES.—These are situated between the extremities of the interplane struts, and between the engine cabanes. They serve at the same time to maintain the distance against the incidence bracing. Given that there are two for the base of each cabane, and a single one for the single summit, there are altogether ten in the lower plane, and eight in the upper plane, a number which is frequently surpassed in the small German aeroplanes.

The tubes are round, 50 mms. in diameter, for those at the summit of the cabane, 45 mms. at the base of the cabane and decreasing, as they get away from the centre of the machine, from 40 mms. down to 12 mms. between the external masts.

Interplane Bracing.

CABANES.—Each of the three cabanes is composed of two A's, of which the bases and summits are fixed by sheaths to the wing spars, or to the fuselage in the case of the base of the central cabane, and they are inter-connected by compression tubes inside the wing and bolted to the sheath.

The width of the engine cabane at the base is 1.2 ms., both front and rear, and the distance between the A's longitudinally is 2.48 ms. Each of the A's is of round tube, 55 × 60 ms., except the rear tubes of the engine cabanes, of which internal and external diameter are 60 × 65 mms. The cross-piece is of 32 mm. tube.

INTERPLANE STRUTS.—These are parallel to one another and vertical : of round steel tube with conical ends stuck inside and welded. They are bolted into lugs on the bottoms of which they press, which lugs are themselves raised on a large steel sheath surrounding the longerons.

Their diameter and thickness diminish from the internal pair (55 × 60 mm.) to the intermediate pair (44 × 48), and the external pair (35 × 38 mm.). These dimensions in each pair are the same for the front and rear struts, contrary to what would have seemed natural and to what exists in the legs of the engine cabanes, and for the front and rear cable bracing.

They are surrounded by fairings of 3-ply with little interior ribs, as on the Bréguet, open at the top and bottom to enclose all attachments.

BRACING.—The cables are disposed in transverse and longitudinal X's. As regards the longitudinal cables, there are two cables from the top of the front strut to the bottom of the rear strut, and one from the top of the rear strut to the bottom of the front strut.

By a disposition peculiar to this machine, and general in the bracing in other directions (except transverse) of its fuselage, each transverse cable of the wings as well as in the stabilising planes is formed of an endless cable. Or, more exactly, after it has passed diagonally round three faces of the wing spar, without having been linked to a fixed point, but passing simply in a groove or gutter welded on to the sheath of the spar, one of the extremities of the cable returns from the opposite side towards the other extremity with which it is linked by the turnbuckle. It is thus, in a sort of way, doubled, but although weighing double, it does not offer double strength or double security.

Undoubtedly this procedure ensures a certain elasticity from which the avion and the cable itself profits, but if a rupture occurs the entire cable ceases to fulfil its functions, because, having no point of attachment, instead of having four, it slacks off and offers no resistance to strain. One can only see in it inconvenience in compensation for very slight and problematic advantages.

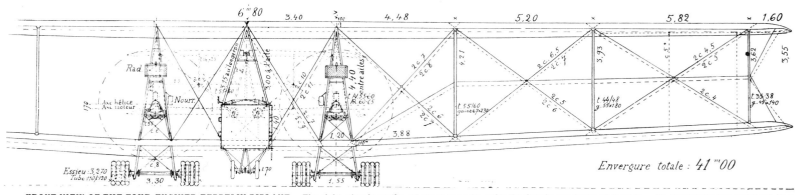

FRONT VIEW OF THE FOUR-ENGINED ZEPPELIN BIPLANE. The right wing is partly cut away so as to make the drawing as large as possible. M. Lagorgette has indicated in a most pains-taking manner the sizes of tubes, cables, and fairings, "t" stands for tube, "g" for "gaine" or fairing, "c" for corde or cable. "Nourr," on the side of the starboard engine stands for "nourrice," or "nurse-tank." The word "longeron" written along the starboard leg of the fuselage cabane refers to the upper plane spar, and not to the fuselage longeron. The symmetrical arrangement of the engine-cabanes and their continuation to the under-carriage struts is noteworthy. The front elevation of the tail is shown in dotted lines behind the fuselage and engine-cabanes.

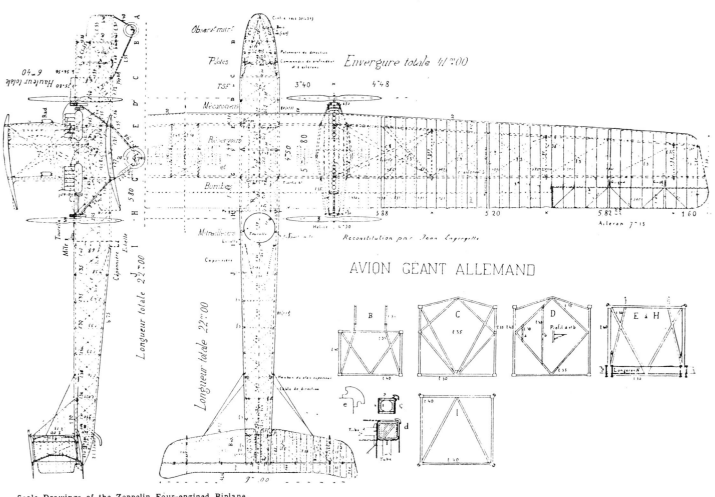

Scale Drawings of the Zeppelin Four-engined Biplane.

An analogous system was applied on the Zeppelin airships in which it was impossible to have absolute rigidity, and if the engineers of this firm have adapted it to avions in the same way as the employment of aluminium, it is undoubtedly because of the psychological influence of tradition not less than for the doubtful technical reason of suppleness.

To avoid distortion of the struts an almost horizontal tube links at mid-height each front strut with the strut behind in the same pair.

Moreover a set of cables of which one extremity is fixed at the intersection of the wing spars with the bases of the engine cabanes runs transversely at half their height from the internal struts to the external struts, and thence terminates .08 or .1 ms. from the extremity of the spars, thus linking up by cable the ends of the horizontal steel tubes already mentioned.

At the crossing of these cables with the transverse bracing cables, the cables are enclosed in a little fairing of poplar profiled in the form of a hollow olive. Over and above this, all the cables, including the double transverse cables, are enveloped in a fairing of light ply wood surrounded by glued fabric.

AILERONS.—As in all German biplanes, except the Albatros. C. type, and the Friedrichshafen, ailerons are only fitted to the upper wings. In spite of the gutter shape form of the third spar it is fairly certain that this would not serve as a hinge fixing ; and that no ailerons exist for the lower wings.

The ailerons are rectangular and do not project. The outer angle is rounded, as are the tips of the lower wings, and is slightly raised towards the rear tip, according to the German habit. They are not balanced, contrary to another habit, and this characteristic seems singular when one recalls the effort necessary to manœuvre the machine even if there were two pilots. And what is more strange the elevators are not balanced either, although there is no servo-motor.

The maximum span of the ailerons is 7.16 ms. and chord 1.02 m., measured from the middle of the 60 mms. tube, which acts as a hinge, and which is imbedded up to that point in the gutter-shaped false spar which supports the ailerons.

Their structure is entirely metallic, being made of steel tubes like those of the ailerons and rudders of all German aeroplanes, though the rudders of the Zeppelin itself are of aluminium. The idea in this is doubtless to give enough strength with slight thickness, and to avoid the warping of the wood.

The ribs, spaced .5 ms. apart, corresponding to those of the wing, are composed of two steel tubes in an elongated V surrounded at half their length by a little band of sheet steel welded to them which maintains their distance. The two rear extremities, to decrease the thickness, are welded one alongside the other, and not one on top of the other, to the trailing edge of the aileron, which is also of steel tube, 25 by 14 mms. Other tubes of 15 mms. are disposed crosswise as bracing. All these

tubes are wrapt with light fabric, on which is stuck that of the ailerons.

The Tail.

CONTROLS.—The tail of the Zeppelin is the least banal part of the machine, on account of its structure, no less than on account of its dimensions. It is remarkable for the turning of its curvature upside-down, and for the large and almost exclusive use of aluminium. Enormous and heavy, each of its planes

would have a surface sufficient to build a monoplane, and, as a whole, they would form a small two-seater biplane, or a large single-seater.

TAIL PLANES.—The tail planes, or longitudinal stabilisers, partly fixed and partly mobile, are biplanes. Not only are they of a surface equal to that of a biplane, but they are a complete biplane in general structure, internal constitution, cabane, struts, bracing, etc. This cellular character permits one to fix the tail

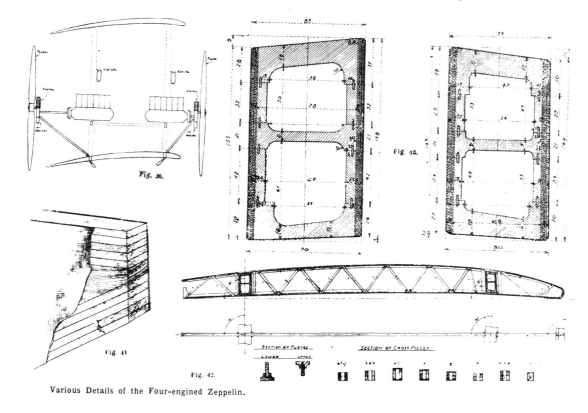

Various Details of the Four-engined Zeppelin.

at suitable horizontal points on the fuselage, which is flattened and raised and built as high as possible to avoid accidents on landing. The directional controls, or rudders, are included between the altitude controls.

The tail planes are of a rounded arrow shape very much accentuated, and their aspect in plan is exactly that of a Taube. The analogy is striking and complete and cannot remain unnoticed.

In spite of the difference in the centre, due to the fact that the lower tail planes are fixed on the sides of the fuselage, they are equal in span (9 ms.) and in chord; 1.6 m. at the centre tapering to 1.5 m. towards the struts, for the fixed tail planes, and .44 ms. to .72 ms. for the mobile flap.

The gap is 2.15 ms. much greater than that of an ordinary biplane, and greater than the chord.

Fixed Portions.—The incidence of the upper surface which is adjustable is sufficiently great (.17 ms.) in a chord of 1.57 ms., or about 1 in 10, which is about the same as that of the wings. That of the lower face is still more marked.

This is made necessary by the weight of the tail, but comparison with ordinary planes would necessitate a special examination, for one characteristic which is peculiar and worthy of remark, is that the curve of the tail planes, which is very much like that of current types, is completely reversed. That is to say, the upper surface is absolutely flat, while the lower surface has a curve similar to that of the upper surface of the wings. That is to say, it is convex instead of concave to the extent of having 112 ms. thickness.

The section of the elevator flap proper is triangular with a slight curve on both faces.

Rudders.—The rudders, which are three in number, are connected to fixed fins, one of them fixed on the axis of the machine, and the others 3.5 ms. out on each side. They are all entirely comprised inside the level of the two tail planes, even to the extent of leaving a slight margin of 8 to 10 cms.

The rudders have a similar form, but the central fixed fin differs from the other two. Mounted on a vertical duralumin tube between the front struts of the cabane, this central fin is prolonged as far as the fifth transverse member of the fuselage, in the middle of which it is fixed at its leading point, while the two other fins mounted on the front struts of the tail are only prolonged forward a little way. At the trailing edge all three of the fins are limited partly by the longitudinal bracing to which they are fixed by their duralumin edges. The rudders are mounted on the rear struts or on the vertical tube (which is a shade shorter)—also of duralumin—which is situated between the rear struts of the cabane. In front of these pivots is a balanced portion which extends to the vicinity of the cross-bracing to which the fixed fins also extend from the other direction.

The fixed fins and the rudders are entirely constructed of aluminium. Their ribs consist of little aluminium girders, analogous to those of the elevators and very similar to the girder work of the Zeppelin airships.

For the rudders the control cables, after passing over horizontal pulleys near the fifth transverse member of the fuselage, set out obliquely, and one cable passes through a window in each of the external fixed fins to a single transverse lever on the outer rudder. It seems then the more necessary that the three rudders should be linked up so as to be movable in both directions.

The Body.

Fuselage.—As on the smallest aeroplanes, there is a single fuselage. Its general characteristics are those of the old German fuselages built in the form of a lattice girder and not, as in the newer types, as a plywood monocoque as in the chaser machines, or in plywood with wooden frames without bracing. The length is 21.35 metres.

The two upper longerons are in a horizontal plane on a level with the axis of the airscrews for practically the whole length, and from 1.8 metres, cross measurement, they approach one another progressively in a straight line from the front of the gun-turret to the rear extremity, where the width is 1.08 metres.

The two lower longerons are horizontal from the front of the machine to the back of the gun-turret, whence they rise in a straight line to the last cross-strut but one, and then rise in a curve, so that the fuselage thins down in a horizontal line as in the Albatros and the early Fokkers. Thus, the maximum section of the fuselage, from behind the pilots to the gun-turret, is 1.8 metres wide by 1.68 metres in height, and thence it flattens out progressively.

These dimensions are concerned with the naked woodwork, but on each angle, so as to fix the fabric on the whole surface and to hold it clear of the cables, turnbuckles and ferrules, which might damage it, there has been added a wooden edging which consists of a strip of poplar, 30 by 40 mm. This strip is cut away frequently to allow for the numerous and somewhat thick ferrules and it forms on each side of the fuselage, a projection of 25 mm. or about 50 mm. to be added to the total width and height of the fuselage.

At 3 metres from the front of the machine, above the leading under-carriage, the longerons are interrupted, and the whole of the front part can, if necessary, be removed. From this point the true upper longerons, which are of ash, 65 × 65 mm. in this vicinity, descend to the summit of two 55 mm. tubes, which come to a point at the leading extremity of the fuselage. The part above these is super-added, and is composed of wood and round light tubing, which is not part of the actual construction.

Cross-Bracing.—As differentiated from the transverse cross-bracing, but in the same way as the cable bracing of the wings, the bracing of the four faces of the fuselage is composed of endless cables.

Internal Arrangements.

Right in the nose of the machine, which is rounded and little raised is a place for at least one gunner-observer who is provided with a handle, probably for the bomb-dropping apparatus.

Behind him and somewhat more elevated so that there is a view behind the "habitacle" (a delightful French word for a cockpit), and protected by a transparent windscreen (partition B general arrangement) are installed the two pilots whose controls will be described later.

Behind them there seems to be a wireless operator. Then on a level with the front of the wings are two mechanics who are certainly not too many for the surveillance of the four engines with their various controls, pumps, and so forth.

From the level of the front spar to the trailing edge the multiple tanks are suspended by girths to the girder frames which have already been mentioned, and the bombs are hung under the fuselage.

Between the tanks a passage is arranged through the partitions B to I, from the front to the cabin behind the gun-turret.

The Zeppelin R.VI production Four-engined Biplane in Flight. (4—250 h.p. Maybach engines.)

Finally, in the turret there are at least two machine-gunners who can fire not only above but under the fuselage from a sort of cabin which is situated behind, and to which they have access by crawling under the partition I.

There are thus a total crew of eight or nine persons. Underneath the gun-turret is a long trap door with the hinges set longitudinally. An external ladder on the left, made of welded tubes, permits the crew to mount into the turret, and another one seems to have been fitted to the front part of the fuselage. The fuselage is covered almost entirely with fabric. The front is three-ply and sundry sheets of aluminium close the roof of the machine towards the front.

The Under-carriages.

In spite of its 18 wheels, the landing system is of the most simple, but not of the most diminished. As on the Friedrichshafen and on the majority of big two-engine machines, it is composed of three parts. One is merely an accessory under the front of the fuselage.

The Front Under-carriage.—This is composed of two widely opened V's, each practically in a longitudinal plane. The after legs, which are 2.6 ms. long, are of 55 mm. tube. They are 1.6 ms. apart and are fixed by bolts under partition C to the lower fuselage longerons at the point where the true longerons are prolonged by false longerons. This entirely detachable part is undoubtedly susceptible to frequent breakage in landing.

The summits of the leading legs, which are short, being 1.1 m. in length, and almost vertical, and made of 40 mm. tube, are joined to the leading extremity of the fuselage by a single bolt in such a fashion that in plan they form a V. The lower ends of these tubes telescope into an elbow of an intermediate diameter, which itself telescopes into a rear tube of 55 mm., the whole being welded together.

Between the elbows of the two V's for a space of about .35 ms. are welded 30 mm. tubes, to which are fixed the rubber shock-absorbers. The two wheels which are .9 ms. apart, have rims of .48 m. diameter by .11 m. wide.

The Main Under-carriage.—This is situated at the level of the motors, under the wings, which particularly, for this reason, have neither a V nor an arrow.

Being subjected always to considerable strains, it is possible that the original under-carriage was miscalculated, which seems to be indicated by the inscription "Verstarkt" ("re-inforced") on each, from which one judges that several modifications have been made in the original arrangements.

Each of them is composed of two longitudinal V's resting under the spars on two 65 mm. bolts, held in a clip which is bolted to another, under the steel sheath which links the engine-cabane to the wing-spar exactly at the level of the foot of the cabane, and not in the prolongation of the leg of the cabane. Thence, where they are 1.2 m. apart, the two V's divide from one another to 1.55 mms. at the base.

The two legs of each V are united by a large hollow steel elbow with rounded angles to avoid cutting the rubber shock-absorbers, and, to hold these "sandows," carry a projection in front and two at the back.

The distance between these bases is maintained by an horizontal tube, one in front and one behind the wheel-axle, and by double-bracing of 8 mm. wire. The axle is held in these V's by sandows in the ordinary manner of an under-carriage, between two bobbins made of several pieces of pressed and welded steel.

This axle, enormous, and fatter than those of railway waggons, is of 110 by 120 mm. tube, and carries at each end two pairs of twin wheels. That is to say, eight wheels for each under-carriage.

The rims are 700 mm. diameter by 120 mm. wide. The tyres appear to be about 1,000 mm. (1 metre) in diameter.

Almost all the pieces of the under-carriage are autogenously welded. The whole thing appears to be strong, but the wheels alone form a cylindrical surface, of which the section is about 2.8 sq. ms., and this must offer considerable resistance to progress.

The Tail Skid.—This is single and of the usual type, pivoted under the middle to a lower fuselage cross-strut.

This tail skid is a single piece of ash, 1.2 ms. long, 70 mm. diameter at its upper part, 110 mm. diameter at the pivot and then square with a side of 110 mm. enlarged at the lower end by a steel sole.

Controls.

For transverse and longitudinal control there are two vertical levers of aluminium tubing, plugged with wood at the base only, permanently mounted on a single transverse axle and each furnished with a wheel.

The levers operate in the ordinary manner for longitudinal control.

The three rudders are controlled by means of two horizontal rudder-bars, and sectors and pulleys guiding the cables along the side of the fuselage as on old L.V.G's and almost all German aeroplanes.

After passing over a horizontal pulley on a level with the fifth partition from the end of the fuselage, the cables divide out horizontally and very obliquely, traverse the outer fixed fins by an opening in their base and thus to the rudder lever.

Armament.

The armament consists of at least four machine-guns, and possibly six. One at least is placed in front of everything.

A huge gun-turret of 1.4 m. internal diameter is situated behind the wings.

On each side, a little behind the middle, a gun-mounting is permanently fixed between the turret and the longeron, to which it is clipped by a collar. The gun-mounting is in the form of a "Z," which can turn on itself, and allows the gun to point downwards outside the fuselage without circulating round the turret. These two mountings make it possible to fire over the sides and upwards, as well as towards the rear.

It is possible that other machine-guns have been installed at the back of the turret to fire backwards and upwards; also the compartment behind the turret makes it possible to fire below the fuselage.

There exists, it seems, only two bomb-carriers, but each is for a bomb of 1,000 kilos. (about 1 ton). They are suspended longitudinally under the fuselage between the wing-spars, to which they are fixed by two collars at each end.

Each bomb-carrier is composed of two triangular girders of steel tubes, braced by crossed tubes, all welded together and cross-braced by piano wire.

This frame, measuring 2 m. in height by .35 m. in width, projects above the longerons into the interior of the fuselage. It carries two longitudinal tubes and two transverse arcs, 1.1 metres apart, under which the bombs would be held by a releasable girth.

It goes without saying that such bombs are not suitable for all sorts of objectives, even if their ratio of action compensates for their small number.

ZEPPELIN.—continued.

Engines.

The four independent engines are placed on the same level, two by two in opposite directions, one being a prolongation of the other with an interval between. Being of the same model they thus turn in opposite directions. The same disposition of engines was tried in France in 1916.

Each of them is held in a rocker between the two legs of a cabane front and rear, half of their length being in front and half behind. Each of their bearers, to which they are bolted direct, is a girder composed of two pieces of ash with a layer of plywood running vertically between them.

The whole is held up by a complex wooden frame—uprights of wood and sheet steel 50 mm. wide by 300 mm. high and 450 mm. apart—which on one part butt against the cabane and on the other part hold up by the intermediary of a cross-strut, the gearbox and the airscrews.

Each cross-strut rests on two tubular sockets of 55 mm., which are adjustable at the base, and rest against the base of the cabane on the wing spar. Cable cross-bracing of a complex nature completes the edifice.

These cabanes are built of two tubular "A's," 55 × 60 mm. in the front, and 60 × 65 mm. on the rear, and not of two "V's," as on the Friedrichshafen. This composition seems quite favourable against smashing, and gives four points of union at the summits of the under-carriage.

Each of the "A's" carries, besides a bracing of 32 mm. under the radiator, a bar of "U" section sheet steel, 100 mm. deep, and .88 to .9 m. in length. At the two extremities of this bar, each front "A" is linked to the rear "A" by two wooden longerons, .9 of a m. apart.

Each base and summit of the cabane is united to the corresponding wing-spar by a clip of 3 mm. sheet steel, 230 mm. wide.

A bonnet of aluminium, at any rate in front, encloses the engines.

These motors are 6-cylinder vertical Maybachs, but their power, which is ordinarily about 250 h.p. in this type, seems to have been forced up to 300 h.p., or 1,200 h.p. in all.

It is worthy of note that the German authorities impose on the engine constructors limited dimensions, lengths of base and other characteristics, which permit the interchangeability of different makes of motors.

Two of the motors are provided with a species of gear, almost destroyed, probably a starting-gear.

AIRSCREW GEARING.—Instead of the airscrew being mounted directly on the shaft, the following arrangement is interposed :—

1. A fly-wheel of cast iron of .4 metres diameter, unlike anything which exists in any other German aeroplane.

2. A connection in aluminium with plates of leather in notches, .36 metres diameter, of which the female part is half engaged in the fly-wheel.

3. A transmission tube, very short indeed for the front engines, but .75 metres long in the rear engines.

4. A gear-box containing two toothed pinions in an aluminium case, made in two parts and bolted together horizontally.

By this gearing the axis of the airscrew is placed 170 mm. above the axis of the motors, and its level corresponds thus with the upper longeron of the fuselage.

Under this one finds an oil reservoir-radiator, semi-cylindrical in shape, .35 by .1 m. thick, with 20 mm. tubes running through it. This has a pump at the base and two electric thermometers.

Airscrews.

The axes of the airscrews are 6.8 metres apart, laterally, and the bosses of the screws are 5.8 m. apart fore and aft. The screws are two-bladed, of 4.3 metres diameter.

From .185 m. towards the boss the thickness changes quickly to .3 m. The maximum width of the blade is .4 m. There are about a dozen laminations, mostly in badly chosen spruce with knots in it, except one which is in mahogany, and the whole length is covered by a thin layer of plywood.

Accessories.

As we have seen, the tanks are suspended to the upper part of the fuselage level with the wings. By each motor there is a gravity tank suspended by two little tubes to the inside leg at the bottom of the cabane at a level with the cylinders. A pump is placed in the fuselage on a level with the front wing spar.

The radiators, of N.I.G. type, and .2 m. thick, .4 m. high and .85 m. wide. Of this width .23 m. consists of a supplementary section, which can be added or taken away as required. The radiators are placed in front and at the top of each "A" of the cabane. They are suspended by two vertical cables.

Electric lighting is installed. Six fire extinguishers were found among the wreckage.

All the fabric is of poor quality, and is camouflaged with dark coloured hexagons, dark blue or violet, on which the black cross does not stand out. The paint used offers little resistance to oil and petrol.

If one reckons on a total weight of 12,600 kilograms, the upper spars must work at a pretty high stress. The most fatigued part, situated immediately outside the engine cabanes, works at 1.7 kilograms per sq. mm. On the same reckoning the spars on the lower plane work at 1.3 kilograms per sq. mm.

The figures for the work of the interplane struts of steel tubes vary from 1.1 kilos to 3.8 kilos per square mm.

Some of the cables vary from 10 kilos. to 25 kilos. per square mm. The cables are flexible and of quite good quality.

If the weight is 12,600 kilograms, the surface 314 square metres and the horse power 1,200 the load would be 40 kilograms per square metre—which is not enormous—and 10.5 kilos. per horse power.

It seems unlikely that the speed of this machine is more than 120-125 kilometres per hour.

THE ZEPPELIN BIPLANE.

Specification.

Type of machine	Four-engined Biplane.
Name or type No. of machine	Zeppelin "Giant" Biplane.
Purpose for which intended	Bombing.
Span	41 m.
Gap, maximum and minimum	4.4 m. ; 3.6 m.
Overall length	22 m.
Maximum height	6.4 m.
Chord, maximum and minimum	4.5 m. ; 3.5 m.
Total surface of wings	314.5 sq. m.
Span of tail	9 m.
Total area of tail	20 sq. m.
Area of elevators	5 sq. m.
Area of rudders (3)	4.2 sq. m.
Area of each aileron and total area	7.25 sq. m. ; 14.55 m.
Engine type and h.p.	4—300 h.p. Maybach.
Airscrew diameter	5.2 m. dia.
Load per sq. metre	40 kgs.
Weight per h.p.	10.5 kgs. per h.p.
Performance.	
Speed low down	120-125 kms. per hr.
Total weight of machine loaded	12,600 kgs.

THE ZEPPELIN FIVE-ENGINED GIANT.

A 5-engined bomber was brought down near Talmas on Aug. 10th, but unfortunately, owing to the explosion of one of its bombs, the machine was damaged beyond hope of reconstruction.

Some of its components have been recovered.

The principal item of interest is the gear box, which is used for all five engines, each of which is a 300-h.p. Maybach of the standard 6-cylinder vertical type.

The power plants are arranged as follows :—In the nose of the machine is one engine driving a tractor screw. On each side of the fuselage, supported by the wings, is a long pair of engine bearers carrying two engines apiece, which drive tractor and pusher screws.

The use of the gear box and driving shafts necessitates the employment of a fly-wheel on the engine, to which is added the female portion of a flexible coupling of the type already described.

Whereas the gear box in the 4-engined Giant, of which notes have already been given in this report, is of a somewhat crude type employing external driving shafts between the gear box and the engine, in the 5-engined machine the gear-box design is considerably improved. The casing consists, as shown in the photograph, of a massive aluminium casting provided with four feet which are bolted to the engine bearers.

Two kinds of gear boxes are employed. These differ only in over-all dimensions and the length of the pusher shaft.

The larger type is used for the pusher screw in order to obviate the necessity of cutting a slice out of the trailing edge of the main planes.

All the gear boxes were very badly damaged except one. This is the longer type, but it would appear that the shorter design is very similar in appearance.

In each case the gear reduction is 21—41.

The over-all dimensions of the gear box is as follows :—

Length, 1,025 mm.
Breadth, 675 mm.
Height, 535 mm.

The weights of the gear box and its attachments are as follows :—

Gear box, long type, 280 lbs.
Fly wheel and female clutch, 44 lbs.
Male clutch, 5 lbs.
Oil radiator, 12¼ lbs.

This it will be seen represents an additional weight of considerably more than 1 lb. per h.p.

The oil radiator in conjunction with each gear box is of a roughly semi-circular shape, and is slung underneath the main transverse members of the engine bearers so that it comes immediately beneath the large feet of the gear box, as shown. The radiator is entirely of steel construction, and embraces 65 tubes of approximately 20 mm. internal diameter. These are expanded and sweated into the end plates, to one of which is fitted a stout flange, against which is bolted a small gear pump which constantly circulates the oil from the gear box case through the radiator.

One of three Zeppelin Type 8300 series Giant Biplane Seaplanes. (4—250 h.p. Maybach engines.)

View Shewing the Pusher Airscrew of the Zeppelin Five-engined Giant.

This gear pump is driven by a flexible shaft from the small pinion, the shaft and its casing being in all respects similar to those employed for engine revolution counters. As shown in the photograph illustrating the complete gear box upside down, this flexible drive is taken off a small worm gear.

It will also be seen that underneath the oil sump of the gear box proper an electrical thermometer is fitted, which communicates with a dial on the dashboard.

Fitted on each gear box and working in connection with the oil circulation is a filter. This is provided with an aluminium case and a detachable gauze cylinder through which the oil passes.

The arrangement of the gear box is such that the axis of the airscrew is raised about 220 mm. above that of the engine crankshaft.

The construction of the long engine bearers is not without interest, as amongst other things, it indicates that German manufacturers are finding themselves short of suitable timber. Each bearer consists of a spruce or pine central portion, to which are applied, top and bottom, five laminations of ash. On each side are glued panels of 3-ply, about $\frac{1}{8}$ in. thick.

The engine bearers taper sharply at each end, and are strengthened by massive steel girders under each gear box.

The screws revolve at approximately half the speed of the engine, and having therefore a moderately light centrifugal load to carry, are made of a common wood that would scarcely be safe for direct driving screws.

Although fitted to 300 h.p. Maybach engines, they are marked 260 p.s. (h.p.) Mercédès. The diameter is 4.30 metres, and the pitch 3.30, for the pusher screw, but unfortunately, owing to the airscrews being badly damaged, not only by the crash, but by fire, it is not possible to state whether the tractor screws are of the same dimensions and pitch.

The construction is very interesting; each screw is made of seventeen laminations of what appears to be soft pine, and these laminations are themselves in pieces, and do not run continuously from tip to tip. They are, of course, staggered, so that the joints in successive layers do not coincide. Two plies of very thin birch veneer are wrapped round the blades. The grain of this veneer runs across the blade instead of along it.

It is difficult to say from the appearance of the screw whether this veneer has been put on in the form of two-ply or as two separate layers, one after the other.

Among other details salved from the wreckage is the engine control. This is a very massive affair. It consists of five stout steel tubular levers, two of which have become unbrazed in the fire which broke out when the machine crashed.

The levers are fitted with rachets so that each one can be operated individually, but the presence of a large single-diameter toothed wheel in the centre of the lever shaft would seem to indicate that all five levers could, when desired, be controlled simultaneously. This fitting had, however, been very badly fused, and it is impossible to give details with certainty.

A smaller fitting recovered from the wreckage consists of a windmill of a type similar to that used on the D.H.9 aeroplane. It is mounted at the top of an aluminium tube, but it is not possible to say for what purpose this mill is employed.

A small and very heavy rotary pump was found in the wreckage. This is possibly the hand-driven petrol pump, though it would appear unusually massive for this purpose.

The Douglas type of engine, carried for the purpose of driving the dynamo of the wireless and heating installation, is a very close copy of the 2¾ h.p. Douglas, and is made by Bosch. The fly-wheel is furnished with radial vanes which induce a draught through a sheet-iron casing, and direct it past cowls on to the cylinder heads and valve chests.

The generator is direct-driven through the medium of a pack of flat leaf springs, which act as dogs, and engage with the slots on the fly-wheel boss.

What appears to be a transformer, used in conjunction with the wireless set, was found.

THE FIVE-ENGINED GIANT.
Specification.

Span	42 m.
Total surface	330 sq. m.
Weight of machine empty	10 tons.
Useful load	4.5 tons.

Three-quarter Front View of a Zeppelin Five-engined "Giant" bomber, probably one of the R.XIVs or XVs of 1918.

The Zeppelin Five-engined "Giant."

Rear View of the Zeppelin "Giant" Biplane. (5—250 h.p. Maybach engines.)

GREEK.

Aerial Societies:—

None.

Aerial Journals:—

None.

Military Aeroplanes:—

Towards the end of 1914, Greece possessed a few dilapidated *Farman* land-going machines and several very workmanlike *Sopwith* seaplanes, these latter being imported by and handled by the British Naval Mission which was then in Greece endeavouring to reform the Greek Navy.

This mission was under the command of Rear-Admiral Mark Kerr, M.V.O., R.N., the late Acting Squadron-Commander Collyns Pizey, R.N., being in command of the Air Service section, with the rank of *Capitaine de Frégate*.

The latter officer died in Athens in 1915, and the whole Mission later left Greece.

Since a part of Greece came into the war on the side of the Allies, a number of Greek officers and men have been trained for aviation service by British and French instructors. Several of them have done good work in the war since then.

Captain H. C. J. A. R. West, late R.N., and late Wing-Commander R.A.F., was until recently in command of the Royal Hellenic Naval Air Service.

Flying Grounds---
Phaleron.
Salonika.

Military Aviators:—

Adamis (824 Ae. C.F.)
Kamberos (744 Ae. C.F.)
Montoussis (839 Ae. C.F.)
Mutassas, Sub-lt,, naval.
Savoff, Lt.
And others.

A Sopwith " Pusher " Seaplane (100 h.p. Anzani engine), in use by the Greek Naval Air Service.

DUTCH.
(HOLLAND)

Aeronautical Journal :—

Periodical (Monthly). *Het Vliegveld,* official organ of the Royal Dutch Aero Club.

Editorial Staff :

J. G. C. Duinker, 1st Flight Lieutenant.

B. Stephan, Engineer L.A.

Dr. H. Wolff, Director of the Government Study Service for aerial locomotion.

A. C. Perk, 1st Lieutenant L.A. (in command of the photo technical service.)

Names of the chief Aviation Centres in the Netherlands :

Soesterberg (near Utrecht) : Chief army flying ground, 21 hangars. Flying school.

Schiphol (near Amsterdam) : Army flying ground. Flying school.

Gilze Ryen (near Breda) : Army flying station. 2 Hangars.

Oldebroek : Artillery camp. 2 Hangars.

De Mok (on Tessel) : Naval flying station for hydroaeroplanes.

De Kooi (near den Helder) : Naval flying ground for land machines. 6 Hangars. Flying school.

Schellingwoude (near Amsterdam) : Naval flying station for hydroplanes.

Veere (Zeeland) : Naval flying station for hydroplanes.

Ede : Private aerodrome.

In Command of the Flying Corps : Major H. Walaardt Sacré.
In Command of the School for Observers : Captain J. C. M. Simon Thomas.
In Command of the Photo-technical service : 1st Lieutenant A. C. Perk.
In Command of the Wireless service : 1st Lieutenant G. M. Claus.

Engineers belonging to the Flying Corps : Ir. H. A. Vreeburg, Ir. H. C. Olivier, Ir. B. Stephan.

Instructors at the flying schools : Capt. F. A. van Heyst. 1st Lieut. W. C. J. Versteegh, 1st Lieut. A. K. Steup, 1st Lieut. C. Land, 1st Lieut. J. G. C. Duinker, 1st Lieut. G. A. Koppen.

Flying Officers in active service : Capt. F. A. van Heyst, 1st Lieut. W. C. J. Versteegh, 1st Lieut. L. J. Roeper Bosch, 1st Lieut. L. F. E. Coblyn, 1st Lieut. A. N. S. W. L. Coblyn, 1st Lieut. M. L. J. Hofstee, A.D.C. to the Commander, 1st Lieut. A. K. Steup, 1st Lieut. G. A. Koppen, 1st Lieut. C. Land, 1st Lieut. J. G. C. Duinker, 1st Lieut. H. Schlimmer, 1st Lieut. A Plesman, 1st Lieut. H. G. van Voorthuysen, 1st Lieut. W. P. van den Abeelen, 1st Lieut. H. van Weerden Poelman, 1st Lieut. G. P. van Hecking Colenbrander, 1st Lieut. M. C. van Dijk, 1st Lieut. W. L. Bisschoff, 1st Lieut. E. J. Hofman, 1st Lieut. W. E. Hoogenboom, 1st Lieut. F. Raland, 2nd Lieut. I. A. Aler.

Flying Officers in reserve now engaged on active service :
1st Lieut. in the Reserve, P. M. van Wulfften Palthe.
", " ,, J. N. Wallast.
2nd Lieut. ,, ,, R. Drost.
" ,, J. Jongbloed.
1st. Lieut. ,, ,, P. ten Zeldam.
2nd. Lieut. ,, ,, J. Balder.
" ,, ,, N. T. van der Stok.
" ,, A. C. Kamerman.
" ,, ,, H. G. B. de Kruyff van Dorssen.
" ,, ,, U. F. M. Dellaert.

2nd Lieut. in the Reserve, W. B. van Doorninck.
", ,, ,, F. M. Copes van Hasselt.
1st Lieut. ,, ,, Ch. J. Graaf Schimmelpenninck.
2nd Lieut. ,, ,, H. J. F. Nab.
", ,, ,, K. Soutendyk.
", ,, ,, C. van Vliet.

Flying Officers of the Naval Flying Service : Lieut.-Comm. D. Vreede, Lieut. A. S. Thomson, Lieut. H. Nieuwenhuis, Lieut. K. W. F. M. Doorman, Lieut. K. Muller, Lieut. Buenink, Lieut. van Hengel, Lieut. Backer, Lieut. Bakker, Lieut. Gauw, Lieut. Scheffelaar, Lieut. Hekman, Lieut. Huese, Lieut. Weemhof, Sub.-Lieut. Anverda, Sub.-Lieut. Akveld, Sub.-Lieut. van der Maesen de Sombreff, Sub.-Lieut. Schmidt Craus, Sub.-Lieut. Verploegh Chassé.

Personal Notes on the Chief Men concerned with the Development of Aviation in the Netherlands.

Major H. Walaardt Sacré, Commandant of the Dutch Flying Corps (Luchtvaartafdeeling), born in 1873. He commenced ballooning in 1909, in Germany, to which country he was commanded several times for instruction, as also to France, where he was trained as airship pilot. He organised the Flying Corps and became commander of the corps in July, 1913, which position he still holds.

F. A. van Heyst, Flight Captain, is the oldest Dutch flying officer. He gained his certificate in 1911, and became an instructor in 1914. Several of the present flying officers were his pupils.

W. C. J. Versteegh, 1st Flight Lieut., also got his brevet in 1911, and is a well-known instructor. Several times he was sent out to buy aeroplanes for the Dutch Government.

Henri Wynmalen, born in 1889, started flying in 1909, first on a *Bleriot-Anzani* Channel type monoplane. Went over to *Farman* biplanes, summer, 1910. Height record, 2,800 metres, 1st October, 1910, on a 50 h.p. *Farman*, at Mourmelon. He won the Grand Prix (100,000 francs) of the Automobile Club de France for the aero race from Paris to Brussels and back, 16th-17th October, 1910. Took part in the European circuit organised by " Le Journal." Established the first aeroplane manufactory in Holland (March, 1914). Took over the Spyker Works in 1915, since when the name of the factory has been changed into " The Netherlands Automobile and Aeroplane Manufacturing Co.,Trompenburg," which, besides the construction of aeroplanes and aircraft motors, continued to build the well-known Spyker motor cars.

Some Officers of the Dutch Flying Corps at Soesterberg. H.R.H. Prince Hendrick centre. On his left is Commandant-Major Walaardt Sacré, and on his right Senior-Instructor Capt. F. Van Heyst.

The N.C.O.'s of the Dutch Flying Corps.

SPYKER.

Netherlands Automobile and Aeroplane Co., Trompenburg. Amsterdam.

Manager, Mr. Henri Wynmalen.

Build for the Dutch Government the following types:—

SPYKER TWO-SEATER SCOUT.

Type of machine	Spyker two-seater Scout.
Name or type No. of machine	V.4.
Purpose for which intended	Reconnaissance.
Span	10.190 m.
Overall length	6.825 m.
Maximum height	3 m.
Engine type and h.p.	Spyker 130 h.p. Rotary.
Load per sq. m.	34 kg.
Petrol tank capacity in gallons	53½ gallons.
Oil tank capacity in gallons	8 gallons.
Performance.	
Speed	160 km. per hour.
Climb.	
To 1,000 ms. in minutes	5½ minutes.

Armament : 2 machine guns and 6 bombs.

SPYKER SINGLE-SEATER FIGHTER.

Type of machine	Spyker single-seater Fighter.
Name or type No. of machine	V.3.
Purpose for which intended	Air Fighting.
Span	8.190 m.
Overall length	6.100 m.
Maximum height	2.6 m.
Engine type and h.p.	Spyker 130 h.p. Rotary.
Load per sq. m.	25 kg.
Petrol tank capacity in gallons	28 gallons.
Oil tank capacity in gallons	4 gallons.
Performance.	
Speed	180 km. per hour.
Climb.	
To 1,000 ms. in minutes	3 minutes with full load

Armament : 2 machine guns.

SPYKER SCHOOL BIPLANE.

Type of machine	Spyker dual control School Biplane.
Name or type No. of machine	V.2.
Purpose for which intended	Training.
Span	10.850 m.
Overall length	6.640 m.
Maximum height	3 m.
Engine type and h.p.	Spyker 80 h.p. Rotary.
Load per sq. m.	23 kg.
Petrol tank capacity in gallons	25 gallons.
Oil tank capacity in gallons	5½ gallons.
Performance.	
Speed, maximum	135 km. per hour.
Speed, minimum	70 km. per hour.
Climb.	
To 1,000 ms. in minutes	8 minutes with full load.

VAN BERKEL'S PATENT Ldt.

Offices :—Boezemsingel, 33, Rotterdam.
Directors :—W. A. van Berkel, C. F. M. Van Berkel.
Aviation Department :—Keilweg, 9, Rotterdam.
Motor Section :—Chief Manager, John Kerner.
Aeroplane Section :—Chief Manager, C. J. Castendijk.

The manufactory is building hydro-aeroplanes for the Dutch Government (Royal Naval and Colonial Service).

The machines are biplanes, two-seater, with two floats and with an engine of 200 h.p.

The speed will be about 160 r.m.p.h.

Further particulars about the machines are :—

Length	9.425 m.
Span	11.20 m.
Height	3.34 m.
Stagger	0.09 m.
Depth of Planes	1.80 m.
Length of Floats	5.65 m.
Breadth	0.71 m.

The type is called " W.A."

A Spyker School Machine used by the Dutch Flying Corps.

Half front view of a Spyker-Trompenburg Two-Seater School Machine, type V.2.

The latest type Spyker-Trompenburg Scout, Holland's leading aeroplane.

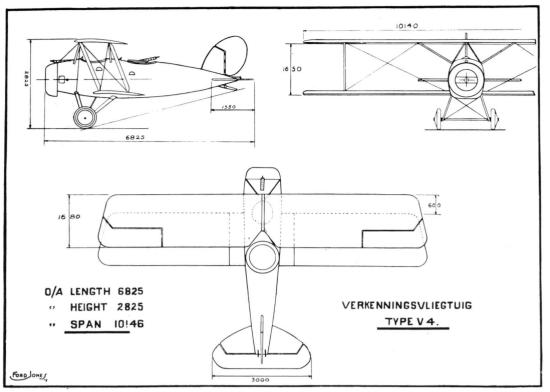

SPYKER—continued.

O/A LENGTH 6825
"   HEIGHT 2825
"   SPAN 10!46

VERKENNINGSVLIEGTUIG
TYPE V 4.

The Spyker-Trompenburg Two-Seater Training Machine.

ITALIAN.

ITALIAN NAVAL AND MILITARY AERONAUTICS.

CHIEFS OF THE ITALIAN MILITARY AVIATION SERVICE.

General Officer Commanding :—Lt. General Morris.
Officer Commanding Personnel :—Maj. General Vincengo Craniello.
Officer Commanding Organisation ⎰ The Under Secretary for
Officer Commanding Supplies ⎱ War.
Chief of Air Staff, Attached G.H.Q. Staff :—Major-General Leone Andrea Maggiorotti.
Director-General of Aeronautical Services :—General M. Rieni.

CHIEFS OF ITALIAN MARINE AVIATION.

General Officer Commanding :—Admiral Orsini.
Second in Command :—Commander Marsiglia.
Officer Commanding Supplies :—Commander Roberti.
Officer Commanding Personnel :—Commander Calderara.
Officer Commanding Dirigible Section :—Commander Valle.

MILITARY AND NAVAL FLYING SERVICES.

Dating from the time of the first Wright flying machine on which Lt. Calderara learnt from the " Master " at Centocelle,—where later Lieuts. Savoia and Ginocchio first left the earth,—Service aviation as in England was for a long time a private but countenanced Military sport which luckily drew its recruits from the more wealthy and scientifically-minded officers.

When flying first became—some little time after the first Brescia meeting in 1909—a recognized Military sideline, these and the other pioneers were classed as a " Specialist " Engineer Brigade, with the balloonists, electrical, and wireless folk.

In the progress of things, the heavier-than-air "specialists" were detached and grew into the Aviation Battalion, with the late Col. Piazza, Capt. Moizo, Lieuts. Falchi and Gavotti in leading parts.

Thus the Tripoli campaign found them mounted on Blériots, Farmans, a few Caproni and Nieuport monoplanes, perhaps even two Bréguets and certainly an Etrich. Even thus, the experience gained opened all Military eyes to possibilities, and things began to move. In spite of ceaseless winds and moving sands, a great deal of flying was done, and albeit the enemy defence was only from below. Captain (as he then was) Moizo was captured and various casualties had to be deplored, though as a whole the Aerial Force was considered to have done all, if not more, than was required of it, and the New Arm was established on the throne to reign.

So in 1914 we find an Aeronautical Corps composed of all things Aerial, learning the lessons as taught in Flanders and other places where men were flying and fighting.

THE NAVAL SECTION.

Meanwhile, the Naval section had some good time before drifted apart and settled to its own element. The Monaco epoch of 1913 was probably the corner stone, or rather the turning point, here as elsewhere.

From then onwards one heard of Lieuts. Calderara, Savoia, Guidoni, Ginocchio and Miraglia, designing and testing their own " seaplanes " while flying foreign types at Venice, Spezia, and other coastal places where seamen are mostly found, and entering into combined manœuvres with airships, what time the Guidoni palette and other national features were on trial.

AIRSHIPS.

It was among the Airship Section (for that period a powerful one) that the Navy's influence was especially felt. The sea-worthy boat-bodies, useful repeatedly on the Tripoli coast,— a feature of the vessels from the very beginning,—and the prominent number of the seamen from among whom the first L. T. A. pilots were recruited, point conclusively to this influence —so natural too and evident when one considers the affinity between the elements and their navigation.

Even were it permitted, it would seem among so many brave pilots invidious to say of anyone that his name stands out. It can not be forgotten that the whole crew of one new vessel perished in flames rather than surrender their secrets to the enemy !

Italian Aviators and Civilian Aviators with an Italian Service machine.

FLYING BOATS.

Curtiss, Italian-built Lohners and later a variety of F.B.A.'s, constructed by the Savoia firm, Messrs. Macchi, and others, were the first craft to be much used by the Italian Marine Aviation in the Great War.

The variety of types still in use may be explained by the extent of fresh water to be patrolled. The inland water boundary on Lake Garda and elsewhere entails large depôts and stations all over Italy, as well as along the coast line, as he who reads maps may see. However, for some time now the use of land-going machines by the Navy has been discontinued, this Service being thus able to confine itself to its element and better co-operation between it and the Army fliers is the result.

EARLY TRAINING.

Though not then much mentioned, a vast amount of squadron flying and cross-country work was being done in 1914. This, and the policy of allowing Military pilots to take part in competitions, is probably one of the causes of the brilliant results obtained from the very first day of Italy's entry into the war.

PERSONNEL.

About six months is about the period normally occupied by a pilot's technical and practical training, during which time, as afterwards, he wears the uniform of the regiment to which he belongs.

Aspirants commence with instruction in the theory of heavier-than-air machines, resistance of material and particular instruction in the various type of aero motors in use. They are taken for flights as passengers.

All then go to the training camp about 80% for monoplane work, the remainder for biplanes.

For the *military brevet* the examination is most comprehensive, special attention is paid to flying in high winds, manœuvring, climbing, good landings without inconvenience to passengers, cross-country flights, etc. The course is generally modelled on war experiences.

FLYING SCHOOLS.

Aviano.—Central school. Size about 5 × 2 kilometres. Sheltered from all winds except westerly, by banks of trees. Workshops capable of any type of repairs. Numerous hangars, both of iron and of wood, as also one of the hexagon type.

Centocelle.—Military school for advanced training. Caudrons and Farmans mostly used.

Miraflori (Turin).—Mixed military and civil school. Repairing shop. Testing shop for motors, chemical laboratory. Arranged for testing all necessary apparatus, motors, lubricants, etc. Acceptance tests of aeroplanes are made here and examinations for pilots' certificates. The whole ground is completely enclosed and admission is only obtained by special permission.

An Italian Seaplane Mother Ship, with her brood of Flying Boats.

Rome.—Aerial acrobatics advanced school.

Varese
Bolsena — Seaplane schools.
Taranto

Pordenone.—School for superior brevets. Five kilometres from Aviano. Treeless plain about 1½ × 1 kilometre, but open in all directions to the wind. Small repairing shop, many spacious hangars, with barracks for both officers and men.

S. Francesco al Campo.—Has two hangars, each suitable for seven *Farman* machines, small repairing shop and carpenters' shop. In July, 1913, it ceased to be a flying school and is now headquarters of the Farman squadron.

Somma Lombardo.—School for *Nieuport* and *Caproni* machines. Large flying grounds, fairly flat with low vegetation only. Buildings adjoining the ground for accommodating the staff and students and with shops capable of every type of repairs and also of constructing machines. Capacious hangars.

Marine Flying School (Venice).—Constituted by Royal Decree, 25th August, 1913.

S. Giusto (Pisa).

Coltano.—(The Vickers-Terni School.)

Padua.—S. Pelagio (Sva H.Q.)

THE ITALIAN AIRCRAFT INDUSTRY.

In spite of restrictions and the difficulty of obtaining raw material, the intense Government demand for aeroplanes in Italy is more than met by the supply.

When the difficulty of getting seasoned wood and tubing before 1915 is remembered, one is at a loss to understand whence now comes all that is needed, and it follows that many bless the war for its revival of those cardinal trade virtues, "push" and goodwill.

Again, when one recollects the conditions under which our pioneers got a machine built—even maybe a copy of an aeroplane which had lowered a world's record—one, after four years of war, is left breathless when he has learnt with what facility aeroplanes in series are turned out nowadays. No one who knew Italy in 1914 would have believed that she could have been in a position to export two or three types of machines after a period of two years of war-régime, as was the case.

ITALIA REDENTA.

The partial explanation of this may be attributed to the fact that formerly chained down by foreign trade oppression, Italy was yet ready for the imprescindable necessity, "the mother, etc.," which has released her. Another reason is that she holds up her head with lawful pride because before the rest of Europe and the world she had used aeroplanes in a first barbaric warfare, and so had learnt what possibilities might be expected before the end of the present one. She therefore started her preparations with a larger and clearer vision than the politicians who ruled in other countries and thought to do here would have voted ample.

Aviation, however, seems to have gone through similar processes in various lands, near and far. So, as in England, Italy's builders had a fight infernal to be recognized as of any good by the authorities.

Luckily, few were felled quite to the ground—the rest propagandered or laid low and were still alive to show when Europe fell on war that Italy could do without Germans, and that she could build war-aeroplanes without the foreign help which had constantly been contracted for by her emissaries afflicted with that mistaken modesty which habitually kept this great people from its place in the hemisphere.

What use was an Italian aeroplane, people asked, when everywhere abroad people were flying foreign machines? This quite regardless of the fact that "people abroad" had never been encouraged to believe that there were Italian flying machines.

GOVERNMENT APATHY.

When the *Asteria* biplane or the *Antoni* monoplane or the *Chiribiri* or any of the *Caproni* early types put up an excellent performance, well ahead of the time, and in spite of untold difficulties, did any financial help or subsidy from the Government henceforward assist that successful firm?

Yet the Dirigible question was tackled thus by the authorities, and these vessels were built under control of Military engineers on Italian lines, with the greatest success. The brains behind the designs were in both cases Italian.

So one is led to conclude the absence of faith in the Heavier-than-Air theory in those days which occasioned scepticism towards even practical manifestations of the principle. Somewhat as England thought to do safely in respect of airships. "Let foreigners do the experimenting, then we can reap the results." She had almost done so!

EARLY DAYS.

This purporting to deal with business, there is unfortunately no room for the most interesting part of flying, to wit, the pioneering days. It was, however, always upheld that the first Italian aeroplane to be sold abroad—I think to a Russian Maecenas—was a *Faccioli* biplane. Now the family of this name built and flew biplanes, etc., at Turin and elsewhere in the remote ages round about 1909. So there the trade began and stopped till the Capronis began to sell to patriotic associations for presentation hints to the State about the time that the pioneer firms were at their last financial gasps and were induced to contemplate agency work, or, in a few rare cases, even the reproduction of foreign types.

Capital for this was found *cela va sans dire*, and we find in 1913 or thereabouts, the leading foreign firms, English and French of course, for the Teutons were not out to let their rather uncertain vassals know the tricks of their trade, disposing themselves to plant their patents in fertile Italian soil. Thus the Bristol, the Blériot, and the Farman—the Voisin Bros.' patents had been under the care of Ing. Thouvenot at Cameri before anything did much serious flying here—were spoken of as the future mounts for Italians.

In reality, shortly the S.I.T. at Turin and the Savoia at Milan, did begin to trade seriously with foreign push and business propensities, the former holding in concession the Blériot and the latter the Farman manufacturing rights.

THE SPUR OF WAR.

It was not till 1914, however, when foreign consignments became no longer hopeful, that the blinded turned to their nearest of kin—for blood is stronger than the strongest foreign water—for wings and more wings for Italy. They were forthcoming, because the designs had been tried and not found wrong, and because the men had faith in themselves, though they might all have taken themselves abroad, as some had done, or to the motor trade, to which some hopeless of the future had returned.

So the war caused an Italian trade renaissance, for the Government, by treaties or entreaties or by mere money, got the materials, and with these two essentials behind it we see the *Caproni* (illustrated in last year's edition) taking the world by storm, the *Gabardinis* finally recognized and ordered to multiply, and an Italian *Voisin*, exhibited ages before, built in series. It is "an ill wind," etc., and by its war blast the fine Italian power producers, the Isotta-Fraschini motor and the F.I.A.T.'s aero-engine, long talked-of hopefully, became live necessities, and flying boats over which laudable enterprise had eaten its heart out were marked "v. urgent," and the goods were delivered.

THE ENTRY OF THE BIG FIRMS.

Big firms like the Ansaldo, the F.I.A.T. mentioned above, and the fast-growing Pomilio, produced types of their own creating, while other companies, such as the Aer and the S.A.M.L. were constituted for definite objects, the reproducing of good Allied or the best enemy aircraft. And so the pre-war firms Caproni, Gabardini, Savoia, Sit, Macchi, Chiribiri, Bossi and others, have seen the rise of many new lights in the firmament.

THE CENTRE OF THE INDUSTRY.

As could be expected, Turin has never been ousted from the place it has held from the earliest days as the centre of things aviatic, as it is that of mechanical traction, but Milan, with its extra facilities, its more central position, and its very character as the Commercial Capital of Italy, has crept up rather close to it. And especially if one includes the big aircraft concerns in the province of Milan and the neighbouring towns.

Now, however, the movement for various and obvious reasons, is towards the south, *via* Genoa and the west coast, as hydro-aero and aero-hydroplanes become of greater importance.

For the big shipping firms are coming in and one might safely prophesy the Spezia-Leghorn district a future Paradise for waterplane builders. When, that is to say, transatlantic liners, aero or marine, will carry flying boats instead of lifeboats—their collapsible wings perhaps spread by engine power in the twinkling of an eye.

Trials of these will be of interest to the shipbuilders, and let us say the insurance agencies, in the early years of peace when stray mines may be met with on the high seas and other floating obstacles be drifting about. Hulls may even have to be converted into flying-boat bodies, a la hydroplanes, if there is a boom in aerial transport. At any rate, large companies have been floated among the sea-going folk down south to be ready to meet these needs, and it is sure that large gun-founders must have foreseen the time when orders will be less brisk, nor will the making of plough-shares occupy their whole output.

FINANCE.

The question of the financial amount that this nation has invested in aviatory enterprises is so vast and complicated owing to war reserve, that even an approximate guess has no chance of getting near the figure. Add the unknown amounts that big engineering works have allocated to experiment—and possibly to adaptation of shops and factories—to the sums dropped by the earliest builders, and the capital of the new expressly-founded companies dealing in commercial aviation, and we get an enormous total. Judging merely by the excess-profits taxes paid in Piedmont alone, of which province Turin is the chief town, one could easily come to a very wrong solution of the matter, even if one did so in strict conjunction with the figures of the various Aero-companies' Share-Price List.

OUTPUT.

In conclusion, one should congratulate the Trade here on the fact that no one has ever heard of a dearth of machines for the front. Everything, not only the carrying out of big flights at home, abroad and across the seas for trade or war propaganda, but the exportation to the Allies advertised by more than one of the big firms, points to the contrary.

It is true that certain types of *Avions* were not used in the numbers thought by some to be necessary or advisable, but the reasons for this are held to be sentential, not commercial. As far as the Trade is concerned, one can rely on Italy's share in international progress in 1919, being up to the standard and warranted efficient and effective.

T. S. HARVEY.

AERIAL COMMERICAL COMPANIES.

The following firms have been formed for commercial purposes, either as traders in parts, or with a view to aerial transport. Some are manufacturers of aircraft in the ordinary :—

SOCIETA TRASPORTI AEREI INTERNAZIONALI. Milan. An international carrier and forwarding agency. Capital : £1,000,000. President : Senator Don Prospero Colonna. Bankers : Banca Commerciale.

SINDACATO INDUSTRIALE AERONAUTICO ITALIANO. Milan. Society of Aeronautical Traders. President : Avv. Goria Gatti. Developed in 1919, into "Locomozione Meccanica."

AGENZIA GENERALE FORNITURE AERONAUTICHE. Via P. Amedeo II. Milan. General Aviation Supply Contractors. A Savoia offshoot.

SOCIETA LAVORAZIONE D'AVIAZIONE. Milan. Capital : £3,000,000.

ING. NICOLO ROMEO e CO. Via Paleocapa, 6, Milan. Nominal capital, 50,000,000 lire. Paid up capital, 30,000,000 lire.

A

ANTONI. Soc. di aviazione Antoni, via Vitt, Emanuele, 46, Pisa. School : S. Guisto, Pisa. Made a name by means of a curious type of monoplane of his own design. No warp to wings. Nearly one-fourth of surface nearest body, and along the trailing edge of wing was left flexibly. A variable camber substituted for warp. Large horizontal empennages, plus usual monoplane rudder and elevators formed tail. Of interest as the first aeroplane to fly from Italy (Pisa) to Corsica. Of late constructing more normal designs. No fresh information available.

"A.E.R." Orbassano, Turin. Offices at Via Governolo No. 4. Turin.

This large new firm dates from practically the beginning of the European war.

Its products have been perhaps the most useful machines turned out in this country, both in the fighting zones and at the home-camps, where they are said to have helped upwards many records, and to have greatly speeded up the perfecting of new pilots.

Commonly credited with building *Caudrons*, used for artillery spotting, and training pilots at Centocelle. No fresh information available.

C

CAPRONI. Società Per Lo Sviluppo Dell'Aviazione in Italia. Taliedo and Vizzola.

Designer : Comm. Gianni Caproni, the Apostle of big planes. Technical Manager—at Taliedo : Ing. Aldredo Fioroili.

The city address of the firm is Corso Venezia 82, Milan.

Commendatore Ing. Gianni Caproni is to the Italian mind all that is rarest in patriotism and aviation.

He was born at Massone, in the Trentino, in 1886, and is thus of that region the release of which, from foreign bondage, Italy ever aspired.

Caproni at 17 was deep in his studies for the diploma of civil engineer at Munich, having obtained which the following years saw him first at Liege studying electrical engineering, then at Paris devoting himself to aeronautics with his contemporary and friend, Coanda.

It was in France that the first of his biplanes was designed ; but the first failure was that met in an attempt to get financial backing to build it somewhere in the early part of 1909, when on a visit to his native country.

So he returned to Belgium and theory, and only in the following year was it found possible to build the machine—which flew at the first trial.

From then onwards, he took up his quarters at Malpensa (Vizzola), on that lonely heath, not unfrequently then used as a manœuvring ground in the summer for cavalry, which was lent him by the War Office.

Little was heard of the brothers Caproni—he had been joined by an elder brother, Dr. Fred. Caproni—by the public, but a quiet and great work was carried through in the following years, culminating in the unavoidable publicity caused by the record-breaking monoplane's performance abroad. (Vienna, 25/6/12.) This was the machine which was used for military purposes by the Italian Government just before the monoplane ban.

Several widely differing types of biplanes had been evolved during 1910 and 1911 ; the last (tractor) with doubly cambered wings and tail-incidence variable during flight, an instructive but not effective machine.

Aero-dynamic experiments of all sorts were tried, e.g., the effects of flexible surfaces, dihedral supporting and control surfaces, side areas, body length, but especially in elicology, a real pleasure to Signor Caproni, this last.

Twin engines, a machine with two engines to be used alternately, dual propeller action, skin friction and indeed every problem that was only to be resolved by experiment on full-sized machines, was gone into in practice, and reliable theory extracted from the results. It is worthy of note, however, that the forward position of the engine was from the beginning the only one for Ing. Caproni.

From these data the first 300 h.p. three-engined biplane rose to conquer in 1914, met, as one might have expected, with some scepticism by the country at first. Now this machine's doings are in everyones' mind, and its potentiality has paled before the prodigious size and perfect controllability of the 1,000 h.p. triplane here illustrated.

The principle of cellular construction, so early propounded by the designer as the only way of guaranteeing the rigidity of large span machines, is the rock of the "CA" triplane's strength.

As it has carried up to 30 passengers, we may take its strength as proved, and the "limit of size" theory held by some to be exploded.

Fore part of an early CAPRONI Ca 3 type biplane with two rotary tractor engines and a pusher Isotta-Fraschini.

Reproduced from " La Guerre Aérienne," from a French military photograph.

Front view of CAPRONI Ca 3 biplane of 1916-18, with the most common arrangement of three 150 h.p. Isotta-Fraschini V4B inline engines. Maximum speed 85 m.p.h. in Ca 33 form.

Reproduced from " La Guerra," the Italian official publication.

THE CAPRONI THREE-ENGINED TRIPLANE. TYPE C.A.4.
(Ca 42 Edition)

	Specification
Type of machine ..	Triplane
Name or type No. of machine ..	Caproni C.A.4
Purpose for which intended ..	Bombing
Span	98 ft. 1 in.
Gap	8 ft.
Overall length	49 ft. 7 in.
Maximum height	20 ft. 8 in.
Chord	7 ft.
Total surface of wings ..	2,223 sq. ft.
Engine type and h.p.	Three Isotta-Fraschini, Fiat or Liberty. Each 270 h.p.
Weight of machine loaded ...	16,534 lbs.
Performance.	
Speed at 6,500 feet ...	87 m.p.h.
Climb.	
To 6,500 feet in minutes ...	14 mins.
Ceiling	9,850 ft.
Disposable load apart from fuel	3,800 lbs.

Three-quarter Front View of the 450 h.p. Caproni experimental Single-engined Triplane. Speed: 200 km. per hour.

A Caproni Ca 47 Seaplane (Ca 5 type). 150 km.p.h. Carrying capacity, 2 tons. Three 300 h.p. Fiat engines.

A 1,000 H.P. CAPRONI TRIPLANE, of 1917, nose to nose with a 100 h.p. Caproni Monoplane of 1915 Type.

Front View of a Caproni Ca 4 type Triplane bomber of 1917.

View from below of a CAPRONI Ca 3 type biplane.

The Pensuti-Caproni in the air.

The Pensuti-Caproni Triplane in the air.

PENSUTI Triplane.

Designed to do what bicycle does for the man on the road, the little vehicle was ready for its trial flight when its builder, the late Emilio Pensuti, was killed in attempting to save a very valuable life for the country.

After the lapse of some months the machine was taken into the air by Lt. L. Montegani and did all that its lamented designer hoped of it.

The Pensuti 2, as it is named, leaves the ground after a run of 20 metres and pulls up in the same distance.

With an Anzani Y, 35 h.p. engine, a speed of 95 kilometres has been attained and a minimum speed of 40 is possible.

Rate of climb : 1000 metres in 1/4 hr.

Span : 4 metres.

Total length : 3.80 metres.

Over all height : 2.40 metres.

Weight in flying trim including pilot : 230 kilos.

Petrol consumption per flying hr. : 2 gallons.

Oil   ..   .. : ½ ..

The Pensuti-Caproni on the ground.

CHIRIBIRI.
A. Chiribiri e C, Borgo S. Paolo, Via Caraglio, and Via Montenegro, Turin, and Stabilimenti già Nazarro ; Borgata Cenisia, Corso Peschiera No. 250, Turin.

Made many interesting experimental monoplanes, on which several Italian Records were broken. Now engaged on motor work exclusively.

G

GABARDINI.
Società Incremento Aviazione, Cameri, Novara.

The *Garbardini* type of monoplane took the competent by storm when it first appeared in 1913 to the public.

With two adult passengers and an 80 h.p. rotary engine, the late Philip Cevasco made a non-stop flight from Milan to Venice, and otherwise proved the powers of the machine to be quite exceptional and unusually well suited for all sorts of general conditions.

With a smaller engine, the *Gabardini* was found to be ideal for training pilots, and so a large school and works were opened at Cameri, in 1914, and were got into swing in time for the work of preparation for war.

Squat and inelegant and built largely of metal, the monoplanes are distinctive, not freakish nor reminiscent of any other aeroplane.

Signor Gabardini, who at one time dedicated himself to art of another sort, is a Piemontese by birth, and cruelly crippled, mental energy alone being in his power of recent years. He has, however, the satisfaction of having produced one of the very few monoplanes which has survived the ban and disfavour into which single-deckers have fallen, and his joy therein is shewn by the pride with which he claims it the best, after trial, in all the world.

The type has had a long testing during four war years of gruelling, with barely a modification, and that in the cockpit, in all that time.

So responsive to control is the *Gabardini* that its designer states that " they answer the intangible helm of the pilot's intention before the material leverage has come into action."

In flight, the *Gabardini* reminded one of the *Antoinettes*, curiously, since the design of the two is so entirely opposite. Up till now radial motors are fitted, with rotaries for school machines.

With a motor less costly in upkeep, the *Gabardini* monoplane is a machine which may, one hopes, become a useful means of commercial transport, being a good lander, a weight-carrier and stable. A commercial traveller's vehicle possibly ?

The work of training some 300 pilots carried on at Cameri has kept Signor Gabardini's designing energy rather in the background necessarily.

A biplane of characteristic design has been produced.

The school claims to have turned out as many pilots as all the others together, and it is to the praise of Machine and Masters that the casualties only average six yearly.

The first aerodrome in Italy to erect a permanent signal-tower for passing air traffic, Cameri may be the first to get its post-war commercial value recognized and realized.

A Garbardini captive monoplane used to teach the use of controls.

GARBARDINI—continued.

THE GARBARDINI BIPLANE.

Type of machine	Single-seater Tractor Biplane.
Name or type No. of machine ..	Garbardini.
Purpose for which intended ..	Advanced Training.
Span	7.20 m.
Maximum height	2.2 m.
Total surface of wings ..	14.81 sq. m.
Engine type and h.p. ..	80 h.p. Le Rhône.
Load per sq. m.	32.07 kgs.
Weight per h.p.	5.9 kgs.

Performance.

Speed low down	180 kms.
Total weight of machine loaded	475 kgs.

A Garbardini Advanced Training Machine (80 h.p. Le Rhône engine).

THE GARBARDINI BIPLANE.

Type of machine	Single-seater Tractor Biplane.
Name or type No. of machine ..	Garbardini.
Purpose for which intended ..	Advanced Training.
Span	7.2 m.
Maximum height	2.25 m.
Total surface of wings ..	15.85 sq. m.
Engine type and h.p. ..	110 h.p. Le Rhône.
Load per sq. m.	33.7 kgs.
Weight per h.p.	4.87 kgs.

Performance.

Speed low down	190 km.p.h.
Total weight of machine loaded.	535 kgs.

A Garbardini biplane with 110 Le Rhône engine.

THE GARBARDINI MONOPLANE.

Type of machine	Tractor Monoplane.
Name or type No. of machine ..	Gabardini.
Purpose for which intended ..	Training Machine.
Span	10 m.
Total surface of wings ..	18 sq. m.
Engine type and h.p. ..	50 h.p. Gnôme.

Performance.

Speed low down	100 km.p.h.

A Garbardini School Machine (50 h.p. Gnôme engine).

Garbardini Monoplane with 50 h.p. Gnôme engine.

Garbardini Monoplane for elementary instruction (35 h.p. Anzani).

A Garbardini Monoplone with 80 h.p. Le Rhône engine.

M

MACCHI. Società Anonima Nieuport-Macchi. Varese.

Well-known as an old coach-building concern, this Company, passing through the motor-body building stage, took up the constructing of *Nieuport* monoplanes some considerable time before the European conflict began.

It had by then produced certain "parasol" types with great success, creating records for Italian aviation about the time other nations were mobilizing.

Naturally, since then enormous strides must have been made, and it seems probable that the Macchi Works could more than meet any demands for machines from their own Government.

But for the preparedness of Ing. Giulio Macchi, and the organization which allowed this firm to construct even more Nieuports than the Italian Army called for, this country's position in the air at the beginning of the war might have been very serious. For one understands that the Allied Forces owe individually a considerable debt to the Macchi concern.

The latter part of the war saw the firnis flying boats in very general use both on active service and on home waters for training purposes. Ing. Macchi is turning his attention to trade on the south American rivers, as soon as the mapping of those immense waterways is completed. In this work his faster boats are, one learns, to take an active part.

MACCHI "5."

Type of machine	Single-seater Waterplane.
Name or type No. of machine	M5.
Purpose for which intended	Hunter.
Span	11.90 m.
Gap	1.90 m.
Overall length	8 m.
Maximum height	2.85 m.
Chord	Upper plane, 1.60 m. ; Lower plane, 1.10 m.
Total surface of wings	29 sq. m.
Span of tail	2.87 m.
Total area of tail	3.95 sq. m.
Elevator, maximum	2.87 × 0.55 m.
Rudder, maximum	1.20 × 0.55 m.
Fin, maximum	2.50 × 0.65 m.
Ailerons, total area	3.75 sq. m.
Fuselage dimensions	1.00 × 0.85 sq. m.
Engine type and h.p.	Isotta Fraschini V4 b., 160 h.p.
Airscrew, diam., pitch and revs.	2.55 m., 15,00.
Weight of machine empty	700 kilos.
Load per sq. m.	35.5 kilos.
Weight per h.p.	6.45 kilos.
Tank capacity in hours	3.15 hours.
Performance.	
Speed low down	189 k.p.h.
Climb.	
To 4,000 metres in minutes	20 mins.
Total useful load	270 kgs.
Total weight of machine fully loaded	970 kgs.

MACCHI "7"

Type of machine	Single-seater Waterplane.
Name or type No. of machine	M7.
Purpose for which intended	Hunter.
Span	9.95 m.
Gap	1.96 m.
Overall length	8.10 m.
Maximum height	2.95 m.
Chord	Upper wing, 1.670 m. ; Lower wing, 1.31 m.
Total surface of wings	26.6 sq. m.
Span of tail	2.84 m.
Total area of tail	2.65 sq. m.
Elevator, maximum	2.84 × 0.6 m.
Rudder, maximum	1.12 × 0.6 m.
Fin, maximum	2.50 × 0.55 m
Ailerons	2.70 sq. m.
Fuselage dimensions, horizontal	1.15 m.
Fuselage dimensions, vertical	0.90 m.
Engine type and h.p.	Isotta Fraschini V6. 260 h.p.
Airscrew, diam. and revs.	2.55 m., 1800.
Weight of machine empty	775 kgs.
Load per sq. m.	41.5 kilos.
Weight per h.p.	4.325 kilos.
Tank capacity in hours	4 hours.
Performance.	
Speed low down	210 k.p.h.
Climb.	
To 5,000 metres in minutes	21 mins.
Total useful load	305 kilos.
Total weight of machine fully loaded	1,080 kgs.

MACCHI "8."

Type of machine	Two-seater Seaplane.
Name or type No. of machine	M8.
Purpose for which intended	Scouting.
Span	13.8 m.
Gap	2 m.
Length	9 m.
Maximum height	3.25 m.
Chord	Upper plane, 1.75 m. ; lower plane, 1.59 m.
Total surface of wings	40 sq. m.
Span of tail	3.270 m.
Area of tail	3 sq. m.
Elevator	3.27 × 0.7 m., 1.70 × 0.7 m.
Fin	3 × 0.58.
Area of ailerons	4.50 sq. m.
Fuselage	1.23 × 1.08.

Engine type and h.p.	Isotta Fraschini V4 B. 160 h.p.
Airscrew, diam. and revs.	2.7 m. 1500 revs.
Weight of machine empty	900 kgs.
Load	35 kgs. per sq. m.
Weight per h.p.	8.75 kgs.
Tank capacity in hours	4 hours.
Performance.	
Speed low down	167 k.p.h.
Climb.	
To 5,000 metres in minutes	55 mins.
Total useful load	500 kgs.
Total weight of machine fully loaded	1,400 kgs.

A Single-seater Macchi-Nieuport M.5 Flying Boat.

Back view of the MACCHI-NIEUPORT, Le Rhône engine.   *Reproduced from "La Guerra," the Italian official publication.*

The Macchi-Nieuport M.9 Boat, with single rudder.

MACCHI "9."

Type of machine	Two-seater Seaplane.
Name or type No. of machine ..	M9.
Purpose for which intended ..	Scouting and Bombing.
Span	15.4 m.
Gap	2 m.
Maximum length	9.4 m.
Maximum height	3.25 m.
Chord	Upper wing, 1.8 m. ; lower wing, 1.6 m.
Total surface of wings	48.5 sq. m.
Elevator	3.50 × 0.65 m.
Rudder	1.75 × 0.70 m.
Fin	3.10 × 0.75 m.
Area of ailerons and total area ..	4.10 × 0.75 m. 6.15 sq. m.
Fuselage, horizontal and vertical	4.10 × 0.75 m.
Engine type and h.p.	Fiat. A 12 bis. 280 h.p.
Airscrew, diam. and revs. ..	2.65 m. 1600 revs.
Weight of machine empty ..	1,250 kgs.
Load per sq. m.	37 kgs.
Weight per h.p.	6.4 kgs.
Tank capacity in hours ..	4 hours
Performance.	
Speed low down	187.5 km.p.h.
Climb.	
To 5,000 m. in minutes ..	40 mins.
Total useful load	550 kgs.
Total weight of machine fully loaded	1800 kgs.

The Macchi-Nieuport Boat, with double rudder.

OFFICINE DI SAVIGLIANO.

Head offices at 23 via Genova, Turin.

One of the largest electrical engineering works in Italy, and also general constructive engineers. Undertook building of dirigible hangars and big aeroplane parts during the war. Among others, *Caproni* biplanes were constructed.

Side View of a Pomilio PC Tractor Biplane for armed reconnaissance from 1917. 260 h.p. Fiat A.12 engine, allowing about 114 m.p.h. Later models became similar but refined PDs and PEs.

P

POMILIO.

Ing. O. Pomilio & Co. Società per Costruzioni Aeronautiche, Corso Francia 366, Turin.

This was a powerful company with a capital of 5,000,000 lire.

Metal biplanes with F.I.A.T. engines were its chief concern.

Capital : Lire 5,000,000. President : Dr. Arnaldo Gussi. Manager : Sig. A. Ricordi.

The firm took a place among the foremost aeroplane builders in the country and constructed two types of pusher biplanes with F.I.A.T. engines and largely of metal. Both speed and weight-carrying powers had been attained, and a big business in war machines had been built up. A large bi-motored craft of this name was illustrated at the Military Exhibit of the Milan Aeroshow (1917). It carried some 75 sq. metres of lifting surface, and I.F. motors were fitted.

The concern is now in the hands of Gia. Ansaldo and Co., of Genova.

The Bros. Pomilio left the country during 1918 to assist the American Trade to create the enormous airfleet which was to have put the fear of the air into the heart of Germany had time permitted.

A Row of Pomilio S.P. (Savoia-Pomilio) Pusher Biplanes. S.P.s in S.P. 2, 3 and 4 versions served from 1915 onwards as reconnaissance and artillery observation biplanes. S.P. 2 version used one 260 h.p. Fiat A.12 engine to achieve 91 m.p.h. Those illustrated are probably 300 h.p. A.12 *bis*-powered S.P.3s.

S

SAVOIA.

Societa Anonima Costruzioni Aeronautiche

City Offices : 5 via Manzoni, Milan.

Works : Bovisio, Milan.

Aerodrome : Mombello, Milan.

School : Cascina Costa, Milan.

This firm claimed, before Italy joined in the war, to have the largest plant in the world, and to produce some 1,000 aeroplanes annually.

The Savoia Co. was founded sometime before the war by Signor Lorenzo Santoni, of the General Aviation Contractors Ltd., London, and has since the war developed enormously.

Farman land and seaplanes are specialised in, by exclusive concession from the inventors of these types, but other machines can be and are built when needed.

Front view of a Savoia-Farman (Maurice type), with water-cooled engine.   *Reproduced from " La Guerra," the Italian official publication.*

The first of the big foreign firms to turn over its drawings to a properly organized Italian company was the Farman Bros., and the "Savoia" was the concern to which they were entrusted, in 1913. How the work of preparing for the wholesale construction of these machines was accomplished is to be learnt from the intimate history of the last five years of Signor Lorenzo Santoni's business life, he being the mainspring of the "Savoia" as of the several satellite companies allied with it.

It is considered that the general public first awoke to the capabilities of the Farman machines when Bille came over the Alps to Milan to do acrobatics on some of the Savoias build of the type. By that time the company was on the point of leaving its first small works at Turro and about to install itself at Bovisio, where it could expand as requirements should arise. That moment, when it came, thus found the Savoia prepared.

The name of its productions tells its technical history from then till now: for all the world knows what may be told of recent Farman progress. Nor can one say more as to proportionate number of the various types of the machines constructed by the firm in these war years. Surely if 1,000 aeroplanes were built in the year before the war, this figure may have been at least tripled since then, year by year? What has been the extent of the help afforded it by the Zari Bros.—an old-established wood-working company who were called to co-operate in the Savoian progress when Bovisio became the company's home—can be imagined more perhaps than judged by those who have handled the delicate egg-shell-in-wood parts turned by Messrs. Zari: things so strong yet so delicate as to seem transparency French-polished.

Signor D. Lorenzo Santoni has had the advantage of a long experience of life abroad, in England and elsewhere, and in the early days when flying was as incredible as miracles his name was in all the newsprints.

It will be remembered that he was the first Italian to fly the Channel—from Paris too—the aeroplane being a Deperdussin with a 70 h.p. Gnôme, the year 1912.

The power of foreseeing the only right moment is undoubtedly his. He is the founder of the following list of thriving trading concerns, and of various societies and institutions for the furthering of aerial aims :—

Societa Generale Imprese Aeronautiche.

Agenzia Generale Forniture Aeronautiche. (Propellers.)

Societa Italo-Orientale Emaillite.

Societa Idrovolanti Alta Italia.

No fresh information is to hand.

SOCIETA ADRIATICA COSTRUZIONI AERONAUTICHE. At Ortona a Mare.

S.A.M.L. Societa Anonima Meccanica Lombarda, Monza, (via Cavalieri) ; Milan, via Broggi, No. 4.

This highly important firm of Military Contractors with its 4,500,000 lire of fully-paid up capital, and employing some 3,000 workmen, decided in 1913 to enter the aeroplane trade, and constructed as almost its first effort that "Amfiplane" which did as well as any of its competitors at the Military Trials of that year.

This machine was a tractor biplane with a S.C.A.T. fixed 4-cylinder motor with automatic starter.

The S.A.M.L., after the entry of Italy into the European war, devoted most of its labour to supplying aeroplanes of its own special type with complete satisfaction to those most competent to judge.

The S. A. M. L. builds a good school machine in large numbers and an *Aviatic* type, which, with Salmson motor, was at one time esteemed a very fast mount.

No fresh information is to hand.

S.I.A. (Societa Italiano Aviazione).

Works at via Nizza 15, Turin.

Flying ground at Lingotto, Turin.

Capital paid-up : Lire 5,000,000.

This title, with its Italian-Latin word-play, must not be confounded with the pre-war firm of the same initials—which produced an excellent monoplane—nor with the S.I.A. an Aero-Club much less with the S.I.A.I. (Societa Idrovolanti Alta Italia) a Savoia offshoot (vide page 397).

This, the Turin S.I.A., builds a large tractor-biplane for the F.I.A.T. engine, with which excellent heart the machine has created many records and places its ceiling some distance farther from the earth's crust than most others.

The firm's growth was abnormal—its machines were flying before the Company was constituted it is claimed—and it is now able to supply aircraft to foreign powers.

The S.I.A. biplane is a tractor type.

The upper and lower wings are united by four pairs of vertical steel struts of oval section. The upper wings are fitted with ailerons.

The fuselage is completely streamlined and consists of four longitudinal wood members with diagonal bracing and canvas covered.

A SAVOIA "HORACE" FARMAN. Three-quarter Front View.

The motor is a F.I.A.T. 300 h.p. 6 cylinders vertical with direct-mounted propeller, carried behind a honeycomb radiator and under a bonnet, as in automobile practice.

It has been officially announced that Lieut. Brach-Papa, Chief Pilot of the S.I.A., has created a new world's altitude record with passenger on a S.I.A. machine of the type illustrated.

This was the third height world's record won by this pilot in 1917. Lieut. Brach-Papa is one of the oldest Italian aeroplane testers. To his credit stands the flying test of more than a thousand machines of twenty different types.

The figures concerning this last record are the following, as issued in all the Italian daily papers :—

Machine : S.I.A. 7.B. No. 5966.

Load (Passengers and fuel) : 350 kgs. (775 lbs.).

1,000 m. in 2 mins. 30 secs.
2,000 m. „ 5 mins.
3,000 m. „ 9 mins.
4,000 m. „ 18 mins.
5,000 m. „ 24 mins.
6,500 m. „ 37 mins. 30 secs.
6,750 m. „ 1 hour 3 mins.
Ground level was .275 metres above the sea.
Height above the sea level reached : 7,025 m. (23,000 ft.).
Military Control Commission at a flying ground near Turin.
Date : 14 Dec., 1917, in the afternoon.

It may be of interest to technical readers to know that the machine was tuned before starting with the "Vibration" method recently adopted by Ingegnere Lerici (See "The Aeroplane," Nov. 7th, page 1342) in order to ensure the highest safety factor to the whole structure under such abnormal conditions of flight.

General View of a S.I.A. 7B Biplane, with F.I.A.T. A.12 *bis* engine, allowing 124 m.p.h.

THE SIA " F.B." AEROPLANE.

The S.I.A. type F.B. biplane, which Captain Laureati flew, in less than seven hours, from Turin to London, is associated with the following officially recorded performance :—

August 26th.—The height of 20,000 ft. (6,165 m.) is reached in 34 minutes with a load of 660 lb. (comprising a pilot and a passenger).

June 28th.—The height of 24,000 ft. (7,310 m.) is reached in 55 minutes, with a load of 600 lb. (pilot alone).

August 26th.—Capt. Laureati flies from Turin to Naples and back without descending, covering in 10 hours a distance of 1,000 miles (1,400 km.).

The world's height records above-mentioned were beaten by the chief pilot of the Società Sia, Lieut. Brach-Papa.

The motor of the SIA 7B reconnaissance-bomber of 1917 is the 250-300 h.p. Fiat "A12" motor, of the standard type widely employed in all the Italian machines.

The aeroplane was designed for being a " jack of all trades " type. Indeed, its carrying capacity, as well as its speed and climbing powers, enable it to be employed as a bomb-dropper as well as a racer.

The machine was built in the workshops for aeronautical construction of the Società Italiana Aviazione, commonly known as the "Sia," a sister company to the famous motor-car firm, F.I.A.T., of Turin.

The designers are the engineers, Torretta and Carlo Maurilio Lerici, of the technical staff of F.I.A.T. Co.

The initials F.I.A.T. stand for Fabbrica Italiana Automobili Torino, and the word " Fiat " in pure Latin, means " Let it Be," or " So Be it "—which, freely translated, indicates that the F.I.A.T. is undoubtedly " It." The word " Sia " in modern Italian also means " Let it be so," with a precisely similar connotation to the word " Fiat." The play on initials is ingenious.

S.I.A.I. Societa Idrovolanti Alta Italia.

Works at Sesto Calende. Offices : 12 via Silvio Pellico, Milan. Flying Water, for testing, etc., at S. Anna, Lago Maggiore. Repair Shops at Castelletto.

Exclusive F.B.A. concessionaires for Italy, and a twin firm to the Savoia.

Joining up with Cape, an old house of wood-workers on Lago Maggiore, in an incredibly short time the S.I.A.I. was able to provide F.B.As. for the defence of Venice, Lago di Garda, and elsewhere, and also to run the regular twice-daily Postal Service to Sardinia. This machine is well-known and has been amply illustrated in " La Guerra."

The Colombo Hispano Suiza and various motors have been fitted to the Company's flying-boats.

Some idea as to the size of this business is provided by the statement that fifty machines can be assembled at the same time at the S. Anna establishment.

The largest hydro-aeroplane factory in Italy, founded also by Signor Lorenzo Santoni. Has been, like the Savoia hydro-aeroplanes, largely used by the Italian Navy for the defence of the Adriatic.

SOCIETÀ INDUSTRIE AEROMARITTIME " GALLINARI." Livorno.

An old-established shipbuilding concern. During the War the firm extended its activities in various ways, and started to construct seaplanes of standard types. A site for testing these was acquired at Marina di Pisa.

FIAT-SIA.

Specification.

Type of machine ..	.. ..	Biplane.
Name or type No. of machine	..	R2.of 1918.
Purpose for which intended	..	Scouting and Bombing.
Span ..	.. ..	12.32 m.
Gap ..	.. ..	1.95 m.
Overall length ..	..	8.75 m.
Maximum height ..	..	3.30 m.
Chord ..	.. ..	1.95 m.
Total surface of wings	..	45.60 sq. m.
Span of tail ..	..	3.40 m.
Total area of tail ..	..	3.05 sq. m.
Area of elevator ..	..	2.00 sq. m.
Area of rudder ..	..	1.05 sq. m.
Area of fin ..	..	2.08 sq. m.
Maximum cross section of body		0.835 m.

Fuselage, vertical and horizontal	1.425 m.	0.835 m.
Engine type and h.p.	Fiat A12 bis.	300 h.p.
Airscrew, diam., pitch and revs..	2.80 m. 1.85 m.	1,500 revs.
Load per sq. m.	36.7 kgs.	
Weight per h.p.	5.56 kgs.	
Tank capacity in hours ..	4 hours.	
Tank capacity in kilograms ..	Petrol, 215 kg. ; Oil, 40 kg.	

Performance.

Speed at 200 metres ..	..	180 k.p.h.
Speed at 2,000 metres ..	..	165 k.p.h.
Landing speed	..	75 k.p.h.

Climb.

To 1,000 metres in minutes	..	6 mins.
To 2,000 metres in minutes	..	14 mins.
To 3,000 metres in minutes	..	23 mins.
To 4,000 metres in minutes	..	38 mins.
Total useful load ..	.. ..	.. ..	450 kgs.
Total weight of machine loaded	.. ..	1,670 kgs.

The S.I.A. Type 9B Two-seater reconnaissance-bomber (700 h.p. Fiat A.14 Engine.)

A S.I.A.I. S.8 reconnaissance and anti-submarine flying-boat, designed in 1917. 172 used by Italian Navy. 170 h.p. Isotta-Fraschini V4B engine, allowing 88 m.p.h. Two machine guns.

A S.I.A.I. S.9 FLYING BOAT of 1918. Bombing Type. Flat A.12 *bis* engine of 300 h.p. Not adopted for service.

S.I.T. Società Italiana Transaerea, Corso Peschiera 251. Turin.

This firm was founded in July, 1912, with a capital of 700,000 lire, under the Directorate of MM. Louis Blériot, Alberto Triaca, Manissero père et fils and Goria-Gatti for the construction of aircraft.

The exclusive manufacturing rights in Italy of the Blériot patents were secured, and these machines formed the greater part of the S.I.T.'s output up to the summer of 1914.

Since then the manufacture of two-deckers of the well-known type (*Voisin*) has been undertaken, and the firm's activities have been enormously extended.

Manager.—Ing. C. Momo.

Late in 1917 the business was incorporated with Gio. Ansaldo & Co., Genoa & Borzoli, ecc. ecc., and so will reap the benefit of that house's firm position in metallurgy and supplies.

The S.I.T. *Voisins* were well tried out in the early war, but then little was heard of even the greatest things. Now the habitual gets no comment.

A certain number of waterplanes issued from this company's works at one time.

S.I.T.-VOISIN III with 130 h.p. Salmson (Canton-Unné) engine.

Front View of the S.V.A.S. Primo Biplane.

S.V.A. Gio. Ansaldo & Co. Borzoli, Bolzaneto, Genoa; and Turin.

Owned by the sons of the late Comm. F. M. Perrone.

This huge engineering firm, with 100,000,000 lire of capital, has recently leapt into the aeroplane business with a record-breaking biplane and other aircraft.

Some 30,000 workpeople are employed.

Ing. G. Brezzi is in charge of the aviation department of the Perrone family's immense business, of which, too, the S.I.T. Co., of Turin, who hold the manufacturing rights of the Blériot and Voisin machines for Italy, is now a part.

The great ramifications of Gio. Ansaldo & Co. entitle the firm to be called the most important of the Allied European Nations handling aircraft.

The rapid reproduction of two types of biplanes, both very speedy, is the Company's chief concern; the S.V.A. series and the A-1 Balilla fighter. The main S.V.A.s are the S.V.A.4 reconnaissance aircraft of 1917 appearance, S.V.A.5 Primo single-seat reconnaissance-bomber, two-seat S.V.A.9 trainer and S.V.A.10 two-seat reconnaissance-bomber.

Spa motors are used on the S.V.A. machines, as the products of the Ansaldo works are named. The name Sva is apparently derived from Spa, Verduzio, Ansaldo, Spa being the engine, Verduzio the designer, and Ansaldo the manufacturers.

The firm advertise their seaplanes extensively, the features of which type are shewn in the illustration herewith.

An early S.V.A. Seaplane.

THE S.V.A. BIPLANE.

The famous engineering and shipbuilding concern, the Societa Gio Ansaldo of Genoa, is now making aircraft upon a very large scale. This firm, which is comparable in this country only with Vickers', Armstrong's, or Beardmore's, or in Germany with Krupps', is governed by the brothers Pio and Mario Perrone. These enterprising men, both of whom are but slightly past forty years of age, have shown enterprise in every department of engineering, and it is not surprising, therefore that their aeronautical products are equally original and successful.

The Ansaldo firm has incorporated the S.I.T. (Societa Italiana Transaerea, Turin) business, which holds the Blèriot and Voisin licenses for Italy, and the F.I.A.T. Saint-Georgio business for the manufacture of aero-engines at Muggiano. In addition an important aircraft works has been established at Borzoli, near Genoa, the whole establishment being raised upon green fields within eight months.

An aerodrome site was purchased about six miles from the works, the surrounding terrain being unsuited to this purpose. A number of houses were pulled down to clear the ground, and a first-class testing depot established.

Owing to the difficulty of procuring steel tube suitable for aircraft work, the firm laid down tube mills to work to make its own. And as first-class wing fabric was scarce, they installed a silk-weaving plant to make special fabric for themselves.

They then commenced to build S.V.A. 5 (Savoia-Verduzio-Ansaldo) aeroplanes, successful examples being single-seater land machines and seaplanes, whose most noteworthy feature is the use of triangularly arranged tubular interplane struts, much after the practice prevailing before the war in certain German biplanes and in the French Clement-Bayard biplane, the object in view being the elimination of unnecessary bracing cables.

On a land machine of this description the military aviator Stoppani flew from Turin to Rome in 2 hr. 50 min. This machine is regarded as a long-distance fighter, and can carry fuel for eight hours, in the course of which it will fly between 1,600 and 1,700 kilometres, which represents the distance from Rome to Paris. When some of the fuel carrying capacity is utilised for bomb loads the machine becomes a formidable raiding unit. The seaplane is a similar machine fitted with long, narrow twin floats of Howard Wright type.

Some idea of the extent of the activities of the Perrone Bros. may be judged from the fact that they employ over 60,000 workmen in their various factories, an important proportion of whom are engaged upon aircraft construction.

During 1918, the firm absorbed the O. Pomilio Aircraft Company, of Turin, mentioned elsewhere in this work.

The principal outstanding work done by S.V.A. in the war was the pacific raid of 7 machines on Vienna, a 700 mile flight done in under 7 hrs. The firm are exclusively fitting the 220

S.P.A. 6-cylinder engines. During the early part of this year most of Italy's crack pilots were flying or in expectation of flying S.V.A. machines. The famous Baracca and Serenissima escadrilles are using them exclusively.

THE S.V.A. 4 BIPLANE.

Type of machine	Single-seater Biplane.
Name or type No. of machine	S.V.A. (Savoia-Verduzio-Ansaldo).
Purpose for which intended	Single-seater reconnaissance.
Span	29 ft. 10 in.
Overall length	26 ft. 7 in.
Maximum height	10 ft. 6 in.
Engine type and h.p.	220 h.p. S.P.A. 6A (Ansaldo).
Weight of machine empty	1,900 lbs
Weight per h.p.	13.2 lbs.
Tank capacity in gallons	75 gallons.

Performance.

Speed low down	140 m.p.h.
Landing speed	45 m.p.h.

Climb.

To 20,000 feet in minutes .. 30 mins.

Total weight of machine loaded .. .. .. 2,900 lbs.

THE S.V.A. 5 BIPLANE.

Type of machine	Single-seater.
Name or type No. of machine	S.V.A. 5 Primo.
Purpose for which intended	Daylight bomber and reconnaissance.
Span	29 ft. 10 in.
Length	26 ft. 7 in.
Height	10 ft. 6 in.
Total lifting surface	261 sq. ft.
Engine type and h.p.	S.P.A. 6A 200 h.p., 6 cyl., vertical. 225 h.p. at 1700 r.p.m.
Tractor screw	Two-bladed.
Weight empty	1450 lbs.
Tank capacity in hours	6-7 hours.

Performance.

Speed at sea level	143 m.p.h.
Landing speed	45 m.p.h.

Climb.

To 10,000 feet in minutes	10 mins.
To 20,000 feet in minutes	28 mins.
Useful load with tanks full	About 450 lbs. has been flown with 650 lbs.

Total weight with tanks full and full load of bombs 2,315 lbs.

Front View of an S.V.A. Biplane

ANSALDO 1, called also the "BALILLA."

Type of machine	Single-seater Biplane.
Name or type No. of machine	Ansaldo 1—nicknamed the "Balilla."
Purpose for which intended	Hunter
Span	25 ft. 2 in.
Length	22 ft. 5 in.
Height	8 ft. 3 in.
Engine type and h.p.	S.P.A. 6A, 200 h.p., 6 cyl., Vertical. 225 h.p. at 1700 r.p.m.
Weight empty	1,823 lbs
Tank capacity in hours	About 2½ hours

Performance.

Speed	137 m.p.h.

Climb.

To 16,000 feet in minutes .. 16 minutes.

Guns fire through propeller.

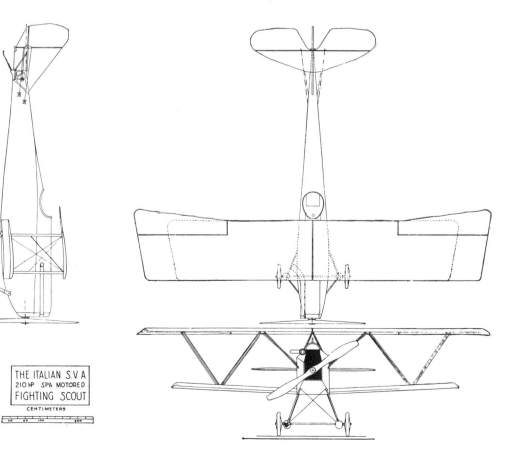

THE ITALIAN S.V.A
210 HP SPA MOTORED
FIGHTING SCOUT
CENTIMETERS

V

VICKERS. (TERNI).

This firm has made recently, a very fast small biplane, known as the *M.V.T.* (*Marchetti-Vickers-Terni*), from the names of the designer, makers and place of production.

The machine is illustrated herewith.

W

WOLSIT-JACCHIA. (LEGNANO).

This firm built a monoplane in two types and was of interest on account of the long, slender, streamlined metal body and absence of nearly all external bracing cables. The machine was also tried as a seaplane with floats, but nothing much was heard of it.

The Wolsit firm, which is allied to the British Wolseley firm, built a bigger model at a later date.

However, such being merely a side line, the war thrust all the firm's activities back into the main stream of its business, and one gathers that many machines have been caused to fly brilliantly by means of the motors flowing from Legnano.

Nothing new, in the way of information is available.

The Marchetti-Vickers-Terni (M.V.T.) biplane.

JAPANESE.

[The first section of this information, and all the photographs have been kindly provided by the Japanese Authorities.—C.G.G.]

Aerial Societies at outbreak of war :—
Teikoku Hiko Kyokai (Hibia Buildings, Kojimochikn, Tokyio).
Kikyu Kenkyu Kai (connected with War Office).

Flying Grounds :—
Oihama. (Naval.)
Tokorozawa. (Army.) Airship shed.

GENERAL MILITARY AVIATION.
This was originally formed as one body without distinction between army and navy. It was subsequently re-modelled on lines somewhat similar to the British Royal Flying Corps with naval and military wings.

NAVY.
The naval section is superintended by Capt. K. Yamaji, I.J.N. The naval headquarters are at Oihama (near Yokosuka).
The naval force in March, 1914, consisted of 10 hydro-aeroplanes (3 *Curtiss*, 2 *Deperdussin* and 5 *Farman*). The available total of qualified naval aviators was 20.

FINANCE.
The total amount granted for aviation of the navy in 1912 (fiscal year) was 100,000 yen (£10,000).
For the year 1914 the estimates amounted was 100,000 yen.

ARMY.
The army wing is responsible for the airships. It has also many aeroplanes (*M. Farman, Nieuport, Jokugawa* (Japanese Military type). *Curtiss, Grade, Bleriot, H. Farman, Rumpler*).
Japanese aeroplanes, chiefly of European make, were used extensively in the siege of Kiau-Chiau early in the war.
Since then it is known that the training of pilots has been carried on vigorously and both naval and military aviators have been produced in fair numbers.

AVIATORS.
The following have been killed :—

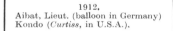

1912.
Aibat, Lieut. (balloon in Germany)
Kondo (*Curtiss*, in U.S.A.).
1913.
Kimura, Lieut.   } *Bleriot.*
Tokuda, Lieut.   }
Takeishi.
Shigematsu, Lieut. (*M. Farman*).
Ogita (*Morane-Saulnier*).

PRIVATE AVIATION.

There are some private aeroplanes being regularly flown in Japan. A number of aeroplanes have from time to time been invented by naval and military officers and private individuals, and some of them are in use. Inventors include Major Hino, naval constructors Narahara and Ushioku, Baron Iga, Baron Shigeno (who was one of the French *Spad* pilots on the Western Front) and Mr. Tsuzuki.

Mr. Yamada's non-rigid type airship was not used in the fighting off Port Arthur, as was formerly reported.

THE AIR SERVICE OF THE IMPERIAL JAPANESE NAVY.

The names of officers controlling Naval Aviation are :—
Rear-Admiral J. Matsumura, I.J.N.
Captain S. Yamanouchi, I.J.N.
Captain S. Harada, I.J.N.

Names of Flying Officers :—
Commanders :—Y. Kaneko and S. Fukuoka.
Lieut.-Commanders :—S. Kono, K. Hiramatsu, C. Yamada, and H. Wada.

A Group of Japanese Naval Air Service Officers.

Lieutenants :—M. Fujise, T. Nanba, N. Osaki, T. Iigura, K. Magoshi, J. Yamamoto, S. Nagamine, T. Kuwabara, M. Kaiya, N. Mikami, A. Beppu, M. Wada, N. Goto, T. Yashima, M Asada, T. Muroi, T. Onishi, T. Shokji, M. Sakamoto, O. Imamura, T. Shirase, M Niwa, and S. Kato.

Sub-Lieutenants :—T. Araki, M. Kani. M. Miki, S. Kira, S. Senda, T. Komaki, M. Sakamaki, Y. Kato, R. Ichinaru, J. Miyake, S. Kadowaki, K. Shirai, K. Uwano, I. Yonesawa, S. Ogura and T. Shimizu.

Engineer-Commander :—S. Yamashita.

Engineer-Lieut.-Commander :—N. Tada.

Engineer-Lieutenants :—K. Hanashima, R. Kuriuo, Y. Takeda, R. Sagisaka, J. Shoda, M. Kido, R Takahashi, K. Sasaki and T. Mogi.

Engineer-Sub-Lieutenants :—S. Kato and Y. Tajiri.

Naval Engineer :—K. Takeuchi

The Japanese Naval Flying School is the Yokosuka Flying School, Yokosuka.

The chief Naval aviation centres in Japan are Yokosuka and Sasebo.

The manufacturers of aircraft are :—

The Imperial Naval Dockyard, Yokosuka.

The Aircraft Engine Factory of the Mitsubishi Shipyard, Kobe.

The Aircraft Factory of the Kawasaki Shipyard, Kobe.

The Japanese Aircraft Factory, Ootamachi.

A Sopwith Schneider type Seaplane (110 h.p. Rotary engine) in the Japanese Naval Air Service.

[The following information is taken from " The Japan Year Book." The Japanese themselves are not anxious to provide detailed information concerning their aviation work.—ED.]

MILITARY AVIATION.

First airmen, two officers, trained in France, who returned home in 1911. There were two others in 1912 and three more in 1915 (names not given). Since then military training courses have been instituted at Tokorozawa (near Tokyo) and Kagamigahara (in Gifuken), and every year a number of young flight officers are turned out.

Decided to create new course in Fukuoka prefecture, Kyushu. Army now has 30 machines and one airship. The fleet (i.e., Air Force) will receive an expansion to make it more "decent and up-to-date."

Gen. Oshima (War Minister) explained in Diet, 1918, that 240 training machines would be built by fiscal year 1923–24. Tokyo Arsenal will be equipped with aircraft plant capable of turning out 120 machines per month (type not specified).

Seven military aviators killed, 1913 to May, 1918. Six civilian aviators killed, 1913-18. (Names not given.)

Machines in Japan mostly *Morris-Farman* and *Newbolt* monoplanes, now out of date and toys compared with Allied and U.S. type.

[Note :—" Newbolt monoplanes " are a novelty. Query *Nieuport*. *Morris-Farman* is obviously *Maurice* Farman.]

Motors are very poor, and best power output is 75 h.p. Two U.S. aviators gave exhibitions in 1916, and stunts by Art Smith showed up the ridiculous development of Japanese military types.

In 1917, Army bought five 125 h.p. biplanes in Europe (type not specified).

In 1915–16 the vote was Y400,000, and in 1916–17, Y600,000. (1916–17 programme was for construction of 30–40 machines.)

In 1918, Diet voted Y1,540,000 for Military Aviation Corps, including establishment of two new " flying battalions."

War Department projects construction of large Y7,000,000 aviation station ; Lake Riva will be the probable site.

The airship is a poor craft of 300 h.p., with maximum speed of 20 m.p.h., but for lack of money construction of modern airships has been deferred for one or two years.

Military flight officers now number about 40, which compose an Aviation Battalion (organised Dec., 1915). In Feb., 1916, Army conducted experimental flights in Manchuria " in a freezing sky."

NAVAL AVIATION.

Naval aviation dates from 1912, when officers trained in France and America came home. Shortly afterwards training ground set up at Oppama, near Yokosuka (Yokosuka is a big, fortified naval base, with navy yard, docks, shipbuilding berths, &c.—M.P.), and experiments were started in real earnest.

Naval Aviation Corps established in 1916 with a first vote of Y35,000. At the same time Y630,000 was granted as an equipment and construction Fund, to be spread over five years.

In 1918–19 fiscal year, Y1,580,000 is voted for Naval Aviation, including cost of creating two more Naval Aviation Corps at the big fleet bases at Sasebo and Kure.

The necessary equipment for Kure and Sasebo aerodromes is to be finished by end of 1819–20 fiscal year.

About 50 flight officers now.

Aviation Corps has built *Farman* machines, with " Runoux " (Renault ?) type motors.

Replying to questions in the Diet, 1918, Admiral Kato (Minister of Marine) said Naval Aviation Repletion Fund included 140 machines, to be finished by end of 1922–23 fiscal year. Five officers and one sailor have been killed up to present.

Mr. K. Yamashita, a new " ship millionaire " (query : ship-building or shipowning ?—Ed.), of Tokyo, contributed in 1918 a million yen towards aviation funds of Army *and* Navy.

A Tellier Flying Boat (200 h.p. engine) in the Japanese Naval Air Service.

A Maurice Farman Seaplane coming alongside a Seaplane Carrier.

A Short Seaplane (320 h.p. Sunbeam engine) in the Japanese Naval Air Service.

The Japanese-built Yokosuka Dockyard type Seaplane (140 h.p.)

ARMY AVIATION.

The Japanese Army has bought a few hundred latest type aeroplanes direct from the French Government recently, and now selected members of the French Aviation Mission, headed by a French Colonel, who are now in Japan, instructing Japanese Army officers. These French flyers were in the battle front, each having brought down a number of Germans, and are among the best flyers (The French Mission consists of 20 Pilots, 20 Mechanics and 5 Observation Officers).

Quite recently the Imperial Air Service has become independent, which is now under direct control of Japanese Government, and a regular aviation school has also been established at Tokorozawa, and number of others are established at different places. Maj.-General Inouye is the head of the Imperial Army Air Service and Maj.-General Arikawa is the chief commanding officer.

AVIATION SCHOOLS.

The Army flyers are first trained in Maurice Farman (Pusher Type) machines and put on Sopwiths for advance training. After finishing their full course, all acrobatic and stunt flying will be taught by expert French flyers. At present, cross-country and formation flights are made almost every day as long as weather permits.

NAVY AVIATION.

The Navy has also bought a considerable number of seaplanes from France recently and is increasing her air force very rapidly.

NUMBER AND TYPE OF MACHINES.

1. ARMY.

	Machines.
Nieuport biplane, one or two seat Le Rhône 120 h.p.	30
Spad biplane, one or two seat Hispano Suiza 200 or 150 h.p.	25
Sopwith biplane, one or two seat Clerget 130 h.p. ..	50
Salmson biplane, two or three seat Salmson 300 h.p.	5
Grahame White biplane, five seat Sunbeam 350 h.p.	2
Grahame White biplane, two seat Salmson 110 h.p.	3
Farman biplane, two or three seat Renault 70 h.p. or Curtiss 100 h.p. and Mercédès Daimler 100 h.p. (Japan make)	200
Seishiki biplane, two seat Mercédès Daimler 100 h.p.	20
Nakajima biplane, two seat Hall Scott 150 or 200 h.p.	20
Another various type	10
Total ..	365

2. NAVY.

	Machines
Farman biplane, two or three seat Renault 70 h.p. or Curtiss 100 h.p. and Salmson 120 h.p., Benz 100 h.p.	150
Short biplane, two seat Sunbeam 150 or 225 h.p. ..	50
Sopwith biplane, one or two seat Gnôme 100 h.p. and 160 h.p.	40
Curtiss Flying Boat and Biplane, Curtiss 100 h.p. ..	10
Another various type	15
Total ..	265

3. CIVILIAN.

	Machines.
Various type machines	30

AVIATORS :—

ARMY.

Tokugawa, Capt.	Katoh, Lieut.	Fujisaki, Sub-Lieut.
Satoh, ,,	Kozawa, ,,	Mori ,,
Oka, ,,	Abe ,,	Oshiba, ,,
Nagasawa, ,,	Sugada ,,	Satoh ,,
Nakazawa, Lieut.	Hishimura, ,,	Otsuka, ,,
Inoue ,,	Watanabe, ,,	Kihaya, ,,
Itoh ,,	Hattori, ,,	Konishi ,,
Sakamoto ,,	Kawabata ,,	Hideshima ,,
Naitoh ,,	Matsuoka ,,	Inoda, ,,
Kozeki, ,,	Nagafuchi, ,,	Yoshida, ,,
Makabe, ,,	Teramoto ,,	Takahashi, ,,
Nomi, ,,	Noguchi, ,,	Kondoh ,,
Mizuta, ,,	Tanaka ,,	Kojima ,,
Takeda ,,	Tatematsu ,	Yamamoto ,,
Nakada, ,,	Tani, ,,	Imamura ,,
Nakamura ,,	Kondoh ,,	Onozaki ,,
Katoh, ,,	Miyazato ,,	Sakeda, ,,
Iba, ,,	Nakaori, ,,	Kondoh ,,
Ashidate ,,	Watanabe ,,	Kawaida, ,,
Seto, ,,	Zintsu, ,,	Totsuka, ,,
Nagao ,,	Tsukikawa, Sub-Lieut.	Ooi, ,,
Tatetomi, ,,	Kawakami, ,,	Tedeshima, ,,
Kinoshita ,,	Shimoda, ,,	Aoki, ,,
Sakaguchi, ,,	Nakayama, ,,	Higuchi, ,,
Niijima ,,	Noda, ,,	Katsumi, ,,
Saitoh, ,,	Wada, ,,	Kasai, ,,
Sone ,,	Kamiya, ,,	
Mitsumura, ,,	Nagada, ,,	

Note :—Other aviators :—

	Officers	80
	Men	55
In School (during training) ..	Officers	150
	Men	80
Total .. 447 persons.		

NAVY.

Yamanouchi, Capt.	Nagamine, Lieut.	Kooji, Sub-Lieut.
Kaneko, Commander	Mikami, ,,	Araki, ,,
Umekita, ,,	Asada, ,,	Sakamoto, ,,
Yamada, Lieut-Comdr.	Kuwabara, ,,	Imamura, ,,
Wada, ,,	Yashima, ,,	Kani, ,,
Tada, ,,	Tsuda, ,,	Yamamua, ,,
Kono, ,,	Shirase, ,,	Miki, ,,
Hanashima, Lieut.	Wada, ,,	Takata, ,,
Nanba, ,,	Umitani, ,,	Mukai, ,,
Umakoshi ,,	Masuda, ,,	Shiose, ,,
Iikura, ,,	Goto, Sub-Lieut.	Katoh, ,,
Fuziki, ,,	Yamaguchi ,,	Kira, ,,
Yamamoto, ,,	Muroi, ,,	Chida, ,,
Bepu, ,,	Asada, ,,	Takeda, ,,
	Onishi, ,,	Mukai, ,,
Shimiza. Sub-Lieut.	Shirato, Sub-Lieut.	Kogami, Sub-Lieut.
Sakami, ,,	Sakakibara, ,,	Katoh, ,,
Tomioka, ,,	Ichimura, ,,	Kadowaki, ,,
Shirai, ,,	Ueno, ,,	Yonezawa, ,,

Note :—Other aviators :—

	Officers	65
	Men	50
In School (during training) ..	Officers	100
	Men	60
Total .. 331 persons.		

CIVILIAN.

Baron Shigeno	Moro	Isobe	Goto
Ozaki	Satoh	Itoh	Shirato
Yamagata	Nakajima	Mazume	Unno
Sakamoto	Tachibana	Oguri	Nakazawa
Nojima	Toteishi	Tamai	Hoshi
Inoue	Kondoh	Iimura	Fujimoto
Yoneda	Takaso	Kawakami	Fujiwara

Other aviators, 20 persons.

KILLED.

The following have been killed up to the end of August, 1919 :—

1913	Kimura, Lieut. Tokuda, Lieut. Takeishi	1919	Inouye, Capt. Yamanouchi, Lieut. Mitsui, Lieut.
1914	Shigematsu, Lieut.		Nishide Masumi, Lieut.
1915	Aoki, Lieut. Adachi, Capt. Takebe, Capt. Yanase Ogita Ohashi		Sasakibara, Lieut. Suga, Lieut. (in Italy) Iwatomi, Lieut. (in Italy) Miyake, Lieut Okada, Lieut. Suho
1916	Abe, Lieut. Tongu, Capt. Higuchi, Lieut.		
1917	Tamai Yugawa Yugawa Sugino, Lieut. Sawada, Capt. Yamamura, Lieut.		
1918	M. Sakamoto, Lieut. Takahashi, Lieut. Tobimatsu, Lieut. Sakamoto, Lieut. Yonezawa, Lieut Tomeoka, Lieut. Sasaki		

MODERN AEROPLANES.

ITOH.

Itoh Aeroplane Works. Inage, Chiba-Ken.

This machine, Sopwith "Baby" type machine, and designed fighting, and fitted with Gnôme Engine (80 or 50 h.p.).

This machine is remarkable for its small size, and range speed. It was made to loop the loop successfully under the pilotage of Mr. Yamagata, at Tokio and Inage.

Details.

Span, upper plane ..	23 ft. 8 in.
Span, lower plane ..	21 ft. 10 in.
Chord	3 ft. 9 in.
Gap	4 ft.
Length	19 ft.
Height	7 ft. 9 in.
Area (Main Wings) ..	157 sq. ft.
Weight (full load) ..	750 lbs.
Engine	Gnôme, 80 or 50 h.p.
Speed	90-100 m.p.h.

NAKAJIMA.

Japan Aeroplane Works Co., Ltd., Oota, Gunma-Ken.

One of the most successful machines made in Japan, and designed for fighting and reconnaissance, and built by Capt. Nakajima, at Japan Aeroplane Works, Oota.

This machine, two-seater biplane and fitted with Hall Scott engine (150 or 200 h.p.), and many of these machines have been supplied to the Army Air Force.

It was made to loop the loop successfully under the pilotage of Lieut. Mizuta, at Oota Aerodrome.

SEISHIKI. (Army Standard Type.)

Japan Aircraft Factory, Tokorozawa, Saitama-Ken.

SEISHIKI No. 1. (1 Go.)

This machine is a two-seater biplane, designed for reconnaissance and fitted with Mercédès Daimler engine (Japanese make). 100 h.p., and built by Lieut. Sawada, who was a famous skilful aviator in Army Air Force.

SEISHIKI No. 2. (2 Go.)

This machine was built by Lieut. Nakazawa and was fitted with Mercédès Daimler engine (Japanese make), 100 h.p. This machine's specification is as follows :—

Span, upper and lower planes ..	9.700 m.
Length	6.700 m.
Chord	1.500 m.
Weight (full load)	850 kg.
Speed	85 m.p.h.

SOGA GO.

Imperial Aero Club, Tokoroazwa, Saitama-Ken.

This machine is a two-seater biplane, designed for reconnaissance, fitted with Austro-Daimler engine, 90 h.p., and built by Mr. Ozaki, who was the most famous civilian aviator in Japan.

TSURUGI GO.

Kishi Aeroplane Works, Akabane, near Tokio.

This manufactory made two types of machines, one of Farman type, two-seater machine; and another, tractor biplane, both fitted with 100 or 150 h.p. Kishi engine (self-made).

MEXICAN.

Aviation Works :—

Military Aviation Factory, Valbuena. Director : Sr. Francisco Santarini. Founded, November, 1915.

The factory is equipped with thoroughly modern machinery and produces training and fighting aeroplanes of its own design.

The engine shop produces a Mexican Anzani type engine, called Aztatl, which is used on the later training machines.

The fighting machines are equipped with Hispano-Suiza engines, production of which will begin in 1918 at Valbuena. Machinery for this purpose appears to have been imported from Spain.

The factory also builds a national type of airscrew, called Anàhuac.

The Government Aircraft Factory is constructing a new monoplane, fitted with the 80 h.p. Aztatl engine. A new engine, called S.S. Mexico, and rated 130 h.p. is also being developed.

AVIATORS.

1912. Salinas, Alberto (Ae. C. A., 170).
       Salinas, Gustavo (Ae. C. A., 172).
       Ruiz, Horacio (Ae. C. A., 182).
       Aldasoro, Juan Pablo (Ae. C. A., 217).
       Aldasoro, Eduardo (Ae. C. A., 218).
1918. Rojas, Samuel C. (Mex. Mil. Cert. No. 1.)

MILITARY AVIATION.

Mexico enjoys the distinction of being the first country to have employed aeroplanes in actual warfare. During the Constitucionalista campaigns against the Diaz *régime,* and, later, against the Villista uprising, a motley assortment of aeroplanes was purchased in the United States and American aviators were engaged to fly them. Four Mexican officers and one civilian were also sent to the United States for training as aviators.

In spite of the questionable quality of the flying *matériel* thus gathered, and the not less doubtful military value of aerial mercenaries, the small Constitucionalista Flying Corps proved quite useful in sundry patrol and reconnaissance work, particularly in the suppression of the Villista guerilla forces.

With the stabilisation of the Constitucionalista regime, the American aviators were discharged and steps were taken to establish a regular Flying Corps.

In 1915, at the instance of Major Alberto Salinas, Mexico's first military aviator and a nephew of President Carranza, an Aviation Department was created in the Mexican War Office, and a military aerodrome and flying school were organised at Valbuena, near Mexico City.

Owing to the difficulty of obtaining a satisfactory type of training machine from Europe, owing also to the then strained relations with the United States, it was at the same time decided to begin the construction of national aeroplanes and thus create an indigenous source of supply.

A group of Mexican Army Pilots, together with Capt. Guillermo Villasana, the Chief of the Technical Department of the Military Aircraft Factory.

A group of Mexican Military Pilots,

The Superintendent of the Government Aircraft Factory, Senor Santarini, with a Mexican pilot and one of the Mexican-built Anzani engines, known as the Aztatl.

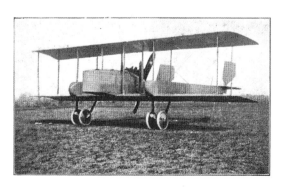

Two Views of a Mexican-built Twin-fuselage Biplane.

An aeroplane factory was organised at Valbuena, and there Blériot and Morane-Saulnier type machines were built and fitted with such aero-engines as had survived the revolutionary campaigns or could be obtained elsewhere.

A number of tractor biplanes were also built, and eventually the factory produced a satisfactory type of airscrew, the Anahuac, and an Anzani type engine, called Aztatl.

In 1917 an arrangement was made with the Hispano-Suiza Co., of Barcelona, whereby the manufacturing rights of their engines were acquired, and the equipment and organisation of a Mexican aero-engine factory was apparently entrusted to Spanish engineers.

In February, 1918, the Military Aviation Factory produced to the designs of its director, Senor Francisco Santarini, and Captain Guillermo Villasana, Chief of the Technical Department, a one-seater fighting-scout fitted with a 150 h.p. Hispano-Suiza engine. The characteristics of this machine, which is officially termed a *Microplano*, are the following :—

Specification.

Type of machine	Mexican Scout Biplane
Name or type No. of Machine .	Microplane Veloz.
Purpose for which intended ..	Single-seater Fighter.
Overall span, upper plane ..	8.00 metres.
Span of lower plane ..	6.88 metres.
Surface area	18 sq. metres.
Interplane gap	1.5 metres.
Overall length	6.60 metres.
Maximum height.. ..	2.55 metres.
Speed, horizontal.. ..	190-220 km.p.h.
Area of elevators ..	1.73 sq. metres.
Area of rudder	.76 sq. metres.
Gross weight	650 kgs.
Net weight	460 kgs.
Useful load	190 kgs.
Engine type and h.p. ..	Hispano-Suiza; 150-160 h.p.
Airscrew, revs.	Anahuac

The Mexican "Microplano Veloz."

Various other types have been constructed, including the training machine described in the following specification :—

MEXICAN GOVERNMENT TWO-SEATER BIPLANE.

(Constructed in the Mexican National Aeronautical Workshops.)

Type of machine..	Mexican Two-seater Biplane
Name or type No. of machine..	Series A.
Purpose for which intended ..	General purposes.
Span	10.15 metres.
Total surface of wings	35.2 sq. metres.
Engine type and h.p.	"Aztatl" 6-cyl. Radial; 80 h.p.
Load per sq. metre	18.76 kgs.
Weight per h.p...	8.2 kgs.
Tank capacity in hours.. ..	40 litres petrol; 20 litres oil.
Performance.	
Speed low down	90 k.p.h.
Disposable load apart from fuel	140 kgs.
Total weight of machine loaded	520 kgs.

The Government-built "Microplano."

A Mexican-built Monoplane.

Group of Mexican Service Machines.

NORWEGIAN.

Aeronautical Journals :—
  Aeroplanet, 6, Kongensgaten, Christiania.

THE NORWEGIAN ARMY FLYING CORPS.

Inspector General :—Colonel G. Grüner.

Staff officer :—Captain H. Norby.

Director of the army aeroplane factory :—Captain E. Sem-Jacobsen.

Assistant officers :—Pr. lieutnant Th. Gulliksen and O. Seippel.

Engine-engineer :—Captain T. Klingenberg.

Chief of the central flying schools :—Pr. Lieut. A. Tellefsen.

Chief pilot :—Pr. lieutnant H. Crawfurd-Jensen.

Chief of Sonnenfjellske squadron :—Captain T. Vetlesen.

Flight commanders :—Pr. lieutnants G. Gottenborg and T. Ibsen.

Chief of Nordenfjellske squadron :—Pr. lieutnant G. Bull.

Chief of Nord-Norges squadron :—Pr. lieutnant E. Haganæs.

Flying officers :—Pr. lieutnants A. Berghoff, E. Boe, K. Sundby, L. Feiring, Chr. Hellesen, Sec. lieutnants E. Herseth. E. D. Meyer, and I. A. Brandt.

AVIATION CENTRES.

Kjeller aerodrome.

Værnes flying ground.

Ovrevand flying ground.

Kjeller aerodrome is situated near Lillestrom (20 km. from the capital, Christiania). This place is the centre of all flying with aeroplanes. Here are the Flying Schools, Sennenfjellske Squadron, and the Army Aeroplane Factory.

Værnes, the flying ground of Nordenfjellske, is situated 20 km. from Trondhjem, near the railway station, Stjordalen.

Ovrevand, the flying ground of Nord-Norges Squadron is situated in Salangen, near the town Harstad.

MANUFACTURERS OF AIRCRAFT.

1. The Army Aeroplane Factory (hærens flyvemaskinfabrik), Kjeller pr. Lillestrom.

2. The Navy Seaplane Factory (marinens flyvebaatfabrik), Horten.

3. A/S. Norsk Aeroplanfabrik, Chr. Hellesen, Tansberg.

FLYING SCHOOLS.

The Army Flying School (hærens flyvevesens skoler), Kjeller pr. Lillestrom.

The Navy Flying School, (marinens flyveskoler), Horten.

The latest organisation of the Army Flying Corps is dated from February, 1917.

COMMERCIAL AVIATION.

1918 saw the formation of the first three Norwegian aircraft enterprises—first, the Nordisk Luftkraft A/S, which arranged the first Scandinavian aero exhibition in Christiania, 1918, and an emergency aerial mail by Lieut. Riiser-Larsen on a Thulin-built Morane monoplane, when the railway service was interrupted by embankment slip.

Secondly, the Norwegian Air Shipping Co., to which the public has been asked to subscribe in small shares, and of which Capt. Dehli, of the Navy, is technical director. So far nothing has been done, but the company will make its chief aim the establishment of national aerial lines, owing to the limits placed upon railway lines on account of the mountainous character of the country ; and, further, will run a North Sea line to Great Britain, and, together with Swedish and Danish firms, a line to Gothenburg and Copenhagen.

The third enterprise is the Norwegian Aeroplane Works, Ltd., in Orsnes per Tonsberg, formed on June 4th, 1918, with a stock capital of towards £30,000. No aircraft have been turned out yet, but scale drawings are shown of a number of contemplated designs. Repairs of automobiles, motors, and boats are undertaken.

MILITARY AND NAVAL AVIATION.

Being the last of the three Scandinavian countries to enter upon aviation activities, Norway leads at present, which fact it owes chiefly to its good connections with England, wherefrom it has during the years of war been successful in drawing equipment, even if not of the very latest active service mounts.

As has been the case, too, in Sweden and Norway, like even the Allied warfaring countries, Henry and Maurice Farman biplanes made the chief composition of both the Army and the Naval Flying Services, both before and while expanding early in the war.

The chief naval air station is by the Royal Dock yard in Horten, and other stations are along the coasts of the North Sea and Skager Rak, like Christiansand, while the main Army flying ground is at Lillestrom, near Christiania.

The respective Government factories are at each of the two centres, under the command of Captain Dehli (Navy), and Captain Sem-Jacobsen (Army), the same officers commanding formerly the flying services. Colonel Grüner is now chief of the Army Corps.

The Army factory has built both Henry and Maurice Farman Longhorn and "Horace" Farman models, for which the Frederiksstad Mechanical Works produced 130 h.p. Renault motors. While of advanced types monocoque scouts with snow-skates for winter flying, equipped with 150 h.p. Hispano-Suiza engines, that were fetched early from Spain, and a two-seater patrol biplane of British influenced outlines and powered by a R.A.F. motor, have been produced. B.E. and Avro biplanes have further been acquired in England.

The Navy long stuck to a twin-float Farman type pusher biplane with F.E. tail fin fashion, equipped first with Curtiss motors, and next with some 170 h.p. Sunbeam engines, obtained from England. Various Naval flying officers, like Lieuts. Lützow-Holm and Rüser-Lassen were allowed to undergo a war instruction course at a British Naval flying school, and some 130 h.p. Clerget-engined Sopwith "Baby" seaplanes were acquired.

Nielsen and Winther, in Copenhagen, built a tractor school seaplane for the Norwegian Naval Air Service, equipped with a 100 h.p. Swedish-built Scania-Vabis Mercédès motor.

Monocoque-bodied Biplane (150 h.p. Hispano-Suiza engine). Built at the Norwegian Army Aircraft Factory, and fitted with ski for use on snow.

PERUVIAN.

MILITARY AEROPLANES.

The Peruvian Government has made a special grant for aviation students, and war machines are projected. Actual order to end of 1912 was one Avro aeroplane, which was not delivered.

MILITARY AVIATION.

The creation of a fifth arm of the Army is seriously contemplated, and although no flying material is presently available, two Peruvian Army officers, 2nd Lieut. Henrique Ruiz and Aspirant Guillerme Proetgel, were sent in 1917 to El Palomar, the Argentine military flying school, wherefrom they successfully graduated.

PORTUGUESE.

Aerial Societies :—
 Ae C. de Portugal (Praça dos Restoradores, 16, Lisbon.

The Portuguese flying service has its earliest roots in 1912, when an agitation in favour of providing the Army with aeroplanes resulted in the subscription by the public of fairly large sums for the purchase of aeroplanes, and a Maurice Farman, a Voisin, and an Avro were actually purchased during that year. Either because the particular political crisis which the agitation for aircraft was intended to conceal was successfully tided over—or for some other reason of State—nothing beyond these purchases and the drawing up of various schemes for a national flying school occurred at that time.

From information contained in "Revista Aeronautica," the official organ of the Aero Club of Portugal, it appears that early in 1916 the proposed flying school was actually inaugurated.

Apparently, the proposals which were drawn up in 1912 by Mr. H. V. Roe, on his visit with the Avro biplane, delivered to the Portuguese Government after tests by the late Mr. Copland Perry, have been to a large extent followed, and the school has started operations on the site recommended by him.

The position—if this is indeed the case—is very nearly ideal, considering the mountainous nature of the country, providing a very large natural aerodrome—a long frontage on to an excellent stretch of water for seaplanes' work. In addition, there is direct railway and water communication with Lisbon.

Previous to the inauguration of the school, a number of officers were sent to France and England to learn to fly.

Of these, Lieut. José Barbosa de Santos Leite, of the Army, and Lieut. Artur de Sacadura Freire Cabral, of the Navy, and Senor Antonio Joaquin Caseiro, a non-executive Naval officer, proceeded to Chartres, in November, 1915.

All these obtained their pilot's certificates by March of 1916, and then proceeded to qualify for their military brevet at various French Army Schools.

Three Army officers, Senors A. Torres, A. Maia, and A. Portela, qualified for their civil brevets at the Ruffy-Baumann School, at Hendon, during June and July, 1916, and qualified as military pilots at one of the R.F.C. schools.

It may be presumed that these officers now form the instructional staff at the Portuguese flying school.

As to the actual organisation of the school, very little can be discovered. "Revista Aeronautica" contains pages of regulations for the conduct of the school, but they are all of the nature of "King's Regulations" of very considerable importance actually, but of very little general interest.

Aerial Journals :—
 Rivista Aeronautica (Ae. C. Journal).

Flying Grounds :—
 Campo do Seigcal. (Military School, 6 hangars.)
 Mounchavo de Pavoa. (Private, 5 hangars.)

The Chief Portuguese Flying School at Villa Nuova della Reinha.

Provision is made in these regulations for training aeroplane pilots, airship pilots, and free balloon pilots, and their appropriate observers, and also for mechanics of all grades.

A commission has been sent to the Higher School of Aeronautics at Lausanne—which may be considered as an aeronautical university—and it may be assumed that this commission has as its object the institution of a fairly thorough course of theoretical training, and it may be fairly safely expected that the technical side of the instruction will be so extremely complete.

At the same time, considering the large number of extremely good horsemen to be found among Portuguese officers, it may be expected that at least a fair proportion of excellent pilots should be turned out.

"Revista Aeronautica," of Lisbon, states further :—
Four officers in training for military pilots were sent to the United States in 1915, to attend the Signal Corps Aviation School in S. Diego, California, but when Portugal declared war, they could no longer be trained in the States, so returned to Europe, finishing their instruction at the Chartres School. All of them obtained their certificates between September and December, 1916, and went on to the Caudron School, at Juvisy, where three of them obtained the School certificate in February, 1917, the fourth having been recalled to the Lisbon War Ministry for organisation work.

A fifth officer took the Caudron courses, which included training in artillery reconnaissance, chasing, fighting, and aerial acrobatics. These officers were from artillery, cavalry, and infantry units.

ROUMANIAN.

Army Aeroplanes.

At end of March, 1915, there were numerous *Bristols*, *Bleriots*, *Nieuports*, *Moranes*, and *Farmans*. The Government school was at Bucharest.

Roumania was, before the war, the only Balkan state possessing an organised Flying Corps, and also able to man it. The Roumanian officers make very fine fliers.

M. Coanda, son of the former Minister for War in Roumania, is one of the most gifted aeroplane designers, and was for some years chief designer of the famous *Bristol* aeroplanes. During the war he has been doing valuable work in France.

When Roumania came into the war it was found that the aeroplanes in possession of the Flying Service were seriously out of date. *Bleriots* of the obsolete side-by-side "fish-tail" type of 1911 were actually put into service, as shown by the accompanying illustration of such a machine with the war identification marks painted thereon, and by the early type *Nieuport* wings in the back-ground.

Just before the fall of Bucharest a number of British aeroplanes manned by R.N.A S. pilots and observers flew from Salonika to Roumania, covering 250 miles of hostile territory in doing so. These machines did good service with the Roumanian Army till worn out by sheer hard work and lack of facilities for repair. Before becoming unfit for service themselves, they reduced somewhat the number of German aeroplanes opposed to them.

VLAICU Monoplane. Designed by Ouvret Vlaicu. First shewn at the Vienna Exhibition, 1911. Modified; it flew very well indeed at Aspern, June, 1912. The 1912 model is of entirely novel type, a tail first monoplane with a propeller either end of the main planes, and a triangular tail aft. Principal details are:—**Length,** 34¾ feet (10·50 m.) **Span,** 30 feet (9·15 m.) **Height,** 12 feet (3·65 m.) Wing frame in three sections with gap between. **Motor,** 50 h.p. Gnome, chain driven. **Fuselage,** old style; landing chassis on three wheels only, with a single ash skid in front. Covered-in engine driving the 31 foot propeller shaft for the 2 propellers. Rear tail consists of 2 fixed planes, a triangular damping plane and a triangular keel plane. Forward an elevator and two semi-circular rudders (double faced). From this combination remarkable results are achieved, and all gyrostatic effect from the propellers eliminated. *Control*, horizontal wheel on column. Elevator depressed or otherwise by action on column. *Note.*—At Vienna, 1912, this machine took first prize for the smallest circle and also for accurate bomb-dropping. The original machine was purchased by the Roumanian Army.

M. Vlaicu was killed in 1913 while flying, and the type has got no further. Two *Farmans* are understood to have been delivered during 1915. (*Maurice* type).

A 1911-12 type BLÉRIOT, bearing war identification marks. An old type *Nieuport* wing, similarly marked, may be seen in the background.

RUSSIAN.

ARMY AVIATION.

Early in 1912, under the presidency of the Grand Duke Alexander, the special school of the Volunteer Aerial Association was finally formed at Sevastopol for the winter and Gatchina for the summer.

June, 1912. Vote of 150 aeroplanes (140 to be built at home). Vote 1,050,000 roubles for new school at Tauride.

November, 1912. Military trials results. (1) Sikorsky in a *Sikorsky*. (2) Haber in a *M. Farman*. (3) Boutmy in a *Nieuport*.

December, 1912. Aeronautical school re-organised. Put under control of one commandant, one assistant, and four juniors. Course made seven months—15 pupils per school at a time. A one month course in aeroplanes, aerial motors, etc. Of the pupils, 10 to be selected for aeroplanes. New flying School established at Tashkend in Turkestan.

March, 1913. New schools established at Moscow, Odessa and Omsk.

At the end of 1913 the total number of machines was about 250, of which about 150 were modern. Principal types : *Albatros, Aviatik, Bristol, Deperdussin, Farman, Nieuport, Rumpler,* there being an average of 20 of each. The majority built under Russian license in Russia. The number of actual military pilots was 72. There was, however, a special volunteer corps of about 36 private aviators, bringing the available total to 108 or thereabouts. In August, 1914, the situation was about the same, except that a few *Sikorskis* had been added. Most other machines were old, and more or less worn out, the effectives did not exceed 50 or so, if that. Aviation was not taken seriously. The *Sikorskis* were still in the "freak stage." In the strict sense of the word Russia did not possess any aerial fleet worthy of the name.

A Russian officer, Lieut. Nestoroff, was actually the first aviator to "loop the loop," doing so on a *Nieuport* monoplane, some months before the Frenchman Pégoud. For this action he was charged with endangering military property and placed under arrest for a month.

NAVY AVIATION.

July, 1912. Lieut. Andreadi, 50 h.p. *Nieuport,* did a flight with stops from Sevastopol to Petersburg.

September, 1912. Special naval aerodrome for hydro-avions ordered for Golodai Island, near Petersburg, bringing total of military and naval aerodromes to 6. *Sikorsky* hydro-avion acquired. Also an *M. Farman* ditto. New naval station projected at Libau.

October, 1912. Naval purchase of several *Curtiss* hydro-avions after trials at Sevastopol.

One of the Four-engined Sikorsky Ilya Mourometz heavy bombers that served so well from 1915. Type B used four Salmson-Canton-Unné radials of 200 h.p. and 135 h.p. (two each), weighed 10,580 lb. could carry 1,102 lb. of bombs. and flew at 60 miles per hour.

Towards the middle of 1914, the approximate effective force was as follows (all hydros. or capable of being so fitted) : 1 *Astra,* 1 *Breguet,* 2 *Donnet-Leveque,* 1 *Farman,* about a dozen *Curtiss,* 2 *Nieuport* (50 h.p.), 1 *Sikorsky.* (A number of others on order.)

At the outbreak of war there were about 50 effective seaplanes mostly of Curtiss make.

GENERAL.

No exact details are available as to progress since the outbreak of war; but it appears to have been considerable. An air service cannot be extemporised at short notice, and constructional facilities in Russia depended on imports of parts which were automatically cut off by the war. Great efforts were made to overcome difficulties. The few aircraft factories worked with commendable energy. Great numbers of land-going aeroplanes and seaplanes were imported from France and America, chiefly the latter via the trans-Siberian railway, so towards the end of 1915, the Russian flying services by land and sea, were by no means badly equipped for their size, but their said size was only enough for quite a small army and navy.

During 1916 and early 1917 the Russian aviators did their best under difficult circumstances. The strain on the Russian roads and railways in feeding the nation's vast armies made the supply of aircraft parts more and more difficult, and consequently worn out aeroplanes and engines were almost impossible to replace.

Russian official reports of German aeroplanes flying a hundred miles or so behind the Russian lines indicated sufficiently clearly the deficiency in the Russian "destroyer" force, and the prominence given in Russian communiqués to single actions of Russian aviators indicate also that there could have been but few well-mounted aviators in the Russian service.

Three officers of the late Imperial Russian Flying Service, accompanied by a French officer.

ALL THIS INFORMATION IS MERELY OF HISTORICAL VALUE, FOR SINCE THE DEPOSITION OF HIS IMPERIAL MAJESTY THE TSAR BY HIS REBELLIOUS SUBJECTS, RUSSIA HAS CEASED TO EXIST. THE BOLSHEVIK ARMIES APPARENTLY POSSESS A FEW AIRCRAFT MANNED AND MAINTAINED BY TRAITORS TO THEIR EMPEROR. THE COUNTER-REVOLUTIONARY ARMIES OF ADMIRAL KOLTCHAK AND GENERAL DENIKIN ARE SUPPLIED WITH AIRCRAFT BY THE ALLIES.

SERVIA.

MILITARY AVIATION.

At the outbreak of war there were about a dozen aeroplanes, mainly obsolete. Since then some modern machines were acquired. Servia did not build, and the war stopped all importation, the machines—imported—having been required elsewhere. A few French aviators were lent, with their machines, to Servia early in the war, among them being MM. Paulhan and Martinet, two of the very earliest French pilots.

After the conquest of Servia, the Servian troops who escaped, and were afterwards re-organised by the Allies in Greece, were equipped with a flying service of their own. This was manned by Servian officers and supplied with French aeroplanes.

Some of these officers, who were taught to fly chiefly by pilots of the late R.N.A.S., did quite good work during the defeat of the Bulgarians and Austrians, but on the whole it appears that the Balkan Slav had not the makings of an aviator nor of an aeroplane or aero-engine mechanic.

A SIAMESE BRÉGUET BIPLANE, used for training.

SIAM.

THE AVIATION SERVICE OF THE ROYAL SIAMESE ARMY.

[The Editor desires to express his indebtedness to Lieut-Colonel Prince Amoradhat, Military Attaché, the Siamese Legation, for the following notes and photographs.]

The Ministry of War having decided in 1911 to adopt aviation for use in the Army, three Officers of the Royal Engineers were selected and sent to France in order to study aviation. These three Officers began their flying instruction in July, 1912, at Villa Coublay, near Paris, and by the following October 22nd Major Luang Sakdi Salyavudh obtained his certificate as a qualified aviator of the French Aero Club, on a Bréguet machine. In May, 1913, Lieutenant Thip obtained his certificate, on a Nieuport, whilst Captain Luang Avudh Sikikorn received his certificate on a similar machine on June 30th of the same year.

Major Luang Sakdi then qualified and obtained the "Brevét d'Aviateur Militaire Française" on the 18th August, 1913.

Having qualified as pilots, all three officers returned to Siam in September, 1913, taking back with them several Nieuport monoplanes and one Bréguet biplane, making their début in flying in Siam in December, 1913.

In April, 1914, His Majesty the King presented to the Army a 100 h.p. Bréguet biplane, which had been offered by Chao Phya Abhai Phubesr as a gift.

Having seen the practical use of aeroplanes and convinced of the great service it could render to the Army, H.R.H. the Prince of Piscnoulok, Chief of the General Staff, decided to form a Flying Corps, which was officially organised on the 23rd March, 1914, officers of the Army being admitted as candidates for the Aviation Service.

A NIEUPORT-TYPE MONOPLANE, built in Siam.

THE ARMY AVIATION CORPS.

The Corps is under the direction of the Inspector General of Royal Engineers, and draws its recruits by voluntary service from officers and men in the Army.

Those who have obtained their certificates as pilots may either be appointed Chief Pilots or are retained for service with the Flying Corps for not more than one year. The latter must then join their former units, returning to the Flying Corps every six months for one month's training.

At present the Corps Aviation School has trained about twenty-five pilots, all of whom are officers, with the exception of ten non-commissioned officers.

The Corps Aviation School and Headquarters is situated at Dorn Muang, a little north of Bangkok, where hangars and workshops have been constructed.

Editorial Note.

During 1916 and 1917 the Siamese aviation corps has taken part in Army Manœuvres and has done good work. As the result of Siam's joining in the war, an aviation contingent composed entirely of volunteers was sent to France, but so far as can be gathered their training for active service was not completed before the Armistice befell.

Officers and Men of the Siamese Royal Flying Corps.

SPANISH.

(By Captain Don Emilio Herrera Linares.)

Aerial Societies:—

Real Aëro Club de España (Carrera de San Jeronimo, 8, Madrid).
Asociacion de Locomocion Aérea (20, Cataluna Sq., Barcelona).
Real Aero Club de Barcelona.
   ,,   ,,   de San Sebastian.
   ,,   ,,   de Santander.
   ..   ..   de Granada.

Aerial Journals:—

Boletin Oficial de la Asociacion de Locomocion Aérea, 20, Cataluna Sq., Barcelona (monthly).
España Automovil, 5, Isabel II Sq., Madrid. Official Organ, Spanish R. Ae. C.
Revista de Locomocion Aerea, 20, Cataluna Sq., Barcelona (monthly).
Heraldo Deportivo, Villalar, 1, Madrid.

The Spanish Royal Flying Service.—A group of the chief aviation officers at a Spanish aerodrome, with a number of " Flecha " type Spanish-built biplanes lined up ready to start.

THE SPANISH AERONAUTICAL SERVICES.

By courtesy of Colonel Señor Don Julio Rodrigeuz Mourelo, formerly Director of Air Services, it is possible to publish the following particulars of the development of the Spanish Flying Services, and the Editor expresses his indebtedness to Captain Don Emilio Herrera Linares, Officer Commanding the Aerodrome of Cuatro Vientos, for sending the information by permission of Colonel Rodriguery.

The Servicio de Aeronautica Militar is commanded by a Colonel-Director and a Second Chief, and has two wings; the Aerostacion Wing, which is concerned with captive and free balloons and airships, and the Aviacion Wing, which is concerned with aeroplanes and hydro-aeroplanes. Both wings are commanded by Comandantes (Majors).

The Parque de Aerostacion (Balloon Yard) is at Guadalajara, and the Aerodromo Central de Aviacion (Main Military Aerodrome) is at Cuatro Vientos (Madrid).

There are five squadrons of land machines in Spain (Madrid, Alcalà, Sevilla, Guadalajara and Cartagena), and one of seaplanes at Cartagena.

In the Spanish part of Morocco are three squadrons (Melilla, Tetouan and Arcila).

THE CHIEFS OF SERVICES.

The following are the Chiefs of the various Aeronautical Services :—

Director of the Air Service : Colonel Senor Don Rafael Moreno y Gil de Borja (Engineers).

Second Chief of the Service : Lieut.-Col. Don Vicente Garcia Del Campo (Engineers).

Chief of Detail of Aerostacion : Lieut.-Col. Don Francisco de Paula Rojas y Rubio (Engineers).

Chief of Aerostacion : Major Don Celestino Garcia Antunez (Engineers).

Chief of Aviacion : Major Don Alfonso Bayo Lucia (Staff).

Chief of Detail of Aviacion : Major Don Carlos Alonso Ilera (Infantry).

Inspector of Aviation Works : Major Don Aristides Fernandez Mathews (Engineers).

Instructor of Observers' School : Staff Major Don Luis Gonzalo Victoria.

CHIEF INSTRUCTORS.

Captain of Engineers, Don Emilio Herrera Linares (Commanding at Cuatro Vientos).

Captain of Infantry, Don Julio Rios Angueso.

Captain of Cavalry, Don Luis Riaño Herrero.

Doctor on Staff, Don Antonio Perez Nuñez.

Lieutenant of Cavalry, Don Angel Martinez de Baños.

Lieutenant of Cavalry, Don Jésus Varela Castro.

THE SPANISH AERODROME.

The following is a list of the Chief Spanish Aerodromes, together with the rank and names of the officers commanding :—

Cuatro Vientos.—Captain of Engineers, Don Emilio Herrera Linares.

Guadalajara.—Major of Engineers, Don Gonzalo Zamora Andreu.

Jetafe (New).—Captain of Infantry, Don Julio Rios Angueso.

Los Alcaceres (Cartagena).—Captain of Infantry, Don José Valencia Fernandez.

Sevilla (New).—Captain of Engineers, Don Alberto Alvarez Rementeria.

The following are the aerodromes in Africa, with their Commanding Officers :

Arcila.—Naval Lieut., Don Pedro Pablo Hernandez.

Tetuan.—Captain of Engineers, Don Emilio Baquera Ruiz.

Zeluan.—Staff Captain, Don José Aymaz.

SPANISH FLYING SCHOOLS

Military School of Aviation.—Cuatro Venitos (Madrid).

National School of Aviation.—Getafe (Madrid).

The Director of the National School of Aviation is Don Alfredo Kindelan Duany.

Civil School of Barcelona.—Pujol y Comabella y Co.

Civilian School also at Santander and Jetafe.

There is also the Aerodrome of the Sociedad Ispañola de Construcciones Aeronauticas at Santander.

MILITARY AEROPLANE.

Various types of Spanish military aeroplanes are published here.

A new fighting machine, called the "Espana," has been evolved. It is not yet permissible to illustrate it.

THE SPANISH AERONAUTICAL INDUSTRY.

The chief manufacturers of aircraft are : Garde y Escoriaza, at Zaragoza ; Pujol y Comabella, at Barcelona ; Sociedad Española de construcciones Aeronauticas, at Santander ; La Hispano-Suiza, at Barcelona (motors) ; Elizalde, at Barcelona (motors) ; Baradal y Ereter, at Barcelona (motors) ; and Amalio Diaz, at Getafe (propellers).

A German KONDOR Taube monoplane in the Spanish Service.

A Spanish military experimental biplane, known as the " Flêcha " type, on generally German lines, but with an original landing gear.

A Spanish military experimental biplane, known as the " W " type, combining a generally German design with apparently a Curtiss engine and radiator and a novel landing gear.

A Spanish-built " Parasol " monoplane, on Morane-Saulnier lines.

A Vendôme Monoplane, used for School Work in the Spanish Army.

Three-quarter Front View of a SPANISH-BUILT SAULNIER BIPLANE, with Hispano-Suiza engine.

A Spanish-built Biplane, apparently a combination of the " Flécha " type with Curtiss influence.   Built by the Spanish Flying Service.

A Spanish military experimental biplane, known as the " Delta " type, combining some Nieuport characteristics with German wing arrangement and curious fins above, which are designed for experiments in lateral stability.

SWEDISH.

CHIEF AVIATION CENTRES IN SWEDEN.

Malmslatt : Military aviation grounds, sheds, works, etc.
Ljungbyhed : Civil aviation grounds, sheds, works, etc.
Furusund : Civil aviation school in the winter, sheds, etc.

SWEDISH FLYING SCHOOLS.

Thulins flying school, Ljungbyhed.
Northern Aviatic Company's flying school, Furusund by Stockholm.

MANUFACTURERS OF AIRCRAFT.

Thulin Aeroplane Manufacturing Company, Ltd., Landskrona.
Northern Aviatic Company, Ltd., Tellusborg, Midsommar-kransen by Stockholm.
Palsons' Aeroplane Manufacturing Company, Ltd., Malmö.

MILITARY AND NAVAL AEROPLANES.

The Army possesses an unknown number of *Albatros*, *Morane* and *Thulin* aeroplanes.

The Navy possesses an unknown number of *Morane* and *Thulin* seaplanes.

The Committee for the Air Defence of Stockholm has six original *Albatros* scouts, which are in case of need to be flown by voluntary civil aviators of yearly training.

Further private aeroplanes are in the possession of the Thulin Flying School at Ljungby Heath (a dozen *Bleriot* and *Morane*, ordinary type, and *Parasol* monoplanes) and of the school of the Northern Aircraft Co., by Stockholm (two *Albatros* biplanes with snowskates for training on ice during the winter, and converted to seaplanes for summer training.)

PERSONAL NOTES ON THE CHIEF MEN CONCERNED WITH THE DEVELOPMENT OF AVIATION IN SWEDEN.

The first aviator in Sweden was Baron Carl Cederström, who took his certificate at the Blériot school at Pau in 1910. When coming back to Sweden, he made a lot of show and exhibition flights at nearly every great place in the country, as well as in certain places in Norway, and did a lot of work to wake the people up to understanding the possibilities of aviation. Being a director of a large automobile concern, he also at once grasped the commercial and business side of the aeroplane movement.

For a long time he was the manager of the aeroplane department of Södertelge Verkstäder, a concern which has now ceased to make aeroplanes.

In 1916 he started a concern for the making of aeroplanes, the Northern Aviatic Company, Ltd., the works of which are situated at Tellusborg, near Stockholm. He was the managing director of this company. The concern has made a great number of machines, both for the Swedish government and civilian persons in Sweden, as well as for the governments of the other neutral states in the North, especially for Finlandia.

In July, 1918, when he was out for a flight from Stockholm to Finland as passenger in an aeroplane, piloted by Captain Krokstedt, one of the best Swedish naval aviators, he met his death. The aeroplane got lost at sea in a thick fog, and both pilot and passenger were drowned.

Another person, who has contributed largely to the development of aviation matters in Sweden, is Mr. Lars Fjällbäck, M.E. Mr. Fjällbäck took his brévet in France in 1911. However, he soon left actual flying and went over to the manufacturing of aeroplanes.

He was the leader of a company which made the first Swedish-built aeroplane for the Swedish army in 1913.

Later he was appointed to the Northern Aviatic Company as chief constructor, and after the death of Baron Cederström he was promoted to managing director of the concern, and is still working as such.

The pilot Phil. Dr. Enoch Thulin's name is also closely connected to the history of the Swedish aviation. Like the foregoing, he also took his brévet at a French flying school. After coming back to Sweden, he made many meritorious long distance flights, and also a great number of exhibition flights.

One of his best known flights was made from Paris to Landskrona, Sweden, in a *Morane* monoplane. On this trip, his friend and constant helper, Lieutenant Ask, accompanied him as passenger.

He also started the Thulins Aeroplane Manufacturing Co., Ltd., in Landskrona, in 1915. These works have developed from a very small scale to one of the biggest industrial concerns in Sweden. They are exclusively intended for the manufacturing of aeroplanes and aero engines, but will after the war also turn their attention to other products.

The concern has sold most of its production to the Swedish and other neutral governments, especially to Holland.

Dr. Thulin has been the managing director of these works from the beginning, but has now left his place to Mr. Hakansson, M.E.

Captain in the Royal Engineers G. von Porat is also one of the more noteworthy persons in the Swedish aviation world. In 1912 he was one of the first three Swedish military aviators, and was sent to the Nieuport school in France, took his brévet and did later a lot of successful flying on *Nieuport* monoplanes.

In 1914 he had a severe accident, and was in hospital for a long time. After that he was appointed as constructor at the Södertelge Verkstäder aeroplane department, and has constructed and built several successful types of aeroplanes.

Meritorious flights made during 1918 by Swedish aviators:— Owing to regulations now in force, no details can be given about flights done in service by military aviators. And owing to well-known causes civil flying has been prohibited, with a very few exceptions. In May, however, Dr. Thulin with a monoplane flew from Christiania, Norway, to Landskrona (near Malmö), Sweden. The distance was 500 km. and was covered in 4 hours. Strong headwind prevailed throughout the trip.

On April 27th, Flight-Lieutenant Kindberg on a private hydro-aeroplane, with a passenger, flew from Stockholm to Abo, Finland and back right across the Baltic Sea. The distance is about 300 kilometres each way, the shortest journey was accomplished in 2 hours and 20 minutes. This flight is noteworthy on account of its being the first flight for a commercial purpose from Sweden to a foreign country.

Three-quarter Front View of Swedish Triplane, used for training.

Side View of a Swedish-built Triplane with Rotary engine.

3 a 2

Swedish Flying Officers and an Aeroplane North of the Arctic Circle.

Front View of Swedish-built Thulin Type K Esant monoplane fighter, built between 1917-19. 90 h.p. Thulin-built Gnôme rotary engine, offering 93 miles per hour.

THE NORTHERN AVIATIC COMPANY.

N.A.B.

1. **Type 9.**

TWO-SEATED RECONNAISSANCE BIPLANE.

Total length	..	..	8·0 metres.
Total width	..	..	13·7 metres.
Total height	..	..	3·5 metres.
Engine ..	..	..	110 h.p. Mercédès fixed.
Load carried	..	..	400 kg.
Speed ..	..	..	120 kil. an hour.

2. **Type 11.**

TWO-SEATED DOUBLE ENGINED RECONNAISSANCE BIPLANE.

Total length	..	..	8·55 metres.
Total width	..	..	16·16 metres.
Total height	..	..	3·6 metres.
Engines..	..	..	Two 110 or 160 h.p. Mercédès, Benz or Scania-Vabis fixed.
Load carried	..	..	800 kg.
Speed for the 160 h.p.	..	140 kil. an hour.	

3. **Type 12.**

TWO-SEATED DOUBLE ENGINED RECONNAISSANCE BIPLANE.

Same as above type, but equipped as hydro.

4. **Type 14.**

TWO-SEATED FLYING-BOAT.

Total length	..	..	8·6 metres.
Total width	..	..	15·0 metres.
Total height	..	..	3·55 metres.
Engine ..	..	..	160 h.p. Benz, Mercédès or Scania-Vabis fixed.
Load carried	..	..	500 kg.
Speed ..	..	..	130 kil. an hour.

5. **Type 17.**

ONE-SEATED SCOUTING BIPLANE.

Total length	..	..	6·7 metres.
Total width	..	..	10·0 metres.
Total height	..	..	3·0 metres.
Engine ..	..	..	110 h.p. Mercédès.
Load carried	..	..	300 kg.
Speed ..	..	..	155 kil. an hour.

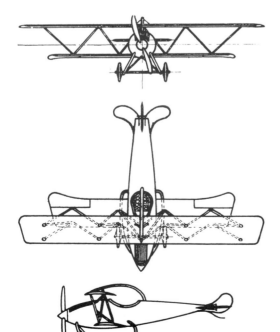

The Palson Single-seater Sporting Biplane.

Three-quarter Front View of Northern Aviatic Co.'s Biplane. Type 9.

Three-quarter Rear View of Northern Aviatic Co.'s Twin-engined Seaplane. Type 12.

Three-quarter Front View of Northern Aviatic Co's Biplane. Type 17.

PALSON Aeroplanes. Malmö.

These aeroplanes are of rather unconventional design, the chief idea of the constructor being a device for altering the position and angle of the top planes.

The aeroplanes are built from three-ply wood, fuselage, wings and rudders

The concern is a new one, machines are under construction, but the value of the special arrangements seems rather doubtful. No tests are yet made.

1. **Type 1.**

ONE-SEATED SPORTING BIPLANE.

Total length	..	..	5·7 metres.
Total width	..	..	8 metres.
Total height	..	..	2·3 metres.
Engine ..	..	..	50 h.p. Gnôme or Palson rotary.

2. **Type 2.**

PASSENGER-CARRYING BIPLANE.

Total length	..	..	11·7 metres.
Total width	..	..	22·3 metres.
Total height	..	..	5·3 metres.
Engine ..	..	..	300 h.p. fixed.
Load carried	..	..	Six passengers and fuel for six hours.

Shaded Sketch of the Palson Single-seater.

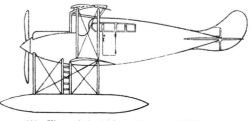

Side View of the Palson Passenger Biplane.

THULIN Aeroplanes. Landskrona.

Since America's entry into the war it is safe to state that the aircraft works of Enoch Thulin in Landskrona, Sweden, are the largest neutral aviation concern left.

When the war broke out there were two small Swedish aeroplane factories, one a department of the well-known Södertelje works, under the management of the Swedish pioneer aviator, Baron Cederström, and holding rights and patterns from the Farman Brothers and the Gnôme engine company, the other one being that of Dr. E. Thulin.

Sundry accidents with the *Henry Farman* biplanes led the Södertelje Works to adopt the *Albatros* model, and to equip the biplanes with original German engines, till the whole Södertelje establishment was taken over by the Government for their important work, when the aircraft department passed into the possession of Dr. Thulin.

His efforts have during the war developed into a concern of imposing Scandinavian dimensions, with a staff of 800 workmen, by the combination of three factors,—personal enterprise, a favourable time and the presence of raw materials in Sweden itself.

The Thulin Aircraft Works have furnished both the Swedish and foreign neutral governments, including Denmark, these being supplied with *Morane-Saulnier* monoplanes and 80/90 h.p. Le Rhône type motors; and Holland getting *Thulin* scout monoplanes and 100/120 h.p. Thulin rotary engines.

The Thulin Aircraft Works run both a flying school with a number of *Bleriot* and *Morane* monoplanes, where more than half of Sweden's aviators have taken their certificates, and an aerodynamical laboratory.

The chief, Dr. Thulin, looks behind on a successful career as an aviator. Among his notable flights were one from Paris to Landskrona in 1914; one from Malmö to Stockholm with photos of the Baltic Exhibition, just opened then, for a newspaper in the Swedish capital; and two days later a flight from Gothenberg to Copenhagen with Baron Blixen-Finecke as passenger that the latter might participate in horse races in both cities, the second time this great feat was done in history, the first being by a German sportsman.

— E. H.

Unfortunately, since these notes were written, Dr. Thulin has been killed in an aeroplane accident on May 14th, 1919.
— C G.G.

1. Type K.
ONE-SEATED SCOUT MONOPLANE.

Total length	..	..	6·5 metres.
Total width	..		9·1 metres.
Total height	..		2·55 metres.
Engine	..	..	90 h.p. rotary Thulin.
Load carried	..	..	185 kg.
Speed	..	..	130—145 kiloms. an hour.

2. Type L.A.
TWO-SEATED RECONNAISSANCE BIPLANE.

Total length	..	..	7·5 metres.
Total width	..		10·4 metres.
Total height	..		3·52 metres.
Engine	..	..	90 or 125 h.p. rotary Thulin.
Load carried	..	..	265 kg.
Speed	..	..	125 to 140 kil. an hour.

3. Type G.A.
TWO-SEATED RECONNAISSANCE BIPLANE.

Total length	..	..	9·48 metres.
Total width	..		17·2 metres.

Total height	..	..	3·54 metres.
Engine	..	..	160 h.p. Benz, Mercédès or Thulin fixed.
Load carried	..	..	400 kg.
Speed	..	..	118 kil. an hour.

4. Type F.A.
TWO-SEATED RECONNAISSANCE BIPLANE.

Total length	..	..	7·9 metres.
Total width	..		11·7 metres.
Total height	..		3·39 metres.
Engine	..		160 h.p. Benz, Mercédès or Thulin fixed.
Load carried	..	..	550 kg.
Speed	..	..	135 kil. an hour.

5. Type N.A.
ONE-SEATED SCOUTING BIPLANE.

Total length	..	..	5·85 metres.
Total width	..		7·9 metres.
Total height	..		2·45 metres.
Engine	..	..	125 h.p. Thulin rotary.
Load carried	..	..	300 kg.
Speed	..	..	165 kil. an hour.

Three-quarter Rear View of Thulin Monoplane.

Front View of Thulin Monoplane.

Three-quarter Front View of Thulin Biplane.

SWISS.

MILITARY AERONAUTICS IN SWITZERLAND.

The Swiss General Staff's Press Bureau published in 1916 a memorandum dealing with the development of aeronautics in the belligerent countries, and referring also to the present status of aeronautics in Switzerland. Regarding the latter it says:—

"The war-born evolution of aircraft cannot but force us greatly to increase our aerial establishment if we want to remain efficient in this field, too. Here it is necessary to consider that, unlike the Great Powers, who can keep large aircraft factories working even in time of peace, Switzerland does not possess a real aircraft industry.

"Therefore, if we have succeeded in building during the war aircraft of our own, it is chiefly due to the fact that our mobilisation recalled a number of engineers who were previously working in foreign countries. The construction of aero-engines, which is of a more exacting nature than that of ordinary petrol engines, has also been successfully undertaken; likewise, the training of pilots, which formerly was entirely dependent on foreign schools, is now satisfactorily done at home.

"Such is, then, briefly the development of national military aeronautics. If some think that the progress realised was not rapid enough, one should keep in mind the great technical difficulties and the corresponding expense of creating and developing this new arm. The Swiss people have— like their neighbours—generously contributed to the national subscription for military aeronautics in order to enable the Army to increase their aerial establishment."

This report permitted one to assume that the fund of the national subscription was then nearly exhausted, as a consequence of which the Confederacy undoubtedly authorised a considerable expenditure for military aviation. It was also proposed to enlarge the kite-balloon branch of the Army, since those craft have proven highly valuable in the great war as fire-control stations.

Thanks to the successful construction of national aeroplanes, the Swiss Flying Corps had then become a reality. Some time ago a squadron of 10 aeroplanes was seen over Zurich, whither it had flown from the Confederate Air Station of Dübendorf. The first of a series of air bases (*points d'appui aérien*), which will be established in the future, had been created at Aarau, and Lt. Bider, the famous cross-Alps aviator, has been made the first Army Aviation Instructor. In order to prevent accidental violations of neutrality, Swiss aviators are under orders not to trespass on the following zone :—Yverdon—Lake of Neufchâtel—Bienne (Biel)—Soleure (Solothurn) —Aar—Lägern—Rorbas—Winterthur—St. Gall—Reichenau—Tödi—St. Gotthard—Berne Alps— Rochers de Nay.

* * *

The war has influenced the situation of Swiss aviators in various ways. The Aero Club had certificated by October, 1916, 61 pilot-aviators; 12 of these lost their lives accidentally, and about as many gave up their profession before the war. Of the latter are Bianchi, Bucher, Gsell, Maffei, Salvioni, Schumacher, and Taddeoli. Nine aviators, namely: Audemars, Bider, Burri, Comte, Cuendet, Durafour, Grandjean, Lugrin, and Parmelin, offered their services to the Army, and are, though mobilised, kept on the reserve list. This enables them to look after their business; thus it was that Audemars broke the world's height record in 1915 in France. Durafour was engaged at Buc, and Burri is with the Franco-British Aviation Cie.

Among the Swiss who are not Service-bound, Domenjoz was on an exhibition tour in South America, and afterwards went to the United States. Favre is chief-pilot of the Levasseur Works, and E. Baumann runs an aviation school at Acton. The youngest Swiss aviator, the 19-year old Pasche, was then testing, apparently with little success, an aeroplane of his own design, at Lavaux. Parmelin was in Geneva, and had to refuse advantageous offers from Russia and England, because the military authorities would not let him leave the country.

Among the Swiss aviators serving with the French *Aviation Militaire*, Blancpain fell on the field of honour.

To his name should be added that of Sergeant Théophile Ingold, of Escadrille N. 23, who died of injuries received during a reconnaissance. He was recipient of a *citation à l'ordre de l'armée* and was proposed for the *Médaille militaire*; he was a cousin of Karl Ingold, serving with the German Flying Corps.

Since the publication of these notes no further information is available. The Swiss Authorities refuse to give any information of any kind. However, as there are no original Swiss aeroplanes or engines of any note little is lost by the refusal.

TURKISH.

Having been without aircraft, as employed by the Italian opponent in the Tripolis war, Turkey had passed through the two Balkan wars with a stock of odd machines left, including the German *Harlan* and *Mars* makes, and the French *Rep, Nieuport*, and others.

When Turkey entered the late war, Germany had to supply both the equipment and organisation beside personnel for the nucleus of th. Turkish Air Services, and very seldom did the name of any Osmanian pilot attain publicity, so that one can take it for granted that German pilots almost exclusively manned the Turkish aircraft. though they had Turkish officer observers on the main fronts of activities, namely, with land machines in the operations against Egypt and the Suez Canal, and employing seaplanes in the Dardanelles campaign.

The German officer who distinguished himself most on this front was Lieut. Buddecke, who fell later, after 12 victories, in the French theatre of war. The officer in command of the naval air station in Constantinople was Captain-Lieut. Langfeld, one of his most active pilots being Captain-Lieut. Liebmann, who has published a book of his experiences under the title " Dardanelles Pilots."

The land aeroplanes to be employed on the Turkish theatres of war included most German types, including modern scouts, contrary to the practice of the opponent in the far-off places, while the Gotha works were the main contractors for seaplanes.

Their first model supplied to Turkey was a re-modelled twin-float two-seater (brought out for the 1914 Warnemünde naval aircraft competition), equipped either with a 150 h.p. motor (Benz or Rapp) better known under its ultimate trade mark, B.M.W. or Bayern (Bavaria) engine, with the gunner observer in front of the pilot, serving the gun, mounted on the top plane in a standing position, as in the early *Nieuport* scouts.

This seaplane was equipped with a float-cum-wheel under-carriage, the shaft with the four wheels, one on each side of each float being mounted below them, and the floats serving as landing brakes by means of an aft extended added skid, as the biplanes had to be sent to Turkey by land, owing to Roumania refusing to grant a transit permit.

So the seaplanes were sent by rail to Herkulesbad, in Hungary, where they were erected and then flew across Roumania and Servia loaded with spares to Lom Polanka, in Bulgaria, whence transport facilities to Constantinople were again available.

That the Turks benefited later from the German experiences of improving speed and performance by paying attention to reducing head resistance from stream-line effect is evident from the later type, supplied in the repeat orders.

URUGUAY.

MILITARY AVIATION.

The government is making a serious effort at creating an aerial arm. For this purpose a number of officers are being trained at the San Fernando Aerodrome, and eight aero-engines have been imported from the Argentine during 1917 for the equipment of training aeroplanes.

No further information is obtainable.

MILITARY AEROPLANES.

Lt. Frigierio was despatched about May, 1914, to Europe to purchase the nucleus of a small aerial fleet. Nothing worth mention has apparently occurred since. One aeroplane was bought for experimental purposes, and was afterwards smashed.

No fresh information is available.

AMERICAN (U. S. A.)

U.S.A. MILITARY AND NAVAL AVIATION IN 1918

Military Aeroplanes.

In March, 1914, there were 15 aeroplanes and seaplanes in service, and about 10 on order.

The machines were :—

1 *Wright B*, 2 *Wright C*, 2 *Wright D*, 1 *Curtiss D*, 2 *Curtiss E*, 2 *Curtiss H*, 1 *Burgess F*, 4 *Burgess H*, 1 *Wright*, 1 *Curtiss* tractor, 1 *Burgess* tractor.

They were mostly stationed at San Diego, Manila, Hawaii and San Antonio.

Naval Aeroplanes.

At the end of March, 1914, the naval force consisted of 10 seaplanes or flying boats (*Benoist, Burgess, Curtiss* and *Wright*), and 30 more were reported on order, with a view to one being supplied to each of the important warships.

The people of the United States during 1915 displayed some desire to possess an Air Fleet, and the Aero Club of America has engineered consider-able newspaper and personal agitation in favour thereof. The U. S. Army and Navy Departments did not display any remarkable solicitude on the subject, but seemed to wait and see with truly British energy.

American aeroplane factories were erected on a huge scale with money paid by the Allies, chiefly for school aeroplanes, and it would appear that the U. S. Government depended on knowledge gained in this way to supply the aircraft (theoretical and actual) which would be required when the United States began to take an active part in the war. The Mexican affair which started early in 1916 provided some useful training for U. S. Service aviators, and demonstrated quite conclusively that the U.S. Army had not even the beginnings of a real Flying Service.

During 1916 some progress was made in building up an Army Flying Service, but it seemingly remained merely an appendix to the Signal Corps, and as such was never likely to be of any serious account. Now that Army flying is being placed on a proper and independent footing, it is becoming evident America has the men and material with which to equal any other country.

Naval flying has been taken rather more seriously of late, a fact largely due to Lieut. John Towers, who was extra Naval Attaché in London for the first two years of war, and who was very closely in touch with the Royal Naval Air Service. He returned to the States late in 1916, and has introduced the best British features produced by active service experience and modified by American freedom from convention. Some interesting and useful experi-mental seaplanes have been built, of which an example is illustrated.

Tenders were invited during 1916 by the U.S. Army and Navy for numerous aeroplanes, but no very large orders were placed, machines being ordered a dozen or so at a time, where the belligerent nations ordered in hundreds.

Much was written in American papers to prove that American aeroplanes were at least equal in every respect to the best European aeroplanes, but Americans of the highest scientific and practical qualifications agreed that America had much to learn from Europe before she could produce war aeroplanes of the best class.

At an American Flying School in France. A review of training machines (French Nieuports) before Mr. Baker, the Secretary for War in the U.S. Government.

On the entry of America into the war in 1917, the U.S. Government very wisely decided to copy the best European machines and output was just beginning early in 1918. During 1917 the "Liberty" motor was produced by a kind of syndicate of designers, who produced a 12-cylinder water-cooled motor of high power in a remarkably short time. This has since been standardised and is being made by the thousand all over the States.

In April, 1918, disclosures in Congress led to the appointment of a Congressional Committee to investigate charges of malfeasance in the output of American aircraft.

It was shown that up till March, at any rate, no American aeroplanes, except a sample or two, had been sent to Europe, and that the only machines of any use in the United States were school machines, unfit for war work.

Meantime many thousands of American troops (totalling 500,000 by April) had been sent to Europe, and a vast number of them were in training as pilots and air mechanics in France and England. Their training was done on French and British machines, and the pilots turned out remarkably well, many of them being on active service by April, and having brought down a number of enemy machines.

Fortunately plenty of European machines were available for the use of the Americans, and so it was possible to use available shipping space for men and stores, instead of for mere school aeroplanes from America, thus the errors of the U. S. Aircraft Production Board happened to work out for the best. However, President Wilson, as the result of the Congressional Enquiry, appointed Mr. John D. Ryan to be over-seer of Aircraft Production. Some members of the former Board remained to work as his subordinates, but the Board itself ceased to have power.

Brigadier-General Squier was removed entirely from all aeronautical duties, and Major-General William Kenly, who had had no previous aeronautical experience, was appointed to re-organise the whole of American Military Aviation.

American Air Mechanics at work on a French Nieuport at an American Flying School in France.

THE ORGANISATION OF THE U.S. AIR SERVICE.

According to "Aerial Age Weekly," New York, of July 30th, 1917, the Intelligence Division of the Aviation Section Signal Corps issued shortly before that date a very comprehensive plan of organisation, which is reproduced hereafter.

In various passages the Aircraft Production Board is referred to as an organisation of purely advisory nature and without power to act, or it is stated that a given Division "may" consult with the Board.

This overlooks the almost unlimited power of the Council of National Defence and unnecessarily gives the impression that the Divisions do not co-operate closely with the Board. There is in fact the closest co-operation between the Aviation Section and the Board.

The statement issued by the Intelligence Division reads as follows :—

Aeronautical work in the Army is conducted directly by the Signal Corps, whether such lies under the heading "Aviation" or "Aerostation."

The Aviation Section (*) of the Signal Corps is composed, originally, of officers and enlisted men of the Regular Army limited by law to a definite number.

Additional personnel is provided through the Signal Officers' Reserve Corps, the Signal Enlisted Reserve Corps, and the employment of civilians in instructive, advisory, administrative or other capacities.

Civilians may be employed(1) as such ; (2) by passing standard physical and mental examinations and going through the routine of joining the Signal Officers' Reserve Corps, in which event, if satisfactory, they may be given commissions therein commensurate in grade with their attainments and duties, as follows : (a) Non-flying duty ; (b) Flying duty or (3) by enlistment in the Signal Enlisted Reserve Corps.

The aeronautical work in the Signal Corps is supplemented by (1) the co-operation of the Navy in the Joint Army and Navy Board of Aero Cognizance,

(2) the Joint Army and Navy Board for Rigid Dirigibles,

(3) and Joint Army and Navy Board for Design and Specifications, which boards are responsible to the Secretary of War and the Secretary of the Navy respectively ; and by co-operation of the

(4) Aircraft Production Board (a subsidiary of the Council of National Defence, and the

(5) National Advisory Committee for Aeronautics, which latter reports to the President of the United States.

The director of the Army aeronautical work is the Chief Signal Officer, acting through his Executive Officer.

The work is divided between various divisions, sections and sub-sections. Following are some notes on the duties of these various branches.

1.—AEROPLANE DIVISION.

Organisation and Training Section.—This Section has to do with the organisation of aviation school squadrons and of standard aero squadrons, the latter composed of graduated Reserve Military Aviators.** It has nothing to do with training of men for aerostatic work, which is handled by the Balloon Division.

Graduates of the Schools of Military Aeronautics (ground schools) are assigned through the Aero Personnel Division in co-operation with the O. and T. Section, to the various aviation school squadrons for instruction in actual flying. From this point on the flying students are in charge of the O. and T. Section.

[Sixteen of these school squadrons were operating when the memorandum was issued. Belleville was to be in operation August 15th (1917).

Following is a list of the location of aviation school squadrons then organised and to be organised in the near future. Doubtless this schedule has been extended.

Mineola, N.Y.—operating.
Mt. Clemens, Mich. (Selfridge Field)—operating.
Fairfield, O. (Wilbur Wright Field)—operating.
Rantoul, Ills. (Chanute Field)—operating.
So. Mississippi Valley—under investigation.
San Antonio, Tex.—operating.
San Diego, Calif.—now operating.
Belleville, Ills.—in operation August 15th.
One station to be in Rocky Mountain Region.
Fort Sill, Okla. (advanced school)—being established.]

At the above schools training is done with as much rapidity as possible. At the conclusion of from fifteen to twenty-five hours' flying it is expected students will be able to pass the tests for certificates as Reserve Military Aviators.

While undergoing this flying instruction, the pupil is required to study radio, telegraphy, gunnery, photography, motors and aeronautical engineering. This study is practical ; the student handling and operating every instrument, assembling and dis-assembling engines, and the construction and repair of aeroplanes to the extent that he must assemble, dis-assemble, line-up, etc. In the gunnery instruction, for instance, the student uses a machine in which a gun is mounted and is given target practice at objects moving in the air.

Upon receiving their certificates, these flying students are commissioned as First Lieutenants, Signal Officers' Reserve Corps, Aviation Section, and when on duty involving frequent or continuous flying, receive twenty-five per cent. increase in pay. The base pay is 2,000 dols. a year. When on foreign duty ten per cent increase on the base pay is allowed. Quarters are also furnished.

Standard aero squadrons of the Army are formed at the aviation school squadrons. The flying and enlisted personnel for these squadrons are furnished from these flying schools. The officers, of course, are Reserve Military Aviators by this time, though some may be Junior Military Aviators. The enlisted men are of the Enlisted Reserve Corps, or of the Regular Army.

These aero squadrons, thus formed, will be fully equipped, save as to aeroplanes, and transported to England or France for advanced training.

These graduated aviators (R.M.A.'s) may also be sent to complete the complement of aero squadrons already in process of formation or partially filled, to be maintained at certain points [Aero squadrons were then located at the following places :

Home.	Overseas.
Columbus, N.M.	Fort Mills, Corregidor, P.I.
San Antonio, Tex.	Honolulu.
Mt. Clemens, Mich.	Ancon, Canal Zone.
Rantoul, Ills.	
Fairfield, O.	
Mineola, N Y. (Reserve).	
Essington, Pa. (Reserve).	

The foregoing, with two exceptions, were Regular Army aero squadrons as distinct from the Reserve Aero Squadron, which were to be composed of Reserve Military Aviators solely.

It was not then expected to utilise civilian training schools as it was planned that the aviation school squadrons should continue to be amply prepared to handle all flying instruction. No civilian schools were then in operation in connection with Army training.]

Applications from officers in the Regular Army for transfer to flying duty are also received and preliminarily acted upon here and then passed to the Personnel Division. If all conditions are met, officers are sent to one of the aviation school squadrons for flying instruction.

These officers, when qualified, are rated as Junior Military Aviators and they receive fifty per cent. increase in pay when on flying duty.

A Junior Military Aviator, having served continuously three years such as on flying duty, may obtain the title of Military Aviator and be then entitled to seventy-five per cent. increase in pay when on duty involving frequent or continuous flying. Foreign service adds ten per cent., as usual.

The Organisation and Training Section, also, handles original applications for commissions in the S.O.R.C. from civilians, Regular Army, or National Guard officers and men, needed as supply, engineer, or field-inspector officers. Opportunity is afforded by personal interview to obtain first-hand knowledge of the particular attainments of each man. If preliminary investigation is satisfactory, the applicant fills out the blank and is turned over to the Personnel Division, which attends to the routine of physical and mental examination. Upon the obtaining of his commission he is assigned to such place as his services are required.

---

*It will be noted in printed matter of this Signal Corps, Aviation Section, that the title "Aviation Section" is used to embrace all aeronautical work in the Army. Since the publication of these pamphlets, the scope has been altered in accordance with this memorandum, as will appear obvious.

**There are but a few officers with the title "Military Aviator" and "Junior Military Aviator." These are in administrative positions. Practically the entire new flying personnel is to be composed of Reserve Military Aviators.

THE ORGANISATION OF THE U.S. AIR SERVICE.

Equipment Section.—This Section makes out all purchase requests for equipment for all aero units, except for local purchases. It adjusts differences between the manufacturers and the Government relative to equipment and determines what equipment shall be shipped to new organisations.

Intelligence Section.—The functions of the Intelligence Section, are, broadly, the collection and filling of data of every nature, and from all sources, relating to military aeronautics and aeronautical engineering and the making of such digests and publications as may be advisable to those interested for confidential and public information.

2.—AIRCRAFT ENGINEERING DIVISION.

The Aircraft Engineering Division, also reporting to the Chief Signal Officer, is divided into the following departments, in charge of an officer and a staff of commissioned assistants and civilian engineers and their assistants.

Aeroplane Section.—In this department is conducted work incident to status, design, specifications for aeroplanes, radio equipment, photographic equipment, instruments and accessories. The testing of units of apparatus, instrumental apparatus, and other, is conducted under the supervision of the officer in charge and commissioned assistants of this department.

Power Plant Section.—In this department is conducted work (a) incident to the investigation and testing of new aircraft engine units in process of development by various manufacturers; (b) incident to standardising of power plant parts, such as propeller bulbs, magneto, couplings, fittings, etc.; (c) incident to special investigations in connection with engine manufacture outside of the field of members of the Inspection Section.

Inspection Section.—This department, although not fully organised, will involve the division of the country into districts, each district in charge of a commissioned officer reporting to the Officer in charge of the Inspection Department. In each district, under the Officer in Charge, will be a commissioned officer in charge of more important factories, with corps of civilian engineers or others qualified for the work. The inspection involves all material and manufactured articles in connection with the Air Service of the Army.

Transport Section.—Within this department the special requirements of transport service incident to both heavier-than-air and lighter-than-air squadron operation are considered, and means adopted whereby the manufacturer of trucks and special equipment to meet all requirements are produced.

Design and Experimentation Section.—This department involves the conduct at Langley Field aeronautical proving ground, of about two thousand acres, near Hampton, Va., of all experiments and tests on (a) aeroplanes of various types; (b) aeroplane engines in production, in development, or of distinctly new types; (c) radio equipment of various types and for various uses in connection with aircraft operations; (d) ordnance—tests under this heading are carried on in conjunction with and under the supervision of the Chief of Ordnance, U.S. Army; (e) photograph experiments with all types of photographic apparatus in aeroplanes; (f) instruments and accessories.

All tests and experiments are carried out on conditions which simulate, as far as possible, the conditions met in actual service.

Langley Field, when completed, will include among other items, the following: administration building, hospital, quartermaster storehouse, commissary buildings, post exchange building, power house, 3 aeroplane hangar units, 2 seaplane hangar units, boat house, garage, truck shed, 2 barracks, laboratory, aeroplane construction shop, machine shop, foundry, three 200-feet observation towers, wind channel building, dynamometer building, engine test house and houses for commissioned, non-commissioned officers and civilians.

3.—FINANCE AND SUPPLY DIVISION.

The functions of the Division are the purchase of aircraft material of every kind in connection with aeronautics in the Signal Corps, and the payment therefor.

4.—AERO PERSONNEL DIVISION.

The duties of the Aero Personnel Division consist in matters affecting the commissioned and enlisted men of the Aviation Section of the Signal Corps, which may be more conveniently termed the Army Air Service. All communications to the Chief Signal Officer, or higher authority, that are concerned with the subject of aviation personnel must pass through this Division, except when such communications deal with civilian employees.

The personnel of the Army Air Service comprises the following groups:—
(a) Enlisted men of the Regular Army.
(b) Signal Enlisted Reserve* (throughout this article referred to as " Enlisted Reserve Proper.")
(c) Men (flying duty) enlisted temporarily in the Signal Enlisted Reserve in order to obtain training for a commission in the Aviation Section of the Signal Officers' Reserve Corps. (Throughout this article referred to as " Enlisted Reserve.")
(d) Reserve Officers (flying duty).
(e) Reserve Officers (non-flying duty).
(f) Officers (of Regular Army).
The Aero Personnel Division is also concerned with two other groups of men:
(g) Enlisted applicants of the Regular Army for transfer to the Air Service.
(h) Commissioned applicants of the Regular Army for detail to the Air Service.
(a) Present provisions in regard to the first of these groups continue as now prescribed by law and Army regulations. The Aero Personnel Division has charge of the records of enlisted men of the Regular Army.

*Inasmuch as all enlistments are for the period of the war and the policy of the office is to accept men for the Regular Army only. Paragraph (b) following is modified to this extent.

(b) The purpose of the " Enlisted Reserve Proper " has been to have a body of trained mechanicians, machinists, electricians, chauffeurs and other qualified men, who may be quickly called in time of need. Cards giving the home addresses and information about the enlistments of such reservists are kept in the Aero Personnel Division. Similar information is in the service record of each reservist, in the hands of the department commander in whose territorial jurisdiction he resides. No more enlistments in this group as reservists are made at present, there being no desirability during war-time in increasing the number of reserves not on active duty. The entire personnel of this group is at the date of writing being called into active service by the department commanders immediately upon enlistment. They are assigned to aviation stations and placed on training.

(c) The enlisted reservists who are applicants for commissions as reserve officers, flying duty, and are enlisted in the Signal Enlisted Reserve Corps simply for the purpose of preliminary training prior to receiving their commissions, comprise an extremely important group. From their numbers will come almost exclusively the aviators of the Army Air Service. The procedure in regard to the enlistment of these men is in the hands of the Aero Personnel Division. All applicants for commission in the Aviation Section of the Signal Officers' Reserve Corps must forward their applications to the Aero Personnel Division for approval or disapproval. If the application is approved, its sender is then given an examination to determine his physical condition, and another to test his moral, professional, and educational qualifications for a commission. Boards to give the complete examinations are situated at each of the Schools of Military Aeronautics, at the several Signal Corps flying schools in the United States and Washington.

If the candidate is successful in passing these examinations, he is re-examined with the view of enlistment as private, first-class, in the Signal Enlisted Reserve, and is then either sent home with a certificate of enlistment to await further orders, or sent immediately to one of the ground schools (Schools of Military Aeronautics) for instruction.

From this time until the receipt of his commission the candidate is under the jurisdiction of, first, the School of Military Aeronautics Division, and later of the Organisation and Training Division—the Aero Personnel Division being simply concerned with keeping his military record.

On recommendation of the Schools of Military Aeronautics Division, the Aero Personnel Division asks for the transfer to the ground schools of suitable students on duty at the Federal Reserve Officers' Training Camps. Such requests, if recommended, are made weekly.

(d) Upon successful completion of the flying school course, the candidate is commissioned as a reserve officer, whereon his relation to the Aero Personnel Division becomes like that of a regular officer of the Air Service.

Competent civilian flyers who pass the physical and mental examinations and are satisfactory otherwise, may be at once commissioned in the Signal Officers' Reserve Corps and ordered to active duty.

(e) Civilian applicants for commissions in the S.O.R.C. for non-flying duty in capacities such as engineers, supply or other officer, may take mental and physical examinations (the latter less rigid than that for flying duty), and if qualifications are satisfactory may be commissioned and ordered to active duty.

(f) All communications in regard to officers of the Army Air Service pass through the Aero Personnel Division. Similarly, all orders for officers of the Air Service that are requested from the Adjutant-General pass through this Division. Complete military records of officers are also kept there.

(g) Applications of enlisted men of the Signal Corps proper, or of other staff corps or departments, or arms, for transfer to the Air Service should be approved by the Aero Personnel Division, before orders are issued for such transfer.

(h) Any officer of the Regular Army who is an applicant for detail in the Air Service, has his military record and correspondence concerning him kept by the Aero Personnel Division while he is undergoing training at the Signal Corps flying schools. Upon detail in the Air Service the status of such an officer in relation to this Division is precisely like that of other officers of the Army Air Service.

In all cases, application for enlistment, transfer, detail or commission, is made direct to the Aero Personnel Division.

5.—SCHOOLS OF MILITARY AERONAUTICS DIVISION.

Successful candidates for flying duty are directed by the Aero Personnel Division to one of the eight ground schools located at the following institutions:

Massachusetts Institute of Technology, Boston, Mass.
Cornell University, Ithaca, N.Y.
Ohio State University, Columbus, O.
University of Illinois, Urbana, Ill.
Texas University, Austin, Texas.
University of California, Berkeley, Cal.
Princeton University, Princeton, N.J.
Georgia Institute of Technology, Atlanta, Ga.

Upon arrival, the S.M.A. Division is advised thereof, with a list, which list is kept by the S.M.A. Division in co-operation with the Organisation and Training Section. Now the students are under the charge of the S.M.A. Division.

Here the students serve eight weeks with the pay of a first-class private, about a dollar a day, and with an allowance of a dollar a day for rations. Quarters are provided in barracks.

Students are given intensive instruction in aeronautical engines, telegraphy, machine guns, bombing and fighting, aerial observation and co-operation with artillery and infantry, including map-reading, contact patrol and reconnaissance; army regulations and military subjects; flying, with meteorology, instruments, compasses, photography and other; rigging, care and repair of aeroplanes, engines and cameras. Guns and other apparatus are provided for practical study. Upon completion

of this course the students are assigned through the Aero Personnel Division to the aviation school squadrons, as noted under " Organisation and Training."

6.—CONSTRUCTION DIVISION.

The functions of the Construction Division are : the locating of the sites for flying schools and squadrons, preparing deeds or leases and entering into contracts for the preparation of the ground and the construction of buildings. This Division may consult other departments, such as the Aircraft Production Board, for instance, but the actual control of these operations is in its hands. Once the field is completed and in shape for the purpose for which it is intended, its operation is taken up by the Aeroplane Division, Organisation and Training Section.

7.—BALLOON DIVISION.

The Balloon Division has charge of all matters pertaining to lighter-than-air craft. Captive ballooning is being developed; first for the reason that observation balloons are urgently needed abroad. The training of pilots and observers for captive balloons involves a preliminary course in free ballooning, using the ordinary spherical type. This is necessary for the reason that when captive balloons break away from their holding cables, they must be manœuvred and landed safely in the same manner as spherical balloons.

The principal army balloon school is at Fort Omaha, Nebr., the entire post being utilised for this purpose. At St. Louis, the Missouri Aeronautical Society is also training balloon pilots as a civilian balloon school in accordance with special regulations No. 50, War Department, and it is possible that one or two additional civilian balloon schools will be utilised in the same way. It is expected that the ballooning instruction at the Fort Omaha school will progress from the captive ballooning to dirigibles as soon as practicable.

The principal function of observation balloons is, first, to keep constant watch of everything of military interest in the sector of the enemy's territory which is assigned to each balloon, and observing and reporting the fall of artillery projectiles. Reports from the balloon to the ground are by telephone connection.

8.—RADIO DIVISION.

The Radio Division deals with the organisation and operation of radio work in completed aero squadrons or aviation school squadrons, and practically applies the results of the work conducted by the Aircraft Engineering Division.

AIRCRAFT PRODUCTION BOARD.

The function of this board, organised by the Council of National Defence, is to consider the situation in relation to the quantity production of aircraft in the United States and to co-operate with the officers of the Army and Navy and of other departments of the Government interested in the production and delivery to these departments of the needed aircraft in accordance with the requirements of each department.

This board has no legal authority and its work is advisory only, but its recommendations are made effective through the Finance and Supply Division, which asks the approval of the Aircraft Production Board as to the qualifications of the manufacturer to whom it is tentatively about to award a contract. The programme is outlined as follows :

Engineering.—To co-operate with the Aircraft Engineering Division of the Army (and with the correlative branch of the Navy), with all manufacturers, engineers and laboratories to advance the science of aviation and aerostation and to stimulate the production of better types of aircraft.

Specifications and Standardisation.—To advise and assist in such standardisation of material and parts, and, as far as practicable, of types of aircraft as will aid in increasing the productive capacity of the industry in the most efficient forms of aircraft.

Production.—To investigate sources of supply of aircraft and their materials and to assist in the formulation and execution of such plans as may be necessary to enable the Government to purchase all kinds of aircraft of the types in the quantities desired. This includes :—

(a) Co-ordination of designs of all aircraft matters through officers of allied countries stationed here for that purpose.

(b) Arrangements with existing American factories as to kinds of aircraft and their component parts best suited to their organisation and facilities and quantities to be built by them.

(c) Suitable arrangements, when necessary, to advance Government funds where larger contracts are considered than can be privately financed, or to make arrangements on a cost-plus basis.

(d) Utilisation of such idle facilities and the erection of such new sources of supply as, in the judgment of the board, are necessary to meet the needs of the Government.

Inspection.—To co-operate with the aeronautic inspection organisation of the Army and the Navy and start to assist in co-ordination of their present systems of inspection to the end that, if possible, there be one system, one standard, and one organisation for the inspection of aircraft in this country.

Aviation Schools.—Following the selection of sites, to advise in regard to buying or leasing the land, the preparing it for use and the erecting of buildings.

Supply Depots.—Following the approval of sites, to advise in regard to the leasing of land and erecting the necessary buildings.

Priority.—To advise regarding the priority of deliveries of aircraft material as between the departments in accordance with the general policy as determined by the Council of National Defence

JOINT ARMY AND NAVY BOARD OF AERONAUTICAL COGNIZANCE.

This joint board was organised with representatives of the Army and Navy as members for the purpose of formulating plans and regulations for joint development and to settle broad questions arising between the two services, distinctive insignia respective responsibilities and spheres of action, methods of co-operation, joint manœuvres and various other allied subjects.

JOINT ARMY AND NAVY BOARD FOR RIGID DIRIGIBLES.
The specific purpose of this board is the design and construction of a rigid dirigible. This work is being prosecuted in the Navy Department.

JOINT ARMY AND NAVY BOARD OF DESIGN AND SPECIFICATIONS.
This is another joint technical board, composed of Army and Navy officers and has to do with the decision as to respective types of aircraft.
*Chief Signal Officer : Brigadier-General George O. Squier.
Executive Officer : Colonel C. McK. Saltzman.

AEROPLANE DIVISION.
Lieut.-Colonel Jno. B. Bennett, Major B. D. Foulois. Organisation and Training Section : Capt. T. D. Milling, Lieut. Philip J. Roosevelt, U.S.R. Intelligence Section : Major H. H. Arnold, Lieut Ernest Jones, U.S.R. Equipment Section : Capt. L. H. Brereton, Capt. J. W Gallagher, U.S.R. ; Lieut. S. Katzman, U.S.R.

AIRCRAFT ENGINEERING DIVISION.
Major Henry Souther, U.S.R. ; Capt. G. R. Wadsworth, U.S.R. Airplane Section : Capt. V. E. Clark, Capt. H. S. Martin. Inspection Section : Capt. H. W. Harms (field), T. W. Mixter (raw material), B. D. Gray (finished material). Power Plant Section : Capt. Howard Marmon, U.S.R. Transport Section : A. J. Slade. Design and Experimentation Section : Capt. H. S. Martin (Aeroplanes), Capt. V. E. Clark (Aeroplanes), Capt. Howard Marmon (Engines), Capt. C. C. Culver (Radio), Capt. R. H. Willis, Jr. (Ordnance), Capt. C. C. Culver (Photography), Capt. H. S. Martin (Instrument and Accessories).

FINANCE AND SUPPLY DIVISION.
Capt. A. G. Gutensohn, Capt. R. M. Jones, Lieut.-Colonel C. S. Wallace, Capt. George H. Brett, Capt. L. R. Evans, Capt H. D. Moore.

AERO PERSONNEL DIVISION.
Capt. Aubrey Lippincott, Capt. W. A. Larned, U.S.R. ; Capt. R. B. Owens, U.S.R. ; Capt. Thomas H. McConnell, U.S.R. ; Lieut. Arthur Hadley, Jr., U.S.R.

SCHOOLS OF MILITARY AERONAUTICS DIVISION.
J. C. Farrar, Major Hiram Bingham, U.S.R. ; Russell MacDonald, Capt. Frank C. Page, U.S.R.

CONSTRUCTION DIVISION.
Capt. C. G. Edgar, U.S.R. ; Capt. C. S. Benton, U.S.R. (Transportation) ; Capt. K. C. Grant, U.S.R. (Engineering) ; Capt. H. Bennington, U.S.R. (Auditing-Accounting).

BALLOON DIVISION.
Lieut.-Colonel Charles DeF. Chandler, Capt. J. C. McCoy, U.S.R. ; Lieut. B. D. Daggett, U.S.R. ; Lieut. Paul Pleiss, U.S.R.

RADIO DIVISION.
Major N. H. Slaughter, U.S.R. ; Capt. C. C. Culver.

AIRCRAFT PRODUCTION BOARD.
Howard E. Coffin, Chairman ; *Brigadier-General G. O. Squier, Rear-Admiral David W. Taylor, Arthur G. Cable, Secretary ; Sidney D. Waldon, E. A. Deeds, R. L. Montgomery.

JOINT ARMY AND NAVY BOARD OF AERO COGNIZANCE.
*Brigadier-General G. O. Squier, U.S.A. ; Capt. J. S. McKean, U.S.N. ; Major S. M. Embick, U.S.A. ; Capt. V. O. Chase, U.S.N. ; Capt. G. S. Marvell, U.S.N. ; Major D. T Moore, U.S.A.

JOINT ARMY AND NAVY BOARD FOR RIGID DIRIGIBLES.
Rear-Admiral David W. Taylor, U.S.N. ; Lieut.-Colonel Chas. DeF. Chandler, U.S.A. ; Capt. V. E. Clark, U.S.A. ; Brigadier-General G. O. Squier, U.S.A. ; Lieut. J. H. Towers, U.S.N ; Lieut. W. G. Child, U.S.N. ; Assistant Naval Constructor. James C. Hunsaker.

JOINT ARMY AND NAVY BOARD OF DESIGN AND SPECIFICATIONS.
Lieut. A. K. Atkins, U.S.N. ; Lieut. J. H. Towers. U.S.N. ; Assistant Naval Constructor, J. C. Hunsaker, U.S.N. ; Major B.D. Foulis, U.S.A., Major Henry Souther, U.S.R. ; Capt. H. W. Harms, U.S.A.

* Brig.-Gen. G. O. Squier ceased to have any connection with aeronautics in May of 1918.

An American Padre in France, attached American Flying Corps, who visits his scattered flocks by aeroplane. In this case on a French Spad.

U.S.A. MILITARY AERONAUTICS.

BY THE BARON LADISLAS DORCY.

THE EARLY BEGINNINGS.

The early development of the American Flying Service rested entirely with the Signal Corps. which had, on December 23rd, 1907, issued specifications for a man-carrying aeroplane that would be capable of remaining in the air for one hour without landing. These conditions were fulfilled the following summer by a *Wright* biplane fitted with a 35 h.p. engine, and the machine was duly purchased ; but in spite of this early start the development of American military aeronautics lagged far behind the other Great Powers until the entry of the States into the war. During the eight years that elapsed in the meanwhile less than one million dollars was appropriated by Congress for military aeronautics, and the Flying Service remained a subsidiary branch of the Signal Corps, known as the Aviation Section, which had been established by Act of Congress on July 18th, 1914.

On April 6th, 1917, when the United States declared war on Germany, the establishment of the Aviation Section comprised 65 officers, 1,120 enlisted men, two small flying fields (Mineola and San Diego), and less than 300 very second-rate training aeroplanes.

Manufacturing facilities were comparatively insignificant and experienced aeroplane designers were lacking, and the latter explains why up to that date no modern service machine had been produced in the States, and why most of the American service aeroplanes produced during the war were of British or French design, with the minor alterations the fitting of the Liberty engine necessitated, if such was fitted.

WAR PROGRAMME OF THE AIRCRAFT PRODUCTION BOARD.

The original American War Programme, based on an army of a million men, made of the air service but a relatively insignificant portion of the military forces, and this was to be met by two appropriations— $10,800,000 on May 21st, 1917, and $43,450,000 on June 5th, 1917. However, after the arrival in the States of a British and a French aviation mission, the General Staff revised their views, and concurred with the recommendations made by the Aircraft Production Board, calling for the construction of 22,500 aeroplanes and as many aero engines. For this purpose Congress was asked to appropriate a sum of $640,000,000—the largest ever asked for one specific item—and this was granted in record time, taking only one week till it became law. From this date—July 24th, 1917—the big American aircraft programme was really launched, largely in response to Allied appeals.

As speed was justly deemed the essential of success, it was decided to concentrate at first upon the production of a few types for which specifications and engines were available ; thus it came that during 1917, the American aircraft industry produced almost exclusively training aeroplanes. Among these were the *Curtiss* J.N 4 (B., C. and D.) and the *Standard* J. 1 for primary training, and the *Curtiss* J.N. H. (Hispano-Suiza) two-seater, and the *Thomas-Morse* S. 4 (B. and C.) and the *Standard* E. 1 single-seaters for advanced training. Some thirty flying fields were created for the training of aviators, and large numbers of Allied (specially French) specialists in military aeronautics were drawn upon for establishing the Flying Service on a thoroughly up-to-date foundation.

After a lengthy controversy as to whether or not the States should entirely concentrate on training, and have their service machines built to the best available Allied designs in France and Great Britain, a decision was arrived at whereby the United States were to standardize three types of service machines (D.H. 4, *Bristol* F. 2 B. and *Spad de chasse*), and modify them so as to allow the fitting of a standardized aero engine, which was to be built in 4, 6, 8, and 12-cyl. models.

This engine, which was to embody the best features of all existing engines, was designed and constructed with a mixed display of secrecy and advertising within a month, in the summer of 1917, and the initial tests having proven, on the surface, successful, orders were placed in August, 1917, for the construction of this so-called Liberty engine with the following firms, for the quantities stated :—Packard Motor Car Co. and Lincoln Motors Co., 6,000 each ; Ford Motor Co., 5,000 ; Nordyke and Marmon, 3,000 ; General Motors Corporation, 2,000 ; Trego Motors Corporation, 500—A total of 22,500 engines. All these were to be of the 12 cyl., 400 h.p. model, for use in the D.H. 4 and the *Bristol* F. 2B. : an 8-cyl. model, rated 225 h.p., was to be developed for use in the modified *Spad*.

A Characteristic Group of U.S. Army Aviators in France.

U.S.A. MILITARY AERONAUTICS.

After some modifications, the Liberty 12 emerged from the experimental stage, and production increased with great rapidity, so that by the time Armistice was signed 13,396 of these engines had been delivered, the output for October, 1918, alone having reached 4,200. The adaptation of the Liberty 12 to the D.H. 4 proved a success, and orders were placed for 9,500 of these machines, of which one-half was delivered during the war; the modification of the *Bristol* F. 2B. and the *Spad* for the fitting of the Liberty 12 and the Liberty 8 respectively was, however, a failure, and the orders had therefore to be cancelled. As a consequence the D.H. 4A. was the only American-built aeroplane that saw service with the American Expeditionary Force, for the war came to an end before the second American aircraft programme could be carried out.

THE ERA OF REORGANISATIONS.

The Aircraft Production Board, which was responsible for the first aircraft programme, was a purely advisory body, which had been appointed after the declaration of war by Howard Coffin, Advisory Commissioner of the Council of National Defence, at the request of the National Advisory Committee for Aeronautics. It consisted of Mr. Coffin, chairman; Brig.-Gen. George O. Squier, Chief Signal Officer, U.S.A.; Rear-Admiral David W. Taylor, Chief Constructor, U.S.N., and Messrs. S. D. Waldon, E. A. Deeds, and R. L. Montgomery.

As the A.P.B. could only make recommendations and had no executive power, there was no assurance that the construction programme it had suggested would be carried out in the most effectual manner. To overcome this drawback, Congress passed, on Sept. 27th, 1917, a bill authorising the creation of an Aircraft Board, consisting of a civilian chairman, the Chief Signal Officer of the Army, the Chief Constructor of the Navy, and two members each taken from the Army, the Navy, and civilian life. This board was empowered, under the direction of the Secretaries of War and the Navy, to supervise and direct the purchase and manufacture of military and naval aircraft. The members, appointed on December 7th, 1917, were:—Howard E. Coffin, chairman; Maj.-Gen. George O. Squier, Rear-Admiral David W. Taylor; Col. E. A. Deeds and Col. R. L. Montgomery, for the Army; Captain H. E. Irwin and Lieut.-Comdr. A. Atkins, for the Navy; and Richard F. Howe.

While the Aircraft Production Board had thus been given, with a new name, a legal status, its usefulness was greatly hampered by the fact that the Flying Service of the Army had remained, in spite of its extraordinary expansion, still a branch of the Signal Corps, which it greatly exceeded in numbers and importance—the tail was actually wagging the dog. This anomaly was responsible for many of the errors and delays which hampered the progress of America's aircraft programme, and eventually the Committee on Military Affairs of the Senate started an investigation with a view to determining responsibilities. This investigation, as well as one conducted independently by Mr. Gutzon Borglum, a sculptor, on behalf of President Wilson, resulted in a total re-organisation of the aeronautical establishment. On April 24th, 1918, the Aviation Section was separated from the Signal Corps and re-named Air Service, which was divided into a Division of Military Aeronautics and a Bureau of Aircraft Production. Brig.-Gen. William L. Kenly was appointed Director of Military Aeronautics, in charge of training operations, and Mr. John D. Ryan became Chief of the Bureau of Aircraft Production, and at the same time, Chairman of the Aircraft Board, Mr. Coffin having resigned in the meanwhile. From then on, the Aircraft Board faded into oblivion, and its existence has become purely nominal; but the Act of Congress which created it fortunately made provision for its automatic deletion six months after the ending of war.

THE AIR SERVICE IN FRANCE.

At the date Armistice was signed, the Air Service forces at the front included 2,161 officers and 22,351 soldiers, and those in the supply service in France, 4,643 officers and 28,353 soldiers. With the French armies there were detailed 8 officers, and with the British Expeditionary Force, 49 officers and 525 soldiers. The total personnel in France consisted of 6,861 officers and 51,229 soldiers.

There were in operation on the front 39 aero squadrons, distributed as follows: 20 pursuit, 1 night bombardment, 6 day bombardment, 5 army observation, twelve corps observation, and one night observation squadrons.

Enemy aeroplanes brought down by American aviators included 491 confirmed and 354 unconfirmed, a total of 845, while 82 enemy observation balloons were reported as destroyed, of which 57 were confirmed. The Air Service lost, on the other hand, only 271 aeroplanes and 45 observation balloons, thus showing its marked superiority over the enemy.

The number of aeroplanes, by type, received from all sources by the American Expeditionary Force between September 12th, 1917, and November 16th, 1918, was as follows:

Pursuit for service, 3,337; pursuit for schools, 90.
Observation for service, 3,421; observation for schools, 664.
Day bombing for service, 421; day bombing for schools, 85.
Night reconnaissance, 31.

Other planes received included 2,285 training planes, 30 experimental planes and 108 miscellaneous, making a total of 10,472.

Eight different schools under American control were established in France and designed for training 3,800 officers and 11,700 men, as follows:—

Tours—Observers: 916 officers and 2,121 soldiers.
Issoudun—General flying: 2,175 officers and 6,100 soldiers.
Clermont-Ferrand—Bombardment: 120 officers and 660 soldiers.
St. Jean de Monte—Aerial gunners: 92 officers and 1,500 soldiers.
Souse—Artillery firing point: 256 officers and 750 soldiers.
Coetquidan—Artillery firing point: 25 officers and 120 soldiers.
Meucon—Artillery firing point: 29 officers and 110 soldiers.
Chatillon sur Seine—Observers: 204 officers and 373 soldiers.

A total of 159 officers and soldiers were killed in training.

Casualties at the front included 109 killed, 103 wounded, 200 missing, 27 prisoners and 3 interned, making a total of 442.

The total strength of the Division of Military Aeronautics, Air Service, on November 11th, 1918, was 18,688 officers, 5,775 cadets, and 133,644 soldiers. At that date the Air Service had trained 8,933 reserve military aviators at home, and about 2,300 had been trained in France, Great Britain and Italy.

The personnel of the Bureau of Aircraft Production, Air Service, comprised 32,520 officers and soldiers.

The ground establishments of the Air Service in the United States comprised 40 flying fields, 8 balloon fields, 3 radio schools, 3 photography schools, 5 schools of military aeronautics, and 14 aircraft depots.

U.S.A. NAVAL AERONAUTICS.

By THE BARON LADISLAS DORCY.

In February, 1915, specifications were issued and bids asked for one small training airship of the non-rigid type and 6 seaplanes, and in August for 3, 6, 9, and 12 seaplanes, respectively. The specifications asked for a high speed of 60-70 m.p.h., a low speed of 40 m.p.h., a climb of 2,500 ft. in 10 minutes, an endurance of 4 hours at full power, and ability to fly in a wind of 35 m.p.h., and to take off, alight, and drift (afloat) in a wind of 25 m.p.h.

During the summer of this year, Naval Constructor H. C. Richardson, U.S.N., who had previously been identified with extensive research work on flying boat hulls, built an experimental twin-engine seaplane of the float type. Experiments were also continued with the Chambers catapult, and apparently gave satisfactory results, for it was suggested at about this time to equip all the capital ships of the Atlantic Fleet with one or two flying boats and launching devices. As a matter of fact, the first U.S. warship to be so equipped was the *North Carolina*, and this took place in 1916.

The real expansion of the N.F.C. dates from the passage of Naval Act, 1916, the provisions of which are referred to elsewhere. On December 1st, 1916, the N.F.C. had in commission 29 seaplanes and 4 kite balloons—the latter having been developed for the U.S. Navy by the Goodyear Tyre and Rubber Co.—and the flying personnel consisted of 9 officer-aviators, 16 student aviators, while 24 officers and 120 enlisted men of the Navy, Marine Corps and Naval Militia were about to be sent for a course of training to Pensacola, Fla.

At the time the United States entered the great war (April, 1917), 21 seaplanes of float and boat types were in commission (out of total of 93 delivered to the N.F.C. since its formation), and 135 seaplanes, mostly of the N-9 and R-6 types, were on order. Air stations were in operation at Pensacola, Fla., Bay Shore, N.Y., and Squantum, Mass; the two latter were later removed to Chatham, Mass., and Rockaway, N.Y., respectively. The training airship ordered in 1915 had also been commissioned. The personnel of the N.F.C. consisted of 30 officers and 300 men.

With the granting of a large appropriation for the fiscal year 1917-18, a comprehensive construction programme was begun, and the Naval Aircraft Factory was established at the Navy Yard of Philadelphia at a cost of $3,750,000 for the manufacture of seaplanes as well as the assembly of parts produced by trade firms and concerns not engaged in other war work. This system gave most excellent results, and the Navy aircraft programme was as a rule well ahead of schedule—an achievement much at variance with the progress of the Army aircraft programme, and for which much praise is due to Naval Constructor F. G. Coburn, U.S.N., under whose direction the factory was built and is operated. In October, 1918, the Naval Aircraft Factory employed 3,700 workers, one-fourth of whom were women, and over 7,000 people were employed by various contractors.

HISTORICAL.

The U.S. Naval Flying Corps was established in 1911, when Congress appropriated the sum of $25,000 for this purpose. With this sum three naval officers (Lieuts. T. G. Ellyson, John Rodgers and J. T. Towers) were trained as aviators, three shore-going machines (two Curtiss and one Wright biplane) were purchased, and an air station was constructed at Greenbury Point, Md. The latter was removed during the same year to Annapolis, Md., where it remained in operation as a flying school till 1913, when the Pensacola air station and flying school was established, except during the winter months, when the training was conducted at the Curtiss School at San Diego, Cal.

During 1912, a considerable volume of research work was done, under the direction of Capt. W I. Chambers, U.S.N., with regard to seaplane floats, flying boat hulls, and general flotation problems, and a catapult launching apparatus, operated by compressed air was developed. Toward the end of this year a temporary air station was established at Guantanamo, Cuba, but this was broken up the following spring. The development of the N.F.C. was greatly hampered by the inadequate funds available.

In 1913, the Office of Naval Aeronautics was created in the Bureau of Operations, with Captain Mark L. Bristol, U.S.N., as Director of Naval Aeronautics, and naval flying school was established at Pensacola, Fla., whither the U.S.S. *Mississippi* was assigned as an "aeronautic station ship." At the end of this year the N.F.C. had 7 flying boats and 2 float seaplanes in commission, and 3 flying boats on order.

In the spring of 1914, the Atlantic Fleet having been mobilised in Mexican waters, an "aeroplane division" (4 machines) was embarked on the U.S.S. *Mississippi* and *Birmingham*, and sent to Vera Cruz and Tampico, respectively. A number of reconnaissance flights were made in this connection over Vera Cruz. In the summer the U.S.S. *Mississippi* was sold to Greece, and her place was taken by the U.S.S. *North Carolina*.

During the war the Naval Flying Corps extensively cooperated with the air forces of the Allies. For this purpose air stations were established in Ireland; in France (Le Havre, Brest, La Pallice, Bordeaux), and in Canada (Halifax), from which stations incoming and outgoing merchant vessels were convoyed for considerable distances in addition to patrol flights and bombing raids made for the purpose of combating the submarine menace. With the ending of the war these stations will be turned over to the respective countries in which they were established—if this has not already been done.

On October 2, 1918, the total strength of the Naval Flying Corps was 40,383 officers and men.

A Characteristic Group of U.S. Naval Aviators on Service in France.

ORGANISATION.

The present organisation of the Naval Flying Corps was laid down in Naval Act, 1916, which fixed the personnel strength at 150 officer-aviators and 350 enlisted airmen, and provided for the creation of the Naval Reserve Flying Corps for qualified civilians, and the yearly appointment, from civil life, of fifteen probationary ensigns, for air duty only, and for a duration of three years.

The Naval Appropriation Bill, of March, 1918, increased the strength of the enlisted personnel of the N.F.C. to 10,000 men.

The Naval Flying Corps sub-divides, as to organisation, into four branches, which are attached to four Bureaus of the Navy Department, respectively. The Director of Naval Aviation, in the Bureau of Operations, is in charge of administration, inspection, training, materiel, personnel, and operations. The Aircraft Division of the Bureau of Construction and Repair is responsible for design, specifications, construction and supply of aircraft, minus their motive apparatus, and research work. The Aviation Division of the Bureau of Steam Engineering is in charge of the production of engines and their parts, airscrews, radiators, and station and school equipment, instruments, and balloon gas. The Aviation Section of the Bureau of Ordnance supplies aircraft armament.

NAVAL AIR EXPENDITURES.

1912-13 : $24,532·79.
1913-14 : $56,032·90.
1914-15 : $194,492·46.
1915-16 : $219,429·20.
1916-17 : $684,679·28.
1917-18 : $61,133,000 (appropriation).
1918-19 : $220,383,119 (appropriation).

In the airship programme, provision is made for 4 rigid airships, 12 large non-rigid airships, and 64 twin-engine coastal airships ; it is not, however, expected to build all these craft during the fiscal year 1919-20.

NAVAL AIRCRAFT STRENGTH.

On Dec. 31, 1918, the following numbers of aircraft were in commission in the United States Navy :

    34 twin-engine service seaplanes ;
    337 single-engine service seaplanes ;
    100 land aeroplanes (Marines, training) ;
    401 training seaplanes ;
    12 experimental seaplanes ;

a total of 884, in addition to which there were shipped abroad, for the war emergency, the following :

    159 twin-engine seaplanes ;
    229 single-engine seaplanes ;
    140 land aeroplanes ;

that is, a total of 528 machines. The grand total of naval seaplanes and aeroplanes commissioned was therefore 1,412. to which must be added 17 airships and 116 kite-balloons, of which latter 42 were shipped to Europe.

SERVICE FLYING BOATS OF THE U.S.N.F.C.

Type	NC. 1.	F. 5 L.	H. 16.	HS. 2 L.
Span, overall ..	126 ft. (38.43 m.)	103 ft. 9 in. (31.92 m.)	95 ft. (29 m.)	74 ft. (22.60. m.)
Length, overall ..	68 ft. 2¼ in. (20.75 m.)	49 ft 3½ in. (15.00 m.)	46 ft. 1½ in. (14·00 m.)	38 ft. 6 in. (11.75 m.)
Height, overall ..	24 ft. 6 in. (7.47 m.)	18 ft. 9 in. (5.78 m.)	17 ft. 8 in. (5.40 m.)	14 ft. 7 in. (3.45 m.)
Chord	12 ft. (3.66 m.)	8 ft. (2.44 m.)	7 ft.. ¾ in. (2·15 m.)	6 ft. 3 in. (1.91 m.)
Wing area ..	2,380 sq. ft. (2,114.2 sq. m.)	1,397 sq. ft. (125.7 sq. m.)	1,164 sq. ft. (104.8 sq. m.)	803 sq. ft. (72.3 sq. m.)
H.P.	1,200	800	800	400
Engines	3 Liberty 12	2 Liberty 12	2 Liberty 12	1 Liberty 12
Airscrews	3 Tractors.	2 Tractors	2 Tractors	1 Pusher
Weight, fully loaded..	22,000 lbs. (9,900 kgs.)	13,000 lbs. (5,850 kgs.)	10,900 lbs. (4,900 kgs.)	6,432 lbs. (2,894 kgs.)
Useful load	7,750 lbs. (3,490 kgs.)	4,750 lbs. (2,140 kgs.)	3,500 lbs. (1,575 kgs.)	2,132 lbs. (960 kgs.)
High speed	81 m.p.h.* (129.6 km.p.h.)	87 m.p.h. (139 km.p.h.)	95 m.p.h. (152 km.p.h.)	91 m.p.h. (145.6 km.p.h.)
Low speed	61 m.p.h.* (97.6 k.m.p.h)	57 m.p.h. (91 km.p.h.)	56 m.p.h. (90 km.p.h.)	55 m.p.h. (88 km.p.h.)
Initial climb .. .··	1,050 ft. 320 m. in 5 mins.	2,625 ft. (800 m.) in 10 mins.	3,000 ft. (915 m.) in 10 mins.	2,500—3,000 ft. (760—915 m.) in 10 mins.
Full speed endurance.	13 hours	10 hours.	hours	hours
Armament	8 M.G.	1 Q.F., 4 M.G. 2—500 lb., or 4—230 lb. bombs	6 M.G.	1 M.G.
Complement	5	5	4	3
Builder	Curtiss	Naval Aircraft Factory	Curtiss	Standard

* Carrying a load of 21,560 lbs. (9,700 kgs).

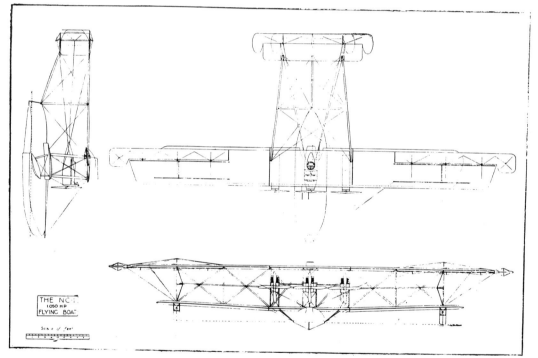

THE N.C.
1050 H.P.
FLYING BOAT

The Curtiss-built N.C.1 Flying Boat, designed by the U.S. Naval Aviation Department.

NAVAL AIR STATIONS.

Atlantic Coast :
  Chatham, Mass.—2 airships, 24 seaplanes, 6 K.B.
  Montauk, L.I., N.Y.—4 airships.
  Rockaway, N.Y.—24 seaplanes, 6 K.B.
  Cape May, Del.—4 airships, 18 seaplanes, 6 K.B.
  Hampton, Va.—4 airships, 24 seaplanes, 6 K.B.
  Yorktown, Va.—6 K.B.
  Moorehead City, N.C.—12 seaplanes.
  Charleston, S.C.—4 airships, 6 K.B.
  Brunswick, Ga.—18 seaplanes, 6 K.B.
  Miami, Fla.—2 airships, 12 seaplanes.

(The General Board of the U.S. Navy recommended the construction of an air station between Rockland and Portland, Me., for 4 airships, and an air station at Narraganset Bay., R.I., for 24 seaplanes and 6 K.B. This item was struck out after the armistice.)

Gulf Coast :
  Key West, Fla.—2 airships, 24 seaplanes, 6 K.B.
  Pensacola, Fla.—6 K.B.
  Galveston, Tex.—24 seaplanes, 6 K.B.
  (An air station at Port Arthur, Tex., for 2 airships, was recommended by the General Board.)

Canal Zone :
  Coco Solo (Colon).—2 airships, 24 seaplanes.

West Indies :
  (The General Board recommended the construction of an air station at St. Thomas, Virgin Islands, for 4 airships, 18 seaplanes, and 6 K.B., and one each at Guantanamo and Samana, Cuba.)

Pacific Coast :
  San. Diego, Cal.—2 airships, 24 seaplanes, 6 K.B.
  (The General Board recommended the construction of air stations at San Francisco, Cal., for 4 airships, 24 seaplanes, and 6 K.B. ; at the mouth of the Columbia River, for 4 airships and 6 K.B. ; at Port Angeles, Wash., for 4 airships and 6 K.B., and at Seward, Alaska, for 4 airships, 6 seaplanes and 4 K.B.)

Hawaian Islands :
  (The General Board recommended the construction of air stations at Pearl Harbor, for 4 airships, 24 seaplanes, 6 K.B., and at Hilo, for 24 seaplanes and 6 K.B.)

Guam :
  (The General Board recommended the construction of an air station at Port Apra, for 4 airships, 24 seaplanes and 6 K.B.)

Phillippine Islands :
  (The General Board recommended the construction of an air station at Cavite, for 4 airships, 12 seaplanes and 6 K.B.)

FACTORIES AND SCHOOLS,

Naval Aircraft Factory, Philadelphia, Pa.—Builds seaplanes of all types, and airship cars ; normal output, 50 twin-engine machines per year. Also engaged in research and experimental work.

Helium Production Plant, Fort Worth, Tex.—Owned by the Linde Air Products Co., but operated for the Navy.

Naval Ground School, Massachussetts Institute of Technology, Cambridge, Mass.

Naval Flying School, Pensacola, Fla.

Naval Balloon School, Arcadia, Fla.

Naval Airship School, Akron, Ohio.

Marine Corps Flying School, Miami, Fla.

Coast Guard Flying School (proposed.)—The U.S. Coast Guard is the result of an amalgamation of the Revenue Cutter and Life Saving Services ; it is proposed to use aircraft for life saving whenever it cannot be done by other means.

Side View of the U.S. Navy's N.C.1 Flying Boat.

U.S.A. POSTAL AVIATION.

The Aerial Mail Service of the Post Office Department was established with an appropriation of $300,000 dollars, on May 15th, 1918, between Washington and New York, with the co-operation of the War Department, which furnished the aeroplanes and the aviators, and conducted the flying and maintenance operations until August 12th, 1918, when the entire service was taken over by the postal authorities.

The Washington-New York route has been in continuous operation ever since, and has functioned quite satisfactorily, even throughout the winter months. It is true the winter of 1918-19 was exceptionally mild and devoid of storms. One round trip daily, except Sunday, is being made without fail. The trip from Washington to New York is performed on an average of 2 hrs. and 30 mins., and from New York to Washington in 2 hrs. and 50 mins., the difference in time being due to the prevailing winds, which are usually from a westerly direction. A stop for the exchange of mail on each trip is made at Philadelphia. An average of 7¾ tons of letter mail is being carried each month.

The cost of the operation of the service since it began, including developments of new routes, is at the rate of 74 cents per mile operated. The cost per ton-mile of mail carried is $5 35. By this service mail between New York and Washington is advanced from 2½ to 3 hours over the train service.

The postage charged on mail carried by aeroplane was originally 24 cents (1s.) for each ounce, but it was soon found that this charge exceeded the cost of the service, and on July 15th, 1918, the aeroplane postage was reduced to 16 cents for the first ounce and six cents for each additional ounce, ten cents of the initial charge being for special-delivery service.

The after-the-war programme of the Post Office Department contemplates the establishment of an aerial mail service which will connect the principal commercial centres of the States by a system of trunk lines and feeders, which in their turn will connect with the West Indies, Central and South America. The trunk and feeder lines decided upon under this programme, for which an appropriation of $860,000 is available in the fiscal year 1918-19, are :—

1. New York to San Francisco, with feeders from—
   (a) Chicago to St. Louis and Kansas City.
   (b) Chicago to St. Paul and Minneapolis.
   (c) Cleveland to Pittsburg.
2. Boston to Key West, with feeders from—
   (a) Philadelphia to Pittsburg.
   (b) Washington to Cincinnati.
   (c) Atlanta to New Orleans.
3. Key West, via Habana, to Panama.
4. Key West, via the West Indies, to South America.

The present American postal fleet consists of six *Standard* E. 4 biplanes (150 h.p. Hispano-Suiza), Six *Curtiss* J.N. 4H. biplanes (150 h.p. Hispano-Suiza), and six *Curtiss* R. 4L.M. biplanes (400 h.p. Liberty).

The U.S. Navy's F.5.L. type Flying Boat ashore.

The U.S. Navy's F.5.L. Flying Boat afloat.

[For the following information the Editor is indebted largely to the Baron Ladislas D'Orcy, and to the two American Journals "Aviation" and "Aeria Age."]

A

AEROMARINE PLANE AND MOTOR COMPANY.
Offices: 1511 Times Building, New York. Factory: Keyport, N.J. President, I. M. Uppercu; Chief Engineer, Charles M. Willard.

Build aeroplanes and seaplanes for naval and sport use. Contractors to the U.S. Navy.

AEROMARINE, SPORT SEAPLANE.

Type of machine	Flying Boat.
Name or type No. of machine	Model 40-T.
Span, upper wing	48 ft. 4 in.
Span, lower wing	37 ft. 4 in.
Stagger	8 in.
Chord	75 in.
Gap	78 in.
Dihedral	2 degrees.
Area, upper panel (with ailerons)	304 sq. ft.
Area, lower panel	200 sq. ft.
Ailerons, each	29 sq. ft.
Elevators, each	12.8 sq. ft.
Stabilizer	39.5 sq. ft.
Vertical stabilizer fin	15 sq. ft.
Rudder	17.5 sq. ft.
Skid fin	5.5 sq. ft.
Length overall	28 ft. 11 in.
Weight, light	1,925 lbs.
Weight, loaded	2,485 lbs.
Gasoline	35 gallons.

Seating Arrangement. Model 40-T is arranged for one operator and one passenger, and is an ideal machine for instruction or sporting purposes.

Performance.
Aeromarine 125-130 h.p. motor:

High speed	80 m.p.h.
Landing speed	38 m.p.h.
Climb	2,500 feet in 10 minutes.

100 h.p. motor:

High speed	70 m.p.h.
Landing speed	38 m.p.h.
Climb	2,100 feet in 10 minutes.

Hull.—The hulls of these boats are constructed in the most modern and durable fashion.

The bottoms are constructed of two-ply, placed diagonally with cloth between and fastened with brass fastenings.

The sides and decks are of three-ply waterproof veneer.

The decks forward of the cockpit and after the rear beam may be removed, as well as the floors in the passenger compartment, and as it is possible to enter the hull between the wing beams through the hatch, the entire bottom and inside of the boat may be inspected and repaired more easily.

50 of these machines have been delivered to the U.S. Navy.
Price : $9,000.

Specifications of Model 50 Flying Boat.

The Aeromarine Plane and Motor Company's Model 50 is of the same general dimensions as that of Model 40-T.

The seating arrangement, however, is for three persons—two passengers side by side and a pilot sitting in a separate cockpit forward of the passengers.

This model will be supplied either with the passenger space enclosed or open, with movable windshield to protect the passengers.
Price : $9,500.

AEROMARINE, PRIMARY TRAINING (ARMY).

Type of machine	Land machine.
Name or type No. of machine	Model M.L.
Span	37 ft. 3 in.
Overall length	25 ft. 11 in.
Overall height	12 ft. 4 in.
Total wing area	430 sq. ft.
Weight, loaded	2,050 lbs.
Dihedral (top and bottom)	1 degree.
Sweep back	None.
Stagger	12 in.
Decalage	1 degree.
Gap	6 ft. 6 in.
Chord	6 ft. 3 in.
Aileron area (two ailerons)	56 sq. ft.
Rudder area	13 ft.
Elevator area (two elevators)	21 sq. ft.
Stabilizer area	33 sq. ft.
Upper plane—span	37 ft. 3 in.
Chord	6 ft. 3 in.
Area (not including ailerons)	194 sq. ft.
Lower plane—span	32 ft. 10 in.
Chord	6 ft. 3 in.
Area	180 sq. ft.

The Aeromarine Model M.L. is a two-place land machine, equipped with the Aeromarine Model L. (6-cylinder) motor.

Seating Arrangement. The seats are arranged in tandem, and controls can be had in either or both cockpits.

Performance.

High speed	90 miles per hour.
Landing speed	42 miles per hour.
Climb	6,000 feet in 10 minutes.

Price : $8,250.

The Aeromarine Sport Seaplane (Curtiss 100 h.p. O.X. 5 engine.

The Aeromarine Central Float Seaplane.

Aeromarine Central Float Seaplane.

AIRCRAFT ENGINEERING CORPORA-
TION, 2, East End Avenue, New York. Sales Offices:
220, West 42nd Street, New York. Factory A: 37, East 79th
Street; factory B: 19, East 93rd Street, New York.

Build a small single-seater sporting aeroplane, the *Ace*, to the
designs of N. W. Dalton, chief engineer of the firm.

Specification.

Span	..	..	..	28 ft. 4 in.
Length overall	..	..	..	16 ft. 1 in.
Chord	..	..	..	4 ft 6 in.
Engine	..	..	..	4-cylinder 40 h.p. B.W.W. (air-cooled).
Tractor airscrew	..	..	..	Direct driven.
High speed	..	..	..	60 m.p.h.
Low speed	..	..	..	30 m.p.h.
Weight, light	..	..	..	600 lbs.
Useful load	..	..	..	225 lbs.

The Aircraft Engineering Corporation's "Ace" (40 h.p B.W.W. engine).

B

BOEING AIRPLANE COMPANY.

Seattle, Wash.

The only seaplane constructors of the Pacific coast. Contractors to the U.S. Navy.

General Description of Model C.L. 4 S.

The model C.L. 4 S. is a modification of the model "C" seaplane. Although the general appearance and characteristics
remain the same, the new engine installation together with a
few minor changes have added to the performance of this
machine.

The wing structure with its center cabane of steel simplifies
assembly and clears the approach to, and vision from, the
cockpits.

The tail unit, consisting of balanced elevators, rudder and
fin, is independently complete, readily assembled and firmly
fixed in place by steel tubing, forming a compact structure in
keeping with the wind surfaces.

The body, although short in appearance, is wholly in keeping
with the aero and hydro conditions met with in this type of
seaplane.

Specification.

Power Plant.

(Hall-Scott Liberty Four)	..	125 h.p.

Wing and Control Surface Areas.

Main planes (including ailerons)	475 sq. ft.
Upper planes (including ailerons)	246 sq. ft.
Lower planes	..	229 sq. ft.
Ailerons	..	36.0 sq. ft.
Number of ailerons	..	2.
Elevators	..	30.0 sq. ft.
Rudder ..	..	12.0 sq. ft.
Vertical fin	..	6.0 sq. ft.

Overall Dimensions.

Span, upper	..	43 ft. 6 in.
Span, lower	..	43 ft. 2 in.
Chord, upper and lower	..	69 in.
Gap	..	72 in.
Length overall..	..	27 ft.

Incidence of Wings with Propeller Axis.

Upper	..	$6\frac{1}{2}$ degrees.
Lower	..	4 degrees.
Dihedral	..	$2\frac{3}{4}$ degrees.
Stagger ..	..	$29\frac{1}{2}$ in.

Performance.

Get away	..	11 sec.
Climb in 10 min. (full load) ..	3,600 ft.
High speed	..	75 m.p.h.
Landing speed ..	..	38 m.p.h.
Endurance at full speed	..	3 hours.
Gasoline consumption (during altitude climb) ..	..	10.5 gallons per hour.
Oil consumption (during altitude climb) ..	..	1.0 gallon per hour.

Weight.

Fully loaded ..	..	2,430 lbs.

The Boeing Seaplane, type C.L. 4 S. (124 h.p. 4-cylinder Liberty engine.)

445a

BREESE AIRCRAFT COMPANY.

New York.

Built "Penguin" training machine for the U.S. Army, and
an experimental seaplane.

No details available.

An Experimental Breese Seaplane.

THE BURGESS COMPANY.

Marblehead, Mass.

Subsidiary company of the Curtiss Aeroplane and Motors Corporation; specialised in the construction of seaplanes to Curtiss designs.

Built *Wright* types under license, also machines of their own. Later adopted the patents of Mr. J. W. Dunne, the British experimenter in inherent stability, and have had considerable success.

The US Navy received single examples of the Burgess-Dunne AH-7 and AH-10 tailless pushers in 1916, used in part for original air gunnery experiments, plus twenty Burgess Type L tractor biplanes as military Model HTs, Ss and Us.

Model and Type.	Flying Boat. B.D.F.	Land Pusher. O.	Navy School Tractor. S.	Tractor Hydro. U.	Burgess Dunne. B.D.	Burgess Dunne B.D.H.
Length	25′ 2″	31′ 6″	30′	30′ 6″	23′	31′
Span ..	53′	45′	46′ 6″	46′	46′	46′ 6″
Useful load lbs.	560	920	750	640	670	350
Motor .. h.p.	100 Curtiss Oxx2	140	125	100 Oxx2	100 Oxx2	140
Fuel capacity ..	3 hours	4 hours	4 hours	4 hours	4 hours	4 hours
Speed, Max. ..	68 m.p.h.	85	73	70	69	70
Speed, Min. ..	43 m.p.h.	47	41	40	45	40
Seating capacity	3	2	2	2	2	2

Type B.D.F. is a Burgess Dunne boat.
  „ B.D.H. „ „ „ reconnaissance biplane with central float.
  „ B.D. „ „ „ sportsman's seaplane.
  „ O is an ordinary land-going " pusher " biplane.
  „ S is a twin-float tractor seaplane.
  „ U is a central-float tractor seaplane.

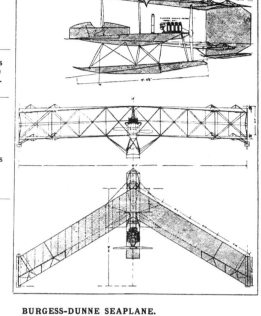

BURGESS-DUNNE SEAPLANE.

BURGESS-DUNNE SEAPLANE ALOFT.

The three types of Burgess Seaplanes: The Training Tractor, type L., the Burgess-Dunne Seaplane, type B.D., and the Burgess-Dunne Reconnaissance Seaplane, type B.D.I.

BURGESS-DUNNE FLYING BOAT, 1916-17 type. Model B.D.F.

C

CANTILEVER AERO COMPANY.

1269 Broadway, New York.

Constructors of the *Christmas* "Bullet," a high-speed single-seater biplane without external wing truss.

THE CHRISTMAS "BULLET."

A single-seater tractor biplane of quaint appearance was tested at the U.S.A. Government Experimental Field No. 1 on Dec. 3rd and 7th.

The machine is named the *Christmas* "Bullet" after its designer, Dr. W. W. Christmas, and is driven by a Liberty "6" engine, which develops 185 h.p. at 1,400 r.p.m. The "Bullet" was reported to have attained a speed of 175 m.p.h. at three-quarter throttle.

The "Bullet" has what is termed one-and-a-half planes, as used in the *Nieuport* biplanes, the upper plane having a span of 28ft., and a chord of 5 ft., the lower plane being 12 ft. in span with a chord of 2½ ft. External bracings and struts do not exist, the upper wing being fitted to the top of the fuselage and the lower wing to the bottom.

The wing curve is one developed by Dr. Christmas, and is of fairly deep section between the main wing spars, but tapers off sharply aft of the rear spar, merging into a flat and thin flexible trailing edge. The wing thus maintains a high angle of incidence and a fair camber at low speeds, and a lower angle and a flatter camber at higher speeds. This system of wing construction is reminiscent in a measure of the earlier *Bréguet* and *Caudron* machines.

Another View of the Christmas "Bullet."

Both upper and lower planes have the same aspect ratio. The upper plane has a maximum thickness of 5 ins. Fuller details of the wing construction cannot at the moment be given, as patents were still pending when the last was heard of the machine.

The car-type radiator and engine are placed in the front part of the fuselage, which is very deep. The two-bladed airscrew has a projecting bullet-shaped hub. The landing carriage struts are of deep section, such as is used in the *Curtiss* land machines and *Burgess* seaplanes. The pilot's cockpit is located behind the upper plane, affording a fairly good view in most directions.

The elevator is not divided, as the rudder is fitted to the vertical fin in such a manner as not to interfere with free elevator movement. This method is similar to that employed in the *Pfalz* single-seater scout. The tail-skid is fixed to the stern-post.

The principal details of the *Christmas* "Bullet" are as follows:

Span, upper plane	28 ft.
Span, lower plane	12 ft.
Chord, upper plane	5 ft.
Chord, lower plane	2 ft. 6 in.
Area, upper plane	140 sq. ft.
Area, lower plane	30 sq. ft.
Length overall	21 ft.
Weight, machine empty	1,820 lbs.
Weight, fully loaded	2,100 lbs.
Minimum speed	50-60 m.p.h.
Maximum speed	175 m.p.h.
Cruising radius	550 miles.
Ceiling	14,700 ft.

THE CONTINENTAL AIRCRAFT CORPORATION.

Office : 120, Liberty Street, New York City. Factory : Amityville, Long Island, New York. Demonstrating ground : Central Park, Long Island.

THE CONTINENTAL KB-3T TRAINING TRACTOR.

The Continental Aircraft Corporation's new training tractor KB-3T recently tested at Amityville, has come up to all expectations of the designer Vincent J. Buranelli. The short "over-all" length of this machine, 23 feet 4 inches, is noteworthy and characteristic of Continental machines.

Mr. Buranelli's chief object in designing the KB-3T was to produce a training machine that could be cheaply constructed. This has been accomplished by an extensive use of one-piece standardized fittings. A very complete list of measurements and weights are given which should prove useful in checking up with other machines.

General Specifications.

Span upper plane	40 ft. 3in.
Span lower plane	34 ft.
Chord both planes	5 ft. 6 in.
Sap	5 ft. 4 in.
Stagger	6 in.
Length over all	23 ft. 4 in.
Height	9 ft. 3 in.
Net weight	1,340 lb.
Useful load	540 lb.
Gross weight	1,880 lb.
Motor. Curtiss..	OX 100 h.p.
Speed range	45-75 m.p.h.
Climb in ten minutes..	3,200 ft.

Weights.

Upper planes	118 lb.
Lower planes	102 lb.
Struts	30 lb.
Wires and turnbuckles	20 lb.
Fittings and bolts	18 lb.
Total	288 lb.
Fuselage	310 lb.
Seats upholstered	12 lb.
Stick controls and mountings	17 lb.
Dash with instruments	13 lb.
Total	352 lb.
Ailerons	24 lb
Elevators	16 lb.
Rudder ..	10 lb.
Vertical stabilizer	3 lb.
Horizontal stabilizer	19 lb.
Control cables ..	16 lb.
Total	88 lb.
Motor complete	390 lb.
Propeller	22 lb.
Radiator and piping ..	53 lb.
Gas tank and gauges ..	22 lb.
Exhaust pipe ..	16 lb.
Total	503 lb.

Landing chassis and incidentals = 109 lb.

Planes.

The wing curve is Eiffel 36. The planes are set with an angle of incidence of 2½ degrees. Top and bottom are the same. The tips of planes are slightly rounded as is in general use on Continental machines. There is no sweepback, but a dihedral of 1 degree and a stagger of 6 in. The upper planes are made in two main sections with a three-foot panel over the body. The lower plane is in two sections and attaching to the body. Wing beams are of "I" section and made of Douglas fir. The overhang is braced by a steel strut made of ⅞ in. seamless tubing with a fairing of spruce.

The struts are of streamline section, the maximum 3¾ in. × 1½ in. occurring at the centre, and tapering in proportion to each end where it sets into a special strut socket. Flying cables are double $\frac{5}{32}$ in. in inner panel, $\frac{1}{8}$ in. outer panel, landing wires are single of the same sizes. Double drift and single trueing wires are used. All control wires are internal.

Ailerons on top plane only, and are 11 ft. × 1 ft. 6 in. Where ailerons are attached, a bevel on the aileron permits the surface to be moved without a space occurring between aileron and wing.

R. A. F. stitching is employed in attaching the fabric to the ribs. To finish four coats of "dope" and two coats of Valspar are used. A factor of safety of 7 is employed. The lift to drag ratio is 12.

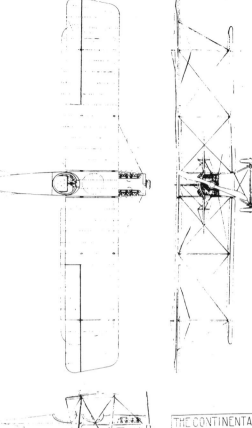

THE CONTINENTAL MODEL KB-3T 100 HP TRAINING TRACTOR

The Christmas "Bullet" (185 h.p. 6-cylinder Liberty engine).

CURTISS AEROPLANE AND MOTORS CORPORATION. 52, Vanderbilt Avenue, New York.

Factories at Buffalo and Hammondsport, N.Y. Flying fields at Buffalo, Hammondsport, Newport News, Va., and Miami, Fla.

The largest American aeronautical construction firm ; their activity ranges from the smallest to the largest aeroplanes and seaplanes, and from aero engines to airship cars. Contractors to the U.S. Army and Navy.

Glenn H. Curtiss in 1907 and 1908 was a member of the Aerial Experiment Association, formed by Dr. and Mrs. Alexander Graham Bell. This Association built four machines, each along the lines of one of the four engineers belonging to the Association, F. W. Baldwin, Lieut. T. E. Selfridge, G. H. Curtiss and J. A. D. McCurdy. The last built was the *June Bug*, designed by Curtiss and was the most successful. In the spring of 1908, the Association was disbanded and The Aeronautical Society gave Curtiss an order for an aeroplane with *carte blanche* as to design. He produced a 4-cyl. machine, with a Curtiss engine, and flew it.

A duplicate was hurriedly built, an 8-cyl. engine installed, and taken to Europe for the first Gordon Bennett, which he won. Returning, the same type was continued with minor improvements. Later the front elevator was brought closer in, finally discarded, and the fan tail adopted. In April, 1913, a military tractor was built and flown.

On January 26th, 1911, first successful flights were made with a hydro-aeroplane, at the Winter camp at San Diego, California. This had two floats tandem. One was finally adopted and great success was achieved. With this machine various experiments were made.

In 1912 he brought out his present type of flying boat. This is being rapidly developed and minor changes in details are made in practically every machine put out.

In May, 1913, he produced a special 4-passenger flying boat for a customer to special order.

In 1914, much attention was paid to flying boats, and a huge two-engined machine was built to the order of Mr. Wanamaker and designed by Lieut. John Porte, R.N., the intention being that it should fly the Atlantic.

Just before the war this machine was fitted with three engines. Later on a big triplane with four 250 h.p. Curtiss engines was built, and was taken over by the British Navy. It was, however, not a success.

Many school biplanes of the "J.N." type were supplied to the belligerent powers, and did remarkably well for their purpose. Late in 1916, a remarkably good flight was made on an "R. 7" type, from Chicago to New York, with one stop, by the late Victor Carlstrom.

CURTISS TYPE 18T. TRIPLANE.

Specification.

General Dimensions.

Wing span, upper plane..	31 ft. 11 in.
Wing span, middle plane	31 ft. 11 in.
Wing span, lower plane ..	31 ft. 11 in.
Depth of wing chord (upper, middle and lower) ..	42 in.
Gap between wings (between upper and middle) ..	42 in.
Gap between wings (between middle and lower)	35 9/16 in.
Stagger ..	None.
Length of machine overall	23 ft. 3 7/16 in.
Height of machine overall	9 ft. 10 3/8 in.
Angle of incidence ..	2½ degrees.
Dihedral angle ..	None.
Sweepback ..	5 degrees.
Wing curve ..	Sloane.
Horizontal stabilizer—angle of incidence ..	0.5 degrees.

Areas.

Wings, upper ..	112.0 sq. ft.
Wings, middle ..	87.71 sq. ft.
Wings, lower ..	87.71 sq. ft.
Ailerons (middle 10.79, lower 10.79) ..	21.58 sq. ft.
Horizontal stabilizer ..	14.3 sq. ft.
Vertical stabilizer ..	5·2 sq. ft.
Elevators (each 6.51) ..	13.02 sq. ft.
Rudder ..	8.66 sq. ft.
Total supporting surface	309.0 sq. ft.
Loading (weight carried per sq. ft. of supporting surface)..	9.4 lbs.
Loading (per r.h.p.) ..	7.25 lbs.

Weights.

Net weight, machine empty ..	..	1,825 lbs.
Gross weight, machine and load..	..	2,901 lbs.
Useful load ..	..	1,076 lbs.
Fuel ..	400 lbs.	
Oil ..	45 lbs.	
Pilot and passenger	330 lbs.	
Useful load ..	301 lbs.	
Total ..	..	1076 lbs.

Performance.

Speed, max. (horizontal flight) ..	163 m.p.h.
Speed, min. (horizontal flight) ..	58 m.p.h.
Climbing speed ..	15,000 ft. in 10 mins.

Motor.

Model K. 12, 12-cylinder, Vee, four-stroke cycle ..	Water cooled.	
Horse power (rated) at 2500 r.p.m.	400.	
Weight per rated h.p. ..	1.70	
Bore and stroke ..	4½ × 6.	
Fuel consumption per hour ..	36.7 galls.	
Fuel tank capacity ..	67 galls.	
Oil capacity provided, crankcase	6 galls.	
Fuel consumption per b.h.p. ..	.55 lbs. per hour.	
Oil consumption per b.h.p. ..	.030 lbs. per hour.	

Propeller.

Material.—Wood.
Pitch.—According to requirements of performance.
Diameter.—According to requirements of performance.
Direction of rotation, as viewed from pilot's seat.—Clockwise.

The Curtiss Triplane, type 18T, Single-seater Fighter (Curtiss K. 12 400 h.p. engine). Two went to US Navy, ordered in March 1918.

Details.

One pressure and one gravity gasoline tank located in fuselage.
Tail skid independent of tail post ; landing gear wheel, size 26 in. × 4 in.
Standard Equipment.—Tachometer, oil gauge, gasoline gauge, complete set of tools ; other equipment on special order.

Maximum Range.

At economic speed, about 550 miles.

CURTISS MODEL J.N. 4D. 2 TRACTOR.

Specification.

General Dimensions.

Wing span, upper plane..	43 ft. 7 3/8 in.
Wing span, lower plane ..	33 ft. 11¼ in.
Depth of wing chord ..	59½ in.
Gap between wings ..	61¼ in.
Stagger ..	16 in.

Length of machine overall		27 ft. 4 in.
Height of machine overall		9 ft. 10 3/8 in.
Angle of incidence ..		2 degrees.
Dihedral angle ..		1 degree.
Sweepback ..		0 degrees.
Wing curve ..		Eiffel No. 6.
Horizontal stabilizer—angle of incidence ..		0 degrees.

Areas.

Wings, upper ..	167.94 sq. ft.
Wings, lower ..	149.42 sq. ft.
Ailerons, upper ..	35.2 sq. ft.
Horizontal stabilizer ..	28.7 sq .ft.
Vertical stabilizer	3.8 sq. ft.
Elevators (each 11 sq. ft.) ..	22 sq. ft.
Rudder ..	12 sq. ft.
Total supporting surface ..	352.56 sq. ft.
Loading (weight carried per sq. ft. of supporting surface) ..	6.04 lbs.
Loading (per r.h.p.) ..	23·65 lbs.

Weights.

Net weight, machine empty ..	..	1,580 lbs.
Gross weight, machine and load ..	..	2,130 lbs.
Useful load ..	..	550 lbs.
Fuel ..	..	130 lbs.
Oil ..	..	38 lbs.
Pilot ..	..	165 lbs.
Passenger and other load..	..	217 lbs.
Total ..	..	550 lbs.

The Standard type Curtiss J.N. 'Jenny' Training Tractor. The type most used by the U.S. Army.

CURTISS MODEL J.N. TRACTOR—*continued*

Performance.

Speed, max. (horizontal flight)	..	75 m.p.h.
Speed, min. (horizontal flight)	..	45 m.p.h.
Climbing speed	.. ..	3,000 ft. in 10 mins.

Motor.

Model O.X. 8-cylinder, Vee, four-stroke cycle	.. ..	Water cooled.
Horse power (rated) at 1400 r.p.m.		90.
Weight per rated h.p.	.. ..	4.33 lbs.
Bore and stroke	.. ..	4 in. × 5 in.
Fuel consumption per hour	..	9 galls.
Fuel tank capacity	.. ..	21 galls.
Oil capacity provided (crankcase)		4 galls.
Fuel consumption per b.h.p	..	0.60 lbs. per hour.
Oil consumption per b.h.p	..	0.030 lbs. per hour.

Propeller.

Material.—Wood.
Pitch.—According to requirements of performance.
Diameter.—According to requirements of performance.
Direction of rotation, viewed from pilot's seat.—Clockwise.

Details.

One gasoline tank located in fuselage.
Tail skid independent of tail post.
Landing gear wheel, size 26 in. × 4 in.
Standard Equipment.—Tachometer, oil gauge, gasoline gauge, complete set of tools.
Other equipment on special order.

Maximum Range.

At economic speed, about 250 miles.

Shipping Data.

Fuselage Box.—Dimensions : 24 ft. 6 in. × 5 ft. 3 in. × 3 ft. 1 in. ; gross weight, 2,380 lbs.
Panel Box.—Dimensions : 20 ft. 9 in. × 5 ft. 8 in. × 3 ft. ; gross weight, 1,450 lbs.

Model R 4 CURTISS.

CURTISS R4

This two-seat bomber appeared in 1915 and was used by the US Army and RNAS for training. Power was provided by a 200 h.p. Curtiss V-2 engine. From it was developed the R6 with the pilot in front (200 h.p. Curtiss or 375-400 h.p. Liberty engine) for observation and training, and the R9 with the same Liberty engine. R6s were the first American produced aircraft to serve abroad in the war (the Azores). The US Navy received examples of all three versions, but the R6 in the greatest number.

General Dimensions.

Span { Upper	48′ 4″
{ Lower	38′ 5″
Chord	6′ 3″
Gap	6′ 2″
Stagger	10′ 1″
Length, overall,	28′ 11¾″
Height	13′ 2¼″
Incidence	2½ degrees
Dehedral	3 degrees
Wing Cvrve	R.A.F. 6
Tail Plane	No incidence

Areas.

Surface (total)	505 sq. ft.
Wings (upper)	257 sq. ft.
„ (lower)	193 sq. ft.
Aileron (upper)	17 sq. ft.
„ (lower)	10¼ sq. ft.

Total Aileron Surface	54½ sq. ft.
Tail Plane	40½ sq. ft.
Elevators (two)	27½ sq. ft.
Fin (vertical)	7 sq. ft.
Rudder	16½ sq. ft.
Load per sq. ft.	6·42 lbs.

Other Figures.

Load per B.H.P.	15·89 lbs.
Net Weight (empty)	2225 lbs.
Gross „ (full)	3245 lbs.
Useful Load	1020 lbs.
Petrol carried	625 lbs. (90 galls.)
Speed (max.)	90 m.p.h.
„ (min.)	48 m.p.h.
Climb	4000 ft. in 10 mins.
Motor (V 2 type)	200 h.p. 8-cyl. Curtiss

The R 7 CURTISS Chicago-New York machine.
Practically an R 4 with an extra bay added to each wing.
Span, 60 feet. Engine, 160 h.p. Curtiss.

A Curtiss experimental Single-Seat Fighter (400 h.p. K.12 Curtiss engine). A very high speed single-seat fighter.

The Curtiss experimental Model 18 B. Two-seater Fighter (400 h.p. K.12 Curtiss engine).

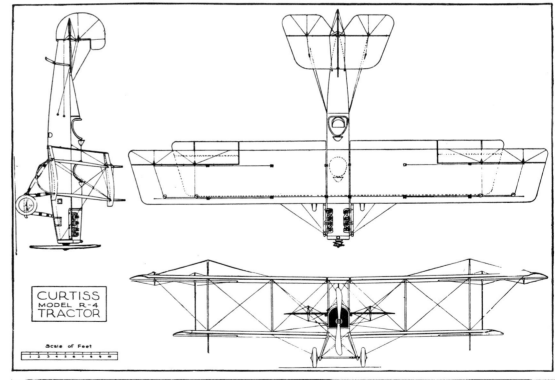

CURTISS MODEL R-4 TRACTOR

Scale of Feet

CURTISS AERODROME

***CURTISS**—continued.*

CURTISS MODEL H. 16A. FLYING BOAT.

Specification.

General Dimensions.

Wing span, upper plane	96 ft. $6\frac{5}{8}$ in.
Wing span, lower plane	68 ft. $11\frac{3}{8}$ in.
Depth of wing chord	$84\frac{49}{64}$ in.
Gap between wings	$96\frac{9}{16}$ in.
Stagger	None.
Length of machine overall ..	46 ft. $1\frac{15}{32}$ in.
Height of machine overall ..	17 ft. $8\frac{5}{8}$ in.
Angle of incidence	4 degrees.
Dihedral angle	1 degree.
Sweepback	None.
Wing curve	R.A.F. No. 6.
Horizontal stabilizer—angle of incidence	2 degrees pos.

Areas.

Wings, upper (without ailerons)	616.2 sq. ft.
Wings, lower	443.1 sq. ft.
Ailerons	131 sq. ft.
Horizontal-stabilizer	108 sq. ft.
Vertical stabilizer	31.1 sq. ft.
Elevators	58.4 sq. ft.
Rudder	27.9 sq. ft.
Non-skids	24 sq. ft.
Total supporting surface ..	119.3 sq. ft.
Loading (weight carried per sq. ft. of supporting surface) ..	8.54 lbs.
Loading (per r.h.p.)	15.42 lbs.

Weights.

Net weight, machine empty		6,956 lbs.
Gross weight, machine and load		10,172 lbs.
Useful load		3,216 lbs.
Fuel and oil	1,527 lbs.	
Crew	660 lbs.	
Useful load	1,029 lbs.	
Total	3,216 lbs.	

Performance.

Speed, max. (horizontal flight) ..	95 m.p.h.
Speed, min. (horizontal flight) ..	55 m.p.h.
Climbing speed	4,000 ft. in 10 mins.

Motor.

Two Liberty 12-cylinder, Vee, four-stroke cycle	Water cooled.
Horse power (each motor 330) ..	660
Weight per rated h.p.	2.55
Bore and stroke	5 in. × 7 in.
Fuel consumption (both motors)	62.8 galls. per hour.
Fuel tank capacity	300 galls.
Oil capacity provided	10 galls.
Fuel consumption per b.h.p. ..	0.57 lbs. per hour.
Oil consumption per b.h.p. ..	0.03 lbs. per hour.

Propeller.

Material.—Wood.
Diameter.—According to requirements of performance.
Pitch.—According to requirements of performance.

Maximum Range.

At economic speed, about 675 miles.

Shipping Data.

Hull Box.—Dimensions: 44 ft. 9 in. × 11 ft. × 9 ft. 4 in.; gross weight, 1,300 lbs.
Panel Box.—Dimensions: 30 ft. 4 in. × 7 ft. 7 in. × 6 ft. 6 in.; gross weight, 4,850 lbs.
Panel Box.—Dimensions: 21 ft. 2 in. × 7 ft. 5 in. × 3 ft. 6 in.; gross weight, 2,170 lbs.
Engine Box.—Dimensions: 6 ft. 2 in. × 4 ft. 4 in. × 2 ft. 9 in.; gross weight, 1,645 lbs.

CURTISS MODEL H.S. 1L and H.S. 2L FLYING BOATS

H.S.1L was a three-seat escort and anti-submarine flying boat of 1917, powered by a 375 h.p. Liberty engine. It was ordered into production and became the only American aircraft to fly with the US Navy in Europe during the war (from May 1918). Of 182 H.S. flying boats received by the USN in Europe, almost all were of this version. Perhaps about 20 were of the later H.S.2L type, with greater wing span to allow carriage of larger bombs. This version is detailed below.

CURTISS MODEL H.S. 2L. FLYING BOAT.

Specification.

General Dimensions.

Wing span, upper plane	74 ft. $0\frac{19}{32}$ in.
Wing span, lower plane	64 ft. $1\frac{21}{32}$ in.
Depth of wing chord	6 ft. $3\frac{5}{32}$ in.
Gap between wings (front) ..	7 ft. $7\frac{1}{8}$ in.
Gap between wings (rear) ..	7 ft. $5\frac{29}{32}$ in.
Stagger	None.
Length of machine overall ..	40 ft.
Height of machine overall ..	14 ft. $7\frac{1}{4}$ in.
Angle of incidence, upper plane .	$5\frac{1}{2}$ degrees.
Angle of incidence, lower plane .	4 degrees.
Dihedral angle	2 degrees.
Sweepback	0 degrees.
Wing curve	R.A.F. No. 6.
Horizontal stabilizer–angle of incidence	0 degrees.

Areas.

Wings, upper	380.32 sq. ft.
Wings, lower	314.92 sq. ft.
Ailerons (upper 62.88, lower 42.48)	105.36 sq. ft.
Horizontal stabilizer	54.8 sq. ft.
Vertical stabilizer	19.6 sq. ft.
Elevators (each 22.8 sq. ft.) ..	45.6 sq. ft.
Rudder	26.5 sq. ft.
Total supporting surface ..	800.6 sq. ft.
Loading (weight carried per sq. ft. of supporting surface) ..	7.77 lbs.
Loading (per r.h.p.)	18.85 lbs.

Weights.

Net weight, machine empty		4,359 lbs.
Gross weight, machine and load		6,223 lbs.
Useful load		1,864 lbs
Fuel	977 lbs.	
Crew	360 lbs.	
Useful load	527 lbs.	
Total	1,864 lbs.	

Performance.

Speed, max. (horizontal flight) ..	91 m.p.h.
Speed, min. (horizontal flight) ..	55 m.p.h.
Climbing speed	1,800 ft. in 10 mins.

Motor.

Liberty 12-cylinder, Vee, four-stroke cycle	Water cooled.
Horse power (rated)	330.
Weight per rated h.p.	2.55 lbs.
Bore and stroke	5 in. × 7 in.
Fuel consumption	32 galls per hour.
Fuel tank capacity	152·8 galls.
Oil tank capacity	8 galls.
Fuel consumption per b.h.p. ..	0.57 lbs. per hour.
Oil consumption per b.h.p. ..	0.03 lbs. per hour.

The Curtiss H. 12 *Large America* flying boat of 1917-18, a larger and more powerful development of the 1914-15 H-4 *America* type. Most especially those used by the RNAS, used two 275 h.p. Rolls-Royce Eagle I engines. This model (illustrated) is one with Curtiss engines. A larger deriative became the H.16.

The Curtiss two-seat HA Dunkirk fighter of 1918, intended for fighter and escort work. Not operational. Maximum speed 132 mph. (Liberty 400 h.p. engine).

A Curtiss N-9 Type Training Seaplane, used by the US Navy from 1917 and also in limited number by the Army. 150 h.p. Hispano-Suiza A engine.

CURTISS MODEL H.S.2 L. FLYING BOAT—*continued.*

Propeller.
Material.—Wood.
Pitch.—According to requirements of performance.
Diameter.—According to requirements of performance.
Direction of rotation, viewed from pilot's seat.—Clockwise.

Maximum Range.
At economic speed, about 575 miles.

Shipping Data.
Hull Box.—Dimensions: 35 ft. 5 in. × 8 ft. 6 in × 6 ft. 4 in.; gross weight, 8,525 lbs.
Panel Box.—Dimensions: 23 ft. 6 in. × 6 ft. 9 in. × 3 ft. 5 in.; gross weight, 2,900 lbs.
Engine Box.—Dimensions: 6 ft. 2 in. × 4 ft. 4 in. × 2 ft. 9 in.; gross weight, 1,645 lbs.

CURTISS MODEL M.F. FLYING BOAT.
Specification.

General Dimensions.

Wing span, upper plane	49 ft. $9\frac{3}{8}$ in.
Wing span, lower plane	38 ft. $7\frac{5}{32}$ in.
Depth of wing chord	60 in.
Gap between wings at engine section	6 ft. $4\frac{5}{64}$ in.
Stagger	None.
Length of machine overall	28 ft. $10\frac{3}{16}$ in.
Height of machine overall	11 ft. $9\frac{3}{8}$ in.
Angle of incidence	6 degrees.
Dihedral angle, lower panels only	2 degrees.
Sweepback	None.
Wing curve	U.S.A. No. 1.
Horizontal stabilizer—angle of incidence	0 degrees.

Areas.

Wings, upper	187.54 sq. ft.
Wings, lower	169.10 sq. ft.
Ailerons (each 22.43 sq. ft.)	44.86 sq. ft.
Horizontal stabilizer	33.36 sq. ft.
Vertical stabilizer	15.74 sq. ft.
Elevators (each 15.165 sq. ft.)	30.33 sq. ft.
Rudder	20.42 sq. ft.
Total supporting surface	401.50 sq. ft.
Loading (weight carried per sq. ft. of supporting surface)	6·05 lbs.
Loading (per r.h.p.)	24.32 lbs.

Weights.

Net weight, machine empty		1,796 lbs.
Gross weight, machine and load		2,432 lbs.
Useful Load		636 lbs.
Fuel	240 lbs.	
Oil	22.5 lbs.	
Water	36 lbs.	
Pilot	165 lbs.	
Passenger	165 lbs.	
Miscellaneous accessories	7·5 lbs.	
Total	636.0 lbs.	

Performance.

Speed, max. (horizontal flight)	69 m.p.h.
Speed, min. (horizontal flight)	45 m.p.h.
Climbing speed	5,000 ft. in 27 mins.

Motor.

Model O.X.X. 8-cylinder, Vee, four-stroke cycle	Water cooled.
Horse power (rated) at 1400 r.p.m.	100.
Weight per r.h.p.	4.01 lbs.
Bore and stroke	$4\frac{1}{4}$ in. × 5 in.
Fuel consumption	10 galls. per hour.
Fuel tank capacity	40 galls.
Oil capacity provided (crankcase)	5 galls.
Fuel consumption per b.h.p.	0.60 lbs. per hour.
Oil consumption per b.h.p.	0.030 lbs. per hour.

Propeller.
Material.—Wood.
Pitch.—According to requirements of performance.
Diameter.—According to requirements of performance.
Direction of rotation, as viewed from pilot's seat.—Clockwise.

Details.
Dual control.
Standard Equipment.—Tachometer, oil gauge, gasoline gauge, complete set of tools.
Other equipment on special order.

Maximum Range.
At economic speed, about 325 miles.

Shipping Data—Foreign Shipment.
Hull Box.—Dimensions: 26 ft. 6 in. × 6 ft 3 in. × 4 ft. 11 in.; gross weight, 2,390 lbs.
Panel Box.—Dimensions: 22 ft. 3 in. × 5 ft. 11 in. × 3 ft. 9 in.; gross weight, 730 lbs.
Engine Box.—Dimensions: 5 ft. 4 in. × 3 ft. 3 in. × 2 ft. 9 in.; gross weight, 680 lbs.
For domestic shipment, sidewalks and engine section are crated with hull; gross weight, 2,680 lbs.

CURTISS ENGINEERING CORPORATION.

Garden City, Long Island, New York.

A company was founded by Mr. Glenn Curtiss and quite distinct from the Curtiss Aeroplane and Motors Corporation. Mainly engaged in experimental work. For this purpose a complete aerodynamical laboratory and a large flying field is available.

The *Curtiss* 18-2 triplane, the 18-B biplane and the N.C-1 flying boat are the most notable achievements of this organisation.

A typical Curtiss F Type Flying Boat used by the US Navy from 1914-18. Curtiss OXX engine (100 h.p.) MF (modified) version was ordered to replace Fs, but only 16 delivered in 1918.

D

THE DAYTON-WRIGHT AIRPLANE COMPANY.

Dayton, Ohio.

President, C. F. Kettering; General Manager, G. M. Williams. Factory: Dayton, Ohio.

This company was organised during the war for the quantity production of aeroplanes to government specifications. On February 1st, 1919, the total number of machines constructed comprised 400 Standard J.1 training aeroplanes and 3,100 D.H. 4 A "battle-planes."

THE AMERICAN D.H. 4 BIPLANE.
(Built by Dayton Wright Aeroplane Co.)

Type of machine	**Two-seater Biplane.**
Name or type No. of machine	**American D.H. 4.**
Purpose for which intended	**Reconnaissance and light bomber.**
Span	**42 ft. $5\frac{3}{4}$ in.**
Overall length	30 ft. $5\frac{1}{64}$ in.
Maximum height	10 ft. $3\frac{9}{32}$ in.
Chord	5 ft. 6 in.
Span of tail	13 ft. 7 in.
Engine type and h.p.	Liberty 12; 400 h.p.
Weight of machine empty	2,391 lbs.
Tank capacity in gallons	88 gallons.

Performance.

Speed low down	124.7 m.p.h.
Speed at 6,500 feet	120 m.p.h.
Speed at 10,000 feet	117 m.p.h.
Speed at 15,000 feet	113 m.p.h.
Landing speed	58 m.p.h.

Climb

To 10,000 feet in minutes	14 minutes.
Ceiling	19,500 feet.
Endurance at 6,500 feet (full throttle)	2 hrs. 13 mins.
Endurance at 6,500 feet (half throttle)	3 hrs. 3 mins.
Track	6 feet.
Total weight of machine loaded	3,582 lbs.

The Dayton-Wright "Honeymoon Express" (400 h.p. Liberty engine). A converted American De H. 4.

G

GALLAUDET AIRCRAFT CORPORATION

East Greenwich, Conn.
New York Office: 15 West 40th Street.

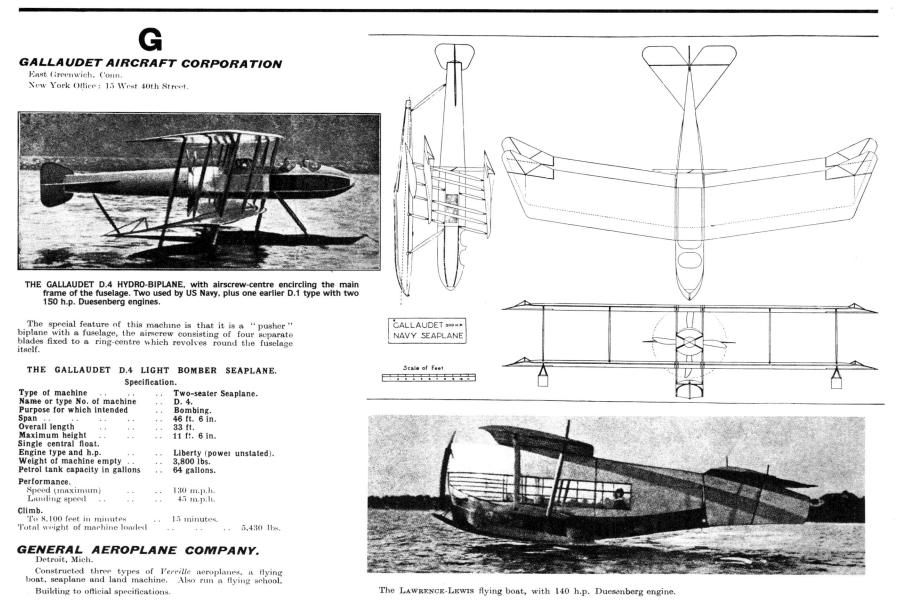

THE GALLAUDET D.4 HYDRO-BIPLANE, with airscrew-centre encircling the main frame of the fuselage. Two used by US Navy, plus one earlier D.1 type with two 150 h.p. Duesenberg engines.

The special feature of this machine is that it is a "pusher" biplane with a fuselage, the airscrew consisting of four separate blades fixed to a ring-centre which revolves round the fuselage itself.

THE GALLAUDET D.4 LIGHT BOMBER SEAPLANE.
Specification.

Type of machine	Two-seater Seaplane.
Name or type No. of machine ..	D. 4.
Purpose for which intended ..	Bombing.
Span	46 ft. 6 in.
Overall length	33 ft.
Maximum height	11 ft. 6 in.
Single central float.	
Engine type and h.p. ..	Liberty (power unstated).
Weight of machine empty ..	3,800 lbs.
Petrol tank capacity in gallons ..	64 gallons.
Performance.	
Speed (maximum)	130 m.p.h.
Landing speed	45 m.p.h.
Climb.	
To 8,100 feet in minutes ..	15 minutes.
Total weight of machine loaded	5,430 lbs.

GENERAL AEROPLANE COMPANY.

Detroit, Mich.

Constructed three types of *Verville* aeroplanes, a flying boat, seaplane and land machine. Also run a flying school.

Building to official specifications.

The following callout appears in the diagram:

GALLAUDET 300 H.P.
NAVY SEAPLANE

Scale of Feet

The LAWRENCE-LEWIS flying boat, with 140 h.p. Duesenberg engine.

		Gamma S.	Beta	Gamma L.
Span (top plane) ..	..	40′ 0″	43′ 0″	40′ 0″
Span (lower plane)..	..	34′ 0″	37′ 0″	34′ 0″
Chord ..	..	5′ 0″	5′ 0″	5′ 0″
Gap ..	..	5′ 0″	6′ 0″	5′ 0″
Length ..	..	25′ 10″	28′ 7″	25′ 0″
Dihedral ..	..	5°	Upper 0° Lower 5°	5°
Stagger ..	..	8″	9″	8″
Total area ..	..	350 sq. ft.	400 sq. ft.	350 sq. ft.
Ailerons ..	..	Top plane only	Top plane only	Top plane only
Airscrew ..	..	Pusher	Pusher	Pusher
Landing gear ..	..	2 floats	Boat	2 Wheels
Engine ..	..	OXX Curtiss 2—100h.p.	100 h.p. Curtiss	100 h.p. Curtiss

K

THE KYLE-SMITH AIRCRAFT COMPANY. Wheeling, West Virginia, U.S.A

Manufactured a two-seater tractor biplane intended for sporting and training purposes, with six cylinder radial engine.

Building to official specifications.

L

LANZIUS AIRCRAFT COMPANY. 149, Broadway,

New York, U.S.A.

Manufacturers of two tractor biplanes with incidence varying from 0° to 15°.

Machines fitted with wheels or floats.

New models to be fitted with 140 h.p. Duesenberg engines.

		L I.	L II.
Span ..	..	38′	38′
Chord ..	..	5′ 6″	4′
Gap ..	..	5′ 3″	4′ 7″
Length ..	..	25′	24′
Total area ..	..	400 sq. ft.	220 sq. ft.
Ailerons ..	..	Patent	Patent
Landing gear ..	..	2 wheels or floats	2 wheels or floats
Engine ..	..	140 h.p. Duesenberg	140 h.p. Duesenberg
Weight with one hour's fuel ..		1400 lbs.	1200 lbs.
Useful load ..		800 lbs.	800 lbs.

LAWRENCE-LEWIS AEROPLANE COMPANY.

Peoples' Gas Building, Chicago, Ill.

Manufacturers of two types of tractor biplane, inherently stable and without ailerons.

		Type AI.	Type BI.
Span ..	..	30′	42′
Gap ..	..	4′ 8″	5′ 8″
Length ..	..	25′	29′
Stagger ..	..	6°	6°
Landing gear	:	Combined land and water	Combined land and water
Engine ..	..	140 h.p. Hall-Scott	140 h.p. Hall-Scott or Duesenberg.
Weight with one hour's fuel ..		1750 lbs.	2200 lbs.
Useful load ..		800 lbs.	1500 lbs.

LAWSON AIRCRAFT CORPORATION.

Green Bay, Wisconsin. President: Alfred W. Lawson.
Manufacturers of a two-seater tractor biplane destined for training and civil flying.

Specifications.

Span, upper plane	39 ft.
Span, lower plane	36 ft.
Chord	5 ft. 2 in.
Gap	5 ft. 1 in.
Stagger	8 in.
Incidence	3 degrees.
Dihedral	1 degree.
Area, upper plane (including ailerons	200 sq. ft.
Area, lower plane	150 sq. ft.
Length, overall	25 ft.
Height, overall	8 ft.
Weight, empty	12,000 lbs.
Weight, loaded	1,900 lbs.
Speed range	40-90 m.p.h.
Climb in 10 minutes	6,000 ft.
Gliding angle, full load	1 in 9.
Engine, Hall-Scott	100 h.p.

The Lawson Aircraft Corporation's Two-seater (100 h.p. Hall-Scott engine).

LOENING ENGINEERING CORPORATION. 351 West 52nd Street, New York.

President : Grover C. Loening.

Aeronautical constructional engineers, engaged during the war in experimental work for the U.S. Army and Navy, as the result of which they produced a fighting monoplane of highly original design and a ship-plane of very small dimensions.

THE LOENING M-8 MONOPLANE

It is stated that in its actual performance the *Loening* monoplane has, with the full two-seater fighter load, not only exceeded all the performances of other machines, but has with this same load equalled, if not exceeded, all of the performances of the very best European single-seaters with the same engine.

In the tests made by the manufacturer at Mineola, the machine showed a high speed of 146 m.p.h., and on one occasion climbed to 24,000 ft. in 43 min. with pilot, passenger, two hours fuel and considerable gun equipment, thus establishing an unofficial height record for two-seaters.

The new monoplane of the same type tested at Dayton by the U.S. Army showed practically the same high speed, and climbed—with a live load almost equal to the weight of the aeroplane—16,000 ft. in 18 min.

The outstanding feature of the machine is the manner in which the wings fasten to the upper body longitudinals, and are braced by two enormous braces to the bottom of the body. This method of wing bracing has so much simplified the construction of the machine, that it has permitted to cut in halves the structure weight.

A very interesting feature of the design proven by the tests made is the slow speed on landing and general buoyancy of the machine, despite the fact that the wing loading has gradually been stepped up to almost 12 lb. per sq. ft.

Construction.

The wings, body, tail surfaces, landing gear, etc., are all built of most approved spruce and metal fitting airplane construction. All metal fittings are of stamped sheet metal, with practically no brazed or welded parts; all joints are pin connected, particularly the joints of the main wing braces to the wings and body, which are free to move in any direction, so that vibration will not fatigue these members. In addition to which, all parts are readily adjustable for alignment.

Safety Factor.

Sand load tests that have been carried on exhaustively to prove the strength of the machine show a safety factor of 14 on drift stresses, and a safety factory of 8 on lift stresses.

All tail surfaces and fin surfaces, stabilizers, rudders, etc., withstand on actual sand test a load of 35 lbs. per sq. ft. area.

Military Features.

It is claimed that the visibility afforded to the pilot is so complete that he has practically no blind spots at all. He can see either above or below the wings or to either side, and in addition to that can see quite well in the front, due to the narrowness of the body.

The Gun Range.

The gun range is also very good, particularly as the gunner can shoot forward, the only obstruction being the arc of the airscrew.

The deep body offers ample room for all kinds of military equipment, oxygen tanks, wireless apparatus, cameras, etc., and in addition to that the arrangement of the cowls is such as to give the occupants ample protection against the wind without interfering with the view.

The construction has everywhere been studied so as to give maximum strength to all of the parts that are vital due to damage from bullets. This is particularly true of the main braces supporting the wings which can be half shot away before they will lose the safety factor of 8 provided.

Performance.

It has been found that the machine lands very slowly, gets off the ground in 4 seconds from a dead start, and that in flight the machine is very easy to handle on all its controls in spirals, loops, barrel rolls, etc.

The performances of the machine with full load are as follows :

Slow speed	48 m.p.h.
High speed	146 m.p.h.
Indicated ceiling, light load	26,000 ft.
heavy load	22,000 ft.

The principal characteristics of the *Loening* monoplane are as follows :—

Areas.

Main planes, total	238.9 sq. ft.
Upper planes, including ailerons	214.9 sq. ft.
Strut planes	24.0 sq. ft.
Ailerons (2)	24.0 sq. ft.
Fins (2)	8.8 sq. ft.
Stabilizer	14.9 sq. ft.
Rudders (2)	9.0 sq. ft.
Elevator	15.0 sq. ft.

Weights.

Weight, empty	1,328 lbs.
Fuel and oil	360 lbs.
Military load	680 lbs.
Total weight	2,368 lbs.

Power Plant.

Engine, Hispano-Suiza, model H, developing 340 h.p. at 1,800 r.p.m. Weight, including airscrew, 618 lbs. Fuel consumption per h.p.-hr., 0.53 lbs.

Performances.

Altitude.	Speed.	Climb.
Sealevel	146 m.p.h.	0 min.
20,000 ft.		20 min.

The Loening M-8 Monoplane (300 h.p. Hispano-Suiza engine).

LOUGHEAD AIRCRAFT.

The machine illustrated herewith was built by the brothers Malcolm and Allan H. Loughead, at Santa Barbara, Cal. Originally built as a seaplane, it flew from Santa Barbara to San Diego with four passengers, and was there fitted with a land chassis in preparation for a flight across America to Washington.

No particulars or specification of this machine are available.

Loughead Model F.I. Seaplane (two 160 h.p. Hall-Scott engines).

The Loughead F.I.A. Machine. This is the Seaplane F.I. fitted with a land chassis.

3 M

THE L.W.F. ENGINEERING COMPANY.

College Point, N.Y.

Constructors of tractor biplanes for training and fighting purposes and of seaplanes and flying boats.

An L.W.F. military biplane flew, late in 1917, with a 200 h.p. Sturtevant engine from Rantoul, Illinois, to San Antonio, Texas, a distance of 1,184 miles, in a total flying time of 9 hrs. 15 mins. This included one non-stop stretch of 620 miles.

The machine carried a U.S. Army Officer and pilot, and made two short stops en route for fuel.

Model V. Thomas 135 h.p. motor. Biplane land machine. Two seater. Speed: 42.2 to 95.5 m.p.h. Climb: 3,750 ft. in 10 mins. Full government load. Wing curve: L.W.F. 1.

Model V1. Same as above machine, but equipped with Sturtevant 140 h.p. motor.

Model V2. Very similar to above machines, but different motor installation and radiator on nose of upper wing. Hall-Scott 165 h.p. motor. Also many minor differences. High speed: 102 m.p.h.

Model V3. Similar to Model V1, except that motor is new Sturtevant 200 h.p. Speed: 42.2 to 110 m.p.h. Climb: 8,000 ft. in 10 mins. Full government load. Made flight from Rantoul, Ill., to San Antonio, Texas.

Model F. New model. Liberty motored.
(First Liberty motor to fly.)

Model G. New model. As detailed below.

L. W. F. Model V 2-seater reconnaissance biplane, with 135 h.p. Thomas motor.

THE L.W.F. MODEL G. FIGHTING AEROPLANE.

Among the most successful of the all-American designs is the L.W.F. machine, the first experimental model of which was in the air early in January, 1918. This first machine, known as Model G., was powered with a Liberty 12 motor and was taken off with the wind, looped and tailspun the first time it was in the air.

Specification.

General.

Type	..	..	..	Two-seater land tractor biplane.
Use	..	..	..	Military reconnaissance, advanced training, or commercial

Dimensions.

Length overall	..	..	..	29 ft. 2 in.
Height overall	..	..	..	10 ft. 7 in.
Width overall	..	..	..	46 ft. 6 in.

Wings.

Wing curve	..	..	..	L.W.F. No. 1.
Chord	..	..	..	80 in.
Gap	..	..	..	80 in.
Stagger	..	..	..	8 in.
Span : Upper wing	..	..	46 ft. 6 in.
Lower wing	..	..	38 ft. 4 in.

Areas.

Total supporting area	..	..	555 sq. ft.
Area of ailerons	..	..	42 sq. ft.
Area of elevators	..	..	22 sq. ft.
Area of horizontal stabilizer	..	29 sq. ft.
Area of vertical stabilizer	..	5.5 sq. ft.
Area of rudder	..	..	11.5 sq. ft.

Control.

Deperdussin control centre column single or dual. Stick control can be furnished if preferred.

Power Plant.

Liberty 12-cylinder engine	..	350 b.h.p.
Gasoline consumption per b.h.p.		.54 lbs. per hour.
Oil consumption per b.h.p.	..	.03 lbs. per hour.
Propeller	.. .. ..	Two blade, 1,650 r.p.m

Weights.

Gross weight, fully loaded	..	..	..	3,522 lbs.
Light weight, empty	..	..	..	2,498 lbs.
Useful load	..	..	..	1,024 lbs.
Water (11 gallons)	..	..	..	92 lbs.
Gasoline capacity (86 gallons)	..	..	532 lbs.
Oil capacity (6 gallons)	..	..	42 lbs.
Two men or equivalent	..	..	330 lbs.
Accessories	..	..	..	28 lbs.

Performance (fully loaded).

High speed	..	..	125 m.p.h.
Low speed (landing)	..	..	47 m.p.h.
Climbing speed	..	..	10,000 ft. in 7½ mins.
Ceiling	..	..	24,000 ft.
Endurance at full speed	..	2¾ hours.

This machine is capable of carrying a cargo of about 1,200 lbs., in addition to the above load.

Model G. 1, an improvement over Model G., was built and flown successfully during the summer of 1918, demonstrating before various government officials its speed, climb and carrying capacity. This machine, loaded as a fighter, with full tanks, seven machine guns, ammunition, pilot and gunner, made 128 m.p.h. and climbed 10,000 feet in ten minutes.

Later in the summer, Model G. 1 was radically changed into Model G. 2 by cutting off the overhang, balancing all control surfaces, doubling the number of wing ribs and later installing a wing curve radiator. The following description refers to the later machine, Model G. 2, which, as before stated, is a modification of Models G. and G. 1.

The L.W.F. "Model G" Two-seater (350 h.p. Liberty engine).

L.W.F.—continued.

General Description.—Model G. 2 is a general service, 425–450 h.p., two man biplane of the land tractor, military type, armoured, and carries an armament of seven machine guns. In addition it can also be equipped with four large bombs. As will be noted, a wing nose radiator was used at the time the photos for the accompanying figures were made. All parts of the machine seen from above are finished in earth brown, while from below it is sky blue. The general specifications follow :—

THE L.W.F. MODEL G. 2 FIGHTING AIRPLANE.
Specification.

Dimensions.

Overall width	..	41 ft. 7½ in.
Overall length	..	29 ft. 1¼ in.
Overall height	..	9 ft. 4¾ in.
Tread of wheels ..	..	5 ft. 6 in.
Wheels ..	..	26 in. × 4 in.

Wings.

Wing curve L.W.F. No. 1 (modified R.A.F. 6) upper and lower wings.

Incidence : lower wing ..	..	0 degrees.
upper wing ..	..	+ 1 degree.
Decalage ..	..	1 degree.
Chord ..	..	80 in., upper and lower.
Dihedral ..	..	0 degrees.
Gap ..	..	72 in., nose to nose on vertical line with body horizontal.
Backsweep ..	..	0 degrees.
Stagger ..	..	7¼ in. (positive).
Span : upper wing, inc. ailerons		41 ft. 7½ in.
lower wing ..		38 ft. 5¾ in.
Aspect ratio : Upper wing, inc. ailerons ..		6.3
Lower wing ..		4.78, average 5.54.

Areas.

Total supporting area, including ailerons) ..	..	515.54 sq. ft.
Net area of main wings, not inc. ailerons ..	..	465·46 sq. ft.
Net area of upper wings, including ailerons ..	..	268.78 sq. ft.
Net area of upper wings, not inc. ailerons ..	..	218.70 sq. ft.
Net area of lower wings..	..	246.76 sq. ft.
Total area of one aileron ..		25·04 sq. ft. balanced area, 1.95 sq. ft.
Total area of both ailerons ..		50.08 sq. ft.
Total area of one elevator ..		13.85 sq. ft. balanced area, 1.5 sq. ft.
Total area of both elevators ..		27.70 sq. ft.
Total area of rudder ..		12·65 sq. ft. balanced area, 1.31 sq. ft.
Total area of horizontal stabilizer (both sides) ..	..	29.15 sq. ft.
Total area of vertical stabilizer..		5.21 sq. ft.

Controls and Control Surfaces.

Dual stick control. Aileron wires enclosed in wings.
Horizontal stabilizer double camber with centre line set at 0 degrees to thrust line.
Elevator curve included in stabilizer curve.
Aileron curve included in wing curve extended.
Rudder and vertical stabilizer flat.

Power Plant.

Liberty 12-cyl. engine, direct connected ..	..	435 hp. at 1,700 r.p.m.
Airscrew, 2 blade, tractor, diam..		9 ft. 7 in ; av. pitch 7.38 ft.
Propeller turned ..	..	1,800 r.p.m.

Weights.

Case 1. Weight of complete machine empty, with

gun mounts, but no guns ..	..	2,675 lbs.

Case 2. Equipped as a fighter.

Weight, light ..	..	2,675.5 lbs.
90 galls. gas ..	..	553.5 lbs.
14 galls. water ..	..	118 lbs.
6 galls. oil ..	..	44 lbs.
Ammunition ..	..	150 lbs.
7 machine guns ..	..	152 lbs.
2 men ..	..	330 lbs.
Total full load ..	..	**4,023 lbs.**

Case 3. Equipped as a bomber.

Weight, light ..	..	2,675.5 lbs.
120 galls. gasoline..	..	752 lbs.
6 galls. oil ..	..	44 lbs.
14 galls. water ..	..	118 lbs.
Ammunition ..	..	150 lbs.
7 machine guns ..	..	152 lbs.
Armour ..	..	66 lbs.
4 bombs, rack and release ..		592 lbs.
2 men ..	..	330 lbs.
Total full load..	..	**4,879.5 lbs.**

Loadings (based on 515.54 sq. ft. area and 435 h.p.)

Case 1.	Loading per sq. ft. ..	5.185 lbs.
	Loading per h.p. ..	6.15 lbs.
Case 2.	Loading per sq. ft. ..	7.82 lbs.
	Loading per h.p. ..	9.25 lbs.
Case 3.	Loading per sq. ft. ..	9.47 lbs.
	Loading per h.p. ..	11.22 lbs.

Performance.

High speed at 10,000 ft.	=	130 m.p.h. (loaded as in Case 2).
High speed at low altitude	=	138 m.p.h. (loaded as in Case 2).
Low speed (landing)	=	50 m.p.h. (loaded as in Case 2).

Climb.

Case 1.	10,000 feet in ..	.. 7 mins. 28 secs.
Case 2.	10,000 feet in ..	.. 9 mins. 18 secs.
Case 3.	10,000 feet in ..	.. 14 mins. 45 secs.

Endurance.

Four hours at full speed.

M

THE GLENN L. MARTIN COMPANY.
Cleveland, Ohio.

This company, which was organised during the war, produced the first successful twin-engined aeroplane of American design. Intended to serve as a night bomber. The *Martin* "Twin" is now being converted into a passenger aeroplane. Four of these machines will be put in operation in California by the Apache Aerial Transportation Company, of Phœnix, Arizona.

Other wartime products, included the S-type seaplane with a 125 h.p. Hall-Scott A-5 engine, of which a small number went to the US Army in 1915-16 for observation work and the US Navy purchased two seaplanes. Earlier T and TT two-seat training seaplanes (1914-15) with 90-135 h.p. engines had also been sold to the Army.

THE MARTIN TWIN-ENGINED BOMBER.

The *Martin* twin-engined bomber constitutes one of the most important developments in bombing airplanes of original American design. In its official test, at Wilbur Wright Field, the all-round performance of this machine, considering the load carried, has easily excelled any other record from a similar bomber, either here or abroad. The machine shows excellent workmanship and such thoroughness of engineering that the organization is to be complimented upon the talent of their personnel. Mr. Martin is proud of the ability of his assistants,

Mr. Lawrence D. Bell, factory manager ; Mr. Eric Springer, pilot ; and Mr. Donald W. Douglas, aeronautical engineer ; and he prophesies important futures in their respective specialties. Lawrence D. Bell, has been with Mr. Martin for seven years, and is noted for his production management. Eric Springer learned to fly at the Martin School five years ago. He is an unusually capable tester and flyer, having made an enviable record in five years of piloting for the Martin Company without an accident. Donald W. Douglas came from the Boston Tech., joining the Martin plant in Los Angeles four years ago, and in that short length of time has grown to be recognised as one of the foremost aeronautical engineers.

The all-round efficiency of the Martin bomber has been proven in its official performance trials. An official high speed at the ground of 118.5 m.p.h. was made on the first trials, with full bombing load on board. This speed has been bettered since, due to the better propeller efficiency arrived at by expensive experiments. With full bomb load, the climbing time to 10,000 feet was 15 minutes, and a service ceiling of between 16,000 and 17,000 feet was attained.

General Description.

As a military machine, the *Martin* "Twin" is built to fulfil the requirements of the four following classes :—(1) Night bomber, (2) day bomber, (3) long-distance photography, (4) gun machine.

(1) As a night bomber it is armed with three flexible Lewis machine guns, one mounted on the front turret, one on the rear, below and to the sides, under the concave lower surface of the body. It carries 1,500 lbs. of bombs and 1,000 rounds

The L.W.F. Model " G. 2 " Two-seater (350 Liberty engine).

The Glenn L. Martin MB-1 Twin-engined Bomber (two 400 h.p. Liberty engines), first flown in August 1918.

The Glenn L. Martin Twin Bomber.

of ammunition. A radio-telephone set and the necessary instruments are carried on all four types. The fuel capacity in all four types is sufficient for four and a half hours' full power at the ground and six hours' full power at 15,000 feet. This gives the machine gasoline for the climb to 15,000 feet, and enough more for about six hundred miles.

(2) As a day bomber two more Lewis guns are carried, one more on each turret. The bomb capacity is cut to 1,000 lbs. to give the higher ceiling necessary for day work.

(3) When equipped as a photography machine, the same number of guns as in the case of the day bomber are carried : but in place of the bombs two cameras are mounted in the rear gunner's cockpit. One camera is a short focal length semi-automatic, and the other is a long focal length hand-operated type.

(4) The gun machine is equipped for the purpose of breaking up enemy formations. In addition to the five machine guns and their ammunition as carried on the photographic machine, a semi-flexible 37 mm. cannon is mounted in the front gun cockpit, firing forward, and with a fairly wide range in elevation and azimuth. This cannon fires either shell or shot, and is a formidable weapon.

The *Martin* "Twin" is easily adaptable to the commercial uses that are now practical. They are :—(1) Mail and express carrying, (2) transportation of passengers, (3) aerial map and survey work.

(1) As a mail or express machine a ton may be carried with comfort, not only because of the ability of the machine to efficiently handle this load, but because generous bulk stowage room is available.

(2) Twelve passengers, in addition to the pilot and mechanic, can be carried for non-stop runs up to six hundred miles.

(3) The photographic machine, as developed for war purposes, is at once adaptable to the aerial mapping of what will become the main flying routes throughout the country. The accuracy that is being obtained in aerial photography should be of vast value in survey and topographical map work. The *Martin* airplane, with its great cruising radius and complete camera installation, presents itself as the logical machine in this field.

General Dimensions and Data.

1,—**Power Plant.**
Two 12-cyl. Liberty engines.

2,—**Wing and Control Surface Areas.**

Main planes, total	1,070 sq. ft.
Upper planes, including ailerons	550 sq. ft.
Lower planes, including ailerons	520 sq. ft.
Ailerons, each	32.5 sq. ft.
No. af ailerons	4
Vertical fins, each	8.8 sq. ft.
No. of fins	2
Stabilizer	62.25 sq. ft.
Elevator	43.20 sq. ft.
Rudders, each	16.50 sq. ft.
No. of rudders	2

3,—**Overall Dimensions.**

Span, upper and lower	71 ft. 5 in.
Chord, upper and lower	7 ft. 10 in.
Gap	8 ft. 6 in.
Length overall	46 ft.
Height overall	14 ft. 7 in.
Incidence of wings with propeller axis	2 degrees.
Dihedral	None.
Sweep back	None.
Decalage, wings	None.
Stabilizer, setting with wing chord	÷ 1 degree.
adjustable between	− 5 degrees.
normal setting	− 2 degrees.

ORDNANCE ENGINEERING CORPORATION.
120, Broadway, New York. Factory : Baldwin, Long Island. Chief Aeronautical Engineer : Walter H. Phipps.

Aeronautical constructional engineers, engaged in experimental work for the U.S. Army.

THE ORDNANCE SCOUT BIPLANE.
Specification.

Type of machine	Single-seater Biplane
Name or type No. of machine	Ordnance Scout.
Purpose for which intended	Advanced training.
Span	26 ft.
Gap	3 ft. 10 in.
Overall length	18 ft. 9 in.
Chord	4 ft. 5 in.
Maximum cross section of body	41½ ins.
Engine type and h.p.	80 h.p. Le Rhône.
Airscrew, diameter	8 ft. 3 in.
Weight of machine empty	335 lbs.

Performance.

Speed low down		98 m.p.h.
Speed at 6,500 feet		94 m.p.h.
Speed at 10,000 feet		84 m.p.h.
Speed at 15,000 feet		70 m.p.h.

Climb.

To 6,500 feet in minutes		9 minutes.
To 10,000 feet in minutes		17 mins. 30 secs.
To 15,000 feet in minutes		55 minutes.
Service ceiling		13,500 feet.
Total weight of machine loaded		1,117 lbs

Side View of the Glenn L. Martin Bomber (two 400 h.p. Liberty engines).

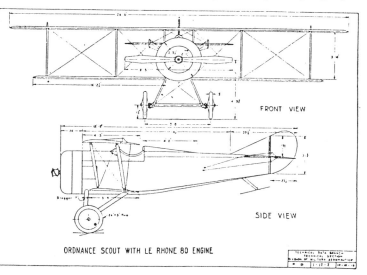

FRONT VIEW

SIDE VIEW

ORDNANCE SCOUT WITH LE RHONE 80 ENGINE

Two Views of the Ordnance Engineering Corporation's Single-seat Scout.

P

PACKARD MOTOR CAR COMPANY.

Detroit, Michigan.

These well-known motor car builders had been experimenting with aero engines for several years when the War Department requested their chief engineer, Mr. J. G. Vincent to collaborate with Mr. E. J. Hall, chief engineer of the Hall-Scott Motor Car Company, of San Francisco, Cal., for the purpose of creating a standardized aero engine of high power. The Liberty engine, which resulted from this collaboration, thus derived at least part of its inspiration from experiments made at the Packard Works.

After the Armistice, this firm produced an 8-cyl. V-type engine, developing 160 h.p., around which a luxuriously-fitted sport aeroplane has been built. This machine was, however, still in the experimental stage when these notes were written.

In the late fall of 1918 a two-seater fighter and day-bomber was also developed to the designs of Captain G. Lepère, of the French Air Service, and was being put into production when the war came to an end.

THE LE PÈRE FIGHTER.

Captain G. Lepère, an aeronautical engineer in the French Air service, designed the Lepère "Fighter" with a Liberty engine for production in the United States. It was intended for use as a fighter or reconnaissance machine, and carried two fixed guns firing forward, synchronized with the engine, and two Lewis guns attached to a movable Scarff ring surrounding the rear cockpit.

General Dimensions.

Span, upper plane	.. ..	39 ft. 0¼ in
Span, lower plane	.. ..	39 ft. 0¼ in.
Chord, both planes	.. ..	5 ft. 6 in.
Gap between planes	.. ..	5 ft. 0⅝ in.
Stagger	.. ..	2 ft. 0¹⁵⁄₁₆ in.
Length over all ..	.. ..	25 ft. 4⅜ in.
Height over all ..	.. ..	9 ft. 10⅞ in.

Weights.

Machine empty ..	.. ..	2,468 lbs.
Pilot and gunner ..	.. .. ..	360 lbs.
Fuel and oil ..	.. .. ..	475 lbs.
Armament..	.. ..	352 lbs.
Total	.. .. ..	3,655 lbs.

Performances.

Height.	Speed.	Time of Climb.
0 ft. ..	136 m.p.h. ..	0 mins. 0 secs.
6,000 ft. ..	132 m.p.h. ..	5 mins. 35 secs.
10,000 ft. ..	127 m.p.h ..	10 mins. 35 secs.
15,000 ft. ..	118 m.p.h. ..	19 mins. 15 secs.
20,000 ft. ..	102 m.p.h. ..	41 mins. 0 secs.

Service ceiling, or height beyond which the machine will not climb 100 feet per minute, 20,800 feet.

Engine Group.

A Liberty "12" 400 h.p. engine is used. It develops 400 h.p. at 1,750 r.p.m. Bore, 5 ins. ; stroke, 7 ins. ; weight, without propeller and water, 858 pounds. Two Zenith Duplex carburetters are used.

The radiator is located in the upper plane centre section, and its location has necessitated some slight modifications in the engine to increase the water circulation.

Propeller, 9 ft. 4 ins. in diameter. Front propeller plate projects 11¾ ins. forward of fuselage nose.

Propeller axis 15⁷⁄₁₆ ins. below top of upper longerons. In flying position the propeller hub is 5 ft. 2⅞ ins. above the ground line ; when at rest on the ground the propeller hub is 6 ft. 1⅝ ins. above ground.

THE PACKARD BIPLANE.

Type of machine	..	Two-seater Biplane.
Name or type No. of machine	..	1 A. Packard.
Span	..	37 ft.
Overall length ..	..	25 ft.
Maximum height ..	..	8 ft. 11 in.

Wing and Control Surface Areas.

Main planes, total	..	387.6 sq. ft.
Ailerons, total ..	..	48.3 sq. ft.
Vertical fin ..	..	7·0 sq. ft.
Rudder ..	..	12·0 sq. ft.
Tail plane ..	..	35.7 sq. ft.
Elevator, total ..	..	21.9 sq. ft.
Engine type.. ..	..	8-cyl. 1 A. Packard ; 160 h.p. at 1,525 r.p.m.
Petrol tank capacity in galls.	..	34 galls.
Fuel consumption per h.p. ..	..	.50 to .54 lbs. per h.p. at sea level.

Side View of the Le Père Fighter (400 h.p. Liberty engine).

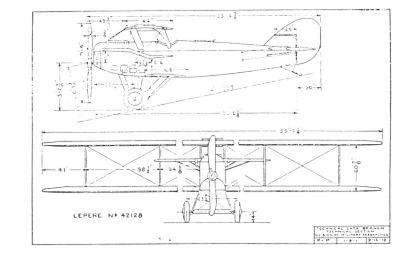

LEPERE Nᵒ 42128

Weight.

Machine empty	..	..	..	..	1,520 lbs.
Gasoline	..	..	..	..	210 lbs.
Oil ..	..	..	..	..	30 lbs.
Water	..	..	..	..	52 lbs.
Tools and extras	..	..	..	..	25 lbs.
Pilot ..	..	..	..	..	165 lbs.
Passenger	..	..	..	..	465 lbs.
Normal flying weight	..	..	..	2,167 lbs.
Weight, lbs. per h.p.	..	..	..	13.5 lbs.
Wing loading per sq. ft..	..	..	..	5.6 lbs.
Permissible extra luggage ..	..	..	100 lbs.

Performance.

High speed near sea level	..	102 m.p.h.
High speed at 5,000 feet	..	100.5 m.p.h
High speed at 10,000 feet	..	98 m.p.h.
High speed at 15,000 feet	..	90.5 m.p.h.

Climb.

To 5,000 feet	..	..	7.5 minutes.
To 10,000 feet	..	..	18.1 minutes.
To 15,000 feet	..	..	34.5 minutes.
Absolute ceiling	..	..	19,500 ft.

Fuel range, wide open, near sea level	2.5 hours.
Fuel range, wide open, at 5,000 ft. .	3 hours.
Fuel range, wide open, at 10,000 ft..	3.5 hours.
Fuel range, wide open, at 15,000 ft..	4 hours.

The Packard Two-seater. (160 h.p. Packard engine.)

S

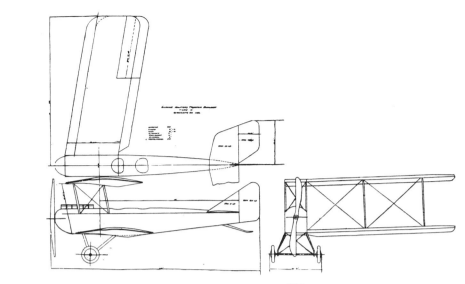

SLOANE. Sloane Aircraft Co., Inc. 1737 Broadway, New York. John E. Sloane, President. M. R. Hutchinson, Vice-President. Daniel L. Menan, jun., Secretary-Treasurer.

The latest type *Sloane* is a military tractor biplane.

This machine is equipped with a 130 h.p. 6-cylinder water-cooled engine.

Climbing speed is 500 feet (*152 metres*) per minute.

The maximum and minimum speeds are 82 m.p.h. (*130 kilometres*) and 47 m.p.h. (*75 kilometres*).

The load carried is 900 lbs. (*410 kilograms*).

Model.				Military Tractor.	
Span	...	...	feet (m.)	38	
Chord	...	...	feet (m.)	6' 6"	Climb 3,000 in 7½ mins.
Length	...	...	...	34	
Area	...	...	sq. feet (m².)	510	
Weight	total	...	lbs. (kgs.)	4300	
	useful	...	lbs. (kgs.)	900	
Motor	...	...	h.p.	125	
Speed	...	...	m.p.h. (km.)	85 to 47	

The SLOANE biplane, with back-swept wings, and 100 h.p. Hall-Scott motor.

STANDARD AIRCRAFT CORPORATION.

Elizabeth, N.J.

President, Mr. Harry Bowers Mingle. Chief Engineer. Charles E. Day. Factories at Elizabeth and Plainfield, N.J.

This, the second largest American aeronautical construction firm, has produced during the war a great variety of machines. Among these is the first postal aeroplane distinctly designed for this purpose, and various numbers of standard J–1 training machines. *Caproni* and *Handley-Page* night bombers fitted with Liberty engines. *DH-4a* two-seater fighters, and *HS* class (Navy) flying boats.

1916-17 Models	H 3. (1916 type).	Model J. Primary Training Type.	Model D. Twin Engined Military Seaplane.	Speed Scout
Span	40'	44' (upper)	62' 4" (upper)	26' 6"
Span	(Both planes)	32' (lower)	49' (lower)	(Both planes)
Chord	6' 6"	6'	7'	5'
Gap	6' 6"	5' 11"	7'	5' 6"
Length	27'	26' 7"	33' 6"	22' 8"
Dihedral	3°	3°	3°	3°
Sweep back	10°	5°	0°	10°
Stagger	1' 3"	10°	0°	15°
Area	491 sq. ft.	433 sq. ft.	760 sq. ft.	225 sq. ft.
Ailerons	Both wings	Upper only	Upper only	Both wings
Landing gear	2 wheels	3 wheels	2 floats	2 wheels
Engine	140 h.p. Hall-Scott (Type A5a)	90 h.p. Hall-Scott (Type A7)	2-140 h.p. Hall-Sct (Type A5a)	125 h.p. Hall-Scott (Type A9)
Weight with 1 hour's fuel	2700 lbs.	1750 lbs.	3300 lbs.	1192 lbs.
Useful load	800 lbs.	500 lbs.	1350 lbs.	425 lbs.

The H 3 type STANDARD AERO CORPORATION's tractor, 140 h.p. Hall-Scott engine.

Front view of Standard Training Tractor.

Rear view of Standard Training Tractor.

THE STANDARD MODEL "J-R" MILITARY TRAINING TRACTOR, WITH HALL-SCOTT 175-H.P. MOTOR.

The Standard Model "J-R" is one of America's recent productions in the way of an advanced training machine. It is similar in general form to the Standard Model "J" Military Preliminary Training Tractor. The 90-h.p. motor has been replaced by a special Hall-Scott 175-h.p. motor, and the R.A.F. No. 3 wing curve has been superseded by the U.S.A. No. 6.

Some leading features of the "J-R" model are as follows :—

(1.) The two-wheeled steel landing gear combines lightness with strength and is perfectly streamlined throughout so as to offer a minimum of head resistance. On landing, the axle rises in vertical guides, and when normal rests in a U-shaped steel case streamlined with aluminium.

(2.) All wing struts are provided with ball and socket fittings.

(3.) An auxiliary fan, driving the gear fuel-pump, projects out from the fuselage, and pumps the fuel from the main tank to the gravity tank.

(4.) The engine-bed is made very rigid by means of steel tube stays which connect the ash engine supports to the longerons.

(5.) There is a single control of the Dep. type in the rear cockpit.

(6.) The radiator is mounted over the motor and is free from vibrations. It strikes one, however, that it produces immense head-resistance.

(7.) There is a single complete manifold for the exhaust.

(8.) The exhaust pipe leads the gases over the top plane.

(9.) Throughout the entire machine, the weight has been kept down and yet none of the strength or air-worthiness has been impaired.

GENERAL SPECIFICATIONS.

GENERAL DIMENSIONS.

Wing span, upper plane	42 ft. 10 in.
Wing span, lower plane	31 ft.
Wing chord	6 ft.
Gap between wings	71 in.
Stagger	10 degs.
Overall length of machine	27 ft. 2½ in.
Overall height of machine	10 ft. 10 in.
Angle of incidence	2½ degs.
Dihedral angle	3 per cent.
Sweepback	5 degs.
Wing curve	U.S.A. No. 6.
Tail plane, angle of incidence	0 deg.

AREAS.

Upper wing	258 sq. ft.
Lower wing	159 sq. ft.
Total supporting surface (wings and ailerons)	417 sq. ft.
Ailerons (each 21 sq. ft.)	42.
Tail plane	23.7 sq. ft.
Fin, vertical	3.7 sq. ft.
Elevators (each 11 sq. ft.)	22.
Rudder	10 sq. ft.
Max. load per sq. ft. supporting surface	5.75 lbs.
Max. load per h.p.	13.7 lbs.

WEIGHT.

Net weight, machine empty	1,764 lbs.
Gross weight, machine loaded	2,400 lbs.

PERFORMANCE.

Max. speed, full load	95 m.p.h.
Min. speed, full load	48 m.p.h.
Gliding angle	1 to 11.
Climbing speed in 10 minutes	5,000 ft.

POWER PLANT.

Hall-Scott A-5A special, 6-cyl. vert. four-stroke cyl. water-cooled.

Horse-power (rated at 1,400 r.p.m.)	175 h.p.
Weight	605 lbs.
Bore on stroke	5¼ in. by 7 in.
Fuel consumption per hour	14 gals.
Fuel tank capacity	51 gals.
Gravity tank capacity	7¾ gals.
Total tank capacity	58¾ gals.
Oil capacity in crank-case	4 gals.

PROPELLER.

Make	"Standard."
Material	Black walnut.
Diameter	8 ft. 4 in.
Pitch	5 ft. 6 in.
Direction of rotation (viewed from pilot's seat)	Clockwise.

LANDING GEAR.

Number of wheels	2.
Size of wheels	26 in. by 4 in.
Thread	68¾ in.

As may be seen from the firm's own figures for performances, the machine cannot be used for war purposes, as the maximum speed would have to be increased by 25 per cent. and the climb by 100 per cent. before it would be safe to send over the lines at all in 1918. Nevertheless, in the advanced stages of training, after a pupil has left the slow preliminary types, and before putting him onto war aeroplanes, the machine should find a distinct field of usefulness.

Seating arrangement of Standard Tractor.

Undercarriage and Engine-mounting of Standard Training Tractor.

THE STANDARD E 1 DEFENCE BIPLANE

Intended, as shown below, for fighter and reconnaissance work, the E 1 was underpowered by 1917 standards. However, over 100 were built with Gnôme and Le Rhône engines for fighter training, delivered from August 1918. With the 100 h.p. Gnôme engine, a speed of 120 m.p.h. was possible.

THE STANDARD E 1 OR M DEFENCE BIPLANE.

Specification.

Type of machine	Single-seater Biplane.
Name or type No. of machine ..	E. 1. (M. Defence)
Purpose for which intended ..	Reconnaissance & fighting.
Span	24 ft.
Gap	4 ft.
Overall length	18 ft. 10¹⁄₁₆ in.
Maximum height	9 ft. 1in.
Chord	42 ins.
Area of elevators	10.3 sq. ft.
Area of rudder	6.8 sq. ft.
Area of fin	2.5 sq. ft.
Total area of ailerons ..	23.2 sq. ft.
Engine type and h.p. ..	80 h.p. Le Rhône,
Airscrew, diameter	8 ft.
Weight of machine empty ..	828 lbs.
Load per sq. ft.	7.5 lbs.
Weight per h.p.	14.3 lbs.
Tank capacity in hours ..	2 hours.
Performance.	
Speed low down	99.8 m.p.h.
Speed at 6,400 feet	94 m.p.h.
Speed at 10,000 feet ..	85 m.p.h.
Landing speed	48 m.p.h.
Climb.	
To 6,000 feet in minutes ..	10 minutes.
To 10 000 feet in minutes ..	22 mins. 20 secs.
Theoretical ceiling	14,800 ft.
Disposable load apart from fuel	201 lbs.
Total weight of machine loaded	1,144 lbs.
Dihedral	3%.
Stagger	13¼ in.
Track	5 ft.

Front View of the Standard Aircraft Corporation's type E.1 Single-seater (80 h.p. Le Rhône engine.)

THE STANDARD J. R. 1 BIPLANE.

(Built by the Standard Aircraft Corporation.)

Specification.

Type of machine	Single-seater Biplane.
Name or type No. of machine ..	J. R. 1.
Span	31 ft. 4¾ in.
Overall length	26 ft. 2 in.
Maximum height	10 ft. 10¹⁵⁄₁₆ in.
Engine type and h.p. ..	170 h.p. Hispano-Suiza engine.
Weight of machine empty ..	1,566 lbs.
Petrol tank capacity in gallons ..	60 gallons.
Performance.	
Speed low down	100 m.p.h.
Landing speed..	48 m.p.h.
Climb.	
To 5,300 feet in minutes ..	10 mins.
Total weight of machine loaded..	2,400 lbs.

THE AMERICAN HANDLEY PAGE TYPE 0-400 BOMBER.

Both in Great Britain and in the United States, the Handley Page has been the principal machine to be put into quantity production for bombing purposes. The American design is similar to the British, except that Liberty " 12 " 400 h.p. engines are employed in the former, and the Rolls-Royce or Sunbeam in the latter.

Side View of The Standard E. 1 Single-seater.

STURTEVANT.

The B. F. Sturtevant Company, Hyde Park, Boston, Massachusetts.

Big engineering firm. Turned out some time ago a "battle" aeroplane of naval type, to designs of Mr. Grover C. Loening, B.Sc., M.A.C.E., former Aeronautic Engineer to U.S. Army.

Machine illustrated has span of 50 feet, length 25 feet, area 700 square feet. Petrol capacity, 150 gallons for 12 hours' flying. Motor, 140 h.p. eight-cylinder V type.

Remarkable for the "gun-turrets" placed one on each side of fuselage, thus given concentrated fire ahead, with fair defensive fire on either side and behind.

The firm's S 4 seaplane is described on the next page.

A *Sturtevant* high-speed scout is in process of production at time of going to press.

STURTEVANT S

The S4 two-seat seaplane was one model of the S series, which found limited favour with the US Navy. Altogether the USN received 12 S machines.

Span	... ...	48 ft. 7½ in.
Chord	...	7'
Gap	...	6' 9"
Length	...	28'
Area	...	620 sq. ft.
Ailerons	...	Both wings
Landing gear	...	Floats or 2 wheels.
Engine	...	5 A Sturtevant (140 h.p.)
Weight	...	2025 lbs. (with 1 hour's fuel)
Useful load	...	525 lbs
Speed range	...	40 to 73 m.p.h.
Climb	...	4000 ft. in 12 mins.

T

THOMAS-MORSE AIRCRAFT CORPORATION.

(Late Thomas Bros.,) Ithaca, New York.

The brothers Thomas began experimenting and flying in 1908 with a machine on the lines of a *Curtiss*. In the winter of 1909-10, a type of their own was produced and was flown during 1911 by Walter Johnson in exhibitions. In 1912 they continued the same type, with refinements. In 1913 they adopted the overhanging top plane type, but of the same general order of construction.

In 1915 the firm supplied various Tractor biplanes to the Allied Governments. In 1916, the firm was reconstructed, and became the Thomas-Morse Aircraft Corporation. It has since supplied numerous machines to the U.S. Government.

The M.B.3, designed in 1918 for war service as a single-seat fighter, was not ordered until 1919.

A U.S. Naval Flying Boat of the H.S. 2 L. type, built by the Standard Aircraft Corporation.

Rear view of STURTEVANT "battle" biplane, with a gun turret on each wing.

Side view of above machine with gunner in near turret.

STURTEVANT S 4 seaplane, with Sturtevant 5 A engine, 140 h.p.

The Thomas-Morse type M.B.3 of 1918 design (300 h.p. Wright-Hispano-Suiza).

THOMAS MILITARY TRACTOR, Type T2. 80-90 horse power.

1. Minimum head resistance and maximum efficiency. Especially adapted to all-round military work—scouting, reconnaissance, range spotting, messenger service, etc.
2. Carries pilot and observer, fuel for four hours, and 285 lbs. (130 kgs.) additional (total useful load is 897 lbs. (405 kgs.) Speed range is 38-82 m.p.h. (60-130 km.) Weight (empty) is 1075 lbs. (487 kgs.) Climb with full load is 4,000 feet (1,220 m.) in 10 minutes, 800 feet (245 m.) in first minute.
3. Over all length, 28 feet (8.50 m.), span, 36 feet (11.00 m.), chord, 5 feet (1.50 m.), gap, 5 feet (1.50 m.) wing area, 350 sq. feet (33 m²), loading, 5.3 lbs. sq. feet.
4. Entirely new model, developed for military purposes.

THOMAS MILITARY RECONNAISSANCE TRACTOR, Type D2. 150-180 horse power.

1. Great power and speed, in addition to all the advantages of Type T2. Also has the most simple and rugged type of landing gear.
2. Carries pilot and observer, fuel for four and a half hours, and 250 lbs. (114 kgs.) additional (total useful load is 1082 lbs. (490 kgs.) Speed range is 40 to 91 m.p.h. 25-145 km.) Weight loaded is 2,250 lbs. (1,020 kg.) Climb is 4,000 feet (1220 m.) in nine minutes.
3. Over all length, 29 feet (8.85 m.), span, 37 feet (11.30 m.), chord, 5 feet 3 ins. (1.50 m.), gap, 5 feet (1.50 m.), total lifting area, 401 sq. feet (37.5 m².), loading, 5.6 lbs. sq. feet.
4. Changed conditions of warfare have shown the need of very powerful, fast, two passenger machines, capable of carrying extra load.

THOMAS NAVY SEAPLANE, Type HS. 140 horse power.

1. Reconnaissance type hydro-aeroplane, capable of manœuvring in rough seas, useful for sea scouting and range correcting work, used by the U.S. Navy for training officers.
2. Carries useful load of 1,200 lbs. (545 kg.) (pilot and observer), fuel for 4 to 6 hours, and additional load. Speed range is 47 to 83 m.p.h. (73-135 km.) Weight (loaded) is 2,200 lbs. (1,000 km.) in 10 minutes; 600 feet (183 m.) in first minute.
3. Over all length, 29 feet (8.85 m.), span, 37 feet (11.30 m.), chord, 5 feet 2 ins. (1.50 m.), gap, 5 feet (150 m.), wing area, 388 sq. feet (36 m².), loading, 5.6 lbs. sq. feet.
4. Completely new design, developed especially for the needs of the naval aviation service.

THOMAS "BATTLE MODEL" SEAPLANE, Type S. Two engines 186 h.p. or 300 h.p.

1. A very powerful fighting seaplane, designed to carry heavy armament, and to be used for offensive warfare.
2. Carries total useful load of 1130 lbs. (515 kgs.) pilot and two passengers, fuel for 4-1/2 hours, gun, ammunition, etc. Speed range with lower power is 47 to 81 m.p.h. (75-130 km.) Weight loaded is 2860 lbs. (1298 kgs.) Climb is 330 feet (100 m.) per minute for first 10 minutes.
3. Over all length, 28.75 feet (8.70 m.), span, 44 feet (13.40 m.), chord, 59 in. (0.90 m.), gap, 6 feet (1.82 m.), wing area, 440 sq. feet (41 m₂).
4. Differs from Type HS in the much greater size and power, (two motors), and in the much greater load carried.

THOMAS PUSHER BIPLANES { Hydroaeroplane, Type SP. Scout Pusher, Type SP 1. Land Machine, Type SP 2. } 150 h.p.

1. For those who prefer the pusher type. It is especially useful for school purposes (the seats are side by side), and also for exhibition work and passenger carrying.
2. Carries pilot and student, fuel for 4 hours, and additional useful load (total useful load is 887 lbs. (402 kgs.) Speed range is 50 to 80 m.p.h. (80-130 kms.) Weight (empty) is 1300 lbs. (590 kgs.) Climb is 3500 feet (1070 m.) in first 10 minutes.

The record-breaking THOMAS tractor biplane, which with 160 h.p. Curtiss engine, was the first American aeroplane to exceed 100 miles an hour.

3. Over all length, 36 feet (11.00 m.), span, 37 feet (11.30 m.), chord, 5 feet 3 ins. (1.50 m.), gap, 5 feet (1.50 m.), wing area, 377 sq. feet (35 m²).
4. This differs completely from the old type of exhibition machine in that it is much more substantially built, and the influence of the military machine is shown in its design.

THOMAS 1915 FLYING BOAT. 90 h.p.

1. Built entirely of mohogany, luxuriously fitted up, hull of best design for water and air use.
2. Carries two or three people, fuel for two to four hours, and additional useful load. Speed is 70 m.p.h. (115 kms.) Weight (empty) is 1250 lbs. (567 kgs.)
3. Over all length, 28 feet 6 ins. (8.65 m.), span-top plane, 38 feet (11.60 m.), lower plane, 28 feet (8.55 m.), chord, 5 feet (1.50 m.), gap (average), 6 feet (1.82 m.), wing area, 360 sq. feet (33.5 m²), loading, 4.3 lbs./sq. feet.
4. Compared with 1914 model, design of wings and hull is much better for the considerations of less resistance, more seaworthiness, and greater air efficiency. The entire construction is of a much higher order, and luxurious comfort is the first consideration.

THOMAS tractor biplane, 90 h.p. Curtiss motor, rising from ground.

THOMAS tractor biplane, 90 h.p. Curtiss engine, just about to land.

The THOMAS flying-boat, 90 h.p. Austro-Daimler engine.

THE THOMAS-MORSE D5

The " D 5 " Thomas Tractor has the following characteristics :

Span	...	52′ 9″ upper plane.	Area	...	... 465 sq. ft.	
		34′ lower plane.	Ailerons	...	... Upper wings only.	
Chord	...	... 5′ 6″	Landing Gear	...	... Two wheels.	
Gap	...	... 5′ 3″	Engine	...	... Thomas 135 h.p., 8-cylinder V	
Length	...	... 29′ 9″	Weight	...	... 2500 lbs. (1 hour's fuel).	
Dihedral	...	... 4 degrees.	Useful load	...	... 1100 lbs.	

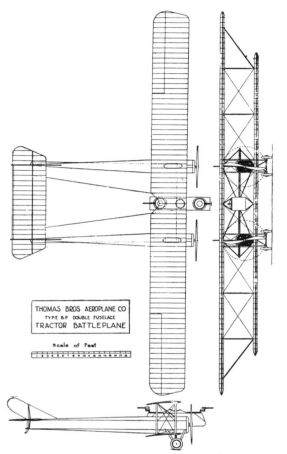

THOMAS BROS AEROPLANE CO
TYPE B.P DOUBLE FUSELAGE
TRACTOR BATTLEPLANE

Scale of Feet

The THOMAS twin tractor biplane, as built for the U.S. Army & Navy.

The " D 5 " Type THOMAS-MORSE military tractor with 135 h.p. Thomas engine.

THE THOMAS-MORSE S.4 SCOUT BIPLANE

The S.4B (100 h.p. Gnôme engine) and S.4C (80 Le Rhône engine) became standard single-seat fighter trainers with the US services from 1917. The details below apply to the S.4C version.

Type of machine	Single-seater Scout trainer.
Name or type No. of machine ..	S.4C.
Purpose for which intended ..	Fighter training.
Span ..	26 ft. 6 in.
Overall length ..	19 ft. 10 in.
Maximum height ..	8 ft. 1 in.
Engine type and h.p. ..	80 h.p. Le Rhône.
Weight of machine empty ..	940 lbs.
Petrol tank capacity in gallons ..	30 gallons.

Performance.

Speed (maximum)	..	97 m.p.h.
Landing speed	..	45 m.p.h.

Climb.

To 7,500 feet in minutes ..	10 minutes
Total weight of machine loaded	1,330 lbs.

THE THOMAS-MORSE S.5 SINGLE SEATER SEAPLANE

Designation of six S.4B seaplanes used by the US Navy from 1917-18.

Type of machine .. .:	Single-seater Seaplane.
Name or type No. of machine ..	S.5.
Purpose for which intended.. ..	Training.
Span	26 ft. 6 in.
Overall length	22 ft. 9 in.
Maximum height	9 ft. 7 in.
Total surface of wings (inc. ailerons)	240 sq. ft.
Total area of fixed tail plane ..	16.8 sq. ft.
Area of elevators ..	22 sq. ft.
Area of rudder ..	8.5 sq. ft.
Area of fin	3.5 sq. ft.
Total area of ailerons ..	30 sq. ft.
Engine type and h.p. ..	100 h.p. Monosoupape
	Gnôme.
Airscrew, diameter and revs. ..	8 ft., 1250 r.p.m.
Load per sq. ft. ..	6.25 lbs.
Weight per h.p. ..	14·3 lbs.
Tank capacity in hours. ..	3 hours.
Tank capacity in gallons ..	30 galls.

Three-quarter Rear View, of the Thomas-Morse type S.4C. (80 h.p. Le Rhône engine).

Performance.

Speed low down	.. ..	95 m.p.h.
Landing speed	.. ..	50 m.p.h.

Climb.

To 5,200 feet in minutes ..	10 minutes.
Total weight of machine loaded	1,500 lbs.

THE THOMAS-MORSE S.H. 4 SEAPLANE

Following the delivery of a number of biplanes of similar but earlier types to the UK from 1915, Curtiss developed the S.H.4. The US Navy received 14 in 1917 for training and observation roles.

Type of machine	..	..	Two-seater Seaplane.
Name or type No. of machine	..	S.H. 4.
Purpose for which intended	..	Training.
Span	..	..	44 ft.
Overall length	..	..	29 ft. 9 in.
Chord	..	..	5 ft. 9 in.
Engine type and h.p.	..	..	100 h.p. Thomas.

The Thomas-Morse S.H. 4 Seaplane.

3 r 2

U

UNITED AIRCRAFT ENGINEERING CORPORATION. 52, Vanderbilt Avenue, New York.

President, F. G. Diffin ; Chief Engineer, M. B. Stout.

This firm was organised early in 1919 for the purpose of promoting commercial aeronautics through the development of aircraft engineering and the construction of aeroplanes to their own designs.

Shortly after their organisation this firm purchased from the Canadian Government a great stock of flying material, valued at $10,000,000, in which were comprised 350 Canadian *Curtiss J.N.* two-seaters, 1,000 Curtiss O.X. engines, hundreds of airscrews and spare parts in proportion. It is intended to sell this material to American sportsmen and others interested in civil aviation.

A number of elementary training machines of various types and conditions were also bought from the British Aircraft Disposal Board.

Single and two-seater monoplanes are being developed to the designs of Mr. Stout.

THE UNITED EASTERN AEROPLANE CORPORATION. 1251, De Kalb Avenue, Brooklyn, New York.

Build three types of tractor biplane.   Factor of safety of 10 claimed for all parts.

Wing curve throughout " Eiffel 36."

Capital recently increased from $30,000 to $1,000,000.

Owns the Eastern School of Aviation.

Were engaged on Military machines for the U. S. Government.

United Eastern Aeroplane Corp aircraft			Military Tractor	Military Tractor (Illustrated)	Seaplane Tractor
Span	..	..	45′	39′	42′
Chord	..	..	6′	5′ 6″	6′
Gap	..	..	6′	6′	6′
Length	..	..	28′ 3″	25′ 6″	29′ 6″
Dihedral	..	..	1°	1°	1°
Sweep back	..	..	None	8°	None
Stagger	..	..	9″	9″	9″
Area	..	..	482 sq. ft.	350 sq. ft.	436 sq. ft.
Ailerons	..	..	Both planes	Upper planes	Upper planes
Landing gear	..	..	2 wheels	2 wheels	Single float
Engine	..	..	125 h.p. Hall-Scott (A5)	Curtiss 100 h.p. (OXX.2)	Curtiss 100 h.p. (OXX.2)
Weight with one hour's fuel	..	..	1550 lbs.	1200 lbs.	1413 lbs.
Useful load	..	..	900 lbs.	800 lbs.	500 lbs.

Top view of EASTERN military tractor.

Side view of EASTERN military tractor, 100 h.p. Curtiss OXX 2 engine.

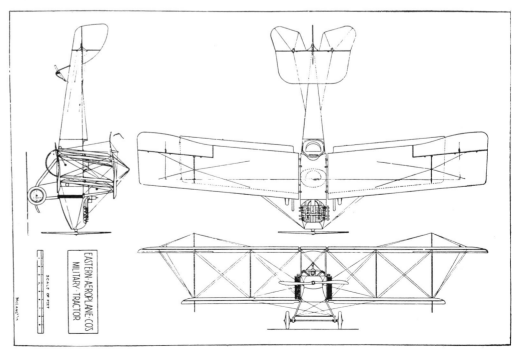

EASTERN AEROPLANE CO'S MILITARY TRACTOR

SCALE OF FEET

V

VOUGHT. Lewis & Vought Corporation, Long Island City, N.Y.

This firm constructs to the designs of Mr. Chance M. Vought, president and chief engineer, a two-seater biplane fitted with a 180 h.p. Hispano-Suiza engine, which is used by the U.S. Army as an advanced training machine. This aeroplane won, in 1918, the Army competition for advanced training machines.

THE V.E.7 "BLUEBIRD" TRAINING MACHINE.

Type of machine	Two-seater Biplane.
Name or type No. of machine ..	V.E. 7 "Bluebird."
Purpose for which intended..	Training.
Span	34 ft. 4 in.
Gap	4 ft. 8 in.
Overall length	24 ft. 5⅜ in.
Maximum height	8 ft. 7½ in.
Chord	4 ft. 7½ in.
Span of tail	10 ft.
Engine type and h.p. ..	150 or 180 h.p. Hispano-Suiza.
Airscrew, diameter	8 ft. 8 in.
Weight of machine empty ..	1,392 lbs.

Performance.

Speed low down.. ..	106 m.p h.
Speed at 6,500 feet	103 m.p.h.
Speed at 10,000 feet ..	97 m.p.h.
Speed at 15,000 feet ..	86 m.p.h.
Landing speed	48 m.p.h.

Climb.

To 6,500 feet in minutes..	8 mins. 50 secs.
To 10,000 feet in minutes ..	15 mins. 15 secs.
To 15,000 feet in minutes ..	29 minutes.
Total weight of machine loaded	1,937 lbs.

Side View of the Lewis & Vought V.E.7 Training Machine (Hispano-Suiza engine).

Three-quarter Rear View of the Lewis & Vought V.E.7 150 h.p. Hispano-Suiza).

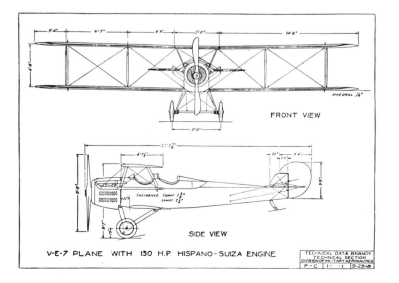

FRONT VIEW

SIDE VIEW

V-E-7 PLANE WITH 150 H.P. HISPANO-SUIZA ENGINE

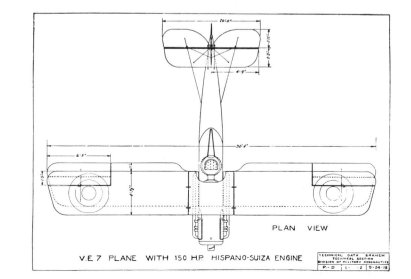

PLAN VIEW

V.E.7 PLANE WITH 150 H.P. HISPANO-SUIZA ENGINE

W

WITTEMAN - LEWIS AIRCRAFT COR-PORATION. Newark, N.J.

Aeronautical constructional engineers, manufacturing to private specifications. Have produced the *Sundstedt* seaplane, which was intended for the trans-Atlantic flight, but crashed in the course of its trials.

Have also produced a reconnaissance tractor biplane of their own design.

THE SUNDSTEDT-HANNEVIG SEAPLANE.

At the plant of the Wittemann-Lewis Aircraft Co., probably one of the largest seaplanes in the United States has been constructed by the prominent Swedish aviator, Captain Hugo Sundstedt, and the well-known Norwegian financier, shipbuilder and shipowner, Mr. Christoffer Hannevig.

Captain Sundstedt is one of the pioneers in aviation, having flown since 1910. In July, 1914, just before the war broke out, he made a non-stop flight from Buc, near Paris, France, to Stockholm, of about 1,200 miles, in a *Henry Farman* biplane, in 13 hours and 20 minutes. During the war Capt. Sundstedt has been about two years in France, and received several decorations. About three years ago he left France for the United States for the purpose of building an aeroplane for a trans-Atlantic flight.

The *Sundstedt-Hannevig* seaplane has been designed for the specific purpose of long-distance flying over the sea. In general, it has been designed with an extra heavy substantial construction, particularly on those parts subjected to the greatest amount of strain during flight and at landings, such as pontoons, wings, and the entire rigging.

In the design, however, only proved aero-dynamical principles have been embodied, assuring a positively efficient machine, and Captain Sundstedt has made a large number of improvements in structural details, affording the utmost strength and lightness of construction.

The seaplane is equipped for two pilots and two passengers in the cabin of the fuselage.

General Dimensions.

Span, upper plane	100 ft.
Span, lower plane	71 ft. 6 in.
Wing chord, lower plane	8 ft.
Wing chord, upper plane	8 ft.
Gap between wings	8 ft. 72 in.
Length of machine overall	50 ft. 6 in.
Height of machine overall	17 ft. 7 in.
Dihedral angle, lower plane	2 degrees.
Wing curve	U.S.A. No. 5.
Total lifting surface	1,587 sq. ft.
Rudder area	22 sq. ft.
Elevator area	54 sq. ft.
Weight	10,000 lbs.
Loading per h.p.	25 lbs.
Loading per sq. ft.	6 lbs.
Speed, estimated, full load	80 m.p.h.
Climbing speed, estimated	3,000 ft. in 10 mins.
Horse power, total	440.

THE WITTEMANN-LEWIS TRACTOR BIPLANE.

Type of machine	Wittemann-Lewis.
Name or type No. of machine	" T. T."
Purpose for which intended	Military training.
Span	42 ft. top; 34 ft. bottom plane.
Gap	5 ft. 6 in.
Overall length	27 ft. 2 in.
Maximum height	11 ft. 6½ in.
Chord	5 ft. 6 in.
Total surface of wings	400 sq. ft.
Total area of tail	28.8 sq. ft.
Area of elevators	21.6 sq. ft.
Area of rudder	12 sq. ft.
Area of fin	5.37 sq. ft.
Area of each aileron & total area	17.44; 38.88 sq. ft.
Engine type and h.p.	Hall-Scott, 100 h.p.
Weight of machine empty	1,560 lbs.
Load per sq. ft.	5.41 lbs.
Weight per h.p.	21.6 lbs.
Tank capacity in hours	3.6 hours.
Tank capacity in gallons	36 gallons.

Performance.

Speed	74 m.p.h. max.; 38 m.p.h. min.

Climb.

To 3,000 feet in 10 minutes.

Disposable load apart from fuel	605 lbs.
Total weight of machine loaded	2,165 lbs.

THE WRIGHT-MARTIN AIRCRAFT CORPORATION. 60, Broadway, New York City.

Western office : 937, S. Los Angelos St. Los Angelos St., Cal. Foreign office : 35, bis Rue d'Anjou, Paris.

The original type of *Wright* machine was mounted on skids only, and started along a rail. Its special features were a biplane elevator forward, main planes with warpable tips to trailing edge, small keel in gap, two propellers, chain driven in rear of planes, double rudder in rear, and no tail. Orville Wright made the first flight worthy of the name on this machine on December 17th, 1903. He flew a machine of this type for 2h. 20m. 23⅘s. in 1908. (For details of early *Wrights* see previous editions of this book.)

During 1916, the Wright Co., represented by Mr. Orville Wright, the surviving brother, formed a " merger " with the Glenn L. Martin Co., the Simplex Automobile Co., the Wright Flying Field Inc., and the General Aeronautic Co., of America.

The Sundstedt-Hannevig Transatlatic Seaplane before complete erection.

The Witteman-Lewis Biplane, type T.T. (100 h.p. Hall-Scott engine).

Mr Orville Wright continued to work as a private experimenter at the experimental factory at Dayton, Ohio.

The firm has factories at Los Angelos, (Cal.), at New York, at Simplex Works, New Brunswick, New Jersey.

The aerodromes are at Los Angelos (Cal.) and at Hempstead Plains, Long Island.

There is a seaplane station at Port Washington, Long Island. 2,400 men were employed in 1916.

The president of the firm is Edward M. Hagar; vice-presidents, Glenn L. Martin and C. S. Jennison; secretary, J. G. Dudley.

Capital, 5,000,000 dollars.

Before the war this firm built biplanes to their own designs, but during the war this work was dropped and most activity centred on the production of Hispano-Suiza engines and on the production of aeroplanes to official designs.

Mr. Glenn L. Martin also started a new concern of his own.

Illustrations of a number of war-period (1914-18) Wright/Wright-Martin experimental aircraft follow, but also built were three Type R seaplanes (150 h.p. Hall-Scott A-5A engine) purchased by the US Navy in 1917.

WRIGHT experimental biplane. Engine in front and two chain-driven propellers.

The Single WRIGHT Model K experimental seaplane taken into service by the US Navy. It was the last Wright aeroplane bought from the original company.

WRIGHT-MARTIN, TYPE V.

Span	... ...	39' 8"
Chord	... ...	5' 10"
Gap	... ...	5' 7"
Stagger	... ...	1'
Dihedral	... ...	$1\frac{1}{4}$ degrees
Span of Tail	... ...	12'
Area	... ...	223·2 sq. ft. (upper plane)
"	... ...	206·8 sq. ft. (lower plane)
Area of Aileron	...	64·6 sq. ft. (total of four)
" Tail	... ...	57·2 sq. ft.
" Fin	... ...	17·37 sq. ft.
Total Area	... ...	430 sq. ft.
Loading per sq. ft.	...	5·86 lbs.
" B.N.P.	...	16·86 lbs.
Weight without engine	...	1130 lbs.
Weight of power plant complete	...	595 lbs.
" useful load	...	445 lbs.
" 6 hrs. fuel	...	460 lbs.
Gross Weight	...	2630 lbs.
Motor—Simplex Model A.		
Hispano-Suiza	...	150 h.p. at 1450 r.p.m.
Propeller, diam.	...	8' 4"
" pitch	...	5' 7½"
Control	... ...	Deperdussin type

Three-quarter front view of the WRIGHT-MARTIN Type V tractor, with 150 h.p. Hispano-Suiza engine.

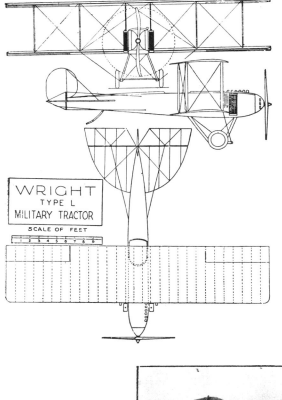

WRIGHT Type L military tractor. As shown in accompanying drawing.

Side view of Model R. Wright-Martin Training Tractor.

THE WORLD'S AERO-ENGINES.

❖

ARRANGED IN THE ALPHABETICAL ORDER OF THEIR NAMES.

❖

A.B.C. (British).

A.B.C. MOTORS, LTD., Walton-on-Thames, formerly the All British Engine Co., Ltd., Hersham, Surrey.

Founded early in 1912 by Mr. Ronald Charteris—later Capt., R F.C.—with Mr. Granville Bradshaw as chief designer. Built many experimental engines in succeeding years.

One of the earliest makers of aero engines. An A.B.C. engine (40 h.p. four-cylinder, vertical, water-cooled) on a *Sopwith* biplane, piloted by Mr. Hawker, beat the British Duration Record, and won the Michelin Cup, in 1912.

Since then the firm has developed air-cooled stationary-cylinder engines, known as the "Gnat," the "Mosquito," the "Wasp," and the "Dragon-fly" respectively, with 2, 6, 7, and 9 cylinders.

THE A.B.C. GNAT II.

Type of engine	2-cylinder horizontally opposed.
Type of cylinder	Steel, fins A.B.C. copper coated.
Bore	4.75 ins.
Stroke	5½ ins.
Normal b.h.p.	45. Max. 50.
Rotation	Anti-clockwise facing propeller.
Normal speed	1800 r.p.m. Max. 2000.
Lubrication	One rotary plunger pump from tank to crankcase and then splash to cylinders.
Oil recommended	Wakefield Castrol "R."
Oil consumption	1.7 pints.
Oil consumption per b.h.p. hour	.037 pints.
Carburetters	1 A.B.C. 48 mm.
Petrol consumption	·56 pints per b.h.p. hour.
Magnetos	1 M.L. Magneto. Type K2.
Speed of Magnetos	½ engine speed.
Mag. rotates	Anti-clockwise facing driving end of armature.
Weight of engine, including prop. boss, but without oil or fuel	115 lbs.
Weight of engine per b.h.p.	2.3 lbs.

THE A.B.C. DRAGON-FLY I.A.

Type of engine	9-cylinder stationary radial
Type of cylinder	Steel, fins A.B.C. copper coated. 3 overhead valves, 2 exhaust and 1 inlet.
Bore	5½ ins. = 139.7 mm.
Stroke	6½ ins. = 165.1 mm.
Normal b.h.p.	340.
Rotation	Anti-clock facing propellor.
Normal speed	1650 r.p.m.

Front and Back View of A.B.C. "Gnat" (45 h.p.)

Cam-ring, Tappets and Big-end Bearing of A.B.C. "Dragon-fly."

Lubrication	2 rotary plunger pumps. 1 feeding through hollow crankshaft to crankpin, centrifugal feed to big end and thence splash. 1 feeding to nose, dropping into cam and forming a permanent sump for gears in bottom of nose	Carburetters .. 2 A.B.C. carburetters.
		Petrol consumption .. .56 pints per b.h.p. hour.
		Magnetos .. 2 A.K. 9 magnetos, 4 spark.
		Speed of magneto .. 1¼ engine speed.
		Mag. rotates .. Clockwise, facing driving end of armature.
Oil recommended	Wakefield Castrol "R."	Rev. counter rotates .. Anti-clock, facing driving shaft.
Oil consumption	7 pints per hour.	Speed of rev. counter drive .. ¼ engine speed.
Oil consumption per b.h.p. hour	.021 pints.	Weight of engine, including prop. boss, but without oil or fuel .. 600 lbs.
		Weight of engine per b.h.p. .. 1.765 lbs.

A.B.C. "Dragon-fly," 330 h.p. (Front View).

A.B.C. "Dragon-fly," 330 h.p. (Back View).

A.B.C.—*continued.*

THE A.B.C. WASP II.

Type of engine	7-cylinder stationary radial.
Type of cylinder	Steel, fins A.B.C. copper coated, 3 overhead valves, 2 exhaust and 1 inlet.
Bore	$4\frac{3}{4}$ ins.
Stroke	$6\frac{1}{4}$ ins.
Normal b.h.p.	200.
Rotation	Anti-clock facing propeller.
Normal speed	1800 r.p.m.
Lubrication	2 rotary plunger pumps, 1 feeding through hollow crankshaft to crankpin, centrifugal feed to big end and thence splash. 1 feeding to nose, dropping into cam and forming a permanent sump for gears in bottom of nose.
Oil recommended	Wakefield Castrol " R."
Oil consumption	4 pints per hour.
Oil consumption per b.h.p. hour	.02 pints.
Carburetters	2 A.B.C. 48 mm.
Petrol consumption	.56 pints per b.h.p. hour.
Magnetos	2 P.L. 7 type. 2 spark.
Speed of magnetos	$1\frac{3}{4}$ engine speed.
Mag. rotates	Clockwise facing driving end of armature
Rev. counter rotates ..	Anti-clock facing driving shaft.
Speed of rev. counter drive ..	$\frac{1}{4}$ engine speed.
Weight of engine, including prop. boss, but without oil or fuel ..	320 lbs.
Weight of engine per b.h.p. ..	1.6 lbs.

A.B.C. " Wasp " (Mark II.), 200 h.p.

Cam-ring and Tappets of A.B.C. " Wasp."

Crankcase Components (two views) of A.B.C. " Wasp."

AERO-MARINE (American).

THE AERO MARINE Co., Times Building, New York.

Mr. J. F. Willard, Engineer.

This firm made in 1917 the following engines.

90 h.p. Model.

Type : Water-cooled vertical.
No. of cylinders : 6.
Bore : $4\frac{5}{16}$ in. $5\frac{1}{8}$ in.
R.P.M. :
Cylinders : Domed heads, cast head jackets, copper side jackets
Valves : Overhead, push rods from crankcase.
Carburetters : 2, each feeding three cylinders.
Lubrication : Forced feed.
Weight : 420 lbs.

150 h.p. Model.

Type : Water-cooled " V "
No. of cylinders : 12.
Bore : $4\frac{5}{16}''$.
Stroke : $5\frac{1}{8}''$.
R.P.M. : 1400.
Cylinders : Separate castings.
Valves : Overhead, push rods.
Carburetters : 2 Zenith.
Ignition : 2—12-spark Dixie.

In 1918 made the 6-cylinder vertical engine illustrated herewith   No details have been vouchsafed by the makers.

The Aero-Marine engine, 125–130 h.p.

ANZANI (British & French).

ANZANI MOTEURS d'AVIATION, 112, Boulevard de Courbevoie, Courbevoie (Seine).

BRITISH ANZANI ENGINE Co., Ltd., 32, Scrubbs Lane, Willesden, London, N.W.

100 h.p. Model.
Type : Radial, air-cooled.
No. of cylinders : 10.
Bore : 105 m/m.   Stroke : 140 m/m.
R.P.M. : 1,100.
Cylinders : Cast iron.
Valves : Inlet and exhaust on cylinder head,
Carburetter : Zenith.
Ignition : Magneto.
Lubrication : Splash and pump.

150 h.p. Model, as above, but :—
No. of cylinders : 14.

60 h.p. Model, as above, but :—
No. of cylinders : 6.
Bore : 105 m/m.   Stroke : 120 m/m.

45 h.p. Model, as above, but :—
Bore : 90 m/m.   Stroke : 120 m/m.

35 h.p. Model, as above, but :—
No. of cylinders : 3.
Bore : 105 m/m.   Stroke : 120 m/m.

Most of the above engines still exist, but no fresh particulars are available.

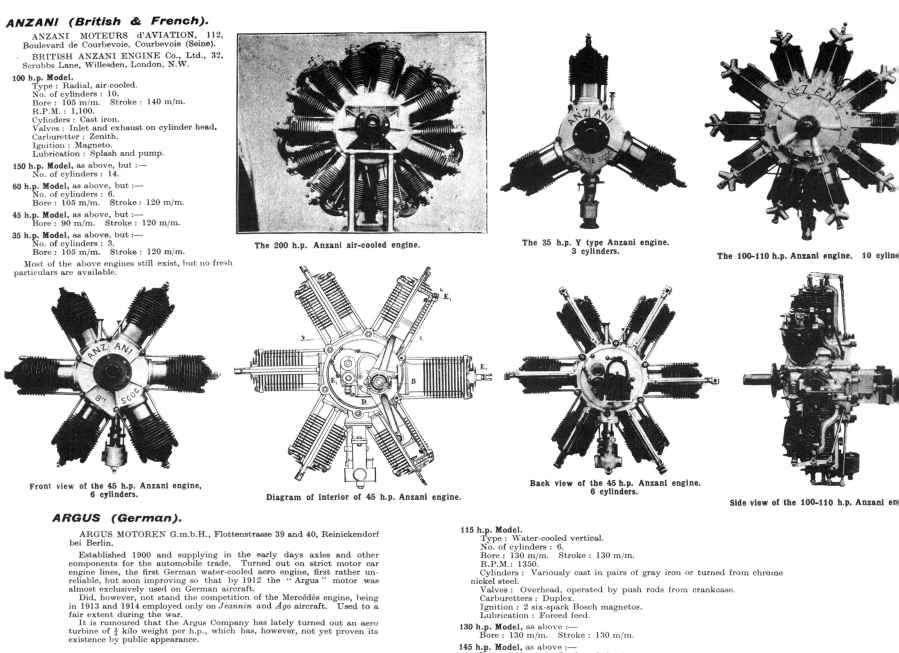

The 200 h.p. Anzani air-cooled engine.

The 35 h.p. Y type Anzani engine.
3 cylinders.

The 100-110 h.p. Anzani engine.   10 cylinders

Front view of the 45 h.p. Anzani engine,
6 cylinders.

Diagram of interior of 45 h.p. Anzani engine.

Back view of the 45 h.p. Anzani engine.
6 cylinders.

Side view of the 100-110 h.p. Anzani engine

ARGUS (German).

ARGUS MOTOREN G.m.b.H., Flottenstrasse 39 and 40, Reinickendorf bei Berlin.

Established 1900 and supplying in the early days axles and other components for the automobile trade. Turned out on strict motor car engine lines, the first German water-cooled aero engine, first rather unreliable, but soon improving so that by 1912 the "Argus" motor was almost exclusively used on German aircraft.

Did, however, not stand the competition of the Mercédès engine, being in 1913 and 1914 employed only on *Jeannin* and *Ago* aircraft. Used to a fair extent during the war.

It is rumoured that the Argus Company has lately turned out an aero turbine of ¾ kilo weight per h.p., which has, however, not yet proven its existence by public appearance.

115 h.p. Model.
Type : Water-cooled vertical.
No. of cylinders : 6.
Bore : 130 m/m.   Stroke : 130 m/m.
R.P.M.: 1350.
Cylinders : Variously cast in pairs of gray iron or turned from chrome nickel steel.
Valves : Overhead, operated by push rods from crankcase.
Carburetters : Duplex.
Ignition : 2 six-spark Bosch magnetos.
Lubrication : Forced feed.

130 h.p. Model, as above :—
Bore : 130 m/m.   Stroke : 130 m/m.

145 h.p. Model, as above :—
Bore : 140 m/m.   Stroke : 140 m/m.

190 h.p. Model, as above :—
Bore : 150 m/m.   Stroke : 145 m/m.

No fresh particulars are available concerning 1918 type engines.

End View of the 190 h.p. Argus engine.

Side View of 190 h.p. Argus engine.

ARMSTRONG-WHITWORTH (British).

Sir W. G. ARMSTRONG. WHITWORTH & Co., Ltd., Newcastle-on-Tyne.

An experimental Vee-type engine. No specification has been supplied.

Side View of the Armstrong–Whitworth Engine.

Front View of the Armstrong-Whitworth Engine.

ASHMUSEN (American).

ASHMUSEN MANUFACTURING Co., 266, Pearl Street, Rhode Island.

Made in 1917 the following model :

105 h.p. Model.

Type : "Self-cooled" (Air-cooled).
No. of cylinders : 12 double-opposed horizontal.
Bore : 3.75 ins.
Stroke : 4.5 ins.
R.P.M. : 1800.
Propeller speed : 900 r.p.m.
Overall length : $42\frac{1}{4}$ in.
Overall width : 34 in.

No fresh information available since America entered into the war.

AUSTRO-DAIMLER MOTOREN GESELL-SCHAFT (Austrian). Wiener Neustadt.

THE 200 H.P. AUSTRO-DAIMLER.

INTRODUCTORY NOTE.

The following report on the design, construction, and general performance of the latest type of Austro-Daimler engine is based on an examination and tests carried out at the R.A.E. on the engine (No. 19,218) taken from a captured Austrian *Berg* scout (R.A.F. No. A.G.6).

This machine, a single-seater biplane brought down on the Italian Front in April, 1918, was captured in very good condition ; the engine had apparently only been in use for a few hours.

With the exception of its high stroke : bore ratio and the construction of a detachable inlet valve seating in each cylinder, the design of this engine shows no great resemblance to the earlier types of Austro-Daimler engines ; generally speaking, the new 200 h.p. Austro-Daimler possesses more than the usual amount of originality in design found in enemy aero engines.

The general construction of the 200 h.p. Austro-Daimler is shown in the two photographs of the complete engine,

Airscrew End of the 200 h.p. Austro-Daimler Engine, 1917-18 type.

AUSTRO-DAIMLER—*continued*.

and also in the accompanying cross sectional and general arrangement drawings.

Following the usual German practice, the engine is of the six-cylinder, vertical, water-cooled type with separate built-up steel cylinders. The principal characteristics of the design and its general performance are given in the following leading particulars of the engine :—

Number of cylinders	.. ..	Six, vertical.
Bore	.. .. ..	135 mm.
Stroke	.. .. ..	175 mm.
Normal b.m.e.ph.	..	123.3 lbs. per sq. in.
Average b.h.p. and speed		200 b.h.p. at 1,400 r.p.m.
Compression ratio	..	5.02 : 1
Petrol consumption per hour..		111.0 pints.
Petrol consumption per b.h.p. hour	.. .. ..	0.555 pints.
Oil consumption per hour	..	7 pints.
Oil consumption per b.h.p. hour		0.035 pints.
Total weight of engine, dry	..	728.5 lbs.
Weight per b.h.p. (normal)	..	3.64 lbs.

The compression ratio is considerably higher than that of any of the enemy engines except the Maybach, and from the complete data published at the end of this report it will be seen that the general efficiency of the engine is good, the h.p. per cu. ft. of stroke volume being 377.3 and the h.p. per sq. ft. of piston area being 216.6.

During calibration and endurance tests carried out at the R.A.E., the running of the engine was very good, being very steady between 700 and 1,700 r.p.m. The engine was remarkably clean, having no trace of oil or water leakages during tests.

Compared with the usual high weight standard of enemy engine design, the weight per b.h.p. of 3.64 is quite normal. From our own standard of weights, however, the weight per b.h.p. is disproportionately high. This is chiefly due to the heavy construction of the crank-chamber and oil base, rather than to the design of the cylinders and reciprocating parts, which are well designed and are of light construction compared with other enemy engines.

GENERAL DESCRIPTION.

As a preliminary survey of the general design of the 200 h.p. Austro-Daimler engine, the principal features of the engine are briefly described in the following summary :—

The six separate cylinders are of the usual built-up steel construction with pressed steel water jackets, and are fitted with twin inlet and exhaust valves in the cylinder heads, which are integral with the cylinder barrels. The valve pockets are welded into position, with the exception of one inlet valve pocket in each cylinder, which is constructed so as to be easily detachable with its valve seating and guide, as in previous Austro-Daimler engines, so that all the valves can be removed without dismounting the cylinder.

Aluminium pistons are adopted, and with the exception of those recently fitted to the 230 h.p. Benz engines, were at the time of capture apparently the only aluminium pistons in use in enemy engines, although since this engine was captured a Rumpler biplane has been brought down fitted with a 270 h.p. Bassé-Selve engine using aluminium pistons. A detailed report of this engine is in course of preparation and will be published very shortly.

The H section connecting rods are of normal design, and the crankshaft runs in seven white metal bearings, which are carried by the top half of the crankcase. The bottom halves of the journal bearing housings are steel forgings and are very deep in cross section, being similar in design to the journal bearings fitted to the Maybach engines.

The design of the valve gear and camshaft drive presents several interesting details. As shown in the illustrations of the engine, the overhead camshaft is driven by a vertical shaft off the front end of the crankshaft. The camshaft runs in four phosphor bronze bearings in the centre of an aluminium camshaft case.

A compression release gear, very similar to the Mercédès type, is provided. The water circulation passage from the cylinders to the top of the radiator is taken through to the front end of the cast aluminium camshaft-casing, just behind the driving bevel gear.

A reciprocating plunger type oil pump is fitted in the front end of the oil base. This pump is driven by bevel and worm gearing directly off the crankshaft and is unusually heavy, but of interesting design.

The lubrication is on normal principles and embodies a large air-cooled oil sump at the bottom of each base chamber, which is supplemented by an auxiliary fresh oil reservoir cast in the front end of the top half of the crank chamber. The fresh oil is delivered by a small auxiliary plunger, working in conjunction with the main oil pump, to the front end of the camshaft, the lubrication of which is well carried out.

A "V" type honeycomb radiator is fitted directly behind the airscrew, and the centrifugal water pump, which is fitted obliquely off the rear end of the camshaft, is of ordinary design.

Two Bosch Z.H.6 magnetos are driven diagonally at 52 degs. off the vertical camshaft driving shaft at the front of the engine, and two plugs are provided in each cylinder. The magneto controls are interconnected with throttle control, so that the ignition is automatically retarded when throttling down.

A heavy duplex carburetter feeds the cylinders through two separate steel induction manifolds, which are galvanised, and lagged with asbestos ; each manifold feeds three cylinders.

The carburetters are water-jacketed and heated by the cylinder water circulation system in the usual way.

Main and slow running jets are fitted, the two annular floats being housed in chambers surrounding the choke tubes. The main air intake is taken through a passage cast in the two halves of the crankcase, leading to the chamber below the false bottom of the oil sump.

Exhaust side of the Austro-Daimler engine.

15b

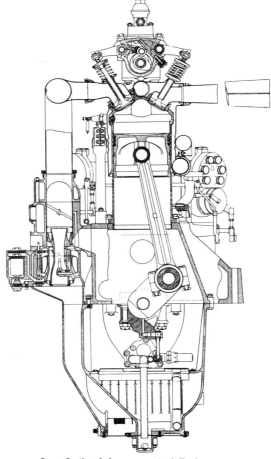

Cross Sectional Arrangement of Engine.

Sectional View of Cylinder.

An air pump of the spring plunger type is driven off the camshaft and is mounted on the top of the camshaft casing towards the rear end of the engine. A transverse shaft driven off the rear end of the crankshaft carries two cams for the synchronised gun interrupter gear.

No exhaust manifold is provided, each cylinder being fitted with a short streamline section exhaust pipe about 12 ins. long, as shown in the illustrations of the engine.

DETAILS OF CRANKSHAFT.

Number and type of main bearings	Seven, bronze cage, lined white metal.
Cylinder centres	166.0 mm. (6.53 in.)

JOURNALS.

Outside diameter	58.0 mm. (2.28 in.)
Inside diameter (front two)	21.0 mm. (0.82 in.)
,, ,, (others)	30.0 mm. (1.18 in.)
Length airscrew end	56.0 mm. (2.20 in.)
,, rear end	43.5 mm. (1.71 in.)
,, centre	50.0 mm. (1.97 in.)
,, intermediate	50.0 mm. (1.97 in.)

CRANKPINS.

Outside diameter	56.0 mm. (2.20 in.)
Inside diameter	30.0 mm. (1.18 in.)
Length	68.0 mm. (2.67 in.)

CRANK WEBS.

Width	74.0 mm. (2.91 in.)
Thickness (front two)	24.5 mm. (0.96 in.)
,, (others)	24.0 mm. (0.94 in.)
Radius at ends of journals and crank pins	4.5 mm. (0.17 in.)
Weight of complete shaft	96.5 lbs.

R.A.E. CALIBRATION AND ENDURANCE TEST REPORT.

The 200 h.p. Austro-Daimler engine was coupled to a Heenan and Foude dynamometer, and run for the usual calibration and one-hour endurance tests. Power, throttle, and comsumption curves are given.

CALIBRATION RESULTS.

R.P.M.	1300	1400	1500	1600
B.H.P.	186	200	212	222
Brake M.E.P.	125.5	123.3	122	119.7
Petrol consump. in pts./B.H.P./ hour	.55	.545	.546	.548

ENDURANCE TEST.

The engine was submitted to an endurance test of one hour's duration at normal revs., i.e., 1400 r.p.m., with the following results :—

Average output	202 B.H.P.
Average speed	1,400 r.p.m.
Petrol consumption per hour	14 gallons.
Petrol consumption B.H.P. hour	0.555 pints/b.h.p./hour
Oil consumption per hour	7 pints.
Oil pressure	5 lbs./sq./inch.
Oil temperature	50° C.
Water temperature (inlet)	54.5° C.
Water temperature (outlet)	60° C.
Total duration of tests	10 hours 25 mins.
Complete weight of engine	728.5 lbs. dry.

WEIGHT PER B.H.P.

At 1,300 r.p.m.	= 3.81 lbs. per B.H.P.
1,400 ,,	= 3.64 ,, ,, ,,
1,500 ,,	= 3.43 ,, ,, ,,
1,600 ,,	= 3.28 ,, ,, ,,

RUNNING DURING ONE HOUR ENDURANCE TEST.

Very steady between 700 and 1,700 r.p.m.

At 500 r.p.m. vibration was bad, and below this speed running was generally unsteady.

DISTRIBUTION.

Very good.

CLEANLINESS.

Throughout the test the engine kept remarkably clean. No trace of oil or water leakage was observed.

TROUBLES EXPERIENCED ON TEST.

The K.L.G. spark plugs fitted for the test gave trouble by shorting internally.

The valve tappets required to be re-adjusted during the test.

TEST OF WATER PUMP.

Speed of the water pump spindle = 1.894 : 1 crankshaft revolution.

The delivery of the water pump under varying pressures has been made the subject of a separate test, the results of which are given in the following test report and delivery curves.

The pump was coupled to an electric motor and run with the following results :—

R.P.M.	Pressure.	Delivery.
1800	2 lbs. sq. in.	42 galls. per. min
1800	4 ,, ,, ,,	35 ,, ,, ,,
1800	6 ,, ,, ,,	28.5 ,, ,, ,,

The weight of the complete water pump = 7.6 lbs.

R.A.E. METALLURGICAL TEST REPORT.

The chemical compositions and the relative material strengths of the principal parts of the engine are given in the following chemical analysis and mechanical test reports :—

(1) CHEMICAL ANALYSIS.

Per Cent.:	C.	Si.	Mn.	S.	P.	Cr.	Ni.
Crankshaft	.14	.27	.43	.030	.006	1.34	3.45
Cylinder	.47	.19	.67	.037	.046	Nil.	Nil.
Connecting Rod	.40	.16	.73	.043	.023	.36	1.50
Camshaft (case-hardened)	—	.21	.43	.035	.012	.57	3.15
Inlet Valve	.46	.24	.42	.023	.022	.47	2.28
Exhaust Valve	.44	.24	.41	.025	.022	.47	2.36
Valve Rocker	.46	.09	.63	.051	.028	.42	1,57
Gudgeon Pin (case-hardened)	—	.12	.49	.028	.011	1.5	3.70

(2) CHEMICAL ANALYSIS.

	Crankcase. Per Cent.	Piston. Per Cent.
Copper	2.79	7.67
Zinc	6.61	1.33
Tin	Nil.	2.21
Silicon	0.76	0.52
Iron	2.06	1.32
Manganese	0.02	Trace
Nickel	—	Nil.
Magnesium	—	0.29
Aluminium (by difference)	87.76	86.66

(3) BEARINGS.

Per Cent. :	Journal Bearings.	Big-End Bearings.	Camshaft Bearings.	Valve Rocker Bearings.
Copper	6.70	5.10	87.51	96.29
Zinc	—	0.28		Trace.
Tin	81.13	81.42	11.34	2.52
Lead	0.71	1.64	0.17	0.28
Antimony	12.00	12.00		
Manganese	—	—	Nil.	0.21
Nickel	—	—	0.35	0.07
Iron	—	—	0.17	0.13
Phosphorus	—	—	0.05	

(4) MECHANICAL TESTS.

		Mark.	No.	Area sq.in.	Y.S T/sq.in.	M.S T/sq.in.	Elong. p.c.	Red: of Area p/c.	Impact ft.lbs.
Journal		A.	1.	.002	66.7	75.1	13.33	57.4	
,,		B.	2.						30.5
Pin		C.	3.	.005	62.7	72.5	15.55	59.8	
,,		D.	4.						33.5
Web, Longitude		E.	5.	.005	71.6	75.8	10.0	35.0	
,,		F.	6.						7.5
,, Transverse		G.	7.	.005	72.9	74.5	7.78	25.1	
,, ,,		H.	8,						(1) 5.0
									(2) 7.0

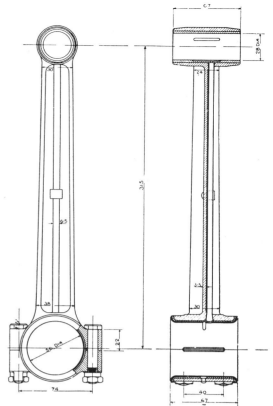

Details of Connecting Rod.

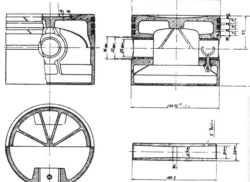

Details of Piston and Gudgeon Pin.

View of Valve Gear.

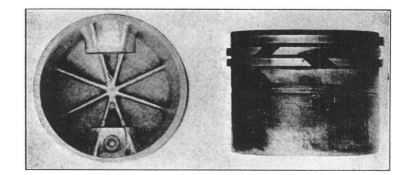

Aluminium Piston.

GENERAL DATA.

Make of engine and rated h.p.	Austro-Daimler 200 h.p.
No. of cylinders	Six.
Type number	8,597
Bore	135.0 mm. (5.31 ins.)
Stroke	175.0 mm. (6.89 ins.)
Stroke/bore ratio	1.29 : 1
Area of one piston	143.1 sq. cm. (22.2 sq. ins.)
Total piston area of engine	858.6 sq.cm.(133.1 sq. ins.)
Swept volume of one cylinder	2504.9 cu. cm. (152.8 cu. ins.)
Total swept volume of engine	15029.7 cu. cm. (916.8 cu. ins.)
Clearance volume of one cylinder	623.1 cu. cm. (38.0 cu.ins.)
Compression ratio	5.02 : 1
Normal b.h.p. and speed	200 b.h.p. at 1400 r.p.m.
Maximum ditto	222 b.h.p. at 1600 r.p.m.
Normal b.m.e.p.	123.3 lbs. per sq. in. at 1400 r.p.m.
Maximum ditto.	123.5 lbs. per sq. in. at 1300 r.p.m.
Piston speed	1607 ft. per min.
Mechanical efficiency (calculated)	89.7 per cent.
Indicated mean pressure (calculated)	137.5 lbs. sq. in.
Fuel consumption per b.h.p. hour.	0.555 pint = 0.499 lb.
Brake thermal efficiency	27.4 per cent.
Indicated thermal efficiency	30.6 per cent.
Air standard efficiency	47.5 per cent.
Relative efficiency	64.4 per cent.
Cub. in. of swept volume per b.h.p.	4.58 cu. ins.
Sq. in. of piston area per b.h.p.	0.665 sq. in.
H.p. per cub. ft. of stroke volume	377.3 b.h.p.
H.p. per sq. ft. of piston area	216.6 b.h.p.
Direction of rotation of crankshaft	Anti-clockwise.
Direction of rotation of airscrew	Ditto.
Type of gear reduction to airscrew	None.
Ratio crankshaft speed/airscrew speed	1 : 1
Type of valve gear	Overhead camshaft.
Type of starting gear	Compression release.

CARBURETTERS.

Number and type of carburetters	One dual Austro-Daimler.
Diameter of choke tube	24.0 mm. (0.945 in.)
Bore of main jets	35.0 c.c. through per min.
Bore of pilot jets	5.8 c.c. through per min.
Fuel consumption per hour	111.0 pints = 100.0 lbs.
Fuel consumption per b.h.p. hour	0.555 pint = 0.499 lb.

GAS VELOCITIES, VALVE AREA, ETC.
Diameters.

Induction pipe	59.0 mm. (2.32 ins.)
Inlet and exhaust effective valve ports (each)	44.0 mm. (1.73 ins.)
Inlet and exhaust cylinder ports (each)	42.0 mm. (1.65 ins.)

CROSS SECTIONAL AREAS.

Induction pipe	27.33 sq. cm. (4.22 sq. ins.)
Inlet valve (π dh) } each	13.69 sq. cm. (2.12 sq. ins.)
Exhaust valve (π dh) }	14.05 sq. cm. (2.18 sq. ins.)
Exhaust branch pipes	38.25 sq. cm. (5.92 sq.ins.)

MEAN GAS VELOCITIES (1400 R.P.M.)

Induction pipe	141.0 ft. per sec.
Inlet valves	140.0 ft. per sec
Exhaust valves	136.0 ft. per sec.
Exhaust branch pipe	100.5 ft. per sec.

INLET VALVES.

Number per cylinder	Two.
Largest diameter	48.0 mm. (1.89 in.)
Effective port valve diameter	44.0 mm. (1.73 in.)
Width of seating	2.5 mm. (0.09 in.)
Angle of seating	45 degs.
Lift of valve	9.9 mm. (0.39 in.)
Diameter of stem	10.0 mm. (0.39 in.)
Length of valve guide	68.0 mm. (2.67 in.)
Overall length of valve	135.0 mm. (5.135 ins.)
Number of springs per valve	One.
Free length of spring	60.0 mm. (2.36 ins.)
Length of spring in position (no lift)	46.0 mm. (1.81 in.)
Mean diameter of coils	34.0 mm. (1.34 in.)
Diameter of wire	4.0 mm. (0.157 in.)
Ratio length of spring/lift of valve	4.61: 1.
Weight of valve complete with spring	0.50 lb.
Weight of spring bare	0.16 lb.
Inlet valve opens	10 degs. early.
Inlet valve closes	30 degs. late.
Period of induction	220 degs.
Inlet valve tappet clearance	0.25 mm. (0.01 in.)

EXHAUST VALVES.

Number per cylinder	Two.
Largest diameter	48.0 mm. (1.89 ins.)
Effective valve port diameter	44.0 mm. = 1.73 in.
Width of seating	2.5 mm. (0.09 in.)
Angle of seating	45 degs.
Lift of valve	10.16 mm. (0.40 in.)
Diameter of stem	10.0 mm. (0.39 in)
Length of valve guide	68.0 mm. (2.67 ins)
Overall length of valve	135.0 mm. (5.315 ins.)
Number of springs per valve	One.

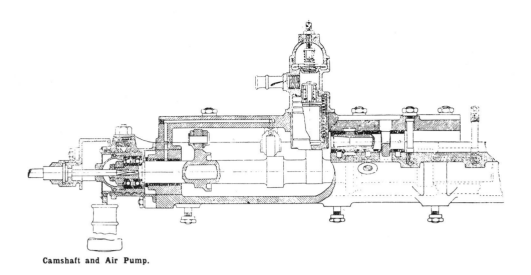

Camshaft and Air Pump.

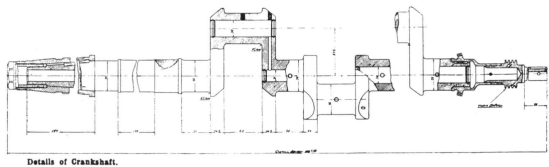

Details of Crankshaft.

Free length of spring	60.0 mm. (2.36 ins.)
Length of spring in position (no lift)	46.00 mm. (1.81 in.)
Mean diameter of coils	34.0 mm. (1.34 in.)
Diameter of wire	4.0 mm. (0.157 in.)
Ratio length of spring/lift of valve	4.6 : 1.
Weight of valve complete with spring	0.5 lb.
Weight of spring bare	0.16 lb.

Exhaust valve opens	45 degs. early.
Exhaust valve closes	7 degs late.
Period of exhaust	232 degs.
Exhaust valve tappet clearance	0.304 mm. (0.012 in.)

INERTIA FORCES, BEARING LOADS, ETC.

Weight of piston complete with rings and gudgeon pin	4.18 lbs.

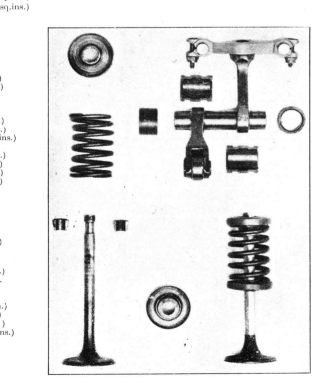

Valves and Rockers.

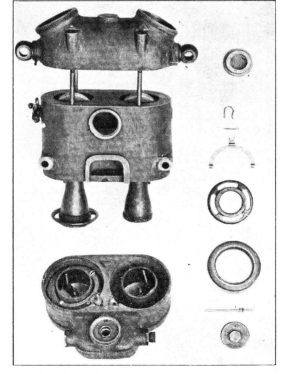

Parts of Carburetter.

Inertia Forces, Bearing Loads, Etc.—*continued.*

Weight per sq. in of piston area ..	0.188 lb.
Weight of connecting-rod complete	4.84 lbs.
Weight of reciprocating part of connecting rod..	1.66 lb.
Total reciprocating weight per cyl. ..	5.84 lbs.
Weight per sq. in. of piston area ..	0.263 lb.
Length of con. rod (centres)	315.0 mm. (12.40 ins.)
Ratio con. rod/crank throw ..	3.6 : 1.
Inertia lbs./sq. in. piston area top centre ..	63.8 lbs./sq. ins.
Inertia lbs./sq. in. piston area bottom centre..	36.2 lbs./sq. ins.
Inertia lbs./sq. in. piston area mean	25.0 lbs./sq. ins.
Weight of rotating mass of con. rod	3.18 lbs.
Total centrifugal pressure ..	610 lbs.
Centrifugal pressure lbs./sq. in. piston area.	27.5 lbs./sq. ins.
Mean average fluid pressure including compression ..	47.0 lbs./sq. ins.
Mean average loading on crank pin bearing, total from all sources in terms of lbs./sq. in. piston area.	91.0 lbs./sq. ins.
Diameter of crank pin ..	56.0 mm. (2.20 ins.)
Rubbing velocity ..	13.42 ft. per sec.
Effective projected area of big-end bearing ..	32.4 sq. cm. (5.02 sq. ins.)
Ratio piston area/projected area of big-end bearing ..	4.42 : 1.
Mean average loading on big-end bearing ..	402 lbs./sq. ins.
Load factor on big-end bearing ..	5400 lbs./ft. sec.

Cylinders.

Overall height of bare cylinder from top of base chamber ..	365.0 mm. (14.370 ins.)
Depth of spigot at base of cylinder	15.0 mm. (0.590 ins.)
Diameter of cylinder over water jacket ..	160.0 mm. (6.29 ins.)
Thickness of flange at base of cylinder ..	11.0 mm. (0.433 in.)
Number of holding-down bolts per cylinder	Eight.
Diameter of holding-down studs ..	4 of 14.0 mm. 4 of 19.0 mm.
Thickness of water jacket ..	1.00 mm. (0.039 in.)
Mean thickness of combustion chamber wall ..	5.0 mm. (0.197 in.)
Thickness of cylinder barrel (top)..	4.0 mm. (0.157 in.)
Thickness of cylinder barrel (centre)	3.0 mm. (0.138 in.)
Thickness of cylinder barrel (bottom)	4.0 mm. (0.157 in.)
Diameter of water connections between cylinders ..	36.0 mm. (1.42 in.)

Piston.

Type of piston	Aluminium ; internal ribs
Diameter at top ..	134.0 mm. (5.275 ins.)
Diameter at bottom..	134.58 mm. (5.277 ins.)
Length	110,5 mm. (4.35 ins.)
Ratio, piston length cylinder bore..	0.82 : 1.
Number of rings per cylinder ..	Three.
Position of rings	Above gudgeon pins.
Width of rings ..	7.0 mm. (0.275 in.)
Gap of rings in cylinder ..	0.48 mm. (0.019 in.)

Connecting-Rod.

Length between centres ..	315.0 mm. (12.40 ins.)
Ratio connecting rod/crank throw..	3.6 : I.
Little-end bearing, type ..	Plain phosphor bronze.
,, ,, ,, diameter	28.0 mm. (1.10 in.)
,, ,, ,, length ..	67.0 mm. (2.64 ins.)
,, ,, ,, projected area..	18.70 sq. cm. (2.90 sq. ins.)
Ratio piston area/projected area little-end bearing	7.66 : 1.
Big-end bearing, type ..	Bronze shell white lined metal.
,, ,, ,, diameter..	56.0 mm. (2.20 ins)
,, ,, ,, length (actual) ..	67.0 mm. (2.63 ins.)
,, ,, ,, length (effective)	58.0 mm. (2.28 ins.)
,, ,, ,, projected area ..	28.4 sq. cm. (5.02 sq. ins.)
Ratio piston area/projected area big end bearing ..	4.42 : 1.
Number of big-end bolts ..	Four.
Full diameter of bolts ..	10.0 mm. (0.39 in.)
Total cross sectional area bottom of threads ..	2.04 sq. cm. (0.316 sq. in.)
Pitch of threads	1.5 metric.
Maximum load due to inertia at 1400 r.p.m... ..	1390 lbs.
Maximum load due to inertia at 1600 r.p.m...	1815 lbs.
Load due to centrifugal force at 1400 r.p.m...	370 lbs.
Load due to centrifugal force at 1600 r.p.m...	485 lbs.
Total load on bolts at 1400 r.p.m.	1760 lbs.
Total load on bolts at 1600 r.p.m.	2300 lbs.
Stress per sq. in. at 1400 r.p.m ..	5570 lbs./sq. ins.
Stress per sq. in. at 1600 r.p.m.	7280 lbs./sq. ins.

Inside view of Base Chamber and Filter Plates.

View of Base Chamber from beneath, showing Air Passages and Cover Plate.

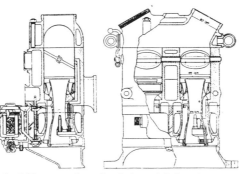

Semi-Diagrammatic sectional views of Carburetter.

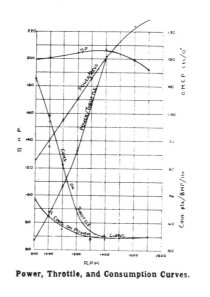

Power, Throttle, and Consumption Curves.

Crankshaft.

Number and type of main bearings	Seven, bronze cage, lined white metal.
Cylinder centres ..	166.0 mm. (6.53 ins.)
Crankpins	
Outside diameter ..	56.0 mm. (2.20 ins.)
Inside diameter ..	30.0 mm. (1.18 in.)
Length	68.0 mm. (2.67 ins.)
Journals.	
Outside diameter ..	58.0 mm. (2.28 ins.)
Inside diameter (front two)	21.0 mm. (0.82 ins.)
,, ,, (others)	30 mm. (1.18 in.)
Length airscrew end..	56.0 mm. (2.20 ins.)
,, rear end ..	43.5 mm. (1.71 in.)
,, centre ..	50.0 mm. (1.97 in.)
,, intermediate	50.0 mm. (1.97 in.)
Crank Webs.	
Width	74.0 mm. (2.91 ins.)
Thickness (front two)	24.5 mm. (0.96 in.)
,, (others)	24.4 mm. (0.94 in.)
Radius at ends of journals and crank pins ..	4.5 mm. (0.17 in.
Weight of complete shaft ..	96.5 lbs.

Working Clearances.

Piston clearance top (total)	1.00 mm. (0.039 in.)
Piston clearance bottom (total)	0.42 mm. (0.016 in.)
Side clearance of con. rod in piston (total) ..	2.50 mm. (0.098 in.)
Side clearance of con. rod on crank-pin (total) ..	1.00 mm. (0.039 in.)
End clearance of crankshaft in main bearings ..	2.00 mm. (0.079 in.)

Lubrication System.

Number and type of oil pumps ..	One plunger.
Oil consumption per hour ..	7.0 pints.
Oil consumption per b.h.p. hour ..	0.035 pt. = 0.039 lb.
Oil pressure	50 degs. C.
Oil temperature ..	5 lbs. per sq. in.
Specific gravity of oil ..	0.899.
Ratio pump speed/crankshaft speed	1 : 15.

Ignition.

Number and type of magnetos	Two Bosch Z.H.6.
Firing sequence of engine ..	Airscrew 1-5-3-6-2-4.
Ignition timing (fully advanced) ..	20 degs. E. to 40 degs. E., variable.
Number of plugs per cylinder ..	Two.
Type of plugs	Bosch.
Ratio magneto speed/crankshaft speed	1.5 : 1

COOLING SYSTEM.

Number and type of water pumps..	One centrifugal.
Diameter of inlet pipe	36.0 mm. (1.42 in.)
Diameter of outlet pipe	36.0 mm. (1.42 in.)
Diameter of rotor	112.0 mm. (4.40 in.)
Number and type of radiators ..	One Honeycomb.
Ratio water pump speed/engine speed	1.894 : 1.
Water temperature inlet ..	54.5 degs. C.
Water temperature outlet ..	60.0 degs. C.

AIR PUMP.

Type of air pump	Cam operated plunger.
Bore	38.0 mm. (1.496 in.)

WEIGHTS.

Weight of complete engine, dry, with airscrew boss and exhaust manifold	720.5 lbs.
Weight per b.h.p. ditto	3.64 lbs.
Weight of fuel per hour ..	100.00.
Weight of oil per hour ..	7.86 lbs.
Total weight of fuel and oil per hour	107.86 lbs.
Gross weight of engine in running order, less fuel and oil (cooling system at 0.65 lb. per b.h.p.) ..	858.50 lbs.
Weight per b.h.p. ditto ..	4.29 lbs.
Gross weight of engine in running order, with fuel and oil for six hours' running (tankage at 10 per cent. weight of fuel and oil) ..	1570.4 lbs.
Weight per b.h.p.	7.85 lbs.

OVERALL DIMENSIONS. .

Height..	1150 mm.
Length	1724 mm.
Width	568 mm.

GENERAL ANALYSIS OF WEIGHTS.

Description of Part.	No. per Set.	Average Unit weight in lbs.	Weight of complete Set in lbs.	Percentage of total weight.
Cylinders, bare ..	6	18.43	110.62	15.30
Detachable Inlet valve pockets	6	1.06	6.37	0.87
Pistons complete with rings	6	3.52	21.12	2.90
Gudgeon pins	6	0.66	4.00	0.54
Connecting rods ..	6	4.84	29.04	3.98
Crankshaft	1	96.50	96.50	13.24
Inlet valves ..	12	0.34	4.12	0.56
Exhaust valves ..	12	0.34	4.12	0.56
Inlet exhaust valve springs	24	0.16	3.88	5.53
Valve collars and locking cones	24	0.09	2.19	0.30
Valve rockers (with bearings)	12	1.25	15.00	2.06
Camshaft	1	10.25	10.25	1.40
Camshaft casing complete	1	34.50	34.50	4.74
Half compression gear	1	2.69	2.69	0.36

Description of Part	No. per Set.	Average Unit weight in lbs.	Weight of complete Set in lbs.	Percentage of total weight.
Vertical camshaft driving spindle (complete)	1	6.81	6.81	0.93
Vertical spindle housing	1	1.62	1.62	0.22
Camshaft bevel sprocket	1	3.15	3.15	0.43
Crankcase, top half ..	1	107.00	107.00	14.68
Crankcase, bottom half	1	73.50	73.50	10.09
Bearing caps	7	2.27	15.93	2.19
Main holding - down bolts	14	0.75	10.50	1.44
Thrust race complete..	1	5.28	5.28	0 72
Airscrew hub	1	11.31	11.31	1.55
Carburetters	1	24.06	24.06	3.30
Induction pipes	2	4.25	8.50	1.16
Exhaust pipes.. ..	6	2.33	14.00	1.92
Oil pump	1	11.81	11.81	1 62
Oil leads with relief valve..	1	4.56	4.56	0.62
Magnetos	2	14.37	28.75	3.94
High tension leads with casing	1	4.75	4.75	0.65
Magneto and throttle controls	1	2.12	2.12	0.29
Water pump	1	7.62	7.62	1.04
Water pipes	1	6.56	6.56	0.90
Air pump	1	1.62	.1.62	0.22
Rev. counter drive ..	1	0.75	0.75	0.10
Gun gear with case ..	1	5.81	5.81	0.80
Miscellaneous parts ..	1	28.09	28.09	3.85
Total.. ..			728.50	100.00

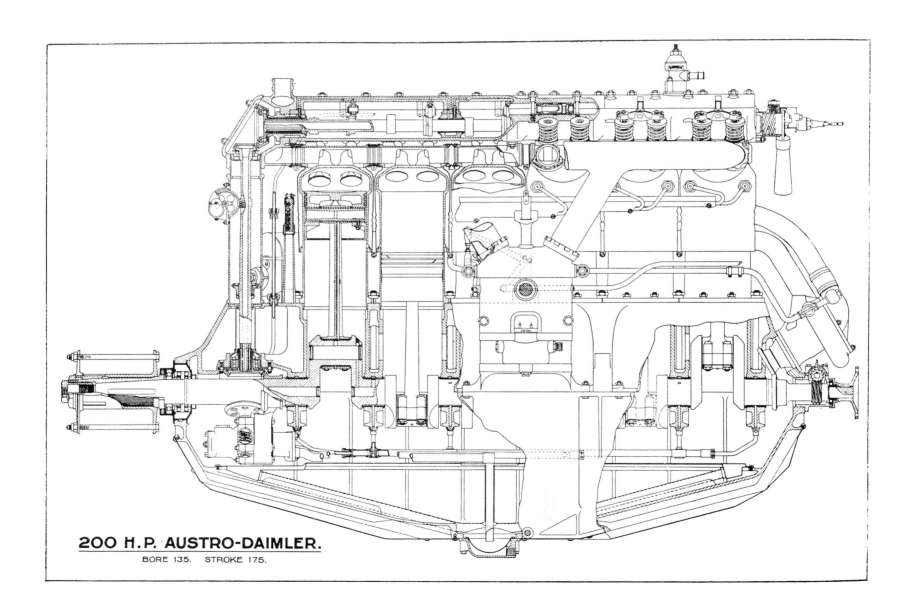

200 H.P. AUSTRO-DAIMLER.

BORE 135. STROKE 175.

BASSÉ & SELVE (German).

BASSE & SELVE, Altena in Westphalia.

THE 270-300 BASSÉ-SELVE AERO-ENGINE.

(This Report is published by courtesy of the Controller, the Technical Department, the Department of Aircraft Production.)

INTRODUCTORY NOTE.

The following report on the design of the 270 h.p. Bassé-Selve engine is based on a detailed examination of the engine (No. 550) taken from the remains of a German Rumpler two-seater biplane (R.A.F. identification No. G/5BD/14), which was shot down and destroyed in France on May 31st, 1918.

Unfortunately, this is the only engine of its type which has been captured up to the time of writing, and as it was seriously damaged, it was impossible to carry out any power and consumption tests of the engine : consequently, the following report deals with design and construction only. Certain figures connected with the performance have, however, been calculated by assuming the engine speed and Brake Mean Effective Pressure to correspond approximately with those of other German engines of about the same capacity. The figures adopted for these items are as follows :—

Normal engine speed .. .. 1,400 r.p.m.
Normal B.M.E.P. at 1,400 r.p.m. 110 lbs. per sq. in.

All the figures in the data at the end of this report, which are based on the above assumption (and therefore only to be accepted with reserve) are marked with an asterisk. Actual figures and test reports on the running of these engines will be issued as soon as an engine of this type is obtained in good condition.

GENERAL DESCRIPTION.

These engines, manufactured by Bassé and Selve, Altena, Westphalia, have but recently appeared in the field. In most of their leading details of construction they closely resemble both the 260-h.p. Mercédès and 230-h.p. Benz engines, on which the design is evidently based. Markings on the engine indicate the year of manufacture to be 1917, the crankshaft being marked "A.G. Krupp, Essen, 1917." The nominal rating of the engine according to a cast plate on the crankcase is 270-h.p., and the normal engine speed would probably be about 1,400 r.p.m. Assuming the B.M.E.P. to be 110 lbs. per sq. in. at 1,400 r.p.m., the power developed would be approximately 269 b.h.p.

The accompanying photographs show the engine to be of the usual six-cylinder water-cooled type, the bore being 155 mm. and the stroke 200 mm., i.e., 5 mm. less in the bore and 20 mm. longer in the stroke than the 260 h.p. Mercédès engines.

Owing to the damaged condition of the cylinders and pistons it has been difficult to ascertain the exact clearance volume. This is approximately 1,130 c.c., giving a compression ratio of 4.34 : 1, which is lower than any of the previous enemy engines.

Twin inlet and exhaust valves are fitted in the head of each cylinder, and the method of water cooling the exhaust valve stems by an annular passage, which completely surrounds the valve stem guides, is a novel detail of construction in enemy engines.

The valves are operated by an overhead camshaft, running in bronze bearings in a cast aluminium casing ; the design of the valve rocker and valve gear is worthy of notice.

An unusual type of compression release gear is used, which is of remarkably simple construction. Aluminium pistons are fitted. These are machined all over, inside and out. The slightly convex crowns are supported by conical pillars which bear upon the centre of the gudgeon pins through the slotted small ends of the connecting rods. This construction, together with the design of the tubular connecting rods, is essentially Benz practice, whilst the construction of the steel cylinders is taken from the 260-h.p. Mercédès design, but incorporates several improvements.

A large oil-cooling radiator is attached to the bottom of the crankcase, and is used in conjunction with a new design of duplex-plunger oil pump, which works vertically at the rear end of the crankcase. The design of the oil pump is somewhat similar to that now used on the new 200-h.p. Austro-Daimler engines.

Two separate two-jet carburetters fitted with annular floats are employed. These are apparently equipped with some form of altitude adjustment. Unfortunately, only one incomplete carburetter was found on the engine.

No details can be given of the construction of the water pump, as this component was missing from the engine.

The crankshaft is of ordinary, but exceptionally heavy design. The main journal bearing shells are machined with a screw-thread bedding for the white metal linings in a similar manner to the 300-h.p. Maybach engines. The propeller hub is fitted to a detachable tapered extension piece, which is bolted by a flange to the end flange of the crankshaft.

Further details of the design are given in the following description, and the leading particulars of the engine are shown in the accompanying data, which are as complete as the condition of the engine allows.

DETAILS OF CONSTRUCTION.

CYLINDERS.

A sectional drawing showing most of the construction of the steel cylinders is given.

This construction is similar to the 260-h.p. Mercédès, as also are the eight ribs machined on the outside of the barrels.

The cylinder heads are of cast steel, and the four valve pockets in each cylinder are cast integrally with the head. The formation of the combustion chamber and the unusual inclination of the valves at 23.5 deg. to the vertical axis of the cylinder are interesting points.

The valve guides are steel tubes lined with phosphor bronze ; they are pressed into the valve pockets, and are acetylene welded in position top and bottom.

The Bassé-Selve Aero-Engine. Three-quarter View from Airscrew End.

View of a Complete Cylinder, from Exhaust Side. The curious gargoyle-face effect of this View is interesting.

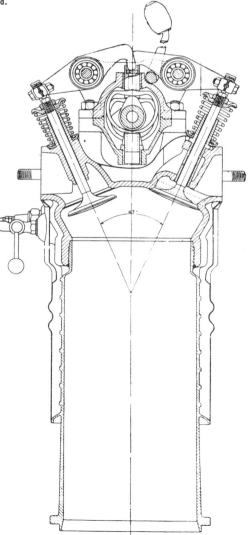

Section of one Cylinder, Bassé-Selve engine.

VALVES.

The inlet and exhaust valves are of the same diameter in the heads and stems, and of similar section.

VALVE GEAR.

The general layout of the valve gear is shown in the cross-sectional arrangement drawing, and presents some interesting details of design. The camshaft runs in eight comparatively short plain bearings of phosphor bronze, which are held in split aluminium housings of hollow section and large diameter. These are carried in the halves of a cast aluminium camshaft casing, and are located by dowel pegs in the usual way. The camshaft is made in two parts, joined together at the centre by two flanges and four short bolts. This valve gear is very similar to that used on the Peugeot racing cars (four valves per cylinder) about seven years ago.

Each pair of valves is depressed by a rocker lever mounted on ball bearings. The inner arm of each rocker lever is operated by its cam through a tappet in the top half of the camshaft casing.

The tappets are made in the form of stirrups which encircle the cams, and are supported in bronze bushes at the top and bottom ends. The cams and their tappets are case-hardened, and the camshaft bearings and tappets are lubricated under pressure through the hollow camshaft.

COMPRESSION RELEASE.

A simple form of compression release gear is used in place of the usual half compression cams and mechanism. This is operated by means of a rod which lies horizontally along the outside of the camshaft casing directly underneath the exhaust valve rocker arms. This rod has slots cut in it which lift the exhaust valve rockers when the rod is partially rotated by means of the hand-lever fixed to the rear end of the horizontal rod. The purpose of this compression release is apparently to facilitate swinging the propeller.

PISTONS.

The pistons are of aluminium.

The crowns are considerably domed and the pistons are machined all over, both inside and out. Both the material and the machining are excellent.

No bushes are provided as liners in the gudgeon pin bosses. The gudgeon pin is fixed in position by a large hollow set-pin which passes through both sides of the boss and gudgeon pin as shown.

CONNECTING RODS.

These are of tubular section, and closely resemble the Benz connecting rods in design, but are of considerably larger proportions throughout. These rods are particularly heavy, the weight of the complete connecting rod being 9.0 lbs.

CRANKSHAFT.

The crankshaft is of normal design, and, apart from its massive proportions, requires no special description.

A large double-thrust ball-race is fitted to the front end of the crankshaft by means of a shoulder machined on a flange just behind the propeller hub ; the thrust races are threaded on over the cranks, and are secured by a large screwed collar and spring locking ring. The main distribution bevel gear floats on the splined rear end of the crankshaft, and is fitted with a thrust ball race between the bevel and the rear end of the journal bearing.

PROPELLER HUB.

This is of the standard 260-h.p. Mercédès type, and fitted to a short tapered extension of the crankshaft. This extension is detachable, being bolted to a flange on the crankshaft. The standard Mercédès locking device is used.

CARBURETTERS AND INDUCTION.

Unfortunately, only one incomplete carburetter was found on the engine. The carburetters, which are quite separate, are of unusually light and simple construction compared with previous German design. The floats and float chambers are of the annular type, and encircle the main air intakes directly below the throttles, which are of the ordinary butterfly type. The body of each carburetter and throttle is made of cast aluminium, and the main jet is formed by a hole drilled in a tube which is screwed diagonally into the water-jacketed body of the carburetter, and lies across the choke tube directly beneath the throttle. The jet tube is open at the bottom end, and projects into the bottom of the annular float chamber, which is made of pressed sheet steel of very light gauge.

The pilot jet is formed by a second tube of small diameter inside the main jet tube. This pilot jet tube is also open at the bottom end, and is drilled radially with a small hole, just above the main jet. It communicates with the mixing chamber just above the throttle by a passage drilled in the carburetter body.

An altitude compensating control is fitted. This takes the form of a pipe opening into a passage drilled in the top of the float chamber.

Each carburetter feeds three cylinders through a branched induction manifold, the vertical part of which is water-jacketed.

The total weight of each carburetter complete should not exceed 2 lbs.

CRANKCASE.

The design of the top half of the crankcase requires no description, being constructed on Mercédès lines. The lower half also closely follows standard Mercédès design, with the exception of the oil reservoir and oil-cooling radiator on the bottom of the rear end. The construction of this cooler may be seen in a photograph. It consists of a cast aluminium oil chamber, having a number of thin aluminium tubes (12 mm. diameter) running longitudinally in three rows, and expanded at the ends. The cooler is bolted to the bottom flange of an oil reservoir below the base chamber, and is not an oil sump, inasmuch as there are no oil connections between it and the base chamber.

Two air intake passages are cast on each side of the crank chamber (see photograph) ; they are arranged to communicate with the carburetter through passages in the top and bottom halves between the transverse box-housings of the main bearings.

OIL PUMP AND LUBRICATION SYSTEM.

The oil pump is attached to the bottom half of the crankcase at the rear end, and driven by a worm gear off the rear end of the crankshaft through a short transverse layshaft.

Most of the details of construction of the oil pump may be seen in the photograph of the pump, which has been specially sectioned to show as much as possible.

The pump consists of two double-acting steel plungers, which work vertically in the barrels formed in the ends of the cast aluminium pump body. In action, the plungers are rotated by means of the worm gear, and are simultaneously reciprocated

View of part of Camshaft and Casing, Bassé-Selve engine.

Three-quarter View from Pump End, showing Clutch and Belt Pulley for Wireless Generator.

by the action of the scroll-cam cut in the spindle, and operated by a hardened steel roller working on a pin screwed into the pump body.

At every stroke of the two double-acting plungers, oil is drawn from the cooler tank and sumps in the base chamber, and is delivered to the main bearings and camshaft or returned to the oil cooler respectively, through the four distributing ports in the pump plungers. These ports when in action coincide with the drilled passages in the body casting of the oil pump, which are connected to the various leads as shown in the lubrication diagram.

The functions of the oil pumps and circuits are as follows :—

1. MAIN PRESSURE CIRCUIT, by the two inner pumps to crankshaft and connecting rod bearings and also to the hollow camshaft, returning by gravity to the two sumps at either end of the base chamber. The oil for this circuit is drawn from the supplementary oil cooler tank, which is replenished by fresh oil from the service oil tank.

2. SCAVENGER CIRCUIT.—Oil is drawn by the two outer pumps from the two oil sumps in the bottom of the base chamber, and is returned to the oil cooler.

The total weight of the oil pump complete is 5 lbs.

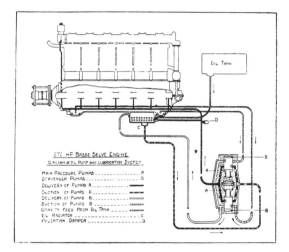

Diagram of the Lubrication System.

High tension leads and case ..	2	2.12	4.24	0.48
*Water pump (estimated) ..	1	8.00	8.00	0.90
*Exhaust manifold (estimated) ..	1	15.00	15.00	1.70
Miscellaneous parts ..	1	27.82	27.82	3.15
Total ..			885.0	100.00

GENERAL DATA.

Type number	No. 550.
Number and arrangement of cylinders	Six, vertical.
Bore	155.0 mm. (6.10 in.).
Stroke	200.0 mm. (7.87 in.).
Stroke/Bore ratio	1.29 : 1.
Area of one piston	188.7 sq.cm. (29.24 sq.in.).
Total piston area of engine ..	1132.2 s.cm. (175.44 s.in.).
Stroke volume of one cylinder ..	3774.0 cu.c. (230.21 cu.in.).

Photograph of the Bassé-Selve Oil Pump sectioned, showing the spiral groove which reciprocates the pistons, and the oil passages in the body.

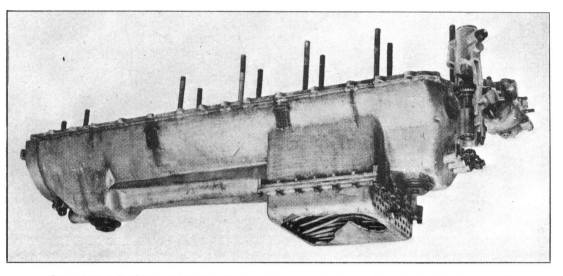

Lower Half of Crankcase, showing the Oil-cooler, Oil-pump in Position, and the Air Vents in Crankcase-side. 270-h.p. Bassé-Selve engine.

The water pump was evidently driven by the short transverse shaft which drives the oil pump at the rear end of the engine.

The air pump, which was driven by a small crank fixed in the front end of the camshaft, was probably similar in design to the 260-h.p. Mercédès.

IGNITION.

Ignition is by two Z.H. 6 magnetos, which are driven obliquely to the crankshaft axis by bevel gears off the camshaft driving spindle at the rear end of the engine.

Two Bosch 3-point plugs are fitted to each cylinder, and are situated just below the induction valves. Provision is also made for fitting one sparking plug on the exhaust side of the cylinders, the holes not in use being plugged.

The machine-gun interrupter-gear triple drive is bolted to the camshaft bevel gear case, and is driven off the rear end of the camshaft as shown in Fig. 2. The wireless dynamo is driven off the rear end of the crankshaft by a standard type of friction-clutch belt pulley described in a previous report

GENERAL ANALYSIS OF WEIGHTS.

Description of Part.	No. per set.	Average unit weight in lbs.	Weight of complete set in lbs.	Percentage of total weight.
Cylinders (bare) ..	6	35.67	214.05	24.20
Pistons, with rings ..	6	5.18	31.12	3.51
Gudgeon pins ..	6	1.00	6.00	0.68
Connecting rods ..	6	9.0	54.0	6.10
Crankshaft	1	138.50	138.50	15.05
Inlet valves	12	0.50	6.00	0.68
Exhaust valves ..	12	0.50	6.00	0.68
Inlet and exhaust valve springs ..	24	0.25	6.00	0.68
Valve collars and locking nuts ..	24	0.03	0.74	0.08
Valve rockers with bearings ..	12	1.43	17.22	1.94
Camshaft, with bearings	1	18.75	18.75	2.12
Camshaft tappets ..	12	0.31	3.75	0.42
Camshaft casing, with air pump and rev. counter drive ..	1	35.77	35.77	4.04
Vertical shaft driving spindle ..	1	4.50	4.50	0.51
Ditto, casing ..	1	2.30	2.30	0.26
Crankcase (top half) ..	1	97.50	97.50	11.00
Crankcase (bottom half)	1	112.00	112.00	12.67
Propeller hub, complete	1	29.43	29.43	3.33
Carburetters ..	2	2.00	4.00	0.45
Induction pipes ..	2	2.00	4.00	0.45
Oil pump ..	1	5.00	5.00	0.56
Oil leads	1	4.56	4.56	0.51
Magnetos	2	14.37	28.75	3.25

Total stroke volume of engine ..	22644.0 c.cm.(1381.28c.in
Clearance volume of cylinder ..	1130 cu.cm. (68.96 cu.in.)
Compression ratio (approx.) ..	*4.34 : 1.
Normal B.H.P. at 1,400 R.P.M. ..	*269 B.H.P.
Maximum B.H.P. at 1,600 R.P.M. ..	*302 B.H.P.
Direction of rotation of crankshaft and propeller	R.H.T.
Type of valve gear	Overhead camshaft.
Type of starting gear ..	Compression release.
Weight of complete engine, dry ..	*885 lbs.
Weight per normal B.H.P., ditto ..	*3.29 lbs.

CARBURETTERS.

Number and type of carburetters ..	Two, 2 jets.
Diameter of choke tube ..	50.0 mm. (1.96 in.).
Bore of main jets	2.59 mm. (0.0102 in.).
Bore of pilot jets	1.17 mm. (0.0046 in.).

VALVE AREAS, GAS VELOCITIES, ETC.

Diameters :—	
Induction pipe	58.0 mm. (2.28 in.).
Inlet and exhaust effective valve ports (each)	56.0 mm. (2.20 in.).

Photograph of the Carburetter of the Bassé-Selve engine. This carburetter appears to be of a type known in Germany as the " Pallas " and manufactured by the German makers of the " Zenith " carburetter.

Cross sectional areas :—	
Induction pipes	10.4 sq. cm. (4.10 sq. in.).
Inlet valve (π dh) and exhaust valve (π dh) (each) ..	17.6 sq. cm. (2.72 sq. in.).

MEAN GAS VELOCITIES (1,400 R.P.M.)

Piston speed	*1837 ft. per min.
Induction pipe	*219 ft. per sec.
Inlet valve	*164 ft. per sec.
Exhaust valve	*164 ft. per sec.

INLET AND EXHAUST VALVES.

Number per cylinder (each) ..	Two.
Largest diameter	61.0 mm. (2.40in.).
Effective valve port diameter ..	56.0 mm. (2.20 in.).
Angle of seating	45 deg.
Lift of valve	10.0 mm. (0.39 in.).
Diameter of stem	11.0 mm. (0.43 in.).
Length of valve guide ..	90.0 mm. (3. 54 in.).
Overall length of valve ..	146.0 mm. (5.74 in.).
Number of springs per valve ..	One.
Free length of spring ..	80.0 mm. (3.14 in.).
Length of spring in position (no lift) inlet	58.0 mm. (2.28 in.).
Length of spring in position (no lift) exhaust	55.0 mm. (2.16 in.).

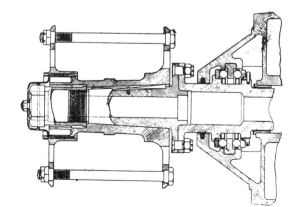

Section of the Airscrew Hub, and of the thrust-bearing of the Bassé-Selve, showing clearly the coupling between the crankshaft and the separate nose-piece.

Mean diameter of coils (top) .. 36.0 mm. (1.41 in.).
Mean diameter of coils (bottom) .. 28.0 mm. (1.10 in.).
Diameter of wire .. .. .. 4.0 mm. (0.157 in.).
Ratio, length of spring/lift of valve
(inlet) .. .. 5.8 : 1.
Ratio, length of spring/lift of valve
(exhaust) .. .. .. 5.5 : 1.
Weight of valve complete with spring 0.75 lb.
Weight of spring .. .. .. 0.25 lb.

INERTIA FORCES, BEARING LOADS, ETC.

Weight of piston, complete with rings
and gudgeon pin .. .. .. 6.187 lbs.
Weight per sq. in. of piston area .. 0.211 lb.
Weight of connecting rod, complete 9.00 lbs.
Weight of reciprocating part of con-
necting rod .. .. .. 2.25 lbs.
Total reciprocating weight per
cylinder .. .. 8.437 lbs.
Weight per sq. in. of piston area .. 0.288 lb.
Length of connecting rod (centres) 360.0 mm. (14.17 in.).
Ratio, connecting rod/crank throw 3.6 : 1.
Inertia lbs./sq. in. piston area :—
top centre .. .. 80.7 lbs. sq. in.
bottom centre .. .. 45.7 lbs. sq. in.
mean .. .. .. 31.6 lbs. sq. in.
Weight of rotating mass of connect-
ing rod .. .. 6.75 lbs.
Total centrifugal pressure .. 1480 lbs.
Centrifugal pressure lbs./sq. in.
piston area .. .. .. 50.7 lbs. sq. in.
Mean average fluid pressure, includ-
ing compression .. .. 44 lbs. sq. in.
Mean average loading on crankpin
bearing, total from all sources in
terms of lbs./sq. in. piston area .. 115.7 lbs. sq. in.
Diameter of crankpin .. .. 70.0 mm. (2.75 in.).
Rubbing velocity .. .. .. 16.8 ft. per sec.
Effective projected area of big-end
bearing .. .. 53.9 sq. cm. (8.35 sq. in.).
Ratio, piston area/projected area of
big-end bearing .. .. .. 3.50 : 1.
Mean average loading on big-end
bearing .. .. 405 lbs. sq. in.
Load factor on big-end bearing .. 6800 lbs. ft. sec.

CYLINDERS.

Depth of spigot at base of cylinder .. 8.0 mm. (0.31 in.).
Thickness of flange at base of cylinder 10.0 mm. (0.39 in.).
Number of holding-down studs per
cylinder .. .. Six.
Diameter of holding-down studs .. Four of 16.0 mm. ;
two of 14.0 mm.
Thickness of water jacket .. 1.0 mm. (0.039 in.).
Mean thickness of combustion cham-
ber wall .. .. 7.0 mm. (0.27 in.).
Mean thickness of cylinder barrel .. 3.0 mm. (0.118 in.).

PISTON.

Types of piston .. .. .. Aluminium (convex
crown).
Diameter of top .. .. .. 154.5 mm. (6.08 in.).
Diameter of bottom .. .. 154.75 mm. (6.09 in.).
Length .. .. 130.0 mm. (5.11 in.).
Ratio, piston length/cylinder bore .. 0.838 : 1.
Number of rings per piston .. Four.
Position of rings .. .. .. 3 above pin, 1 below.
Width of rings .. .. .. 6.0 mm. (0.23 in.).
Type of joint in rings .. .. Stepped.

CONNECTING ROD.

Length between centres .. .. 360 mm. (14.17 in.).
Ratio, connecting/crank throw .. 3.6 : 1.
Little-end bearing, type .. .. Phosphor bronze.
Little-end bearing, diameter .. 35.0 mm. (1.37 in.).
Little-end bearing, length .. 80.0 mm. (3.14 in.).
Little-end bearing, projected area .. 28.0 sq. cm. (4.34 sq. in.)
Ratio, piston area/projected area of
little-end bearing .. .. 6.74 : 1.
Big-end bearing, type .. .. Bronze shell lind.wh.met.
Big-end bearing, diameter .. 70.0 mm. (2.75 in.).
Big-end bearing, length (effective) .. 77.0 mm. (3.03 in.).
Big-end bearing, projected area .. 53.9 sq. cm. (8.35 sq. in.).
Ratio, piston area/projected area of
big-end bearing .. .. .. 3.50 : 1.
Number of big-end bolts .. .. Four.
Full diameter of bolts .. .. 12.0 mm. (0.47 in.).
Total cross-sectional area bottom of
threads .. .. 0.460 sq. in.
Pitch of threads .. .. .. 1.75 mm.
Weight of big-end cap, with two bolts
and bearing shell .. .. 2.562 lbs.
Total load on bolts at 1,400 R.P.M. 3460 lbs.
Total load on bolts at 1,600 R.P.M. 4530 lbs.
Stress per sq. in. at 1,400 R.P.M. 7500 lbs. sq. in.
Stress per sq. in. at 1,600 R.P.M. 9850 lbs. sq. in.

CRANKSHAFT.

Number and type of main bearings 7,br'ze shell lin'd wh.met.
Cylinder centres .. .. .. 210.0 mm. (8.26 in.).
Crankpins :—
Outside diameter .. .. 70.0 mm. (2.75 in.).
Inside diameter .. .. 40.0 mm. (1.57 in.).
Length .. .. .. 85.0 mm. (3.34 m.).
Journals :—
Outside diameter .. .. 70.0 mm. (2.75 in.).
Inside diameter .. .. 40.0 mm. (1.57 in.).
Length (propeller end) .. 60.0 mm. (2.36 in.).
Length (rear end) .. .. 95.0 mm. (3.74 in.).
Length (intermediate) .. 63.0 mm. (2.48 in.).

Webs :—
Width .. .. 84.0 mm. (3.30 in.).
Thickness (front one) .. 37.0 mm. (1.45 in.).
Thickness (others) .. .. 31.0 mm. (1.22 in.).
Radius at ends of crankpins and
journals .. .. .. 4.0 mm. (0.158 in.).
Weight of complete shaft .. 138.5 lbs.
Length of complete shaft .. 820 mm. (38.28 in.).

IGNITION.

Number and type of magnetos .. Two, Bosch Z.H. 6.
Firing sequence of engines .. Prop. 1, 5, 3, 6, 2, 4.
Number of plugs per cylinder .. Two.
Type of plugs .. .. .. Bosch 3-point.
Ratio, magneto speed/engine speed 1.5 : 1.

LUBRICATION.

Number and type of oil pumps .. One, duplex(double actg.)
Bore .. .. 45.0 mm. (1.77 in.).
Stroke .. .. 12.0 mm. (0.47 in.).
F.G.C., Ap.D. L.

J. G. WEIR, Brigadier-General,
October, 1918.   Controller, Technical Department.

R.A.E. METALLURGICAL REPORT.

CHEMICAL ANALYSIS.

The chemical compositions of the crankshaft and piston are as
follows :—

Crankshaft.		A 1. Piston.	
Carbon ..	0.48 per cent.	Silicon ..	0.45 per cent.
Silicon ..	0.32 per cent.	Iron ..	1.06 per cent.
Sulphur ..	0.061 per cent.	Copper ..	1.90 per cent.
Phosphorus ..	0.016 per cent.	Tin ..	Nil.
Manganese ..	0.32 per cent.	Zinc ..	15.62 per cent.
Nickel ..	2.59 per cent.	Manganese ..	Nil.
Chromium ..	1.17 per cent.	Aluminium	
Vanadium ..	Nil.	(by diff.)	80.97 per cent.

MECHANICAL TESTS.

Mechanical tests on the crankshaft gave values stated below :—

Mark.	A Web Longitudinal.	B Web Transverse.	C Pin.
Diameter	.249 in.	.253 in.	.249 in.
Yield Point, Tons/sq. in. ..	44.6	44.5	46.3
Ultimate Stress, Tons/sq. in.	55.5	54.4	56.4
Elongation on 4 √A	19.5 p.c.	12.8 p.c.	20.8 p.c.
Reduction of Area ..	48 p.c.	24 p.c.	56 p.c.
Impact, ft. lbs. .. .. {	28	26	41
	25	25	41

R.A.E., Dec. 5th, 1918.

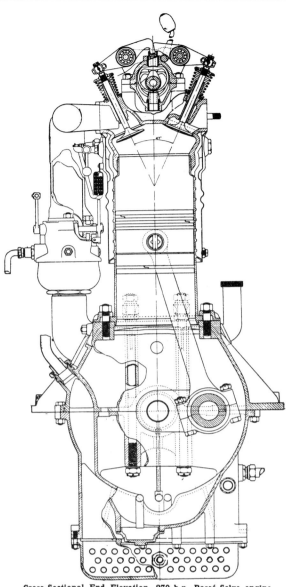

Cross-Sectional End Elevation, 270-h.p. Bassé-Selve engine.

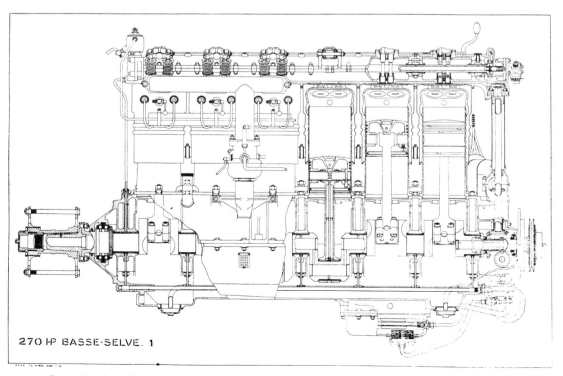

270 HP BASSE-SELVE. 1

Part sectional side Elevation, the Bassé-Selve engine.

BEARDMORE (British).

THE BEARDMORE AERO ENGINE, Ltd.

Chief Office : Parkhead, Glasgow, Scotland.

Registered Office : 36, Victoria Street, Westminster, London, S.W. London Agency and Show Rooms : 112, Great Portland Street, W.

Manufactured by : Arrol-Johnston, Ltd., Dumfries, Scotland, and by various sub-contractors.

Have concentrated on the 160 h.p. type engine illustrated herewith.

160 h.p. type.

B.H.P. at normal revs. : 166 h.p.
Normal R.P.M. : 1250.
Bore : 142 m/m.
Stroke : 175 m/m.
No. of cylinders : 6.
(Set desaxé 18 m/m.)

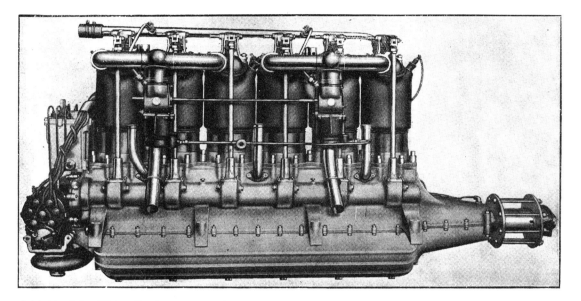

Inlet side of the 160 h.p. Beardmore aero engine.

Petrol consumption, pints per B.H.P. hour : .57.
Oil consumption, pints per B.H.P. hour : .03.
Weight complete with magnetos, carburetters, piping, oil and water pumps, propeller boss, hand starting magneto and switch. } 600 lbs.
Weight of water in cylinder jackets : 4 lbs. 7 ozs.
(But without radiators and water therein.)

This engine is a greatly improved and refined version of the pre-war Austro-Daimler, which itself was in its time one of the most efficient engines in being.

BENZ (German).

BENZ. & CIE, Mannheim.

THE 230-H.P. BENZ ENGINE.

[The following particulars of the 1917 Benz Engine, together with photographs and drawings, have been kindly supplied by the Technical Department of the Air Ministry, to whom the Editor desires to express his thanks.]

This detailed description of the 230-h.p. Benz engines is based on an investigation and tests of the engine (No. 30127) taken from the German Aviatik biplane G.40, captured on May 20th, 1917, and includes a report on the power and consumption tests carried out at the Royal Aircraft Factory, together with chemical analyses of the principal parts of the engine.

LEADING FEATURES OF THE ENGINE.

Following the usual German aero-engine practice, the 230-h.p. Benz is of the six cylinder-vertical water-cooled type. Each separate cylinder is bolted to the crankcase by long studs, which pass through the crank-chamber top half and secure the crankshaft bearings between the top and bottom halves of the crank-chamber.

Two inlet and two exhaust valves are fitted in the head of each cylinder. The valves are operated by overhead valve rockers working on ball bearings and by push rods on either side of the cylinders. The two camshafts, which run on plain bearings, are neatly arranged inside the top half of the crankcase, and the floating exhaust camshaft is provided with half compression cams.

The pistons are of cast-iron, fitted with three exceptionally wide rings, and the piston heads, following usual Benz practice, are supported by conical steel forgings riveted and welded to the piston crown, which bear on the centre portion of the gudgeon pins, through slots cut in the connecting rod small ends.

As in the 160-h.p. Benz engines, two separate two-jet carburetters are fitted, each having their air intake passages through the top half of the crankcase casting. Each carburetter supplies three cylinders through an independent branched induction pipe, built up of light aluminium tube.

The lubrication of the crankshaft and connecting rod bearings is effected by a very neatly designed gear pump working in an auxiliary oil reservoir formed in the bottom of the air-cooled base chamber.

An oil-sealed petrol pump of interesting design supplies petrol to the carburetters in conjunction with a supplementary pressure reservoir enclosed in the main petrol tank. The petrol pump is driven off the rear end of the inlet camshaft. The same driving spindle also operates the machine-gun interrupter gear and the tachometer drive.

CONSTRUCTIONAL DETAILS.

CYLINDERS.—Except for the steel water-jackets, the cylinders are made entirely of cast-iron. The water-jacketed heads, including the twin inlet and exhaust valve passages, are cast

End View of the 160 h.p. Beardmore aero engine.

integral with the cylinder castings.

The bore of the cylinders is 145 mm. and the thickness of the cylinder walls tapers from 5.5 mm. at the base flanges to 6.5 mm. at the top of the cylinder barrels. The water-jackets are of die-pressed sheet steel, built up from half sections and welded both at the vertical joints and at the bottom of the water-jackets to flanges machined on the outside of the cylinder barrels. The water-jackets are exceptionally long, extending to within .45 millimetres of the cylinder base flanges. Seven annular corrugations are formed in the water-jackets to allow for expansion, and three transversely in the sheet steel crown of the water-jackets. The general construction of the cylinders and water jackets with their water connections is clearly shown in the photographic views of the cylinders and in the sectional drawings. Figs. 3 and 4.

The water spaces formed in the cylinder-heads and the cooling of the valve pockets are well carried out. Dished plates are welded in position in the water space above the crown of each

Fig. 1.—Inlet Side of the 230 h.p. Benz Engine.—145 mm. Bore × 190 mm. Stroke.

cylinder to deflect the flow of water onto the exhaust valve pockets. The diameter of the cylinder-head water connections is 60 mm.

The cylinder registers extend to 10 mm. below the base flanges into the crank-chamber, and are held down by four 12-mm. studs, and also by dogs at four points. The dogs are secured by long studs which pass through the top half of the crank-chamber and are screwed into the bottom halves of the main bearing housings, which are cast integral with the bottom half of the base chamber. The parts of the holding-down studs which screw into the aluminium are of larger diameter and of coarser pitch. The nuts which secure the cylinder holding-down clamps are of interesting design, being of circular cupped formation and drilled radially with four 12-mm. holes for screwing up with a "Tommy Bar."

The total weight of each cylinder complete with valves, valve springs and valve rocker-supports = 44.25 lbs.

PISTONS.—The pistons, with the exception of the small conical pillars, are made entirely of cast-iron, and weigh 7.62 lbs. each, complete with rings and gudgeon pin.

Three rings are provided above the gudgeon pin, the lower one being a scraper ring. The width of each ring is 8 mm. and the width of gap in cylinder = 0.45 mm. The space between the two top rings is 4.25 mm., whilst the scraper ring is 10 mm. below the middle ring; 4-mm. pegs are provided to locate the radial position of each ring, and six 2-mm. holes are drilled in the piston below the scraper ring.

The slightly domed head of each piston is supported by a hollow conical pillar, which is machined from a steel forging and is riveted onto the under side of the piston, as shown in the sectional drawings of the piston, Figs. 6 and 7. The lower end of the conical pillar, which is machined at the same time as the holes in the gudgeon-pin bosses are bored, bears on the centre part of the gudgeon-pin, and to allow for this the centre portion of the top of the connecting rod small end and gudgeon-pin bush is cut away. By this construction the greater part of the force of the explosion is transmitted from the head of the piston directly to the connecting rod.

The gudgeon pins are 38 mm. diameter and are bored 30 mm. inside diameter. The centre portion of the gudgeon pin is 25 mm. bore for a length of 20 mm., where the conical piston head support bears on the centre of the gudgeon pin. The piston ring side clearance = 0.004 in. The diameter at the top of the piston = 144.15 mm. The diameter at the bottom of the piston = 144.67 mm.

CONNECTING RODS.—The very clean design of the tubular connecting rods is apparent in the photographic views.

The whole of the connecting rod, including the lugs for the four bolts securing the halves of the big end, is machined all over from a steel forging. The outside diameter of the tubular

rod is 36 mm. and the inside is bored with a 30 mm. hole from the crank-pin end to within 6 mm. of the gudgeon-pin bush—the bottom end of the bore being fitted with a screwed plug.

A 6 mm. steel pipe, for lubricating the gudgeon pin, is fixed inside the centre of the connecting rod and the pipe is supported in the centre by two flanged discs, as shown in the drawing. The weight of the big end is lightened by four 12-mm. holes and one 30-mm. hole drilled radially through the big end. Two

semi-circular oil grooves are machined in the white metal of the big end bearing caps and one lateral groove is cut in the top portion of the big end bearing. The total weight of the complete connecting rod is 7 lbs. 1 oz.; the big end weighing 4 lbs. 12 ozs., and the small end 2 lbs. 5 ozs.

Total big end side clearance = 0.15 mm. and the float of the small end bush between the gudgeon-pin bosses = 14 mm.

Fig. 2.—Exhaust Side of the 230 h.p. Benz Engine.

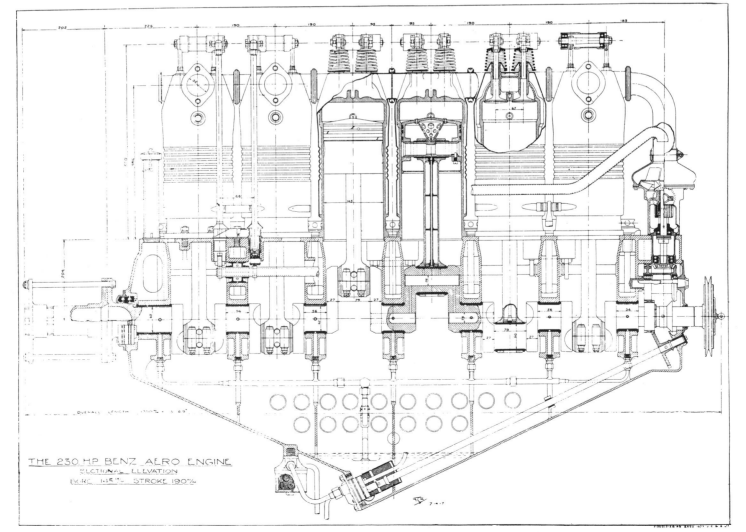

Fig. 3.—Sectional General Arrangement.

BENZ—*continued.*

CRANKSHAFT.—The six-throw crankshaft runs in seven plain bearings, and weighs 109.25 lbs., including the airscrew boss.

The cranks are, of course, set at 120°, and the diameter of all the journals is 62 mm., whilst that of the crank-pins is 60 mm. The length of the front journal bearing (propeller end) = 79 mm., and the length of the other journal bearings = 54 mm., with the exception of the rear end bearing, which is 55 mm.

The crankshaft journals and crank-pins are bored for lubrication, the webs being drilled with communicating holes in the

VALVES AND VALVE GEAR.—The twin inlet and exhaust valves work vertically in the cylinder heads, and are operated as previously mentioned by rockers mounted on ball bearings, carried by supports screwed into the cylinder head. The general design of the complete valve-gear is clearly shown in the sectional drawings (Figs. 3 and 4), and the arrangement of the valves and valve springs, etc., on the cylinder head in Fig. 9.

The rocker levers operate the valve stems through hardened steel rollers which are mounted on eccentric bolts. These, in conjunction with adjustable spherical joints screwed into the

case. The camshaft gears are bolted to the camshafts by drilled flanges, which provide a vernier adjustment for setting the camshafts.

Half compression cams are arranged on the exhaust camshaft in the usual manner. The lateral movement of the floating camshaft is effected by a small lever at the rear end of the crankcase which operates a two start square thread screw of

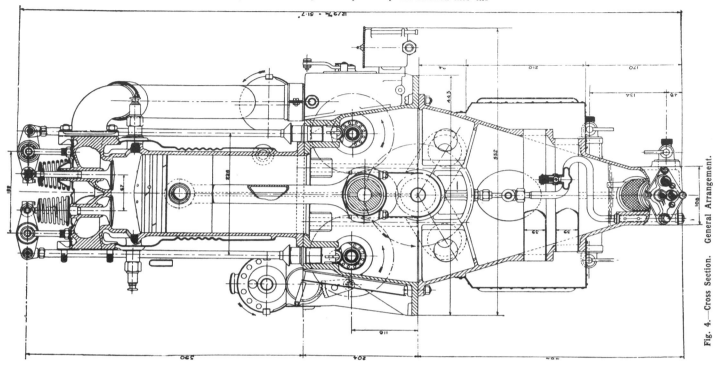

Fig. 4.—Cross Section. General Arrangement.

usual manner. The internal diameter of the holes bored in both crank-pins and journals is 27 mm. The ends of the holes are plugged with sheet-steel discs sweated into the recessed ends, and all the discs which plug the rear ends of the holes in both the crank-pins and journals are drilled with a central 5-mm. hole presumably with the idea of lubricating the camshafts with the oil thrown out by the cranks.

A double-thrust ball race, 120 mm. diameter, is fitted at the front end of the crankshaft behind the front flange to which the propeller hub is bolted. The thrust races are large enough to be assembled over the cranks, and are secured in position by a split collar which is screwed on to the crankshaft. The halves of the split collar are held together on the screw thread on the shaft by a recess cut in the split collar. This recess holds a corresponding flange turned on the crankshaft.

Fitted to the rear end of the crankshaft is a friction clutch for operating the wireless drive, which is designed so that the driving brake-shoes of the clutch can be thrown in or out of engagement with the driving pulley from the pilot's seat, through the action of two wedges, which operate the friction shoes through ball-ended levers.

The propeller boss is attached to the crankshaft by a flange which is bolted to a corresponding flange on the end of the crankshaft by eight 14-mm. bolts.

top ends of the vertical push rods on each side of the cylinders, give a fine adjustment for the tappet clearances. The spherical joints on the valve rockers are evidently provided to simplify the alignment of the valve rocker supports which are screwed into the cylinder heads.

Semi-spherical joints are also provided at the bottom ends of the push rods, which work in steel cups inside the hollow tappets, and it should be noted that the hardened steel rollers of the tappets, are slightly off-set from the camshaft centres and each pair of tappet guides is held in position by a steel bridge clamp.

The dimensions of both the inlet and exhaust valves are the same, each valve weighing 1.25 lbs. The lift of the inlet valve = 0.465 in. and lift of the exhaust valve = 0.443 in. Clearance of inlet tappet = 0.009 in., exhaust 0.015 in.

CAMSHAFTS.—The hollow camshafts each run in three plain phosphor-bronze bearings, and are arranged inside the top half of the crank-chamber. The camshaft bearing bushes, which are hollow, are 53 mm. outside diameter, and are split on the camshaft axis and held together by wire rings on either side to allow the camshafts to be easily inserted in the crankcase. The bearings are located by grub screws screwed in from the outside of the crank-chamber.

The camshafts are driven by gears from the intermediate gear wheel which meshes with the crankshaft distribution pinion, and arranged inside a casing formed at the rear end of the crank

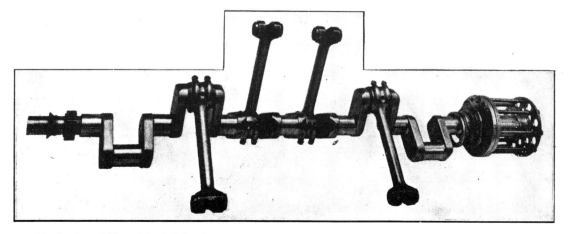

Fig. 8.—General View of Crankshaft, with Connecting Rods and Airscrew Boss.

Fig. 9.—Top of Cylinder Showing General Arrangement of Valve Gear.

BENZ—*continued.*

24 mm. pitch. The camshaft is returned to its normal running position by a spring arranged inside the front end of the hollow camshaft.

The half compression cams open the exhaust valves at 35° E., and close 22° L.

CRANKCASE. The general design of the crankcase is shown in the longitudinal and cross sectional drawings of the engine (Figs. 3 and 4.)

The method of cooling the interior of the crank-chamber and sump indicates the fact that this matter has received most careful consideration in design. In the top half of the crankcase six of the seven main bearing housings are cast so that the webs form air passages transversely across the engine. Two of these passages form the air intake passages for the two carburetters—similarly to those of the 160-h.p. Benz engines—as already stated.

The bottom half of the crank-chamber is extended to form an oil sump and is of unusual design. The lower portion is cooled by eighteen 30-mm. aluminium tubes fixed transversely across the base chamber. the air being scooped into the cooling tubes by a large sheet aluminium louvred cowl on the induction side of the engine. A corresponding but reversed cowl is fitted on the exhaust side.

Breathers are also fitted into the top half of the crank-chamber. The simple type of wire spring clip fitted to the breathers should be noted.

CARBURATION SYSTEM.—Two separate carburetters are fitted each feeding three cylinders. These are attached by flanges to the side of the top half of the crank-chamber.

The combined jet is screwed obliquely into the bottom of the float chamber casting and not into the body of the carburetter. The float chamber is attached to the body of the carburetter by two bolts, and the throttle is of the horizontal barrel type.

September 4th, 1917.

ROYAL AIRCRAFT FACTORY TEST REPORT ON 230-H.P. BENZ ENGINE.

The engine was run up to 1700 r.p.m., the peak of the power curve occurring at 1650 r.p.m., at which 250 h.p. was developed.

The maximum brake m.e.p. reached 119 lbs. per square inch at 1100 r.p.m.

The results of a one-hour test run were as follows :—

R.P.M.	.. .. ..	1400
B.H.P.	.. .. ..	229
Petrol Consumption	.. ..	150 pints.
Oil Consumption	.. ..	4.5 pints.
Water Inlet Temperature (average)		62°C.
Water Outlet Temperature (average)		71°C.
Oil Temperature (Max.)	..	50°C.
Oil Pressure (Min.)	.. ..	28 lbs. sq. in. steady.

The engine was erected on a test bed and coupled to a Heenan and Froude Water Dynamometer.

230-H.P. BENZ ENGINE DATA.

Number and arrangement of cylinders	.. ..	6 vertical.
Bore ..	.. .. ..	145 mm. (5.71 ins.).
Stroke	.. .. ..	190 mm. (7.48 ins.).
Stroke/bore ratio	.. ..	1.31-1.
Stroke volume of one cylinder	..	3137.476 cub.cms.(191.386 cub. ins.).
Total stroke volume of engine	..	18824.856 cub. cms. 1148.316 cub. ins.).
Area of one piston	.. ..	165.13 sq. cms. (25.59 sq. ins.).
Total piston area of engine	..	990.78 sq. cms. (153.57 sq. ins.).
Clearance volume of one cylinder	..	796 cub. cms. (48.66 cub. ins.).
Compression ratio. ..	..	4.91-1.
Normal B.H.P. and speed ..	..	230 B.H.P at 1,400 r.p.m.
Piston speed	.. ..	1,744 ft. per min.
Brake mean effective pressure	..	113 lbs. per sq. inch at 1,400 r.p.m. : 119 lbs. per sq. inch at 1,100 r.p.m.
Cub. inches of stroke volume per B.H.P.	.. .. ..	4.99.
Sq. inches of piston area per B.H.P.		.667.
H.P. per cub. ft. of stroke volume		346.3 h.p.
H.P. per sq. ft. of piston area	..	215.9 h.p.
Direction of rotation of crank	..	R.H.T.
Direction of rotation of propeller	..	R.H.T.
Normal speed of propeller ..	..	Engine speed.
Lubrication system ..	..	Forced to main bearings from reservoir in sump.
Brand of oil	.. ..	50 per cent. Vacuum Heavy and 50 per cent. Sternol.
Oil pressure ..	..	28 lbs. normal, 50 lbs. max.
Oil temperature	..	50° C., max.
Oil consumption per hour ..	..	4.5 pints.
Oil consumption per B.H.P. hour		.02 pints.
Specific gravity of oil	..	.9.
Type of carburetter	..	2 Benz each feeding 3 cylinders (2 jet)
Mixture control	..	Automatic
Fuel consumption per hour	..	150 pints.
Fuel consumption per B.H.P. hour		.65 pint.
Specific gravity of fuel	..	.720.
Type of Magneto ..	..	2 Bosch Z.H.6.
Firing sequence of engine ..		Prop. : 1-5-3-6-2-4.
Numbering of cylinders	..	Prop. : 1-2-3-4-5-6.
Speed of magneto ..	..	2/3rds. engine speed.

Direction of rotation of magneto, facing driving end of armature ..		Anti-clockwise.
Magneto timing		30° E. 18 mm. on stroke.
Inlet valve opens. Deg. on crank		10° E.
Inlet valve closes. Deg. on crank		55° L.
Maximum lift of inlet valve = h ..		11.8 mm. (.465 in.)
Diameter of inlet valve = d (smallest diam.)		Two of 52 mm.
Area of inlet valve port = π × d × h		19.27 sq. cms. each.
Mean gas velocity through inlet valve		124 ft. per sec.
Clearance of inlet tappet ..		.009 in.
Exhaust valve opens. Deg. on crank		60° E.
Exhaust valve closes. Deg. on crank		20° L.
Maximum lift of exhaust valve = h		11.25 mm. (.443 in.)
Diameter of exhaust valve ports=d (smallest diam.)		Two of 52 mm. dia.
Area of exhaust valve ports = π × d × h		18.37 sq. cms. (each) = 2.84 sq. ins.
Clearance of exhaust tappet ..		.015 in.
Direction of rotation of revolution counter drive, facing driving shaft on engine		Anti-clockwise.
Speed of revolution counter drive		½ E.S.
Weight of engine complete with propeller hub, less water, fuel and oil and exhaust manifold ..		848.32 lbs.
Weight per B.H.P. ditto ..		3.68 lbs.
Weight of exhaust manifold ..		15 lbs.
Weight of oil carried in engine ..		18 lbs.
Jacket capacity of one cylinder ..		1873 c.c.
Weight of water carried in engine..		30.9 lbs.
Weight of radiators, less water ..		136 lbs.
Weight of fuel per hour ..		135 lbs.
Weight of oil per hour ..		5.06 lbs.
Total weight of fuel and oil per hour		140.06 lbs.
Gross weight of engine in running order, less fuel and oil. Cooling system at 0.65 lbs. per B.H.P. ..		996 lbs.
Weight per B.H.P. ditto ..		4.33 lbs.
Gross weight of engine in running order with fuel and oil for six hours. (Tankage reckoned at 10 per cent. weight of fuel and oil)		1920.89 lbs.
Weight per B.H.P. with fuel and oil for six hours.		8.35 lbs.

B.H.P. (British).

Initials stand for Beardmore-Halford-Pullinger.
Made by :—

The Galloway Engine Co., Ltd., Dumfries.
The Siddeley-Deasy Motor Co., Ltd., Coventry.

The original design of 6 cylinder water-cooled engine was produced by Major (then Captain) F. B. Halford, in collaboration with Sir William Beardmore, Bart. and Mr. T. C. Pullinger (Managing Director of Arrol Johnston & Co. Ltd.)

The work was started in the Spring of 1916, when the situation on the Western Front made it vital that the Royal Flying Corps should have machines with engines of considerably higher power than had been used to that date. Although the

Germans had adopted the 6 cylinder type of engine as their standard, the only engine of the same type which had been consistently used by the British Flying Services up to that time, was the 120 h.p. Beardmore.

As the situation was serious, it was considered that there was insufficient time to design and try out and produce an entirely new design of engine. Arrol Johnston & Co. Ltd. then set to work to modify the 120 h.p. Beardmore to give over 160, as was eventually proved. This latter engine completely replaced the 120 h.p. and has done extraordinarily good work on long distance bombing and reconnaissance machines.

A new Company, the Galloway Engineering Co. Ltd., was formed to exploit the new B.H.P. Engine, and a new factory was built to assist it's production. The size of the cylinder proposed, i.e. 145 m/m bore was considered by many to be too

large to embody in a 6 cylinder engine, but as has been happily proved, the critics proved wrong.

The first engine was running in June, 1916, and after satisfactory non-stop endurance tests on the bench, was fitted into a D.H.4 Aeroplane, which had been specially designed for the engine by Captain Geoffrey de Haviland, of the Aircraft Manufacturing Company.

The results in the air with this combination proved extremely satisfactory, in that although the best performance of this type of machine had been approximately 95 m.p.h. the D.H.4 resulted in 115½ m.p.h. at 1000 feet.

The machine was officially tested by the Central Flying School and decision made by the Authorities to order the engine in larger numbers than had been proposed before with any other type.

Realising the facilities that would be required to produce 100 engines per week and spares, which was the figure suggested, and in view of the important part played by the Beardmore engine (which occupied the whole production of Arrol Johnston and Co. Ltd.), Siddeley-Deasy, of Coventry, were asked to take over the production of the B.H.P. and to take such steps as would ensure the maximum output per week.

Although this Firm was only then producing some 25 to 30 engines per week, the results of their efforts are best realised

Induction Side of the B.H.P. Galloway " Adriatic " engine.

when it is stated that at the time of the Armistice the production of Siddeley-Deasy's Works of the B.H.P. Engine, better known as the "Puma," was equivalent, including spares, to 200 engines per week.

The engine was made the standard 6 cylinder water-cooled used by the Royal Air Force, and has been consistently used by the Independent Air Force in the bombing of Rhine Towns.

Before the aluminium cylinder block reached the satisfactory stage the Galloway Engineering Co. Ltd., tried out a cast iron construction, in order to ensure engines being turned out in the quickest possible time. This type was dropped when the Siddeley engines reached the production stage.

Realising again the necessity for considerably higher powered engines, the Galloway Engineering Co. Ltd. set to work to design and produce a 12 cylinder B.H.P. Engine.

To eliminate as many experimental features as possible a double B.H.P. was made, incorporating two pairs of cylinder blocks with cast iron construction. This engine was known as the "Atlantic" B.H.P. and gave 500 h.p. at 1500 r.p.m.

As in the case of the 6 cylinder B.H.P. no gear reduction was fitted, and the fact that the weight per h.p. of 2¼ lbs. was obtained with an engine running at only 1400-1500 r.p.m. was very creditable This engine, the "Atlantic" was tested out on the bench, and also flown in another of the Aircraft Manufacturing Company's machines, the D.H. 9A, which was designed for the "Liberty."

A short time before the Armistice when it became imperative that a high power engine should be standardised for bombing machines, one of the engines chosen for mass production was the "Atlantic"; but for production purposes as the "Puma" cylinder blocks were then on the satisfactory production basis and being turned out in very large numbers, it was decided to pool the resources of several of our largest firms in the mass production of the engine, which was then rechristened the "Siddeley Pacific." Some thousands were ordered, and but for the Armistice no doubt would have been produced. It is thus interesting to see the order in which the four engines came forward.

THE 500 H.P. B.H.P. "ATLANTIC" AERO ENGINE.

Specification.

Bore	145 mm.
Stroke	190 mm.
Normal b.h.p.	500.
Direction	Right hand tractor.
Petrol consumption per b.h.p. hour	.588 pints.
Oil consumption per b.h.p. hour ..	.060 pints.
Weight (dry)	1210 lbs.
Weight per b.h.p. (dry)	2.42 lbs.
Weight in running order with 6 hours fuel and oil	3508 lbs.
Weight per b.h.p. ditto	7.02 lbs.
Compression ratio	4.9 : 1.
Maximum lift of exhaust valve ..	12 mm.
Clearance of inlet tappet	.25 mm.

Front End of the Galloway "Atlantic" engine, 500 h.p.

Side View of the Siddeley "Pacific" engine, 500 h.p.

Front View of the Siddeley "Pacific" engine, 500 h.p.

Connecting Rod Arrangement of the Siddeley "Pacific" engine.

B.H.P.—continued.

THE 230 H.P. SIDDELEY "PUMA."
Specification.

Type : 6 cylinder water-cooled vertical. Aluminium, with steel liners.
Bore : 145 mm.
Stroke : 190 mm.
B.H.P. : 230 at 1400 r.p.m.
Weight (dry) : 680 lbs. (including airscrew boss, carburetters magnetos, etc.).
Fuel consumption : .55 pints per B.H.P. hour.
Oil consumption : .025 pints per B.H.P. hour.
Lubrication : Force feed at 30 lbs. per sq. in. to main bearings.

        Force feed at 10 lbs. per sq. in. to camshaft.
Dry sump : One suction pump, one pressure pump.
Ignition : Dual magnetos. 2 plugs per cylinder. Hand starter magneto.
Carburetters : 2 Zeniths, with altitude control.
Valve gear : 2 exhaust, and 1 inlet.
Camshaft set *désaxé*, operating direct on exhaust valves and by overhead rockers to inlet valves.

B.M.W. (German).

Bayerische Motor Werke, Munich.

The motor appears to follow general Mercédès design with overhead camshaft.

B. R. (British).

Bentley Rotary.

Designed by Mr. W. R. Bentley for the Air Department, Admiralty. Originally known as the A.R. (Admiralty Rotary) and afterwards as the B.R. (as above).

Generally very similar to the Clergét Rotaries, from which it differed in having cylinders of aluminium alloy with pressed-in steel liners.

Made in two types—B R. 1, 150 h.p., and B.R. 2, 250 h.p.

Manufactured by Humber, Ltd., Coventry; Gwynne's, Ltd., Hammersmith.

THE B.R. 1 ROTARY AERO ENGINE.
Specification.

No of cylinders	..	..	..	9.
Bore	..	..	..	120 m/m.
Stroke	..	..	..	170 m/m,
Normal b.h.p.	..	..	..	150
Normal r.p.m.	..	..	..	1250
Weight per b.h.p.	..	..	2 67 lbs.
Fuel consumption	..	..	11 galls. per hour.
Oil consumption ..	..	..	12 pints per hour.

THE B.R. 2 ROTARY AERO ENGINE.
Specification.

No of cylinders	..		..	9
Bore	..	..	..	140 m/m.
Stroke	..	..	..	180 m/m.
Normal b.h.p.	..	..	..	250
Normal r.p.m.	..	..	...	1250
Weight per b.h.p.	..	..	1.9 lbs.
Fuel consumption	..	..	20 galls. per hour.
Oil consumption	..	..	16 pints per hour.

Rear End of the B.H.P. Siddeley " Puma " Engine 230 h.p.

Front View of the B.R. 1 engine, 150 h.p.   (*From a photograph supplied by Humber, Ltd.*

Front View of the B.R. 2 engine, 250 h.p.   (*From a photograph supplied by Humber, Ltd.*)

KING-BUGATTI (Italo-American).

BUGATTI ENGINE.

The American version of the engine designed and built in France by Signor Bugatti and made in America by the Duesenberg Motor Corporation, Edgewater, N.J., Chicago, Ill.

The following particulars of the Americanised version of the 400-h.p. Bugatti aero-engine are due to the "Aerial Age Weekly," of New York.

Generally speaking, the main features and dimensions of the American engine and of the original appear to be very similar.

The cylinders are in two vertical rows, each of eight cylinders, each row driving a separate crankshaft revolving in the same direction. Each crankshaft drives through a pinion at its end a spur-wheel on the common airscrew shaft.

The crankshaft of each row of cylinders is made in two halves, each half being of the standard type for a four-cylinder vertical engine. That is to say, the two central crank-pins of each set of four are in line one with the other, and the two outer crank-pins are also in line one with each other, but displaced 180 deg. from the two central pins. The pair of four-throw shafts for each line of eight cylinders are coupled together 90 deg. out of phase, and the two lines are geared together with an angular displacement between them of 45 deg.

The engine is, therefore, so far as regularity of turning movement is concerned, equivalent to four four-cylinder engines coupled together with a displacement of 45 deg. between each crankshaft, and gives eight equally-spaced impulses per revolution.

The following general specification is given :—

GENERAL DATA.

No. and arrangement of cylinders ..	16 vertical, 2 rows of 8 in blocks of 4.
Material	Cast iron.
Bore	4.33 ins. (110 mm.).
Stroke	6.3 ins. (160 mm.).
Stroke-bore ratio	1.455 : 1.
Area of one piston	14.725 sq. ins.
Total piston area	235.6 cu. ins.
Swept volume of one cylinder ..	92.768 cu. ins.
Displacement of motor	1484.288 cu. ins.
Compression ratio	5 : 1.
Normal brake h.p.	410 at 2,000 r.p.m.
Ratio propeller to crankshaft speed	2 : 3.

Three-quarter view from Airscrew end, 410-h.p. Bugatti Engine.

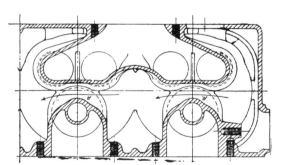

Section through cylinder head, showing valve ports.

VALVES.

Number per cylinder	Two inlet and one exhaust.
Outside diameter, inlet	1.535.
Outside diameter, exhaust	2.263.
Port diameter, inlet	1 27/64 in.
Port diameter, exhaust	2 3/64 ins.
Angle of seat	10 deg.
Valve lift, inlet	.653 ins.
Valve lift, exhaust	.700 ins.
Number of springs per valve, inlet and exhaust	2 concentric.
Length of spring in position, inlet (small)	2 7/64 ins.
Length of spring in position, inlet (large)	2 15/64 ins.
Length of spring in position, exhaust (small)	2 27/64 ins.
Length of spring in position, exhaust (large)	2 27/64 ins.

Valves parallel to centre line of cylinder bore.

CYLINDERS.

Overall height of cylinders ..	10 27/64 ins.
Length of projection in crankcase ..	3 1/16 ins.
Thickness of flange (base) ..	7/16 in.
Number of studs per block of four cylinders	20.
Diameter of stud	5/16 in.
Thickness of water-jacket wall side and head	5/32 in.
Thickness of combustion chamber wall	13/64 in.
Thickness of cylinder barrel, above flange at water-jacket ..	3/16 in.
Thickness of cylinder barrel, above flange below water-jacket ..	7/32 in.

PISTONS.

Length	4 1/16 ins.
Length to diameter ratio ..	0.938 : 1.
Width of rings	1/8 in.
Distance from bottom to centre of gudgeon pin	2 1/6 ins.
Thickness of head at centre ..	1/4 in.
Thickness of head at edge ..	3/8 in.
Thickness of wall at bottom ..	1/8 in.

GUDGEON PIN.

Diameter of gudgeon pin	1 5/64 in.
Thickness of wall	0.164

CONNECTING ROD.

Length between centres	10 7/16 ins.
Ratio length to crank throw ..	3.313 : 1.
Width	5/8 in.

CRANKSHAFT.

Number of crankshafts	2.
Number of bearings (Plain) per crankshaft ..	9.
Number of bearings (Ball) per crankshaft ..	1.
Cylinder centres (in block) ..	4 17/32 ins.
Cylinder centres (between blocks) ..	7 15/32 ins.
Crank pins, outside diameter ..	2 3/16 ins.
Inside diameter	1 1/8 ins.
Length	2 11/64 ins.
Main Bearings :	
Outside diameter Nos. 1, 2, 3, 4, 6, 7, 8, 9	2 3/16 ins.
Outside diameter No. 5 ..	2 5/8 ins.
Inside diameter, Nos. 1, 2, 3, 4, 6, 7, 8, 9	1 1/8 in.
Length, Nos. 1, 2, 3, 4, 6, 7, 8 Bearing Bushings	1 9/16 in.

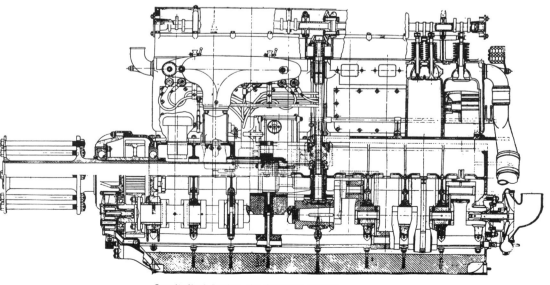

Longitudinal Section, the American Bugatti.

Length No. 9 Bearing Bushing	2 19/32 in.
Length No. 5 Bearing Bushing	1 31/32 ins.
Ball Bearing	Hess-Bright Monarch No. 6211.

Crank Webs :

Width	3 17/32 ins.
Thickness	43/64 in.
Radius of fillets	3/32 in.
Weight of one complete shaft, for 8 cylinders, with propeller drive gear bolts and nuts, bevel gear and oil passage shells	96½ lbs.

CAMSHAFT.

Diameter of shaft	1 in.
Inside diameter	11/16 in.
Number of bearings	10.
Number of cams per cylinder	3.

CAMSHAFT BEVEL GEAR.

Pitch diameter	3 3/4 ins.
Number of teeth	30.
Pitch	8.
Width of face	3/4 in.

CAMSHAFT DRIVING SHAFT.

Diameter	3/4 in.
Wall thickness	1/8 in.

CRANKSHAFT UPPER HALF.

Material	Aluminium.
Thickness of wall	3/16 to 5/16 in.
Thickness of supporting flange	3/8 to 7/16 in.
Centre distance of support bolts	24 3/4 ins.
Number of support bolts	12.
Diameter of support bolts	3/8 in.
Centre to centre of crankshaft	10 1/4 ins.
Height of case	9.055 ins.

CRANKCASE LOWER HALF.

Material	Aluminium.
Thickness of wall	3/16 in.

IGNITION.

Type	Magneto.
Number	4.
Make	" Dixie 800."
Firing order	1L, 7R, 5L, 4R, 3L, 8R, 7L, 2R, 4L, 6R, 8L, 1R, 2L, 5R, 6L, 3R.
Advance	38 deg.

REDUCTION GEARS.

Crankshaft airscrew drive gear :

Pitch diameter	5.6 ins.
Pitch	5.
Number of teeth	28.
Width face	2 3/8 ins.
Diameter bolt circle	3 17/32 ins.
Number of bolts	9.
Diameter of bolts	7/16 in.

Airscrew shaft gear :

Pitch diameter	8.4 ins.
Pitch	5.
Number of teeth	42.
Width face	2 3/8 ins.
Number of splines	8.
Width of splines	0.405.
Height of splines	0.094.

PROPELLER SHAFT.

Number of bearings	3.
Type of bearings	Two ball, one plain.
Plain bearing	Bronze babbitt lined.
Outside diameter at gear (over splines)	3 3/4 ins.
Outside diameter at rear end	3 5/16 ins.

VALVE GEAR.

The valves are driven through rocking levers by overhead camshafts, one centrally over each row of cylinders.

Actually there are four separate shafts, one for each block of four cylinders, but the pair of camshafts for each line of cylinders are coupled together between the two cylinder blocks.

At this coupling a bevel wheel is attached, which engages with a gear at the head of a vertical shaft, which is in turn driven by the centre of the crankshaft.

Outside diameter at propeller	3 31/64 ins.
Inside diameter	2 61/64 ins.
Diameter airscrew flange	9 3/4 ins.
Diameter of bolt circle	7 7/8 ins.
Diameter of bolts	5/8 in.
Number of bolts	8.

The following further details have been extracted from the same source :—

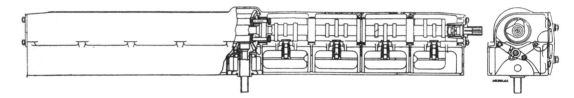

Crankshaft assembled, 410-h.p. American Bugatto.

Camshaft and Casing Assembly.

Each camshaft with its gear and the attendant rocking levers is carried in a cast aluminium housing, which completely encloses the valve gearing.

PISTONS.

These are aluminium castings, with cut-away skirts.

CONNECTING RODS.

The connecting rods are steel forgings of I section, machined all over. The small ends have bronze bushes pressed in. The big ends are bronze-bushed and white metal lined.

CRANKSHAFTS.

As has already been stated, each of the two crankshafts is made in two pieces coupled together.

The junction is a fine taper cone, keyed and held tight by a nut on the small end. At this junction is a bevel wheel which drives a vertical shaft from which the magnetos and the camshaft of that line of cylinders are both driven.

Upper half of crankcase, American Bugatti engine.

CYLINDERS.

The cylinders are of cast iron in blocks of four. The water jackets are integral with the cylinder blocks, but open on each side below the inlet and exhaust ports. These openings are covered by screwed-on aluminium plates.

Three vertical valves are used per cylinder. The relative positions of these valves are shown in a figure, from which it is seen that each of the large exhaust valves is provided with a separate port, and that the four inlet valves of each pair of cylinders have a common inlet port.

All valve stems and seatings are amply water-jacketed.

Two ignition plug sockets are fitted to each cylinder in the side of the combustion chamber on the inlet side.

Cross-section showing Oiling System of the American Bugatti.

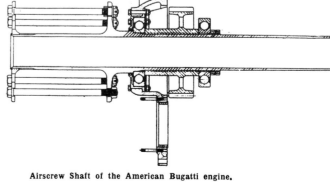

Airscrew Shaft of the American Bugatti engine.

CRANKCASE.

Both upper and lower halves are aluminium castings. All crankshaft bearings are carried entirely by the upper half of the crankcase.

The lower bearing caps are carried by bridge pieces which pass nearly across the crankcase and support both crankshafts. The central bridge is a steel forging, as the bearings at this point are arranged to take any end thrust which may come on the crankshafts. All the other crankshaft bearings have end play, and the corresponding bridge pieces are aluminium castings.

All the main bearings are plain, bronze-bushed and white metal lined, but at the airscrew end of each shaft, beyond the pinion for the airscrew drive one ball-race journal is used.

THE AIRSCREW SHAFT.

This is a steel forging, with one airscrew hub flange solid with the shaft.

This shaft is bored out to a sufficient diameter to permit of firing a 37 m/m. Q.F. gun through it, and a clear passage through the crankcase in line with it is provided for the same purpose.

The spur wheel through which the shaft is driven from the crankshafts is carried by 9 bolts passing through a flange on the shaft.

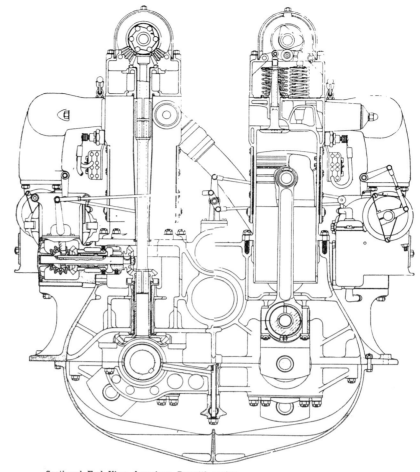

Bugatti engine with Exhaust Pipes.

Sectional End View American Bugatti engine.

Deep grooved ball-races support the shaft on each side of the spur wheel and these races take the whole of the airscrew thrust.

IGNITION.

Four magnetos, each firing eight cylinders, are fitted. Two are placed on each side of the engine between the carburetters, with their shafts parallel to the crankshafts. Upon the vertical shaft driving the camshaft a bevel wheel is mounted inside the crankcase, and this drives a horizontal shaft at right angles to the crankshaft, passing out through the side of the crankcase. At its outer end this shaft carries another bevel wheel which drives the two magnetos on its own side of the engine. The magnetos appear to be fitted with an advance and retard mechanism of the spiral coupling type, which secures maximum spark intensity at all magneto timings.

LUBRICATION.

The oiling system is arranged on the dry sump system, with one pressure and one scavenging oil pump. One of these pumps is driven from the airscrew end of each crankshaft.

CARBURATION.

A separate carburetter is provided for each block of four cylinders. Gas is led to the inlet ports through water-jacketed manifolds.

The modifications from the original model are solely to points of detail design, the most important probably being an alteration to the cylinder head, providing freer water circulation, better valve cooling, and a slight increase in the distance between valve centres.

The original engine was fitted with an overhung airscrew shaft, with bearings inside the spur gear only, and the adoption of bearings on both sides of the gear should undoubtedly improve the engine.

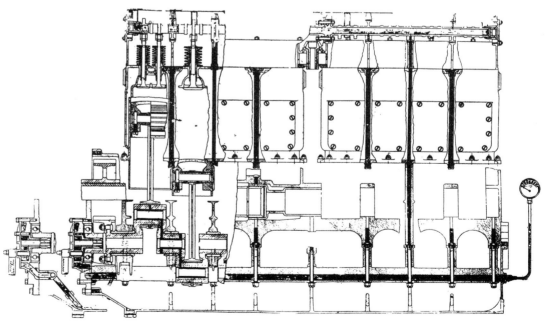

Longitudinal Section of the Bugatti engine, showing the Oiling System.

CLERGÊT (French & British).

France :—CLERGÊT BLIN ET CIE, 37, Rue Cavé, Levallois (Seine).

Great Britain :—GWYNNES, Ltd., Hammersmith Iron Works, London, W.

THE CLERGET ENGINE.

This successful engine of the rotary type is the outcome of years of investigation and experiment carried out by the firm of Clerget Blin & Cie, of Paris, who, working from the lesser to the greater, have successively perfected more and more powerful models.

Owing to the decelerated rotary motion of the cam tooth during the short period it is in contact with the tappet, and to the special form of the tooth and tappet foot, there is very little sliding motion between them, friction and wear being reduced to a minimum.

CYLINDERS AND PISTONS.

The steel cylinders and connecting rods and aluminium pistons are all carefully proportioned in accordance with the demands of experience in order to obtain the desired results ; the crankshaft is more amply proportioned than is usual in rotary engines.

THE CLERGET ENGINE. TYPE 7Z. 80 H.P.

Specification.

No. of cylinders	7.
Bore	120 mm.
Stroke	150 mm.
Weight complete	234 lbs.
Compression ratio	4 : 1.
Normal h.p.	80.
Effective h.p.	85.
R.P.M.	1200.
Oil consumption per h.p. hour	.10 pints.
Petrol consumption per h.p. hour	.74 pints.

Front View of the Gwynne-Clerget engine. Type 7 Z. 80 h.p.

Front View of the Gwynne-Clerget engine. Type 9 Z. 110 h.p.

The sole licence and manufacturing rights for the British Empire are held by Gwynnes Ltd., of Hammersmith and Chiswick, who have the distinction of being the first constructors in this country, after the outbreak of war, to lay down the necessary and suitable plant, in entirely new works, for the manufacture of aeroplane engines.

The earlier types of Clerget engines being of small power, have now become obsolete, except for demonstration purposes, and the smallest engine now manufactured is an 80 h.p. with seven cylinders, which was at the time of its introduction a distinct advance upon previous models. It has done excellent service, and is still a useful and reliable engine for purposes where greater power is not demanded.

The advent of the 9-cylinder 110 h.p. type immediately placed the Clerget in a high position amongst engines of the rotary class, a position it has deservedly maintained by subsequent improvements introduced in the 130 h.p. and one later model.

The 110 h.p. and higher power motors have the advantage of great accessibility, the whole of the working parts being easily removable from the front end without the necessity of disconnecting the engine from the aeroplane. A trained mechanic can easily open up the engine for examination of the pistons, rods, valve cam gear, etc., and re-assemble the parts removed ready for flight well within 30 minutes.

From a cursory glance at the accompanying illustrations, the Clerget appears to have a strong family likeness to other engines of the rotary type, but a more careful examination will disclose distinctive features peculiar to this particular engine.

Whilst the success it has attained is partly due to its mechanical construction, there can be no doubt it has been rendered more certain by the great care and attention bestowed on the design of the various details, to make them particularly suitable for the duties they have to perform under the special flying conditions demanded of light high-speed aeroplanes ; quite a different matter to designing a showy test bench engine.

VALVE GEAR.

As to details, an essential feature of the Clerget design is the valve tappet driving gear, which is distinctly ingenious.

The inlet and exhaust tappets are actuated independently by two cam gear wheels which run on ball bearings centred on fixed eccentrics ; the cam gear wheels are driven by crown wheels fixed in the cam gear box, each crown wheel having twice as many teeth as the number of tappets to be operated. The cam gear wheel has two teeth less than its driving crown wheel, and one tooth in every four in the cam gear wheel is extended to form a cam tooth for actuating the tappets.

It is interesting to note in this connection that in cases where machines driven by Clerget engines have crashed or had bad landings, the crankshafts have given a good account of themselves. The thrust has been calculated on sound mechanical principles, and the thrust bearing is of ample proportion and quite independent of either of the journal bearings.

The main particulars of the various types are given below in list form, and they show that the Clerget is an excellent example of modern rotary engines.

THE CLERGET ENGINE. TYPE 9Z. 110 H.P.

Specification.

No. of cylinders	9.
Bore	120 mm.
Stroke	160 mm.
Weight complete	397 lbs.
Compression ratio	4 : 1.
Normal h.p.	110.
Effective h.p.	115.
R.P.M.	1180.
Oil consumption per h.p. hour	.14 pints.
Petrol consumption per h.p. hour	.75 pints.

Front View of the Clerget engine. Type 9 B.F. 140 h.p.

THE CLERGET ENGINE. TYPE 9B. 130 H.P.
Specification.

No. of cylinders	9.
Bore	120 mm
Stroke	160 mm
Weight complete	381 lbs.
Compression ratio	4 : 1.
Normal h.p.	130.
Effective h.p.	135.
R.P.M.	1250.
Oil consumption per h.p. hour	.09 pints.
Petrol consumption per h.p. hour	.74 pints.

THE CLERGET ENGINE. TYPE 9BF. 140 H.P.
Specification.

No. of cylinders	9.
Bore	120 mm.
Stroke	172 mm.
Weight complete	381 lbs.
Compression ratio	5.3 : 1.
Normal h.p.	140.
Effective h.p.	153.
R.P.M.	1250.
Oil consumption per h.p. hour	.11 pints.
Petrol consumption per h.p. hour	.59 pints.

THE CLERGET ENGINE. TYPE 11EB. 200 H.P.
Specification.

No. of cylinders	11.
Bore	120 mm.
Stroke	190 mm.
Weight complete	507 lbs.
Compression ratio	5 : 1.
Normal h.p.	200.
Effective h.p.	210.
R.P.M.	1300.
Oil consumption per h.p. hour	.11 pints.
Petrol consumption per h.p. hour	.68 pints.

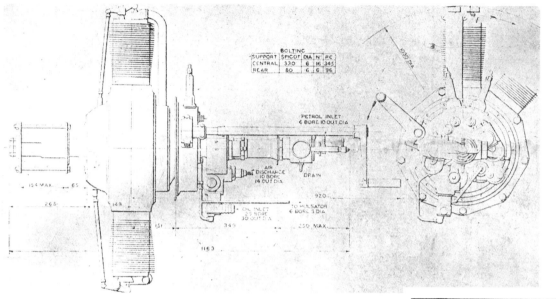

General Arrangement Diagram of the Clerget engine. Type 9 B.F. 140 h.p.

THE CLERGET ENGINE. TYPE 16X. RADIAL. 400 H.P.
Specification.

No. of cylinders	16.
Bore	130 mm.
Stroke	130 mm.
Weight complete	750 lbs.
Compression ratio	5 : 1.
Normal h.p.	400.
Effective h.p.	420.
R.P.M.	1600.
Oil consumption per h.p. hour	.05 pints.
Petrol consumption per h.p. hour	.63 pints.

Half-Front View of the Gwynne-Clerget engine. Type 11 E.B. 200 h.p.

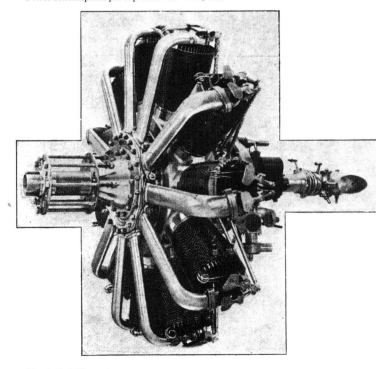

Front End View of the Gwynne-Clerget engine. Type 11 E.B. 200 h.p.

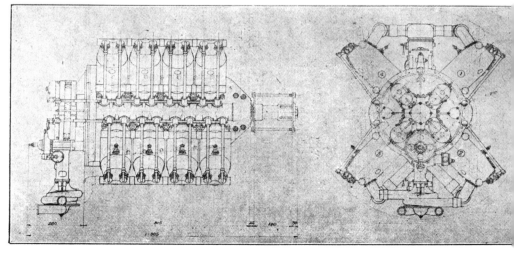

General Arrangement Diagram of the Water-cooled Clerget engine. Type 16 x. 400 h.p.

THE COSMOS (British).

THE COSMOS ENGINEERING Co., Ltd. Offices :—Orient House, 42, 45, New Broad Street, London, E.C.2. Works :— Fishponds, Bristol.

One of the firms who have specialised in the radial engine and have pinned their faith to the type is the Cosmos Engineering Co., Ltd., of Bristol, formerly known as Brazil, Straker & Co., Ltd. To those who know their car histories little more need be

THE "MERCURY" ENGINE.

The "Mercury" engine—two rows of seven cylinders each—was introduced to satisfy Air Board Scheme A issued in April, 1917. Its main details are :—Maximum diameter, 41⅜ ins. ; bore, 4¾ ins. ; stroke, 5 13-16 ins. ; power output, 315 b.h.p. at 1,800 r.p.m. (normal) and 347 at 2,000 r.p.m. (maximum) ; total weight, without fuel and oil tanks, but with the engine absolutely complete, even to the gun synchronising gear, 582 lbs.

view of the engine ; the tappet gear is of the roller type arranged in a circular unit, which can be assembled complete before attachment to the crankcase.

As regards constructional details not apparent in the illustrations, the cylinders are turned from a solid billet, the fins integral with the barrel. Separate aluminium heads are bolted onto the cylinder barrels. These heads are so designed as to obtain effective cooling of the valve seatings and ports, and to avoid all distortion. The crankshaft is of the two-throw type on roller bearings throughout. The rollers of the big-end

Front View. "Mercury" engine.

Rear View. "Mercury" engine.

said. The Cosmos Co. is not entirely identical with the car people, but it is not far removed, as offspring go.

Research and experiment have led to the production of two radial engines by the firm—the "Mercury" of 315 h.p. and the "Jupiter" of 500 h.p., of fourteen and nine cylinders respectively. Other engines will be, and, indeed, are being, designed and produced, but upon the success of these two engines the makers have decided to commit themselves definitely to a programme of peace-time production.

Front and rear view illustrations are reproduced herewith, which make quite clear the general lay-out of the unit, including the ignition apparatus of two 7-cylinder M.L. magnetos and Remy 14-cylinder distributor and the two carburetters bolted to circular induction chambers on the crankcase. The mixture is conducted from these chambers by separate induction pipes to each cylinder and admitted through one inlet valve. The three overhead valves per cylinder may be seen in the front

bearings run direct on the crank-pin, and each connecting-rod has its own crankshaft bearing, so that the seven rods of each row of cylinders lie side by side on their respective crank-pins. An interesting feature of this part of the engine is that the whole crankshaft assembly can be withdrawn complete, with the connecting-rods in position. The tappet gear is of the roller type, the tappets operated by two cam rings, each having three cams and working at one-sixth engine speed.

Front View. "Jupiter" engine.

Rear View. "Jupiter" engine.

Lubrication is on the dry sump principle, and the oil is drawn by one pump from the tank mounted in the fuselage, delivered under pressure to the hollow crankshaft, and, after being led by separate leads to all necessary parts, is returned to the tank by another pump.

On this engine the airscrew is ungeared, the airscrew boss being driven direct through serrations on the crankshaft. The airscrew boss is to Air Board standard design.

On the Bristol Scout Type "F" this engine has been given exhaustive flying tests, and has given extremely satisfying results.

THE 300 H.P. "MERCURY" RADIAL AERO-ENGINE.

Specification.

No. of cylinders	14.
Bore	4⅔ ins.
Stroke	5¹³⁄₁₆ ins.
Normal b.h.p.	315 b.h.p.
Maximum b.h.p.	347 h.p.
Normal revs. per min.	1800.
Maximum revs. per min.	2000.
Total weight	587 lbs.
Maximum dia. of engine	41¾ ins.
Ignition	2 M.L. magnetos and a 14-cylinder Remy distributor and coil.

THE "JUPITER" ENGINE.

The rear view of the "Jupiter" engine makes clear many of its constructional features. There are nine cylinders made on lines similar to those of the "Mercury," but the bore and stroke are 5¾ ins. and 7½ ins. respectively, while the power output is 450 h.p. at 1,800 r.p.m. as an ungeared engine or 500 at 2,000 r.p.m. with a geared down airscrew. The weight of the ungeared model is 662 lbs. complete, including electric starter, but without fuel and oil tanks.

AN IMPORTANT FEATURE.

From the illustration the engine might be taken to be of the rotary type, owing to the arrangement of the inlet pipes, which form part of a very interesting induction system. As will be seen, three carburetters are bolted to the crankcase cover, which also forms one side of the induction chamber.

This induction chamber is annular, and into it is fitted a spiral fluted aluminium casting which acts as a gas distributor to the cylinders. Each of the three carburetters supplies three cylinders *via* the spiral, which delivers the carburetted charge to the correct cylinder in turn, with the advantage that each cylinder is more efficiently supplied with mixture, and, if one cuts out, none of the others is affected. On bench tests the arrangement has proved itself a success.

Two inlet and two exhaust valves are fitted per cylinder, operated by two cam rings, each with four cams running at one-eighth engine speed, through tappets mounted in the front of the engine. Ignition is by two 9-cylinder Thompson Bennet magnetos driven by bevel gearing from the crankshaft and mounted on the back cover of the crankcase—i.e., the cover of the induction chamber—in such a position that the contact breakers are readily accessible.

With the exception of the connecting-rod assembly, the engine is, in essentials, similar to the "Mercury." A master connecting-rod with articulated rods is used. The bearing of the master rod is white metal lined, all other bearings in the engine are of the roller type. It is hardly necessary to point out that the crankshaft in the "Jupiter" engine is of the single throw type.

THE 500 H.P. "JUPITER" RADIAL AERO-ENGINE.

Specification.

No. of cylinders	9.
Bore	5¾ ins.
Stroke	7½ ins.
Normal b.h.p.	450 h.p. (Mark i). 500 h.p. (Mark ii geared).
Normal revs. per min.	1800 (Mark i). 1300 (Mark ii geared).
Total weight	662 lbs. (Mark i).
Ignition	2 9-cylinder Thompson Bennett magnetos.

In addition to these engines, the Cosmos firm are to manufacture a light cheap 3-cylinder engine, to be known as the "Lucifer," and are experimenting with a much larger engine than the two already described.

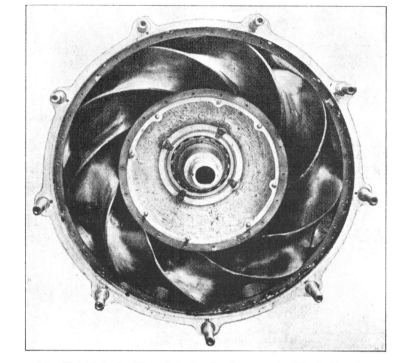

Spiral Fluted Induction Ring. Induction chamber removed. "Jupiter" engine.

Back Cover Unit, "Jupiter" engine.

CURTISS (American).

THE CURTISS AEROPLANE CO., Buffalo, New York.

British Representative : Clun House, Surrey Street, Strand, W.C.

250 h.p. Model.

Type : Water-cooled "V."
No. of cylinders : 12.
Bore : 5 in.   Stroke : 7 in.
R.P.M. : 1,400–1,500.
Cylinders : High carbon steel, cast separately.
Valves : Overhead.   Inlet, nickel steel ; exhaust, tungsten steel.
Carburetters : 4 Zenith, each supplying 3 cylinders.
Ignition : Two 12-spark magnetos.
Lubrication : Pressure feed from reservoir.
Weight : Engine, 1,125 lbs.   Radiator, 120 lbs.   Water : 100 lbs.

Dimensions : Length, 84⅝ in. ; width, 34⅛ in. ; depth, —— in. ; width at bed, 30½ in. ; height from bed, 21⅛ in. ; depth from bed, 18½ in.

Other models on same lines, but with only eight cylinders, with the following bores and strokes :—

	Bore.	Stroke.	r.p.m.	Wt. in lbs.
90 h.p.	100 m/m.	125 m/m.	1,200	325
100 h.p.	105 m/m.	125 m/m.	1,250	340
160 h.p.	125 m/m.	180 m/m.	1,100	700

In 1918 produced the K–6 and K–12 models, designed by Mr. Kirkham.

The feature of this engine is that the cylinders and the top part of the crank-case are cast of aluminium alloy in one unit.

Pressed steel cylinder-liners are used.   The cylinder heads are cast in one unit and bolted to the top of the other casting.

Made in two models :—

K–6—6 cylinder vertical—150 h.p. direct drive.
K–12—12 cylinder Vee—375 h.p. gear drive.

The 250 h.p. Curtiss engine.

Side View of the Curtiss K–12, minus exhaust manifold.

Side View of the Curtiss engine, Type K-6.   150 h.p.

Front End of the Curtiss engine, Type K–6. 150 h.p.

Side View of the Curtiss engine, Type O X–5. 100 h.p.

THE 150 h.p. CURTISS-KIRKHAM AERO ENGINE.

Specification :

Type	K–6
No. of cylinders	6
Bore	4¼ in.
Stroke..	6 in.
B.H.P.	150
Engine speed	1700 r.p.m,

THE 375 h.p. CURTISS-KIRKHAM AERO ENGINE.

Specification :

Type	K–12
No. of cylinders	12
Bore	4½ in.
Stroke..	6 in.
B.H.P.	375
Engine speed..	2250 r.p.m.

DUESENBERG (American).

THE DUESENBERG MOTORS CORPORATION
Edgewater, New Jersey and Chicago, Ill.

Made the following types in 1917-18 :—

4 Cylinder Vertical.
Bore : 4¾ in. Stroke : 7 in.
Weight (all on) : 509 lbs.
(Without demultiplication gear 436 lbs.)
H.P. : 125 at 2,100 r.p.m. (propeller speed 1,210 r.p.m.)
Also 300 h.p. "V" type, as shown in end view drawing.

Have recently produced the 16-cylinder Vee engine, stated to
be of 850 h.p. Illustrated herewith.

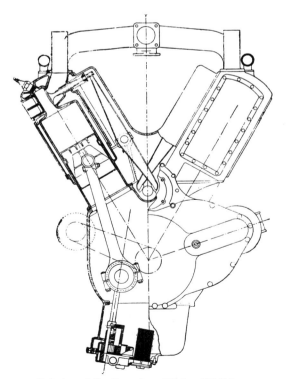

End view of the Duesenberg 300 h.p. "V" type
engine showing valve-rockers and horizontal valves.

The 850 h.p. Model H. Duesenberg 16-cylinder Aero engine.

FIAT (Italian).

Societa Anonyma F.I.A.T., Turin.

The Fiat 300 h.p. aviation engine, officially known as the A-12, is a 6-cylinder water-cooled vertical type of 160 × 180 mm. bore and stroke.

The cylinders are separate steel forgings, each one carrying four inclined valves in the head and fitted with a welded-on sheet steel water-jacket, having a patented flexible joint at the base.

The cylinders are mounted on an aluminium crank chamber with detachable "dry" sump, all the oil, which is delivered to the bearings under pressure, being contained in a tank independent of the engine.

Valves are inclined in the head and are operated by an overhead enclosed camshaft.

There is a single cam with forked rocker for each pair of valves—two inlets, or two exhausts.

Pistons are aluminium, and connecting rods are I-section.

All the valve operating mechanism is at the rear of the engine. This consists of an enclosed vertical shaft, driven by bevel gearing from the crankshaft, and operating the camshaft by means of a pair of bevel pinions.

At the base of the vertical shaft, and to left and right of it are two 6-cylinder magnetos. Thus the charge in each cylinder is fired by a pair of plugs.

At the base of a downward extension of the magneto driving shaft is the centrifugal water pump contained with an aluminium housing.

The carburetter is a dual Fiat type, with independent float chambers and mixing chambers, but forming a common aluminium casting and having a common water-jacket around the mixing chamber.

The airscrew is mounted direct on the crankshaft and rotates anti-clockwise at a normal speed of 1,700 revolutions a minute.

The 300 h.p. Fiat engine is used by all the Allied air services. Among its most notable performances are the non-stop flight of 1,040 miles from Turin to Naples and return, and a flight from Turin to London with passenger, guns, ammunition, provisions and mail.

In addition to the 300 h.p. 6-cylinder vertical engine, the Fiat Company produces a 12-cylinder V-engine of 700 h.p.

Fiat 300 h.p.
Bore : 160 m/m.
Stroke : 180 m/m.
No of cylinders : 6.
R.P.M. : 1,700.
H.P. : 300.

No details are available as to the Specifications of the 400 h.p., and 700 h.p. Engines.

Rear End of the Fiat 300 h.p. 6-cylinder engine (1918 type).

THE FIAT AIRSHIP ENGINES.

The majority of Italian airships were equipped with Fiat engines. The size and type of engine varied with the airship, but a very popular installation was a twin group composed of two four cylinder engines placed side by side, and as close together as possible, in a channel section frame.

These engines have a bore and stroke of 110 by 190 mm.

The cylinders are a block casting, with enclosed valves in the head, and large aluminium water jacket plates on the sides and the ends.

The overhead camshaft is operated by means of an enclosed vertical shaft and bevel gearing, and advantage is taken of this shaft to mount the starting gear by means of a lever and bevel gearing.

The carburetter is placed on the outside of each engine, and the exhaust is on the inside.

At the base of the vertical shaft the water pump and the high-tension magneto are driven by means of bevel gearing. These two organs are opposed, so that the magneto distributors and contact breakers are on the outside in each case.

Each engine is fitted with a light fly-wheel and a spiral spring clutch, the control of which is by means of a lever at the forward end of the engine.

From the clutch shaft the airscrew shaft is driven by means of bevel gearing, this shaft having an inclination of about 45 deg. from the vertical.

Front end of the 12-cylinder Fiat engine. 400 h.p.

Rear View of the 12 cylinder Fiat engine. 700 h.p.

Rear end of the 12 cylinder Fiat engine. 700 h.p.

Front View of the Fiat Twin Airship engines.

Rear end of Fiat Twin Airship Engines.

GANZ-FIAT AERO MOTOR CO. LTD. (Austrian)

Formed in 1916 with a capital of £100,000 by the Anglo-Austrian Bank, the Maschinen-und-Schiffbau A.G., Ganz-Danubius, at Budapest, and the Austrian Fiat Motor Works, Ltd., originally a branch of the Italian Fiat company.

It may in this respect further be mentioned that the rest of the Austrian-Hungarian automobile industry (Laurin & Clement, Alpha, M.A.G.F.A., Hungarian Benz Co.) has, similarly to the conditions of the other belligerent countries too, supplied aero engines (all of vertical, water-cooled type and general automobile engine features).

GENERAL ORDNANCE (American).

THE GENERAL ORDNANCE COMPANY, Derby, Connecticut.
Were constructors in 1917 of a new engine of water-cooled "V" type.
No. of cylinders : 8.
Bore : 4¾ in.   Stroke : 6½ in.
H.P. : 200.
Weight all on : 876¼ lbs.

GNÔME & RHÔNE (French & British).

SOCIÉTÉ DES MOTEURS GNÔME & RHÔNE, 3, Rue la Boétie, Paris.

GNÔME & LE RHÔNE ENGINE Co., Ltd., 47, Victoria St., S.W.

Also made by THE GENERAL VEHICLE CO., Long Island City, Long Island, U.S.A.

Also made by LA SOCIETA ITALIANA MOTORI GNÔME & RHÔNE, 73, Strada Veneria, Madonna di Compagna, Italy.

GNÔME ENGINES.
Monosoupape type :—
(Type A)   80 h.p. 7 cylinders, 110×150 m/m (1200 r.p.m.).
(Type B 2) 100 h.p. 9 cylinders, 110×150 m/m (1200 r.p.m.), 260 lbs.
(Type N) 160 h.p. 9 cylinders, 150×170 m/m (1350 r.p.m.), 340 lbs.
Petrol consumption of Type B Mono. giving 106 h.p. at 1230 revs., is ·778 pints per h.p. per hour.

LE RHÔNE ENGINES.
80 h.p. 7 cylinders, 105×140 m/m (1200 r.p.m.), 199 lbs.
120 h.p. 9 cylinders, 112×175 m/m (1200 r.p.m.), 308 lbs.

Side and front view of 100 h.p. Monosoupape Gnôme engine.

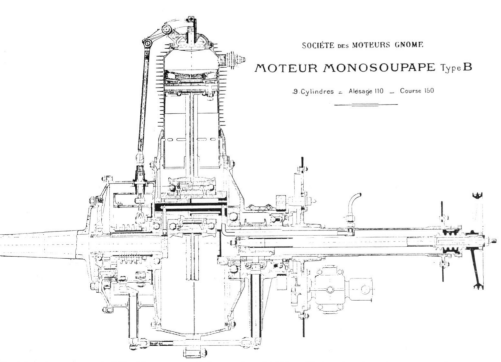

SOCIÉTÉ DES MOTEURS GNOME

MOTEUR MONOSOUPAPE Type B

9 Cylindres ═ Alésage 110 ═ Course 150

The internal arrangement of the Monosoupape Gnôme engine of 1914. This has since been improved by altering the valve gear and removing the hand-control device.

Side view of 110 h.p. Le Rhône engine, showing valve rockers and attachment of inlet pipes ; also arrangement of magneto and main shaft.

Front view of 110 h.p. Le Rhône engine.

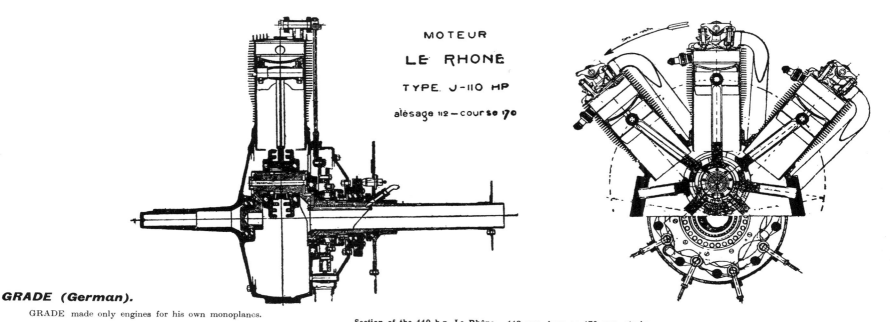

MOTEUR

LE RHONE

TYPE J-110 HP

alèsage 112 — course 170

Section of the 110 h.p. Le Rhône. 112 mm. bore × 170 mm. stroke.

GRADE (German).

GRADE made only engines for his own monoplanes.

GREEN (British).

THE GREEN ENGINE Co., Ltd., 166, Piccadilly, W.

100 h.p. Model.
Type : Water-cooled vertical.
No. of cylinders : 6.
Bore : 140 m/m.   Stroke : 152 m/m.
R.P.M. : 1,200.
Cylinders : Steel, copper water jackets.
Valves : Overhead camshaft.

150 h.p. Model.
Type : Water-cooled vertical.
No. of cylinders : 6.
Bore : 142 m/m.   Stroke : 178 m/m.
R.P.M. : 1,200.
Cylinders : Steel, copper water jackets.
Valves : Overhead camshaft with vertical gear drive.

300 h.p. Model.
Type : Water-cooled " V."
No. of cylinders : 12
Bore : 142 m/m.   Stroke : 178 m/m.
R.P.M. : 1,200.
Cylinders : Steel, copper waterjackets.
Valves : Overhead camshafts with vertical gear drive.
Carburetter : Twin.
Ignition : Twin magnetos.
Lubrication : Forced feed.

A batch of the 300 h.p. Green engines ready for delivery.

Rear End of the 450 h.p. Green engine, which is practically a " Broad Arrow " version of the 300 h.p. type.

HALL-SCOTT (American).

THE HALL-SCOTT MOTOR CAR Co., Inc. Gen. Offices : Crocker Building, San Francisco.

Built in 1917, the following model. No further information available.

212 b.h.p., at 1,666 r.p.m.
Bore and stroke, 5 in. and 7 in.
Weight, 502 lbs.

HIERONYMUS (Austrian and German).

ESSLER, WARSCHALOWSKI & Co., Vienna.

Designed by Hieronymus, the famous racing motor driver. The Warschalowski Brothers were early pilots and manufacturers of the *Autopian* biplanes (*Henry Farman* box kite type with steel-tube landing chassis).

Also made under license by the Loeb Motor Works in Berlin.

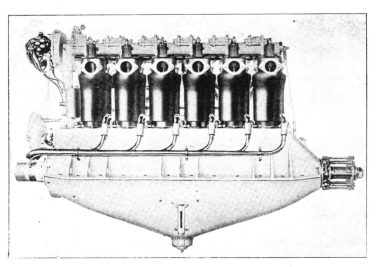

Exhaust-side View of the L. 6 type Hall-Scott 6-cylinder engine.

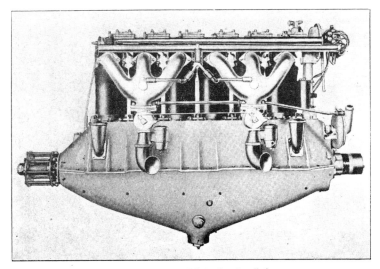

Inlet-side View of the L. 6 type Hall-Scott. 6 cylinder.

HISPANO-SUIZA (Spanish, French, British and American).

Head Office :—LA SOCIEDAD HISPANO-SUIZA, Barcelona. Spain.

U.S.A :—THE WRIGHT-MARTIN AIRCRAFT CORPORATION Simplex Works, New Brunswick, New Jersey, U.S.A.

Also manufactured in France and in England

One of the most successful engines in the world, being light for its weight, reliable, and designed so as to fit neatly into an aeroplane.

The distinguishing feature of the engine is the use of aluminium Monobloc cylinder castings into which steel liners are screwed.

Made in three sizes :—

180 h.p. 8-cylinder. V-type, direct drive.
220 h.p. 8-cylinder. V-type, geared drive.
300 h.p. 8-cylinder. V-type, geared drive.

Model A. 180 h.p.

Bore : 4.7245" ⎫ 4 cylinders in each block of the " V."
Stroke : 5.1182" ⎭
Piston Displacement : 718 cubic inches.
H.P. : 180, at 1750 r.p.m.
Weight, without radiator, water, oil or exhaust pipes: 445 lbs.
Fuel consumption : .5 lbs. per h.p. per hour.
Oil consumption : 3 quarts per hour.

The 220 h.p. type is the same as the 180 h.p., but running at 2,200 r.p.m.

The 300 h.p. type is as the 220 h.p., but with bigger bore and longer stroke.

THE WRIGHT-MARTIN HISPANO-SUIZA AERO ENGINE.

Specification :

Type	..	..	Model 1.
No. of cylinders	..	..	8 (Vee type)
Bore	..	..	120 m/m. (4.724 in.)
Stroke	..	..	130 m/m. (5.118 in.)
Normal b.h.p.	..	..	150
Normal r.p.m.	..	..	1,500
Maximum b.h.p.	..	..	170
Maximum r.p.m.	..	..	1,700
Weight (with airscrew)	..	..	455 lbs.
Fuel Consumption	..	..	.51 lbs. per h.p. per hour
Oil ,,	..	..	.03 lbs. per h.p. per hour

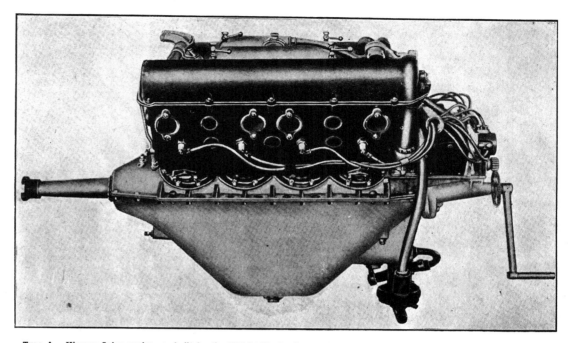

Type A. Hispano-Suiza engine, as built by the Wright-Martin Corporation at the New Brunswick Works, New Jersey, U.S.A.

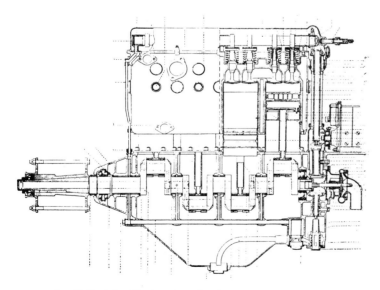

Longitudinal Part Section of the Standard Hispano-Suiza engine.

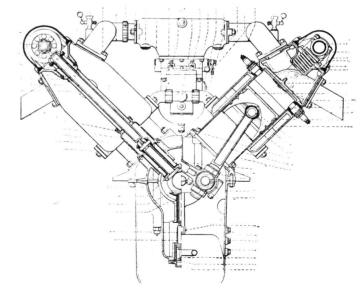

Cross-Section of the Hispano-Suiza Engine.

ISOTTA-FRASCHINI (Italian).

IL FABRICA AUTOMOBILI ISOTTA FRASCHINI, Via Monte Rosa 79, Milan.

The Isotta Fraschini firm are famous as motor car, aero-motor and big marine motor builders. Their aeromotors were used first on the hydro-aeroplanes of the Italian Navy, and later on biplanes of *Voisin* type before Italy came into the war, and they have since been used successfully on *Caproni* triple engine biplanes. The newer Isotta-Fraschini engines, type V6 have been adopted also in the Italian " chaser " aeroplanes. Moreover, the Isotta-Fraschini is the only Italian firm that has made a speciality in the manufacture of big marine motors from 300 to 800 h.p. which have been adopted in a large scale by the Italian Navy on the " chaser " boats against submarines.

No fresh particulars are available since last year.

190 h.p. Model.—Type V4B.

Type : Water-cooled vertical.
No. of cylinders : 6.
R.P.M. : 1,450 (direct drive).
Cylinders : In pairs—steel water-jackets.
Valves : Overhead camshafts and valves.
Carburetters : Twin.
Ignition : 2 six-spark magnetos.
Lubrication : Forced feed.

245 h.p. Model.

Type : Water-cooled vertical.
No. of cylinders : 8.
Bore : 130 × 190 m/m.
R.P.M. : 1,300 (direct drive).
Cylinders : In pairs—copper water-jackets
Valves : Overhead camshafts.
Carburetter : Twin.
Ignition : 2 eight-spark magnetos.
Lubrication : Forced feed.

245 h.p. Model.—Type V5.

Type : Water-cooled vertical.
No. of cylinders : 8.
R.P.M. : 1,400 (direct drive).
Cylinders : In pairs—steel water-jackets.
Valves : Overhead camshafts and valves.
Carburetter : Twin.
Ignition : 2 eight-spark magnetos.
Lubrication : Forced feed.

A Later type Isotta-Fraschini 6-cylinder model.

LAWRENCE (American).

LAWRENCE MOTOR Co.,

Make the engine described and illustrated herewith.

THE LAWRENCE 60 h.p. RADIAL ENGINE.

Specification :

Type						L-1.
No. of cylinders ..		..	..	..	..	3 (Y–type).
Bore	..	..	..	..	..	4.25 in.
Stroke	..	..	..	..	..	5.25 in.
Normal B.H.P.	..		..	..	..	60.
Maximum B.H.P.	..		..	..	..	63.
Normal r.p.m.	..		..	..	..	1900
Maximum r.p m. ..		..	..	..	..	2100
Weight complete (with air-screw hub)			..	..	..	130 lbs.

LOEB & CO. AUTOMOBILE WORKS.

Berlin, Charlottenburg.

Manufacturers of the Austrian Hiero aero engines by licence. Said to have made aeroplanes also.

Side View of the Lawrence 60 h.p. Air-cooled Radial engine

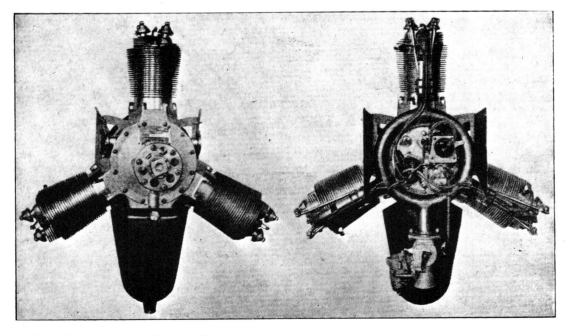

Front and Rear View of the Lawrence 60 h.p. engine.

LIBERTY (American).

Manufactured wholly and in part by a number of automobile firms in the U.S.A.

The Liberty engine, or parts of it, is being made by every motor factory in the United States. It is an officially designed engine, intended to fulfil all purposes in air war.

THE OFFICIAL ACCOUNT.

The following account of the origin of the engine was published officially in 1917.

It was designed by Major Vincent, of the Packard Co., and Major Hall, of the Hall-Scott Co., under circumstances hereinafter officially related.

The first hand-made engines have given good results and good weight for power.

The successful completion of the U.S.A. or Liberty aircraft engine was announced in an official statement issued by the Secretary of War, on August 12th, 1917. The statement reads :—

" The United States aviation engine has passed its final tests. They were successful and gratifying. The new engine, designated by the Signal Service as the 'Liberty engine,' is now the main reliance of the United States in the rapid production in large numbers of high-powered battle planes for service in the war. In power, speed, serviceability and minimum weight the new engine invites comparison with the best that the European war has produced.

" I regard the invention and rapid development of this engine as one of the really big accomplishments of the United States since its entry into the war. The engine was brought about through the co-operation of more than a score of engineers, who pooled their skill and trade secrets in the war emergency, working with the encouragement of the Aircraft Production Board, the War Department and the Bureau of Standards.

" The story of the production of this engine is a remarkable one. Probably the war has produced no greater single achievement.

" One of the first problems which confronted the War Department and the Aircraft Production Board after the declaration of hostilities was to produce a dependable engine. Two courses were open. One was to encourage manufacturers to develop their own types, the other to bring the best of all types together and develop a standard.

" The necessity for speed and quantity of production resulted in a choice of the latter course, and a standard engine became our engineering objective.

" Two of the best engineers in the country, who had never before seen each other, were brought together at Washington, and the problem of producing an all-American engine at the earliest possible moment was presented to them. Their first conference, on June 3rd, lasted from the afternoon until half-past two o'clock in the morning.

" These two engineers were figuratively locked in a room in a Washington hotel and charged with the development of an aeroplane engine for use by American aviators over the battle-fields of Europe. For five days neither man left the suite of rooms engaged for them. Consulting engineers and draughtsmen from various sections of the country were brought to Washington to assist them. The work in the draughting room proceeded continuously, day and night. Each of the two engineers in immediate charge of engine development alternately worked a twenty-four hour shift.

" An inspiring feature of this work was the aid rendered by consulting engineers and motor manufacturers, who gave up their trade secrets under the emergency of war needs. Realising that the new design would be a Government design and no firm or individual would reap selfish benefit because of its making, the motor manufacturers patriotically revealed their trade secrets and made available trade processes of great commercial value. These industries have also contributed the services of approximately 200 of their best draughtsmen.

" The two engineers locked together in a hotel room in this city promised the Government, if given an opportunity, they would design a satisfactory aero-engine before a working model could be brought from Europe.

" A remarkable American engine was actually produced three weeks before any model could have been brought from Europe. It was promised that this engine would be developed before the Fourth of July. Twenty-eight days after the drawings were started the new engine was set up. This was on July 3rd.

" In order to have the engine in Washington and in actual running order at the nation's capital on Independence Day the perfected engine was sent from a Western city in a special express car. The journey was made in twenty-one hours, and four young men guarded the engine en route to Washington and personally attended to its transfer from one railroad to another.

" With the need for speed as an incentive, tools for building the first engine were made even before the drawings were finished —on the assumption that they would be correct.

" Parts of the first engine were turned out at twelve different factories, located all the way from Connecticut to California. When the parts were assembled the adjustment was perfect and the performance of the engine was wonderfully gratifying. This in itself demonstrated the capabilities of American factories when put to the test and when thoroughly organised for emergency work of this sort.

" One of the chief rules outlined at the beginning of the designing work was that no engineer should be permitted to introduce construction which had not been tried out. There was no time for theorising. The new engine is successful because it embodies the best thought of engineering experience to date. Not only did this country furnish ideas through celebrated consulting engineers, but the representatives in the United States, of England, France and Italy co-operated in the development of this motor.

The Liberty Engine. Three-quarter View—Airscrew End. *(Photograph by courtesy of the Technical Department (Aircraft), Ministry of Munitions.)*

(Photograph by courtesy of the Technical Department (Aircraft), Ministry of Munitions.)

The Liberty Engine—Ignition End.

" Thirty days after the assembling of the first engine, preliminary tests justified the Government in formally accepting the engine as the best aircraft engine produced in any country. The final tests confirmed our faith in the new engine in every degree.

" Both the flying and altitude tests of the new engine have been gratifying. One test was conducted at Pike's Peak, where the United States aviation engine performed satisfactorily at this high altitude. One of the engines in an aeroplane broke the American altitude record in a recent flying test.

" While it is not deemed expedient to discuss in detail the performances and mechanics of the new engine, it may be said that standardisation is a chief factor in the development of the

Government's engine. Cylinders, pistons and every other part of the engine have been standardised. They may be produced rapidly and economically by a great many factories operating under Government contracts. They may be as rapidly assembled, either by these plants or at a central assembly plant.

"The new engine amounts practically to an international model. It embodies the best there is in American engineering and the best features of European models, so far as it has been possible to adapt the latter to American manufacturing methods.

"The two engineers most directly connected with the production of the United States aviation engine had before them not only the blueprints and models of the most successful engines the war has produced, but also every available American suggestion. Men skilled in the invention of motors, both automobile and aeroplane, advised these engineers, who were charged with the duty of providing rapidly and unerringly an engine which would embody every essential of war-time use. Non-essential complexities were consistently discarded by these engineers. The result was a composite design of maximum power, minimum weight, great speed capability and adaptability to quick production.

"The standardisation of parts materially simplifies the problem of repair and maintenance. Spare parts will be promptly available at all times. Even the cylinders are designed separately. It is possible to build the new engine in four models, ranging from four to twelve cylinders, and under the standardisation plan now worked out an eight-cylinder or a twelve-cylinder model can be made, using the same standard cylinders, pistons, valves, cam shafts, and so on.

"With the completion of final tests of the engine—tests which satisfied and gratified both expert engineers and army officers—progress already has been made toward organising industry for the manufacture of the new machines and deliveries will begin within a comparatively short time."

THE LIBERTY ENGINE.

The first official technical announcement concerning the Liberty was made by the War Department on May 15th, 1918. The statement read :—

"The design of the parts of the Liberty engine were based on the following :—

"Cylinder.—The designers of the cylinders for the Liberty engine followed the practice used in the German Mercédès, English Rolls-Royce, French Lorraine Dietrich, and Italian Isotta Fraschini before the war and during the war. The cylinders are made of steel inner shells, surrounded by pressed steel water jackets. The Packard Company by long experiment had developed a method of applying these steel water jackets. The valve cages are drop forgings welded into the cylinder heads. The principal departure from European practice is in the location of the hold-down flange, which is several inches above the mouth of the cylinder, and the unique method of manufacture evolved by the Ford Company. The output is now approximately 1,700 cylinder forgings per day.

"Cam Shaft and Valve Mechanism Above Cylinder Heads.—The design for the above is based on the Mercédès, but was improved for automatic lubrication, without wasting oil, by the Packard Motor Car Company.

"Cam Shaft Drive.—The cam shaft drive was copied almost entirely from the Hall-Scott motor ; in fact, several of the gears used in the first sample engine were supplied by the Hall-Scott Motor Car Company. This type of drive is used by Mercédès, Hispano-Suiza, and others.

"Angle Between Cylinders.—In the Liberty engine the included angle between the cylinders is 45 degrees ; in all other existing 12-cylinder engines it is 60 degrees. This feature is new with the Liberty engine, and was adopted for the purpose of bringing each row of cylinders nearer the vertical and closer together, so as to save width and head resistance. By the narrow angle greater strength is given to the crank case and vibration is reduced.

"Electric Generator and Ignition.—A Delco ignition system is used. It was especially designed for the Liberty engine, to save weight and to meet the special conditions due to firing 12 cylinders with an included angle of 45 degrees.

"Pistons.—The pistons of the Liberty engine are of Hall-Scott designs.

"Connecting Rods.—Forked or straddle type connecting rods, first used on the French De Dion car and on the Cadillac motor cars in this country, are used.

"Crank Shaft.—Crank shaft design followed the standard 12-cylinder practice, except as to oiling. Crank case follows standard practice. The 45 degree angle and the flange location on the cylinders made possible a very strong box section.

"Lubrication.—The first system of lubrication followed the German practice of using one pump to keep the crank case empty, delivering into an outside reservoir, and another pump forcing oil under pressure to the main crank shaft bearings. This lubrication system also followed the German practice in allowing the overflow in the main bearings to travel out the face of the crank cheeks to a scupper, which collected this excess of crankpin lubrication. This is very economical in the use of oil and is still the standard German practice.

"The present system is similar to the first practice, except that the oil, while under pressure, is not only fed to main bearings, but through holes inside of crank cheeks to crank pins, instead of feeding these crank pins through scuppers. The difference between the two oiling systems consists of carrying oil for the crank pins through a hole inside the crank cheek, instead of up the outside face of the crank cheek.

"Propeller Hub.—The Hall-Scott propeller hub design was adapted to the power for the Liberty engine.

"Water Pump.—The Packard type of water pump was adapted to the Liberty.

"Carburetter.—A Carburetter was developed by the Zenith Carburetter Company for the Liberty engine.

"Bore and Stroke.—The bore and stroke of the Liberty engine is 5 by 7 ins., the same as the Hall-Scott A5 and A7 engines, and as in the Hall-Scott 12-cylinder engine.

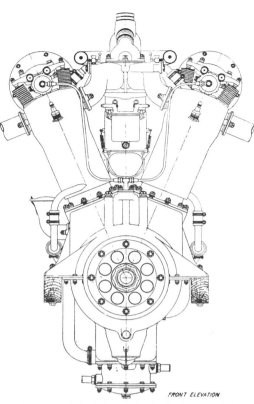

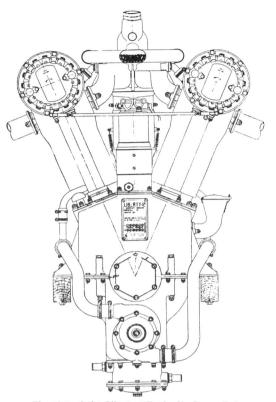

FRONT ELEVATION

Elevation of the Liberty "Twelve"—Airscrew End.

Elevation of the Liberty "Twelve"—Pump End.

"Remarks.—The idea of developing Liberty engines of 4, 6, 8, and 12 cylinders with the above characteristics was first thought of about May 25th, 1917. The idea was developed in conference with representatives of the British and French missions, May 28th to June 1st, was submitted in the form of sketches at a joint meeting of the Aircraft (Production) Board and the joint Army and Navy Technical Board, June 4th. The first sample was an 8-cylinder model, delivered to the Bureau of Standards, July 3rd, 1917. The 8-cylinder model, however, was never put into production, as advices from France indicated that demands for increased power would make the 8-cylinder model obsolete before it could be produced.

"Work was then concentrated on the 12-cylinder engine, and one of the experimental engines passed the fifty-hour test August 25th, 1917.

"After the preliminary drawings were made, engineers from the leading engine builders were brought to the Bureau of Standards, where they inspected the new designs and made suggestions, most of which were incorporated in the final design. At the same time expert production men were making suggesstions that would facilitate production.

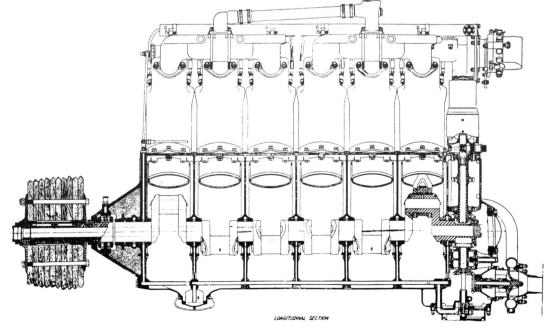

LONGITUDINAL SECTION

Longitudinal section of the Liberty Twelve

"The Liberty 12-cylinder engine passed the fifty-hour test, showing, as the official report of August 25th, 1917 records, that the fundamental construction is such that very satisfactory service, with a long life and high order of efficiency, will be given by this power plant, and that the design has passed from the experimental stage into the field of proven engines.

"An engine committee was organised informally, consisting of engineers and production managers of the Packard, Ford, Cadillac, Lincoln, Marmon and Trego companies. This committee met at frequent intervals, and it is to this group of men that the final development of the Liberty engine is largely due."

The prime consideration of the designing engineers was to have a motor that would be efficient from every modern standpoint, and at the same time suitable for production on a rapid basis. Both results have apparently been achieved.

The following dimensions and characteristics are of interest :—

General Data.

Number and arrangement of cylinders	Twelve-Vee
Included angle	45 deg.
Bore	5 in.
Stroke	7 in.
Stroke-bore ratio	1.4 : 1
Area of one piston	19.635 sq. in.
Total piston area	234.62 sq. in.
Swept volume of one cylinder	137.445 cu. ins.
Displacement of motor	1649.5 cu. in.
Compression ratio (Army)	5 4 : 1
Compression ratio (Navy)	5. : 1
Normal brake h.p.	400 at 1750 r.p.m.
Type of Valve gear	Overhead cam shaft and valve rockets
Number of carburettors	Two Duplex Zenith

Valves.

Number per cylinder	One inlet and one exhaust
Outside diameter	$2\frac{3}{4}$ in.
Port diameter	$2\frac{1}{2}$ in.
Width of seat	$\frac{1}{8}$ in.
Angle of seat	30 deg.
Valve lift (inlet)	7/16 in.
Valve lift (exhaust)	$\frac{3}{8}$ in.
Diameter of stem	7/16 in.
Length of valve	6 3/16 in.
Number of springs per valve	2 concentric
Length of spring in position	2 3/16 in.
Mean diameter of coils (large spring)	1 7/16 in.
Mean diameter of coils (small spring)	1 in.
Inlet rocker clearance	015 in.
Exhaust rocker clearance	020 in.
Included angles of valves	27 deg.

Cylinders.

Overall height of cylinders	16 13/16 in.
Length of projection in crankcase	57/64 in.
Diameter of cylinder over water-jacket	$6\frac{3}{8}$ in. max.
Diameter of cylinder over water-jacket	5 13/16 in. min.
Thickness of flange (base)	$\frac{1}{4}$ in.
Number of studs	10
Diameter of stud	$\frac{3}{8}$ in.
Thickness of water-jacket	3/64 in.
Thickness of cylinder head	3/16 in.
Thickness of combustion chamber-wall	5/32 in.
Thickness of cylinder barrel	$\frac{1}{8}$ in.
Number of reinforcing ribs	8
Thickness of valve ports	$\frac{1}{8}$ in.
Diameter of port at valve	$2\frac{1}{2}$ in.
Diameter of port at flange	$2\frac{1}{8}$ in.
Number of spark plugs	2 per cylinder

Pistons.

Type of piston (Army)	Crowned
Type of piston (Navy)	Flat
Material	Aluminium
Length of piston	5 in.
Length to diameter ratio	1 : 1
Number of rings per piston	3
Position of rings	Above gudgeon pin
Width of rings	$\frac{1}{4}$ in.
Width of lands	$\frac{1}{8}$ in.
Distance from bottom to centre of gudgeon pin	2 in.
Thickness of head	$\frac{3}{8}$ in.
Thickness of wall at bottom	3/16 in.
Diameter of gudgeon pin	$1\frac{1}{4}$ in.
Thickness of gudgeon pin wall	$\frac{1}{8}$ in.

Connecting Rods.

Type	Forked
Length between centres	$11\frac{7}{8}$ in.
Ratio length to crank throw	3.49 : 1
Small end bearing	Bronze bushing
Outside diameter of bushing	$1\frac{3}{8}$ in.
Outside diameter	1 11/16 in.
Type of section	"I"
Depth	1 5/16 in.
Width	15/16 in.
Thickness of flange	3/32 in.
Large end bearing	Bronze, babbit lined
Inside diameter	$2\frac{3}{8}$ in.
Outside diameter	2 13/16 in.
Length	$2\frac{1}{2}$ in.
Thickness of babbit	1/16 in.

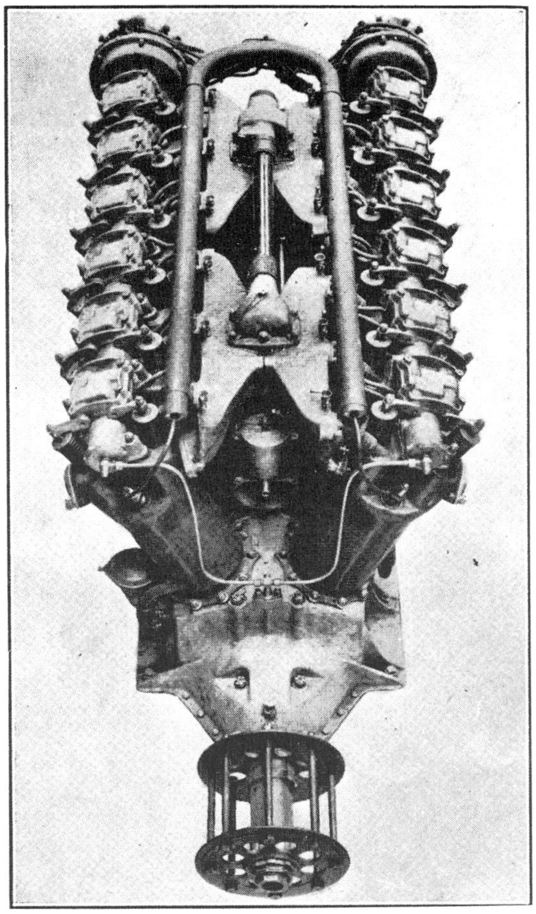

Three-quarter Top View from Airscrew End, Liberty Engine.

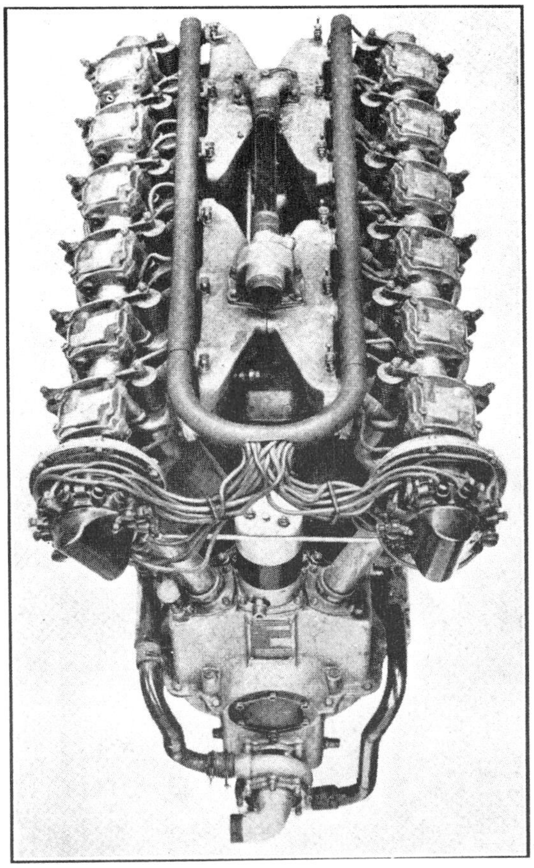

Three-quarter Top View from Pump End, Liberty Engine.

Crankshaft.

Number of bearings (Main)	7
Cylinder centres	$6\frac{1}{2}$ in.
Crank pins :	
Outside diameter	$2\frac{3}{8}$ in.
Inside diameter	$1\frac{1}{4}$ in.
Length diameter	$2\frac{1}{2}$ in.
Main bearings :	
Outside diameter	$2\frac{5}{8}$ in.
Inside diameter	$1\frac{3}{8}$ in.
Length	2 in.
Length (propeller end)	$4\frac{1}{2}$ in.
Crank Webs :	
Width	$2\frac{3}{4}$ in.
Thickness	1 in.
Radius of fillets	$\frac{1}{8}$ in.
Weight of shaft	103 lbs.

Camshaft.

Diameter of shaft	1 in.
Inside diameter	11/16 in.
Number of bearings	7
Length of bearing (5 intermediate)	$3\frac{1}{8}$ in.
Length of bearing (gear end)	$2\frac{3}{4}$ in.
Length of bearing (front end)	$3\frac{1}{4}$ in.
Width of cam face	$\frac{3}{8}$ in.
Number of cams per cylinder	1 inlet and 1 exhaust
Diameter of gear flange	$2\frac{5}{8}$ in.
Thickness of gear flange	3/16 in.
Diameter of bolt circle	2 in.
Number of bolts	7
Diameter of bolts	$\frac{1}{4}$ in.
P. D. of gear	6 in.
Number of teeth	48
Width of face	$\frac{1}{2}$ in
Camshaft housing	Barrel type
Material	Aluminium
P. D. of pinion	2 in.
Number of teeth	16
Width of face	$\frac{1}{2}$ in.
Diameter of inclined drive shaft	$\frac{3}{4}$ in.

Crankcase (upper).

Material	Aluminium
Thickness of wall	3/16
Thickness of cylinder pads	$\frac{1}{2}$ in.
Thickness of supporting flange	3/16 in.
Centre distance of motor support bolts	$16\frac{3}{4}$ in.

Crankcase (lower).

Material	Aluminium
Thickness of wall	$\frac{1}{8}$ in.

Lubrication.

Type	Forced feed
Type of pumps	Rotary gear
No. of pumps	1 double pressure and 1 scavenging
Ratio of pump speed to crankshaft speed	1.5 : 1

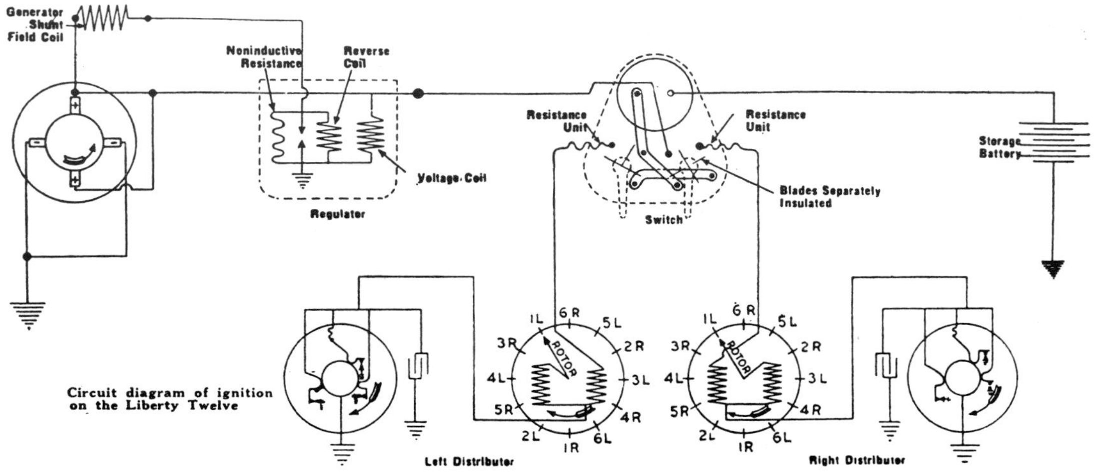

Circuit diagram of ignition on the Liberty Twelve

LIBERTY—*continued.*

IGNITION.					
Type	..	..	..		Battery and generator
Firing order	..	..	..		L 1-9-5-11-3-7,
					R 8-4-12-6-10-2
Number of plugs per cylinder			..		2
Type of plug	..	..	..		A, C.
Ratio of generator speed to crank-					
shaft speed..		..			1.5 : 1

COOLING SYSTEM.					
Type	..	..	..		Water cooled
Pump	..	..	..		1 centrifugal

Diameter of inlet pipe	..	..	2 in.
Diameter of outlet pipe	..		$1\frac{3}{4}$ in.
Number of outlets	..	..	2
Diameter of rotor	..	..	$3\frac{1}{8}$ in.
Ratio of pump speed to crankshaft			
speed	..	..	1.5 : 1
Water temperature inlet	..		155° F.
Water temperature outlet	..		175° F.

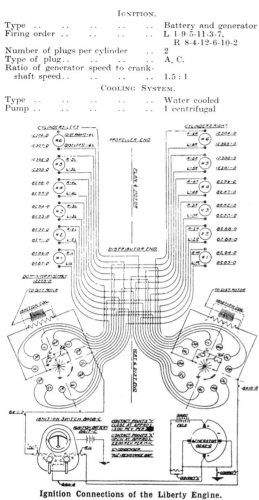

Ignition Connections of the Liberty Engine.

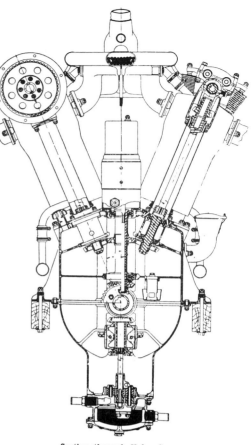

Transverse Section through Cylinders.

Section through Valve Gears.

MAYBACH (German).

MAYBACH MOTORENBAU G.m.b.H., Friedrichshafen.

Constructed by the Canstatt-Daimler Co., Canstatt.

Herr Maybach was formerly of the Daimler Motor Co., and collaborateur of Gottlieb Daimler. Maybach developed and specialized in the German airship engine, which is exclusively used on the *Zeppelin*, *Schütte-Lanz* and *Parseval* craft.

THE 300 H.P. MAYBACH ENGINE.

The following is extracted from the Official Report on the 300 h.p Maybach engine and is published by courtesy of Technical Department of the Air Ministry, to whom the thanks of the Editor are due.

INTRODUCTORY NOTE.

The general distinctive features of the design of the Maybach Aero Engines are comparatively speaking, as well known amongst aeronautical engineers in this country as any of the enemy aero engines in service ; firstly, by reason of the adoption of the old Wolseley-Maybach aero engines, the designs of which was acquired before the war for airship work, and which was based on the design of the original Maybach engine ; and, secondly, through the publication of the somewhat incomplete details of construction of the Zeppelin-Maybach engines and their installation, which were collected under great difficulties from the remains of the several Zeppelin airships brought down during the war.

These engines, in almost every case, were so badly damaged by fire that it was found almost impossible at the time to compile any really detailed report on their design, or of their power and general performance.

A new and more powerful type of Maybach engine is now being used in service by the enemy, which, according to French reports, develops over 300 h.p., and which possesses great efficiency.

During the past few months several of the latest type of Rumpler machines have been captured fitted with the new 300 h.p. Maybach engines. These engines in their general design follow more or less the principle of the Zeppelin-Maybach 240 h.p. engines, and a detailed report, together with a full description of the constructional details and the general running performance of the new engine, is herewith given.

The following report on the design of the 260/300 h.p. Maybach engines is based on a detailed examination of the engine (No. 1261) taken from a Rumpler two-seater biplane (G. 120), known as the C.4 type. This machine was brought down in France by a shot which perforated the carburetter and water pump, on Jan. 18th, 1918. The machine was, unfortunately, completely destroyed by fire on landing, but the engine was captured intact and little damaged. After slight repairs this

Induction side view of Engine

(Note.—The Airscrew Hub Flange Bolts are not those normally used.)

engine has been put into running condition and tested for power, consumption, etc., at R.A.E. The results of these tests are given in the following report, together with metallurgical analyses and mechanical tests of materials and alloys used in the principal parts of the engine.

Compared with the 260 h.p. Mercédès engines, fitted in these machines, the new Maybach engines are credited with attaining an increase of 200 r.p.m. at altitudes above 2,000 ft., and also possess greater efficiency in speed and climb in the Rumpler biplanes.

Total weight of machine fully loaded, approx. = 3,439 lbs.

GENERAL FEATURES.

The 300 h.p. Maybach presents several unusual and interesting details, and as compared with the old 240 h.p. Zeppelin-Maybach design, the new engines are undoubtedly a great improvement in general design and efficiency. The quality of the workmanship of every part, including the exterior finish throughout, is exceptionally good, and the working clearances are carried to very fine limits. Compared with any other of the types of enemy engines, the workmanship is undoubtedly of a very much more finished nature ; every part, nevertheless, shows the usual German characteristics of strength and reliability, combined with standardisation of parts and ease of manufacturing, in preference to the saving of weight

The general lay-out of this engine follows the usual German six-cylinder vertical type. The compression ratio is exceptionally high, viz., 5.94 : 1, which necessitates the use of very heavy pistons and connecting rods ; in these particulars this engine follows the previous Maybach practice, but the adoption of a cast-iron floating bush in the little end bearing is an interesting development.

Four overhead valves per cylinder are fitted—*i.e.*, two inlet and two exhaust. These are operated by rocker levers mounted on roller bearings in brackets fixed to the cylinder heads, as shown in Fig. 2, and by push rods on each side of the cylinders actuated by separate inlet and exhaust camshafts.

The camshafts run in plain bronze bearings in the crank-chamber, and are splash lubricated.

Little alteration has been made in the design of the massive crankshaft, which runs on plain white-metal lined bearings throughout, and is provided with the well-known Maybach type centrifugal pressure lubrication system to the crank-pins, thence to the gudgeons pins through small pipes, inside the hollow connecting rods.

The three separate and detachable gear oil pumps, which are situated in the bottom of the base chamber, are of new design.

Exhaust side view of Engine, showing rear end carburetter and throttle indicator, water pump, magnetos, wireless dynamo clutch-pulley, petrol pump and gun gear, and also the crankcase ventilator, which has been cut open to show oil trap.

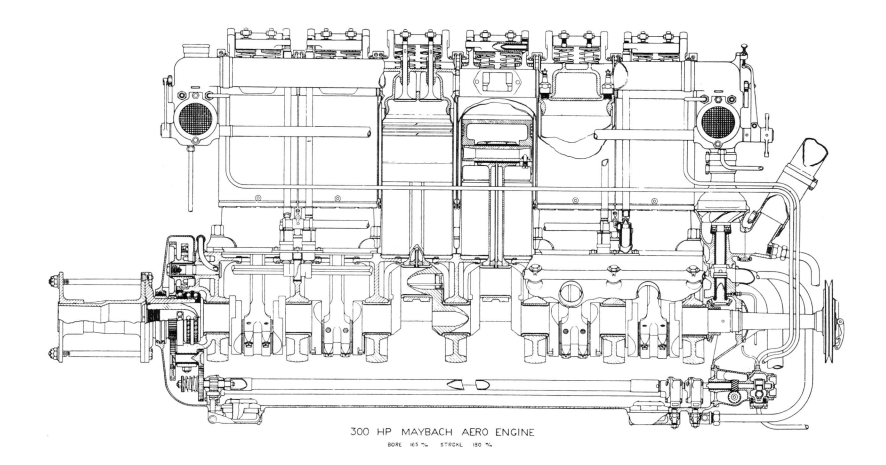

300 HP MAYBACH AERO ENGINE

BORE 165 ⁒ STROKE 180 ⁒

The pump driving shaft at the front end is driven through a ratchet gear on the front scavenger pump, apparently with the object of preventing an air lock in the lubrication system in the event of back-firing.

A double-acting, oil-sealed petrol pump of unusual design is now fitted. This is driven off an extension of the main oil pump spindle at the rear end of the base chamber, and works, of course, in conjunction with the two separate carburetters. These are of the well-known Maybach type, and have been only slightly modified; as shown in Figs. 1 and 2, they are attached, as in the Zeppelin engines, to the front and rear cylinder water jackets. A full description of the functions and workings of this interesting type of carburetter is given towards the end of this report.

The well-known Maybach induction type starting gear is fitted, but is slightly modified in design.

The whole of the induction system and the oil-condensing crankcase ventilating system is an interesting point in the design of this engine, as is also the method of attaching the airscrew-hub driving flange on the tapered front end of the crankshaft.

Practically no alteration has been made to the general design of the very simple and efficient type of water pump, which delivers directly into the bottom of the rear end carburetter water jacket as in the old Maybach engines. Ignition is by two Z.H.6 type Bosch magnetos, which are driven directly off the rear ends of the camshafts; the position of the sparking plugs in the cylinder heads is a point of interest dealt with in detail in the following description.

ENGINE TEST REPORT AT ROYAL AIRCRAFT ESTABLISHMENT. 5-4-18.

CALIBRATION AND ENDURANCE TESTS.

The Maybach engine (No. 1261), after several slight repairs had been carried out to the cylinders and propeller hub flange and coupling, was erected on a test bed, coupled to a Heenan and Froude dynamometer, and submitted to the following power and consumption tests, including a one hour's duration test at normal speed. The results of the calibration tests are as follows :—

R.P.M.	1,200	1,300	1,400	1,500
B.H.P.	258	279	294.5	304.5
Brake, M.E.P.	120.5	120.3	118	113.9
Petrol consumption in pints b.h.p. hour	0.53	0.52	0.526	0.545

The results of these tests are shown graphically on the diagram.

ONE HOUR TEST.

At the conclusion of the above tests a run of one hour's duration at normal revolutions (1,400 r.p.m.) was carried out with the following results :—

Cylinder, complete.

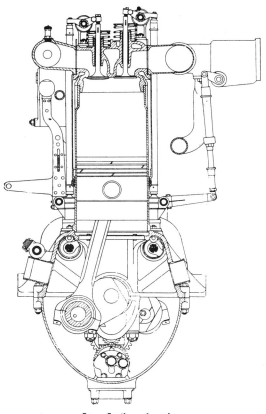

Cross Section of engine.

Calibration Curves. R.A.E. Tests.

Average b.h.p.	290
Petrol consumption	20 gallons = 0.55 points per b.h.p. hour.
Oil consumption	11 pints = 0.038 pints per b.h.p. hour.
Oil pressure	5 lbs./sq. in.
Oil temperature	67°C.
Water temperature (inlet)	57°C.
Water temperature (outlet)	68°C

VALVE TIMING DURING TESTS.

Inlet.	Exhaust.
O. 8°E.	O. 33°E.
C. 35°L.	C. 7°L.
Magneto advance	38°E.

Running was steady at all speeds between 900 and 1,400 r.p.m., but owing to the fact that the propeller hub flange on the crank-shaft was damaged, and was running slightly out of truth, the vibration became excessive above 1,400 r.p.m.

Considerable trouble was experienced with the water connection between the cylinders on the exhaust side. The running became unsteady below 900 r.p.m.

DISTRIBUTION.

Owing to the exhaust manifold being fitted as part of the engine starting gear, it was not possible to form an idea of the distribution.

GENERAL DATA.

Make of engine and rated h.p.	Maybach 300 h.p.
Type number	1261
Number and arrangement of cylinders	Six vertical
Bore	165.0 mm. = 6.50 ins.
Stroke	180.0 mm. = 7.09 ins.
Stroke/Bore ratio	1.09 : 1.
Area of one piston	213.825 sq. cm. = 33.2 sq. ins.
Total piston area of engine	1282.95 sq. cm. = 199.2 sq. ins.
Swept volume of one cylinder	3848.85 cu. cm. = 235.3 cu. ins.
Total swept volume of engine	23093.1 cu. cm. = 1412.0 cu. ins.
Clearance volume of one cylinder	778.9 cu. cm. = 47.54 cu. ins.
Compression ratio	5.95 : 1.
Normal b.h.p. and speed	294.0 b.h.p. at 1400 r.p.m.
Maximum b.h.p. and speed	304.5 b.h.p. at 1500 r.p.m.
Normal b.m.e.p.	117.7 lbs. per sq. in. at 1400 r.p.m.

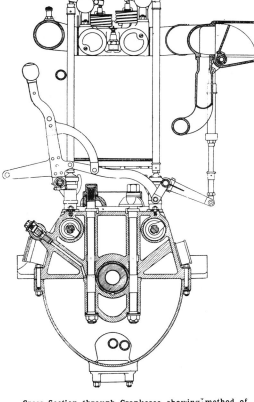

Cross Section through Crankcase, showing method of holding Cylinders and Journal Bearings.

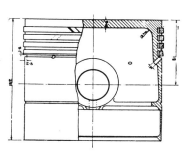
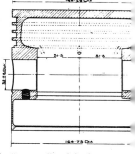

Details of Pistons, gudgeon pins and floating small-end bushes.

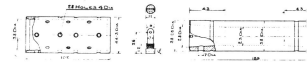

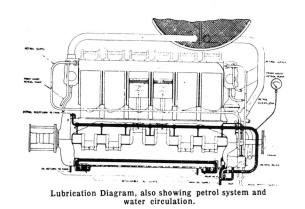

Lubrication Diagram, also showing petrol system and water circulation.

Maximum b.m.e.p.	120.5 lbs. per. sq. in. at 1200 r.p.m.
Piston speed	1654.0 ft. per min. at 1400 r.p.m.
Mechanical efficiency (calculated)	86.0%
Indicated mean pressure (calculated)	137.0 lbs. sq. in.
Fuel consumption per b.h.p. hour	0.526 pint = 0.473 lbs.
Brake thermal efficiency	28.9%
Indicated thermal efficiency	33.6%
Air standard efficiency	51.0%
Relative efficiency	65.9%
Cu. in. of swept volume per b.h.p.	4.80 cu. ins.
Sq in. of piston area b.h.p.	0.678 sq. ins.
H.p. per cu. ft. of swept volume	360.0 b.h.p.
H.p. per sq. ft. of piston area	212.4 b.h.p.
Direction of rotation of crankshaft	Anti-clockwise (facing propeller).
Direction of rotation of propeller	Anti-clockwise (facing propeller).
Type of Valve gear	Overhead valve rockers and push-rods
Type of starting gear	Maybach of special design.
Number of Carburetters	Two Maybach.
Bore of main jets	Variable from 0.0 to 2.5 mm.
Bore of pilot jets	Variable from 0.0 to 1.1 mm.
Fuel consumption per hour	19.33 gallons

VALVE AREAS AND GAS VELOCITIES.

Diameters.

Induction Pipe	62.0 min. = 2.44 ins.
Inlet port	45 × 67 mm. = 1.77 × 2.64 ins.
Exhaust port	45 × 67 mm. = 1.77 × 2.64 ins.
Exhaust branch pipes	66.0 mm. = 2.60 ins. (approx.).

Cross Sectional Areas.

Induction pipe	29·26 sq. cm. = 4.67 sq. ins.
Inlet port	30.15 sq. cm. = 4.67 sq. ins.
Inlet valve (π dh.)	4.416 sq. ins. (total).
Exhaust valve (π d·h.)	4.366 sq. ins. (total).
Exhast port	30.15 sq. cm. = 4.67 sq. ins.
Exhaust branch pipes	34.11 sq. cm. = 5.31 sq. ins.

Gas Velocities.

Induction pipe	196.1 ft. per sec.
Inlet port	196.1 ft. per sec.
Inlet valve	208.0 ft. per sec.
Exhaust valve	210.0 ft. per sec.
Exhaust port	196.1 ft. per sec.
Exhaust branch pipes	172.5 ft. per sec.

INLET VALVES (Two per cylinder).

Outside diameter	54.0 mm. = 2.126 ins.
Port diameter (in cylinder head)	48.0 mm. = 1.89 in.
Width of seating	3.5 mm. = 0.137 in.
Angle of seating	30°
Radius under valve head	20.0 mm. = 0.787 in.
Lift of valve	9.45 mm. = 0.372 in.
Diameter of stem	11.0 mm. = 0.433 in.
Over-all length of valve	136.5 mm. = 5.373 ins.
Number of springs per valve	One.
Free length of spring	52.5 mm. = 2.066 in.
Length of spring in position (no lift)	39.5 mm. = 1.55 in.
Mean diameter of coils	51.0 mm. = 2.00 in.
Gauge of wire	No. 6 B.W.G.
Ratio length of spring/lift of valve	4.21 : 1.
Weight of valve complete with spring	0.843 lb.
Weight of spring bare	0.281 lb.
Inlet valve opens, deg. on crank	8° early.
Inlet valve closes, deg. on crank	35° late.
Period of induction	223°
Inlet tappet clearance	0.3 mm. = 0.012 in.

EXHAUST VALVES (Two per cylinder).

Outside diameter	54.0 mm. = 2.126 ins.
Port diameter (in cylinder head)	48.0 mm. = 1.89 in.
Width of seating	3.5 mm. = 0.127 in.
Angle of seating	30°.
Radius under valve head	9.0 mm. = 0.354 in.
Lift of valve	9.34 mm. = 0.368 in
Diameter of stem	11.0 mm. = 0.433 in.
Length of valve guide	80.0 mm. = 3.149 ins.
Over-all length of valve	152.5 mm. = 6.00 ins.
Number of springs per valve	One.
Free length of spring	52.5 mm. = 2.06 ins.
Length of spring in position (no lift)	39.5 mm. = 1.55 in.
Mean diameter of coils	51.0 mm. = 2.00 ins.
Gauge of wire	No. 6 B.W.G.
Ratio length of spring/lift of valve	4.21 : 1.
Weight of valve complete with spring	0.881 lb.
Weight of spring bare	0.281 lb.
Exhaust valve opens, deg. on crank	33° early.
Exhaust valve closes, deg. on crank	7° late.
Period of exhaust	220°.
Exhaust tappet clearance	0.4 mm.

INERTIA FORCES, BEARING LOADS, ETC.

Weight of piston, complete with rings and gudgeon-pin	14.05 lbs.
Weight per sq. in. of piston area	0.4235 lb.
Weight of connecting-rod complete	8.93 lbs.
Weight reciprocating part of connecting-rod	3.305 lbs.
Total reciprocating weight per cylinder	17.355 lbs.

Weight per sq. in. piston area	0.538 lb.
Length of connecting-rod (centres)	310.0 mm. = 12.20 ins.
Ratio. Connecting-rod/crank throw	3.445 : 1.
Inertia, lbs. sq. in. piston area, top centre	137.0 lbs. sq. in.
Inertia, lbs. sq. in. piston area, bottom centre	75.5 lb. sq. in.
Inertia, lbs. sq. in. piston area, mean	53.25 lbs. sq. in.
Weight of rotating mass of connecting rod	5.625 lbs.
Total centrifugal pressure	1106 lbs.
Centrifugal pressure, lbs. sq. in. piston area	34.4 lbs. sq. in.
Mean average fluid pressure, including compression	48.0 lb. sq. in.
Mean average loading on crankpin bearing, total from all sources in terms of lbs. sq. in. piston area	118.0 lbs. sq. in.
Diameter of crankpin	66.0 mm. = 2.598 ins.
Rubbing velocity	15.85 ft. sec.
Effective projected area of big end bearing	43.23 sq. cm. = 6.70 sq. ins.
Ratio. Piston. area/projected area of big end bearing	4.96 : 1.
Mean average loading on big end bearing	585 lbs. sq. in.
Load factor on big end bearing	9270 lbs. ft. sec.

CYLINDERS.

Over-all height of bare cylinder from top of base chamber	479.5 mm. = 18.87 ins.
Depth of spigot at base of cylinder	3.5 mm. = 0.13 in.
Diameter of cylinder over water jacket	185.0 mm. = 7.28 ins.
Valve centres (between inlet and exhaust)	63.0 mm. = 2.48 ins.

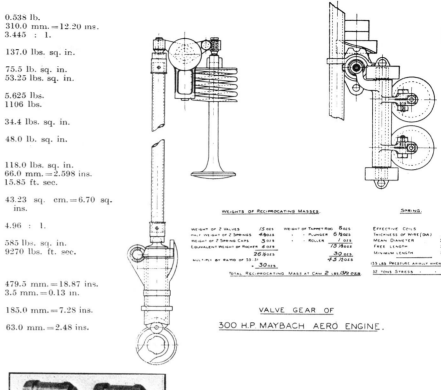

VALVE GEAR OF
300 H.P. MAYBACH AERO ENGINE.

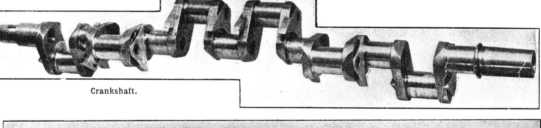

Crankshaft.

Top half of Crankcase.

Inside view of Crankcase, top half, shown upside down

MAYBACH—*continued*.

Thickness of flange at base of cylinders	12.0 mm. = 0.47 in.
Number of holding-down studs per cylinder	Four.
Diameter of holding-down studs	19.0 mm. = 0.74 in.
Thickness of water jacket	1.0 mm. = 0.039 in.
Mean thickness of combustion chamber wall	8.0 mm. = 0.31 in.
Mean thickness of cylinder barrel	3.0 mm. = 0.11 in.
Tensile stress	6.640 lbs. sq. in. (approx.) (Assumed maximum pressure 450 lbs. sq. in.)

PISTON.

Type of piston	Cast-iron (flat crown.)
Diameter at top	164.25 mm. = 6.466 ins.
Diameter at bottom	164.75 mm. = 6.486 ins.
Length	151.00 mm. = 5.944 ins.
Ratio. Piston length/cylinder bore	0.914 : 1
Number of rings per piston	Three piston rings, one scraper ring.
Position of rings	All above gudgeon-pin.
Width of rings	6.5 mm. = 0.255 in.
Gap of rings in cylinder	1.39 mm. = 0.055 in.

CONNECTING ROD.

Length between centres	310.0 mm. = 12.205 ins.
Ratio. Connecting rod/crank throw	3.44 : 1.
Little end bearing type	Floating cast iron bush.
Floating bush, diameter, inside	38.0 mm. = 1.496 in.
Floating bush, diameter, outside	44.3 mm. = 1.743 in.
Floating bush, effective length inside	93.0 mm. = 3.661 ins.
Floating bush, projected area of bearing on gudgeon-pin	35.35. sq. cm. = 5.48 sq. ins.
Ratio. Piston area/projected area of little end bearing	6.06 : 1.
Big end bearing. Type	Bronze shell lined white metal.
Big end bearing. Diameter	66.0 mm. = 2.598 ins.
Big end bearing. Length (actual).	73.56 mm. = 2.893 ins.
Big end bearing. Length (effective)	65.5 mm. = 2.580 ins.
Big end bearings. Projected area.	43.23 sq. cm. = 6.700 sq. ins.
Ratio. Piston area/projected area of big end bearing	4.96 : 1.
Number of big end bolts	Four.
Full diameter of bolts	14.0 mm. = 0.551 in.
Diameter at bottom of threads	12.0 mm. = 0.472 in.
Total cross sectional area, bottom of threads	4.520 sq. cm. = 0.70 sq. in.
Pitch of threads	1.5 mm.
Total load on bolts at 1,400 r.p.m.	5,824 lbs.
Total load on bolts at 1,600 r.p.m.	7,602 lbs.
Stress per sq. in. at 1,400 r.p.m.	8.320 lbs. sq. in.
Stress per sq. in. at 1,600 r.p.m.	10.860 lbs. sq. in.

CRANKSHAFT.

Number and type of main bearings	Seven bronze shell lined white metal
Cylinder centres	187.0 mm. = 7,362 ins.
Crank-pins—	
Outside diameter	66.0 mm. = 2.598 ins.
Inside diameter	38.0 mm. = 1.496 in.
Length	74.0 mm. = 2.913 ins.
Journals—	
Outside diameter	66.0 mm. = 2.598 ins.
Inside diameter	36.0 mm. = 1.417 in.
Length, propeller end	68.0 mm. = 2.638 ins.
Length, rear end	67.0 mm. = 2.638 ins.
Length, centre	67.0 mm. = 2.638 ins.
Length, intermediate	67.0 mm. = 2.638 ins.
Crank Webs—	
Width	95.0 mm. = 3,740 ins.
Thickness	23.0 mm. = 0.906 in.
Radius at ends of Journals and crank-pins	4.5 mm. = 0.171 in.
Weight of complete shaft	99.9 lbs.

WORKING CLEARANCES.

Piston clearance, top (total)	0.75 mm. = 0.029 in.
Piston clearance, bottom (total)	0.25 mm. = 0.009 in.
Side clearance of connecting rod in piston (total)	11.8 mm. = 0.464 in.
Side clearance of big end on crank-pin (total)	0.44 mm. = 0.0173 in.
End clearance of crankshaft in main bearings	3.0 mm. = 0.118 in.
Clearance of valve stem in guide (inlet)	0.12 mm. = 0.00472 in.
Clearance of valve stem in guide (exhaust)	0.15 mm. = 0.0059 in.

LUBRICATION SYSTEM.

Number and type of oil pumps	Three, rotary gear.
Oil consumption per hour	11.0 pints.
Oil consumption per b.h.p. hour	0.037 pint.
Oil temperature	65° Centigrade.
Oil pressure	5.0 lbs. per sq. in.
Specific gravity of oil	0.899 s p.g.
Ratio, Pump speed/crankshaft speek	1 : 2.
Pump delivery (calculated at 100% volumetric efficiency	91 gallons per hour of normal engine revs.

IGNITION.

Number and type of magnetos	Two Bosch.
Firing sequence of engine	1-5-3-6-2-4.
Ignition timing (fully advanced)	38° early.
Number of plugs per cylinder	Two.
Type or plugs	Bosch 3 point.
Ratio. Magneto speed/engine speed	1.5 : 1.

COOLING SYSTEM.

Number and type of water pumps.	One centrifugal.
Diameter of inlet pipe	54.0 mm. = 2.126 ins.
Diameter of outlet pipe	50.0 mm. = 1.966 ins.
Diameter of rotor	111.0 mm. = 4.36 ins.
Water capacity of one cylinder	1284.0 cu. cm.
Number and type of radiators	One semicircular honey-comb.
Ratio. Water pump speed/engine speed	2 : 1.
Water temperature, inlet	57° Centigrade.
Water temperature, outlet	68° Centigrade.

PETROL PUMP.

Number and type of petrol pumps	One Maybach double acting.
Bore	15.0 mm. = 0.59 in.
Stroke	17.0 mm. = 0.66 in.
Normal delivery	264 pints per hour at 800 r.p.m.
Maximum delivery	630 pints per hour at 1.275 r.p.m.
Ratio. Pump speed/crankshaft speed	1. : 2.

WEIGHTS.

Weight of complete engine, dry, with propeller boss & exhaust manifold .	911 lbs.
Weight per b.h.p., ditto	3.10 lbs.
Weight of fuel per hour	139 lbs.
Weight of oil per hour (s.p.g. 0.899).	12.36 lbs.
Total weight of fuel and oil per hour	151.36 lbs.
Gross weight of engine in running order, less fuel and oil (cooling system at 0·65 lbs. per b.h.p.	1102.0 lbs.
Weight per b.h.p., ditto	3.79 lbs.
Gross weight of engine in running order, with fuel and oil for six hours (tankage at 10% weight of fuel and oil)	2100.9 lbs.
Weight per b h.p., ditto	7.14 lbs.

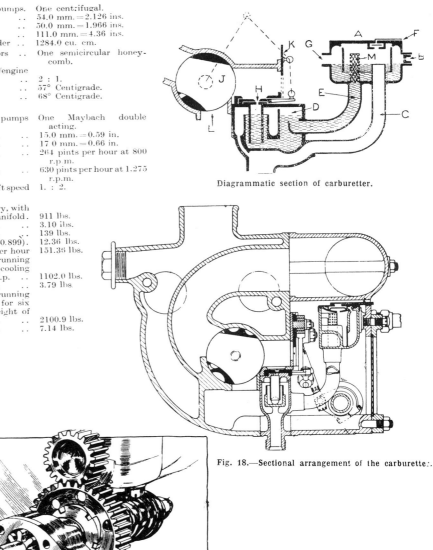

Diagrammatic section of carburetter.

Fig. 18.—Sectional arrangement of the carburetter.

The front oil pump, showing ratchet drive and section of detachable oil sump in Chamber.

Radiator fitted to centre section of Rumpler biplanes, as used with 300 h.p. Maybach and 260 h.p. Mercédès engines.

MERCÉDÈS (German).

MERCÉDÈS-DAIMLER MOTOREN GESELLSCHAFT.
Stuttgart-Untertürkheim.

Turned out early an aviation engine, which was not favoured by the German aviators, though excellent design work—for which the engine was awarded the prize of the Automobile Technic Society, as best in the B-Z £5.000 competition, 1911.

Was brought into limelight by Hirth in numerous flights, and universally adopted from 1912 even to 85-90 per cent. Is a very reliable motor.

Daimler engines were employed in the first *Zeppelin* and other early German airships, but the former Oberingenier of the company and collaborateur of Daimler, Maybach, catered for special airship wants, and Maybach airship motors are now exclusively used (see later).

The 100 h.p. Model won the chief prize in the Kaiser engine Competition, and an upside-down hanging cylinder type, never further developed, was once tried.

TYPES.

100 h.p., 6-cyl.	220 h.p. 6-cyl.
160 h.p., 6-cyl.	250 h.p. 8-cyl.
180 h.p., 6-cyl.	260 h.p. 6-cyl.
200 h.p., 6-cyl.	

160-70 h.p. Mercédès engine :

No. of cylinders : 6.
Bore : 140 m/m.
Stroke : 160 m/m.
Cylinders : Steel, cast in single units, with integral water-jackets.
Ignition : Twin Bosch magnetos.
Valves : Overhead, with overhead camshaft, bevel driven from mainshaft.
Lubrication : Forced feed.
H.P. : 160 at 1250 r.p.m.

THE 260-H.P. MERCÉDÈS ENGINE.

[The following details of the 260-h.p. Mercédès Engine have been supplied, together with the photographs and drawings, by the Technical Department of the Air Ministry, to whom the Editor desires to express his thanks.]

INTRODUCTORY NOTE.

The details of the following report on the latest type Mercédès engines and the accompanying scale sectional drawings have been collected from an investigation of the twin engines taken from the captured German aeroplane G 23, a three-seater "Gotha" biplane of the pusher type, which was brought down near Vron by Lieut. Breadner on April 23rd, 1917.

The machine was set on fire by the occupants after landing and partially destroyed, one engine being scrapped and the crankcase melted. The other engine, No. 29870, however, was little damaged, with the result that after certain repairs had been carried out, this engine was able to be put through a bench test at the Royal Aircraft Factory, where the following particulars regarding B.H.P., consumption, etc., were taken.

LEADING PARTICULARS OF THE 260-H.P. MERCÉDÈS ENGINE.

Number and arrangement of cylinders	6, vertical
Bore	160 mm., 6.30 in.
Stroke	180 mm., 7.09 in.
Stroke/Bore ratio	1.125—1.
Stroke volume of one cylinder	3.620 cub. cms., 220.82 cub. in.
Total stroke volume of engine..	21,720 cub. cms., 1.324.92 cub. in.
Area of one piston	20.1062 sq. cms., 31.164 sq. in.
Total piston area of engine	1,206.372 sq. cms., 186.984 sq. in.
Clearance volume of one cylinder	920 cub. cms., 56.12 cub. in.
Compression ratio	4.94—1.
Normal b.h.p. and speed	252 at 1,400.
Piston speed	1,653 ft. per min. at 1,400. 1,775 ft. per min. at 1,500.
Brake mean effective pressure..	107.5 lbs. per sq. in.
Cub. in. of stroke volume per b.h.p. ..	5.25.
Sq. in. of piston area per b.h.p.	0.74
H.P. per cub. ft. of stroke volume	329.14 h.p.
H.P. per sq. ft. of piston area	194.6.
Direction of rotation of crank	Anti-clock.
Direction of rotation of propeller	,,
Normal speed of propeller	E.S.
Lubrication system	Forced feed to all bearings and camshaft.
Brand of oil recommended	Sternoil (air cooled) on test.
Oil pressure recommended	No indicator.
Oil temperature recommended	Not above 60° C.
Oil consumption per hour	8.125 pints.
,, ,, ,, b.h.p. hour	.032 pints.
Specific gravity of oil ..	.9.
Type of carburetter	1 twin jet Mercédès.
Mixture control ..	Automatic.
Fuel consumption per hour	125 pints.
,, ,, ,, b.h.p. hour	.605 pints.
Specific gravity of fuel	.720.
Type of magneto	2 Z H 6.
Firing sequence of engine	Prop. 1 5 3 6 2 4.
Numbering of cylinders	Prop. 1 2 3 4 5 6.
Speed of magneto	1.5 engine speed.
Direction of rotation of magneto, facing driving end of armature	Anti-clock.
Magneto timing	31° E.
Inlet valve opens, degree on crank	1° L

Inlet valve closes, degree on crank	49° 3' L.
Maximum lift of inlet valve	10.125 mm
Diameter inlet valve ..	55.25 mm.
Area of inlet valve opening (2 valves)	35.12 sq. cm., 5.44 sq. in.
Mean gas velocity through inlet valve	151.1 ft. per second.
Clearance of inlet tappet	.018 in.
Exhaust valve opens, degrees on crank ..	50.6° E.
Exhaust valve closes, degrees on crank	17.6° E

Maximum lift of exhaust valve	10 mm.
Diameter exhaust valve	55.25 mm.
Area of exhaust valve opening (2 valves)	34.70 sq. cm., 5.4 sq. in.
Clearance of exhaust tappet	.018 in.
Speed of revolution counter drive	Camshaft speed.
Weight of engine complete without water, fuel or oil	936 lbs.
Weight per b.h.p. without water, fuel or oil	3.71 lbs.
Weight of exhaust manifold	26 lbs.

Weight of starting gear not integral with engine ..	Nil.
Weight of fuel per hour	136.8 lbs.
,, of oil per hour	9.14 lbs.
Total weight of fuel and oil per hour	145.94 lbs.
Gross weight of engine in running order, less fuel and oil	1,099 lbs. approx.
Weight per b.h.p., less fuel and oil	4.36 lbs

Fig. 1.—Inlet Side of 260-h.p. Mercédès engine.

Fig. 2.—Exhaust Side of 260-h.p. Mercédès engine.

MERCÉDÈS—*continued*.

Gross weight of engine in running order, with fuel and oil for six hours	2,072 lbs.
Weight per b.h.p., with fuel and oil for six hours	8.2 lbs.
Period of induction	228°.
,, exhaust	247°.

Fig. 3.—Magneto and Carburetter End.

Half compression cam opens exhaust	12° A.B.C.
Half compression cam closes exhaust	44° B.T.C.
Diameter of induction pipe branch	75 mm.
Diameter of induction pipe main	100 mm.
Diameter of choke tube	32 mm.
Length of connecting rod between centres	326 mm.
Diameter of crank pin	64 mm.
Length of crank pin bearing	80 mm.
Diameter of journals	64 mm.
Length of journal bearings	64 mm.
Length of front journal bearing	104 mm.
Connecting rod side-clearance (total) in piston	2.25 mm.
Total capacity of each petrol tank	95 galls.
,, ,, oil tank	7.25 galls.
,, ,, water in system	6 5 galls.
Weight of complete cylinder with valves and springs	34.25 lbs.
Weight of complete piston with rings and gudgeon pin	10.725 lbs.
Total weight of complete connecting rod with gudgeon pin bush	7 lbs.
Weight of connecting rod, big-end, complete	4 lbs. 14 oz.
Weight of connecting rod, small-end, with bush	2 lbs. 2 ozs.
Weight complete valve with spring washer and nut (inlet and exhaust)	.759 lbs.
Weight of valve rocker complete	1.246 lbs
Total weight of engine with water, including radiator, etc.	1,099 lbs. approx.
Weight of crankshaft with propeller boss	139.5 lbs.
Diameter of piston at top	159.258 mm.
,, ,, ,, bottom	159.715 mm.
Width of rings	5 mm.
Width of gap in rings in cylinder	16/1000 mm.
Diameter of water pump inlet	44 mm.
Diameter of water pump outlet	44 mm.

GENERAL DESCRIPTION.

In many respects these engines resemble the 160-h.p. Mercédès and are of the usual German aero-engine design, being of the six-cylinder vertical type, water cooled, with a massive six-throw crankshaft running in plain bearings, the design throughout aiming at strength and reliability combined with ease of manufacture in preference to the consideration of weight per b.h.p. as the primary factor in design.

The salient features of the 260-h.p. Mercédès are briefly as follows :—Notwithstanding its abnormal size, the whole engine is of very proportionate and clean design throughout, as shown in the accompanying photographs and detail drawings of the engine. The complete engine, including the propeller boss,

Fig. 4.—Airscrew End.

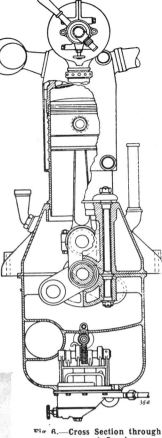

Fig 6.—Cross Section through Crankcase.

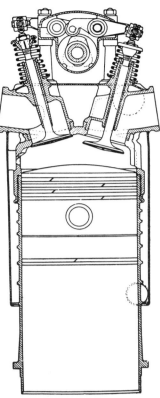

Fig. 7.—Cross Section through Cylinder and Valve Gear.

measures 6 ft. 5½ in. overall, and from the bottom of the sump to the top of the overhead camshaft casing measures approximately 3 ft. 10 in. The bore of each cylinder is 160 mm. and the stroke 180 mm. Four valves, *i.e.*, two inlet and two exhaust, are fitted in the head of each cylinder, and are operated by an overhead camshaft, running in a detachable casing of malleable cast iron supported on brackets screwed into the head of each cylinder. All the valves are interchangeable.

A half compression gear, employing a sliding camshaft device similar to that in the 160-h.p. Mercédès, is fitted to the rear end of the shaft casing.

A single carburetter employing a main jet and a slow running jet is attached to the rear end of the base chamber, taking its air supply from the interior of the base chamber through a 4-in. diameter passage cast in the bottom of the crank chamber, which is constructed with a false bottom.

The bottom halves of the crankshaft main bearing housings, or bearing caps, are cast integral with the bottom half of the crankcase ; the long bolts which secure the bearing caps pass

Fig. 5.—The Mercédès Cylinder.

through the top half of the crankcase, and are used to secure the cylinders in position by triangular clamps, a design of questionable merit, but a method which undoubtedly adds increased stiffness to the crankcase construction.

The lubrication system is forced to all bearings through the drilled crankshaft from a four-throw eccentric-driven plunger pump, which is an improved design on the 160-h.p. form of Mercédès type. The scheme embodies an "auxiliary" sump in the front end of the crankcase, and small supplementary pump plungers, which work in conjunction with the main oil pump for the purpose of feeding fresh oil into the system from the service oil tank.

Full details of this lubrication system, and also of the somewhat complicated Mercédès oil pump, are given in the following description. Two Bosch Z.H. 6 magnetos are used, driven off the camshaft vertical driving shaft, one being a starter magneto. All plugs are fitted on the induction side of the cylinders.

The water-pump driving spindle is lubricated whilst in flight by a rachet-driven grease lubricator worked by a cable and lever from the pilot's seat. An electric tachometer is driven at engine speed from the rear end of the camshaft through a flexible shaft.

DETAILS OF CONSTRUCTION.

CYLINDERS (Fig. 5).—The construction of the built-up cylinders, which are composed entirely of steel forgings and sheet steel, pressed to the form of the water jackets, is an interesting example of expert acetylene steel welding.

The method of building up the cylinders, and their general construction, is shown in the scale cross-sectional drawing. (Fig. 7).

Fig. 10.—Valves and Valve-Springs.

Fig. 8.—Double Branch Valve Tappets and Rockers.

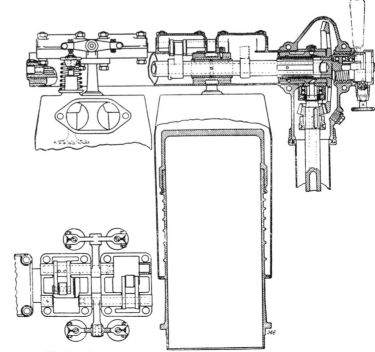

Fig. 9.—Connecting Rod, Piston, Gudgeon Pin, and Bush.

The steel cylinder barrels are screwed into the cylinder head, the pitch of the thread being 1.75 mm.

The cylinder barrels are machined from steel forgings, the thickness of the cylinder walls being 3.5 mm., this dimension being increased to 6 mm. at the holding-down base flange.

Six rectangular ribs are machined on the outer diameter of the cylinder barrel, the distance between the ribs increasing towards the base of the cylinder. The cylinder barrels extend 35 mm. below the base flanges and are of 3 mm. thickness for a depth of 12 mm.; the extension is reduced to 2.75 in thickness at the lowest part (Fig. 7).

The cylinder heads are machined from steel forgings, into which are built the four valve pockets and inlet and exhaust ports.

The valve face seatings are machined in the cylinder heads, the thickness of the crown of the cylinder head being 11 mm. The valve pockets, which are machined from steel forgings, are acetylene welded into the cylinder heads, and steel valve stem guides are pressed into the valve pockets and welded.

The valve stem guides are bushed with phosphor-bronze liners, which are pressed into the guides.

It will be noticed that the exhaust valve stem guide is considerably longer than the inlet valve stem guide.

The water-jackets are built up in four sections from sheet steel pressings 1.25 mm. in thickness, the lower section of the jacket being of barrel formation, and welded to the flange joint on the cylinder walls.

The top sections are in halves, and encircle the valve pockets, the joints being welded vertically on the centre line of the valve ports.

The top of the water-jacket is a sheet steel disc which is welded on to the flanged top sections, and the water circulation pipe connections are welded into the top and bottom of the jackets on the exhaust side.

The sparking plug bosses are fitted and welded into the cylinder barrels on the induction side just below the inlet valves.

As in the 160-h.p. Mercédès engines, the exhaust valve stem guides are water-cooled by recesses formed in each of the exhaust valve pockets, so that the water is led right up to the valve stem guides.

Considering the size of the cylinders, they are remarkably light in weight. The complete cylinder with valves, valve springs, etc., including the two brackets screwed into the cylinder head to carry the camshaft, weighs 34.25 lbs.

The PISTONS are constructed in two parts, the head which carries the gudgeon pin in projecting lugs, and the skirt of the piston, into which the head is screwed.

The head of the piston is a steel forging machined all over, the thickness of the crown being 8.5 mm. The skirt of the piston is screwed onto the head and acetylene welded at the joint; the head of the piston is slightly domed.

The skirt of the piston is of cast-iron. Three compression rings are fitted in grooves cut in the cast-iron skirt above the gudgeon pin, and a scraper ring at the base of the piston, the width of the rings being 5 mm.

All the rings are split at a diagonal gap of 45° and no locating pegs are fitted to maintain the positions of the rings. The gudgeon pin, which is 37 mm. in diameter, projects through the lugs on the piston head, and fits into the piston skirt, flush with the outside diameter. The gudgeon pin is fixed by an 8 mm. set screw, screwed into the end of the gudgeon pin through the boss and locked with a split pin on the inside.

The weight of the complete piston with gudgeon pin and bush is 10.93 lbs.

VALVES AND VALVE GEAR.—As previously mentioned, the twin inlet and exhaust valves are interchangeable. The maximum diameter of the head of all valves is 60 mm.; the lift of both the inlet and exhaust valves is 10 mm.; and the clearance between the end of valve stem and adjustment screw of the arm rocker is 0.018 in. The general arrangement of the valves and rocker arms is clearly shown in the cross-sectional scale drawing (Fig. 7). In this drawing the section is taken through the centre of the cylinder as far as the top of the cylinder barrel,

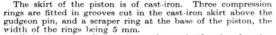

Fig. 11.—Arrangement of Camshaft and Half Compression Gear.

MERCÉDÈS *continued.*

and above this point the section is shown through one inlet and one exhaust valve, and valve gear.

The valves are operated by a single overhead camshaft, working in a detachable casing of special alloy machined all over, which is supported on twin T brackets which are screwed into the head of each cylinder.

The camshaft runs on seven phosphor-bronze plain bearings, which are mounted in aluminium bushes fitted into the bore of the camshaft casing, each bush being located by a tapered grub-screw.

The method of operating the twin valves off one cam and the general design of the camshaft and camshaft casing is of interesting design. The details of this are shown in the sectional drawings (Fig. 11).

The spindle of each rocker lever is mounted on three bearings in the camshaft casing, and so designed that the cam operates the arm of the rocker lever inside the camshaft casing, whilst the other arm of the rocker operates the valve outside the casing. This arm works between two outer bearings of the rocker spindle and is situated between the separated compartments of the camshaft casing.

On the end of the outer rocker arm a double branch tappet arm is fixed which operates the twin valves (Fig. 8).

Although these branch arms do not swivel upon the valve rocker, they are not secured by a set screw or pin, being merely pressed on to the ends of the rocker arm and easily driven off.

The spindles of the valve rockers are carried directly in the camshaft casing, no gun-metal bearing liners being fitted.

The inner arms of the rocker levers, which are worked by the cams, are fitted with hardened steel rollers. The diameter of the valve stem is 11 mm., and each valve works in a phosphor-bronze bush in the valve stem guide, as already mentioned. Each valve works at an angle of 15° to the perpendicular axis of the cylinder centre line. Single helical valve springs are fitted and measure 39 mm. at the base of the coil, tapering to 31 mm. at the top.

Conical based adjusting nuts are provided inside the valve spring washers for adjusting the valve springs. Details of these are shown in the sectional drawings.

Camshaft Drive and Half Compression Gear.—The camshaft is driven through a vertical shaft by the main distribution bevel gear mounted on the end of the crankshaft by four splines.

The method of attaching the small driving bevel gear to the top end of the vertical driving shaft is interesting. The bevel gear pinion is detachable from the shaft, and is designed so that it may be adjusted for the correct mesh in the teeth of the camshaft-driven bevel wheel. Full details of this gear are shown in the sketch Fig. 11.

The driving end of the shaft is machined and ground parallel to 23 mm. diameter, and is fitted with a key, onto which is driven a ground taper on the bottom extension of the bevel pinion, which is split by four saw-cuts. A collar, screwing on to the lower extension of the bevel pinion, locks it securely on the vertical driving shaft.

Half Compression Gear.—In order to allow these large engines to be more easily turned over, a half compression gear is provided.

This is similar in design to that fitted on the 160-h.p. Mercédès engines.

In this type of compression release gear the camshaft is designed to slide longitudinally in its bearings, and in doing so, it brings into operation a small cam situated on the mid neutral axis of the exhaust cam, but not of course on the actual cam face.

To allow for the sliding movement of the camshaft in its bearings without disturbing the mesh of the driving bevel gears, the large driven bevel gear is provided with six rectangular serrations, which engage with corresponding serrations cut in the end of the camshaft. The bevel gear is mounted in a split

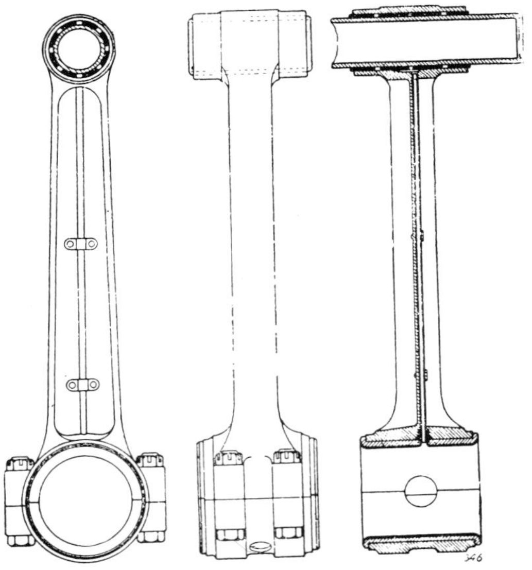

Fig. 12.—Details of Connecting Rods.

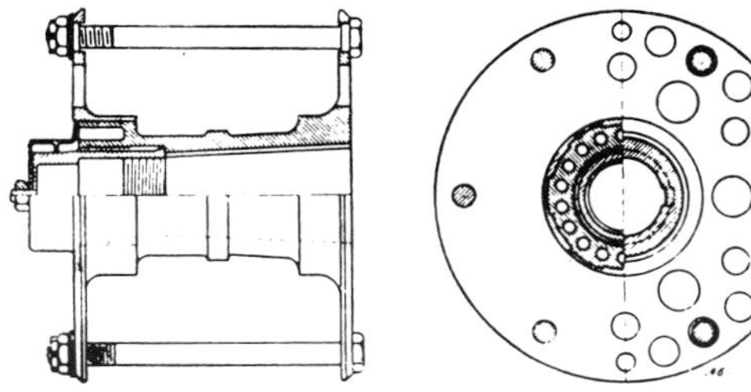

Fig. 13.—Airscrew Boss and Locking Device.

gun-metal bearing which is driven into the rear end of the camshaft casing. The sliding movement of the camshaft is effected by means of a hand lever, which is set at right angles to the axis of the camshaft, and attached to a gun-metal collar, having a five start square-thread screw of 23-mm. pitch cut on its inner diameter.

This collar, which is located in an aluminium housing, operates a corresponding screw thread cut on the outer diameter of a steel sleeve, and inside the sleeve is contained a double thrust ball race and collar, which is fixed to the rear end of the camshaft. (See Fig. 11.)

In action the partial rotation of the half compression lever on the axis of the camshaft rotates the quick-thread screw of the sleeve, which pulls or pushes the end of the camshaft in its bearings through the serrated bore of the driven bevel gear. When the camshaft is drawn to its limit of movement towards the rear, the half compression cam is drawn into line with the roller end of the exhaust valve rocker arm, thus giving a slight lift to the exhaust valve as the camshaft rotates.

The half compression cam is so positioned on the camshaft as to open the exhaust valve 12° after bottom dead centre on the compression stroke, and to close it 44° before top dead centre.

The hardened steel rollers on the cam rocker arms are bevelled off at 45° on one side to allow of easy engagement of the half compression cam, which is also bevelled at 45°.

The details of this gear are clearly shown in the scale longitudinal sectional drawing of the rear end of the camshaft driving gear (Fig. 11).

Connecting Rods.—The connecting rods are of normal design and are of H section forgings machined from steel forgings, and measure 326 mm. between centres. The total weight of the complete connecting rod, including the small-end bush, is 7 lb. The weight of the big end complete is 4 lb. 14 oz., and the weight of the small end 2 lb. 2 oz. [Presumably the connecting rod was cut exactly midway and the weights represent each half of the rod.—Ed.]

The thickness of the centre web of the H section is 2.5 mm., and that of the two outer webs is 3.5 mm. The diameter of the big end bearings is 64 mm., and the length 80 mm. These are split in the usual manner and held by four 12-mm. bolts.

The distinctive feature of the connecting rods is the floating gudgeon pin bush, the design of which is similar to that used on the 160-h.p. Mercédès. The bush is of hardened steel ground 2.5 mm. in thickness, the outside diameter being 42 mm., and the inner diameter 37 mm. The bush is a perfect working fit in the small end, and also on the gudgeon pin; and is lubricated by 14 holes of .5 mm. drilled radially in the bush, oil being supplied by a 6-mm. pipe leading upwards from the big end bearing. The pipe, which is of soft mild steel, is attached to the central web of the connecting rod by two riveted clips. Details of the connecting rods and floating gudgeon pin bush are given in Fig. 12.

Crankshaft.—The six-throw crankshaft, which is of very massive design, weighs no less than 139 lb., including the propeller boss. The cranks are set at 120°, and the diameter of both crankpins and journals is 64 mm. The length of the front journal bearing next to the propeller is 140 mm., and the other crankshaft bearings is 64 mm.

The thickness and the width of the crank webs increase towards the front end of the crankshaft. The thickness of the front web is 29 mm., that of the second is 28 mm., whilst the remainder are all 27 mm. in thickness.

The crankshaft is bored and the webs drilled with oil passages leading from the hollow journals to the crankpins for lubricating the big end bearings in the usual manner. The holes bored in the journals and crankpins are of decreasing diameters, according to their distance from the oil pump and main delivery, as follows :—

Internal diameter of Hollow Crankshaft Journals.

Prop. end. 1	2	3	4	5	6
35 mm.	35 mm.	35 mm.	38 mm.	40 mm.	41 mm. Oil pump.

Internal diameter of Hollow Crankpins.

Prop. end. 1	2	3	4	5	6
32 mm.	33 mm.	35 mm.	38 mm.	41 mm.	43 mm. Oil pump.

The ends of the hollow journals and crankpins are plugged with sheet steel caps which are driven into the cranks, and then expanded into an annular groove cut inside the holes bored in the cranks.

To take the propeller thrust, a single thrust ball race 110 mm. in diameter is provided on the front end of the front journal bearing, and mounted in a split cage which is held in the housing of the crankcase halves.

Propeller Boss.—The propeller boss, which is mounted on a taper of the crankshaft, is secured by a single key 120 mm. long and 13 mm. wide, which is sunk in the crankshaft parallel to the taper.

The front flange is fitted on to the boss by six stepped serrations or grooves, each 29 mm. wide, and is clamped to the propeller by six 18-mm. bolts on a 230 mm. diameter circle.

The propeller boss and the front flange are both locked on the shaft by the usual Mercédès locking device, shown in the drawings of the boss (Fig. 13).

Crankcase.—The very clean design of the crankcase casting is evident in the photographic views of the engine. It is of very light section considering the size of the engine, the average thickness of the walls of the casing being 6 mm. The top and bottom halves are bolted together in the usual way by 26 10-mm. hollow bolts through the flange on the centre level of the crankshaft.

The crankshaft main bearing caps are cast as part of the bottom half of the crank chamber. The long 20-mm. bolts which secure the bearing caps at the bottom pass through the top half of the crankcase and act as the holding-down bolts for the cylinders, which are held in position by triangular bridge clamps.

The bottom ends of the cylinder barrels extend past the base flanges, and fit into the top of the crankcase; the holding-down bolts clamp each cylinder base flange at four points by the bridge pieces between each pair of cylinders.

Below the crank chamber, at the rear end is situated the main oil sump, which contains the oil pump. In the front end of the base chamber casting below the false bottom is an auxiliary service oil sump, into which the return oil from the circulation system drains through a wire gauze filter.

The central chamber of the base chamber casting between the two sumps is used as an air chamber for the dual purpose of cooling the oil and warming the air supply to the carburetter.

Air is led by two ventilating funnels on each side of the crankcase into two oval ports in the base chamber casting, and a number of fins are cast on the under side of the false bottom inside the base chamber for cooling purposes.

The air intake to the carburetter is a large passage 4 in. in diameter, cast in the left-hand side of the crank chamber and base, as shown in the sectional arrangement drawings of the engine.

Cooling fins are also cast on the under side of the sump, and four breathers are fitted into the top half of the crank chamber between the webs of the main-bearing housings.

Lubrication.

Although the general lubrication system of the 260-h.p. Mercédès engines is arranged on normal principles it is necessary to deal with the various details of the somewhat complicated construction of the plunger type oil pump, and to describe their different functions and the method of lubricating the engine as a whole.

The system of lubrication may be subdivided into three circuits :—

(*a*) The main pressure circuit, in which oil is drawn from the main oil sump at the rear of the engine and forced to the main crankshaft and connecting rod bearings, and also to the camshaft bearings.

(*b*) The supplementary pressure system, in which two auxiliary plungers of the main oil pump draw a small charge of fresh oil from the service oil tank at every stroke, and supply the main circulation with fresh oil.

(*c*) A suction "scavenger" circuit, which supplies the main oil sump from the auxiliary drain sump at the front of the base chamber. The working oil level is maintained in the rear sump by a secondary suction pump, which draws off the oil above the oil level through an overflow pipe and returns it to the service oil tank.

Oil Pump.—The oil pump is attached to the bottom of the oil sump and is of the plunger type, being somewhat similar in design to that used on the 160-h.p. Mercédès.

Two main plunger pumps for suction and delivery are employed, and three auxiliary needle plunger pumps, suspended from one of the main pump plungers, work in conjunction with piston valves on plungers at the sides of the main pumps.

Each pump and valve plunger is operated by an eccentric, and the eccentric spindle is driven transversely to the engine crankshaft by a worm gear from a lay shaft, which is driven by bevel gearing from the vertical driving shaft of the water pump; this shaft is in turn driven from the main distribution gear pinion on the rear end of the crankshaft, as shown in the sectional elevation of the engine (Fig. 6).

In its passage through the hollow camshaft the oil under pressure is fed through small holes and oil grooves cut in each of the camshaft bearings.

The camshaft rocker arm spindles are lubricated by oil thrown off the revolving cams, which deliver oil into two holes drilled side by side in the upper portion of the hollow rocker arm spindles and communicating with the bearings by small holes drilled radially in the spindle.

The lubrication of the rocker arm does not appear to have been very efficiently carried out, as it was noticed that one or more of the spindles had commenced to seize in their cast-iron brackets in the camshaft casing.

No outlet holes are provided in the rear end of the camshaft for the egress of oil, consequently the camshaft is entirely under a constant oil pressure, which finds its way through the bearings into the troughs in the bottom of the camshaft casing. The overflow oil returns to the crankcase through a 12-mm. pipe at the front end of the engine from the bottom of the air pump crankcase, and also at the rear end of the camshaft casing down the hollow vertical shaft, oil channels being cut in the under side of each of the camshaft bearing bushes.

The oil which has returned by gravity to the crankcase is led into the oil sump at the rear through two holes 30 mm. in diameter drilled in the false bottom of the base. At the forward end of the crank-chamber the oil flows into the front auxiliary sump through a wire gauze filter, already mentioned.

In action, the pulsations of the oil pump plungers are damped out in the delivery pipe by the cushioning effect of the spring loaded plunger, which communicates direct with the pump on its under side. The bottom face of the plunger is prevented from touching the bottom of the barrel by a small set screw in the base.

The lubrication of the crankshaft and connecting rod bearings is standard practice and has already been referred to. Details of this are shown in the sectional elevation of the engine.

Carburetter and Induction System.—Notwithstanding the large size of these engines only one carburetter is employed; this is situated low down at the rear end of the crankcase.

Below the float chamber is attached a petrol filter chamber, the petrol entering through a gauze cylindrical filter tube, which is screwed into the top filter chamber.

Petrol enters the bottom of the float chamber, which is of the ordinary balanced needle valve type.

The main jet, which is a plain tube with an orifice of 2.33 mm. diameter, is situated in the centre of the intake pipe, inside the choke tube. The choke tube is 32 mm. in diameter at the waist and 45 mm. at the largest diameter, top and bottom.

The throttle valve, which is of the barrel type, is 80 mm. in diameter and is mounted on ball bearings at each end; the races are 35 mm. in diameter, and are supported in recesses turned in the end covers of the gun-metal throttle valve liner, which is pressed into the cast aluminium body of the carburetter.

The dimensions of the semi-elliptical ports in the throttle valve are 80 mm. long by 50 mm. wide at the bottom side and 80 mm. × 55 mm. at the top.

The pilot jet, which is the same length as the main jet, is .89 mm. bore at the orifice. It is situated at the side of the intake passage, and communicates with an annular groove machined around the outer end of the throttle valve liner in the body of the carburetter. From this annular channel a passage communicates with the induction pipe just above the throttle valve, which when closed draws air through a V slot cut in the barrel of the throttle.

A conical suction valve supplies extra air automatically through eight holes 14 mm. in diameter drilled in the annular seating which surrounds the base of the choke tube.

Air is taken into the carburetter, as already mentioned, from the interior of the air chamber cast in the base chamber. The diameter of the air intake passage is 100 mm., and it extends inside the crankcase to the centre of the engine.

Induction Pipe.—The diameter of the induction pipe at its joint with the carburetter is 70 mm.; this diameter increases to 100 mm. as it leads upwards to the engine in a right angle bend, which is lagged with asbestos cord.

The throttle valve is water heated by pipes leading from the main water circulation pipe to a water space cast in the body of the carburetter around the throttle valve.

No device for altitude adjustment is provided on the engines examined.

The design of the induction pipe is interesting; the gas is led to the centre of the engine by the 100-mm. pipe; the gas then enters a branch pipe 70 mm. in diameter through a port 100 mm. in diameter. Thence the two branch induction pipes lead outwards to the six inlet ports of the cylinders, which are 85 mm. long and 50 mm. wide.

Ignition.—Two Bosch magnetos, type Z.H.6, are mounted on a transverse bracket at the rear end of the crankcase, one being a starter magneto, used in conjunction with a hand starter dynamo.

The magnetos are driven direct by bevel gears off the vertical camshaft driving shaft, the direction of rotation being anti-clockwise in both cases.

All 12 sparking plugs are fitted on the inlet side of the engine, and are situated directly below the inlet valves; the H.T. wires are carried in two fibre tubes attached to the sides of the cylinders on the inlet side.

Air Pump.—The air pump is driven off the front end of the camshaft, the bore being 26 mm. and the stroke 27 mm.

An adjusting screw is fitted above the release valve of the pump for regulating the strength of the spring, the released pressure being taken through the hollow stem of the adjusting screw. An oil trap is provided just below the air pump to retain any surplus oil which may find its way past the air pump valve and into the pressure pipe.

Water Pump.—The water pump extension shaft is driven through a vertical shaft off a bevel gear on the end of the crankshaft, and in the same vertical axis as the camshaft driving shaft; it is attached by a flange to the bottom of the sump, next to the oil pump.

The pump is of the centrifugal type, employing a rotary vane disc, the water entering below the bottom flanged cover through a 44-mm. port, below the rotor, and the water is delivered centrifugally from the vanes between the top and bottom of the rotor, which is also fitted with vanes upon its top side to throw the water away from the spindle.

Instead of packing glands, a hardened steel friction washer is let into a recess machined in the upper face of the rotor, and is kept in uniform contact with the face of the phosphor-bronze spindle bush by the action of a light spring, which is fitted under a ball thrust race at the driving end of the spindle.

The diameter of the outlet passages from the water pump to the cylinders is 44 mm.

Double inlet water connections between each of the six cylinders supply the water-jackets at top and bottom, the diameter of the circulation hole in the steel water-jacket being 40 mm.

[The figures in the following columns are exactly as given in the official document.—Ed.]

Tests on 260-h.p. Mercédès Engines at R.A.F. 14.7.17.

Power readings were taken at full throttle from 950 r.p.m. to 1600 r.p.m., simultaneous fuel consumption readings being taken. During this test the water outlet temperature varied from 75° to 81° C.

The water brake was then set to absorb full power at 1400 r.p.m. and the engine was gradually throttled down to 900 r.p.m. power and consumption readings being taken.

The results of these tests are shown graphically on the appended chart (C. 335).

At the conclusion of the above tests, a run of one hour's duration at 1400 r.p.m., full throttle, was made with the following results :—

Average b.h.p.	252
Petrol—pints per hour	15.25
pints per h.p. hour	0.605
Oil—pints per hour	8.125
pints per h.p. hour	0.032
Oil temperature at end of run	54.5° C.
Water outlet temperature	80° C.

It was noticed that at speeds below 1150 r.p.m. the vibration was rather excessive.

No adjustments were made to the engine during these tests.

Material Specification of Parts of 260 h.p. Mercédès Engine, No. 30111.

Analysis shows the chemical composition of the parts to be as follows :—

Gear Wheel.

Carbon	0.30 per cent.
Silicon	0.27 ,,
Manganese	0.74 ,,
Sulphur	0.025 ,,
Phosphorus	0.030 ,,
Nickel	4.17 ,,
Chromium	1.39 ,,
Vanadium	Nil. ,,

Mechanical Tests.

Mechanical tests on the valve spring gave the following results :—

Outside diameter of spring	1.250 to 1.352 in.
Diameter of wire	1.56 in.
	[Probably a misprint for .156.—Ed.]
Number of free coils	7
Length of spring	3 in.

Compression in inches.	*Load in lbs.*	*Unloading.*
0	0	0
.1	6	4¾
.2	12	10¾
.3	18	16¾
.4	24	23
.5	30	29⅛
.6	36	35⅛
.7	42	41
.8	48	47
.9	54⅜	53⅛
1.0	60⅜	59⅝
1.1	66¾	65⅞
1.2	73½	72½
1.3	81	79¾
1.4	88½	88
Closed 1.5	97⅛	—

Permanent Set, Nil.

Crankcase.

Tensile Tests :—

Yield point	8.7 tons per sq. in.
Maximum stress	9.35 ,, ,,
Elongation	3.55 per cent. on 2 in.
Reduction of area	3.5 per cent.
Specific gravity	2.867

Crankshaft.

Tensile Test :—

Yield point	55.7 tons per sq. in.
Maximum stress	62.0 ,, ,,
Elongation	13.5 per cent. on 2 in.
Reduction of area	23.5 per cent.

Impact Test on Crankshaft :—
23 ft. lbs. } on boss in direction
16 ft. lbs. } of shaft.

B. M. Department, R.A.F.

July 16th, 1917.

ENGINE DATA.

Number and arrangement of cylinders	6 (vertical, separate).
Bore	6.30 in.
Stroke	7.09 in.
Stroke/Bore ratio	1.125—1.
Normal b.h.p.	252.
Normal speed	1,400 r.p.m.
Piston speed	1,655 ft. min. (27.6 ft. sec.)
Area of one piston	31.17 sq. in.
Total piston area of engine	187.02 sq. in.
Swept volume of one cylinder	221 cub. in.
Total swept volume of engine	1,326 cub. in.
Volume of clearance space	56.10 cub. in.
Compression ratio, total vol./clearance vol.	4.94—1.
Air standard efficiency	47.30 per cent.
Brake mean pressure	107.50 lbs.
Mechanical efficiency (calculated)	87.90 per cent.
Indicated mean pressure (calculated)	122.35 lbs. sq. in.
Fuel consumption (lb. per b.h.p. hour)	0.541 lb.
Brake thermal efficiency (18,500 B.T.U.'s lb.)	25.46 per cent.
Indicated thermal efficiency	28.96 ,,
Relative efficiency	61.20 ,,

FRICTION LOSSES (CALCULATED).

(*In terms of lbs. per sq. in. of piston area.*)

Bearings, valve gear and auxiliaries	2.50 lbs. per sq. in
Fluid pumping losses	4.50 ,, ,,
Piston friction	7.85 ,, ,,
Total losses	14.85 ,, ,,
Brake mean pressure	107.50 ,, ,,
Mechanical efficiency, 107.50/122.35	87.90 per cent.

GAS VELOCITIES, VALVE AREAS, ETC.

Gas Velocity.

Choke tube	302.0 ft. per sec.
Vertical induction pipe	70.2 ,,
Induction manifold	125.6 ,,
Inlet port	115.6 ,,
Inlet valve	158.0 ,,
Exhaust valve	158.0 ,,
Exhaust port	115.6 ,,

Cross Section Area.

Choke tube	Total, 2,850 sq. in.
	[Probably a misprint for 2.850.—Ed.]
Vertical induction pipe	12.18 sq. in.
Induction manifold	6.86 ,,
Inlet port (total)	7.44 ,,
Inlet valve (total) (d.h.) ..	5.45 ,,
Exhaust valve (total) (d.h.) ..	5.38 ,,
Exhaust port (total) ..	7.44 ,,

Diameter.

Choke tube	
Vertical induction pipe	3.937 in.
Induction manifold	2.953 ,,
Inlet port (each)	2.175 ,,
Exhaust port (each)	2.175 ,,

Inlet valve (two per cylinder):—

Outside diameter of valve ..	2.362 in.
Lift of valve	0.398 ,,
Width of seating	0.0787 ,,
Diameter of stem, in guide ..	0.433 in.
Diameter of stem, below guide ..	0.433 ,,
Radius under valve head ..	0.394 ,,
Length of valve guide ..	3.818 ,,
Length of spring, valve closed ..	2.362 in.
Ratio—Length of spring lift of valve	5.95—1

Exhaust Valve (two per cylinder):—

Outside diameter of valve ..	2.362 in.
Lift of valve	0.394 ,,
[Compare with inlet lift. Possibly a micrometer error of 0.004 in.—Ed.]	
Width of seating	0.0787 in.
Diameter of stem, in guide ..	0.433 ,,
Diameter of stem, below guide ..	0.433 ,,
Radius under valve head ..	0.394 ,,
Length of valve guide ..	3.818 ,,
Length of spring, valve closed ..	2.362 ,,
Ratio—Length of spring lift of valve	5.99—1.

INERTIA STRESSES.
LOADING ON CRANK-PIN BEARINGS, ETC.

Weight of piston, complete with rings, gudgeon pin, etc.	10.725 lbs.
Weight per sq. in. piston area ..	0.344 lb.
Weight of connecting rod, complete with bearings	7.00 lbs.
Total reciprocating weight per cylinder	13.225 lbs.
Weight per sq. in. piston area	0.424 lb.
Length of connecting rod between centres	12.835 in.
Ratio, connecting rod / crank-throw (l./r.)	3.62—1.
Inertia pressure, lbs. per sq. in. piston area—	
Top centre	106.70 lbs. sq. in.
Bottom centre	60.50 lbs. sq. in.
Mean	83.60 lbs. sq. in.
Weight of rotating mass of connecting rod	4.50 lbs.
Total centrifugal pressure ..	887 lbs.
Centrifugal pressure, lbs. sq. in. piston area	28.45 lbs. sq. in.
Total loading due to inertia and centrifugal pressures ..	112.05 lbs. sq. in.
Mean average fluid pressure, including compression and pumping strokes ..	44.00 lbs. sq. in.
Mean average loading on connecting rod bearing, total from all sources in terms of lbs. per sq. in. on piston area (⅔ inertia)	128,120 lbs. sq. in. [?—Ed.]
Diameter of crank-pin	2 520 lbs. [?—Ed.]
Rubbing velocity	15.40 ft. per sec.
Projected area of big-end bearing ..	8.80 sq. in.
Ratio, piston area/projected area big-end bearing	3.545—1.
Mean average pressure on big-end bearing	454.00 lbs. sq. in.
Loading on connecting rod big-end bolts :—	
Maximum load due to inertia at 1,400 r.p.m.	3,328 lbs.
Maximum load due to inertia at 1,600 r.p.m.	4,338 lbs.
Maximum [!—Ed.] load due to centrifugal force at 1,400 r.p.m. ..	887 lbs.
Maximum loads due to centrifugal force at 1,600 r.p.m. ..	1,163 lbs.
Total load on bolts at 1,400 r.p.m. ..	4,215 lbs.
Total load on bolts at 1,600 r.p.m. ..	5,501 lbs.
Number of bolts	Four.
Full diameter of bolts ..	0.4724 in.
Total cross-sectional area at bottom of thread	0.580 sq. in.
Stress per sq. in. at 1,400 r.p.m. ..	7,270 lbs. sq. in.
Stress per sq. in. at 1,600 r.p.m. ..	9,990 lbs. sq. in.

THE 180 H.P. MERCÉDÈS ENGINE.

ENGINE DATA.

Number and arrangement of cylinders	Six, vertical, separate.
Bore	140 mms. = 5.51 ins.
Stroke	160 mms. = 6.30 ins.
Stroke/bore ratio	1.142 : 1.
Area of one piston	23.84 sq. ins. = 153.9 sq. cms.
Total piston area of engine ..	143.04 sq. ins. = 924 sq. cms.
Stroke volume of one cylinder ..	150.28 cu. ins. = 2463 cu. cms.
Total stroke volume of engine ..	901.68 cu. ins. = 14778 cu. cms.
Volume of clearance space ..	41.3 cu. ins. = 676.64 cu cms.
Compression ratio. Total volume/ Clearance volume	4.64 : 1.
Normal B.H.P. and speed ..	174 B.H.P. at 1400 r.p.m.
Piston speed	1470 ft. per min.
Brake mean pressure	109.1 lbs. sq. in.
Cu. ins. of stroke volume per B.H.P.	5.18 cu. ins.
Sq. in. of piston area per B.H.P. ..	0.823 sq. in.
B.H.P. per cu. ft. of stroke volume	334.0
B.H.P. per sq. ft. of piston area ..	175.0.
Direction of rotation of crank and airscrew	Anti-clockwise facing airscrew.
Lubrication system	Forced, multiple plunger pumps.

Oil consumption per hour	7.3 pints = 8.21 lbs.
Oil consumption per B.H.P. hour ..	0.642 pint = 0.047 lb.
Oil pressure	20 lbs. sq. in.
Volume of oil carried in base chamber	17 pints.
Number and type of carburetters ..	One dual Mercédès, twin-jet.
Diameter of chokes	0.945 in. = 24 mms.
Bore of main jets	0.058 in. = 1.472 mms.
Bore of pilot jets	0.022 in. = 0.559 mms.
Fuel consumption per hour ..	94.83 pints = 85.32 lbs.
Fuel consumption per B.H.P. hour	0.545 pint = 0.491 lb.
Inside diameter of induction pipes	2.126 ins. = 54 mms.
Number and type of magnetos ..	Two, Bosch, Z.L.6.
Firing sequence of engine ..	1, 5, 3, 6, 2, 4.
Ignition timing (fully advanced) ..	30 deg. early.
Speed of magnetos	1.5 engine speed.
Inlet valve opens	Top dead centre.
Inlet valve closes	40 deg. late.
Diameter of inlet valve (smallest diam.) = d	2.677 ins. = 68 mms.
Lift of inlet valve = h	0.453 in. = 11.5 mms.
Area of inlet valve opening (π.d.h.)	3.81 sq. in. = 24.58 sq. cms.
Mean gas velocity through inlet valve	153.4 ft. per sec.
Clearance of inlet tappet ..	0.017 in. = 0.432 mms.
Exhaust valve opens	40 deg. early.
Exhaust valve closes	10 deg. late.
Diameter of exhaust valve (smallest diam.) = d	2.677 ins. = 68 mms.
Lift of exhaust valve = h ..	0.453 in. = 11.5 mms.

Magneto end of the 180 h.p. Six Cylinder Mercédès. High Compression Type.

Description of Part.	No. per set.	Average unit weight.	Weight of complete set.	Percentage of total weight.
Area of exhaust valve opening (π.d.h.)			3.81 sq. ins. = 24.58 sq. cms.	

Area of exhaust valve opening
(π.d.h.) .. .. 3.81 sq. ins. = 24.58 sq. cms.
Clearance of exhaust tappet .. 0.014 in. = 0.355 mms.
Diameter of inlet and exhaust ports 2.165 in. = 55 mms.
Diameter of water-pump inlet .. 1.692 in. = 43 mms.
Diameter of water-pump outlet .. 1.575 in. = 40 mms.
Ratio of water-pump speed to crank-
shaft speed .. .. .. 1.5 .1.
Delivery of water-pump at normal
speed .. .. .. 41.4 gallons per min.
Inlet water temperature .. .. 64 deg. Cent.
Outlet water temperature .. .. 64 deg. Cent.
Outlet water temperature .. .. 74 deg. Cent.
Water-jacket capacity of one cylinder 1280 cu. cms.

GENERAL ANALYSIS OF WEIGHTS.

Description of Part.	No. per set.	Average unit weight.	Weight of complete set.	Percentage of total weight.
Cylinders (bare) ..	6	19.25	115.50	17.5
Pistons, complete with rings and gudgeon pins	6	6.85	41.10	6.23
Connecting rods, with gudgeon pin bushes	6	5.00	30.00	4.55
Valves, complete with springs, etc. ..	12	1.31	15.74	2.39
Crankshaft (bare) ..	1	70.00	70.00	10.60
Camshaft (bare) ..	1	7.75	7.75	1.17
Camshaft casing with bearings and covers	1	27.63	27.63	4.18
Valve rockers	12	.87	10.50	1.59
Half compression gear (complete) ..	1	7.00	7.00	1.06
Vertical driving shaft (complete, including casing, oil pump, drive, and floating bevel) ..	1	17.50	17.50	2.66
Base chamber (top half)	1	72.25	72.25	10.92
Base chamber (bottom half)	1	100.00	100.00	15.16
Carburetters	one dual	16.75	16.75	2.54
Induction pipes (lagged asbestos) ..	2	5.00	10.00	1.52
Water pump (complete)	1	7.75	7.75	1.17
Oil pump (complete) ..	1	13.25	13.25	2.00
Air pump (complete) ..	1	4.75	4.75	.72
Magnetos (complete) ..	2	14.00	28.00	4.25
Water piping	—	3.25	3.25	.49
Propeller hub (complete)	1	12.50	12.50	1.90
Ignition wiring (complete)	2	2.00	4.00	.61
Exhaust manifold ..	1	13.00	13.00	1.97
Miscellaneous parts ..	—	31.78	31.78	4.82
Total weight of complete engine (dry) (with propeller hub and exhaust manifold)		660 lbs.		100.00

WEIGHTS.

Weight of engine complete, dry, including propeller
hub and exhaust manifold .. .. .. 660.0 lbs.
Weight per B.H.P. .. .. 3.79 lbs.
Weight of exhaust manifold.. .. .. 13.0 lbs.
Weight of oil carried in engine .. .. 19.125 lbs.
Weight of fuel and oil per hour .. .. 93.53 lbs.
Gross weight of engine in running order, less fuel,
oil and tanks, but including cooling system at
0.65 lbs. per B.H.P. .. .. .. 773.0 lbs.
Weight per B.H.P. .. .. 4.44 lbs.
Gross weight of engine in running order, with fuel,
oil and tanks for six hours. (Tanks at 10 per
cent. weight of fuel and oil) .. .. 1390.3 lbs.
Weight per B.H.P. .. .. 8.00 lbs.

THE 200 H.P. HIGH COMPRESSION MERCÉDÈS ENGINE.

The following particulars are published by courtesy of the Controller, Technical Department, Department of Aircraft Production :—

The following report on the running performance of the 200-h.p. High Compression Mercédès Engine is based on an examination and tests carried out at R.A.E. on the engine (No. 775) taken from a *Fokker D.7* biplane (*G/2 B/14*) brought down in France on June 6th, 1918.

It is of interest to note that this is the first Mercédès engine to be fitted with an altitude compensator carburetter. This compensator, which is here fully described, is so arranged that it is impossible to run the engine all out on the ground.

In most respects this engine is identical in design with the standard 180-h.p. Mercédès engine already reported on, except as to the following points :—

1. New design of pistons giving increased compression.
2. Carburetter—fitted with altitude control.
3. Induction manifolds—water-jacketed.
4. Duplex horizontally opposed air pumps.
5. Wireless dynamo mounted on induction side of crankcase, driven by gearing from rear end of crankshaft.

PISTON DESIGN AND COMPRESSION RATIO.

The pistons used in these engines are of the usual Mercédès construction, being built up with steel crowns which carry the gudgeon pins. The crowns are screwed and welded into their cast-iron skirts, and, as shown in the sectional drawing (Fig. 2), are considerably domed as compared with the concave heads used in the standard 180-h.p. Mercédès engines, thus giving a compression ratio of 5.73 : 1, *i.e.*, an increase of 23.54 per cent.

Standard 180-h.p. Mercédès connecting rods are fitted, and the distance from the gudgeon-pin centre to the top of piston is the same as before.

CARBURETTER.

The carburetter fitted to this engine is of the standard Mercédès type, with the exception of the throttle barrel, which is slightly modified to provide the automatic altitude control. This device consists of two extensions on the bottom of the barrel diametrically opposite to each other, of the shape shown in the sketch.

A section of the complete carburetter is shown diagrammatically in a figure.

Slots are cut in the sliding air valve to correspond with the extensions on the throttle barrel. The throttle control lever is marked for opening out to its maximum ground level position,

and at all throttle openings up to this mark the lift of the sliding air valve is restricted, owing to its coming in contact with the extensions on the throttle barrel. Immediately the throttle is opened past the mark on the control lever, the extensions on the throttle barrel come in line with the slots in the

Airscrew end of the 180 h.p. (High Compression) 6 Cylinder Mercédès. *Photograph by courtesy of the Technical Department, R.A.F.*

Three-quarter View from Airscrew End, 200 h.p. High Compression Mercédès engine.

MERCÉDÈS—continued.

sliding air valve, allowing the air valve to lift to its maximum position and uncover extra air holes, thus weakening the mixture to such an extent that the engine stops if the throttle is fully opened on the ground.

INDUCTION MANIFOLDS.

The induction manifolds are fitted with welded steel water jackets in place of the usual asbestos lagging. The jackets are each in direct communication with a feed from the water pump to the carburetter, the respective outlets being connected to the rear end cylinder jacket. Circulation is controlled by a cock on the return pipe (presumably for use in hot weather) which does not affect the water supply to the carburetter jackets.

AIR PUMP.

A double acting air pump of the usual plunger type is now fitted in place of the standard Mercédès air pump used hitherto on these engines. Both plungers are operated by a small common crank attached to the front end of the camshaft, the construction of which is shown in a sketch.

COMPARATIVE DATA.

In view of the similarity of design of the 160-h.p., 180-h.p. and 200 h.p. (high compression) Mercédès engines, the following brief comparison of the leading data is interesting :—

	160 H.P.	180 H.P.	200 H.P. (H.C.)
Bore	140 mm.	140 mm.	140 mm.
Stroke	160 mm.	160 mm.	160 mm.
Compression ratio	4.5 : 1	4.64 : 1	5.73 : 1
Normal B.H.P. and speed	162.5 at 1,400 r.p.m.	174 at 1,400 r.p.m.	204 at 1,600 r.p.m.
B.H.P. per c.f. Stroke vol.	312 B.H.P.	334 B.H.P.	391 B.H.P.
B.H.P. per sq. in. Piston area	163.5 B.H.P.	175 B.H.P.	205.4 B.H.P.
Normal B.M.E.P.	102 lbs. sq. in.	109 lbs. sq. in.	112 lbs. sq. in.
Fuel consumption per B.H.P. per hour	0.58 pt. =0.522 lb.	0.545 pt. =0.491 lb.	0.629 pt. =0.566 lb.
Diameter of choke tube	24.0 mm.	24.0 mm.	24.0 mm.
Capacity of main jets	355 cc. per min.	355 cc. per min.	450 cc. per min. (test jet) 250 cc. per min. (standard jet)
Oil consumption per B.H.P. per hour	0.031 pt. =0.025 lb.	0.042 pt. =0.047 lb.	0.029 pt. =0.032 lb.

VALVE TIMING.

	160 H.P.	180 H.P.	200 H.P.
Inlet opens	2 deg. L.	Top dead centre.	1 deg. L.
Inlet closes	35 deg. L.	40 deg. L.	40 deg. L.
Exhaust opens	63 deg. E.	40 deg. L.	46 deg. E.
Exhaust closes	13 deg. L.	10 deg. L.	8 deg. L.

TAPPET CLEARANCES.

Inlet		0.017 in.	0.017 in.
Exhaust		0.014 in.	0.015 in.
Magneto timing	30 deg. E.	30 deg. E.	30 deg. E.

TESTS.

Three sets of calibration curves were taken in the following order :—

(a) With the carburetter opened out to its maximum position for ground level running.

(b) With the sliding air valves fixed at the base of the choke tubes and the throttle fully opened.

(c) With a 180-h.p. Mercédès carburetter (which had no altitude control) fitted in place of the standard carburetter, the jets being opened out to suit the engine, and the curves being taken with the throttle fully opened.

Subsequently two one hour duration tests were carried out—
1 at 1,500 r.p.m.
1 at 1,600 r.p.m.

R.P.M.	1,500	1,600
Average B.H.P.	168	171
Average water inlet temperature	60 deg. C.	58 deg. C.
Average water outlet temperature	67 deg. C.	63 deg. C.
Average oil pressure	20 lbs. sq. in.	20 lbs. sq. in
Average oil temperature in tank	23 deg. C.	20 deg. C.
Oil consumption	4 pts. per hour = .024 pt./h.p./hr.	5 pts. per hour = .029 pt./h.p./hr.
Petrol consumption	91 pts./hr. = 35 pt./h.p./hr.	96.5 pts./hr. = .565 pt./h.p./hr.

F.G.C., Lieut., R.A.F. Ap.D. (L.).
J. G. WEIR, Brigadier-General, Controller, Technical Department.

In the last test a fair amount of trouble was experienced with over-heating, due to the high compression ratio employed, but this was overcome at the expense of petrol consumption.

From the general running it is assumed that the normal speed of the engine is in the region of 1,500-1,600 r.p.m., as these are the best running speeds. Below 1,400 r.p.m. the engine is very rough, and it has a very bad period between 1,000-1,200 r.p.m.

SUMMARY OF POWER CURVES.

R.P.M.	1,200			1,400			1,600		
Para. as above	(a)	(b)	(c)	(a)	(b)	(c)	(a)	(b)	(c)
B.H.P.	148.5	144.5	151	164	174	180	171	186	204
B.M.E.P. lbs./in.	108.5	105.5	110	102.5	109	112.5	94	102	111.9
Petrol consumption pt. B.H.P./hr.	.515	.650	.680	.511	.590	.645	.520	.590	.629

Maximum power recorded—217 B.H.P. at 1,750 r.p.m.
Induction pipe depressions were taken between Nos. 1 and 2 cylinders.

NAPIER (British).

D. NAPIER & SON, LTD., 14, New Burlington Street, London, W. 1. Works, Acton, London, W.

THE 450 H.P. NAPIER "LION."

The all-British "Lion" aero engine has many points of interest. The most noticeable novelty in the latest model is the new type of water jacket. There is now a separate jacket to each cylinder instead of a multiple jacket for each block of four cylinders. Undoubtedly, this is an improvement. Weight is saved, and the new method of making a water-tight joint between the cylinder and jacket is preferable to the old method which was used in the type produced in 1917, which could not then be described owing to the war. In the war former models the lower joint was made by a rubber ring; in the latest type the jackets are welded to the cylinders.

The "Lion" engine, which develops 450 B.H.P. at 2,000 r.p.m., and weighs only 1.86 lbs. per B.H.P. (without water, fuel, or oil), is in its entirety a highly creditable British production. Its twelve cylinders are arranged in three sets in the "broad arrow" method. Each cylinder has two inlet and two exhaust valves, the seatings of which are screwed through the head of the cylinder into the head casting. The valves are operated by two overhead camshafts, and the cams act directly upon the tappet heads, the stems of which are screwed into the valve stems so that the clearance may be adjusted. A spring locking ring secures the tappet head when the adjustment has been made.

THE SELF-STARTING DEVICE.

The engine is started by pumping an explosive mixture into the cylinders and firing it by means of a hand-starting magneto. By means of linked control levers the two forward valves of each cylinder are opened by hand pressure. The air-pump is mounted in the cockpit, and by means of a two-way cock it can be used first to pump pure air to the cylinders to expel any foul gasses that there may be in the combustion chambers, and then the explosive mixture is ready for firing. The mixture is formed by pumping air through a petrol vaporiser which is a form of spray carburetter.

The three rows of cylinders are supplied with mixture, when running, by two carburetters, a single and a duplex type. The gas passages are water-jacketed. So far as the throttles, diffusion jets and altitude control cocks are concerned the carburetters resemble the H.C.7 type, but modifications have been made to adapt them to the "Lion" engine.

The altitude control system is that of reducing the supply of petrol as the machine climbs. This is, of course, necessary, because as the air becomes rarified the percentage of air to petrol would become incorrect if the flow of fuel were not

View of complete Engine from Airscrew End.

[The Editor desires to express his indebtedness to the Technical Department of the Air Ministry for assistance in compiling this description.]

checked. There is a safety device, which causes the control when open to shut automatically when the throttle is closed. This prevents the mixture being too weak when the pilot makes a long dive and flattens out.

LUBRICATION.

Oil pumps of the spur wheel type are fitted and the lubricant is fed under pressure to both ends of the crankshaft and from thence along the inside of the shaft to the crank-pins and to the big-ends and gudgeon pins. Oil is also supplied under pressure to one of the camshafts on each set of cylinders and to the reduction gears. The cylinders are lubricated by oil splashed from the connecting-rod big-end bearings and gudgeon. Two scraper rings are fitted to each piston and the oil from the upper scraper ring is drained through holes cut in the piston,

IGNITION.

Two 12-cylinder magnetos are fitted. They are of the A.V.12 type manufactured by the British Thomson-Houston Co., Ltd. Both rotate anti-clockwise and one has a special distributer rotor for starting purposes. They are driven at one-and-a-half times the speed of the crankshaft in order to give six sparks for each revolution of the engine, as this type of magneto gives four sparks to each revolution. Two plugs are, of course, fitted to each cylinder. Those recommended by Messrs. Napier and Sons are the K.L.G. type F.10.

THE CRANKCASE.

The crankcase of the "Lion" is a fine casting of aluminium alloy. The top halves of the housings for the crankshaft plain and roller bearings are contained in the two ends and four internal cross-webs. The lower halves of the housings for the roller bearings are steel caps carried in studs in the rear and crosswebs.

The casing for the reduction gear is formed at the front end of the crankcase. The gearing is clearly shown in one of the diagrams. It will be seen that the arrangement is extremely neat. There are six camshafts—two for each set of cylinders, one operating the exhaust and one the inlet valves. Only one camshaft on each set of cylinders is driven by the reduction gear, the other camshaft is geared to this. Consequently, there are three shafts driven by the bevel gear wheel attached to the crankshaft. The diagram also shows how one shaft has two bevel wheels, one of which engages with the bevel wheel that drives the centre shaft. The compact arrangement by which the six camshafts, water pumps, oil pumps, and two magnetos are driven is clearly shown.

The following general particulars and dimensions are of interest :—

CYLINDERS.

Steel forgings machined all over. Water-jackets of steel. Detachable aluminium cylinder head, containing inlet and exhaust passages, valves and valve-actuating mechanism.

PISTONS.

Of aluminium alloy, fitted with two gas and two scraper rings. Gudgeon pins of large dimensions and hollow, working in steel bushes.

CONNECTING RODS.

Machined from special high-grade steel. The master rod, coupled to the pistons of the vertical block of cylinders, is formed with lugs on either side, to which are attached the short auxiliary rods for the pistons of the right and left groups of cylinders. The big ends are white metal lined, anchor pins and other parts work in bushes of ample size.

CRANKSHAFT.

Machined from a solid steel forging. The four throws are in one plane, and all journal bearings and crank pins are of large diameter and bored out. The shaft is carried in five substantial roller bearings and a large plain bearing at the forward end.

The new type Water Jacket in Place.

Upper Half of Crankcase—The Napier "Lion."

Crankshaft and Bearing Components of the Napier "Lion."

WATER-PUMP.

Centrifugal type, mounted to rear end of engine and running at half crankshaft speed. The spindle is fitted with a metallic packed gland and a screw-down greaser. Water is delivered through a separate outlet to each of the three cylinder blocks.

Specification.

Number of cylinders	Twelve
Arrangement	Three sets of four each, one vertical, two at 60 deg.
Bore	5¼ in.
Stroke	5⅛ in.
Horse-power, normal	450 at 1925 revs.
Direction of rotation of propeller shaft	Clockwise viewed from propeller end.
Speed of ditto	Reduction ratio 1 to 1.52 of crankshaft.
Ignition	Two special dual magnetos; anti-clockwise rotation.
Oil consumption	0.02 pint approximately per B.H.P. hour, at full load.
Fuel Consumption	6.51 pint approximately per B.H.P. hour, full load.
Self Starter	Napier Patent Air Petrol System
Weight of engine	850 lbs. approximately, complete with propeller boss, carburetters, induction pipes, etc.
Weight per h.p.	1.89 lbs.
Length over-all to centre of propeller	4 ft. 8 in. approximately.
Width over-all	5 ft. 6 in. approximately.
Height over-all	3 ft. approximately.

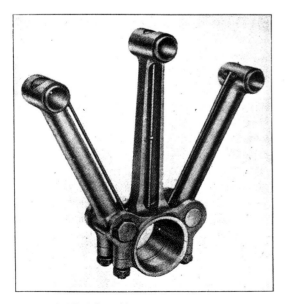

Connecting Rod Assembly.

The 450 h.p. Napier "Lion" engine.

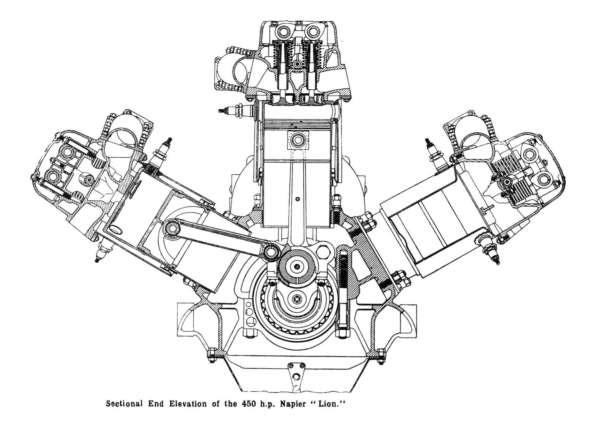

Sectional End Elevation of the 450 h.p. Napier "Lion."

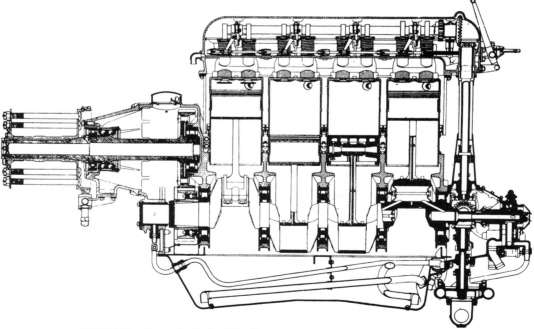

Sectional Elevation of the Napier "Lion."

NEILSEN & WINTHER (Danish).

NEILSEN & WINTHER, A/S. Presundsvej, Copenhagen.

The only Danish aero-engine makers. Have produced the engine illustrated herewith. It appears to be almost purely Mercédès in type, plus a Benz arrangement of carburetters and inlet pipes.

OBERURSEL (German).

OBERURSEL MOTOREN GESELLSCHAFT, Oberursel by Frankfurt. German licensees for the Gnôme engine.

The fate of the Gnôme motor in Germany is an interesting record. The well-known automobile manufacturer and sportsman, Mathis—an early owner and pilot of an *Antoinette*—being the first agent. The Gnôme was used to a large extent on early German aircraft—*Albatros* constructed *Farman* box-kites and *Antoinette* monoplanes, some "Taubes," and *Euler* aircraft. Owing to national competition conditions, Gnôme disappeared but from Euler, who stuck faithfully to it as pure manufacturer and never entering competitions.

Later agents got small profits from the agency till the Oberurseler Motor Co. took up Gnôme manufacture by license, likely because they constructed already a stationary motor for agriculture service named Gnôme. The Deutsche Motoren Bebricles Gesellschaft were selling agents and found brisk business before and during the war for fighting aircraft of the star turn pilots, as *Ago*, *Fokker*, *Pfalz* and *Rex* mounts.

Same models as the French Gnôme Co. and later as the Le Rhône.

OPEL (German.)

OPEL MOTOR Co., Berlin.

Well-known motor-car firm now making aero-engines of more or less conventional Mercédès type. The Opel engine captured early in 1918 by the R.F.C. gives good results but particulars are not yet available.

OTTO (German).

OTTO-WERKE, Munchen.
200 h.p., 8-cyl. vertical water-cooled.

PACKARD (American).

THE PACKARD MOTOR COMPANY, Detroit, Mich.

This well-known motorcar firm devoted their aeroplane engine department to manufacturing engines for the U.S. Government, and consequently no information is available as to the most recent developments. However, the firm has made an 8-cylinder V engine, of alleged 160 h.p. which is illustrated herewith.

Side View of the 160 h.p. Packard Engine.

R. A. F. (British).

ROYAL AIRCRAFT FACTORY (Now "Royal Aircraft Establishment" to avoid confusion with initials of the Royal Air Force), South Farnborough, Hampshire.

Have experimented with engines for many years. Produced various types at various times.

Best known are the 8-cylinder 70 h.p., 8-cylinder 90 h.p. and 12-cylinder 140 h.p. All air-cooled. V type. General design and layout very similar to *Renault*.

R.A.F.—*continued*.

Later types have been built in large numbers by motor manufacturers in various parts of Great Britain.

Have also experimented with water-cooled V-type engines, and obtained interesting and educative results. A certain number of the water-cooled type had been manufactured for active service use, up to the end of 1917, but the engine is now obsolescent.

RAPP (German).

RAPP MOTORENWERKE G.m.b.H., München. Schleissheimerstrasse 211.

Started aero engine manufacture shortly befor and have extended during the war. One of the first samples of this sound-looking design was the power of the well-known German aviator, Bruno Büchner's *Pfalz* biplane, brought to German East Africa for attaining colonial experience before the war and active during the campaign there.

6-cyl., 125 h.p. Weight : 474 lbs.
6-cyl., 150 h.p.
And higher powers.

Features :—
Vertical, water-cooled.
Steel cylinders in pairs.
Detachable inlet and exhaust valves.
Petrol consumption (150 h.p. Model) : 40 litres per hour.

REX (German).

REX Flugmaschine Rex Gesellschaft G.m.b.H., Kölln on Rhine, 1, Antwerpenerstrasse. Has turned out a single-valved rotary engine for their own light aircraft.

RHEINISCHE (German).

RHEINISCHE AEROWERKE G.m.b.H., Euskirchen. Never constructed their own types, but in few copies, and selling to experimenters.

RHENANIA MOTOR WORKS, Ltd.,
Mannheim.

Manufacturers of apparently 11-cylinder rotary engines for fighting aeroplanes.

RICHARD & HERING (German).

RICHARD & HERING (Rex-Simplex Automobile Works) have likely dropped their own designs, or may manufacture on small quantity scale for school machines or even the leading types under royalty.

RENAULT (French & British).

France :—LOUIS RENAULT, 15, Rue Gustav-Sandoz,
Billancourt (Seine).

These engines are made in the types illustrated hereafter but
the firm has not vouchsafed any specifications.

Side View of the Renault engine, 190 h.p.

Rear View of the 300 h.p. Renault engine.

Side View of the Renault engine, 300 h.p.

Side View of the Renault Aero engine, 450 h.p.

Rear View of the Renault engine. 450 h.p.

THE ROBERTS (American).

THE ROBERTS MOTOR MANUFACTURING Co., 151, Roberts Building, Sandusky, Ohio.

Two-stroke engines, made in two models, 6-cylinder, 100 h.p. and 12-cylinder, 350 h.p., as follows :—

	Model 6-X	Model E-12
Number of cylinders	6	12 V Type
H.P.	100	350
Bore and stroke	5″ × 5½″	6″ × 6¼″
Speed (r.p.m.)	400 to 1500	400 to 1500
Speed (normal)............	1200	1200
Weight	368 lbs.	990 lbs.
Propeller	8′3″ × 5′	as required
Piston pins (hollow)	1⅛″ dia.	1⅜″
Bearings (number of)	7	13
Bearings (size of crankshaft)	2¼″ × 2½″ dia.	1¾″ × 3½″ dia.
Crankpin bearings	1¾″ × 2½″	2″ × 3½″

No fresh particulars have been received.

Roberts engine, type 6X, 100 h.p. Inlet side, with carburetters and one magneto.

ROLLS-ROYCE

ROLLS-ROYCE, Ltd., Derby, and Conduit Street, London, W.

Four types are made, the " Hawk," 100 h.p. ; the " Falcon," 280 h.p ; the " Eagle," 360 h.p. ; and the " Condor," 600 h.p.

The makers have kindly supplied the specifications and installation diagrams which follow hereafter.

One is permitted by courtesy of the Technical Department of the Air Ministry, to publish the accompanying photographs of the " Eagle " type.

Photographs of the other engines and of details are not available.

THE 100-H.P. ROLLS-ROYCE " HAWK."

Type	..	..	..	..	6-cylinder ungeared vertical water-cooled.
Bore	..	..	..	..	4 ins.
Stroke	..	..	..	..	6 ins.

The airscrew is carried by a shaft bolted to the crankshaft. This shaft runs in a nose bearing carried by an extension of the crankcase. By this means the heavy stresses due to the re-action of the porpeller when the machine is turning or diving, which occur in the end crank where the propeller is carried directly on the crankshaft, are avoided.

NORMAL POWER AND SPEED, AND FUEL CONSUMPTION.

Normal b.h.p.	..	..	..	100.
Normal engine speed	..	..	1500 r.p.m.
The maximum speed of the engine should not exceed ..	..	..	1700 r.p.m.
Fuel consumption at normal power and speed, using a mixture of 80% petrol and 20% benzole ..	6.5 gallons per hour.
Weight, including airscrew hub, carburetter, magneto, engine feet, etc., but excluding exhaust boxes, radiator, oil, fuel, and water	405 lbs.

IGNITION.—The ignition is provided by a 6-cylinder magneto serving one ignition plug in each cylinder.

Owing to the simple fact that the engine has only one single carburetter, it is capable of easy starting and of throttling down on slow running, more reliably and efficiently than is obtained by the common arrangement.

The oil consumption should be taken as ½ gallon per hour.

The quantity of water carried in the cylinder water-jackets, water pipes, and pump is 1.4 gallons.

The water system is completed to two points, at which pipes or couplings joining to the radiator may be affixed. These consist of one inlet connection to the water pump, and one outlet connection from the cylinders.

STARTING OF ENGINE.

It is usual, when starting this small engine, to turn it by means of the propeller for filling the cylinders after the induction pipes have been primed. The operation of the hand magneto (supplied by Messrs. Rolls-Royce) then starts the engine.

The Rolls-Royce Patented Device is supplied for priming. This is a light and simple apparatus, embodying a hand pump, which can be fixed in any convenient position near the pilot's seat, or as desired. One priming device may serve two or more engines with the use of a change-over cock.

When required, a starting handle can be supplied, arranged in line with the crankshaft at the timing gearcase end of engine, and connected thereto by a reduction gear. This apparatus is specially suitable for airship installations.

AIRSCREW HUB.

The airscrew hub is a specially Rolls-Royce design, but it conforms as far as the dimensions of the propeller boss to the design standardised by the Engineering Standards Committee. To overcome the troubles which are known to occur with propeller hubs on 6-cylinder engines, due to the comparatively irregular turning moment of this type of engine, Messrs. Rolls-Royce use a taper serration for connecting the hub to the propeller shaft, which is entirely successful in action.

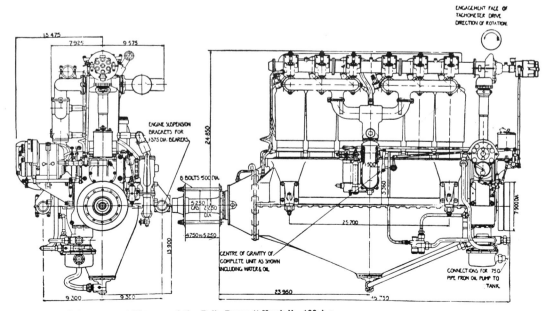

General Arrangement Diagram of the Rolls-Royce " Hawk." 100 h.p.

THE 280 H.P. ROLLS-ROYCE "FALCON."

Type .. .. 12-cylinder vee water-
cooled.
Bore .. .. 4 ins.
Stroke .. .. 5.75 ins.
With an epicyclic reduction gear driving the airscrew at the
most efficient speed.

NORMAL POWER AND SPEED, AND FUEL CONSUMPTION.

Normal b.h.p. .. .. .. 280.
Normal engine speed .. .. 2250 r.p.m.
Normal airscrew speed with reduction gear of 56/95 ratio .. .. 1327 r.p.m.
The maximum speed of the engine
should not exceed .. .. .. 2500 r.p.m
Fuel consumption at normal power
and speed, using a mixture of 80%
petrol and 20% benzole .. 18.5 gallons per hour.

WEIGHT.

Weight of engine, including airscrew
hub, carburetters, magnetos, engine
feet, etc., but excluding reduction
gear, exhaust boxes, radiator, oil,
fuel and water .. .. 630 lbs.
Weight of engine as above, but including reduction gear of 56/95 ratio 686 lbs.

IGNITION.

The ignition is effected by two six-cylinder magnetos, one
firing each side of the engine, each cylinder being provided with
one ignition plug.

OIL CONSUMPTION.

The oil consumption should be taken as .75 gallons per hour.

WATER COOLING SYSTEM.

The quantity of water carried in the cylinder water-jackets,
water pipes, and pump is 2.5 gallons.

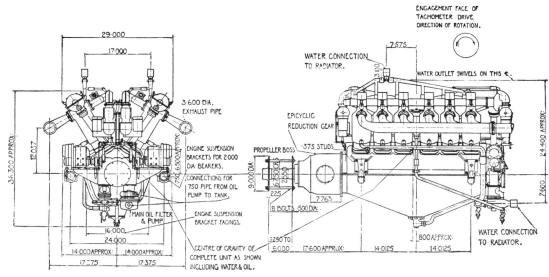

General Arrangement Diagram of the Rolls-Royce "Falcon." 280 h.p.

THE 360 H.P. ROLLS-ROYCE "EAGLE."

Type .. .. 12-cylinder vee water-
cooled.
Bore .. .. 4.5 ins.
Stroke .. .. 6.5 ins.
With an epicyclic reduction gear driving the airscrew at the
most efficient speed.

NORMAL POWER AND SPEED, AND FUEL CONSUMPTION.

Normal b.h.p. .. .. .. 360.
Normal engine speed .. .. 1800 r.p.m.
Normal airscrew speed, with reduction gear of .6 ratio .. .. 1080 r.p.m.
The maximum speed of the engine
should not exceed .. .. .. 2000 r.p.m.
Fuel consumption at normal power
and speed, using a mixture of 80%
petrol and 20% benzole .. .. 24 gallons per hour.

WEIGHT.

Weight of engine, including airscrew
hub, carburetters, magnetos, engine
feet, etc., but excluding reduction
gear, exhaust boxes, radiator, oil,
fuel, water, and starter battery .. 836 lbs.
Weight of engine as above, but including reduction gear of .6 ratio 900 lbs.

VIRTUES OF THE 12-CYLINDER VEE ENGINE.

The 12-cylinder vee, having an angle of 60° is the type " par
excellence " for high-power aero-engines. It possesses a superior
mechanical balance, and an evenness of turning moment not
found in any other known arrangement of cylinders at present
in use. These factors, combined with the excellent power for
weight ratio of this type of engine, enables it to excel over all
others in meeting commercial requirements.

CYLINDERS.

The cylinders are such an essentially important feature of the
engine that there should be no doubt about the reliability of
the materials used in their construction.
The Rolls-Royce Cylinders are made entirely of wrought
steel to a special patented design, the most reliable and efficient
construction yet known for light aero-engines.

OTHER ENGINE PARTS.

The unmeasured attention which has been given to the other
parts of the engine, such as pistons, connecting rods, crankshaft, etc., in respect to design, has resulted in great strength
and reliability for the minimum weight and complication.
All material used in the manufacture of these pieces is
rigorously tested to see that it is of consistent quality and
conforms to the requisite standards.

The "Eagle" Rolls.

IGNITION.

The ignition is effected by four six-cylinder magnetos, two firing each side of the engine, each cylinder being provided with two ignition plugs.

It is generally known that magneto ignition is to be preferred where economy in running cost is required, as it is capable of firing those mixtures which are found to give the least fuel consumption.

This ignition being in duplicate and independent of a battery or a single electric conductor is arranged to give the greatest degree of reliability.

SAFETY FROM FIRE.

The four carburetters are specially arranged so as to be particularly free from risk of fire. No petrol can accumulate anywhere internally or externally in the engine, and the carburetters are arranged to drain away from the engine to a point outside of the cowling in the best known manner.

ROLLS-ROYCE REDUCTION GEAR.

With the epicyclic gear, as arranged on the Rolls-Royce Aero-Engines, there is no pressure on the crankshaft bearings due to reaction of the drive, and an efficiency is obtained which is far greater than can be got with any other type of gear, principally owing to the direction of motion not being reversed, and owing also to the gear only having to convert part of the horse power. This arrangement also avoids a great many heavy stresses in the casing.

FUEL, FUEL FEED AND CONNECTIONS.

It is specially recommended that the "Eagle" Engine be run on a mixture of 80% petrol and 20% benzole. This mixture gives slightly more power, and its characteristic manner of burning is specially suitable for an engine of this size.

Fuel is fed to the carburetters through the medium of the usual float feed, which performs satisfactorily through a pressure range of 1 to 4 lbs. per square inch, correspondingly, roughly, to a head variation of 3 to 12 feet.

The fuel feed connections to the carburetters are joined together by a system of piping having flexible joints which connects them to one single point on the engine. A suitable nipple and nut is provided at this main connection, for fixing the petrol pipe from the tank when completing the installation.

OIL CONSUMPTION, OIL FEED SYSTEM AND CONNECTIONS.

The oil consumption should be taken as 1 gallon per hour. The quantity of oil carried in the engine is negligible. The lubrication system of the "Eagle" Engine is of the type in which one oil pump supplies pressure oil to the main bearings, and other parts, while one scavenger pump evacuates the accumulation of oil in the crankcase to the oil tank, which should be provided in the installation. Each oil pump is protected by a strainer, which can be easily detached and cleaned. Connections, for which suitable nuts and nipples are provided, should be made at two points on the engine from the oil tank.

WATER COOLING SYSTEM.

The quantity of water carried in the cylinder water-jackets, water pipes, and pump is 3.1 gallons.

The water system is completed to three points, at which pipes or couplings joining to the radiator may be affixed. These consist of one inlet connection to the water pump, and two outlet connections, one from each group of six cylinders.

HIGH ALTITUDES.

The Rolls-Royce Carburetters are fitted with a control so that the delivery of petrol may be adjusted from the pilot's seat. This not only serves as a means of correcting the effects of decreasing atmospheric pressure with increasing altitude, but can also be used to obtain extremely economical running, and also to obtain a rich mixture for starting. Furthermore, the adjustable jet of the control serves as a very easy means of setting the carburetters for correct running on the bench.

CONTROL GEAR FOR CARBURETTERS AND MAGNETOS.

All controls, e.g., throttle, altitude, and magneto, are brought to one common location on the engine, to facilitate connection to the plane. Only those control connections and levers which are fitted to the engine are supplied. If it is desired to operate the engine from a distance, control wire pulleys instead of levers may be supplied on the final engine connections.

The carburetter throttles are fitted with springs, which, in the event of a breakage of the control, are intended to open the throttles to the full extent.

ENGINE FEET.

The engine feet are designed for use with tubular bearers. One pair of feet should be located endways on the bearers, with suitable collars, while the other pair should be allowed to remain free.

STARTING GEAR.

An electric motor is fitted, arranged to turn the engine at about 25 r.p.m. through a reduction of 100 to 1 after the induction pipes have been primed. The operation of the hand magneto (supplied by Messrs. Rolls-Royce) then starts the engine.

The control gear operating the starter, finishes with a wire pulley on the engine, so that connection can be made to it from a distance, if desired.

The Rolls-Royce Patented Device is supplied for priming. This is a light and simple apparatus embodying a hand pump, which can be fixed in any convenient position near the pilot's seat, or as desired. One priming device may serve two or more engines with the use of a change-over cock.

A detachable handle is incorporated for turning the engine over by hand, through part of the reduction gear which serves the electric motor.

The electrical starting gear is complete in every way, except for the battery, which is not supplied.

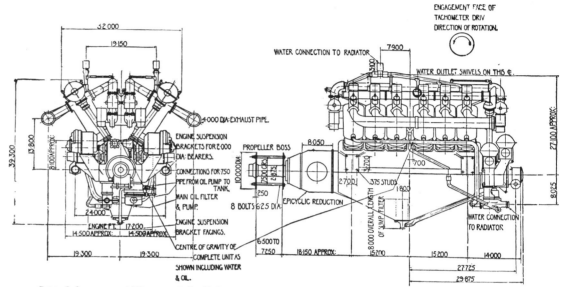

General Arrangement Diagram of the Rolls-Royce "Eagle." 360 h.p.

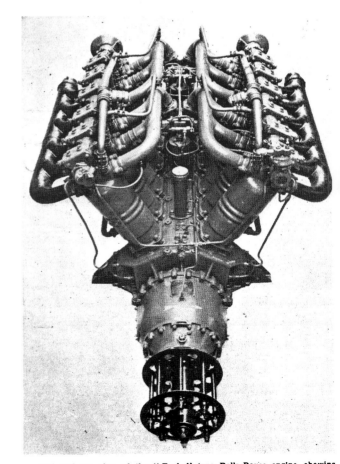

End and top view of the "Eagle" type Rolls-Royce engine, showing gear-box of air-screw shaft.

ROLLS-ROYCE—continued.

THE 600 H.P. ROLLS-ROYCE " CONDOR."

Type	12-cylinder vee water-cooled type.
Bore	5.5 ins.
Stroke	7.5 ins.

With an epicyclic reduction gear driving the airscrew at the most efficient speed.

NORMAL POWER AND SPEED, AND FUEL CONSUMPTION.

Normal b.h.p.	600.
Normal engine speed	1750 r.p.m.
Normal airscrew speed, with reduction gear of .666 ratio suitable for machines of moderate size and high speed	1167 r.p.m.
Normal airscrew speed, with reduction gear of .554 ratio, suitable for large machines of moderate speed	970 r.p.m.
The maximum speed of the engine should not exceed	1900 r.p.m.
Fuel consumption at normal power and speed, using a mixture of 80% petrol and 20% benzole	39 gallons per hour.

WEIGHT.

Weight of engine, including airscrew hub, carburetters, magnetos, engine feet, etc., but excluding reduction gear, exhaust boxes, radiator, oil, fuel, water, and starting battery ..	1200 lbs.
Weight of engine as above, but including reduction gear of .666 ratio	1300 lbs.

CRANKCASE.

The crankcase is of Rolls-Royce patented cellular construction, which increases the strength and simplicity of the cylinder attachments, and has not the weak points which appear in vee engine crankcases of conventional design.

IGNITION.

The ignition is effected by two complete and independent magnetos, each of which fires the whole of the cylinders.

SAFETY FROM FIRE.

The two carburetters are specially arranged in position and form so as to be particularly free from risk of fire.

Owing to the simple fact that this engine has only two single carburetters, it is capable of easy starting and of throttling down on slow running more reliably and efficiently than is obtained by the more common arrangement.

OIL CONSUMPTION.

The oil consumption should be taken as 1.6 gallons per hour.

WATER COOLING SYSTEM.

The quantity of water carried in the cylinder water-jackets, water pipes, and pump is 5 gallons.

SALMSON (French & British).

SOCIÉTÉ DES MOTEURS SALMSON, 9, Avenue des Moulineaux, Billancourt.

British Address :—THE DUDBRIDGE IRON WORKS, Ltd., 37, Victoria Street, London, S.W.

(Salmson engines are built under the Canton-Unné Patents, and are in consequence frequently called Cantons, or Unnés.)

THE 250 H.P. SALMSON AERO-ENGINE.

Compared with the former Canton-Unné motor of radial type, dropped in 1917 and 1918, the new edition of the Salmson shows improvements and simplicity in many ways.

The development of high performance engines for war aeroplanes leads, undoubtedly, from the vertical model to the radial edition. Because of this development the new Salmson aero engine is very suggestive, and thus worth while to describe at some length.

The engine in question has a normal number of r.p.m. of 1400-1500 with nine cylinders of 125 mm. bore by 170 mm. stroke, and a nominal performance of 250 h.p.

The connecting-rods are attached to a master rod on the well-known principle of the Gnôme rotary engine. The great length of the connecting-rods favours this arrangement without any drawback in respect to the uniformity of the stroke, and offers good balancing of the masses.

The number of r.p.m. has been chosen as high as is possible with direct airscrew drive. Yet measures appear to have been provided for a possible use of the reduction gear, to increase the number of revolutions, as is intimated by the performance curve in Fig. 1.

The cylinders, arranged radially, are mounted round a two-part crankcase. The crankshaft rests on each side in a ball-bearing, and is at the rear end provided with a double-thrust bearing to take the airscrew pressure. On the front side of the crankcase the timing gear wheel box is mounted, enclosing a second bearing for the support of the airscrew shaft. The back half of the crankcase is provided with brackets for the mounting of the water and oil pumps and of the two magnetos.

The carburetter is arranged below the two pumps and is connected with a gas distributing channel, cast in the rear part of the crankcase, by means of two tubes, heated by the radiator water. From the gas channel nine suction tubes lead to the single inlet valves.

Nine tubes bring the exhaust tangentially to a collector, formed as a ring and arranged in front of the cylinders, which corresponds well with the circular fuselage form.

The engine is mounted by means of a centre plate with fixing eyes on the back part of the crankcase.

The general arrangement is evident from the Figs. 2 and 3. Further, it is apparent that the total apparatus is made very compact by the use of a ring-form exhaust collector, and of a round front radiator, long tubes, and other projections being thus avoided.

Figs. 4 to 6 give the general dimensions, which come out very favourably in relation to performance, as well as in regard to diameter and even more in respect to length.

Further details are shown in Figs. 7 and 8.

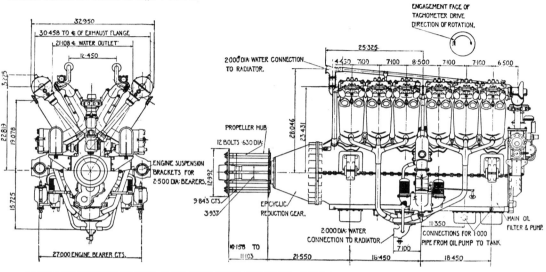

General Arrangement Diagram of the Rolls-Royce " Condor." 600 h.p.

THE CRANKCASE.

The crankcase is made of an aluminium alloy, and is divided at the level of the connecting rods. Though it should apparently receive no greater strains than a single-cylindered engine, many ribs are provided as well as long guides for the centring of the cylinders. The housings for the ball bearings are strengthened by linings of a harder material. The front part has a centring for the mounting of the gear-wheel case and of an oil sump for the return suction pump.

Fig. 2.   Fig. 3.

The 1917 Salmson Engine showing how the exhaust manifold is arranged to fit the front of a fuselage of circular form.

The back half has inside an arrangement for supporting the thrust-block with double ball bearings and its lubrication system. Outside is the centering with fixing eyes for the mounting in the aeroplane. The gas collector has been cast in one piece with the back half of the crankcase.

THE CYLINDERS.

The cylinders are made of steel, and are provided with welded water jackets of sheet steel. Much attention has been paid to giving the compression space the right form, and the valves sufficient area. The valve spindle guides are partly cooled.

The plugs are specially protected against oiling and overheating.

The cylinders rest in the crankcase by means of a base with large jointing surfaces, and are secured by stay bands of key section.

The pistons are cast of a special aluminium alloy, suitable for this purpose in respect to lightness, strength and anti-friction. The inner ribs are reduced to a minimum number, but are of specially large dimensions to avoid any deformation. Four cast iron piston rings, 3 mm. thick, are provided, the fourth being arranged in the opposite end of the piston as a scraper.

The gudgeon pin turns in the piston bearings, so that the pin cannot cause a deformation of the piston. The connecting rods are made of compensated silver steel. Their length is sufficiently great to give a small deviation. Only the main connecting rod turns on the crank pin, while the eight others are attached in the well-known way. The section of the main connecting rod is a double-T form, that of the other ones circular.

THE CRANKSHAFT.

The crankshaft is made of chrome nickel steel in two pieces. The airscrew hub is mounted on the front part. The coned front part is connected with the rear part by means of a sort of head screw through a cone ground in at the crank pin.

The diameter has been very amply chosen, and drilling is employed to a fair extent for the purpose of lightening. To attain a balancing of the masses minutely counter weights are arranged on the crank webs. Each engine is specially tested with all its moving masses for complete balancing.

All main bearings are amply dimensioned and are on ball bearings.

Though this arrangement turns out heavier than journal bearings it has been preferred owing to its smaller sensibility to insufficient lubrication and because of the smaller oil consumption.

The connecting-rod bottom end bearings have ball-races with a special form of cage, and are tested separately under double load before the mounting. The thrust ball-bearing mounted on the stern end of the crankshaft will take up the load of either a propeller or tractor airscrew.

THE VALVE GEAR.

As is evident from Fig. 8, one valve each is provided in the cylinder head for the inlet and the exhaust, being manipulated by means of rocker levers and adjustable tappets from one single camplate. The latter is mounted free on the front crankshaft pin, and is provided with six cams, each two of which lie in one level. Each pair of cams operate in turn the inlet and exhaust valves of three cylinders. During one turn of a pair of cams each valve of the group of three cylinders is operated twice. As two valve openings correspond in the four cycle operation with four turns of the crankshaft, the gear ratio is thus 1 to 4 between cam and crankshaft. The cam is driven by means of a gearing cut in the crankshaft and two intermediate gear-wheels, mounted on the crankcase.

The transmission of the lift of the tappets by the cams is carried out by means of rocker levers and well-supported valve guides, all of which is housed in an aluminium chamber on the front side of the crankcase.

As the cams are accurately cut in the machining operation, it suffices to adjust one cylinder to regulate the whole cam operation.

LUBRICATION.

The lubrication takes place by means of oil circulating under pressure from a piston pump, mounted on the rear side of the engine below the water pump.

This pump has two cylinders, one to force the oil into the crankshaft and a second to bring the oil back to the oil tank from the sump cast in the front part of the crankcase. The oil-pump operates completely immersed in oil in an enclosed chamber that is connected with the oil tank by an amply dimensioned pipe from which the one piston sucks direct. The drive takes place by means of a worm-drive, lying inside the pump through an outer gear drive from the water-pump gear driving wheel. The wheel engaging in the worm is provided with a crankpin that operates direct on the two pistons, the pistons developing with the corresponding cylinders an oscillating movement whereby the inlet and outlet sections are operated. Thus valves and slides are avoided.

The motor is supplied with oil through the back crankshaft pin by means of a sort of casing running therefrom to the connecting pins wherefrom it is distributed farther on by the centrifugal force.

The inner drilling of the main connecting-rod big end bearing head is, in spite of the ball-bearing, formed as a journal surface, provided at the points of the main and auxiliary rods with drillings, through which the oil gets to the connecting and piston pins, as is usual with stationary engines. The oil coming out by the various bearings is slung round by the moving parts in the crankcase and lubricates in this way the cylinders.

The oil flung by the crankshaft and the pistons is again picked up by corresponding pockets to lubricate the cams, the crankshaft bearings and the thrust bearing. The supply of the camshaft case with the oil from the corresponding oil-catching pocket goes through two lines of piping.

The excess supply of oil from the pump is sucked away from the oil sump, cast in the front half part of the crankcase, and returned to the oil tank.

WATER CIRCULATION.

The water is circulated by means of the usual centrifugal pump, which is mounted on the back half of the crankcase and

driven by gears from the crankshaft. In leaving the radiator the water enters the pump through the cap, disperses through tube branches to the two lower cylinders 1 and 9, and therefrom flows through the rest of the cylinders, which are connected with each other by means of rubber sockets. This connection between the various cylinders is so worked out that the formation of steam-pockets is impossible.

The two water currents meet in the top cylinder No. 5, from which the water goes to the radiator. An exchangeable filter is provided between the motor and the radiator to prevent incrustation.

The tachometer is driven from the crankshaft by a gearing reduction of 2 : 11, and is mounted on the water-pump cap.

IGNITION.

There are two magnetos for the ignition, of Salmson manufacture, having stationary armatures and rotating casing. As the magnetos produce four sparks in one revolution, the relation of the revolution number to that of the crankshaft is 9 : 8. The magnetos are driven by a spur wheel transmission gear from the crankshaft. No spark variation arrangement is provided. Further details of this simple and interesting magneto are to be seen in the wiring diagram.

Finally, a combined drive for the timing the fixed machine-gun and for an alternating current generator is provided on the rear crankcase half appearing pretty voluminous, so far as the

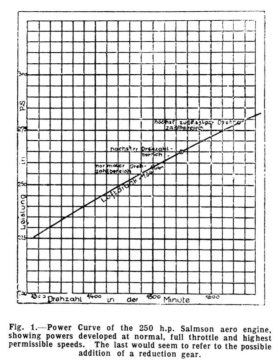

Fig. 1.—Power Curve of the 250 h.p. Salmson aero engine, showing powers developed at normal, full throttle and highest permissible speeds. The last would seem to refer to the possible addition of a reduction gear.

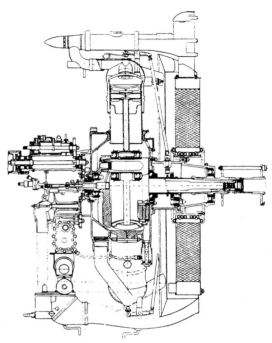

Fig. 7.—Sectional side view.

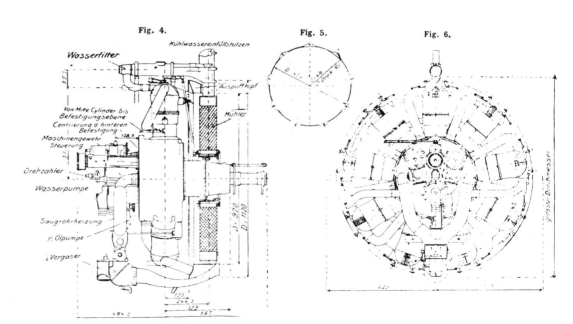

Fig. 4. Fig. 5. Fig. 6.

GENERAL ARRANGEMENT DRAWING.—Kühlwasserein füllstutzen = Water inlet pipe connections. Wasserfilter = Water filter. Von Mitte, etc. = From middle of cylinder to backplate level. Centrierung etc. = Centring of rear mounting. Maschinengewehr Steuerung = Machine-gun timing. Auspuffkopf = Exhaust head. Kühler = Radiator. Drehzähler = Tachometer. Wasserpumpe = Waterpump. Saugrohrheizung = Hot water jacket on inlet pipe. Olpumpe = Oilpump. Vergaser = Carburetter. Grösster Durchmesser = Greatest diameter.

SALMSON—*continued*.

machine-gun timing is concerned, while the drive of the wireless generator is by means of a simple belt pulley with a cone friction clutch.

CARBURATION.

The carburetter is a Zenith twin model with gas regulation for great altitudes, and with a common float chamber. The method of operation is the same as in the rest of the well-known Zenith carburetters with main and slow-running jets and compensator. The arrangement of these jets has been chosen so that the various positions of the aircraft do not influence the ratio of mixture. At the same time the jet arrangement permits a very simple adjustment of the carburettor without dismantling.

Besides the above-mentioned jet arrangement, the carburetter is further provided with an equipment for the regulation of the ratio of mixture for altitude, a simple cock effecting connection

of the channel between the fuel jets and the inner air nozzle with the air pressure outside. When this cock is opened the pressure at the mouths of the jets rises, i.e., the pressure gradient between the float chamber and the jet mouths is reduced ; less fuel therefore leaving and the mixture becoming thereby weaker. This cock remains closed on the ground and is opened in relation to the climb of the aeroplane up to a greater altitude. As this cock to some degree reduces the fuel supply in the jets, it may well be called a mixture reduction cock. Similar is the effect of the German Pallas carburetter, only in this case the air reduction section provided with a calibrated nozzle has a fixed adjustment. The piping scheme for petrol and oil is of interest, and will be understood without further explanation. It seems only worth mentioning how a pressure-free supply of the fuel has been attempted, to which end the somewhat elaborate installation of an air-pump in connection with a membrane petrol pump has been made.

Fig. 17.

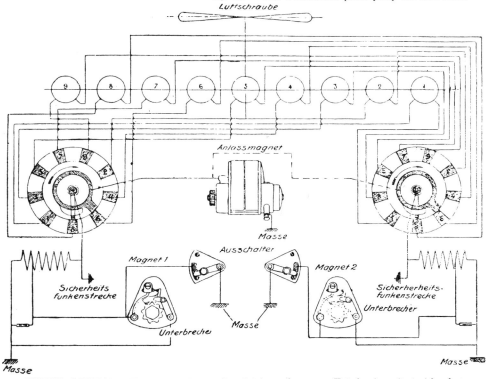

WIRING DIAGRAM.—Sicherheitsfunkenstrecke = Safety-spark gap.　　Unterbrecher = Contact-breaker.
Ausschalter = Switch.　　Masse = Earth.　　Anlassmagnet = Starting magneto.

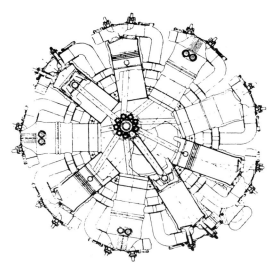

Fig. 8.—Part sectional diagram of engine.

Fig. 9.—Sectional view of Valve-timing gear.

SCHWADE (German).

OTTO SCHWADE & Co., of Erfurt, made Gnôme-copied Stahlherz motors for his *Henry Farman* type biplanes.

S.P.A. (Italian).

SOCIETA PIEMONTESE AUTOMOBILI, Turin.

200 h.p. Model (6A).

Type : Water-cooled vertical.
No. of cylinders . 6.
Bore : 5.31 in.
Stroke : 6.69 in.
R P.M. : 1,600.
H.P. : 220.
Valves : Overhead. Overhead camshaft.
Carburetters : Two Zenith.
Ignition : Two type N2 Marelli magnetos.

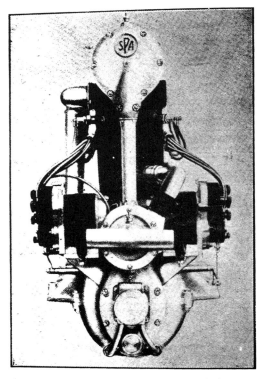

The S.P.A. 200 h.p. aero engine.　Magneto end view.

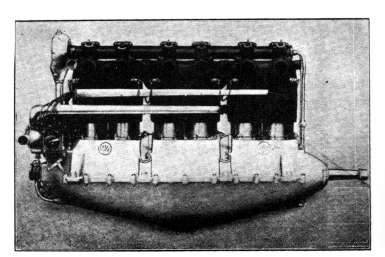

The S.P.A. 200 h.p. aero engine.　Exhaust side.

SPYKER (Dutch).

TROMPENBURG-SPYKER WORKS, Amsterdam, Holland.

Make a 9-cylinder Rotary Engine of Clergèt type.

Specification.
9 Cylinders.
135 h.p. at 1100/1200 revolutions per minute.
Bore 120.

Stroke 160 m/m.
Mechanically operated valves by push rods, one exhaust, one inlet.
Aluminium pistons. Hollow connecting rods with fixed gudgeon pins floating in bronze bushings in piston.
Cylinders all steel with ribs integrally machined.
Dual ignition.
Total weight 138 K.G.

STŒWER AUTOMOBILE WORKS (German.)

Stettin.

Manufacturers of 6-cylinder vertical aero-engines of 125, 150 and 180 h.p. to own design.

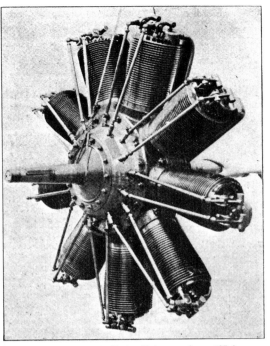

Front End View of the Spyker Rotary engine. 135 h.p.

Front View of the Spyker Rotary engine. 135 h.p.

Rear view of the Sturtevant Model 5A.

STURTEVANT (American).

THE B. F. STURTEVANT Co., Hyde Park, Boston, Mass., U.S.A.

210 h.p. Model 5A—4-1/2.

Type : Watercooled V.
Bore : $4\frac{1}{2}$ in. = 114 m/m.
Stroke : $5\frac{1}{2}$ in. = 140 m/m.
Cylinder capacity : 700 cub. in.
No. of cylinders : 8.
Arrangement of cylinders : " V."
Cooling : Water circulation by centrifugal pump.
Cycle : 4 stroke.

Ignition : Double.
Magnetos : 2—8-cylinder " Dixie " magnetos.
Carburetter : Zenith Duplex, water-jacketed manifold.
Oiling system : Semi dry sump, complete forced feed.
Normal engine speed : 2,250 r.p.m.
Propeller speed : 1,350 r.p.m.
Rated H.P. : 210. Maximum H.P. 240.
Weight, with all accessories, but without water, petrol or oil : 480 lbs.
Weight of water contained in engine : 35 lbs. = 16 kilos.
Weight per B.H.P. dry : 2.4 lbs. = 1.09 kilos.
Fuel consumption, full speed, full load : .55 lbs. per H.P. hr.
Oil consumption : 8 lbs. per hr.

Front End view of Sturtevant Model 7. 300 h.p.

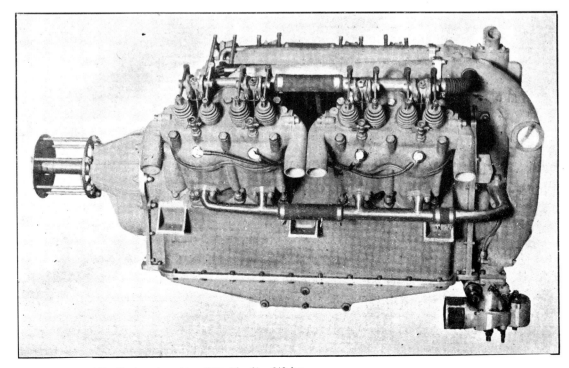

Side View of the Sturtevant engine. Type 5A—4½. 210 h.p.

SUNBEAM (British).

THE SUNBEAM MOTOR CAR Co., Ltd., Wolverhampton.

THE SUNBEAM "ARAB" ENGINE.

The issue of Dec. 20th, 1918, of the German motor and aero paper, "Der Motorwagen," contains an illustrated article by Civil Engineer Otto Schwager, of Charlottenburg, on "A New English Aero Motor of Unknown Manufacture," of which an abstract follows.

An eight-cylinder high-speed engine, resembling the Hispano-Suiza engine in appearance and arrangement, made its appearance some time ago on the Western Front. The engine is apparently made by the English Sunbeam firm at Wolverhampton.

The main data of this new motor are as follows :—

Cylinder bore = 120 mm.
Stroke = 130 mm.
Total cylinder capacity = 11.8 litres.
Compression ratio = 5.39.

The engine appears to be designed for a similar rotation speed to the Hispano-Suiza 2,000 r.p.m., and the performance, assuming mean effective pressure of 8.4 kg. per sq. cm., works out at 220 h.p. Between the camshaft and the airscrew a spur-gear has been installed with a reduction ratio of 5.3, the airscrew running thus at 1,200 r.p.m. for 2,000 r.p.m. at the crankshaft. The weight of the motor without water and oil, airscrew boss and exhaust manifold amounts to 240 kg., which corresponds with 1.09 kg. h.p.

All these figures correspond almost exactly with those of the 220 h.p. Hispano-Suiza engine, with which latter its exterior has much in common. Yet it shows quite a number of novel features, some being improvements upon the Hispano-Suiza, although, taken on a whole, it cannot be considered a serious development of its prototype. Its creation must rather be considered a superfluous increase of the types. Nevertheless, this engine possesses many noteworthy details, distinguishing it from its model and affording the designer many hints.

The engine is mounted on an aluminium crankcase, fundamentally different from that of the Hispano-Suiza. The crankshaft is carried entirely by the upper half, as is the practice in various German motors. There is even more reason for choosing this design, as with each set of four cylinders cast together in a block and bolted to the crankcase, an arrangement giving the greatest resistance to torsional stresses can be used. Furthermore, the designer has displaced the joint between the top and bottom parts of the case as far as possible below the crankshaft, still further stiffening the upper half against such stresses, which are always pretty low in V-type motors with block cylinders. The bearing brasses are lined with white metal and bolted to the top part of the case, through cast aluminium covers.

The bearing covers are further supported by fish-plates of a rolled aluminium alloy, apparently duralumin, and the whole is bolted to the top part of the crankcase.

There is less reason for this design than for that of the upper crankcase, as it should be possible to make the bearing covers considerably more torsion-proof for the same weight. The gear-casing is well strengthened by ribs cast direct on the front part of the case. For mounting in aircraft a continuous ledge, cross-ribbed upwards and downwards, is cast level with the crankshaft centre line. Immediately above this ledge a channel for the oil-supply to the crank bearing is cast in, thus dispensing with oil-pipings, but making the oil-supply depend on accurate moulding. The bottom part of the crankcase is formed mainly as a light oil sump, and is divided from the top part by means of an oil-filter for most of its length. Thus cleaning the oil-filter is only possible when the motor is taken down, which is apparently unimportant, owing to the large free section of the filter. The weight of the whole crankcase amounts to about 47½ kg. against only 36 kg. by the Hispani-Suiza engine. The advantages of the original design seem thus not to have been turned to full effect.

Including the support in front of the small gear wheel the crankshaft has six main bearings. The diameter of these main journals is 59 mm., that of the connecting-rod bearings is 50 mm. The centre crankshaft bearing is much longer than the rest. Though the crankshaft appears stronger than that of the Hispano-Suiza one, its weight is only 16.2 kg., against 23 kilos. of the Hispano-Suiza shaft. This result is achieved by ample boring of the shaft to the extent of 38 mm. diameter between the gear wheel and the first crank, to 42 mm. in the rest of the crankshaft bearing, and to 32 mm. in the crank-pins.

Taking the most unfavourable condition that the piston pressure is distributed on two main bearings 48 mm. long, the surface load = 72 kg. sq. cm. at 30 atmospheres maximum explosion pressure, which corresponds at n = 2,000 r.p.m. to a value for the friction loss x of = 436 m. kg. per sq. cm. per sec.

[1] The connecting rods (illustrated here), contrary to the Hispano-Suiza, have been formed as articulated rods. In spite of the resulting uneven piston movement the articulated rod is to be preferred to the forked rod on the score of reliability, though the latter represents undoubtedly a more elegant design. It renders possible a strong design of connecting-rod bearing cap; and, secondly, the friction at these bearing connecting-rods can be better dealt with, though care must be taken not to attain this advantage at the cost of too heavy a main connecting-rod. In the present case weight is saved by leaving out brasses in the connecting-rod bearing and casting the white metal in the rod head, with the attendant risk of greater damage to the crankshaft if a bearing runs. The auxiliary connecting-rod is attached to the main rod in the usual way by a bolt 30 mm. diameter and 40 mm. bearing length. The two rods are both of double

T-section. The rod end for the bronze gudgeon-pin bush of 30 mm. diameter and 51 mm. bearing length shows the usual form, and is provided with a number of weight-reduction holes. The lubrication of the gudgeon-pin, contrary to the Hispano-Suiza practice and to the rest of the well-known motor designs, is by oil splashing, which simplifies the lubrication system, but does not increase the reliability.

Assuming the maximum explosion pressure, but neglecting the inertia forces, the various bearing loads will be as shown in the following table :—

Bearing	Diameter. Cm.	Bearing length. Cm.	Surface load. kg. per cm.
Main connecting rod pin	5.0	5.2	130.5
Joint pin	3.0	4.0	283
Gudgeon-pin	—	5.1	222

The friction losses for the connecting-rods at 2,000 r.p.m. work out at 681 kgm. per sq. cm. sec. Taken altogether, the design and construction of the connecting-rods must be considered successful, especially considering their weight, which for a complete set of two is 2.075 kg. against 2.57 kg. in the Hispano-Suiza motor.

An astonishing feature of the piston design is its small height, amounting only to 73 mm. against 105 mm. in the Hispano-Suiza motor. This small height has been chosen to reduce the weight of the reciprocating masses and thereby keep the horizontal inertia forces low. The weight of the finished piston with rings and pin amounts only to 1.165 kg., against 1.4 kg. in the Hispano-Suiza, or 10.2 grammes per sq. cm. of piston surface, as against 12.3 in the prototype. The piston is an aluminium die casting, which practice appears to play an increasing part in foreign aero-motor manufacture, and justifiably so. Firstly, the die casting produces a most exact blank, thus relieving the designer from providing a margin to cover core eccentricities, allowing him to choose the dimensions, giving the necessary stiffness; and, secondly, die-cast metal possesses better strength qualities than usual sand-castings (about 20-22 kg. sq. mm. and 4-4½ per cent. extension against 10-15 kg. sq. mm. and 1-2 per cent. extension), thus permitting a further reduction of the wall thicknesses, which are reasons for the greater employment in Germany of this casting process. The piston-head is stiffened by two cross-ribs reaching nearly to the bottom of the piston-skirt. Furthermore, a support reaching to the gudgeon-pin has been provided in the middle of the head, a practice employed in some German engines.

Three piston rings are provided above the gudgeon-pin. A fourth ring at the other end of the piston is fitted to scrape off surplus oil. The gudgeon-pin is locked against side displacement by spring rings and studs resist turning. Where the gudgeon-pin bearings penetrate the body of the piston, the latter has been milled flat to avoid seizing caused by distortion of the piston.

The cylinder block is another interesting design item. As in the Hispano-Suiza motor the four cylinders are united in a single aluminium casting. In this case the cylinder casing is extended to the crankcase to which it is fixed through very strong flanges, which renders the whole construction rigid indeed. The steel liners of 2 mm. wall thickness are not screwed in, but are held and prevented from moving by a collar, turned at the bottom. Two small exhaust valves and one large inlet valve are mounted in the cylinder head, inclined slightly in relation to the cylinder shaft, with bronze seats screwed into the aluminium casing. Inserted cast iron bushes serve as valve-stem guides. Special steel bushes are provided on both sides for the plug-threads. Below the plug socket the water-jacket casting is open, with aluminium sheet covers, strengthened by pressed ribs, and fixed with 16 screws to flanges on the block. The top side of the cylinder block is provided with a straight through tunnel carrying the camshaft bearings.

The "Arab 2" Sunbeam-Coatalen with ungeared airscrew drive. End View.

The weight of the cylinder block, ready for erection, with all studs is 35.6 kg., somewhat heavier than in the Hispano-Suiza engine.

The valve gearing differs fundamentally from that of the Hispano-Suiza, this motor being equipped, as already mentioned, with two small exhaust valves of 36 mm. diameter, and one large inlet valve of 53 mm. diameter per cylinder. The valves are operated by the camshaft through twin-armed levers for the exhaust valves, and single-armed ones for the inlet valve. There are no cam-rollers, the rocking levers bear direct on the cams. The lever end does not press direct on the head of the valve stem, but on an inserted thrust-jacket. The play between the latter and the lever can only be readjusted by inserting thrust discs in the jacket. A better arrangement might have been devised here. The whole valve-gearings is enclosed in an oil and dust-proof casing as in the Hispano-Suiza. The lubrication takes place through the hollow camshaft.

The camshaft drive is by an auxiliary shaft, running in a casing cast on at the end of each cylinder block parallel to the cylinder.

The twin-carburetter, mounted between the cylinder blocks, is a Claudel-Hobson, with altitude regulation, much used by enemy aero-motors, with no special features. As in the Hispano-Suiza the incoming air is pre-heated by the radiator, the carburetter intake is fitted with a heating jacket, and the induction pipes are without any heating device. With induction pipes of greater area, combined with the amply dimensioned inlet valve, the charging of the cylinders is better provided for than in the Hispano-Suiza, and the performance, stated at the beginning of the article, should be surpassed.

The "Arab" Sunbeam-Coatalen engine, 235 b.h.p. at 2,000 r.p.m.

The ignition arrangements correspond both as regards to position and drive with Hispano-Suiza practice.

The circulating pump is of the usual centrifugal type, and is driven direct from the rear end of the crankshaft. From the pump the cooling water enters the water-jacket of each cylinder block on the inner side of the cylinders between the third and fourth cylinder in each block. To obtain an equal distribution of the water inside the water-jacket, each cylinder block is provided with three gutters, any steam pocket formation being avoided by their favourable position.

4 overhead valves per cylinder.
2 overhead camshafts per block of cylinders, driven by a train of gears.
Volume of cylinders : 12,270 ccs.
Direct drive to propeller shaft. A flywheel is also fitted to these engines.
Articulating connecting rod system.
Normal revolutions 2100 per minute.
275 B.H.P. at normal revolutions of engine.
Approximate weight per h.p. : 3.3 lbs.
4 Claudel Hobson carburetters B.Z.S. 38.

Pressure feed to carburetters.
Ignition is by two 12 cylinder magnetos.
A hand starter and electric starter are fitted.
The exhaust pipes are provided with a special arrangement for water cooling.
The water pumps are of specially large dimensions, and a governor is fitted to the engine to prevent over-running. When the engine speed reaches 2,500, the governor automatically comes into operation, and similarly when the oil pressure falls below 20 lbs. per square inch.

Airscrew end of " Arab " Sunbeam engine.

Magneto end of " Arab " Sunbeam engine.

The lubrication system is a simple circulation system with a pump extracting the oil from the lowest point of the very deep sump. The oil is pumped by a circulating pump into the already described oil ways in the upper half of the crankcase, thence distributed to the different bearings. At the front end of this oil channel a branch pipe to the gear box leads oil to the gear wheels. The oil collected in the lower part of the crankcase is then returned by the suction pump to the oil tank, which may be replaced by an oil radiator.

The reduction gear is of the usual spur wheel type, and of the following main dimensions :—

Gear ratio, 2,000/1,500 ; gear teeth, 27/45 ; gear diameters, 110.97 m./194.95 mm.

The shaft of the large wheel serves at the same time as airscrew hub, the rear flange of which is in one piece with the shaft. A cam ring, operating the machine-gun control, is screwed to the hub.

Briefly, it may be said that the motor is a somewhat belated, partly improved, edition of the Hispano-Suiza motor, but shows no great development of the original, though in many details it can give German aero-motor designers hints. Specially the use of aluminium die castings should be emphasised.

Specification.

8 cylinders.
120 m/m bore by 130 m/m stroke.
90 degrees Vee.
3 valves per cylinder.
Volume of cylinders : 12,260 ccs.
The camshaft drive is by means of bevel gearing.
Approximate weight per horse power : 2.3 lbs.
Normal revolutions 2,000 per minute.
Articulating connecting rod system.
Maximum B.H.P. is 235 at 2,000 R.P.M.
Variable ignition by two 8 cylinder magnetos.
Claudel Hobson carburetter type H.C.7 set inside.
Lubricant consumption : average 6.5 pints of castor oil per hour.
Normal oil pressure to main engine details at full power : 45 lbs. per square inch.
Some of these engines are fitted with hand starters.
Propeller shaft driven direct from the crankshaft.

THE " MAORI 4 " SUNBEAM-COATALEN AIRCRAFT ENGINE.

(Specially designed for airship use.)

12 cylinders.
100 m/m. bore by 135 m/m. stroke.
60 degrees Vee.

The " Maori 4 " Sunbeam-Coatalen engine (Direct Drive for Airships). 275 Nominal h.p.

SUNBEAM—*continued.*

THE "COSSACK" SUNBEAM-COATALEN AIRCRAFT ENGINE.

12 cylinders.
110 m/m bore by 160 m/m stroke.
60 degrees Vee.
4 valves per cylinder.
Volume of cylinders : 18,246 cubic centimeters.

Articulating connecting rod system.
Normal revolutions 2,000 per minute.
Geared drive to propeller shaft.
Reduction ratio : 2 to 1.
Approximate weight per h.p. : 3.7 lbs.
350 B.H.P. at 2,000 R.P.M.
Average petrol consumption : 0.54 per h.p. per hour.
4 Claudel Hobson carburetters, type C.Z.S. 42, set outside cylinder blocks.

Pressure feed to carburetters.
Ignition is by two 12 cylinder magnetos.
Lubricant consumption : average 6.5 pints of castor oil per hour.
Normal oil pressure to main engine details at full power : 45 lbs. per square inch.
A compressed air starter and hand starter are fitted to these engines.

The "Cossack" Sunbeam-Coatalen engine, 350 b.h.p. at 2,000 r.p.m.

End View of the "Cossack" Sunbeam-Coatalen engine.

THOMAS (American).

THE THOMAS AEROMOTOR COMPANY, Inc., Ithaca, New York.

150 h.p. Model 88.
Type : Water-cooled "V."
No. of cylinders : 8.
Bore : 4 ins.   Stroke : 5½ ins.
R.P.M. : 2,100.   (Propeller shaft : 1,200 r.p.m.)
Cylinders : Cast in pairs, integral jackets, with detachable heads.   Cylinders and heads of aluminium alloy, with steel liners to cylinders.

Valves : Side by side, central valve gear.
Carburetters : Duplex Zenith, hot air intake, water heated.
Ignition : 2 four-spark magnetos.
Lubrication : High pressure.
Water feed : Pump operated.
Weight : 525 lbs., including self-starter.
Oil consumption : 1½ gals. per hour.
Petrol consumption : 15 gals. per hour.

UNION (American).

THE UNION GAS ENGINE COMPANY, Oakland, California, U.S.A.

Produce the 6-cylinder engine illustrated, which is believed to have been used on certain small American Airships.   No data available.

Exhaust Side of the Union Aero engine.

Pump End of the Union Aero engine.

Inlet Side of the Union Aero engine.

WISCONSIN (American).

WISCONSIN MOTOR MFG. Co., Sta. A.. Dept. 335, Milwaukee, Wis.
Engaged entirely on aero engines for U.S. Government. No fresh details available.

140 h.p. Model.
Type : Water-cooled vertical.
No. of cylinders : 6.
Bore : 5 in.   Stroke : 6½ in.
R.P.M. : 1,400.
Cylinders : Cast in pairs.
Valves : Overhead.   Overhead camshaft.

Carburetter : Single
Ignition : 2 six-spark magnetos.
Lubrication : Forced feed.
Weight (claimed) : 600 lbs.

250 h.p Model, as above, but :—
No. of cylinders : 12.
Weight (claimed) : 1,000 lbs.